CONSTITUTIONS
of
NATIONS

VOLUME III – EUROPE

CONSTITUTIONS

of

NATIONS

VOLUME III – EUROPE

by

AMOS J. PEASLEE

Formerly Ambassador of the United States of America to Australia, Secretary-General of the International Bar Association, Member of the American Council of Learned Societies, President of the American Branch of the International Law Association, Representative of the American Society of International Law at the San Francisco Conference of 1945, Associate of the American Commission to Negotiate Peace at Versailles in 1919

Author of INTERNATIONAL GOVERNMENTAL ORGANIZATIONS THEIR CONSTITUTIONAL DOCUMENTS (*Martinus Nijhoff, The Hague; and Justice House, New York, 2nd Ed., 1961*), A PERMANENT UNITED NATIONS (*Putnams, 1942*), UNITED NATIONS GOVERNMENT (*Putnams, 1945*), *and co-author of* THREE WARS WITH GERMANY (*Putnams, 1944*)

✶

REVISED THIRD EDITION

In four Volumes

Prepared by Dorothy Peaslee Xydis

Formerly officer in the Secretariat of the General Agreement on Tariffs and Trade

Originally published by Martinus Nijhoff, The Hague, Netherlands in 1968
Softcover reprint of the hardcover 3rd edition 1968

ISBN 978-94-017-7077-4 *ISBN 978-94-017-7102-3 (eBook)*
DOI 10.1007/978-94-017-7102-3

NETHERLANDS

SUMMARY

INTERNATIONAL STATUS

The Netherlands is a member of the United Nations (December 10, 1945).[1] It is a member of the European Economic Community, Benelux, and other international organizations. It was a member of the League of Nations.

The Seven United Provinces constituted themselves as the Dutch Republic by the Union of Utrecht in 1579, and renounced Spanish sovereignty

[1] The Netherlands has accepted the compulsory jurisdiction of the International Court under Article 36 of its Statute.

in 1581. The Peace of Westphalia in 1648 entailed unqualified recognition of their independence by Spain. In 1810, Holland was annexed to France. In 1814, all the provinces of Holland and Belgium were united to form the United Kingdom of the Netherlands under the King of Holland. The 1815 constitution provided for an autocratic monarchy which lasted until the reforms of 1848 instituted a parliamentary monarchy. In 1830, the southern provinces broke away and relations between Belgium and the Netherlands were regulated by the Treaty of London of 1839. The Dutch government assumed full control of the Netherlands East Indies in 1819 from the Dutch East India Company. Holland was invaded and occupied by Germany in 1940, and the Dutch East Indies by Japan in 1942. The Benelux agreements were signed between Holland, Belgium and Luxembourg on September 5, 1944, the customs union came into force on January 1, 1948, and the economic union on February 3, 1958. On December 27, 1949, Indonesia became independent, remaining in union with the Netherlands until 1954.

FORM OF NATIONAL GOVERNMENT

The Constitution of the Kingdom of the Netherlands of August 24, 1815, as amended to 1963, describes the territory of the Kingdom and states that the Constitution is binding only for the territory in Europe.[1] The King may not wear a foreign crown and the seat of government may in no case be removed outside the Kingdom.[2] The source of sovereign power is not stated.

RIGHT OF THE PEOPLE

There is no section devoted to rights but the Constitution provides the equal rights of all to protection of their persons and goods, the rights of the press, petition and assembly,[3] due process of law, inviolability of the dwelling, secrecy of communication,[4] freedom of religion.[5] All Netherlanders must participate in the defense of the land.[6] A section relates to education and poor relief.[7]

LEGISLATIVE DEPARTMENT

Legislative power is exercised jointly by the King and the States General.[8] The States General are bicameral, composed of a first and a second chamber, representing the whole people.[9] The 150 members of the Second Chamber are elected by universal suffrage and proportional representation

[1] Const., Art. 1, 2. [2] Id., Art. 21. [3] Id., Art. 4, 7–9.
[4] Id., Art. 171, 172, 173. [5] Id., Art. 181–187. [6] Id., Art. 194.
[7] Id., Art. 208, 209. [8] Id., Art. 119. [9] Id., Art. 88, 89.

for a term of four years.[1] The First Chamber is composed of 75 members chosen by the provincial States on the basis of proportional representation for a term of six years.[2] Immunities of deputies are provided.[3] The States General meet in one ordinary session a year and are subject to dissolution.[4] There are provisions regarding finances,[5] provincial and municipal government,[6] regulatory public bodies.[7]

EXECUTIVE DEPARTMENT

There are provisions concerning the succession to the throne, the income of the Crown, guardianship and regency.[8] The executive power is vested in the King who is inviolable.[9] He conducts foreign relations, commands the Armed Forces, grants honors and pardons.[10] The Constitution provides for a Council of State and for Ministers who are responsible.[11] Ministers may not be members of the States General but may take part in its sessions.[12] A section deals with Water Affairs which are under the supreme control of the King.[13]

JUDICIAL DEPARTMENT

Judicial power is exercised solely by judges designated by law.[14] Persons may not be withdrawn from their natural judge.[15] A Supreme Court of the Netherlands is provided with power to try high officials for indictable offences, and to supervise the judicial power.[16]

AREA, POPULATION, ETC.

The area of the Netherlands is 33,491.46 square kilometres, irs population (1965) 12,362,000. The capital is Amsterdam.

[1] Id., Art. 90, 91, 95.
[2] Id., Art. 92, 101.
[3] Id., Art. 107.
[4] Id., Art. 110, 82, 114.
[5] Id., Art. 133–136, 188–193.
[6] Id., Art. 137–158.
[7] Id., Art. 159–162.
[8] Id., Art. 10–54.
[9] Id., Art. 55, 56.
[10] Id., Art. 58, 68, 74, 77, 78.
[11] Id., Art. 83, 86, 55.
[12] Id., Art. 104, 106.
[13] Id., Art. 204–207.
[14] Id., Art. 169.
[15] Id., Art. 170.
[16] Id., Art. 176–179.

CONSTITUTION of THE NETHERLANDS[1]

August 24, 1815, as amended to 1963

FIRST CHAPTER

OF THE KINGDOM AND ITS INHABITANTS

Art. 1. The Kingdom of the Netherlands comprises the territory of the Netherlands, Surinam and the Netherlands Antilles.

Art. 2. The Constitution shall be binding only for the territory of the Kingdom in Europe, in so far as the contrary does not appear therefrom.

Wherever the Kingdom is mentioned in the following articles, only the territory of the Kingdom in Europe shall be understood.

Paragraph 3 (*repealed*).

Art. 3. Provinces and municipalities may be united and divided and new ones formed, by law.

The boundaries of the Kingdom, provinces, and municipalities may be changed by law.

Art. 4. All persons who are on the territory of the Kingdom shall have equal rights to protection of their persons and goods.

The admission and expulsion of aliens and the general conditions under which, in respect of their extradition, treaties may be concluded with foreign powers shall be regulated by law.

Art. 5. Every Netherlands subject shall be eligible for appointment to any office in the service of the State. No alien shall be eligible for such appointment save in accordance with the provisions of the law.

Art. 6. It shall be declared by law who are Netherlanders and who are residents.

Naturalization shall take place by virtue of a law. The consequence of naturalization in respect of the wife and children under age of the naturalized person shall be regulated by law.

Art. 7. No person shall require previous permission to publish thoughts or feelings by means of the printing press, without prejudice to every person's responsibility according to law.

[1] **English translation supplied by the Ministry of Foreign Affairs in July 1966. Ed.**

Art. 8. Every person shall have the right to present petitions to the competent authority, always provided he does so in writing.

Every petition must be signed by the petitioner. It may only be signed in the name of another person by virtue of a written power of attorney submitted with the petition. Incorporated bodies may present petitions to the competent authority, but only on matters appertaining to their particular sphere of activity.

Art. 9. The right of association and assembly of residents is recognized.

The exercise of this right shall, in the interests of public order, be regulated and limited by law.

SECOND CHAPTER

OF THE KING

First Section. Of Succession to the Throne

Art. 10. The Crown of the Netherlands is and shall remain vested in His Majesty William Frederick, Prince of Orange-Nassau, to be possessed by him and his legitimate descendants.

Art. 11. The Crown shall pass by hereditary succession to the deceased King's descendants, sons taking precedence of daughters; the older child then taking precedence of the younger. Substitution shall taken place under the same rules; if there are no descendants of the deceased King the crown shall pass in like manner to the descendants, first of his parent, then of his grandparent in the line of succession, but not further removed from the deceased King than the third degree of consanguinity.

Art. 12. Repealed.

Art. 13. Repealed.

Art. 14. Repealed.

Art. 15. In respect of succession, abdication of the crown shall have the same consequences as death. Without prejudice to the provisions of the next Article, children born after the abdication shall be excluded from hereditary succession.

Art. 16. The unborn child of a woman pregnant at the moment of the death of the King shall, in respect of the right to the crown, be regarded as already born. If still-born, it shall be deemed never to have existed.

Art. 17. All the children born of a marriage contracted by a King without consulting the States-General, or contracted without legal sanction by a male or female person capable of inheriting the crown from the reigning King shall be excluded from hereditary succession, as shall the descendants of any such children.

As far as the possession of and the succession to the crown are concerned the contracting of such a marriage shall have the same consequence as death.

Art. 18. If prospects exist that there will be no successor competent according to the Constitution, such a successor may be appointed by a law, the draft of which shall be introduced by the King.

The States-General, being convoked in double numbers to that end, shall deliberate and decide thereon in united assembly.

Art. 19. If, on the death of the King, no successor competent according to the Constitution exists, the States-General shall be convoked by the Council of State in double numbers, within four months of the King's decease, in order to appoint a king in united assembly.

Art. 20. As far as the succession is concerned, a King invested with the crown by appointment shall take the place of His Majesty William Frederick, Prince of Orange Nassau.

Art. 21. The King cannot wear a foreign crown.

In no case can the seat of government be removed outside of the Kingdom.

Second Section. Of the Income of the Crown

Art. 22. Besides the income from the domains ceded by the law of the 26th August, 1822, and returned to the State in 1848 as Crown Domains by the late King William II, the King shall receive from the Exchequer of the Kingdom an annual income of 2,500,000 florins.

Art. 23. Summer and winter residences shall be prepared for the King for his use, for the maintenance of which, however, not more than 100,000 florins may be annually charged to the account of the Kingdom.

Art. 24. The King and the members of the Royal House named in Articles 26, 28 and 29 shall be free from all personal imposts.

They shall not be exempt from any other tax.

Art. 25. The King shall organize his household according as he shall think fit.

Art. 26. The Consort of a reigning Queen shall enjoy from the Exchequer of the Kingdom an annual income of 200,000 florins; he shall continue to enjoy this income after the decease of the Queen, as long as he is a widower and retains the status of Netherlander.

A Queen shall enjoy, after the decease of the King, an annual income of 200,000 florins from the Exchequer of the Kingdom during her state of widowhood.

An annual income from the Exchequer of the Kingdom may be bestowed by law upon a King or a Queen who has relinquished the Crown.

Art. 27. The eldest of the King's sons, or further male descendants, who is the heir presumptive to the crown, shall be the King's first subject and shall carry the title of Prince of Orange.

Art. 28. The Prince of Orange shall receive from the Exchequer of the Kingdom an annual income of 200,000 florins from the time when he shall have completed the age of eighteen years. This income shall be increased to 400,000 florins after the solemnization of a marriage for which sanction has been granted by law.

After the death of the Prince of Orange, his widow shall receive from the Exchequer of the Kingdom an annual income of 200,000 florins during her widowhood.

Art. 29. The daughter of the King who is heir presumptive to the Crown shall enjoy from the Exchequer of the Kingdom an annual income of 200,000 florins from the time she has reached the age of eighteen years. If she contracts a marriage, for which sanction has been granted by law, her consort shall enjoy equally from the Exchequer of the Kingdom an annual income of 200,000 florins; he shall continue to enjoy this income after the decease of the Princess, as long as he is a widower and retains the status of Netherlander.

After the decease of her consort the Princess shall receive as long as she remains unmarried, an annual income of 400,000 florins. The incomes mentioned in this article shall continue to exist in the event that a Prince of Orange is born subsequently.

Art. 30. The amounts fixed in this Section may be changed by a law.

The Chambers of the States-General cannot pass such a law, nor any law to amend or repeal such a law, except with the votes of two thirds of the number of members constituting each of the Chambers.

Third Section. Of Guardianship over the King

Art. 31. The King shall attain his majority on completing his eighteenth year.

This shall also apply to the Prince of Orange and to the King's daughter who is the heiress presumptive to the crown, should they become regent.

Art. 32. The guardianship over the King whilst a minor shall be regulated, and the guardian or guardians appointed by a law.

The States-General shall deliberate and decide in united assembly upon the draft of that law.

Art. 33. This law shall be enacted during the lifetime of the King for the event of his successor being a minor. Should this not have been done, some of the nearest relations by consanguinity of the minor King shall be consulted, if practicable, about the regulation of the guardianship.

Art. 34. Before assuming the guardianship, every guardian shall take the following oath or make the following promise at a united assembly of the States-General, which oath or promise shall be administered by the president:

"I swear (promise) fealty to the King; I swear (promise) that I will sacredly perform all the duties which the guardianship lays upon me, and that I will particularly endeavor to inculcate upon the King attachment to the Constitution and love for his people. So help me, God Almighty! (That I promise!).

Art. 35. In the event of the disability of the King to exercise government, the necessary supervision of his person shall be provided for in accordance with the rules respecting the guardianship over a minor King laid down in Article 32.

The oath or promise to be taken or made by the guardian or guardians appointed to this end shall be formulated by law.

Fourth Section. Of the Regency

Art. 36. During the King's minority, royal authority shall be exercised by a regent.

Art. 37. The regent shall be appointed by a law which may at the same time regulate the succession in the regency until the King's majority.

The States-General shall deliberate and decide upon the draft of this law in united assembly.

The law shall be enacted during the lifetime of the King for the event of his successor being a minor.

Art. 38. Royal authority shall also be committed to a regent in the event of the disability of the King to exercise government.

Should the heads of the ministerial departments assembled in council consider that this case exists, they shall notify their findings to the Council of State and invite that council to give its advice within a specified time.

Art. 39. If after the termination of the appointed period, they maintain their opinion, they shall convoke the States-General in united assembly in order to report the case to them, at the same time submitting the advice of the Council of State if this has been received.

Art. 40. If the States-General in united assembly are of opinion that the case described in the first paragraph of Article 38 exists, they shall so declare in a resolution which shall be promulgated by order of the President designated in the second paragraph of Article 118 and which shall enter into operation on the day of its promulgation. Failing such a President, the assembly shall appoint one.

Art. 41. In the case provided for in Article 40, the Prince of Orange, or the King's daughter who is the heiress presumptive to the crown shall be regent according to law when they shall have completed their eighteenth year.

Art. 42. Failing a Prince of Orange and a King's daughter who is the heiress presumptive to the crown, or if they have not completed their eighteenth year, the regency shall be provided for in the manner determined in Article 37; in the latter case until they shall have completed their eighteenth year.

Art. 43. Royal authority shall also be exercised by a regent in case the King has temporarily relinquished the exercise of royal authority by virtue of a law of which he has submitted the draft. The States-General shall deliberate and decide in united assembly upon the draft of this law, which shall at the same time provide for the appointment of a regent.

Art. 44. On assuming the regency the regent shall take the following oath or make the following promise at a united assembly of the States-General, which oath or promise shall be administered by the president:

"I swear (promise) fealty to the King; I swear (promise) that in exercising royal authority, as long as the King is a minor (as long as the King is unable to exercise government, or as long as the exercise of royal authority has been relinquished), I will always observe and uphold the Constitution.

I swear (promise) that I will defend and preserve, with all my power the independence and the territory of the State; that I will protect the general and particular liberty and the rights of all and each of the King's subjects, and will employ, for the maintenance and promotion of the general and particular welfare, all the means which the laws place at my disposal, as a good and true regent should do. So help me, God Almighty! (That I promise!)."

Art. 45. If a regent becomes unable to exercise the regency, Articles 38, second paragraph, 39 and 40 shall apply. If the succession in the regency has not been regulated, then the first paragraph of Article 37 shall be applied.

Art. 46. Royal authority shall be exercised by the Council of State:

(1) On the death of the King, as long as succession to the throne has not been provided for according to Article 19, as long as no regent has been appointed for the minor successor to the throne, or as long as the successor to the throne, or the regent is absent.

(2) In the cases provided for in Articles 40 and 45, as long as there is on regent or as long as the regent is absent; and on the death of the regent, as long as his successor has not been appointed and has not assumed the regency.

(3) In case succession to the throne is uncertain and there is no regent, or the regent is absent.

Such exercise of royal authority shall cease according to law as soon as the competent successor to the throne or the regent has assumed his dignity. If the regency has to be provided for, the Council of State shall introduce the draft of the law for that purpose:

In the cases mentioned in paragraphs (1) and (2), within a period of one month after the assumption of the exercise of royal authority;

In the case mentioned in paragraph (3), within a period of one month after the succession to the throne has ceased to be uncertain.

Art. 47. On the appointment of the regent or on the assumption of the regency by the Prince of Orange or by the King's daughter who is the heiress presumptive to the crown, a law shall determine the sum which shall be taken from the annual income of the crown for the cost of the regency. This provision may not be changed during the regency.

Art. 48. As soon as the case described in Article 38 has ceased to exist, the States-General shall so declare in united assembly, by a resolution which shall be promulgated by order of the President mentioned in Article 40.

Art. 49. This resolution shall be adopted on the proposal of the regent, or of at least twenty members of the States General. These members shall lodge their proposal with the President of the First Chamber, who shall immediately convoke the two chambers in united assembly.

If the session of the Chambers is closed, those members shall have the power themselves so to convoke the meeting of the Chambers.

Art. 50. The heads of the ministerial departments and the guardian or guardians shall personally be bound to make a report to the Chambers of the States-General on the condition of the King or regent, as often as they are asked to do so.

Article 104, third paragraph, shall in this matter also apply to the guardians.

Art. 51. Immediately after the promulgation of the resolution described in Article 48, the King shall resume the exercise of government.

Fifth Section. Of the Inauguration of the King

Art. 52. The King, having assumed government, shall be solemnly sworn and inaugurated as soon as possible within the city of Amsterdam, at a public and united assembly of the States-General.

Art. 53. At this assembly the King shall take the following oath, or make the following promise, on the Constitution:

"I swear (promise) to the Netherlands people that I will always observe and uphold the Constitution.

I swear (promise) that I will defend and preserve, with all my power, the independence and territory of the State; that I will protect the general and particular liberty and the rights of all and each of my subjects, and will employ for the maintenance and promotion of the general and particular welfare, all the means which the laws place at my disposal, as a good King should do.

So help me, God Almighty! (That I promise!)."

Art. 54. After taking his oath or making the promise, homage shall be done to the King at the same assembly by the States-General, whose

President shall pronounce the following solemn declaration, which shall then be sworn or confirmed by him and by each of the members individually:

"We receive you and do homage to you as King, in the name of the Netherlands people and by virtue of the Constitution; we swear (promise) that we will uphold your inviolability and the rights of your crown; we swear (promise) that we will do everything that good and true States-General should do.

So help us, God Almighty! (That we promise!)."

Sixth Section. Of the Power of the King

Art. 55. The King shall be inviolable; the ministers shall be responsible.

Art. 56. The executive power shall be vested in the King.

Art. 57. The King shall fix general administrative measures. Provisions which are to be maintained by means of penalties shall not be made in such measures otherwise than by virtue of the law.

The penalties which are to be inflicted shall be regulated by law.

Art. 58. The King shall have the supreme direction of foreign relations.

He shall promote the development of the international legal order.

Art. 59. The King shall not declare the Kingdom to be at war with another Power except with the previous consent of the States-General. This consent shall not be required when as a result of an actual state of war consultation with the States-General has appeared to be impossible.

The States-General shall discuss and decide on these matters in united assembly.

The King shall not declare a war between the Kingdom and another Power to be terminated except with the previous consent of the States-General.

Art. 60. Agreements with other Powers and with organizations based on international law shall be concluded by or by authority of the King. If required by such agreements they shall be ratified by the King.

The agreements shall be communicated to the States-General as soon as possible; they shall not be ratified and they shall not enter into force until they have received the approval of the States-General.

The judges shall not be competent to judge of the constitutionality of agreements.

Art. 61. Approval shall be given either explicitly or implicitly.

Explicit approval shall be given by an Act.

Implicit approval has been given if, within thirty days after the agreement has been submitted for that purpose to both Chambers of the States-General, no statement has been made by or on behalf of either Chamber or by at least one fifth of the constitutional number of members of either

Chamber, expressing the wish that the agreement shall be subject to explicit approval.

The period referred to in the previous paragraph shall be suspended for the time of adjournment of the States-General.

Art. 62. Except in the case referred to in Article 63, the approval shall not be required:

(a) if the agreement is one with respect to which this has been laid down by law;

(b) if the agreement is exclusively concerned with the execution of an approved agreement, provided the Act regulating the approval does not contain any reservations in this respect;

(c) if the agreement does not impose considerable pecuniary obligations on the Kingdom and if it has been concluded for a period not exceeding one year;

(d) if in exceptional cases of a compelling nature it would be decidedly detrimental to the interests of the Kingdom if the agreement were not to enter into force before it has been approved.

An agreement as referred to under (d) shall, however, be submitted to the approval of the States-General without delay. In this case Article 61 applies. If the States-General withold their approval, the agreement shall be terminated as soon as shall be compatible with the provisions of the agreement.

An agreement shall not be concluded but subject to the reservation that it shall be terminated if the States-General withold their approval, provided this should be decidedly detrimental to the interests of the Kingdom.

Art. 63. If the development of the international legal order requires this, the contents of an agreement may deviate from certain provisions of the Constitution.

In such cases only explicit approval can be given; the Chambers of the States-General shall not approve a Bill to that effect but with a two-thirds majority of the votes cast.

Art. 64. The provisions of the four preceding articles shall similarly apply to any accession to or any denunciation of agreements.

Art. 65. The provisions of agreements the contents of which may be binding on anyone shall have this binding effect as from the time of publication. Rules with regard to the publication of agreements shall be laid down by law.

Art. 66. Legal regulations in force within the Kingdom shall not apply if this application should be incompatible with provisions—binding on anyone—of agreements entered into either before or after the enactment of the regulations.

Art. 67. Subject, where necessary, to the provisions of Article 63, certain powers with respect to legislation, administration and jurisdiction may by or in virtue of an agreement be conferred on organizations based on international law.

With regard to decisions made by organizations based on international law, Articles 65 and 66 shall similarly apply.

Art. 68. The King shall have supreme authority over the Armed Forces.

Military officers shall be appointed by him. They shall be promoted, discharged or pensioned by him, according to rules to be laid down by law. Pensions shall be regulated by law.

Art. 69–71. Repealed.

Art. 72. The King shall have the supreme direction of general finances. He shall fix the remuneration of all boards and officials who are paid from the exchequer of the Kingdom.

The law shall fix the remuneration of the Council of State, of the General Auditing Court, and of the judicial power.

The King shall include the remunerations in the estimates of expenditure of the Kingdom. The pensions of officials shall be fixed by law.

Art. 73. The King shall have the right of mintage. He may cause his image to be impressed on the coins.

Art. 74. The King confers nobility. Foreign nobility may not be accepted by any Netherlands subject.

Art. 75. Orders of Knighthood shall be founded by a law upon the King's proposal.

Art. 76. Foreign orders to which no obligations are attached may be accepted by the King, and with his consent, by the princes of his House.

In no case may other Netherlands subjects or those aliens who are in the service of the Netherlands State accept foreign insignia of orders, titles, rank, or dignity, without the King's special leave.

Art. 77. The King shall have the right to grant pardon in respect of penalties inflicted by judicial sentence.

He shall exercise this right after having ascertained the opinion of the judge designated for the purpose by general administrative measure.

Amnesty or annulment may not be granted except by a law.

Art. 78. Dispensation from legal provisions may only be granted by the King with the authorization of the law.

The law granting such authorization shall name the provisions to which the right of dispensation shall extend.

Dispensation from the provisions of general administrative measures shall be permitted in so far as in that measure the King shall have explicitly reserved to himself power to do so.

Art. 79. Disputes between provinces; between provinces and municipalities; between municipalities; and also between provinces or municipalities and drainage districts, peat-districts and peat-polders, not included among those referred to in Article 167 or those the settlement of which is committed by virtue of Article 168 to the ordinary judge or to a board entrusted with the adjustment of disputes arising from administrative law, shall be adjusted by the King.

Art. 80. The King shall submit drafts of laws to the States-General and shall make such other proposals to them as he shall deem necessary.

He shall have the right to approve or disapprove the bills passed by the States-General.

Art. 81. The manner of promulgating laws and general administrative measures and the time when they shall commence to be binding shall be regulated by law.

The form of promulgating laws shall be as follows:

We, &c., King of the Netherlands, &c.,

To all who shall see this or hear it read, greeting!

Be it known:

Whereas we have taken into consideration that, &c., (The reasons of the law)

Now therefore, we, having heard the Council of State, and with the joint deliberation of the States-General, have decreed and ordained, as we hereby do decree and ordain, &c. (The contents of the law)

Given, &c.

In case a Queen reigns or royal authority is exercised by a regent or by the Council of State, the modification necessary in consequence thereof shall be made in this form.

Art. 82. The King shall have the right to dissolve the Chambers of the States-General, each one seperately or both together. The decree whereby such dissolution is pronounced shall at the same time order the election of new chambers within forty days, and the assembly of the newly elected chambers within three months.

For the Chambers elected after dissolution, the duration of the session may be fixed by law for a period other than that appointed by Articles 95 and 101.

The Council of State, exercising royal authority, shall not exercise the right of dissolution.

Seventh Section. Of the Council of State, the Ministers, the Under-Secretaries of State, and the Permanent Boards of Advice and Collaboration

Art. 83. There is a Council of State, whose composition and powers shall be regulated by law.

The King shall be the President of the Council, and appoint the members.

The Prince of Orange and the King's daughter who is the heiress presumptive to the crown shall, by law, sit on the Council after they shall have completed their eighteenth year.

Art. 84. The King shall submit to the consideration of the Council all the proposals to be made by him to the States-General or made by the States-General to him, and also all general administrative measures.

It shall be stated at the head of the decrees to be issued that the Council of State has been heard concerning them.

The King shall moreover consult the council of state on all agreements with other powers and organizations based on international law requiring the approval of the States-General, as well as on all matters in which he deems it necessary to do so.

The King, alone, decides and he shall in each instance notify his decision to the Council of State.

Art. 85. The adjustment of disputes may be entrusted by law to the Council of State, or to a section of that Council.

Art. 86. The King shall constitute ministerial departments.

He shall appoint Ministers thereof, and remove them from office at will. He may appoint ministers without portfolio.

He may appoint to a department one or more Under-Secretaries of State, who in all cases in which the Minister, Head of the Department, deems this necessary, may act as Minister in his place observant of his directions. The Under-Secretary of State is responsible on that account without prejudice to the responsibility of the Minister, Head of the Department.

The provisions on Ministers in this article and in Articles 55, 104, 106, 107, 120 and 178 are of similar application to him.

The Ministers shall provide for the enforcement of the Constitution and of other laws, in so far as such enforcement depends on the crown.

Their responsibility shall be regulated by law.

On assuming office they shall take the following oath or make the following promise, which oath or promise shall be administered by the King:

> "I swear (promise) fidelity to the King and to the Constitution; I swear (promise) that I will faithfully perform all the duties which the office of a minister lays upon me.
>
> So help me, God Almighty! (That I promise!)."

Before being permitted to take this oath or make this promise, they shall take the following oath (make the following declaration and promise) of vindication:

> "I swear (declare) that in order to be appointed minister, I have not promised or given, directly or indirectly, any gifts or presents to any person under whatsoever name or pretext.
>
> I swear (promise) that in order to do or refrain from doing anything whatsoever in this office, I will not accept, directly or indirectly, any promises or presents from anyone whomsoever.
>
> So help me, God Almighty! (That I declare and promise!)."

All royal decrees and decisions shall be countersigned by one or more of the heads of the ministerial departments.

Art. 87. The constitution of permanent boards of advice and collaboration with the government shall be regulated by virtue of laws which shall also contain rules and regulations respecting their appointment, composition, procedure, and powers.

THIRD CHAPTER

OF THE STATES-GENERAL

First Section. Of the Composition of the States-General

Art. 88. The States-General shall represent the whole Netherlands people.

Art. 89. The States-General shall be divided into a First Chamber and a Second Chamber.

Art. 90. The members of the Second Chamber shall be elected direct by the inhabitants, the latter being Netherlanders or recognized by law as Netherlands subjects, who have reached an age to be fixed by law, which age shall not be under twenty-one years. Each elector shall have one vote only.

It shall be determined by law what extent the exercise of elective franchise shall be suspended for military personnel, for the time during they are performing military service.

Those persons shall be debarred from the right of exercising elective franchise to whom that right has been denied by irrevocable sentence of a court of law; those who are lawfully deprived of their liberty; those, who, by virtue of an irrevocable sentence of a court of law have lost the right to dispose of or administer their property on account of insanity or imbecility; and those who have been deprived of parental authority or guardianship over one more of their children. Temporary or permanent loss of elective franchise shall be connected by law with irrevocable condemnation to a penalty involving loss of liberty for more than one year, or on account of mendicancy or vagrancy, as well as with more than two irrevocable sentences of a court of law for drunkenness in public, occurring within a period to be fixed by law.

Art. 91. The Second Chamber shall consist of one hundred and fifty members, chosen on the basis of proportional representation within the limits to be determined by law.

All further matters relating to elective franchise and the method of election shall be regulated by law.

Art. 92. The First Chamber shall consist of seventy-five members. They shall be chosen by the members or the provincial states, on the basis of proportional representation within the limits to be imposed by law.

Art. 93. When the States-General are convoked in double numbers, the number of ordinary members of each chamber shall be increased by that number of extraordinary members, to be chosen in the same manner as the ordinary members.

The convoking decree shall at the same time indicate the day on which the election shall take place.

Second Section. Of the Second Chamber of the States-General

Art. 94. To be eligible as a member of the Second Chamber a person must be a Netherlander or recognized by law as a Netherlands subject, must have reached the age of twenty-five years, and must not have ceased to be eligible or have been deprived of the right to vote by virtue of the regulation in the third paragraph of Article 90, with the exception of the judicial deprivation of liberty and the condemnation to a penalty involving loss of liberty other than on account of mendicancy or vagrancy or on account of drunkeness in public.

Art. 95. The members of the Second Chamber shall be chosen for four years.

They shall vacate their seats simultaneously, and shall be re-eligible immediately.

Art. 96. The members shall vote without mandate or instructions from the electors.

Art. 97. When assuming office they shall take the following oath or make the following promise:

"I swear (promise) fidelity to the Constitution. So help me, God Almighty! (That I promise!)."

Before being permitted to take that oath or make that promise, they shall take the following oath (make the following declaration and promise) of vindication:

"I swear (declare) that in order to be appointed a member of the States-General, I have not promised or given, directly or indirectly, any gifts or presents to any person under whatsoever name or pretext.

I swear (promise) that in order to do or refrain from doing anything whatsoever in this office, I will not accept any promises or presents, directly or indirectly, from any person whomsoever.

So help me, God Almighty! (That I declare and promise!)."

These oaths (promises and declaration) shall be taken and made before the King or at the assembly of the Second Chamber before the president, authorized there to by the King.

Art. 98. The President shall be appointed by the King for the duration of a session, from a list of three members submitted by the Chamber.

Art. 99. The members shall receive an indemnity and a compensation for expenses incurred in the exercise of their functions according to rules to be fixed by law.

The President shall, in addition, be granted an annual allowance, the amount of which shall be fixed by law.

To the laws referred to in the preceding clause the provisions of the last paragraph of Article 30 shall apply. The members' pensions shall be regulated by law.

Rules may also be laid down by law regarding the granting of a temporary allowance on retirement. The pensions of widows and orphans of members or retired members shall be regulated by law.

Third Section. Of the First Chamber of the States-General

Art. 100. To be eligible as a member of the First Chamber, the same requirements must be fulfilled as for membership of the Second Chamber.

Art. 101. The members of the First Chamber shall be chosen for six years. Article 96 shall apply to them.

On assuming office they shall take similar oaths (make similar promises and declarations) as have been fixed for members of the Second Chamber, either before the King or at assembly of the First Chamber, before the President thereto authorized by the King.

Every three years thirty-eight and thirty-seven members shall retire alternately. The retiring members shall be re-eligible immediately. The members shall receive a compensation for expenses incurred in the exercise of their functions according to rules to be fixed by law. The President shall, in addition, be granted an annual allowance, the amount of which shall be fixed by law.

To the law regarding the allowance the provisions of the last paragraph of Article 30 shall apply.

Art. 102. The President shall be appointed by the King from among the members, for the duration of a session.

Fourth Section. Provisions Relating to Both Chambers

Art. 103. No person can be a member of both Chambers simultaneously. Any person chosen simultaneously as a member of both Chambers shall declare which of those appointments he accepts.

Art. 104. The ministers shall sit in both Chambers. They shall have as such only an advisory voice. They may arrange to be assisted at the assembly by such officials as they have designated for the purpose.

They shall furnish the Chambers, either orally or in writing, with any information desired, the furnishing of which cannot be regarded as being contrary to the interests of the State.

They may be invited by each of the Chambers to attend the assembly for that purpose.

Art. 105. Both Chambers, each one separately or in united assembly, shall have the right of investigation to be regulated by law.

Art. 106. A member of the States-General cannot simultaneously be a Minister, vice-president or member of the Council of State, President, Vice-President or member of, or Attorney-General or Solicitor-General to, the High Court, or President or member of the General Auditing Court, or King's commissioner in a province.

Nevertheless, a Minister who is chosen a member of the States-General on election may for a period of not more than three months hold both his ministerial post and his membership in the States-General. The law shall regulate, as far as necessary, the consequences of the union of membership of either of the Chambers with offices salaried from the Exchequer of the Kingdom, other than those excluded by the first paragraph. Military personnel on active service accepting membership of either of the two Chambers shall, during such membership, be regarded by law as not on active service. On ceasing to be members, they shall return to active service.

Art. 107. The members of the States-General, as well as the Minister the commissioners referred to in the second paragraph of Article 120, and the officials referred to in the first paragraph of Article 104, shall be exempt from prosecution for anything they have said at the assembly or have submitted to it in writing.

Art. 108. In so far as is not otherwise provided for by law, each Chamber shall examine the credentials of its newly elected members, and shall decide differences of opinion arising concerning those credentials or the election itself, according to rules to be laid down by law.

Art. 109. Each Chamber shall appoint its clerk.

The clerk may not at the same time be a member of one of the Chambers.

Art. 110. The States-General shall assemble at least once a year. Their ordinary session shall be opened on the third Tuesday in September.

The King shall convoke an extraordinary session as often as he shall consider necessary.

Art. 111. The separate meetings of the two Chambers, and likewise the united meetings, shall be held in public .

The doors shall be closed when a tenth part of the members present require this, or when the President considers it necessary to do so.

The meeting shall decide whether it will debate with closed doors.

Regarding points dealt with at a meeting held with closed doors, a decision may be taken at that meeting.

Art. 112. If on the death of the King or on the abdication of the crown the session is closed, the States-General shall meet without previous convocation.

This extraordinary meeting shall be held on the fifth day after the death or abdication. If the Chambers had been dissolved, this period shall begin to run as from the termination of the new elections.

Art. 113. The session of the States-General shall be opened in a united assembly of the two Chambers by the King or by a commission acting on his behalf. It shall be closed in the same manner when he considers that the interests of the State do not require its continuation.

The ordinary annual session shall last at least twenty days, unless the King avails himself of the right described in Article 82.

Art. 114. In dissolving either or both Chambers, the King shall at the same time close the session of the States-General.

Art. 115. The Chambers may not deliberate or decide either separately or in united assembly if there are not more than one half of the members present.

Art. 116. All decision about matters shall be taken by an absolute majority of the members voting.

In the event of the votes being equally divided, the taking of the decision shall be postponed until a subsequent meeting.

If at this meeting, and likewise at a meeting attended by all the members, the votes are equally divided, the proposal shall be regarded as not having been passed.

Voting shall take place by calling over the names of the members, if one of the members so desires, and orally in that case.

Art. 117. Voting for persons for the appointments or nominations mentioned in the Constitution shall take place by closed and unsigned voting papers.

The absolute majority of the voting members shall decide.

If the votes are equally divided, decision shall be by lot.

Art. 118. In the case of a united assembly, the two Chambers shall be regarded as being only one, and their members shall take their seats, at will.

The President of the First Chamber shall conduct the meeting.

First Section. Of the Legislature

Art. 119. The legislative power shall be exercised jointly by the King and the States-General.

Art. 120. The King shall send his proposals, either of law or others, to the Second Chamber in a written message or by a commission.

He may direct special commissioners designated by him to assist the Ministers in dealing with these proposals at the meetings of the States-General.

Art. 121. The public debate on any of the King's proposals' which have been received shall always be preceded by an examination of that proposal.

In its by-laws the Chamber shall determine the manner in which such examination shall be made.

Art. 122. The Second Chamber, and also the united assembly of the States-General, shall have the right to introduce changes in a proposal submitted by the King.

Art. 123. If the Second Chamber resolves to pass the proposal, either unchanged or changed, it shall send it to the First Chamber accompanied by the following form:

The Second Chamber of the States-General sends to the First Chamber the enclosed proposal of the King, and is of opinion that it should be passed by the States-General in its present form.

If the Second Chamber resolves not to pass the proposal, it shall give notice thereof to the King, by means of the following form:

The Second Chamber of the States-General expresses to the King its thanks for his zeal in promoting the interests of the State, and respectfully requests him to consider the proposal which he has made.

Art. 124. The First Chamber, duly observing Article 121, shall consider the proposal in the form in which it has been passed by the Second Chamber.

If it resolves to pass the proposal, it shall give notice thereof to the King and Second Chamber by means of the following forms.

To the King,

The States-General express to the King their thanks for his zeal in promoting the interests of the State, and agree to that proposal in its present form.

To the Second Chamber,

The First Chamber of the States-General notifies the Second Chamber that it has agreed to the proposal relative to . . ., which was sent to it by the Second Chamber on the . . .

If the First Chamber resolves not to pass the proposal, it shall give notice thereof to the King and to the Second Chamber by means of the following forms:

To the King,

The First Chamber of the States-General expresses to the King its thanks for his zeal in promoting the interests of the State, and respectfully requests him to reconsider the proposal which has been made.

To the Second Chamber.

To the Second Chamber.

The First Chamber of the States-General notifies the Second Chamber that it has respectfully requested the King to reconsider the proposal relative to . . ., which was sent to it by the Second Chamber on the . . .

Art. 125. As long as the First Chamber has not taken a decision, the King shall continue to have the power to withdraw the proposal which he has made.

Art. 126. The States-General shall have the right to make proposals of law to the King.

Art. 127. The right of initiative in respect of such a bill shall belong exclusively to the Second Chamber, which shall consider the bill in the same manner as the King's bills, and after passing it shall send to the First Chamber by means of the following form:

The Second Chamber of the States-General sends to the First Chamber the enclosed bill, and is of opinion that the States-General should request the King's assent thereto.

It shall have the power to entrust one or more of its members with the written and oral defence of its bill in the First Chamber.

Art. 128. If the First Chamber, after having deliberated on the bill in the usual manner, approves it, it shall send it to the King by means of the following form:

The States-General, considering that the enclosed bill might serve to promote the interests of the State, respectfully request the King's assent thereto.

It shall, furthermore, give notice thereof to the Second Chamber, by means of the following form:

The First Chamber of the States-General notifies the Second Chamber that it has agreed to the bill relative to . . . received form the Second Chamber on the . . ., and in the name of the States-General has requested the King's assent thereto.

If the First Chamber does not approve the bill, it shall give notice thereof to the Second Chamber by means of the following form:

The First Chamber of the States-General has not found sufficient reason to request the King's assent to the bill returned herewith.

Art. 129. Other proposals than drafts of laws may be made to the King by each chamber separately.

Art. 130. The King shall notify the States-General as soon as possible whether he approves or disapproves a bill which has been passed by them. Such notification shall take place by means of one of the following forms:

The King agrees to the bill,

or

The King is keeping the bill under consideration.

Art. 131. All bills passed by the States-General and approved by the King shall acquire the force of law and shall be promulgated by the King.

The laws shall be inviolable.

Art. 132. Repealed.

Sixth Section. Of the Budget

Art. 133. The estimates of all expenditure of the Kingdom, and the means for the defrayal thereof, shall be fixed by law.

Art. 134. The drafts of the general budget laws shall be submitted by the King to the Second Chamber, immediately after the opening of the ordinary session of the States-General before the commencement of the period for which the estimates are intended. This period may not exceed two years.

Art. 135. No chapter of the estimates of expenditure may comprise more than those for one department of general administration. Each chapter shall be comprised in one or more bills. Transference may be allowed by such a law.

Art. 136. The rendering of account of state expenditure and revenue for each (branch of) service shall be made to the legislature in accordance with the provisions of the law, accompanied by the account approved by the auditing court.

FOURTH CHAPTER

OF THE PROVINCIAL STATES

AND MUNICIPAL GOVERNMENTS

First Section. Of the composition of the Provincial States

Art. 137. The members of the Provincial States shall be elected direct for a number of years to be fixed by law by the inhabitants of the province, the latter being Netherlanders or recognized by law as Netherlands subjects, who have reached an age to be fixed by law, which age shall shall not be under twenty-one years.

Election shall take place in accordance with the proportional representation principle within the limits to be determined by law.

The last sentence of the first paragraph and the second and third paragraphs of Article 90 shall apply.

They shall vacate their seats simultaneously, and shall be re-eligible immediately. To be eligible as a member of the provincial states a person is required to be a Netherlander or recognized by law as a Netherlands subject and an inhabitant of the province, to have completed the age of twenty-five years, not to be deprived of eligibility, or excluded from exercising elective franchise by virtue of the regulations made on the subject pursuant to the third paragraph of Article 90, with the exception of judicial deprivation of liberty and condemnation to a penalty involving loss of liberty otherwise than on account of mendicancy or vagrancy or on account of a fact showing drunkenness in public. The election of the members of the provincial states shall take place in the manner to be regulated by law.

Art. 138. Repealed.

Art. 139. The meetings of the states shall be public, with the same reservation as provided for in Article 111 in respect of the meetings of the Chambers of the States-General.

Art. 140. The members of the states shall vote without mandate or instructions from the electors.

Art. 141. With regard to deliberations and voting, the rules shall apply which are laid down in Articles 115, 116, 117, first paragraph, in respect of the Chambers of the States-General.

Second Section. Of the Powers of the Provincial States

Art. 142. The authority and powers of the states shall be regulated by law with due observance of the provisions contained in the following Articles of this section.

Art. 143. To the states shall be left the regulation and administration of the domestic affairs of the province. They shall make the ordinances which they consider necessary in the provincial interests.

Art. 144. Whenever the laws or general administrative measures so require, the states shall afford their co-operation in giving effect thereto.

Art. 145. Each resolution of the states to introduce, modify or abolish a provincial tax shall require the King's approval. It may be laid down by law that also other ordinances shall, according to rules to be fixed by law, require the King's approval; the approval of such ordinances may not be refused otherwise than by means of a decree setting forth the reasons therefore, after the Council of State has been heard.

General rules with regard to provincial taxes shall be laid down by law.

Such taxes may not obstruct conveyance in transit, exportation to, or importation from, other provinces.

Art. 146. The estimates of provincial revenue and expenditure to be drawn up annually by the states shall require the King's approval.

The fixation of the provincial account shall be regulated by law.

Art. 147. The states may advocate the interests of their provinces and inhabitants to the King and to the States-General.

Art. 148. The states shall appoint from their midst a board of deputies to which, according to rules to be laid down by law, the daily conduct and execution of affairs shall be entrusted, whether the states are assembled or not.

Art. 149. The power of the King to suspend and annul the resolutions of the provincial states and of boards of deputies which are contrary to law or general interests shall be regulated by law.

Art. 150. The King shall appoint in each province a commissioner entrusted with the execution of his commands.

This commissioner shall be the president of the meeting of the provincial states and of that of boards of deputies, and shall have a vote in the latter board.

His salary and the cost of his official residence shall be included in the estimates of expenditure of the Kingdom. It shall be decided by law whether other expenditure of the provincial government shall be for the account of the Kingdom.

Third Section. Of Municipal Government

Art. 151. The composition, organization, and powers of municipal governments shall be regulated by law with due observance of the rules contained in the following Articles of this Section.

Art. 152. At the head of the municipality there shall be a council whose members shall be elected direct for a specified number of years by the inhabitants of the municipality, the latter being Netherlanders or recognized by law as Netherlands subjects, who have reached an age to be fixed by law, which age shall not be under twenty-one years.

Election shall take place in accordance with the proportional representation principle within the limits to be determined by law.

The last sentence of the first paragraph and the second and third paragraphs of Article 90 shall apply.

To be eligible as a member of the council, a person is required to be a Netherlander or recognized by law as a Netherlands subject and an inhabitant of the municipality, to have completed the age of twenty-three years, not to be deprived of eligibility or excluded from exercising the elective franchise by virtue of the regulations made on the subject pursuant to the third paragraph of Article 90, with the exception of judicial deprivation of liberty and condemnation to a penalty involving a loss of liberty otherwise than on account of mendicancy or vagrancy or on account of a fact showing drunkeness in public.

The election of the council shall take place in the manner to be regulated by law.

The president shall be appointed by the King from amongst members of the council or from amongst non-members, and shall be removed from office by the King.

Art. 153. To the council shall be left the regulation and administration of domestic affairs of the municipality.

With due observance of rules to be laid down, the council may, in certain cases to be specified, entrust to other organs, under the council's supervision, the whole or a part of the administration of certain branchess of domestic affairs of the municipality, which branches are to be specified. It shall make the ordinances which it considers necessary in the interests of the municipality.

When laws, general administrative measures, or provincial ordinances so require, municipal governments shall afford their co-operation in giving effect thereto.

Should the regulation and administration of the municipal affairs be grossly neglected, a law may determine the manner in which the government of that municipality shall be provided for in deviation from the first and second paragraphs of this Article.

It shall be determined by law which authority shall replace the municipal government in the event of its failing to give effect to laws, general administrative measures, or provincial ordinances.

Art. 154. The King's power to suspend and annul resolutions of municipal governments which are contrary to law or the general interests shall be regulated by law.

Art. 155. The resolutions of municipal governments concerning such disposal of municipal property, or such other actions under civil law as are designated by law, as well as estimates of revenue and expenditure, shall be submitted to the approval of the boards of deputies.

The compilation of the estimates and the drawing up of the accounts shall be regulated by law.

Art. 156. Resolutions of municipal governments concerning the introduction, modification, or abolition of a local tax shall require the King's approval. General rules regarding local taxes shall be laid down by law.

These taxes may not obstruct conveyance in transit, exportation to, or importation from, other municipalities.

Art. 157. Municipal governments may advocate the interests of their municipalities and inhabitants to the King, States-General and states of the province to which they belong.

Art. 158. Provision shall be made by law in affairs, interests , establishments, or works in which two or more municipalities are involved.

FIFTH CHAPTER

OF PUBLIC BODIES

FOR PROFESSIONS AND TRADES

Art. 159. Bodies for certain professions and trades and groups thereof, and also for professional and economic life in general, may be instituted by law in order to take regulatory action. The composition, institution and powers of these bodies shall be regulated by law.

Art. 160. To these bodies regulatory powers may be granted by law.

Art. 161. The decisions of these bodies which conflict with the law or public interest may be suspended and annulled in accordance with regulations to be determined by law.

The law may render certain decisions of these bodies subject to approval in accordance with regulations to be determined by the law.

SIXTH CHAPTER

OF OTHER BODIES WITH REGULATORY POWERS

Art. 162. The law may give the power to issue orders to bodies other those mentioned in the Constitution.

SEVENTH CHAPTER

OF THE JUDICIAL POWER

First Section. General Provisions

Art. 163. Throughout the Kingdom justice shall be administered in the name of the King.

Art. 164. Civil and commercial law, civil and military penal law, procedure, and the organization of the judicial power, shall be regulated by law in general codes, without prejudice to the power of the legislature to regulate certain subjects in separate laws.

Art. 165. Expropriation for reasons of public utility cannot take place except after a previous declaration by law that public utility requires expropriation and against previously received or previously assured compensation, all in accordance with rules laid down by law.

It shall be determined by law in which cases the previous declaration by law shall not be required. The requirement that the compensation shall be paid or assured beforehand shall not apply if war, danger of war, riot, fire, or flood require that possession be taken immediately.

This Article shall not apply to rights of fetching soil which existed in 1886.

Art. 166. When in the public interests the public authority has to destroy property or render it unserviceable either permanently or temporarily, this shall take place against compensation, unless the contrary is stipulated by law.

The use of property for the preparation and effecting of military inundations, if required on account of war or danger of war, shall be regulated by law.

Art. 167. All lawsuits about property or rights arising therefrom, about claims on account of debt and other civil rights, shall belong exclusively to the cognizance of the judicial power.

Art. 168. The decision of lawsuits not connected with those referred to in Article 167 may be referred by law either to the ordinary judge or to a board entrusted with the decision of disputes arising from administrative law; such law shall regulate the procedure and the consequences of the decisions.

Art. 169. The judicial power shall be exercised solely by judges designated by law. Such law may provide that persons not belonging to the judicial power shall also take part in the settlement of the lawsuits referred to in Article 167 and designated by that law.

Art. 170. No person may be withdrawn against his will from the judge whom the law assigns to him.

The manner in which disputes about competency which have arisen between the administrative power and the judicial power shall be decided shall be regulated by law.

Art. 171. Except in the cases determined by law, no person may be arrested otherwise than under an order of the judge stating the reasons for the arrest. This order must be served on the person against whom it is directed either at the moment of arrest or immediately afterwards.

The form of this order and the time within which all arrested persons must be heard shall be fixed by law.

Art. 172. To enter a dwelling against the occupant's will shall only be permitted in the cases determined by law, by virtue of a special or general order given by an authority designated by law. The forms to which the exercise of this power shall be bound shall be regulated by law.

Art. 173. The secrecy of letters entrusted to the postal service or to other public institutions of conveyance shall be inviolable, except by order of a judge in the cases described by law.

Art. 174. The general forfeiture of the goods belonging to an offender may not be inflicted as a penalty for any crime.

Art. 175. All judgments shall state the grounds upon which they are based, and in penal cases they shall indicate the legal provisions upon which the condemnation is based.

The pronouncement of sentence shall take place with open doors.

Without prejudice to the exceptions made by law, the hearings shall be public.

In the interests of public order and morality, the judge may depart from this rule.

For punishable acts designated by law, the provisions of the first and second paragraphs may also be departed from.

Second Section. Of the Judicial Power

Art. 176. There is a supreme court of justice called the High Court of the Netherlands, the members of which shall be appointed by the King in conformity with the following Article.

Art. 177. The occurrence of a vacancy shall be notified by the High tCour to the Second Chamber of the States-General which, for the purpose of filling the vacancy, shall submit the names of three persons to the King in order that a selection may be made therefrom.

The King shall appoint the President and Vice-President from amongst the members of the High Court.

Art. 178. The members of the States-General, the heads of the ministerial departments, the governors of Surinam and of the Netherlands Antilles, the members of the Council of State and the King's Commissioners in the provinces shall be liable to trial by the High Court, even after their retirement, for indictable acts committed in discharging their official duties, proceedings having been entered against them by the King or by the Second Chamber.

It may be determined by law that other officials and members of high boards shall be liable to trial by the High Court for punishable acts committed in the exercise of their functions.

Art. 179. The High Court shall supervise the regular course and settlement of lawsuits, as well as the observance of the laws by the members of the judicial power and by those persons referred to at the conclusion of Article 169. If their proceedings, orders, and sentences are contrary to the laws, the High Court may annul them and render them inoperative according to the provisions to be made on the subject by law and without prejudice to the exceptions made by law.

The further powers of the High Court shall be regulated by law.

Art. 180. The members of the judicial power shall be appointed by the King.

The members of the judicial power entrusted with the administration of justice, and the attorney-general to the High Court, shall be appointed for life.

It may be determined by law that on attaining a certain age they shall be retired.

They shall be deposed or removed from office by a verdict of the High Court in the cases designated by law.

At their own request the King may retire them.

If a board is entrusted with the decision of disputes arising from administrative law in the highest instance for the Kingdom, the first, second, third, and fifth paragraphs of this Article apply to the members thereof. They may be deposed or removed from office in the manner and cases designated by law.

This Article shall not apply to those who are entrusted exclusively with the administration of justice over persons belonging to the Armed Forces or with the decision of disciplinary cases.

EIGHTH CHAPTER

OF RELIGION

Art. 181. Every person shall profess his religious opinions with perfect liberty, without prejudice to the protection of society and its members against the violation of the penal laws.

Art. 182. All religious communities in the Kingdom shall be afforded equal protection.

Art. 183. The professors of the several religions shall all enjoy the same civil and civic rights, and shall have equal claim to the holding of dignities, offices, and employment.

Art. 184. All public divine services within buildings and enclosed places shall be permitted, without prejudice to the measures required to ensure public order and peace. Subject to the same provision, public divine services outside buildings and enclosed places shall continue to be permitted where they are at present allowed according to laws and regulations.

Art. 185. The stipends, pensions, and other revenues of whatsoever kind, which are at present received by the several religious denominations or by their ministers, shall remain assured to those denominations.

Those ministers who, up to the present, have not received any stipend or who have received an insufficient stipend from the Exchequer of the Kingdom, may be granted stipends or their existing stipends may be increased.

Art. 186. The King shall see that all religious communities keep within the limits of obedience to the laws of the State.

Art. 187. The government's intermediary shall not be required in corresponding with the heads of the several religious communities, or, without prejudice to responsibility according to law, in publishing ecclesiastical rules.

NINTH CHAPTER

OF FINANCE

Art. 188. No taxes may be levied on behalf of the Exchequer of the Kingdom, except by virtue of a law.

This provision shall also apply to imposts for the use of works and establishments of the Kingdom, in so far as the regulation of such imposts has not been reserved to the King.

Art. 189. No privileges may be granted in the matter of taxes.

Art. 190. The obligations of the State towards its creditors shall be guaranteed. The debt shall be considered every year for the purpose of promoting the interests of the creditors of the State.

Art. 191. The weight, fineness, and value of the coinage shall be regulated by law.

Art. 192. The supervision and direction of the affairs of the mint and the decision of disputes about alloy, assay and other matters shall be regulated by law.

Art. 193. There is a General Auditing Court, the composition and duties of which shall be regulated by law.

On the occurrence of a vacancy in this court, the Second Chamber of the States-General shall send the names of three persons to the King, who shall appoint therefrom.

The members of the Auditing Court shall be appointed for life.

The third, fourth and fifth paragraphs of Article 180 shall apply to them.

TENTH CHAPTER

OF DEFENCE

Art. 194. All Netherlanders who are able shall be bound to collaborate for the maintenance of the independence of the Kingdom and for the defence of its territory. This obligation may also be laid upon residents who are not Netherlanders.

Art. 195. For the protection of the interests of the State there are the Armed Forces, composed of volunteers and conscripts. Obligatory military service shall be regulated by law. Such law shall also regulate the obligations in respect of the defence of the Kingdom which may be laid upon those persons who do not belong to the Armed Forces.

Art. 196. The conditions upon which exemption from military service may be granted on account of serious conscientious objections shall be stated by law.

Art. 197. Foreign troops may not be employed except by virtue of a law.

Art. 198 and 199. Repealed.

Art. 200. When, in the case of war, danger of war, or other exceptional circumstances, those conscripts who are not on active service are called up by the King to join the colors either wholly or partly "extra-ordinarily," a draft of law shall be submitted without delay to the States-General for the purpose of enacting that the conscripts shall remain with the colors as long as necessary.

Art. 201. All the expenditure for the armies of the Kingdom shall be defrayed from the Exchequer of the Kingdom. The billeting and maintenance of the troops, the transports and supplies of whatsoever nature required for the armies and works of defence of the Kingdom, cannot be laid upon one or more inhabitants or municipalities, except according to general rules to be laid down by law and against compensation. The exceptions to these general rules for the event of war, danger of war, or other exceptional circumstances shall be fixed by law.

The King shall decide whether danger of war exists in the sense in which that term occurs in the laws of the Kingdom.

Art. 202. For the maintenance of external or internal security, every part of the territory of the Kingdom may be declared by, or in name of, the King to be in a state of war or siege. The manner and cases in which this may be done shall be determined, and the consequences thereof regulated, by law. Such regulation may enact that the constitutional powers of the civil authority in respect of public order and police shall pass wholly or in part to the military authority, and that the civil authorities shall become subordinate to the military.

Moreover, the provisions of Articles 7, and 9, 172, and 173 of the Constitution may, in that case, be departed from. In the event of war, the first paragraph of Article 170 may also be departed from.

Art. 203. For the maintenance of exernal or internal security, in extraordinary circumstances, it may be decreed by, or in the name of, the King, for any part of the territory of the Kingdom, that the constitutional powers of organs of civil authority in respect of public order and the police are transferred in whole or in part to other organs of civil authority. The manner in which such may take place and the occasions on which such may happen, shall be laid down by statute, which also provides the consequences. The provision of the third paragraph of Article 202 is thereby of equal application.

ELEVENTH CHAPTER

OF THE WATER AFFAIRS ADMINISTRATION

Art. 204. Rules regarding the administration of water affairs ("*Waterstaat*"), including supreme control and superintendence, shall be laid down by law with due observance of the provisions contained in the following Articles of the chapter.

Art. 205. The King shall have the supreme control of everything that concerns water affairs ("*Waterstaat*"), irrespective of whether the cost thereof is paid from the Exchequer of the Kingdom or defrayed in some other manner.

Art. 206. The provincial states shall have the superintendence of all works relating to water affairs, drainage districts, peat districts, and peat polders. Nevertheless the superintendence of certain works may be entrusted to others by law. The states shall have the power, subject to the King's approval, to make changes in existing organizations and regulations of drainage districts, peat districts, and peat polders to abolish drainage districts, peat districts, and peat polders and to establish new ones, and to fix new regulations for such institutions. The boards of such institutions, may submit to the provincial states proposals for the alteration of the organizations or regulations.

Art. 207. The boards of drainage districts, peat districts, and peat polders may make ordinances in the domestic interests of those institutions in accordance with rules to be laid down by law.

TWELFTH CHAPTER

OF EDUCATION AND POOR RELIEF

Art. 208. Education shall be an object of constant solicitude on the part of the government.

The imparting of education shall be free, saving superintendence by the government, and moreover, in so far as general education, elementary as well as secondary, is concerned, saving the examination with regard to the ability and morality of the teacher, the whole to be regulated by law. Public education shall be regulated by law, every person's religious views being duly respected.

In each municipality the authorities shall impart sufficient public general elementary education in an adequate number of schools. According to rules to be laid down by law, deviation from this provision may be permitted, provided that opportunity is given for such education to be received. The standards of efficiency to be prescribed for education to be defrayed wholly or in part from public funds shall be regulated by law, with due observance in so far as private education is concerned, of ideological freedom.

These standards shall be regulated for general elementary education in such a manner as to guarantee equally well the efficiency of the private education defrayed entirely from public funds and public education. In these regulations the freedom of private education concerning the choice of means of instruction and that appointment of teachers shall, particularly, be respected.

Private general elementary education fulfilling conditions to be imposed by law shall be defrayed from public funds according to the same standards as public education.

The education upon which private general secondary education and preparatory university education shall be granted contributions from public funds shall be fixed by law.

The King shall cause a report of the condition on education to be made annually to the States-General.

Art. 209. Poor relief shall be an object of constant solicitude on the part of the government, and shall be regulated by law. The King shall cause a detailed report of the relevant activities to be made annually to the States-General.

THIRTEENTH CHAPTER

OF CHANGES

Art. 210. Every proposal for the alteration of the Constitution shall explicitly indicate the proposed change. It shall be declared by a law that grounds exist for considering the proposal in the form in which that law fixes it.

Art. 211. After the promulgation of this law, the chambers shall be dissolved. The new chambers shall consider that proposal, and cannot pass the alteration proposed to them in conformity with the aforesaid, law otherwise than by two thirds of the votes given.

Art. 212. The changes in the Constitution fixed by the King and States-General shall be solemnly promulgated and added to the Constitution.

Art. 213. The text of the Constitution may be brought into line by law with the Charter for the Kingdom of the Netherlands as it now reads or as it should subsequently come to read.

The provisions of Articles 210, 211 and 212 shall not apply in this respect.

Art. 214. The text of the revised Constitution shall be promulgated by the King. The chapters, the sections of each chapter and the articles may be numbered consecutively by him; he shall, in so far as necessary, alter the references.

Art. 215. The authorities, binding laws, rules and decrees existing at the moment of promulgation of a change in the Constitution shall continue to be maintained until they have been replaced by others in pursuance of the Constitution.

ADDITIONAL ARTICLES

Art. I. The seignorial rights concerning nomination or appointment of persons to public or ecclesiastical offices are hereby abolished.

The abolition of the remaining seignorial rights and indemnification of the owners may be determined upon and regulated by law.

Art. II. The first paragraph of Article 166 shall not be applied until the coming into force of the legal regulations respecting the cases in which no compensation shall be granted in case of the destruction of property or the rendering unserviceable, permanently or temporarily, of property.

Art. III. The law mentioned in the fourth paragraph of Article 99 shall ensure no pensions to widows and orphans of ex-members of the Chamber who retired or died prior to January 1, 1921.

Art. IV. (1) Indemnity as referred to in Article 99, to which claim may be laid under the regulations maintained in virtue of Article 215 of the Constitution, shall not be received by those members who hold the office of Minister, nor by those members who, in accordance with the standing orders of the Chamber, are excluded from attending its sessions.
(2) The following provisions shall apply to a pension received by retired and retiring members of the Second Chamber of the States-General, under the regulations maintained in virtue of Article 215 of the Constitution, until such time as the entry into force of an enactment as referred to in the first sentence of the third paragraph of Article 99.
(3) The pension shall not be received as long as a retired member holds office as Minister or if such member, after re-election, receives the indemnity referred to in Article 99.
(4) The amounts of the pension and of its maximum may be modified by a law. Until such time as the entry into force of an enactment as referred to in the first sentence of the third paragraph of Article 99, the Chambers of the States-General may pass the relevant bill, including the bill amending or repealing such enactment, only by a two-thirds vote of the total membership of each Chamber.
(5) The enactment referred to in the first sentence of the third paragraph of Article 99 shall provide that the regulations which it contains shall not apply and that, instead, the provisions concerning the pension referred to in the second paragraph of this article shall continue to be in force in respect of:
(a) any person who on the day preceding the date of the entry into force of that enactment is entitled to a pension as a retired member of the Second Chamber of the States-General and who, within a period of three months after the date of the entry into force of that enactment, expresses a wish to that effect in writing;
(b) any person who on the day preceding the date of the entry into force of that enactment is a member of the Second Chamber of the States-General and who, within a period of three months after the date on which he retired without being immediately re-elected and admitted, expresses a wish to that effect in writing.

Art. V. Unless the Second Chamber of the States-General has in the meantime been dissolved, the *Centraal Stembureau* (i.e. Central Election Office) for the election of members of the Second Chamber of the States-General shall, within two months after the solemn promulgation of the amendment to the Constitution for increasing the number of members of the Chamber, on a day to be fixed by the King, declare fifty new members appointed to fill the new vacancies, in accordance with the following provisions. The Central Election Office shall, on the basis of the results of the latest election for the Second Chamber, ascertain how many seats should, in view of the increased number of members of the Chamber, be allocated to each list, on the proviso that no seats will be allocated to a group of lists, a set of identical lists, a or single list to which no seats were allocated as a result of the latest election. The number of seats already allocated to a certain list is then deducted from the number of seats thus allocated to the list. The vacancies thereafter remaining for a list are filled by corresponding application of the provisions of Chapter V of the Franchise Act, after the order of the names of the candidates on the list, referred to in Article N 19 of that Act, has been altered in so far as necessary and with due observance of the new list quota to be determined. If a candidate should have to be declared appointed on more than one list, the provisions of Article N 18 of the Franchise Act shall apply correspondingly.

As from the twenty-first day after the new members have been declared appointed, the Chamber shall be regarded as being composed in accordance with Article 91.

The new members shall retire simultaneously with the sitting members.

Art. VI. Unless the First Chamber of the States-General has in the meantime been dissolved, an election for a new First Chamber shall be held within two months of the solemn promulgation of the amendment to the Constitution for increasing the number of members of the Chamber. As from the twenty-first day after the result of this election becomes known, the sitting members shall retire and the new members shall take their seats.

Article P 2, Article P 5 and the second paragraph of Article S 1 of the Franchise Act shall apply correspondingly.

Until further provisions have been laid down in this respect by law, the following amendments shall be made to the Franchise Act:

(a) In the second paragraph of Article P 1, the numbers 13, 13, 12 and 12 shall be replaced by 21, 19, 17 and 18.

(b) The fourth paragraph of Article P 1 shall read:

(4) Every three years thirty-eight and thirty-seven members of the First Chamber shall retire alternately, namely the thirty-eight members elected in the provinces of North Brabant, Zeeland, Utrecht, Limburg, North Holland and Friesland and the thirty-seven members elected in the provinces of Gelderland, Overijssel, Groningen, Drenthe and South Holland alternately. The retiring members shall be immediately eligible for re-election.

(c) Article P 2 shall read:

When the First Chamber is dissolved it shall be decided by lot whether the thirty-eight or thirty-seven members referred to in the fourth paragraph of Article P 1 shall retire as from the third Tuesday in September in the third calendar year after the next third Tuesday in September. Members not drawing this lot shall retire as from the third Tuesday in September in the sixth calendar year after the next third Tuesday in

September. The retiring members shall be immediately eligible for re-election.

(d) In the second paragraph of Article Q 3 the words "ten candidates" shall be replaced by "fifteen candidates."

Art. VII. The supervision of the municipalities in reclaimed areas not yet apportioned to any province shall be regulated by law.

NORWAY

SUMMARY

INTERNATIONAL STATUS

Norway is a member of the United Nations (November 27, 1945).[1] It is a member of the Nordic Council, the European Free Trade Association and other international organizations. It was a member of the League of Nations.

Norway was united to Denmark until 1814 when it was ceded to Sweden by the Treaty of Kiel of January 14, 1814. It declared itself independent

[1] Norway has accepted to the compulsory jurisdiction of the International Court under Article 36 of its Statute.

under a Danish prince. A convention of August 14, 1814, provided for the independence of Norway in union with Sweden under the Swedish king. Its constitution was promulgated on May 17, 1814, and vested supreme authority in Parliament with suffrage extended to all persons paying taxes. In 1884 cabinet responsibility was accepted by the King. In June 1905, the union with Sweden was dissolved. Norway was invaded and occupied by Germany in the Second World War.

FORM OF NATIONAL GOVERNMENT

The Constitution of Norway, formerly the Fundamental Act, of May 17, 1814, as amended to 1964, states that Norway is a free, independent, individual and inalienable realm with a limited and hereditary monarchy.[1] The Evangelical Lutheran religion is the religion of the State.[2] The Storting may, by a three-fourths majority, consent that an international organization of which Norway is a member shall have the right to exercise powers normally vested in Norwegian authorities, exclusive of the power to alter the Constitution.[3]

RIGHTS OF THE PEOPLE

The Constitution guarantees due process of law and forbids torture, retroactive laws and unlawful detention, guarantees freedom of press and speech, inviolability of the domicile, forbids any privileges implying restrictions on the freedom of trade, forbids forfeiture of land and goods, forbids the creation of titles, states that the governmental authority must provide conditions for all the earn their living by work.[4] All citizens are bound to defend the State.[5]

LEGISLATIVE DEPARTMENT

Legislative power is exercised by the people through the Parliament or Storting, composed of two divisions, the Lagting and the Odelsting.[6] The 150 deputies are elected by universal suffrage and proportional representation for a term of four years.[7] They then nominate from among themselves one quarter of the total to constitute the Lagting and the remaining three quarters constitutes the Odelsting[8] Immunities of representatives are provided.[9] The Storting meets in one regular session a year.[10]

[1] Const., Art. 1. [2] Id., Art. 2. [3] Id., Art. 93. [4] Id., Art. 96–110.
[5] Id., Art. 109. [6] Id., Art. 49. [7] Id., Art. 50, 54, 57, 59, 71.
[8] Id., Art. 73. [9] Id., Art. 66. [10] Id., Art. 68.

EXECUTIVE DEPARTMENT

Executive power is vested in the King who must be of the Evangelical Lutheran religion and whose person is sacred and inviolable.[1] He has the power of appointment, right of pardon, grants honors, commands the Armed Forces.[2] The Council, composed of a Prime Minister and other ministers is responsible.[3] Ministers may not be members of the Storting.[4]

JUDICIAL DEPARTMENT

The Constitution provides for a Constitutional Court of the Realm to act in cases of impeachment.[5] There is provision for a Supreme Court of Justice which is a court of final appeal.[6] Its opinion may be demanded on points of law by the Storting.[7] It is an established constitutional practise that courts refuse to pass judicial sentence according to laws which are at variance with the Constitution.[8]

AREA, POPULATION, ETC.

The area of Norway is 323,884.54 square kilometres, its population (1965) 3,723,000. The capital is Oslo.

[1] Id., Art. 3–5. [2] Id., Art. 12, 20–23, 25. [3] Id., Art. 5, 12.
[4] Id., Act., 62. [5] Id., Art. 86. [6] Id., Art. 88. [7] Id., Art. 83.
[8] See note to Art. 49, 88.

CONSTITUTION of NORWAY[1]

May 17, 1814, as amended to May 4, 1964

A. FORM OF GOVERNMENT AND RELIGION

1. The Kingdom of Norway[2] is a free, independent, indivisible and inalienable [3] realm. Its form of Government is a limited and hereditary monarchy.

2. All inhabitants of the realm have the right to freedom of religion.

The Evangelical-Lutheran religion shall remain the public religion of the State. The inhabitants professing it shall be bound to bring up their children in the same.

B. THE EXECUTIVE POWER,

THE KING, AND THE ROYAL FAMILY

3. The Executive Power is vested in the King.

4. The King shall always profess the Evangelical-Lutheran religion, and maintain and protect the same.

5. The King's person shall be sacred; he cannot be blamed nor accused. The responsibility shall rest with his Council.

6. The order of succession shall be lineal and agnatic, whereby only male, born in lawful wedlock, may succeed male; the nearer line shall pass before the more remote, and the elder in the line before the younger.

Among those entitled to the succession shall be considered also an unborn child, who shall immediately take his proper place in the line of

[1] Published in English by Norwegian Universities Press, Oslo, 1962 (third revised edition). Supplied, together with latest amendments, by Ministry of Foreign Affairs in February 1966. Ed.

[2] Norwegian Mainland, Svalbard (Spitsbergen) with Bear Island and the island of Jan Mayen.

[3] Norway's Antarctic possessions (Bouvet Island, Peter I's Island and the Antarctic Sector (Queen Maud Land) between the Falkand Islands Dependencies and the Australian Antarctic Dependencies) are *not* regarded as a constitutional part of the motherland.

succession the moment he is born into the world after the death of his father.

When a Prince entitled to succeed to the Crown of Norway is born, his name and the time of his birth shall be notified to the first Storting thereafter held, and be entered in the record of its proceedings.

7. If there is no Prince entitled to the succession, the King may propose his successor to the Storting, which has the right to elect another candidate if the King's nominee is not acceptable.

8. The age of majority of the King shall be fixed by law.[1]

As soon as the King has attained the age of majority fixed by law, he shall make a public declaration that he has arrived at his majority.

9. As soon as the King, being of full age, assumes the authority of Government, he shall make to the Storting the following oath:

"I promise and swear that I will govern the Kingdom of Norway in accordance with its Constitution and Laws, so truly help me God, the Almighty and Omniscient!"

If the Storting is not in session at the time, the oath shall be made in writing to the Council of State, and be repeated solemnly by the King at the next ensuing session of the Storting.

10. (*Repealed*).

11. The King shall reside in the Kingdom and may not, without the consent of the Storting, stay outside the Kingdom for more than six months at a time; otherwise he shall have forfeited, for his person, his right to the Crown.

The King may not accept any other crown or government without the consent of the Storting, a majority of two thirds of the votes being required.

12. The King himself [2] chooses a Council of Norwegian citizens, who must not be under thirty years of age. The Council shall consist of a Prime Minister and at least seven other members.

More than half the number of the members of the Council of State shall profess the public religion of the State.

The King shall apportion the business among the members of the Council of State, as he deems suitable. On extraordinary occasions, the King may summon other Norwegian citizens to take a seat in the Council of State, beside the ordinary members of the Council of the State, but no member of the Storting may be summoned thus.

Husband and wife, parents and children, or brothers and sisters, may not, at the same time, have a seat in the Council of State.

13. During his travels within the Kingdom, the King may leave the

[1] 21 years of age.

[2] Since 1884 the King has always chosen Councils which have enjoyed the confidence of the Storting. It must be considered a firm constitutional custom that a Government is bound to resign if the Storting makes clear that it desires a change of government.

Government to the Council of State. The Council of State shall conduct the Government in the King's name and on his behalf. They shall inviolably observe the provisions of this Constitution as well as the particular constitutionally valid directions which the King may give by Instruction.

The matters of business shall be decided by vote; in the case of an equality of votes, the Prime Minister, or, in his absence, the next highest ranking member present of the Council of State, shall have two votes.

The Council of State shall make a report to the King of the matters of the business which have been dealt with thus.

14. (*Repealed*).

15. (*Repealed*).

16. The King shall give directions for all public Church services and public worship, all meetings and conventions dealing with religious matters, and shall ensure that the public teachers of religion follow the rules prescribed for them.

17. The King may issue and repeal Ordinances concerning commerce, tariffs, trade and industry, and police; they must not, however, be at variance with the Constitution or the laws passed by the Storting (as hereinafter prescribed in sections 77, 78 and 79). They shall be in force provisionally until the next Storting.

18. The King shall, as an ordinary rule, cause the taxes and duties imposed by the Storting to be collected.

19. The King shall watch over the management of the estates belonging to the State, and its privileged controls and monopolies, to ensure that they are administered in the manner determined by the Storting and to the best advantage of the community.

20. The King in the Council of State shall have the right to pardon criminals after sentence has been passed. The criminal shall have the choice whether he will accept the King's grace or submit to the punishment imposed.

In the actions which the *Odelsting* [1] causes to be brought before the Constitutional Court of the Realm [2] (*Riksrett*) no other pardon than exemption from capital punishment may be granted.

21. The King, with the advice of his Council of State, shall choose and appoint all civil, ecclesiastical, and military officials (*embetsmenn*) [3]. Such officials shall swear, or, if by law exempted from taking the oath, solemnly declare obedience and allegiance to the Constitution and the King. The Royal Princes must not hold civil offices.

22. The Prime Minister and the other members of the Council of State, as well as officials attached to the Government offices or to the Diplomatic

[1] A Division of the Storting, See § 73.
[2] Deals with impeachment for political offences.
[3] Only a few per cent of the public servants are *embetsmenn*.

or Consular services, Chief civil and ecclesiastical officials,[1] Commanders of regiments and other military forces, Commandants of forts and Officers Commanding warships, may, without any preceding judicial sentence, be dismissed by the King, who shall previously have heard the opinion of the Council of State on the subject. Whether pensions should be granted to officials thus dismissed, shall be determined by the next Storting. In the meantime they shall receive two thirds of their previous pay.

Other officials may only be suspended by the King, and shall then at once be prosecuted before the Courts; but they may not, unless judgment has been pronounced against them, be dismissed, nor may they, against their will, be transferred to another place.

All officials (*embetsmenn*) may, without any preceding judicial sentence, be dismissed when they have attained an age-limit determined by law.[2]

23. The King may confer decorations on whomsoever he pleases as a reward for distinguished services, which must be publicly announced; but he must not confer any other rank or title than such as each office carries with it. The decoration exempts no one from the common duties and burdens of the citizens, nor does it carry with it any preferential admission to the offices of the State. Officials who are released from office with the King's favour, retain the title and rank of the office they have filled. This does not, however, apply to the members of the Council of State.

No personal or mixed hereditary privileges must henceforth be granted to any one.[3]

24. The King chooses and dismisses at his own discretion his Royal household and Court attendants.

25. The King is Commander-in-Chief of the Army and the Navy of the Kingdom. These forces may not be increased or reduced without the consent of the Storting. They may not be transferred to the service of foreign powers, nor may any military forces of foreign powers, except auxiliary forces against hostile attacks, be brought into the Kingdom without the consent of the Storting.

The territorial contingent (*landevern*) and the other troops that cannot be classed as belonging to the line troops may never, without the consent of the Storting, be employed outside the borders of the Kingdom.

26. The King shall have the right to assemble troops, to commence war in the defence of the Kingdom and to make peace, to conclude and denounce treaties, to send and to receive diplomatic envoys.

Treaties on matters of special importance, and, in any case, treaties the implementation of which, according to the Constitution, necessitates a new

[1] "Chief civil in official" in practice means the chief administrative authority in a province (governor of a province, *fylkesmann*); "chief ecclesiastical official" in practice means the bishop.

[2] The present limit is usually 70 years of age.

[3] Titled ranks were abolished in 1821.

law or a decision on the part of the Storting, shall not be binding until the Storting has given its consent thereunto.

27. All members of the Council of State shall, unless prevented by lawful impediment from attending, be present in the Council of State. No decision must be taken in the Council unless more than half the number of its members are present.

Members of the Council of State who do not profess the public religion of the State, do not take part in the consideration of matters which concern the State Church.

28. Proposals regarding appointments to offices (*embeter*) and other matters of importance shall be presented in the Council of State by the member to whose department they belong, and the matters in question shall be dispatched by him in accordance with the decisions of the Council of State. Matters strictly relating to military command may, however, to the extent determined by the King, be excepted from being dealt with in the Council of State.

29. If a member of the Council of State is prevented by lawful impediment from attending the meeting and from presenting the matters belonging to his department, these may be presented by another member whom the King may depute for the purpose.

If, by lawful impediment, so many members are prevented from attending that not more than half of the fixed number are present, other men or women shall, to the number required, be deputed to take seats in the Council of State.

30. All the proceedings of the Council of State shall be entered in the records of the Council. Diplomatic matters which the Council of State have decided to keep secret shall be entered in a special record. The same applies to matters relating to military command which the Council of State has decided to keep secret.

Everyone who holds a seat in the Council of State is in duty bound to express with frankness his opinion, to which the King is bound to listen. But it remains with the King to make a decision according to his own judgment.

If any member of the Council of State is of the opinion that the King's decision is at variance with the form of government or the laws of the Kingdom, or is prejudicial to the Kingdom, it is his duty to make strong remonstrances against it, and also to have his opinion entered in the record. A member who has not thus protested, shall be deemed to have been in agreement with the King, and shall be answerable in such manner as may be subsequently decided, and may be impeached by the Odelsting before the Constitutional Court of the Realm (*Riksrett*).

31. All decisions made by the King shall, in order to become valid, be countersigned. The decisions relating to military command shall be countersigned by the person who has presented the matter; other decisions shall be countersigned by the Prime Minister or, if he has not been present, by the next highest ranking member of the Council of State present.

32. The decisions made by the Government during the absence of the King shall be drawn up in the King's name and be signed by the Council of State.

33. (*Repealed*).

34. The nearest heir to the Throne, if he is the son of the reigning King, shall bear the title of Crown Prince. The other persons entitled to succeed to the Crown are to be called Princes, and the daughters of the Royal House, Princesses.

35. As soon as the heir to the Throne has completed his eighteenth year, he is entitled to take a seat in the Council of State, but without vote or responsibility.

36. No Prince of the Royal House may marry without the consent of the King. Nor may he accept any other crown or government without the consent of the King and the Storting; to obtain the consent of the Storting, two thirds of the votes are required.

If he acts contrary to this rule, he, as well as his descendants, forfeit their right to the Norwegian Throne.

37. The Royal Princes and Princesses shall not be answerable personally to any other than the King, or to such person as he may appoint to sit in judgment on them.

38. (*Repealed*).

39. If the King dies, and the heir to the Throne is still under age, the Council of State shall immediately summon the Storting.

40. Until the Storting has assembled and made provisions for the Government during the minority of the King, the Council of State shall be responsible for the administration of the Kingdom in accordance with the Constitutiton.

41. If the King is absent from the Kingdom, and not in the field, or if he is prevented by illness from attending to the Government, the Prince next entitled to succeed to the Throne shall conduct the Government as being temporarily invested with the Royal power, provided that he has attained the age fixed for the King's majority.[1] If that is not the case, the Council of State shall be responsible for the administration of the Kingdom.

42. (*Repealed*).

43. The election of guardians to conduct the Government on behalf of the King during his minority shall be made by the Storting.

44. The Prince who in the cases mentioned in section 41 conducts the Government, shall make to the Storting in writing the following oath: "I promise and swear that I will conduct the Government in accordance with

[1] Twenty-one years of age.

the Constitution and the Laws, so truly help me God, the Almighty and Omniscient!"

If the Storting is not in session at the time, the oath shall be delivered to the Council of State and afterwards be transmitted to the next Storting.

The Prince who has once made the oath shall not repeat it later on.

45. As soon as their conduct of the Government has ceased, the guardians shall submit to the King and the Storting an account of the same.

46. If the persons in question neglect to summon the Storting immediately in accordance with section 39, it becomes the unconditional duty of the Supreme Court of Justice (*Høyesterett*), as soon as four weeks have elapsed, to cause this summons to be issued.

47. The superintendence of the education of the King during his minority shall, if his father has left no written directions, be determined by the Storting.

48. If the male line of the Royal family has become extinct, and no successor to the Throne has been designated, then a new King shall be chosen by the Storting. Meanwhile the Executive Power shall be exercised in accordance with section 40.

C. CITIZENSHIP AND THE LEGISLATIVE POWER

49. The people shall exercise the Legislative Power through the *Storting*, which consists of two divisions, the *Lagting* and the *Odelsting*.[1]

50. Those entitled to vote are Norwegian citizens, men and women, who have completed their 21st year, who have been domiciled in the Kingdom for five years, and are living there.

Norwegian civil servants holding positions in the Diplomatic and Consular Services, and members of their household, are, if otherwise meeting the above-mentioned requirements, entitled to vote in the electoral district in Norway where they last had their domicile.

51. The rules concerning the electoral registers and the registration of the persons entitled to vote shall be determined by law.

52. (*Repealed*).

53. The right of voting shall be lost in the case of any person who:

(a) is sentenced for criminal offences, subject to such provisions as may be laid down by law;

(b) enters the service of a foreign power without the consent of the Government;

(c) (*repealed*);

[1] It is an established constitutional custom that the courts refuse to pass judicial sentence according to laws which are at variance with the Constitution. See the note to section 88.

(d) is found guilty of having bought votes, or sold his/her own vote, or of having voted at more than one poll;

(e) is declared incapable of managing his or her own affairs.

54. Elections shall be held every four years. They shall be completed by the end of September.

55. Elections shall be conducted in such manner as shall be determined by law. Disputes as to the right of voting shall be settled by the polling officers, against whose decision an appeal may be brought to the Storting.

56. Before the elections commence, sections 50–64 of the Constitution shall be read out aloud by the presiding officer of the poll.

57. The number of representatives to be elected as members of the Storting shall be one hundred and fifty.

58. Every province with its town shall be a constituency.[1]

Representatives from the Kingdom's constituencies shall be divided as follows:

The province of Østfold shall elect eight; the city of Oslo thirteen; the province of Akershus seven; the province of Hedmark eight; the province of Opland seven; the province of Buskerud seven; the province of Vestfold seven; the province of Telemark six; the province of Aust-Agder four; the province of Vest-Agder five; the province of Rogaland ten; the province of Hordaland ten; the city of Bergen five; the province of Sogn og Fjordane five; the province of Møre og Romsdal ten; the province of Sør-Trøndelag ten; the province of Nord-Trøndelag six; the province of Nordland twelve; the province of Troms six; and the province of Finnmark four.

59. Every town and, in the country districts, every municipality, as well as every non-chartered town (*ladested*) possessing a municipal council[2] of its own, shall constitute a separate polling district. The towns may, by law, be divided into several polling districts.

The elections shall be held separately for each polling district. At the poll the votes are cast, by the method of direct election, for the representatives in the Storting of the whole electoral district and their substitutes.

[1] Svalbard (with Bear Island) and Jan Mayen are not included in any special polling districts. The inhabitants of these islands are entitled to vote in the polling district on the Norwegian Mainland in which they had their last residence.

[2] Norway is divided into 64 urban and 679 rural municipalities. The municipalities have had extensive local self-government since 1837. The election period for the municipal councils is now 4 years. Each council consists of not less than 13 and not more than 85 members.

The municipalities have extensive taxation rights to enable them to undertake their numerous tasks, the most important being school and health services, social welfare, and building and maintenance of roads and streets. The funds required by the municipalities are mainly obtained by direct taxation, and in some parts by State subsidies.

Svalbard (Spitsbergen) and the other Arctic islands are administered directly from the Ministry of Industry, Handicrafts and Shipping in Oslo. The Governor of the province of Svalbard is called the *sysselmann*.

The system of election is proportional. The rules to be applied hereunto, as well as the particular regulations concerning the elections, shall be determined by law, subject to the provisions laid down in the Constitution.

60. How far and in what manner qualified voters may be allowed to deliver their ballot papers without going personally to the poll, shall be determined by law.[1]

61. No one shall be qualified for election as a representative to the Storting unless he is 21 years old, has been domiciled 10 years in the Kingdom, and has the right to vote.

62. Officials employed in the Government offices and attendants or servants and pensioners of the Court are debarred from being nominated as representatives. The same applies to persons attached to the Diplomatic or Consular services.

The members of the Council of State must not attend at the Storting as representatives as long as they have a seat in the Council of State.

63. Everyone who is elected as a representative shall be in duty bound to accept the election, unless elected outside the electoral district in which he has the right to vote, or is prevented by an impediment which the Storting judges to be valid. If any one has attended as a representative at each ordinary session of the Storting following one election, he shall not be obliged to accept election at the next election for the Storting.

If anyone is elected as a representative without being obliged to accept such election, he must, within the time and in the manner prescribed by law, make a declaration stating whether he accepts the election or not.

The time within which a person returned for two or more electoral districts shall state which election he accepts, and the manner in which this shall be done, shall likewise be fixed by law.

64. The representatives elected shall be furnished with certificates, the validity of which shall be submitted to the judgment of the Storting.

65. Every representative and every substitute called to the Storting shall be entitled to receive, as fixed by law, reimbursement from the treasury for travelling expenses to and from the Storting, and from the Storting to his home and back again, during vacations lasting at least fourteen days, and also for expenses for medical treatment in the case of illness.

He shall further be entitled to receive compensation, as determined by law, for attending sittings of the Storting.

66. The representatives shall be exempt from personal arrest while on their way to and from the Storting, as well as during their stay there, unless they are apprehended in public crimes; nor shall they be called to account outside the meetings of the Storting for the opinions they have

[1] If a voter is going to be absent from his polling district on election day, he can deliver his ballot paper in advance; but if he is in his polling district on the day of election he must vote personally at the poll.

expressed there. Every representative shall be bound to conform to the rules of the Storting.

67. The representatives elected in the aforesaid manner shall constitute the *Storting* of the Kingdom of Norway.

68. The Storting shall as a rule assemble on the first weekday in October every year in the capital of the Kingdom, unless the King, by reason of extraordinary circumstances, such as hostile invasion or infectious disease, shall appoint for the purpose another town in the Kingdom. Such an appointment must then be publicly notified in good time.

69. In extraordinary cases the King shall have the right to summon the Storting at a time other than the ordinary one.[1]

70. Such an extraordinary Storting may be dismissed by the King when he thinks fit.

71. The members of the Storting shall act as such for four successive years in extraordinary as well as in ordinary Storting held during that period.

72. If an extraordinary Storting is still sitting at the time when an ordinary Storting is due to open, the former shall be dismissed before the latter assembles.

73. The Storting shall nominate from among its members one fourth to constitute the *Lagting*; the remaining three fourths shall constitute the *Odelsting*. This nomination shall take place at the first ordinary Storting that assemblies after a new general election, and thereafter the *Lagting* shall remain unchanged at all *Storting* that meet after the same election, except in so far as any vacancy which may occur among its members has to be filled by special nomination.

Each *Ting* shall hold its meetings separately, and nominate its own President and Secretary. Neither of the *Ting* may hold a meeting unless at least one half of its members are present. Bills concerning amendments to the Constitution may not be dealt with unless at least two thirds of the members of the Storting are present.

74. As soon as the Storting is constituted, the King or the person he appoints for the purpose shall open its proceedings with a speech, in which he shall inform it of the state of the Kingdom and of the subjects to which he particularly desires to call the attention of the Storting. No deliberations may take place in the presence of the King.

When the proceedings of the Storting are opened, the Prime Minister and the members of the Council of State have the right to attend at the Storting, as well as at both of its divisions, and have the same rights as the members of the Storting to take part in the proceedings in so far as these are conducted in open session, without, however, having the right to vote.

[1] An extraordinary Storting has been summoned nine times (1814, 1822, 1828, 1836 1858, 1864, 1882, 1918 and 1939).

They may take part in matters which are discussed in private session only in so far as permission is granted by the Ting concerned.

75. The duties and prerogatives of the Storting are:

(a) to enact and to repeal laws; to impose taxes, duties, customs, and other public charges, which, however, shall not remain operative longer than 31 December of the following year, unless they are expressly renewed by a new ordinary Storting;

(b) to open loans on the credit of the Kingdom;

(c) to control the finances of the Kingdom;

(d) to appropriate the sums of money necessary to meet the expenditure of the State;

(e) to decide how much shall be paid annually to the King for his Royal household, and to determine the apanage of the Royal family, which may not, however, consist of real estate;

(f) to have laid before it the records of the Council of State, and all public reports and documents; the records of such diplomatic matters and of such matters relating to military command as, in pursuance of a decision to that effect, are to be kept secret, shall, however, be laid before a committee consisting of at the most nine members chosen from among the members of the Odelsting, and may further be brought before the Odelsting if any member of the committee moves that the Odelsting give its opinion on the subject, or that an action be brought in the Constitutional Court of the Realm (*Riksrett*).

(g) to have communicated to it the treaties and agreements which the King, on behalf of the State, has concluded with foreign powers; the provisions contained in paragraph (f) concerning such matters as are to be kept secret, shall apply equally to secret clauses which, however, must not be at variance with the public ones;

(h) to have power to summon anyone to meet before it in matters of State, the King and the Royal family excepted, this exception, however, does not apply to the Royal Princes if they hold any public office;

(i) to revise the lists of salaries and pensions temporarily granted, and to make therein such alterations as it finds necessary;

(k) to appoint five auditors, who shall annually examine the accounts of the State and publish extracts of the same in print, which accounts shall for this purpose be delivered to the auditors within six months of the expiration of the year for which the appropriations of the Storting are made; and to provide for the organization of an office to approve the accounts of the State accountants;

(l) to naturalize aliens.

76. Every bill shall first be introduced in the Odelsting, either by one of its own members, or by the Government through a member of the Council of State.

If the bill is passed, it is sent to the Lagting, which either approves or rejects it, and in the latter case sends it back with comments appended. These are taken into consideration by the Odelsting, which either lets the bill fall or again sends it to the Lagting, with or without alteration.

When a bill from the Odelsting has twice been laid before the Lagting and has been a second time rejected by it, the whole Storting shall meet in joint session, and the bill is then disposed of by a majority of two thirds of the votes.

Between any two of these deliberations there shall be an interval of at least three days.

77. When a bill passed by the Odelsting has been approved by the Lagting or by the Storting in joint session, it shall be sent to the King, with a request that it may receive the King's assent.

78. If the King assents to the bill, he shall attach to it his signature, whereby it becomes law.

If he does not assent to it, he shall return it to the Odelsting with the declaration that he does not for the time being find it expedient to give his assent to it. In this case the bill must not again be submitted to the King by the Storting then assembled.

79. If a bill has been passed unaltered by two ordinary sessions of the Storting, constituted after two separate successive elections and separated from each other by at least two intervening ordinary sessions of the Storting, without any divergent bill having been passed by the Storting in the period between the first and the last passing, and it is then submitted to the King with the petition that His Majesty shall not refuse his assent to a bill which, after the most mature deliberation, the Storting considers to be for the benefit of the country, it becomes law, even if the Royal assent is not accorded before the Storting dissolves.

80. The Storting shall remain in session as long as it may find necessary. When, having finished its business, it is dismissed by the King, he shall at the same time communicate his decision with regard to the bills that have not already been disposed of (see sections 77–79), either by assenting to them or by rejecting them. All such bills as he does not expressly assent to, are considered as having been rejected by him.

81. All Acts (with the exception of those mentioned in section 79) shall be drawn up in the King's name, under the seal of the Kingdom of Norway, and in the following terms: "We, X, make it publicly known that the following decision of the Storting of (such and such a date) in the following terms has been laid before Us (here follows the decision). In consequence whereof We have assented to and confirmed, as We hereby assent to and confirm the same as a law under Our hand and the seal of the Kingdom."

82. (*Repealed*).

83. The Storting may demand the opinion of the Supreme Court of Justice (*Høyesterett*) on questions of law.

84. The Storting shall meet in open session, and its proceedings shall be published in print, except in those cases in which a majority decides to the contrary.

85. Any person who obeys an order the purpose of which is to disturb the liberty and the security of the Storting, shall thereby be guilty of treason against the country.

D. THE JUDICIAL POWER

86. The Constitutional Court of the Realm (*Riksrett*) shall pronounce judgment in the first and last instance in such actions as are brought by the Odelsting against members of the Council of State, or against members of the Supreme Court of Justice (*Høyesterett*), or against members of the Storting for criminal offences which they may have committed in that capacity.

The particular rules concerning impeachment by the Odelsting, according to this section, shall be determined by law. The period within which a prosecution may be instituted in the Constitutional Court of the Realm shall not, however, be fixed at less than fifteen years.

The ordinary members of the Lagting and the permanent members of the Supreme Court of Justice shall be judges of the Constitutional Court of the Realm. The provisions contained in section 87 shall apply to the constitution of the Constitutional Court of the Realm in each particular case. In the Constitutional Court of the Realm the President of the Lagting takes the chair.

A person sitting in the Constitutional Court of the Realm as a member of the Lagting does not vacate his seat in the Court if the period for which he is elected a member of the Storting should expire before the Constitutional Court of the Realm has terminated the trial of the case. If, for any other reason, he ceases to be a member of the Storting, he shall resign as a judge of the Constitutional Court of the Realm. The same shall apply if a judge of the Supreme Court of Justice, sitting as a member of the Constitutional Court of the Realm, retires as a member of the Supreme Court of Justice.

87. The accused and the person prosecuting on behalf of the Odelsting have the right to challenge members of the Lagting and the Supreme Court of Justice (*Høyesterett*), provided that fourteen of the members of the Lagting and seven members of the Supreme Court of Justice remain as judges in the Constitutional Court of the Realm (*Riksrett*). Each party has the right to challenge an equal number of the members of the Lagting, the accused having, however, the preferential right of challenging one more, if the number to be challenged is not divisible into two equal parts. The same shall apply to the challenging of the members of the Supreme Court of Justice. If, in an action, there are more than one accused, they shall exercise the right of challenge collectively in accordance with rules to be determined by law. If challenge is not made to the extent permitted, members of the Lagting and of the Supreme Court of Justice in excess of fourteen and seven respectively shall withdraw as determined by ballot.

When the action comes up for judgment, the members of the Court in excess of fifteen shall withdraw from the Court, the selection being made by ballot; the remaining judges who are to pass judgment, shall number ten members at most of the Lagting and five of the Judges of the Supreme Court of Justice.

The President of the Constitutional Court of the Realm and the President of the Supreme Court of Justice shall not in any case retire as a result of a ballot.

If the Constitutional Court of the Realm cannot be constituted so as to contain the number of members of the Lagting and the Supreme Court of Justice prescribed in the preceding paragraphs, the case may nevertheless be tried and judgment be passed provided that the Court numbers at least ten judges.

Further provisions as to the manner in which the Constitutional Court of the Realm shall be constituted shall be laid down by law.

88. The Supreme Court of Justice shall pronounce judgment in the last instance. The right to bring an action in the Supreme Court of Justice may, however, be limited as determined by law.

The Supreme Court of Justice shall consist of a President and at least four other members.[1]

89. (*Repealed*).

90. The judgments of the Supreme Court of Justice may not in any case be appealed against.

91. No one may be appointed a member of the Supreme Court of Justice before he is 30 years of age:

E. GENERAL PROVISIONS

92. To official posts (*embeter*) in the State shall be appointed [2] only Norwegian citizens, men and women, who speak the language of the country, and who at the same time:

(a) were born in the Kingdom of parents who at that time were subjects of the State;

[1] The Supreme Court consists of one President (*Justitiarius*) and about 20 permanent judges. In each case the court is made up of 5 judges, the senior judge of each section acting as chairman. In cases where two of the judges are of the opinion that the case must be decided in a way which is not in accordance with the interpretation of law previously laid down by the Supreme Court of Justice, or if two judges consider that *a provision laid down by an Act, by decision of the Storting or by decree given by the administration, is at variance with the Constitution,* then the case must be decided by the complete court. The same applies in other cases where questions of a particularly doubtful nature have been raised.

[2] Only a few per cent of the public servants are *embetsmenn*.

(b) or were born in a foreign country of Norwegian parents who were not at that time subjects of another state;

(c) or shall hereafter have resided ten years in the Kingdom;

(d) or are naturalized by the Storting.

Others may, however, be appointed as teachers at the University and the secondary schools, as physicians and as consuls in foreign places.

93. In order to secure international peace and security, or in order to promote international law and order and co-operation between nations, the Storting may, by a three-fourths majority, consent that an international organization of which Norway is or becomes a member, shall have the right, within a functionally limited field, to exercise powers which in accordance with this Constitution are normally vested in the Norwegian authorities, exclusive of the power to alter this Constitution. For such consent as provided above at least two thirds of the members of the Storting—the same quorum as is required for changes in or amendments to this Constitution—shall be present.

The provisions of the preceding paragraph do not apply in cases of membership in an international organization, the decisions of which are not binding on Norway except as obligations under international law.

94. The first, or if this is not possible, the second ordinary Storting, shall make provision for the publication of a new general civil [1] and criminal [2] code. In the meantime the laws of the State now in operation shall remain in force, provided that they are not at variance with this Constitution or the provisional ordinances that may be issued in the meantime.

The existing permanent taxes shall likewise continue in operation until the next Storting.

95. No dispensations, protections, postponements of payments or redresses must be granted after the new general code has come into operation.[3]

96. No one must be convicted expect according to law, or be punished except according to judicial sentence. Interrogation by torture must not take place.

97. No law must be given retroactive effect.

98. When special fees are paid to officials of the Courts of Justice, the payer shall be exempt from further payment to the Public Treasury in respect of the same matter.

99. No one must be arrested and committed to prison except in the cases determined by law and in the manner prescribed by law. For un-

[1] A civil code has never been published.

[2] A criminal code was first published in 1842. The present criminal code is from 1902 with later amendments.

[3] A general code has never been published. To-day the Constitution is construed in such a way that it forbids dispensation granted by the administration unless authorized by law.

warranted arrest and illegal detention the officer concerned shall be responsible to the person imprisoned.

The Government is not entitled to employ military force against subjects of the State, except in accordance with the forms prescribed by law, unless any meeting should disturb the public peace and not immediately disperse after the articles of the Statute-book relating to riots have been read out loud three times by the civil authority.

100. There shall be liberty of the press. No person must be punished for any writing, whatever its contents may be, which he has caused to be printed or published, unless he wilfully and manifestly has either himself shown or incited others to disobedience to the laws, contempt of religion or morality or the constitutional powers, or resistance to their orders, or has advanced false and defamatory accusations against any other person. Everyone shall be free to speak his mind frankly on the administration of the State or on any other subject whatsoever.

101. New and permanent privileges implying restrictions on the freedom of trade and industry must not be granted to any one in future.

102. Search of private homes shall not be made except in criminal cases.

103. Asylum for the protection of debtors shall not be granted to such persons as hereafter become bankrupt.

104. Forfeiture of lands and goods shall be abolished.

105. If the welfare of the State requires that any person shall surrender his movable or immovable property for the public use, he shall receive full compensation from the public treasury.

106. The purchase-money, as well as the revenues of the landed property constituting ecclesiastical benefices, shall be applied solely to the benefit of the clergy and to the promotion of education. The property of charitable institutions shall be applied solely for their own benefit.

107. The *Odel* and *Åsete* rights shall not be abolished.[1] The further conditions under which these rights shall continue for the greatest benefit of the State and the best advantage of the rural population, shall be determined by the first or second Storting following.

108. No earldoms, baronies, *majorats* or *fideicommissa* must be created in the future.

109. Every citizen of the State is in general equally bound to defend his native country during a certain time, without any regard to birth or fortune.

The application of this principle and the restrictions it may become subject to, shall be determined by law.

[1] The *Odel* (right of allodial possession) is the ancient right of complete ownership of land in the country districts, including the right of redemption by the family if it has been sold.

The *Åseterett* (right of succession to landed property) is the right of the eldest son to retain possession of the property at a moderate price.

The *Odel* and *Åsete* rights are excluded from Svalbard.

110. It is incumbent on the authorities of the State to create conditions which make it possible for every person who is able to work to earn his living by his work.

111. The form and the colours of the Norwegian Flag shall be determined by law.

112. If experience proves that any part of the Constitution of the Kingdom of Norway ought to be changed, a proposal to this effect shall be submitted to the first, second or third ordinary Storting after a General Election, and be published in print. But it shall be left to the first, second or third ordinary Storting after the following General Election to decide whether or not the proposed amendment shall be adopted. Such amendment must, however, never contradict the principles embodied in this Constitution, but merely relate to modifications of particular provisions which do not alter the spirit of this Constitution, and should receive the support of two thirds of the members of the Storting.

An amendment of the Constitution adopted in the manner aforesaid shall be signed by the President and the Secretary of the Storting, and be sent to the King for public notification in print, as forming an integral part of the Constitution of the Kingdom of Norway.

POLAND

SUMMARY

INTERNATIONAL STATUS

Poland is a member of the United Nations (October 24, 1945). It is a member of the Council of Mutual Economic Assistance, the Warsaw Treaty and other international organizations. It was a member of the League of Nations.

Poland's first constitution was promulgated in 1572 and provided for an elective monarchy and curtailed royal power. The first partition of Poland by Prussia, Russia and Austria was in 1772. A new constitution in 1791, abolished the *liberum veto* and made Poland a hereditary monarchy but by the second partition in 1793, Prussia and Russia took further Polish territory and by the third in 1795, after a national insurrection, Poland ceased to exist. The struggle for independence consumed the entire nineteenth century and insurrections occurred in 1830, 1846, 1848, and 1863. Modern Polish political life began with the formation in Galicia of the National Democratic and Polish Socialist parties. The 1904–1905 Russian Revolution had its counterpart in Poland. The German and Austrian emperors proclaimed the independence of Poland on November 5, 1916 and its independence was part of Wilson's Fourteen Points. On October 7, 1918, the Regency Council in Poland announced the formation of an independent Polish Government and independence was proclaimed on November 10, 1918 Boundary questions led to war with Russia and the Treaty of Riga of 1921 gave Poland territory east of the Curzon line. The 1939 Pact between Germany and the USSR partitioned Poland between the two countries and from 1941, Poland was entirely occupied by Germany. In 1944, Warsaw was razed after the city's insurrection. On January 5, 1945, the USSR recognized the Communist Political Committee of National Liberation as the provisional government of Poland and on July 5, 1945, the United States and United Kingdom recognized the Polish Provisional Government of National Unity established in Moscow, which included some members of the London government in exile.

Following the 1947 elections, sovietization of the country was accelerated. The treaty of 1950 with the German Democratic Republic recognized the frontier of Poland on the Oder-Neisse line. After the Poznan insurrection in 1956, nationalist elements gained control of the Communist Party and gave it a greater independence.

FORM OF NATIONAL GOVERNMENT

The Constitution of July 22, 1952, as amended in 1954, 1957, 1960, 1961 and 1963, replaces the fundamental laws which were the legal foundation of the political system of the Polish People's Republic from 1947 to 1952. Before that, the basic principles of the Constitution of March 17, 1921 had been declared by the Manifesto of the Polish Committee of National Liberation of July 22, 1944, to be in force. The Preamble of the 1952 Constitution states that the Polish People's Republic is a republic of the working people and a state of People's Democracy.[1] Sovereign power belongs to the working people of town and country.[2] A section describes the economic and social structure.[3]

RIGHTS OF THE PEOPLE

The Constitution provides the right to work, rest and leisure, health protection, education, protection and development of science, literature

[1] Const., Art. 1, Preamble. [2] Id., Art. 1. [3] Id., Art. 7–14.

and art, equal rights for women and special care for marriage, the family and young people; it stipulates equal rights, freedom of conscience and religion, speech, press, association and assembly, petition, inviolability of the person, inviolability of the home and correspondence, the right of asylum.[1] All citizens must safeguard and strengthen social property, defend the country and be vigilant against enemies of the nation.[2]

LEGISLATIVE DEPARTMENT

The highest organ of State power is the legislative body, the Seym.[3] It is composed of 460 deputies elected for a term of four years by universal, direct, equal, and secret ballot.[4] It meets in two regular sessions a year.[5] Immunities of deputies are provided.[6] Provision is made for a Supreme Control Chamber which supervises the economic, financial and organizational-administrative activity of higher and local organs of State administration and presents its opinion to the Seym on the execution of the budget and the fulfilment of the national economic plan.[7]

EXECUTIVE DEPARTMENT

The Council of State fulfils the function of a collective Head of State; it is elected by the Seym from among its members and has the power of appointment, convenes the Seym, awards orders and honors, exercises the right of pardon.[8] The Government, consisting of the Council of Ministers, is appointed and revoked by the Seym and responsible thereto, and is the supreme executive and administrative organ of State power.[9] Provision is made for Peoples Councils as local organs of State power.[10]

JUDICIAL DEPARTMENT

Judges are independent and subject only to the law.[11] The Courts are the custodians of the political and social system of the Republic.[12] The highest judicial organ is the Supreme Court, elected by the Council of State for a term of five years.[13] Provision is made for a Prosecutor General accountable to the Council of State.[14]

AREA, POPULATION, ETC.

The area of Poland is 312,520 square kilometres, its population (1965) 31,496,000. The capital is Warsaw.[15]

[1] Id., Art. 57–75. [2] Id., Art. 76–79. [3] Id., Art. 15.
[4] Id., Art. 16, 23, 80. [5] Id., Art. 17. [6] Id., Art. 16.
[7] Id., Art. 28A–28D. [8] Id., Art. 24, 25. [9] Id., Art. 29, 30.
[10] Id., Art. 34–45. [11] Id., Art. 52. [12] Id., Art. 48. [13] Id., Art. 51.
[14] Id., Art. 54–56. [15] Id., Art. 90.

CONSTITUTION
of
POLAND[1]

July 22, 1952, as amended September 25, 1954, December 13, 1957, December 22, 1960, May 15, 1961, December 19, 1963

The Polish Peoples' Republic is a republic of the working people.

The Polish People's Republic carries on the most glorious progressive traditions of the Polish nation and gives effect to the liberation ideals of the working masses.

The Polish working people under the leadership of the heroic working class, and on the basis of the alliance between workers and peasants, fought for many decades for the liberation from national enslavement imposed upon the nation by the Prussian, Austrian and Russian conquerors and colonizers, just as they fought for the abolition of exploitation by the Polish capitalists and landlords.

During the occupation, the Polish nation waged an unflinching heroic fight against the murderous Nazi invasion. The historic victory of the Union of Soviet Socialist Republics over fascism liberated Polish soil, enabled the Polish working people to take power into their own hands, and established conditions for the national re-birth of Poland within new and just frontiers. The Regained Territories were restored to Poland forever.

By carrying out the memorable directives of the Manifesto of the Polish Committee of National Liberation of July 22, 1944, and by developing the principles laid down in the program of that Manifesto, people's power—thanks to the selfless and creative efforts of the Polish working people in the fight against the bitter resistance of the remnants of the old capitalist-landlord system—has accomplished great social changes. As a result of revolutionary struggles and transformations, the power of the capitalists and landlords has been overthrown, a State of People's Democracy has been firmly established, and a new social system, in accord with the interests and aspirations of the great majority of the people, is taking shape and growing in strength.

[1] *Constitution of the Polish People's Republic.* Polonia Publishing House, Warsaw, 1964; Introduction by Professor Andrzej Burda. Supplied by Ministry of Foreign Affairs in January 1966. Ed.

The legal principles of this system are laid down by the Constitution of the Polish People's Republic.

The basis of people's power in Poland today is the alliance between the working class and the working peasants. In this alliance, the leading role belongs to the working class—the leading class of the people, the class based on the revolutionary gains of the Polish and international working class movement, and on the historic experience of victorious socialist construction in the Union of Soviet Socialist Republics, the first State of workers and peasants.

Implementing the will of the Polish nation, the Legislative Seym of the Republic of Poland, in accordance with its purpose, solemnly adopts the present Constitution as the fundamental law by which the Polish nation and all organs of power of the Polish working people shall be guided, in order:

to consolidate the People's State as the fundamental power assuring to the Polish nation the highest degree of prosperity, its independence and sovereignty;

to accelerate the political, economic and cultural development of the Fatherland, and the growth of its resources;

to strengthen the patriotic feelings, the unity and solidarity of the Polish nation in its struggle still further to improve social conditions, to eliminate completely the exploitation of man by man, and to put into effect the great ideals of Socialism;

to strengthen friendship and co-operation between nations, on the basis of the alliance and brotherhood which today link the Polish nation with the peaceloving nations of the world for the attainment of their common aim—to make aggression impossible and to consolidate world peace.

CHAPTER 1

POLITICAL STRUCTURE

Art. 1. 1. The Polish People's Republic is a State of People's Democracy.

2. In the Polish People's Republic the power belongs to the working people of town and country.

Art. 2. 1. The working people exercise the authority of the State through their representatives elected to the Seym of the Polish People's Republic, and to the People's Councils, on the basis of universal, equal and direct suffrage by secret ballot.

2. The people's representatives in the Seym of the Polish People's Republic, and in the People's Councils, are responsible to their constituents and may be recalled by them.

Art. 3. The Polish People's Republic:

(1) safeguards the achievements of the Polish working people of town and country and secures their power and freedom against forces hostile to the people;

(2) secures the development and continuous growth of the productive forces of the country through its industrialization and through elimination of economic, technical and cultural backwardness;

(3) organizes a planned economy on the basis of undertakings constituting social property;

(4) places restrictions on, gradually ejects and abolishes those classes of society which live by exploiting the workers and peasants;

(5) ensures a continual rise in the level of the well-being, health and cultural standards of the people;

(6) secures the development of national culture in all its aspects.

Art. 4. 1. The laws of the Polish People's Republic express the interests and the will of the working people.

2. Strict compliance with the laws of the Polish People's Republic is the fundamental duty of every organ of the State and of every citizen.

3. All organs of State power and administration act on the basis of law.

Art. 5. All organs of State power and administration are supported in the exercise of their functions by the conscious and active co-operation of the broadest masses of the people, and they are bound:

(1) to account to the nation for their work;

(2) to examine carefully and take into consideration, in accordance with existing legislation, reasonable proposals, complaints and wishes of the citizens;

(3) to interpret to the working people the basic aims and guiding principles of the policy of the people's authorities in the various fields of State, economic and cultural activity.

Art. 6. The Armed Forces of the Polish People's Republic safeguard the sovereignty and independence of the Polish nation, its security and peace.

CHAPTER 2

SOCIAL AND ECONOMIC STRUCTURE

Art. 7. 1. The Polish People's Republic promotes, on the basis of socialized means of production, trade, transportation and credit, the economic and cultural life of the country in accordance with the national economic plan and, in particular, through the expansion of Socialist State industry, which is the decisive factor in the transformation of social and economic relations.

2. The State has the monopoly of foreign trade.

3. The principal aim of the planned economic policy of the Polish

People's Republic is the constant development of the productive forces of the country, the continuous raising of the standard of living of the working people, and the strengthening of the power, defence capacity and independence of the Fatherland.

Art. 8. The national wealth, that is, the mineral deposits, waters, State forests, mines, roads, rail, water and air transport, means of communication, banks, State industrial establishments, State farms and State machine stations, State commercial enterprises and communal enterprises and utilities, is the subject of special care and protection by the State and by all citizens.

Art. 9. 1. The Polish People's Republic strengthens, according to plan, the economic bond between town and country founded on brotherly co-operation between workers and peasants.

2. For this purpose, the Polish People's Republic secures a continuous increase in the output of State industry, serving to meet the all-round needs of the rural population in their capacity as producers and consumers, at the same time exerting a planned influence on the constant growth of production of agricultural commodities which supplies industry with raw materials and the urban population with foodstuffs.

Art. 10. 1. The Polish People's Republic protects the individual farms of working peasants and assists them with a view to safeguarding them against capitalist exploitation, to increasing production, to raising the technical level of agriculture and to improving their welfare.

2. The Polish People's Republic gives special support and all-round aid to the co-operative farms, set up on the basis of voluntary membership, as forms of collective economy. By applying methods of the most efficient collective cultivation and mechanized work, collective farming enables the working peasants to reach a turning point in production and contributes to the complete elimination of exploitation in the countryside and to a rapid and considerable improvement in the level of its wellbeing and culture.

3. The principal forms of State support and help for co-operative farms are the State machine stations, which make it possible to employ modern technology, and low-interest State credits.

Art. 11. The Polish People's Republic promotes the development of various forms of the co-operative movement in town and country and gives it every help in the fulfilment of its tasks, while extending special care and protection to co-operative property constituting social property.

Art. 12. The Polish People's Republic recognizes and protects, on the basis of existing laws, individual property and the right to inherit land, buildings and other means of production belonging to peasants, craftsmen and home-workers.

Art. 13. The Polish People's Republic guarantees to citizens full protection of personal property and the right to inherit such property.

Art. 14. 1. Work is the right, the duty and a matter of honor of every citizen. By their work, by the observance of work discipline, by work emulation and the perfecting of methods of work, the working people of town and country add to the strength and power of the Fatherland, raise the level of prosperity of the people and expedite the full realization of the Socialist system.

2. Exemplary workers enjoy the respect of the whole nation.

3. The Polish People's Republic gives increasing practical effect to the principle: "From each according to his ability, to each according to his work."

CHAPTER 3

THE SUPREME ORGANS OF STATE POWER

Art. 15. 1. The highest organ of State power is the Seym of the Polish People's Republic.

2. The Seym, which is the highest representative of the will of the working people of town and country, realizes the sovereign rights of the Nation.

3. The Seym passes laws and exercises control over the functioning of other organs of State power and administration.

Art. 16. 1. The Seym is made up of 460 Deputies.

2. The validity of the election of a Deputy is confirmed by the Seym.

3. No deputy may be either prosecuted or arrested, without the consent of the Seym, and when the Seym is not in session, without the consent of the Council of State.

Art. 17. 1. The Seym meets in sessions. The sessions of the Seym are convened by the Council of State at least twice a year. The Council of State is also bound to convene a session on a written motion by one third of the total number of Deputies.

2. The first session of a newly elected Seym must be convened within a period of one month after the date of the elections.

Art. 18. 1. The Seym elects from among its members a Marshal, Deputy Marshals and committees.

2. The Marshal or his deputy presides over the debates and supervises the course of the work of the Seym.

3. The debates of the Seym are open to the public. The Seym may vote the holding of a secret meeting if the interests of the State require it.

4. The order of work of the Seym, the nature and number of committees, are defined by rules of procedure adopted by the Seym.

Art. 19. 1. The Seym adopts the national economic plans for a period of a number of years.

2. The Seym adopts every year the State budget.

Art. 20. 1. The right to propose legislation is vested in the Council of State, the Government and the Deputies.

2. Laws passed by the Seym are signed by the Chairman of the Council of State and its Secretary. Laws are published in the Journal of Laws by order of the Chairman of the Council of State.

Art. 21. The Seym may appoint a commission to examine a specified matter. The terms of reference and the procedure of the commission are determined by the Seym.

Art. 22. The Chairman of the Council of Ministers or individual Ministers are bound to give an answer within seven days to an interpellation by a Deputy.

Art. 23. 1. The Seym is elected for a term of four years.

2. The Council of State orders the holding of elections to the Seym not later than one month before the expiry of the term of office of the Seym, the date of elections to be fixed on a work-free day within two months after the expiry of the term of office of the Seym.

Art. 24. 1. At its first sitting, the Seym elects from among its members the Council of State, consisting of:

the Chairman of the Council of State;

four Deputy Chairmen;

the Secretary of the Council of State;

eleven Members.

2. The Marshal and Deputy Marshal of the Seym may be elected to the Council of State as Deputy Chairmen or as Members.

3. After the expiry of the term of office of the Seym, the Council of State acts until the election of a Council of State by the newly elected Seym.

Art. 25. 1. The Council of State:

(1) orders the holding of elections to the Seym;

(2) convenes sessions of the Seym;

(3) lays down universally binding interpretation of laws;

(4) issues decrees having the force of law;

(5) appoints and recalls plenipotentiary representatives of the Polish Republic in other States;

(6) receives letters of credence and of recall of diplomatic representatives of other States accredited to the Council of State;

(7) ratifies and denounces international treaties;

(8) fills civilian and military posts specified by law.

(9) awards orders and decorations, and confers titles of honor;

(10) exercises the right of pardon;

(11) exercises other functions vested in the Council of State by the Constitution or assigned to it by law.

2. The Council of State is accountable to the Seym for all its activities.

3. The Council of State acts as a collective body.

4. The Council of State is represented by its Chairman or his Deputy.

Art. 26. 1. In the intervals between the sessions of the Seym, the Council of State issues decrees having the force of law. The Council of State submits its decrees for approval to the next session of the Seym.

2. Decrees issued by the Council of State are signed by the Chairman of the Council of State and its Secretary. Decrees are published in the Journal of Laws by order of the Chairman of the Council of State.

Art. 27. The Council of State exercises ultimate supervision over the People's Councils. Specific powers of the Council of State in this respect are determined by law.

Art. 28. 1. A decision concerning the declaration of a state of war may be adopted only in the event of armed aggression having been committed against the Polish People's Republic, or if, in pursuance of international agreements, the necessity of common defence against aggression should arise. Such a decision is voted by the Seym or, if the Seym is not in session, by the Council of State.

2. The Council of State may, should considerations of the defence or security of the State so require, proclaim martial law in parts or in the entire territory of the Polish People's Republic. For similar reasons the Council of State may proclaim partial or general mobilization.

CHAPTER 3a

THE SUPREME CONTROL CHAMBER

Art. 28a. 1. The function of the Supreme Control Chamber is to exercise supervision over the economic, financial and organizational-administrative activity of the higher and local organs of State administration, as well as of agencies subordinate to them, from the point of view of legality, good management, utility and honesty.

2. The Supreme Control Chamber may also carry out supervision over social organizations and institutions as well as non-socialized units of the economy with regard to tasks indicated by the State, and also in other cases defined by law.

Art. 28b. 1. The Supreme Control Chamber comes under the jurisdiction of the Seym.

2. The Council of State exercises supervision over the Supreme Control Chamber in the realm specified by law.

Art. 28c. 1. The Chairman of the Supreme Control Chamber is appointed and recalled by the Seym.

2. The Supreme Control Chamber functions as a collective body, in accordance with the provisions of the law.

3. The organizational structure and the way of operation of the Supreme Control Chamber are defined by law.

Art. 28d. The Supreme Control Chamber present its opinions to the

Seym regarding the execution of the State Budget and of the National Economic Plan, and submits motions of approval for the Government in this regard.

CHAPTER 4

THE SUPREME ORGANS OF STATE ADMINISTRATION

Art. 29. 1. The Seym appoints and recalls the Government of the Polish People's Republic—the Council of Ministers or its individual members.

2. In the intervals between sessions of the Seym, the Council of State, on the motion of the Chairman of the Council of Ministers, appoints and recalls members of the Council of Ministers. The Council of State submits its decisions for approval to the next session of the Seym.

Art. 30. 1. The Council of Ministers is the supreme executive and administrative organ of State power.

2. The Council of Ministers is responsible and accountable to the Seym for its work, and when the Seym is not in session, to the Council of State.

Art. 31. The Council of Ministers consists of:

the Chairman of the Council of Ministers, who presides;

the Vice-Chairmen of the Council of Ministers;

the Chairmen of such Commissions and Committees as are specified by law, and fulfil the functions of the highest organs of State administration.

Art. 32. The Council of Ministers:

(1) co-ordinates the activities of Ministries and other organs under its jurisdiction and gives directives as to their work;

(2) adopts yearly and submits to the Seym the State budget estimates, adopts and submits to the Seym the draft of the national economic plan for a period of a number of years;

(3) adopts the yearly national economic plans;

(4) ensures the execution of laws;

(5) supervises the execution of the national economic plan and of the State budget;

(6) presents to the Seym an annual report on the execution of the State budget;

(7) ensures the protection of public order, of the interests of State and of the rights of citizens;

(8) in pursuance of laws and in order to give them effect, issues regulations, adopts decisions and supervises their execution;

(9) exercises general guidance in the sphere of relations with other States;

(10) exercises general guidance regarding the defence capacity of the country and the organization of the Armed Forces of the Polish People's Republic, and establishes the annual contingent of citizens to be called up for military service;

(11) directs the work of the Presidia of the People's Councils.

Art. 33. 1. Ministers direct specified branches of State administration. The sphere of competence of Ministers is determined by law.

2. Ministers issue orders and regulations in pursuance of laws and for the execution of laws.

3. The Council of Ministers may rescind an order or a regulation issued by a Minister.

CHAPTER 5

THE LOCAL ORGANS OF STATE POWER

Art. 34. 1. The organs of State power in rural communities in towns, in boroughs of larger towns, in settlements and voivodeships are the People's Councils.

2. The People's Councils are elected by the population for a term of four years.

Art. 35. The People's Councils express the will of the working people, and develop their creative initiative and activity in order to increase the strength, prosperity and culture of the nation.

Art. 36. The People's Councils strengthen the links between the State authorities and working people of town and country, drawing increasing numbers of the working people into participation in governing the State.

Art. 37. The People's Councils direct, within the limits of their jurisdiction, economic, social and cultural activities, linking local requirements with the general tasks of the State.

Art. 38. The People's Councils take constant care of the everyday needs and interests of the population, combat any manifestations of arbitrary and bureaucratic attitude towards citizens, exercise and promote social supervision over the activities of offices, enterprises, establishments and institutions.

Art. 39. The People's Councils ensure the maintenance of public order and watch over the observance of the people's rule of law, protect social property, safeguard the rights of citizens and co-operate in strengthening the defence capacity and security of the State.

Art. 40. The People's Councils fully exploit all local resources and possibilities for the general economic and cultural development of the area, for meeting to an increasing extent the needs of the population, with regard to supply and services, as well as for the expansion of communal institutions and facilities connected with public services, education, culture, sanitation and sport.

Art. 41. The People's Councils adopt local economic plans and local budgets.

Art. 42. 1. The People's Councils meet in sessions.

2. The Presidia elected by the People's Councils are the executive and administrative organs of those Councils.

3. The Presidium of a People's Council is responsible to the People's Council by which it has been elected, and to the Presidium of the People's Council of a higher level.

Art. 43. The People's Councils appoint committees for various spheres of their activity. The committees of the People's Councils maintain constant and close links with the population, mobilize it for co-operation in implementing the Council's tasks, exercise social supervision on behalf of the Council and submit proposals to the Council and its organs.

Art. 44. 1. A People's Council rescinds the decision of a People's Council of a lower level or of the Presidium of such Council, if that decision is at variance with the law or incompatible with the basic line of the policy of the State.

2. The Presidium of a People's Council may suspend the execution of a decision of a People's Council of a lower level and submit the case for decision at the next meeting of its own People's Council.

Art. 45. The details of composition as well as the terms of reference and the rules of procedure of the People's Councils and their organs are established by law.

CHAPTER 6

THE COURTS AND THE PUBLIC PROSECUTOR'S OFFICE

Art. 46. 1. The administration of justice in the Polish People's Republic is carried out by the Supreme Court, Voivodeship Courts, District Courts and Special Courts.

2. Organization, jurisdiction and procedure of the Courts are established by law.

Art. 47. The Courts pronounce judgment in the name of the Polish People's Republic.

Art. 48. The Courts are the custodians of the political and social system of the Polish People's Republic; they protect the achievements of the Polish working people, safeguard the people's rule of law, social property and the rights of citizens, and punish offenders.

Art. 49. People's assessors take part in the hearing of cases and the pronouncement of judgment, except in cases specified by law.

Art. 50. 1. Judges and people's assessors are elected.

2. The procedure of election and the term of office of judges and assessors of Voivodeship and District Courts are established by law.

3. The procedure of appointment of judges of Special Courts is established by law.

Art. 51. 1. The Supreme Court is the highest judicial organ and supervises the activity of all other courts concerning the pronouncement of judgment.

2. The procedure for the exercise of supervision by the Supreme Court is established by law.

3. The Supreme Court is elected by the Council of State for a term of five years.

Art. 52. Judges are independent and subject only to the law.

Art. 53. 1. Cases in all courts of the Polish People's Republic are heard in public. The law may specify exceptions to this principle.

2. The accused is guaranteed the right to legal defence. He may have a defence counsel, either of his own choice or appointed by the Court.

Art. 54. 1. The Prosecutor General of the Polish People's Republic safeguards the people's rule of law, watches over the protection of social property and ensures that the rights of citizens are respected.

2. The Prosecutor General supervises, in particular, the prosecution of offences endangering the political and social system, security and independence of the Polish People's Republic.

3. The limits of jurisdiction and the scope of activity of the Prosecutor General are established by law.

Art. 55. 1. The Prosecutor General of the Polish People's Republic is appointed and recalled by the Council of State.

2. The mode of appointing and recalling Prosecutors subordinate to the Prosecutor General, is, together with the principles of the organization and procedure of organs of the Prosecutor's Office, established by law.

3. The Prosecutor General is accountable to the Council of State for the activity of the Prosecutor's Office.

Art. 56. The organs of the Prosecutor's Office are subordinate to the Prosecutor General of the Polish People's Republic and in the exercise of their functions are independent of local organs.

CHAPTER 7

FUNDAMENTAL RIGHTS AND DUTIES OF CITIZENS

Art. 57. The Polish People's Republic, by consolidating and multiplying the gains of the working people, strengthens and extends the rights and liberties of the citizens.

Art. 58. 1. Citizens of the Polish People's Republic have the right to work, that is, the right to employment paid in accordance with the quanti ty and quality of work done.

2. The right to work is ensured by the social ownership of the basic means of production, by the development of a social and co-operative system in the countryside, free from exploitation; by the planned growth of the productive forces; by the elimination of sources of economic crises and by the abolition of unemployment.

Art. 59. 1. Citizens of the Polish People's Republic have the right to rest and leisure.

2. The right to rest and leisure is assured to manual and office workers by reduction of working hours through the application of the 8-hour working day and shorter work time in cases specified by law, by the institution according to law of days off work and by annual holidays with pay.

3. The organization of workers' holiday schemes, the development of the tourist movement, of health resorts, sports facilities, houses of culture, clubs, recreation rooms, parks and other leisure time facilities, create possibilities for healthy and cultural relaxation for an increasing number of working people in town and country.

Art. 60. 1. Citizens of the Polish People's Republic have the right to health protection and to aid in the event of sickness or incapacity for work.

2. Effect is being given to this right on an increasing scale through:

(1) the development of social insurance for manual and office workers to cover sickness, old age and incapacity for work, as well as through the expansion of various forms of social assistance;

(2) the development of the State organized protection of the health of the population, the expansion of sanitation services and the raising of the health standards in town and country, consistent improvement of safety conditions, protection and hygiene of work, a wide campaign for the prevention of and fighting disease, increasing access to free medical attention, the development of hospitals, sanatoria, medical aid centres, rural health centres, and care for the disabled.

Art. 61. 1. Citizens of the Polish People's Republic have the right to education.

2. This right is ensured on an increasing scale by:

(1) universal, free and compulsory primary schools;

(2) a constant development of secondary schools, providing general or vocational education, and of schools of academic level;

3. the help of the State in raising the skill of citizens employed in industrial establishments and other places of employment in town and country;

(4) a scheme of State scholarship, the development of hostels, boarding schools and students' homes, together with other forms of material aid for the children of workers, working peasants and intelligentsia.

Art. 62. 1. Citizens of the Polish People's Republic have the right to benefit from cultural achievements and to participate in the development of national culture.

2. This right is ensured on an increasing scale by developing and making accessible to the working people in town and country libraries, books, press, radio, cinemas, theatres, museums and exhibitions, houses of culture, clubs and recreation rooms; by a general fostering and promoting of the cultural creative activity of the people and of the development of creative talents.

Art. 63. The Polish People's Republic fosters the all-round development of science and learning based on the achievements of the most advanced thought of mankind and of Polish progressive thought—the development of science and learning in the service of the nation.

Art. 64. The Polish People's Republic encourages the development of literature and art which express the needs and aspirations of the nation and which are in accord with the best progressive traditions of Polish creative thought.

Art. 65. The Polish People's Republic extends special protection to the creative intelligentsia—to those working in science, education, literature and art, as well as to pioneers of technical progress, to rationalizers and inventors.

Art. 66. 1. Women in the Polish People's Republic have equal rights with men in all spheres of public, political, economic, social and cultural life.

2. The equality of rights of women is guaranteed by:

(1) equal rights with men to work and pay according to the principle "equal pay for equal work," the right to rest and leisure, to social insurance, to education, to honors and decorations, to hold public office;

(2) mother-and-child care, protection of expectant mothers, paid holidays during the period before and after confinement, the development of a network of maternity homes, crèches and nursery schools, the extension of a network of service establishments and restaurants and canteens.

Art. 67. 1. Marriage and the family are under the care and protection of the Polish People's Republic. The State gives particular care to families with many children.

2. A child born out of wedlock suffers no loss of rights.

Art. 68. The Polish People's Republic gives particularly careful attention to the education of youth and guarantees them the most extensive possibilities for development.

Art. 69. 1. Citizens of the Polish People's Republic, irrespective of nationality, race or religion, enjoy equal rights in all spheres of public, political, economic, social and cultural life. Infringement of this principle by any direct or indirect granting of privileges or restriction of rights, on account of nationality, race or religion, is punishable by law.

2. The spreading of hatred or contempt, the provocation of strife or the humiliation of man on account of national, racial or religious differences are forbidden.

Art. 70. 1. The Polish People's Republic guarantees freedom of conscience and religion to citizens. The Church and other religious bodies may freely exercise their religious functions. It is forbidden to prevent citizens from taking part in religious activities or rites. It is also forbidden to coerce anybody to participate in religious activities or rites.

2. The Church is separated from the State. The principles of the relationship between Church and State are, together with the legal and patrimonial position of religious bodies, determined by law.

3. The abuse of the freedom of conscience and religion for purposes prejudicial to the interests of the Polish People's Republic is punishable.

Art. 71. 1. The Polish People's Republic guarantees its citizens freedom of speech, of the press, of meetings and assemblies, of processions and demonstrations.

2. The making available to the working people and their organizations of the use of printing shops, stocks of paper, public buildings and halls, means of communication, the radio and other indispensable material means, serves to give effect to this freedom.

Art. 72. 1. In order to promote the political, social, economic and cultural activity of the working people of town and country, the Polish People's Republic guarantees to citizens the right of association.

2. Political organizations, trade unions, associations of working peasants, co-operative associations, youth, women's, sports and defence organizations, cultural, technical and scientific associations, as well as other working people's social organizations unite the citizens for active participation in political, social, economic and cultural life.

3. The setting up of, and participation, in associations the aims or activities of which are directed against the political or social system or against the legal order of the Polish People's Republic are forbidden.

Art. 73. 1. Citizens have the right to approach all organs of the State with complaints and grievances.

2. Citizens' complaints and grievances are to be examined and settled in an expeditious and just manner. Those guilty of protraction or of displaying a soulless and bureaucratic attitude towards citizens' complaints and grievances will be called to responsibility.

Art. 74. 1. The Polish People's Republic guarantees to citizens inviolability of the person. A citizen may be deprived of his freedom only in cases specified by law. A detained person must be set free unless, within forty-eight hours from the moment of his detention, a warrant of arrest issued by the Court or the Prosecutor has been served on him.

2. The law protects the inviolability of the home and the privacy of correspondence. Search of the home is permissible only in cases specified by law.

3. Property may be seized only in cases established by law, by virtue of a final judgment.

Art. 75. The Polish People's Republic grants asylum to citizens of foreign countries persecuted for defending the interests of the working people, for struggling for social progress, for activity in defence of peace, for fighting for national liberation or for scienctific activity.

Art. 76. It is the duty of every citizen of the Polish People's Republic to abide by the provisions of the Constitution and of the laws, to maintain socialist work discipline, to respect the rules of social intercourse and to discharge conscientiously their duties towards the State.

Art. 77. 1. It is the duty of every citizen of the Polish People's Republic to safeguard and strengthen social property, which is the unshakable foundation of the development of the State, the source of the wealth and might of the country.

2. Persons who commit sabotage, subsversion, inflict damage or who otherwise injure social property, are punishable with all the severity of law.

Art. 78. 1. To defend the country is the most sacred duty of every citizen.

2. Military service is an honorable patriotic duty of citizens of the Polish People's Republic.

Art. 79. 1. Vigilance against the enemies of the nation and the diligent guarding of State secrets is the duty of every citizen of the Polish People's Republic.

2. High treason—espionage, undermining of the Armed Forces, desertion to the enemy—is punishable as the gravest of crimes with all the severity of law.

CHAPTER 8

PRINCIPLES OF ELECTORAL LAW

Art. 80. Elections to the Seym and to the People's Councils are universal, equal, direct and carried out by secret ballot.

Art. 81. Every citizen who has reached the age of eighteen has, irrespective of sex, nationality and race, religion, education, length of residence, social origin, profession or property, the right to vote.

Art. 82. Every citizen who has reached the age of eighteen is eligible for election to the People's Councils, and every citizen who has reached the age of twenty-one is eligible for election to the Seym.

Art. 83. Women have all electoral rights on equal terms with men.

Art. 84. Citizens serving in the Armed Forces have all electoral rights on equal terms with civilians.

Art. 85. Electoral rights are denied only to insane persons and to persons deprived by Court decision of public rights.

Art. 86. Candidates for the Seym and candidates for the People's Councils are nominated by political and social organizations in town and country.

Art. 87. It is the duty of Deputies to the Seym and of members of People's Councils to report to the electors on their work and on the activity of the body to which they have been elected.

Art. 88. The procedure for nomination of candidates and for holding elections, as well as the procedure for the recall of Deputies to the Seym and of members of People's Councils, are established by law.

CHAPTER 9

COAT-OF-ARMS, COLORS AND CAPITAL OF THE POLISH PEOPLE'S REPUBLIC

Art. 89. 1. The Coat-of-Arms of the Polish People's Republic is the image of a white eagle on a red field.

2. The colors of the Polish People's Republic are white and red.

3. The details are established by law.

Art. 90. The capital of the Polish People's Republic is Warsaw—city of heroic traditions of the Polish nation.

CHAPTER 10

PROCEDURE FOR AMENDING THE CONSTITUTION

Art. 91. The Constitution may be amended only by an Act of the Seym of the Polish People's Republic, passed by a majority of not less than two thirds of the votes, not less than half the total number of Deputies being present.

PORTUGAL

SUMMARY

INTERNATIONAL STATUS

Portugal is a member of the United Nations (December 14, 1955).[1] It is a member of other international organizations. It was a member of the League of Nations.

Portugal resumed its independence in 1668 after a period of dual monarchy with Spain from 1580 to 1640. Following the invasion by Napoleon in 1807, the capital was transferred to Brazil. In 1820, occurred the first

[1] Portugal has accepted the compulsory jurisdiction of the International Court under Article 36 of its Statute.

liberal revolution. In 1822, Brazil became independent. In 1834, a representative system was established. The republic was proclaimed on October 5, 1910. Sixteen years of party struggles, government changes, economic and administrative crises led, in 1926, to a military *coup d'état* which established a non-parliamentary régime entitled the "New State." Dr. Salazar, minister of finance, became President in 1932 and in 1933 promulgated a constitution for a corporative state.

FORM OF NATIONAL GOVERNMENT

The Constitution of April 11, 1933, as amended in 1935, 1936, 1937, 1938, 1945, 1951 and 1959, describes the territory of Portugal [1] and states that Portugal is a unitary and corporative republic.[2] There are provisions concerning corporative bodies,[3] and the economic and social order.[4] The Catholic religion is the religion of the Portuguese nation and church and State are separate.[5] Sovereignty is vested in the nation.[6]

RIGHTS OF THE PEOPLE

The Constitution provides for equality before the law, the right to life and personal safety, to work, good name and reputation, freedom of religion, expression, teaching, association and assembly (subject to special laws governing their exercise), inviolability of residence and privacy of correspondence, freedom of profession, personal liberty, right of property, the right of petition.[7] There are provisions concerning protection of the family and its political status.[8] Primary education is obligatory.[9] Military service is general and compulsory.[10]

LEGISLATIVE DEPARTMENT

The legislature is composed of the National Assembly and the Corporative Chamber. The National Assembly consists of 130 deputies elected by direct vote for a term of four years subject to dissolution.[11] Immunities of members are provided.[12] It meets in one regular session a year.[13] The Corporative Chamber is composed of representatives of local autonomous bodies and social interests; it has the same term as the National Assembly; its duty is to give its opinion on all bills and international conventions and treaties submitted to the National Assembly before discussion thereon by the latter begins.[14] There are provisions concerning finance.[15]

[1] Const., Art. 1. [2] Id., Art. 5. [3] Id., Art. 16–21. [4] Id., Art. 29–41.
[5] Id., Art. 45. [6] Id., Art. 71. [7] Id., Art. 5, 8, 46.
[8] Id., Art. 12–15, 19–21. [9] Id., Art. 43. [10] Id., Art. 54.
[11] Id., Art. 85, 87, 81. [12] Id., Art. 89. [13] Id., Art. 94.
[14] Id., Art. 102, 103. [15] Id., Art. 63–70.

EXECUTIVE DEPARTMENT

The President of the Republic is elected by an electoral college composed of the members of the National Assembly and the Corporative Chamber, municipal representatives of each district or overseas province, and representatives of the legislative councils and government councils of the provinces, for a term of seven years which may not be renewed.[1] Relatives of Kings of Portugal are not eligible.[2] The President has the power of appointment, convenes and dissolves the National Assembly, promulgates laws, has the right of pardon.[3] He acts in conjunction with the Council of State, composed of the Presidents of the Council of Ministers, of the National Assembly, of the Corporative Chamber, of the Supreme Court, the Procurator General and ten public men chosen by the President.[4] The Government consists of the President of the Council of Ministers and of Ministers who are responsible to the President; they do not forfeit their mandates as members of the National Assembly or Corporative Chamber but may not sit in their respective Chambers.[5] A section relates to local government,[6] and another to overseas Portugal.[7]

JUDICIAL DEPARTMENT

The exercise of judicial functions belongs to the ordinary courts, consisting of the Supreme Court of Justice and courts of the first and second instance, and to special courts for fiscal or social crimes or crimes against the safety of the State.[8] Judges of ordinary courts are appointed for life.[9] The constitutionality or legality of ordinances promulgated by the President may be called into question only by the National Assembly which determines its effects.[10]

AREA, POPULATION, ETC.

The area of Portugal is 91,531 square kilometres, its population (1965) 9,199,000. The capital is Lisbon.

1 Id., Art. 72.
2 Id., Art. 74.
3 Id., Art. 81.
4 Id., Art. 83.
5 Id., Art. 107, 108, 110.
6 Id., Art. 125–132.
7 Id., Art. 133–175.
8 Id., Art. 116, 117.
9 Id., Art. 119.
10 Id., Art. 123.

CONSTITUTION of PORTUGAL[1]

April 11, 1933, as amended 1935, 1936, 1937, 1938, 1945, 1951 and 1959

PART I

ON THE FUNDAMENTAL GUARANTEES

CHAPTER I – ON THE PORTUGUESE NATION

Art. 1. The territory of Portugal is that which at present belongs to it and comprises:

(I) in Europe: the mainland and the archipelagoes of Madeira and the Azores;

(II) in West Africa: the Cape Verde archipelago, Guinea, S. Tomé and Principe and their dependencies, S. João Baptista de Ajudá, Cabinda and Angola;

(III) in East Africa: Mozambique;

(IV) in Asia: the State of India and Macau and their respective dependencies.

(V) in Oceania: Timor and its dependencies.

Sole. §. The nation does not renounce the rights which it has or may hereafter acquire over any other territory.

Art. 2. The State shall not in any way alienate part of the national territory or the sovereign rights it exercises over it, except in so far as concerns the rectification of frontiers when approved by the National Assembly.

§ 1. No part of national territory may be acquired by the Government or public legal entity of a foreign country, except for the installation of diplomatic or consular representation where there is reciprocity in favor of the Portuguese State.

§ 2. In the Overseas Territories the acquisition by a foreign Government

[1] *Political Constitution of the Portuguese Republic.* S.N. 1. Lisbon, 1957. Supplied, together with 1959 amendments, by the Ministry of Foreign Affairs in December 1965. Ed.

of land or buildings for the installation of consular representation shall be subject to the approval of the choice of the site in question by the Minister of Overseas Territories.

Art. 3. The nation consists of all Portuguese citizens resident within or outside its territory and they shall be considered as subject to the State and Portuguese law, without prejudice to the rules of international law which may be applicable.

Sole §. Foreigners sojourning or resident in Portugal are also subject to the State and Portuguese laws, without prejudice to the provisions of international law.

Art. 4. The Portuguese nation is an independent State. Its sovereignty recognises in the internal sphere morality and law as the only limitations; in the international field it recognizes only those limitations which are derived from conventions or treaties freely entered into, or from customary law freely accepted. It is the duty of the nation to co-operate with other states in preparing and adopting measures making for peace among people and for the progress of mankind.

Sole §. Portugal advocates arbitration as a means of settling international disputes.

Art. 5. The Portuguese State is a unitary and corporative republic founded upon the equality of all its citizens in the eyes of the law, upon the free access for all classes to the benefits of civilization, and upon the participation of all the constituent forces of the nation in its administrative life and in the making of laws.

Sole §. Equality before the law implies the right to be employed in public service according to ability or services rendered; it also involves no recognition of privilege of birth, nobility, title, sex or social position, save only the distinction due to women by reason of their nature and in the interest of the family; in regard to the obligations and benefits of citizens, it involves those differences imposed by diversity of circumstances or arising out of natural conditions.

Art. 6. It is the duty of the State:

(I) To promote the unity and establish the juridical order of the nation by defining and enforcing respect for the rights and guarantees of morality, justice or the law, in the interest of the individual, of families, and local autonomous and public or private bodies;

(II) To co-ordinate, stimulate and direct all social activities in order to promote a proper harmony of interests within the lawful subordination of private interests to the general good;

(III) To strive to improve the conditions of the least favored social classes, endeavoring to secure for them a standard of living compatible with human dignity;

(IV) To protect public health.

CHAPTER II – ON CITIZENS

Art. 7. Civil law defines how Portuguese citizenship is acquired and lost. A Portuguese citizen enjoys the rights and guarantees provided by the Constitution; naturalized citizens, however, are subject to the restrictions prescribed by law.

Sole §. Foreigners resident in Portugal enjoy the same rights and guarantees, unless the law determines otherwise. This does not apply to political rights or to public rights which involve a duty towards the State, although, as regards public rights, reciprocal privileges granted to Portuguese nationals by other states shall be observed.

Art. 8. Portuguese citizens shall enjoy the following rights, liberties and individual guarantees:

(I) The right to life and personal safety;

(I-*A*) The right to work within the terms prescribed by law;

(II) The right to good name and reputation;

(III) Liberty and inviolability of religious beliefs and practices, on the ground of holding which nobody may be persecuted, deprived of a right or exempted from any obligation or civic duty. Nobody shall be compelled to answer questions concerning the religion he professes, except in a legally conducted census;

(IV) The free expression of thought in any form;

(V) Freedom of teaching;

(VI) The inviolability of residence and the privacy of correspondence, as may be determined by law;

(VII) Freedom of choice of profession or nature of work, art or trade, subject to such legal restrictions as may be necessary in the interests of public welfare and to monopolies which, by law, can only be granted by the State and administrative bodies for reasons of recognised public utility;

(VIII) Nobody shall be deprived of personal liberty or arrested without being charged except for cases coming under paragraphs 3 and 4 hereof;

(IX) Nobody shall be sentenced for a criminal offence unless there is an existing law which declares the act or omission to be punishable;

(X) To prepare a case in defence, the accused being given the necessary guarantees to this end both before and after being formally charged;

(XI) Nobody shall be punished by imprisonment for an unlimited term or by death, except however, as regards the latter, during a state of war with a foreign country, in which case the sentence must be carried out in the theatre of war;

(XII) There shall be no confiscation of goods nor can any personal punishment be inflicted except upon the delinquent;

(XIII) Nobody shall suffer imprisonment for failure to pay costs or stamp duties;

(XIV) Freedom of meeting and association;
(XV) The right of property and its transmission during life or by death, as provided by the civil law;
(XVI) Freedom from the payment of taxes not decreed in accordance with the Constitution;
(XVII) The right to reparation for all actual damage in accordance with the provisions of the law, which may prescribe pecuniary reparation for damages of a moral character;
(XVIII) The right of making representation or petition, claim or complaint, to sovereign or other public authority, on matters affecting personal rights or the general good;
(XIX) The right of resistance to any order which may infringe individual guarantees, unless legally suspended, and of repelling by force private aggression when recourse to public authority is impossible;
(XX) Sentences for criminal offences shall be open to revision, and the right to an indemnity from the State for loss and damage shall be assured to the convicted person or his heirs by measures to be defined by law.

§ 1. The enumeration of the above rights and guarantees shall not exclude any others derived from the Constitution or the law, it being understood that citizens should always exercise them without injuring the rights of third parties, or damaging the interests of society or moral principles.

§ 2. Special laws shall govern the exercise of the freedom of expression of opinion, education, meeting and of association. As regards the first item, they shall prevent, by precautionary or restrictive measures, the perversion of public opinion in its function as a social force, and shall protect the character of citizens, who, when libelled or abused in a periodical publication, shall have the right to have a correction or reply inserted in the same, free of charge, without prejudice to any other right or to such proceedings as may be determined by law.

§ 3. Imprisonment without formal charge is permitted in cases of *flagrante delicto* and in cases of the following actually committed, prevented or attempted crimes: those against the safety of the State; the counterfeiting of money, bank-notes and government bonds; wilful homicide; burglary or robbery; larceny, fraud or embezzlement, when perpetrated by a habitual criminal; fraudulent bankruptcy; arson; the manufacture, possession, or use of explosive bombs and other similar appliances.

§ 4. Except in the cases specified in the preceding paragraph, imprisonment in a public goal, or detention in a private residence, or institution for lunatics, is only permitted on a written order from the competent authorities, and shall not be continued on the accused offering proper bail or bond in regard to residence, when allowed by law.

The exceptional safeguard of *habeas corpus* may be used against an abuse of authority in the circumstances prescribed in a special law.

Art. 9. No one shall be prejudiced in his situation or permanent employment by virtue of the obligation to undergo military service or in consequence of his services in the civil defence of the territory.

Art. 10. The State shall bestow distinctions of honor or rewards on those citizens who distinguish themselves by reason of personal merit or civic or military deeds, and likewise on foreigners when there is an international interest; the law prescribing the orders, decorations, medals and diplomas which may be used for this purpose.

Art. 11. All authorities are jointly and severally precluded from suspending the Constitution or limiting the rights therein established except in the cases therein provided.

CHAPTER III – ON THE FAMILY

Art. 12. The State shall ensure the formation and protection of the family as the source of preservation and development of the Portuguese people, as the first basis of education, social discipline and harmony, and as the foundation of all political and administrative order through family grouping and representation in the parish and the municipality.

Art. 13. The constitution of the family is based upon:

(I) marriage and legitimate offspring;

(II) equality of rights and duties of husband and wife in regard to the maintenance and education of their legitimate children;

(III) the obligation to register the marriage and birth of children.

§ 1. The civil law shall determine the rules governing the persons and goods of husband and wife, parental authority and its substitution, the rights of succession in direct or collateral line, and the right of maintenance.

§ 2. Legitimate children shall be guaranteed those full rights necessary for the order and unity of the family, and rights corresponding to their position shall also be recognised in the case of illegitimate children who can be recognised as offspring, and likewise unborn children, particularly the right to maintenance which shall be the liability of those upon whom, after investigation, the duty is found to fall.

Art. 14. With the object of protecting the family it is the duty of the State and local bodies:

(I) to encourage the establishment of separate homes under healthy conditions, and the institution of the family household;

(II) to protect maternity;

(III) to adjust taxation to the legitimate obligations of the family, and to promote the adoption of a family wage;

(IV) to assist parents in the discharge of their duty of instructing and educating their children, and to co-operate with them by means of public institutions for education and correction, or by encouraging private establishments having the same objects;

(V) to take all measures necessary to prevent the corruption of morals.

Art. 15. The registration of the civil status of citizens is a matter proper to the State.

CHAPTER IV – ON CORPORATIVE BODIES

Art. 16. It is the duty of the State to authorise, unless otherwise provided by law to the contrary, all corporative, collective, intellectual or economic bodies, and to promote and assist their formation.

Art. 17. The principal aims of the corporative bodies, referred to in the preceding article, shall be scientific, literary or artistic, or physical training, relief, alms, or charity; technical improvement or solidarity of interests.

Sole §. The constitution of these bodies and the way in which they function shall be governed by special regulations.

Art. 18. Foreigners domiciled in Portugal may be members of the corporative organizations referred to, on such conditions as may be determined by law; they shall not be allowed a share in the exercise of the political rights granted to these bodies.

CHAPTER V – ON THE FAMILY, CORPORATIVE ORGANIZATION AND AUTONOMOUS BODIES AS POLITICAL UNITS

Art. 19. It is the particular privilege of families to elect the parish councils.

Sole §. This right is exercised by the head of the family.

Art. 20. All the activities of the nation shall be organically represented in corporative bodies, and it shall be their duty to participate in the election of town councils and district boards and the constitution of the Corporative Chamber.

Art. 21. In the political organization of the State, the parish boards take part in the election of town councils, and the latter in that of district boards. Representatives of local authorities shall sit in the Corporative Chamber.

CHAPTER VI – ON PUBLIC OPINION

Art. 22. Public opinion is a fundamental part of the policy and administration of the country; it shall be the duty of the State to protect it against all those influences which distort it from the truth, justice, good administration, and the common weal.

Art. 23. The press exercises functions public in nature, and by virtue of this cannot refuse to print official news sent to it by the Government on matters of national interest. A special law shall define the rights and duties both of newspaper companies and of professional journalists so as to safeguard the independence and dignity of both.

CHAPTER VII – ON THE ADMINISTRATIVE ORDER

Art. 24. Civil servants are for the service of the community and not for that of any party or association of private interests; it is their duty to respect the authority of the State and cause others to do so.

Art. 25. The employees and servants of local autonomous authorities, of the corporative bodies and organizations for economic co-ordination, of bodies engaged in administrative public utilities and of firms which conduct services of public interest, are subject to the discipline prescribed in the previous article.

Art. 26. Planned interruption of public services or of those of interest to the community shall involve the dismissal of the offenders, without prejudice to any other liability at law.

Art. 27. Nobody shall be allowed to hold more than one office in the employment either of the State or local bodies, or of both, except on such conditions as may be laid down by law.

Sole §. Rules as to incompatibility, whether in regard to public offices or to the exercise of other professions in conjunction with same, shall be determined by a special law.

Art. 28. All citizens are bound to lend their services and co-operation to the State and local bodies as established by law and to contribute towards public expenditure according to their means.

CHAPTER VIII – ON THE ECONOMIC AND SOCIAL ORDER

Art. 29. The economic organization of the nation must provide the maximum production and wealth for the benefit of society, and shall create a collective existence from which shall flow power to the State and justice to its citizens.

Art. 30. The State shall conduct its economic relations with other countries according to the principle of proper co-operation, without prejudice to the commercial advantages to be obtained from any particular country, or the necessity for protection against external threats or attacks.

Art. 31. It shall be the right and duty of the State to co-ordinate and control economic and social life with the following objects:

(I) to establish a proper balance of the population, of professions, of occupations, of capital and of labor;

(II) to protect the national economic system from agricultural, industrial and commercial ventures of a parasitic nature, or those incompatible with the higher interests of human life;

(III) to secure the lowest price and the highest wage consistent with fair remuneration for other factors of production, by means of improved technical methods, services and credit;

(IV) To prevent exaggerated profits for capital, not allowing the latter to diverge from its humane and christian purpose.

(V) to develop the settlement of the national territories, to protect emigrants and to regulate emigration.

Art. 32. The State shall encourage those private economic activities which are the most profitable, relative costs being equal, but without detriment to the social benefit conferred and to the protection due to small home industries.

Art. 33. The State may only intervene directly in the management of private economic ventures when it has to finance them and for the purpose of securing a larger measure of social benefit than would otherwise be the case.

Sole §. State undertakings carried on for profit, even if working on the basis of free competition, are likewise subject to the provisions laid down in the latter part of the present article.

Art. 34. The State shall promote the formation and development of the national corporative economic system, taking care to prevent any tendency among its constituent bodies to indulge in unrestricted competition with each other, contrary to their own proper aims and those of society, and shall encourage them to collaborate as members of the same community.

Art. 35. Property, capital and labor have a social function in the field of economic co-operation and common interest, and the law may determine the conditions of their use or exploitation in accordance with the community aim in view.

Art. 36. Labor, whether unskilled, skilled, or technical, may be associated with an undertaking in any form that circumstances render advisable.

Art. 37. Only economic corporations which are recognised by the State may conclude collective labor contracts, in accordance with the law, and those made without their intervention shall be null and void.

Art. 38. Disputes arising out of labor contracts shall be the concern of special tribunals.

Art. 39. In their economic relations with each another, neither capital nor labor shall be allowed to suspend operations with the object of imposing their respective claims.

Art. 40. Obstacles will be placed in the way of the accumulation of posts in private enterprises, as being contrary to public economy and morality.

Art. 41. The State shall promote and encourage community concerns and provident, co-operative, and mutual benefit institutions.

CHAPTER IX – ON EDUCATION, INSTRUCTION AND NATIONAL CULTURE

Art. 42. Education and instruction are obligatory and are the concern of the family and of public or private institutions in co-operation with the same.

Art. 43. The State shall officially maintain primary, secondary middle and high schools, and institutions for advanced education.

§ 1. Elementary primary instruction is obligatory and may be given at home, or in private or state schools.

§ 2. The arts and sciences shall be encouraged and their development, teaching and dissemination favored, provided that respect is maintained for the Constitution, the authorities and the co-ordinating functions of the State.

§ 3. The instruction provided by the State, in addition to aiming at physical fitness and the improvement of intellectual faculties, has as its object the formation of character and of professional ability as well as the development of all moral and civic qualities, the former according to the traditional principles of the country and to Christian doctrine and morality.

§ 4. No permission shall be required for the teaching of religion in private schools.

Art. 44. The establishment of private schools on the lines of the State schools shall be free, but subject to State inspection; schools may be subsidised by the State or authorized to grant diplomas if their *curricula* and standard of their teaching staff are not inferior to those of the corresponding public institutions.

CHAPTER X – ON THE RELATIONS OF THE STATE WITH THE CATHOLIC CHURCH AND OF THE REGIME OF WORSHIP

Art. 45. The Catholic religion may be freely practised, in public or in private, as the religion of the Portuguese Nation. The Catholic Church shall enjoy juridical personality and may organize itself in conformity with canon law and create thereunder associations or organizations, the juridical personality of which shall equally be recognized. The relationship between the State and the Catholic Church shall be one of separation, with diplomatic relations maintained between the Holy See and Portugal by means of reciprocal representation, and concordats or agreements entered into in the sphere of the *Padroado* (Patronage) and where other matters of common interest are, or need to be, regulated.

Art. 46. The State shall also ensure freedom of worship and organization for all other religious faiths practised on Portuguese territory, their outward manifestations being regulated by law, and it may grant juridical personality to associations constituted in conformity with the creeds in question.

Sole §. These provisions shall not apply to creeds incompatible with the life and physical integrity of the human person and with good behavior, or to the dissemination of doctrines contrary to the established social order.

Art. 47. The State may not assign to any other purpose any chapel, building, or article belonging to a religious body.

Art. 48. Public cemeteries shall be secular in character and ministers of any religions may freely practise their respective rites therein.

CHAPTER XI – ON THE PUBLIC AND PRIVATE DOMAINS OF THE STATE

Art. 49. The public domain of the State shall comprise the following:

(I) mineral deposits, medicinal mineral springs and other natural wealth below the surface;

(II) sea waters and their shores;

(III) lakes, lagoons, and watercourses navigable to ships or rafts, their respective beds or channels, and also any others recognised by special decree to be of public utility as suitable for the production of electric power, national or regional, or for irrigation;

(IV) dykes opened up by the State;

(V) the air over the land beyond such limits as the law fixes in favor of the owner of the surface;

(VI) railways of public interests of any kind, public highways and roads;

(VII) territorial areas reserved for military defence;

(VIII) any other property placed by law under the régime of public domain.

§ 1. The authority of the State over the property of the public domain and the use of it by citizens shall be governed by law and by the international conventions concluded by Portugal, without prejudice to the prior rights of the State and the acquired private rights of individuals. The latter rights, however, shall be subject to expropriation as may be determined by the public interest and upon payment of reasonable indemnity.

§ 3. Rocks and common earths, and materials commonly employed in building are expressly excepted from the natural riches specified in (I) above.

§ 3. The State shall undertake the demarcation of those private lands which abut on any property of public domain.

Art. 50. The administration on the mainland and on the adjacent islands of property owned by the State in a private capacity pertains to the Ministry of Finance, except when it is expressly attributed to any other Ministry.

Art. 51. No State property or rights which affect its prestige or the more important national interests may be alienated.

Art. 52. Artistic, historical and natural monuments, and artistic objects officially recognized as such, are under the protection of the State, and their alienation in favor of foreigners is prohibited.

CHAPTER XII – ON NATIONAL DEFENCE

Art. 53. The State shall guarantee the existence of the military land, sea and air institutions which are required by the supreme defence needs of national integrity and the keeping of order and public peace.

Sole §. There shall be a single military organization for the entire territory.

Art. 54. Military service shall be general and compulsory. The law shall determine the conditions of service.

Art. 55. The law shall regulate the general organization of the nation in wartime in accordance with the principle of a nation in arms.

Art. 56. The State shall promote, encourage and assist civil institutions whose aim is to teach and discipline young persons in preparation for the fulfilment of their military and patriotic duties.

Art. 57. No citizen may hold or obtain employment from the State or local autonomous bodies unless he has fulfilled the duties to which he is liable under military law.

Art. 58. The State guarantees protection and pensions to persons who incapacitated on military service in defence of the country or of order, and likewise to the families of individuals who lose their lives in such service.

CHAPTER XIII – ON THE ADMINISTRATION OF UNDERTAKINGS OF PUBLIC INTEREST

Art. 59. All undertakings, the object of which is the utilization or exploitation of anything forming part of the State public domain, are regarded as being of collective interest and are subject to a special State régime of administration, competition, supervision, or control, in accordance with the needs of public security, national defence and economic and social relations.

Art. 60. The following shall conform to uniform rules, without prejudice to special circumstances when necessary in matters of secondary importance:

(I) the establishment or alteration of land, river, sea or air communications, whatever their nature or purpose;

(II) the construction of works for the utilization of water or coal for the production of electric power; the construction of grid systems for its transmission, supply or distribution, and also in general works for agricultural drainage and irrigation purposes.

(III) the exploitation of public services in connection with above mentioned communications, works and grid system.

Art. 61. The State will promote the development of the public improvements mentioned in the previous article, above all the development of the national merchant navy, having particularly in view connections with the overseas territories and with those countries where Portuguese are numerous.

Art. 62. The tariffs for the exploitation of public services in respect of which concessions have been granted are subject to control and legal inspection by the State.

CHAPTER XIV – ON STATE FINANCE

Art. 63. There shall be a single general State budget for the mainland and adjacent islands, showing the sum total of public receipts and expenditure and likewise those of the autonomous services. Detailed explanations of these may be published separately.

Art. 64. The general State budget shall be drawn up annually and put into effect by the Government, in conformity with the legal provisions in force and particularly the law of authorization mentioned in Article 91 (IV).

Art. 65. Expenditure corresponding to the legal or contractual obligations of the State, or that which is permanent by reason of its nature or purpose, including interest charges and redemption of the Public Debt, shall be taken as the basis for fixing taxation and other State revenue.

Art. 66. The budget shall state the measures which are essential for meeting total expenditure.

Art. 67. The State may only borrow for extraordinary expenditure for economic expansion, for redemption of other loans, and for essential increase of State patrimony, or vital requirements for the defence and preservation of the nation.

Sole §. Essential supplementary revenue may however be obtained by means of floating debt, representing receipts of the current administrative period, at the end of which the amount must be liquidated, or the Treasury placed in a position to liquidate it through its funds.

Art. 68. The State may not reduce the capital or interest of the funded public debt to the detriment of the bondholders, but may convert it on equitable terms.

Art. 69. Sums due on account of deposits placed in State funds or its credit institutions may not be subjected to compulsory consolidation.

Art. 70. The law shall fix general principles in regard to the following matters:

(I) taxation;

(II) rates chargeable on public services;

(III) administration and exploitation of State property and undertakings.

§ 1. In the matter of taxation the law shall determine the liability, rate, exemptions where proper, and the claims and reliefs to be allowd to the taxpayer.

§ 2. The collection of taxes established for an indefinite time, or for a fixed period exceeding a single administrative period shall be subject to the authorization of the National Assembly.

PART II

ON THE POLITICAL ORGANIZATION OF THE STATE

CHAPTER I – ON SOVEREIGNTY

Art. 71. Sovereignty is vested in the nation; its representatives are the Head of the State, the National Assembly, the Government and the Courts of Justice.

CHAPTER II – ON THE HEAD OF THE STATE

Section I. On the election of the President of the Republic and of his Prerogatives

Art. 72. The Head of the State is the President of the Republic elected by the Nation through an electoral college. This college consists of acting members of the National Assembly and of the Corporative Chamber, by the municipal representatives of each district or of each overseas province that is not divided into districts, and also of the representatives of the legislative councils and of the governing councils of the provinces possessing a governor-general or possessing an ordinary governor, respectively.

The municipal representatives will be nominated by elected town councils according to the law, which will establish the number of representatives for each district or overseas province, to correspond to the number of town councils in each case. The representatives of the legislative councils and governing councils will be nominated by these bodies in the terms of the law, which will lay down the number falling to each council, to correspond to its representative character.

§ 1. The President is elected for seven years, not prolongable except when events make it inpossible for the electoral college to meet, in which case the term of office shall end as soon as his successor takes office.

§ 2. For the purposes of election the electoral college meets of its own right, under the chairmanship of the Chairman of the National Assembly, on the fifteenth day preceding the end of a president's term of office.

§ 3. Election shall fall on candidates proposed by a minimum of twenty electors and a maximum of fifty.

§ 4. The election shall be effected without previous debate by secret vote. That candidate shall be considered to be elected and shall be so proclaimed who receives two thirds of the votes cast by the legal number of members of the electoral college in the first poll.

§ 5. Should no candidate receive the majority of votes established in the preceding clause, a second poll shall be cast, and the candidate elected who receives an absolute majority of the votes referred to in that clause.

§ 6. If it be necessary to proceed to a third poll, that candidate who receives the largest number of votes shall be elected.

Art. 72A. If the date of election established in § 2 of the previous article should fall after the period of presentation of candidatures for a new legislature, than the electoral college shall meet after the new National Assembly has been elected, and the election shall take place on the fifteenth day following the commencement of the term of office of the new Members of the National Assembly.

If the same circumstances should refer to a period following the dissolution of the National Assembly, then the presidential election shall take place on the thirtieth day following the close of the election period.

Art. 73. Only a Portuguese citizen over thirty-five years of age, who has always possessed Portuguese nationality, and is in full enjoyment of his civil and political rights, may be elected President of the Republic.

Sole §. If the candidate elected is a member of the National Assembly or of the Corporative Chamber he shall forfeit his seat.

Art. 74. Relatives of the kings of Portugal, up to the sixth degree, are ineligible for the office of President of the Republic.

Art. 75. The President elect shall take up office on the day on which the term of office of his predecessor expires. He shall assume his functions before the National Assembly and the Corporative Chamber, met in joint session, and the following formula of oath shall be used.

> "I swear to maintain and loyally and faithfully to carry out the Constitution of the Republic, to observe the laws, to promote the general welfare of the nation and to uphold and protect the integrity and independence of the Portugeuse fatherland."

Art. 76. The President of the Republic may only leave the country with the assent of the National Assembly and of the Government. Such assent is not called for in cases of mere transit or non-official journeys lasting not longer than five days.

Sole §. Failure to observe the provisions of this article shall in the full meaning of the law involve loss of office.

Art. 77. The President of the Republic shall receive a salary, fixed before his election, and he may choose two State properties for use as the

Presidential Secretariat and as a private residence for himself and the members of his family.

Art. 78. The President of the Republic shall be directly and exclusively responsible to the nation for actions performed in the exercise of his duties. Both the exercise of the latter and his office as magistrate shall be independent of any vote of the National Assembly.

Sole §. For crimes unconnected with the exercise of his functions the President shall be answerable to ordinary courts of law but only after conclusion of his mandate.

Art. 79. The President of the Republic may resign his office in a message addressed to the nation and published in the *Diário do Governo* (Official Gazette).

Art. 80. In the case of a vacancy in the office of President of the Republic due to death, resignation, permanent physical unfitness of the President, or absence abroad without the assent of the National Assembly, and of the Government, the new President shall be elected on the thirtieth day following the declaration of the vacancy.

§ 1. The President's permanent physical disability must be recognised by the Council of State summoned for the purpose by the President of the Council of Ministers who, if the disability is confirmed, shall publish in the *Diário do Governo* an announcement of the presidential vacancy.

§ 2. Until the election provided for in this article takes place or when for any reason there is a temporary interruption in the exercise of the presidential function, the President of the Council shall be invested with the attributes of the Chief of State in addition to those of his office.

Art. 80A. In those cases where it is impossible for the electoral college to meet, such impossibility to be checked by the Council of State, the election of the new President of the Republic shall be carried out on the fifteenth day after that on which the Council of State considers the situation of *force majeure* to have terminated.

Section II. On the Attributes of the President of the Republic

Art. 81. It shall be the business of the President of the Republic:

(I) to appoint the President of the Council of Ministers and the Ministers, Secretaries and Under-Secretaries of State, from among Portuguese citizens, and to release them from office;

(II) solemnly to open the first meeting of each legislative session and to address messages to the National Assembly, directing them to its Chairman, who shall read them at the first meeting to be held after their receipt;

(III) to fix a day, in accordance with the electoral law, for a general election or by-election of deputies;

(IV) to confer constituent powers upon the National Assembly and to submit to a National Plebiscite such alterations of the Constitution as may refer to the legislative functions or to public bodies charged therewith, in accordance with Article 135 (I) and (II);

(V) to convene the National Assembly in extraordinary session, in time of urgent public emergency, for the consideration of specified matters, and to adjourn its sessions, without prejudice to the duration fixed for the Legislative Session in each year;

(VI) to dissolve the National Assembly when the supreme interests of the nation so require;

(VII) to represent the nation and direct the foreign policy of the State; to conclude international conventions and negotiate treaties of peace, alliance, arbitration and commerce, submitting them through the government to the National Assembly for approval;

(VIII) to grant pardons and commute punishments. No pardon may be granted until half the sentence has been served;

(IX) to promulgate and cause to be published the law and resolutions of the National Assembly as well as the Decree laying down regulations, and to sign all individual decrees in default of which they shall be considered as non-existent.

Art. 82. The acts of the President of the Republic must be countersigned by the President of the Council and by the appropriate Minister or Ministers; in default of this they shall be non-existent.

Sole §. Counter-signatures are not required for:

(I) the appointment and dismissal of the Council of Ministers;

(II) messages addressed to the National Assembly;

(III) the message of resignation from office.

Section III. On the Council of State

Art. 83. The President of the Republic shall perform his functions in conjunction with the Council of State, composed of the following members:

(I) the President of the Council of Ministers;

(II) the President of the National Assembly;

(III) the President of the Corporative Chamber;

(IV) the President of the Supreme Court of Justice;

(V) the Procurator General of the Republic;

(VI) ten public men of outstanding ability, appointed for life by the Chief of State.

Art. 84. The Council of State shall be obliged to discharge the following functions:

(a) to check the situation making impossible a meeting of the electoral college referred to in Article 72 and the termination of that situation for the purposes of Article 80A.

(b) to assist the Chief of State when exercising certain of the functions assigned to him by paragraphs 4, 5, 6 of Article 81 and § sole of Article 87;

(c) to deliver its opinion, in the manner laid down by § 1, of Article 80, in all emergencies threatening the life of the Nation and whenever the President of the Republic deems it necessary to summon it.

Sole §. The Council shall meet in its own right to exercise the power laid down in sub-clause (a).

CHAPTER III – ON THE NATIONAL ASSEMBLY AND THE CORPORATIVE CHAMBER

Section I. On the National Assembly

Art. 85. The National Assembly shall be composed of one hundred and thirty Deputies, elected by the direct suffrage of the citizen electors. Their term of office shall be four years, which may not be prolonged save in the case of events which make it impossible to effect the election.

§ 1. The necessary qualification for deputies, and the organization of the electoral colleges and procedure, shall be governed by a special law.

§ 2. Nobody may be a member of the National Assembly and of the Corporative Chamber at the same time.

§ 3. Vacancies occurring in the National Assembly, provided they attain the number fixed by the electoral law and not exceeding one fifth of the total number of deputies required by law, shall be filled by means of by-elections, the respective mandates expiring with the life of the legislature.

§ 4. Deputies may resign their mandates, but such resignation shall not be effective unless accepted by the Assembly or its Chairman, according to whether it is presented during or in an interval between sessions.

Art. 86. It shall be the duty of the National Assembly to examine and recognise the powers of its members, to elect its board, to draw up its own internal rules, and to regulate its police.

Art. 87. If the National Assembly is dissolved, elections shall be held within sixty days, under the electoral law in force at the time of the dissolution. The new Chambers shall meet within the thirty days following the closing of the electoral proceedings; if the legislative session of that year has not been concluded, they shall continue for the full legislative period without reckoning the time during which they functioned in completion of the previous legislative session, and without prejudice to the right of dissolution.

Sole §. If the supreme interests of the country render it advisable, the period of sixty days mentioned in this article may be extended to six months.

Art. 88. After the final ordinary legislative session of the four-year period, the National Assembly shall remain in being until the results of the new general election have been ascertained.

Section II. On the members of the National Assembly

Art. 89. The members of the National Assembly shall enjoy the following immunities and privileges:

(a) they may not be attacked for the opinion and votes they give in the exercise of their mandates, subject to the limitations laid down in § 1 and 2;

(b) they may not be called upon to serve on juries, or as experts or witnesses, without the sanction of the Assembly;

(c) they may not be detained or arrested without the consent of the Assembly, except in cases of crimes punishable by the maximum sentence or its equivalent in the penal scale, provided that in the latter case they are arrested *in flagrante delicto* or under a warrant of the Court;

(d) if criminal proceedings are taken against any deputy and he is formally charged, the judge shall notify the Assembly of the fact; the Assembly (save in the case mentioned in the latter part of paragraph c) of this article) shall then decide whether or not the deputy shall be suspended to enable the proceedings to take their course;

(e) they shall have the right to be remunerated as may be determined by the electoral law.

§ 1. Freedom from attack in respect of their opinions and votes does not exempt members of the National Assembly from civil and criminal liability for defamation, calumny and abuse, outrage of public morals, or open incitement to crime.

§ 2. The National Assembly may withdraw the mandates of those deputies who express opinions opposed to the existence of Portugal as an independent state, or who in any way instigate the violent overthrow of social and political order.

§ 3. The immunities and privileges set out in (b), (d) and (e) shall only be effective during the actual exercise of legislative functions.

Art. 90. Members of the National Assembly shall forfeit their seats in the following circumstances:

(I) if they should accept any remunerated employment or commission by way of subsidy from the Government or from any foreign government;

(II) if, being civil or military officers, they should exercise these functions during the actual session of the National Assembly;

(III) if they occupy posts of an administrative, executive or inspectional nature otherwise than by government appointment; or as legal or technical advisers in undertakings or companies formed under special

State contract or concession, or which enjoy a State privilege not conferred by general law, or which receive a subsidy or guarantee of revenue or interest;

(IV) if they should enter into contracts with the government;

(V) if they should act as concessionaires, contractors or partners in firms contracting for public concessions, public adjudicated contracts or contracts subject to public tender; and also if they should participate in State financial operations.

§ 1. The following are excepted from the provision laid down in no. 1 above:

(a) temporary diplomatic missions and military commissions or military commands which do not involve residence away from the mainland;

(b) appointments by advancement, legal promotions, acts which confirm temporary appointments as definitive and appointments to equivalent posts arising out of the reorganization of services;

(c) competitive appointments made by the government in pursuance of regulations, or on the recommendation of bodies legally entitled to recommend or choose officials; as also the appointments to posts and commissions only open to a certain class or category of officials.

§ 2. The recognition by the President of the facts referred to in (I) and (II) shall have the same effect as the acceptance of resignation.

§ 3. The circumstances mentioned in (IV) and (V), further, render the contracts and acts in question null and void.

Section III. On the Attributes of the National Assembly

Art. 91. The functions of the National Assembly are:

(I) to make, interpret, suspend and revoke laws;

(II) to safeguard the observance of the Constitution and the laws and to examine the acts of the government or the administration;

(III) to receive the accounts for each economic year, both for metropolitan Portugal and the overseas territories. These shall be laid before it with the report and resolution of the Court of Accounts, if the accounts have been examined by this Court, and such other information as may be necessary for their appreciation;

(IV) to authorize the government up to December 15th of each year to collect State revenues and to meet public expenditure for the ensuing financial period; also to determine in the appropriate authorizing enactment the principles which shall govern that part of the budget dealing with expenditure of sums not fixed by previously existing laws;

(V) to authorize the government to float loans or other similar operations not included in the floating debt, and to fix the general conditions of the same;

(VI) except in the case of actual or imminent aggression by foreign forces, to authorize the Head of the State to make war (should recourse to arbitration be impossible or of no avail) and to make peace;

(VII) in accordance with the provisions of Article 81 (VII), to approve all international conventions and treaties;

(VIII) to declare martial law with total or partial suspension of the constitutional guarantees, in one or more places on national territory, in the case of actual or imminent agression by foreign forces, or when public order and safety are seriously disturbed or threatened;

(IX) to define the boundaries of national territories;

(X) to grant amnesties;

(XI) to receive addresses from the Head of the State;

(XII) to discuss the revision of the Constitution.

(XIII) to bestow legislative authority on the government.

Art. 92. Laws voted by the National Assembly must be confined to the examination of the general legal principles of the enactments, but the constitutional legality of any provisions contained therein may not be impugned on the ground of violation of such principles.

Art. 93. The approval of the general principles of the following shall be the exclusive concern of the National Assembly:

(a) the organization of national defence;

(b) the weight, value and denomination of coinage in currency;

(c) the standards of weights and measures;

(d) the creation of banks or issuing institutions;

(e) the organization of the law-courts.

(f) The exercise of the liberties to which § 2 of Article 8 refers and the conditions of use of the exceptional measure of *habeas corpus;*

(g) the life-long, irremovable and non-responsible nature of the office of judges of ordinary courts and the terms in which the respective application for permanent and temporary commissions may be made.

Section IV. On the activities of the National Assembly and of the promulgation of Laws and Orders

Art. 94. The National Assembly shall be in session for a period of three months, beginning on November 25th of each year, without prejudice to the provisions of articles 75, 76 and 81 (V).

Sole §. The President of the National Assembly, if he considers it proper, may extend the session of the National Assembly for one month and interrupt it without prejudice to the period fixed in this article for the same, provided always that its closure shall not be later than April 30th.

Art. 95. The National Assembly shall meet in full session and its decisions shall be taken by absolute majority vote provided there is a quorum; it may set up permanent committees of its members or form special committees for specific purposes.

§ 1. Plenary sessions are public, unless otherwise resolved by the Assembly or by its President.

§ 2. The commissions and committees shall only function during the periods when the Assembly is functioning, except when their activity be prolonged by the nature of their functions or because of the special purpose for which they were set up, or, furthermore, in the case of eventual commissions set up by the President outside the effective period of activity of the Assembly.

§ 3. The Ministers, Secretaries and Under-Secretaries of State may take part in the sessions of the commissions. In those sessions held to discuss alterations suggested by the Corporative Chamber a delegate from that Chamber may take part.

Art. 96. The Members may:

§ 1. Put written questions on any acts of the Government or the Administration, in order to enlighten public opinion;

§ 2. Independently of the effective functioning of the National Assembly, hear, consult or solicit information from any corporation or official sphere. The official spheres, however, cannot reply without previous authorization from the Minister concerned.

Sole §. In both cases it is only licit to refuse a reply on the grounds of State secret.

Art. 97. The right to introduce legislation is vested equally in the government, and in any member of the National Assembly; individual members, however, may not introduce bills nor propose amendments involving any increase in State expenditure, or any reductions of State revenue created by former laws.

Sole §. During the discussion of proposals or bills, the Government may submit amendments for the consideration of the Assembly provided those amendments deal with matters on which a vote has not yet been taken.

Art. 98. The proposals and bills approved by the National Assembly are called decrees of the National Assembly and are sent to the Presidency of the Republic to be made law within a period of fifteen days.

Sole §. The decrees not declared to be law within that period shall be resubmitted to the National Assembly. If they are then approved by a majority of two thirds of its members in active discharge of their functions the Head of State cannot refuse to make them law.

Art. 99. Promulgation of laws shall be in the following form:

"In the name of the Nation, the National Assembly decrees and I promulgate the following Law (or Order)."

Sole §. The following shall be promulgated as Orders:

(a) the ratification of decree-laws;

(b) the decisions referred to in Articles 2, 80 and nos. 3, 6, 7 and 12 of Article 91 and other like Articles.

Art. 100. Any motions or bills brought before the National Assembly but not discussed during that session shall be reintroduced during the next session of the Assembly; should they finally be rejected they may not be introduced again in the same Legislative Session, except in the case of a motion for dissolution of the National Assembly.

Art. 101. The regulations of the Assembly shall contain:

(a) a prohibition to alter the agenda by introduction of fresh matter without at least twenty-four hours previous notice;

(b) the conditions for introducing bills;

(c) the conditions on which the questions referred to in paragraph 1 of Article 96 may be put.

Section V. On the Corporative Chamber

Art. 102. There shall be a Corporative Chamber, equal in length of term with the National Assembly, composed of representatives of local autonomous bodies and social interests, the latter being those of an administrative, moral, cultural and economic order; the law shall designate those bodies on which such representation falls, the manner of their selection and the duration of their mandate.

§ 1. When vacancies occur in offices whose holders as such have a seat in the Corporative Chamber, the representation of such offices devolves upon those who properly substitute them according to law or by statute. The same principle applies to cases of impediment.

§ 2. Except in the case mentioned in the preceding paragraph, vacancies occurring in the Corporative Chamber shall be filled in the same manner as the original officer was appointed.

§ 3. The provisions of Article 89 and its subsections shall apply to the members of this Chamber; but the action envisaged in (b), (c) and (d) of that article shall be taken on the authority, or by the decision, of the President. The amount of the remuneration mentioned in (e) (of Article 89) and the conditions on which it is granted shall be regulated by law.

Art. 103. It is the duty of the Corporative Chamber to report and gave its opinion on all proposals or draft bills and on all international conventions or treaties submitted to the National Assembly, before discussion thereof is commenced by the latter.

§ 1. The report shall be given within thirty days or within such period as the Government or the Assembly shall fix if the matter concerned is considered urgent.

§ 2. Should the time limit referred to in the preceding subsection expire before the report has been sent to the National Assembly discussion may proceed immediately.

§ 3. If the Corporative Chamber, while advising on general grounds the rejection of a bill, recommends that it be replaced by another, the Government or any Deputy may adopt the bill in question and it shall then be considered jointly with the original bill, independently of further reference to the Corporative Chamber. If the latter suggests alterations of detail in a proposal or bill, the National Assembly may decide that a vote be taken first on the text proposed by the Corporative Chamber and any Deputy may always move such amendments as his own.

Art. 104. The Corporative Chamber shall function in plenary sessions or in committees and sub-committees.

§ 1. There will be committees for administrative, moral, cultural and economic questions and sub-committees for specialized questions within each committee.

§ 2. When the matter under discussion so requires, two or more committees or sub-committees may meet jointly.

§ 3. In the discussion of proposals or bills the Chairman of the Council of Ministers and the Ministers, Secretaries and Under-Secretaries of State concerned may take part, as may their representatives and the Member who was the author of the proposal or bill.

§ 4. Sessions of the committees and sub-committees of the Corporative Chamber shall not be held in public, but plenary sessions may be.

Art. 105. The Government may consult the Corporative Chamber on enactments to be published or on draft bills to be presented to be National Assembly; it may decide that the work of the committees or sub-committees shall continue or take place during adjournments, interruptions or intervals between legislative sessions; and it may request the convo cation of all or any of the committees or sub-committees in order to make a communication to them.

§ 1. The discussion of draft bills in the National Assembly shall not be dependent on fresh reference to the Corporative Chamber if the latter has already been consulted by the Government.

§ 2. During the legislative session of the National Assembly the Corporative Chamber may suggest to the Government such measures as it considers advisable or necessary.

Art. 106. The Provisions of Article 86 apply to the Corporative Chamber, except insofar as concerns the verification of powers. This duty shall be entrusted to a special commission elected by the Chamber, and in Article 101 (a) and (b) the respective Committees and Sub-Committees shall also enjoy the facilities conferred by Article 96 on the members of the National Assembly.

CHAPTER IV – ON THE GOVERNMENT

Art. 107. The Government consists of the President the of Council of Ministers who may administer the affairs of one or more Ministries, and of the Ministers. The latter shall always be substituted by the former in acts within their sphere of competence when they are absent abroad, or unable to appear, when, that is, interim Ministers have not been appointed.

§ 1. The President of the Council of Ministers is freely appointed and released from his duties by the President of the Republic. The Ministers, Secretaries and Under-Secretaries of State as appointed by the President of the Republic on the proposal of the President of the Council of Ministers. The latter countersigns the President's appointments of Ministers as well as the release from duties of outgoing Ministers.

§ 2. The functions of the Secretaries and Under-Secretaries of State cease with the release from duties of the respective Minister.

Art. 108. The President of the Council shall be responsible to the President of the Republic for the general policy of the government and shall co-ordinate and direct the activities of all the Ministers, who shall be responsible to him politically for their acts.

Art. 109. It shall be the duty of the Government:

(I) to countersign the acts of the President of the Republic;

(II) to draw up decree-laws and, in cases of urgency, to approve international conventions and treaties;

(III) to draw up decrees, regulations and instructions for the proper carrying out of laws;

(IV) to superintend public administration as a whole, ensuring that the laws and resolutions of the National Assembly are carried out, controlling the acts of administrative bodies and of corporate entities of public administrative utility, and doing whatever may be necessary in relation to the appointment, transfer, resignation, retirement, superannuation, dismissal or reinstatement of civil or military officers, subject to the right of recourse of the parties concerned to the competent courts.

§ 1. Any action by the President of the Republic and the Government which involves an increase or decrease of revenue or expenditure shall be countersigned by the Minister of Finance.

§ 2. Legislative authorizations may not be utilized more than once, except those which by their nature are for repeated use. The Government may however utilize them in stages until they expire.

§ 3. Decree-laws published by the Government while the National Assembly is sitting, if they fall outside the scope authorized by law, shall be subject to ratification. This will be held to have been granted if, during the first ten sessions after publication, at least ten Deputies have not required that such decree-laws be submitted to the Assembly for its consideration.

Should ratification be refused, the decree-law will cease to have effect from the day on which the appropriate notice, issued by the President of the Assembly, is published in the Official Gazette.

The ratification may be granted subject to amendments; in this case the decree-law will be sent to the Corporative Chamber, if it has not already been consulted, but will continue in force unless the National Assembly, by a majority of two thirds of the Deputies actually functioning, suspends its effect insofar as concerns the creation or re-organization of services involving an increase of personnel or alteration of their respective ranks in relation to the existing staffs.

§ 4. If the law by itself is not capable of practical application the Government will issue appropriate decrees within six months unless the law itself establishes some other period.

§ 5. The appointment of Governors of the Overseas Provinces shall be made by the Council of Ministers.

§ 6. The appointment, transfer, removal, retirement, pensioning, dismissal or reinstatement of the President of the Supreme Court of Justice, of the Procurator-General of the Republic, of diplomatic and consular agents and of Governors-General and Governors of the Overseas Provinces, shall be made by decree.

Art. 110. Ministers may not exercise any other public duties, or any private employment, in addition to their ministerial offices.

§ 1. Ministers shall be subject to the other prohibitions and provisions contained in Art. 90.

§ 2. Those members of the National Assembly or of the Corporative Chamber who accept the office of Minister, Secretary or Under-Secretary of State shall not forfeit their mandates but they may not sit in the Chambers concerned.

Art. 111. The Council of Ministers shall meet when its President or the Head of State considers it necessary. When the said President or the Head of the State thinks fit, the meeting shall take place under the presidency of the latter and it shall be obligatory for the Head of the State to preside, when he has to use the powers conferred upon him in Article 81 (II), (III), (IV), (V), (VI) and (VIII).

Art. 112. The Government depends exclusively upon possessing the confidence of the President of the Republic, and its continuance in office shall not depend upon the fate of its draft bills, or upon any vote of the National Assembly.

Art. 113. The President of the Council shall transmit to the President of the National Assembly the draft bills to be submitted to the latter, together with any explanations requested of the government or which the government may deem it appropriate to give.

Sole §. In the case of matters that are of recognized national importance, the Chairman of the Council of Ministers or a Minister authorized by him may attend the National Assembly to deal with them.

Art. 114. Each Minister is responsible politically, civilly and criminally for any acts which he may legalise or carry out; Ministers shall be tried in the ordinary courts for acts involving civil or criminal liability.

Sole §. If any M inister be prosecuted for a criminal offence, the Supreme

Court of Justice in full session, the Attorney General of the Republic being present, shall, provided the proceedings have not gone beyond the stage of formally charging the offender, decide whether the Minister shall be tried immediately, in which case his suspension shall be decided on, or whether the trial shall be conducted on the completion of his tenure of office.

Art. 115. Criminal liability attaches to Ministers, Secretaries and Under-Secretaries of State and government agents in respect of any acts directed:

(I) against the political existence of the nation;

(II) against the Constitution and the established political system;

(III) against the free exercise of their functions by the representatives of national sovereignty;

(IV) against the enjoyment and exercise of political and individual rights;

(V) against the internal security of the country;

(VI) against the integrity of the administration;

(VII) against the custody and constitutional employment of public moneys;

(VIII) against the law dealing with public accounts.

Sole §. Conviction for any of those crimes involves loss of office and exclusion from holding public office.

CHAPTER V – ON THE COURTS

Art. 116. The exercise of judicial functions belongs to the ordinary courts and special tribunals.

The Supreme Court of Justice and the judicial courts of first and second instance are the ordinary courts, and they shall have such material and territorial jurisdiction as is determined by law.

Art. 117. The establishment of special courts with exclusive jurisdiction to try a certain category of crime or certain categories of crimes, is forbidden, unless the crimes are fiscal or social by nature or are against the safety of the State.

Art. 118. The State shall be represented in the courts by the Public Attorney.

Art. 119. Judges of the ordinary courts are appointed for life, and cannot be removed; the conditions of their appointment, promotion, dismissal, suspension, transfer and nomination outside the cadre shall be fixed by law and they may not accept any other office of profit from the government; this shall not however prejudice their being requisitioned for permanent or temporary commissions.

Art. 120. Judges shall not be held responsible for the judgments pronounced by them, except in cases specified by law.

Art. 121. The sittings of the courts shall be public, except in special cases prescribed by law, and whenever publicity would be contrary to good order, the interests of the State, or morality.

Art. 122. In the execution of their decisions and judgements, the courts shall have a right to the collaboration of other authorities whenever required.

Art. 123. In cases submitted for judgement the courts may not apply laws, decrees or any other ordinances which transgress the provisions of this constitution or violate the principles herein contained.

Sole §. The organic or formal constitutional illegality of ordinances promulgated by the President of the Republic may only be called into question by the National Assembly either on its own initiative or on that of the Government, and the National Assembly shall determine the effects of such constitutional illegality, without prejudice however to situations created by *causae judicatae.*

Art. 124. As a means of preventing and suppressing crime, penalties and precautionary measures shall be introduced for the protection of society and as far as possible for the social rehabilitation of the offender.

CHAPTER VI – ON THE ADMINISTRATIVE DIVISION AND LOCAL AUTONOMOUS AUTHORITIES IN METROPOLITAN PORTUGAL

Art. 125. Without detriment to the regional designation of "province," the territory of the Continent (Continental Portugal) is divided into municipalities, comprising parishes and grouped into districts. The law shall establish the limits of all these divisions.

§ 1. The boroughs of Lisbon and Oporto are subdivided into wards, and the latter into parishes.

§ 2. The territorial division of the adjacent islands and their administrative organization shall be the subject of a special law.

Art. 126. The administrative authorities are the Town Councils, the Parish and District Boards.

Art. 127. The administrative activities of local autonomous authorities are subject to scrutiny by government inspectors and the resolutions of their executive committees may be subject to confirmation or require the approval of other bodies or authorities and be submitted to examination.

Art. 128. In order to give effect to their resolutions, and for other purposes specified by law, administrative authorities shall appoint a President or special sub-committees in accordance with the said law.

Art. 129. Resolutions of administrative authorities can only be amended or annulled in the cases and in the manner prescribed by administrative enactments.

Art. 130. Administrative authorities enjoy financial autonomy under conditions to be determined by law but town councils are bound to divide among the parishes for the purpose of rural improvements such part of their revenues as is fixed by law.

Art. 131. Systems of local taxation shall be organized in such a manner as to avoid interfering with the general tax or financial organization of the State, and the circulation of produce and merchandise between different districts of the country.

Art. 132. Administrative authorities may only be dissolved in such cases and in such manner as prescribed by administrative enactments.

CHAPTER VII – OVERSEAS PORTUGAL

Section I. On the Fundamental Principles

Art. 133. It is intrinsic in the Portuguese Nation to fulfil its historic mission of colonization in the lands of the Discoveries under their sovereignty and to diffuse among the populations inhabiting them the benefits of their civilization, as also to exercise the moral influence enjoined upon it by the Patronage of the East.

Art. 134. The law shall define the general régime of government of the territories given the generic denomination of provinces, which will enjoy a political and administrative organization suited to their geographical situation and the conditions of their social environment. The political and administrative organization shall tend to integration in the general régime of administration of other national territories.

Art. 135. The Overseas Provinces, as an integral part of the Portuguese State, are united as between themselves and with Metropolitan Portugal.

Art. 136. This unity between the Overseas Provinces and Metropolitan Portugal involves in particular the obligation to contribute in an adequate manner to the preservation of the integrity and defence of the whole Nation and the aims of the national policy as defined in the common interest, by the bodies in which sovereignty resides.

Section II. General guarantees

Art. 137. The rights, liberties and individual guarantees enshrined in the Constitution are assured to nationals and foreigners alike in the Overseas Provinces, within the terms of the law, but without prejudice to the right to refuse entry to both nationals and foreigners into any Overseas Province or to order their expulsion, in accordance with the regulations, if grave inconvenience of a domestic or international character should be caused by their presence. Appeals against such decisions may be made to the Government alone.

Art. 138. Regard shall be had in the overseas territories to the state of development of the native inhabitants. To this end and where necessary there shall be established, by special statutes, in the spirit of Portuguese public and private law, systems in keeping with native usage and customs, provided that these are not incompatible with morality, the dictates of humanity or the free exercise of Portuguese sovereignty.

Art. 139. The State shall ensure, in its overseas territories, liberty of conscience and the free exercise of the various religions, subject only to such restrictions as may be required for the preservation of the rights and interests of Portuguese sovereignty, for the maintenance of public order and in conformity with international treaties and conventions.

Art. 140. The Portuguese Catholic missions overseas and the establishments for training personnel for their services and for those of the *padroado* (Patronage) shall, in conformity with the Concordat and other agreements concluded with the Holy See, enjoy juridical personality and shall be protected and assisted by the State, as being institutions of education and assistance and instrument sof civilization.

Section III. On special guarantees for native

Art. 141. The State guarantees, through special measures in the stage of transition, the protection and defence of the natives living in the provinces, in accordance with the principles of humanity and sovereignty, the provisions of this chapter and international conventions.

The authorities and the law-courts shall prevent and punish in accordance with the law all abuses against the persons and property of the natives.

Art. 142. The State shall establish public Portuguese institutions and encourage the establishment of private Portuguese institutions to uphold the rights of the natives and to give them assistance.

Art. 143. The natives are confirmed, in accordance with the law, in their property and in the possession of their lands and crops and this principle shall be respected in all concessions made by the State.

Art. 144. Natives contracted for the service of the State or for administrative bodies shall be paid for their work.

Art. 145. The following are prohibited:

(I) Systems whereby the State undertakes to provide native labor for any firms working for their own profit.

(II) Systems whereby the natives in any territorial area are compelled to work for such firms, whatever the pretext.

Art. 146. The State may only compel the natives to work on public works of general interest to the community, on tasks of which the finished product will belong to them, in the execution of judicial sentences of a penal character or for the discharge of fiscal liabilities.

Art. 147. The system of native contract labor shall be based on individual liberty and on the right to a fair wage and assistance, the public authorities intervening only for the purpose of regulation.

Section IV. On the political and administrative system

Art. 148. The Overseas Provinces shall be guaranteed the right of administrative decentralization and financial autonomy in conformity with the Constitution and with their state of development and resources, without prejudice to the provisions of Article 175.

Sole §. Political unity shall be maintained in each overseas province by the establishment of a single capital and government of the province.

Art. 149. The Overseas Provinces shall, as a rule, be governed by special legislation passed by the legislative bodies of Metropolitan Portugal or, according to circumstances in each Province, by the provincial legislative bodies, within the legislative limits established by law.

Art. 150. The following bodies in Metropolitan Portugal shall have the right to legislate for the Portuguese Overseas Provinces:

(I) The National Assembly, at the instance of the Minister of the Overseas Provinces, on matters on which of necessity legislation is required by the terms of Article 93, and also in the following:

(a) The general system of government of the Overseas Provinces;

(b) The definition of the powers of the Metropolitan Government and of the governments of the Overseas Provinces in matters relating to the area and duration of territorial concessions or to others which involve exclusive rights or special privileges;

(c) Authorization for contracts, not being loans, when they require special security or guarantees.

(II) The Government when, under the terms of the Constitution, it has by decree-law to take action affecting the whole national territory; or when an executive measure provides for questions of common concern both to Metropolitan Portugal and one or more of the Overseas Provinces.

(III) The Minister for the Overseas Provinces, whose authority covers all matters involving the higher or general interests of national policy in the Overseas Provinces or which are common to more than one Overseas Province, as specified in the legal system described in 1(a) of this article.

§ 1. The legislative power of the Minister for the Overseas Provinces shall be exercised after consultation with the Council for the Overseas Territories, except in cases of urgency and others prescribed by law, as also in those cases where the Council delays for more than thirty days in delivering its opinion on the matter referred to it by the Minister. The executive measures taken in the exercise of his legislative power shall be published in the form of decrees, promulgated and countersigned as provided for by the Constitution. The form of a ministerial legislative enactment shall be adopted when the Minister is exercising his functions in any of the Overseas Provinces and that of an order in the other cases provided for in law.

§ 2. All enactments to be enforced in the Overseas Provinces shall contain an instruction from the Minister of the Overseas Provinces, to the effect that they must be published in the Official Bulletin of the Province or Provinces concerned.

§ 3. The constitutional validity of the provisions contained in such enactments shall not be contested on the grounds that they violate this article, save as provided in Article 123, sole §.

Art. 151. All matters of exclusive concerns to an Overseas Province and outside the scope, as defined in the previous Article, of the National Assembly, the Government or the Minister for the Overseas Provinces, shall be dealt with by the legislative bodies of the Overseas Provinces prescribed by law.

§ 1. Agreements and conventions outside the terms of Articles 81 (VII) and 91 (VII) which the governments of the Overseas Provinces, duly authorized, negotiate with the governments of other provinces or territories, national or foreign, shall require the approval of the Overseas Minister.

§ 2. The enactments of the Overseas governments cannot revoke, suspend or run contrary to the provisions of the Constitution or of any other enactments passed by the legislative bodies of Metropolitan Portugal.

Art. 152. The legislative functions of each of the governments of the Overseas Provinces, within their jurisdiction, shall be exercised under the supervision of the bodies in which sovereignty resides and shall be, as a rule, in accordance with the vote of a council in which representation is suited to local social conditions.

Art. 153. The Government shall superintend and control the whole administration of the Overseas Provinces, according to the Constitution and the organic law or laws referred to in Article 150 1(a) through the bodies prescribed by those laws.

Art. 154. In each of the Overseas Provinces there shall be, as the supreme authority, a Governor or Governor-General, with powers and prerogatives defined by law. They shall not be entrusted in any way with powers which, under the Constitution, belong to the National Assembly, to the Government or to the Minister for the Overseas Provinces, save such limited powers as may be granted by the proper authority, for specified matters and in exceptional circumstances.

Sole §. No person connected with the direction or management of enterprises which have their head offices or sphere of activity in a Province may be appointed governor of that province.

Art. 155. The executive functions in each Overseas Province shall be discharged by the Governor, who, in the cases provided for by law, shall be assisted by a consultative body.

Art. 156. The administrative division of the Overseas Provinces and the conditions on which local autonomous bodies may be established shall be decided by law, having regard to the importance, the development and the population of each area.

Sole §. Without prejudice to the provision of the sole § of Article 7, foreigners permanently resident in a territory for not less than five years and who are able to read and write Portuguese may be members of administrative bodies up to a maximum of one third of the total number of members.

Art. 157. It is the supreme duty and honor of the Governor, in each of the Overseas Provinces, to uphold the sovereign rights of the Nation and to promote the welfare of the province, in accordance with the principles enshrined in the Constitution and in the laws.

Section V. On the economic order

Art. 158. The economic organization of the Portuguese Overseas Provinces shall form part of the general economic organization of the Portuguese Nation and shall thereby take its place in the world economy.

Sole §. To attain the ends indicated in this Article the free circulation of products within the whole national territory shall be facilitated by suitable means, including the gradual reduction or suspension of customs duties. The same principle shall be applied as far as possible to the movement of persons and capital.

Art. 159. The economic systems of the Overseas Provinces shall be established in harmony with the needs of their development and the well-being of their population, with fair reciprocity between them and the neighbouring countries, and with the rights and legitimate advantages of the Portuguese Nation, of which they are an integral part.

Art. 160. Without prejudice to the decentralization prescribed by Article 148, it is for Metropolitan Portugal to secure, through measures taken by the competent bodies, a proper balance in the interests which, under the previous Article, should be considered as a whole in the economic systems of the Overseas Territories.

Art. 161. The law shall specify those areas of land and other properties overseas, which, because they are used or intended for use as public property or involve the prestige of the State or are required for supreme national purposes, cannot be ceded or in any way alienated.

Sole §. The law shall also regulate the use or occupation of such areas of land by public or private bodies when it is in the interest of the State and on a temporary basis.

Art. 162. The concessions granted by the State or by the local autonomous bodies in the sphere of their competence shall always be subject to conditions which ensure the national interest and other requirements of the national economy even when they are to be effected with the aid of foreign capital.

To this end special measures will be taken to govern the situation.

Art. 163. The administration and operation of ports and airports in the Portuguese Overseas Provinces shall in future be reserved to the State. Exceptions to this allowed in each port or airport in connection with certain installations or services shall be regulated by special law.

Art. 164. Neither the State nor local autonomous bodies may, in the Portuguese Overseas Provinces, grant to private or collective enterprise:

(I) The exercise of the prerogatives of public administration;

(II) The right to levy or fix any charge or tax. This does not include the collection of public revenue the sale of which by auction is allowed by law;

(III) The possessions of land or the exclusive right of prospecting for minerals, with the right of sub-lease to other enterprises.

Sole §. In Overseas Territories where concessions of the nature of those mentioned in this article exist, the following will be observed:

(a) They may not be renewed, in whole or in part;

(b) The State will exercise its right of cancellation or redemption, in accordance with the relevant laws or contracts.

Section VI. On the financial system

Art. 165. The Overseas Provinces shall have collective personality in public law, with the right to acquire, contract and take legal proceedings.

Art. 166. Each of the Overseas Provinces has its own assets and liabilities, with the right to dispose of its property and revenue and the responsibility for its expenditure and debts and its acts and contracts, in conformity with the law.

Art. 167. The following are state property in each of the Overseas Provinces within the limits of its territory: waste lands and those lands in respect of which neither public or private title has been finally established; unclaimed inheritances and other real or personal property which do not belong to anybody; real or personal property which the Overseas Province acquires, or which belong to it legally, outside its territory, including shares of profits or of any other kind which may be due to it.

§ 1. The administration of those properties of the Overseas Provinces which are situated in Metropolitan Portugal shall be carried out by the Ministry for the Overseas Provinces.

§ 2. The shares and bonds of concessionary companies belonging to an Overseas Province may be made over or mortgaged only to the Public

Treasury or to such credit establishments as the Government may designate; and the proceeds derived therefrom as a result of any financial operation may likewise by made over to the said institutions alone.

Art. 168. Each Overseas Province shall have its own separate budget, drawn up in accordance with a uniform plan and in harmony with the principles contained in Articles 63 and 66, and approved in the appropriate Provincial bodies in accordance with such terms as may be enjoined by the law.

§ 1. The budget of each Overseas Province shall include only such revenue and expenditure as is authorized by legal enactments.

§ 2. If the budget cannot be put into effect by the beginning of the financial year, the budget of the previous year and the credits sanctioned to meet new permanent charges shall continue in force provisionally, on a monthly basis, but only in respect of ordinary expenditure.

Art. 169. The general system described in Article 150 (a) shall provide for:

(I) The expenditure and revenue which belong to the Overseas Provinces, separately or in common, as well as those pertaining to Metropolitan Portugal;

(II) The rules of control or superintendence to which the Governments of the Overseas Provinces shall be subject by way of safeguard for their finances.

Art. 170. The accounting of the Overseas Provinces shall be organized like that of continental Portugal with such modifications as may be necessitated by special circumstances.

Art. 171. The annual accounts of the Overseas Provinces shall be sent to the Ministry for the Overseas Provinces for submission, after audit and check by the Court of Accounts, for their examination in the manner and within the time limit fixed by law; and for consideration by the National Assembly in accordance with Article 91 (3).

Art. 172. Continental Portugal shall give financial assistance to the Overseas Provinces, against the necessary guarantees.

Art. 173. The Overseas Provinces may not contract loans in foreign countries.

Sole §. When it is necessary to have recourse to foreign markets to obtain capital intended for the government of any Overseas Province, the financial operation shall be made exclusively to the account of Metropolitan Portugal, without the Province assuming any responsibility towards those markets. The Province in question shall, however, assume full responsibility with regard to Metropolitan Portugal.

Art. 174. The rights of the Public Treasury or of the credit establishments described in Article 167 (2) as regards the past or future debts of the Overseas Provinces shall not be subject to prescription.

Art. 175. The financial autonomy of the Overseas Provinces shall be subject to such temporary restrictions as may be inevitable should a serious situation arise in connection with their finances or should there be danger of their affecting the finances of Metropolitan Portugal.

SUPPLEMENTARY PROVISIONS

(a) *Revision of the Constitution*

Art. 176. The Constitution may be revised every ten years, counted from the date of the last law of revision; and the National Assembly whose life includes the last year of the decade or the National Assemblies which follow the tenth year, shall, for this purpose, enjoy constituent powers until the law of revision is published.

§ 1. Constitutional revision may be anticipated by five years if, at the beginning of the legislative session corresponding to the last year of the five-year term, it is so decided by two thirds of the Deputies in effective exercise of their mandate.

In this case the ten year period shall likewise be counted from the date of the law of revision then voted.

§ 2. Once a proposal or draft bill for constitutional revision has been presented, others may only be presented within twenty days from the date of the first presentation.

§ 3. Proposals or draft bills for constitutional revision shall not be accepted for consideration unless the proposed amendments are clearly defined.

§ 4. The bills for constitutional revision shall be signed by a minimum of ten and a maximum of fifteen Deputies in the effective discharge of their duties.

§ 5. As soon as the law of revision has been published the constituent powers of the National Assembly shall cease.

Art. 177. Notwithstanding the provisions of the preceding article, should public interest urgently demand it, the Head of the State, after consulting the Council of State, may by a decree signed by all the Ministers:

(I) determine that the National Assembly to be elected shall assume constituent powers and revise the Constitution in such parts as are specified in the relative decree;

(II) submit to a national plebiscite the alterations of the Constitution referring to the legislature or its instruments; such approved alterations shall enter into effect as soon as the final results of the plebiscite are published in the *Diário do Governo* (Official Gazette).

Art. 177A. The law shall establish the method of substitution of the organs of sovereignty and the conditions of their activity when, in case of need and to safeguard the free exercise of power in the face of an external enemy, they cannot function or act freely.

(*b*) *Special and Temporary Provisions*

Art. 178. A transitional régime shall be adopted for carrying into effect the sole § of Art. 53, with such temporary restrictions as are deemed essential.

Art. 179. Until such time as the corporative organization of the Nation is completed, temporary measures shall be adopted to give effect to the principle of organic representation laid down in Chapter V of Part I.

Art. 180. Laws, and decrees having the force of law, that have been or may be published not later than the first meeting of the National Assembly shall continue in operation and remain in force as laws insofar as they contain nothing explicitly or implicitly contrary to the principles contained in the present Constitution.

Art. 181. The laws and decree-laws referred to in the preceding article may nevertheless be revoked by regulating decrees in all matters concerning internal service organisation provided the juridical position of private individuals at law and the statute of Civil Servants are unaffected.

Sole §. The restrictions laid down in this article do not include laws and decree-laws defining what constitutes legislative matter, nor the exceptions under § 1 of Art. 70 and Art. 93.

RUMANIA

SUMMARY

INTERNATIONAL STATUS

Rumania is a member of the United Nations (December 14, 1955). It is a member of the Council for Mutual Economic Assistance, the Warsaw Treaty and other international organizations. It was a member of the League of Nations.

The principalities of Moldavia and Wallachia were part of the Ottoman Empire rules by Phanariot[1] governors. They were occupied by Russia in 1806–1812, in 1828–1829 and again in 1856. After revolts organized by the

[1] Greeks from the Constantinople quarter of the Phanar.

governors in 1821, these were replaced by local princes. An organic statute in 1834 attempted to regulate relations between boyars and peasants. In September 1857, the councils of the two principalities voted to unite under a hereditary prince and became Rumania in 1861. A constitution was promulgated in 1866. Turkey granted Rumanian independence in 1878, by the Treaty of San Stefano and this was confirmed by the Congress of Berlin. Rumania took part in the second Balkan War and remained neutral until 1916 in the First World War. In 1923, a new constitution was proclaimed. With the return of King Carol in 1931, the government became fascist, in 1938 all political parties were abolished and a corporate constitution promulgated. In June 1940, Bessarabia, which had voted to join Rumania in 1918, was occupied by the USSR. In October 1940, Rumania was occupied by Germany. The country was liberated by Soviet troops in 1945 and in March of that year a Communist government was formed. The 1946 elections gave the majority to the Communist party. The peace treaty was signed in February 1947. In 1947, the king abdicated and Rumania was proclaimed a People's Republic on December 30, 1947. A constitution was promulgated on April 13, 1948.

FORM OF NATIONAL GOVERNMENT

The Constitution of 1965 replaces that of September 24, 1952, and states that Rumania is a socialist republic, a sovereign, independent and unitary state of the working people of the towns and villages.[1] Sovereign power belongs to the people.[2] The leading political force of the whole of society is the Rumanian Cummunist Party.[3] The economic system is described.[4]

RIGHTS OF THE PEOPLE

The Constitution provides equality, the right to work, leisure, material security, education, the free use of their languages for other nationalities, equal rights for women, the right of association, freedom of speech, press, assembly, provided these are not used for aims hostile to the socialist system, freedom of conscience, inviolability of the person, inviolability of the domicile, secrecy of correspondence, the rights of petition, personal property, inheritance, asylum.[5] Citizens are bound to defend socialist property and the development of the socialist system and to defend their homeland.[6]

LEGISLATIVE DEPARTMENT

The Grand National Assembly is the supreme body of state power and the sole legislative body.[7] Deputies are elected by universal, direct and

[1] Const., Art. 1. [2] Id., Art. 2. [3] Id., Art. 3. [4] Id., Art. 5–13.
[5] Id., Art. 17–24, 27–38. [6] Id., Art. 39–41. [7] Id., Art. 4, 42.

secret suffrage for a term of four years.[1] It meets in ordinary session twice a year.[2] Immunities of deputies are provided.[3]

EXECUTIVE DEPARTMENT

The State Council, subordinate to the Grand National Assembly is the supreme body of state power with permanent activity.[4] It has the power of appointment, grants honors and pardons, represents Rumania in international relations through its President, and convenes the legislature.[5] It is elected by the Grand National Assembly from among its members and for the same term and it is responsible to it; it is composed of a President, three Vice-Presidents and fifteen members.[6] The Council of Ministers is the supreme body of state administration and is elected by the Grand National Assembly and responsible to it.[7] There are provisions concerning local bodies.[8]

JUDICIAL DEPARTMENT

The law is administered by the Supreme Court, regular courts, people's and military courts.[9] The Supreme Court is elected by the Grand National Assembly for the same term and is responsible to it.[10] Judges are independent and subject only to law.[11] A Procurator's Office under a Procurator-General is provided.[12]

AREA, POPULATION, ETC.

The area of Rumania is 237,428 square kilometres, its population (1965) 19,027,000. The capital is Bucharest. The language is Rumanian, the cohabiting nationalities having the right to free use of their native languages.[13]

[1] Id., Art. 25, 44, 45. [2] Id., Art. 54. [3] Id., Art. 61.
[4] Id., Art. 62. [5] Id., Art., 63, 64. [6] Id., Art. 65, 66, 69.
[7] Id., Art. 70–78. [8] Id., Art. 79–93. [9] Id., Art. 94. [10] Id., Art. 98, 99.
[11] Id., Art. 104. [12] Id., Art. 105, 106. [13] Id., Art. 22.

CONSTITUTION of RUMANIA[1]

1965

CHAPTER I

THE SOCIALIST REPUBLIC OF RUMANIA

Art. 1. Rumania is a socialist republic.

The Socialist Republic of Rumania is a sovereign, independent and unitary state of the working people of the towns and villages. Its territory is inalienable and indivisible.

Art. 2. The whole power in the Socialist Republic of Rumania belongs to the people, free and masters of their destiny.

People's power is based on the worker-peasant alliance. In close union, the working class—the leading class of society—the peasantry, the intelligentsia and the other categories of working people, regardless of nationality, build the socialist system, creating the conditions for transition to communism.

Art. 3. In the Socialist Republic of Rumania, the leading political force of the whole of society is the Rumanian Communist Party.

Art. 4. The sovereign holder of power, the people exercise this power through the Grand National Assembly and the People's Councils, bodies elected by universal, equal, direct and secret vote.

The Grand National Assembly and the People's Councils are the basis of the whole system of state bodies.

The Grand National Assembly is the supreme body of state power, under whose conduct and control all the other state bodies carry on their activities.

Art. 5. The national economy of Rumania is a socialist economy, based on the socialist ownership of the means of production.

In the Socialist Republic of Rumania, man's exploitation by man has been abolished for ever and the socialist principle of distribution according to the quantity and quality of work is implemented.

[1] *Constitution of the Socialist Republic of Rumania.* Meridiane Publishing House, Bucharest, 1965. Supplied by the Ministry of Foreign Affairs in March 1966. Ed.

Work is a duty of honor for each citizen of the country.

Art. 6. Socialist ownership of the means of production is either state property—goods belonging to the whole people, or co-operative property—goods belonging to each co-operative organization.

Art. 7. The wealth of the subsoil, whatever its nature, the mines, the state land, the forests, waters, sources of natural power, the factories and mills, the banks, the state farms, the machine-and-tractor stations, the means of communication, the state means of transport and telecommunication, the state buildings and dwellings, the material basis of state socio-cultural institutions belong to the whole people and are state property.

Art. 8. Foreign trade is a state monopoly.

Art. 9. The land of the agricultural production co-operatives, the animals, implements, installations and buildings belonging to them are co-operative property.

The plot of land which according to the rules of the agricultural production co-operatives is being used by the family household of the co-operative farmers, is co-operative property.

The dwelling and the ancillary farm buildings, the land on which they stand and, according to the rules of the agricultural production co-operatives, the production livestock and small agricultural dead stock are the personal property of the co-operative farmers.

The tools, machines, installations and constructions of the handicraft co-operatives and of the consumer co-operatives are co-operative property.

Art. 10. The agricultural production co-operatives, a socialist form of agricultural organization, secure the conditions for the intensive cultivation of the land and the application of advanced science and contribute, by increasing output, to the development of the national economy, to the continuous raising of the living standard of the peasantry and of the whole people.

The state gives support to the agricultural production co-operatives and protects their property. The state also gives support to the other co-operative organizations and protects their property.

Art. 11. In the conditions of co-operativized agriculture, the state guarantees to the peasants who cannot associate themselves in agricultural production co-operatives, ownership of the land which they themselves and their families are working as well as ownership of the animals they use for work and for production.

The handicraftsmen are also guaranteed ownership of their own workshops.

Art. 12. Land and buildings can be expropriated only for work of public interest and on payment of an equitable compensation.

Art. 13. In the Socialist Republic of Rumania the whole of state activity has as its purpose the development of the socialist system and the prosperity of the nation, the continuous growth of the people's living standard and cultural level, the ensurance of the freedom and dignity of man, the many-sided affirmation of the human person.

For this purpose, the Rumanian socialist state:

organizes, plans and conducts the national economy;

defends the socialist property;

guarantees the full exercise of citizen rights, assures socialist legality and defends the rule of law;

develops education at all levels, ensures the conditions for the development of science, the arts and culture, carries out public health protection;

ensures defence of the country and organizes its Armed Forces;

organizes relations with other states.

Art. 14. The Socialist Republic of Rumania maintains and develops relations of friendship and fraternal collaboration with the socialist countries, in the spirit of socialist internationalism, promotes relations of collaboration with countries having other socio-political systems, is active in international organizations with a view to ensuring peace and understanding among the peoples.

The foreign relations of the Socialist Republic of Rumania are based on the principles of observance of sovereignty and national independence, equal rights and mutual advantages, non-interference in internal affairs.

Art. 15. The territory of the Socialist Republic of Rumania is organized in territorial-administrative units: regions, districts, towns and villages.

The regions of the Socialist Republic of Rumania are:

Argeş, Bacău, Banat, Braşov, Bucharest, Cluj, Crişana, Dobruja, Gatati, Hunedoara, Jassy, Maramureş, Mureş-Magyar Autonomous, Oltenia, Ploieşti and Suceava.

The capital of the Socialist Republic of Rumania is the city of Bucharest.

Art. 16. Rumanian citizenship is acquired and lost according to the law.

CHAPTER II

THE FUNDAMENTAL RIGHTS AND DUTIES OF THE CITIZENS

Art. 17. The citizens of the Socialist Republic of Rumania, irrespective of nationality, race, sex or religion, have equal rights in all fields of economic, political, juridical, social and cultural life.

The state guarantees the equal rights of the citizens. No restriction of these rights and no difference in their exercise on the gounds of nationality, race, sex or religion are permitted.

Any expression aiming to establish such restrictions, nationalist-chauvinist propaganda, the fanning of racial or national hatred are punished by the law.

Art. 18. In the Socialist Republic of Rumania, the citizens have the right to work. Each citizen is given the possibility to carry on, according to his training, an activity in the economic, administrative, social or cultural field and is remunerated according to its quantity and quality. For equal work there is equal pay.

The law establishes the measures for the protection and safety of labor as well as special measures for the protection of the work of women and young people.

Art. 19. The citizens of the Socialist Republic of Rumania have the right to leisure.

The right to leisure is guaranteed to those who work by the establishment of the maximum duration of the working day at eight hours, of weekly rest and of annual paid holidays.

In the sectors of arduous and very arduous work, the working day is reduced to less than eight hours, without any reduction in pay.

Art. 20. The citizens of the Socialist Republic of Rumania have the right to material security in case of old age, sickness or incapacity to work.

The right to material security is implemented for factory and office workers through pensions and sickness benefits paid by the state social insurance system, and for the members of the co-operative organizations or of other public organizations through the forms of insurance organized by these organizations. The state ensures medical assistance through its health units.

Paid maternity leave is guaranteed.

Art. 21. The citizens of the Socialist Republic of Rumania have the right to education.

The right to education is ensured by compulsory general education, by the fact that education at all levels is free and by the system of state scholarships.

Education in the Socialist Republic of Rumania is state education.

Art. 22. In the Socialist Republic of Rumania the co-inhabiting nationalities are ensured the free utilization of their native language as well as books, papers, magazines, theatres and education at all levels in their own language. In districts also inhabited by a population of non-Rumanian nationality, all the bodies and institutions use the language of the respective nationality in speech and in writing and appoint officials from its ranks or from the ranks of other citizens who know the language and way of life of the local population.

Art. 23. In the Socialist Republic of Rumania women have equal rights with men.

The state protects marriage and the family and defends the interests of mother and child.

Art. 24. The Socialist Republic of Rumania ensures to young people the conditions required for the development of their physical and intellectual aptitudes.

Art. 25. The citizens of the Socialist Republic of Rumania have the right to elect and to be elected to the Grand National Assembly and the People's Councils.

The vote is universal, equal, direct and secret. All citizens who have reached the age of 18 years have the right to vote.

Citizens with the right to vote who have reached the age of 23 years can be elected as deputies to the Grand National Assembly and to the People's Councils.

The right to nominate candidates is ensured to all organizations of the working people: the organizations of the Rumanian Communist Party, the trade unions, the co-operatives, the youth and women's organizations, the cultural associations and other mass and public organizations.

The electors have the right to recall their deputy at any time, according to the same procedure under which he has been nominated and elected.

Mentally alienated and deficient people have no right to elect and to be elected, also persons deprived of these rights during the period laid down by a court of law in its sentence.

Art. 26. The most advanced and conscious citizens from the ranks of the workers, peasants, intellectuals and other categories of working people unite in the Rumanian Communist Party, the highest form of organization of the working class, its vanguard detachment.

The Rumanian Communist Party expresses and loyally serves the aspirations and vital interests of the people, implements the role of leader in all the fields of socialist construction, and directs the activity of the mass and public organizations and of the state bodies.

Art. 27. The citizens of the Socialist Republic of Rumania have the right to associate themselves in trade union, co-operative, youth, women's and socio-cultural organizations, in creative unions, scientific, technical, sports associations and other public organizations.

The state gives support to the activity of the mass and public organizations, creates conditions for the development of the material basis of these organizations and defends their property

The mass and public organizations ensure the large participation of the mass of the people in the political, economic, social and cultural life of the Socialist Republic of Rumania and in the exercise of public control—an expression of the democratic spirit of the socialist system. Through the mass and public organizations the Rumanian Communist Party achieves an organized link with the working class, the peasantry, the intelligentsia and the other categories of working people, mobilizes them in the struggle for the completion of the building of socialism.

Art. 28. The citizens of the Socialist Republic of Rumania are guaranteed freedom of speech, of the Press, of reunion, of meeting and demonstration.

Art. 29. The freedom of speech, of the Press, reunion, meeting and demonstration cannot be used for aims hostile to the socialist system and to the interests of the working people.

Any association of a fascist or anti-democratic character is prohibited. Participation in such associations and propaganda of a fascist or anti-democratic character are punished by the law.

Art. 30. Freedom of conscience is guaranteed to all the citizens of the Socialist Republic of Rumania.

Anybody is free to share or not to share a religious belief. The freedom of exercising a religious cult is guaranteed. The religious cults organize and function freely, The way of organization and functioning of the religious cults is regulated by law.

The school is separated from the Church. No religious confession, congregation or community can open or maintain any other teaching establishments than special schools for the training of servants of the Church.

Art. 31. The citizens of the Socialist Republic of Rumania are guaranteed inviolability of the person.

No person can be detained or arrested if there are no well-grounded proofs or indications that he has committed a deed listed and punished by the law. The organs of inquiry can order the detention of a person for a maximum of 24 hours. No one can be arrested except on the basis of an order of arrest issued by a court or the Procurator.

The right to defence is guaranteed throughout the lawsuit.

Art. 32. The domicile is inviolable.

No one can enter the dwelling of a person without the latter's consent, except in the cases and conditions specially laid down by the law.

Art. 33. The secrecy of correspondence and of telephone conversations is guaranteed.

Art. 34. The right to petition is guaranteed. The state bodies have the obligation to resolve the petitions of the citizens concerning personal or public rights and interests.

Art. 35. Those harmed in a right of theirs by an illegal act of a state body can ask the competent bodies, in the conditions provided by the law, to annul the act and repair the damage.

Art. 36. The right to personal property is protected by the law.

Objects of the right to personal property can be income and savings derived from work, the dwelling house, the household around it and the land on which they stand, as well as the goods of personal use and comfort.

Art. 37. The right to inheritance is protected by the law.

Art. 38. The Socialist Republic of Rumania grants the right of refuge to foreign citizens persecuted for their activity in defence of the interests of the working people, for their participation in the fight for national liberation or in defence of peace.

Art. 39. Every citizen of the Socialist Republic of Rumania is bound to respect the Constitution and the laws, to defend socialist property, to contribute to the strengthening and development of the socialist system.

Art. 40. Military service in the ranks of the Armed Forces of the Socialist Republic of Rumania is compulsory and is a duty of honor of the citizens of the Socialist Republic of Rumania.

Art. 41. To defend the homeland is the sacred duty of each citizen of the Socialist Republic of Rumania. Violation of the military oath, treason to the homeland, desertion to the enemy, prejudice to the defensive capacity of the state are the greatest crimes against the people and are punished by the law with the utmost severity.

CHAPTER III

THE SUPREME BODIES OF STATE POWER

The Grand National Assembly

Art. 42. The Grand National Assembly, the supreme body of state power, is the sole legislative body of the Socialist Republic of Rumania.

Art. 43. The Grand National Assembly has the following main attributions:

(1) it adopts and amends the Constitution of the Socialist Republic of Rumania;

(2) it regulates the electoral system;

(3) it adopts the State Plan of the National Economy, the State Budget and the general final account of the budgetary exercise;

(4) it organizes the Council of Ministers, the ministries, and the other central bodies of state administration;

(5) it regulates the organization of courts and the Procurator's Office;

(6) it establishes the norms for the organization and functioning of the people's councils;

(7) it establishes the administrative organization of the territory;

(8) it grants amnesty;

(9) it ratifies and denounces international treaties that imply modification of laws;

(10) it elects and recalls the State Council;

(11) it elects and recalls the Council of Ministers;

(12) it elects and recalls the Supreme Court and the Procurator General;

(13) it exercises general control of the application of the Constitution. It is only the Grand National Assembly that decides on the constitutionality of the laws;

(14) it controls the activity of the State Council;

(15) it controls the activity of the Council of Ministers, of the ministries and of the other central bodies of state administration;

(16) it hears reports on the activity of the Supreme Court and controls its directive decisions;

(17) it controls the activity of the Procurator's Office;

(18) it exercises general control of the activity of the People's Councils;

(19) it establishes the general line of foreign policy;

(20) it proclaims, in the interest of the country's defence, of public order or state security, the state of urgency in some localities, or throughout the country's territory;

(21) it orders partial or general mobilization;

(22) it declares the state of war. The state of war can be declared only in case of armed aggression directed against the Socialist Republic of Rumania or against another state towards which the Socialist Republic of Rumania has mutual defence obligations arising from international treaties, if a situation has come about for which the obligation of declaring a state of war has been laid down;

(23) it appoints and recalls the Supreme Commander of the Armed Forces.

Art. 44. The deputies to the Grand National Assembly are elected in constituencies with the same number of inhabitants. The constituencies are established by decrees of the State Council.

One deputy is elected for every constituency.

The Grand National Assembly is made up of 465 deputies.

Art. 45. The Grand National Assembly is elected for a term of four years, reckoned from the date the mandate of the previous Grand National Assembly has expired.

The mandate of the Grand National Assembly cannot cease before the term it has been elected for has expired.

In case it finds that there are circumstances which make impossible to hold elections, the Grand National Assembly can decide to prolong its mandate for the duration of these circumstances.

Art. 46. Elections to the Grand National Assembly are held on one non-working day in the last month of every legislature. The date of elections is established at least 60 days before.

The newly-elected Grand National Assembly is convened during the three months following the expiration of the mandate of the previous Grand National Assembly.

Art. 47. The Grand National Assembly verifies the legality of the election of every deputy, deciding on the validation or annulment of his election.

In the case of an annulled election, the rights and duties of the deputy cease from the moment of annulment.

Art. 48. The Grand National Assembly adopts its rules of functioning.

Art. 49. The Grand National Assembly establishes its annual budget which is included in the State Budget.

Art. 50. The Grand National Assembly elects, for the duration of the legislature, the Bureau of the Grand National Assembly, formed of the Chairman of the Grand National Assembly and four Vice-Chairmen.

Art. 51. The Chairman of the Grand National Assembly conducts the proceedings of the sessions of the Grand National Assembly.

The Chairman of the Grand National Assembly can designate any one of the four Vice-Chairmen to fulfil some of his attributions.

Art. 52. The Grand National Assembly elects standing commissions formed of deputies.

The standing commissions draw up reports or opinions on bills or matters sent to them for study, according to their competence, by the Chairman of the Grand National Assembly.

At the request of the State Council, the standing commissions draw up opinions on the draft of decrees with the power of law.

In keeping with its competence, each standing commission can hear informations—periodically or according to problems—presented by the leaders of any body of the state administration, of the Procurator's Office and of the Supreme Court on the activities of these bodies. The standing commissions submit to the Grand National Assembly their findings and proposals.

The Grand National Assembly can elect temporary commissions for any problem or field of activity, establishing the authority and mode of activity for each of these commissions.

All the state bodies and officials are obliged to put at the disposal of the commissions of the Grand National Assembly the requested information and documents.

Art. 53. In exercising control of the constitutionality of laws, the Grand National Assembly elects a Constitutional Commission for the duration of the legislature.

Experts who are not deputies, can be elected to the Constitutional Commission; their number must not exceed one third of the total membership of the Commission.

The Commission presents to the Grand National Assembly reports and opinions at its own initiative or at the intimation of the bodies provided for by the rules of the Grand National Assembly.

Art. 54. The Grand National Assembly works in sessions.

Ordinary sessions of the Grand National Assembly are convened twice a year.

The Grand National Assembly is convened whenever, necessary, in special sessions, at the initiative of the State Council or of at least one third of the total number of deputies'

Art. 55. The Grand National Assembly works only if at least one half plus one of the total number of deputies are present.

Art. 56. The Grand National Assembly adopts laws and decisions.

The laws and decisions are adopted by a majority vote of the deputies to the Grand National Assembly.

The Constitution is adopted and amended by the vote of at least two thirds of the total number of deputies to the Grand National Assembly.

The laws and decisions of the Grand National Assembly are signed by the Chairman or Vice-Chairman of the Grand National Assembly who conducted the meeting.

Art. 57. After their adoption by the Grand National Assembly, the laws are published in the Official Bulletin of the Socialist Republic of Rumania within a maximum of ten days, signed by the President of the State Council.

Art. 58. Every deputy to the Grand National Assembly has the right to put questions and address interpellations to the Council of Ministers or to any of its members.

Within the framework of the control exercised by the Grand National Assembly, a deputy can put questions and address interpellations to the president of the Supreme Court and to the Procurator General.

The person to whom a question or interpellation has been put is obliged to reply orally or in writing in a maximum of three days, and in any case during the same session.

Art. 59. In preparation of the discussions of the Grand National Assembly or of interpellations the deputy has the right to ask for the necessary information from any state body applying for this purpose to the Bureau of the Grand National Assembly.

Art. 60. Every deputy is obliged to periodically report to the electorate on his activity and on that of the Grand National Assembly.

Art. 61. No deputy to the Grand National Assembly can be detained, arrested or sent for trial without the previous consent of the Grand National Assembly during session and of the State Council between sessions.

Only in case of flagrant infraction can a deputy be detained without this consent.

The State Council

Art. 62. The State Council of the Socialist Republic of Rumania is the supreme body of state power with a permanent activity; it is subordinated to the Grand National Assembly.

Art. 63. The State Council permanently exercises the following main attributions:

(1) it establishes the date of elections to the Grand National Assembly and People's Councils;

(2) it appoints and recalls the heads of central bodies of state administration who are not on the Council of Ministers;

(3) it establishes the military ranks; it grants the ranks of general, admiral and marshal;

(4) it institutes and confers decorations and honorary titles; it authorizes the wearing of decorations conferred by other states;

(5) it grants pardon;

(6) it grants citizenship, approves renunciation of citizenship and withdraws the Rumanian citizenship;

(7) it grants the right of refuge;

(8) it ratifies and denounces international treaties with the exception of those whose ratification and denouncement is within the competence of the Grand National Assembly;

(9) it establishes the ranks of diplomatic missions, appoints and recalls diplomatic representatives of the Socialist Republic of Rumania;

(10) it receives letters of credence and of recall of diplomatic representatives of other states;

(11) in international relations the State Council, through its President, represents the Socialist Republic of Rumania.

Art. 64. The State Council exercises, in the interval between the sessions of the Grand National Assembly, the following main attributions:

(1) it convenes the sessions of the Grand National Assembly:

(2) it establishes, without being able to change the Constitution, norms with the power of law. The norms with the power of law are tabled, at the first session, for discussion to the Grand National Assembly according to the procedure for the adoption of laws. The State Plan of the National Economy, the State Budget as well as the general final account of the budgetary exercise can be adopted by the State Council if the Grand National Assembly cannot meet due to exceptional circumstances;

(3) it appoints and recalls the Council of Ministers, the Supreme Court and the Procurator General if the Grand National Assembly cannot meet because of exceptional circumstances;

(4) it appoints and recalls the members of the Council of Ministers at the proposal of its Chairman;

(5) it appoints and recalls the President and members of the Supreme Court;

(6) it gives the laws in force a general and compulsory interpretation;

(7) it grants amnesty;

(8) it controls the application of laws and decisions of the Grand National Assembly, the activity of the Council of Ministers, of the ministries and of the other central bodies of state administration as well as the activity of the Procurator's Office; it listens to the reports of the Supreme Court and controls its directive decisions; it controls the decisions of the people's councils;

(9) in the interest of defending the Socialist Republic of Rumania, of ensuring public order or state security, it proclaims in case of emergency, in some localities or throughout the country's territory, the state of urgency;

(10) it orders, in case of emergency, partial or general mobilization;

(11) it declares, in case of emergency, the state of war. The state of war can be declared only in the event of armed aggression directed against the Socialist Republic of Rumania or against another state towards which the Socialist Republic of Rumania has mutual defence obligations, arising from international treaties, if a situation has come about for which the obligation of declaring a state of war has been laid down;

(12) it appoints and recalls the Supreme Commander of the Armed Forces.

Art. 65. The State Council is elected by the Grand National Assembly from among its members for the duration of the legislature in its first session. The State Council functions up to the election of the new State Council in the following legislature.

Art. 66. The State Council is formed of the President of the State Council, three Vice-Presidents and fifteen members.

The State Council elects a secretary from among its members.

Art. 67. The State Council carries on its activity according to the principle of collective leadership.

Art. 68. The State Council issues decrees and adopts decisions.

The decrees and decisions are signed by the President of the State Council. The decrees with the power of law are published in the Official Bulletin of the Socialist Republic of Rumania.

Art. 69. The State Council reports to the Grand National Assembly on the exercise of its attributions, as well as on the observance and execution in state activity of the laws and decisions of the Grand National Assembly.

The State Council as a whole and every one of its members are responsible to the Grand National Assembly for the entire activity of the State Council.

CHAPTER IV

THE CENTRAL BODIES OF STATE ADMINISTRATION

Art. 70. The Council of Ministers is the supreme body of state administration.

The Council of Ministers exercises the general conduct of the executive activity for the whole territory of the country and has the following main attributions:

(1) it establishes general measures for the implementation of the state's home and foreign policy;

(2) it organizes and ensures the application of the laws;

(3) it guides, co-ordinates and controls the activity of the ministries and of the other central bodies of state administration;

(4) it takes measures with a view to ensuring public order, defending the interests of the state and protecting the rights of the citizens;

(5) it works out the draft of the State Plan and the draft State Budget; it draws up the general final account of the budgetary exercise;

(6) it establishes measures for the implementation of the State Plan and the State Budget;

(7) it sets up enterprises, economic organizations and state institutions of republican interest;

(8) it establishes the annual contingents of citizens to be called up for military service; it takes measures for the general organization of the Armed Forces;

(9) it exercises the general conduct in relations with other states and takes measures for the conclusion of international agreements;

(10) it suspends the decisions of the regional people's councils which are not in accordance with the law;

(11) it exercises the conduct, direction and general control of the activity of the Executive Committees of all People's Councils.

Art. 71. The Council of Ministers is elected by the Grand National Assembly for the duration of the legislature in its first session. The Council of Ministers functions up to the election of the new Council of Ministers in the following legislature.

Art. 72. In the fulfilment of its attributions the, Council of Ministers adopts decisions on the basis and in view of the application of the laws.

The decisions of a normative character are published in the Official Bulletin of the Socialist Republic of Rumania.

Art. 73. The Council of Ministers is formed of the Chairman of the Council of Ministers, the Vice-Chairmen of the Council of Ministers, of whom one or more can be First Vice-Chairmen; ministers as well as heads of other central bodies of state administration provided for by law.

The Chairman, the First Vice-Chairmen and the Vice-Chairmen of the Council of Ministers form the Permanent Bureau of the Council of Ministers.

Art. 74. The Council of Ministers carries on its activity according to the principle of collective leadership, ensuring the unity of political and administrative action of the ministries and of the other central bodies of state administration.

Art. 75. The Council of Ministers as a whole and everyone of its members is responsible to the Grand National Assembly and in the interval between sessions to the State Council. Every member of the Council of Ministers is answerable both for his own activity and for the entire activity of the Council of Ministers.

Art. 76. The ministries and the other central bodies of state administration implement the state policy in the branches or fields of activity for which they have been set up.

They manage, guide and control the enterprises, economic organizations and state institutions subordinated to them.

Art. 77. The ministers and the heads of the other central bodies of state administration issue, on the basis and in view of applying the laws and the decisions of the Council of Ministers, instructions and orders as well as other acts provided for by law; their acts of a normative character are published in the Official Bulletin of the Socialist Republic of Rumania.

Art. 78. The ministers and the other heads of central bodies of state administration are responsible to the Council of Ministers for the activity of the body which they lead.

CHAPTER V

THE LOCAL BODIES OF STATE POWER AND THE LOCAL BODIES OF STATE ADMINISTRATION

Art. 79. The People's Councils are the local bodies of state power in the regions, districts, towns, and villages.

The People's Councils conduct the local activity, securing the economic, socio-cultural and administrative development of the territorial-administrative units in which they have been elected, the maintaining of public order, socialist legality and the protection of citizen rights.

The People's Councils organize the participation of the citizens in the solution of state and public affairs on the local level.

Art. 80. The People's Council exercises the following main attributions:

(1) it adopts the local budget and economic plan, approves the final account of the budgetary exercise;

(2) it elects and recalls the Executive Committee of the People's Council;

(3) it establishes enterprises, economic organizations and state institutions of local interest;

(4) it conducts, directs and controls the activity of its Executive Committee, of the specialized sections of state administration, of the subordinated enterprises, economic organizations and institutions;

(5) it controls the decisions of hierarchically inferior People's Councils.

Art. 81. The People's Councils are formed of deputies elected by the constituencies, one deputy being elected for each constituency.

The constituencies formed for the election of the deputies to a People's Council have the same number of inhabitants.

The mandate of the People's Council is of four years, except that of the village People's Council which is of two years. The mandate is reckoned from the date of the end of the mandate of the preceding People's Council.

The new elections are held on the one of the non-working days during the last month of the mandate of the People's Council.

Art. 82. The People's Councils elect from among the deputies standing commissions which help them in the fulfilment of their tasks.

Art. 83. The People's Councils work in sessions; the convocation of sessions is made by the Executive Committee of the People's Council.

Special sessions are called at the initiative of the Executive Committee or at the demand of at least one third of the total number of deputies.

Art. 84. The People's Councils work in the presence of at least one half plus one member of the total number of deputies. At each session the People's Council elects a presidium to conduct its proceedings.

Art. 85. Each deputy is obliged to periodically present to the electorate reports on his activity and on that of the People's Council to which he has been elected.

Art. 86. The People's Councils adopt decisions.

A decision is adopted if it receives the vote of the majority of the People's Council deputies.

Decisions of a normative character are communicated to the citizens in the forms provided for by the law.

Art. 87. The Executive Committee of the People's Council is the local body of state administration with general competence in the territorial-administrative unit in which the People's Council has been elected.

Art. 88. The Executive Committee of the People's Council has the following principal attributions:

(1) it carries out the laws, decrees and decisions of the Council of Ministers and the other acts of the superior bodies;

(2) it applies the decisions of the People's Council which has elected it;

(3) it works out the drafts of the local budget and economic plan; it elaborates the final account of the budgetary exercise;

(4) it carries out the local budget and economic plan;

(5) it conducts, directs and controls the activity of the specialized sections of the state administration and of the subordinated enterprises, economic organizations and institutions;

(6) it conducts, directs and controls the activity of the Executive Committees of the People's Councils which are hierarchically inferior to the People's Council which has elected it;

(7) it suspends the decisions of the People's Councils subordinated to the People's Council that has elected it which are not in accordance with the law.

Art. 89. The members of the Executive Committee are elected by the People's Council from among its deputies at the first session after the elections for the duration of the mandate of the People's Council.

After the expiry of the mandate of the People's Council the Executive Committee continues to function up to the election of the new Executive Committee.

Art. 90. The Executive Committee of the People's Council is formed of a chairman, vice-chairmen and a number of members established by the law.

The Executive Committee carries on its activity according to the principle of collective leadership.

Art. 91. In the exercise of its attributions, the Executive Committee of the People's Council issues decisions on the basis of and with a view to the implementation of the law.

Decisions of a normative character are communicated to the citizens in the forms provided for by the law.

Art. 92. The Executive Committee is responsible for its activity to the People's Council which has elected it.

The Executive Committee is also responsible to the Executive Committee of the hierarchically superior People's Council; the Executive Committee of the Regional People's Council is responsible to the Council of Ministers.

Art. 93. The regional, district and city People's Councils organize, attached to their Executive Committees, specialized sections of the state administration.

CHAPTER VI

THE COURTS

Art. 94. In the Socialist Republic of Rumania the law is administered by the Supreme Court, regional courts, people's courts and by military courts established according to the law.

Art. 95. By their judiciary activity, the courts defend the socialist system and the rights of persons, educating the citizens in the spirit of respect for the law.

In applying penal sanctions, the courts aim to reform and re-educate infractors and to prevent the commission of new infractions.

Art. 96. The courts try civil, penal and any other cases in their competence.

In the cases provided for by the law, the courts exercise control over the decisions of administrative or public bodies having a jurisdictional activity.

The courts try the demands of those harmed in their rights by administrative acts and can, in the conditions provided for by the law, also give their views on the legality of these acts.

Art. 97. The Supreme Court exercises general control over the judicial activity of all the courts. The way of exercising this control is established by law.

With a view to the uniform application of the laws in judicial activity, the Supreme Court, in its plenum, issues decisions of direction.

Art. 98. The Supreme Court is elected by the Grand National Assembly for the duration of the legislature in its first session.

The Supreme Court functions up to the election of the new Supreme Court in the following legislature.

Art. 99. The Supreme Court is responsible for its activity to the Grand National Assembly, and between sessions to the State Council.

Art. 100. The organization of the courts, their competence and judicial procedure are established by law.

Cases in the first instance at the people's courts, the regional courts and the military courts are tried with the participation of people's jurors, unless otherwise provided for by law.

Art. 101. Judges and people's jurors are elected in accordance with the procedure established by law.

Art. 102. In the Socialist Republic of Rumania judicial procedure is in the Rumanian language and, in the regions and districts inhabited by a population of another nationality than Rumanian, the use of the mother tongue of that population is assured.

The parties who do not speak the language in which the trial is held, are given the possibility of becoming acquainted through an interpreter with the files and the right to speak in court and to sum up in the mother tongue.

Art. 103. Trials are held in public sessions, unless otherwise provided for by law.

Art. 104. In their judicial activity the judges and the people's jurors are independent and only subject to the law.

CHAPTER VII

THE ORGANS OF THE PROCURATOR'S OFFICE

Art. 105. The Procurator's Office of the Socialist Republic of Rumania exercises the supervision of the observance of the law by the ministries and the other central bodies of the state administration, the local bodies of the state administration, the penal prosecution organs and the courts as well as by the officials and other citizens.

Art. 106. The Procurator's Office is conducted by the Procurator General. The organs of the Procurator's Office are the Procurator General's Office, the Procurator's regional, district and city offices and the Procurator's military office.

The organs of the Procurator's Office are hierarchically subordinated.

Art. 107. The Procurator General is elected by the Grand National Assembly for the duration of the legislature in its first session and functions up to the election of the new Procurator General in the first session of the following legislature.

The procurators are appointed by the Procurator General.

Art. 108. The Procurator General is responsible to the Grand National Assembly for the activity of the Procurator's Office, and between sessions to the State Council.

CHAPTER VIII

THE INSIGNIA OF THE SOCIALIST REPUBLIC OF RUMANIA

Art. 109. The emblem of the Socialist Republic of Rumania represents wooded mountains over which the sun is rising. In the left part of the emblem there is an oil derrick. The emblem is surrounded by a wreath of wheat ears. The emblem is surmounted by a five-pointed star. At the base of the emblem the sheaves are bound with a tricolour ribbon bearing the words "Republica Socialistă România."

Art. 110. The State Seal bears the country's emblem, around which are are the words "REPUBLICA SOCIALISTĂ ROMÂNIA."

Art. 111. The flag of the Socialist Republic of Rumania bears the colors red, yellow and blue, placed vertically, with the blue stripe next to the flag-staff. The emblem of the Socialist Republic of Rumania is placed in the centre.

Art. 112. The Anthem of the Socialist Republic of Rumania is approved by the Grand National Assembly.

CHAPTER IX

FINAL PROVISIONS

Art. 113. The present Constitution comes into force on the date of its adoption.

Art. 114. The Constitution of September 24, 1952 and any provisions of laws, decrees and other normative acts that are contrary to the provisions of the present Constitution are abrogated on the same date.

SAN MARINO

SUMMARY

INTERNATIONAL STATUS

San Marino is not a member of the United Nations. It is a party to the Statute of the International Court of Justice and a member of other international organizations.

Independent for sixteen hundred years, the Republic of San Marino maintained a policy of isolation from its neighbours. The first treaties of friendship and commerce were in 1798 with the Roman Republic and with the Cisalpine Republic. After the unification of Italy it concluded on March 22, 1862 a Convention of Good Neighborliness and Friendship, the first of the four general Conventions (the others on March 27, 1872, June 28, 1897, as amended to 1924, and March 31, 1939, as amended to 1963) regulating relations with Italy and preserving the independence of San Marino.

FORM OF NATIONAL GOVERNMENT [1]

San Marino has a constitution written in Book I of the "*Leges Statutae,*" or "*Statuti,*" approved by the Grand and General Council on October 8, 1600, and codifying earlier San Marino statutes compiled from 1295. The organs laid down at that time and still existing are the Arengo, the Grand and General Council, the Captains-Regents, the Council of XII and the *Sindaci di Governo* (Syndics of Government). Reforms and developments have taken place to bring the structure of government up to date. In accordance with a law of 1906, the source of sovereign power lies in the people.

LEGISLATIVE DEPARTMENT

The legislative, jurisdictional and administrative powers are held by the Grand and General Council, composed of 60 members elected by universal suffrage for a term of five years by proportional representation.[2] It passes laws, ratifies international treaties, appoints diplomatic representatives, has the right of pardon, approves the budget, grants naturalizations and has the power of appointment.

The Grand and General Council elects (1) the Council of XII for the duration of the legislature with functions in questions of alienation of state property and acquisition of property by foreigners and in questions of administrative justice; (2) the *Sindaci di Governo* from among its members for the duration of the legislature who represent the state in justice and in all financial matters.

EXECUTIVE DEPARTMENT

The executive power is exercised by the Congress of State which, in pursuance of a law of May 15, 1945, has become the central executive organ and the government of the country. Together with the Regents, it carries on the activities of government and administration and gives force to the decisions of the Grand and General Council. The Congress of State is composed of ten members elected by the Grand and General Council from among its midst for the duration of the legislature. The two Captains-

[1] Information regarding the system of government from the *Annuario di San Marino 1966*, 1665 d.F.R., supplied by the Secretariat of State for Foreign Affairs.

[2] Electoral Law, Article 8.

Regents are elected every six months by the Grand and General Council from among its members and represent the State as heads of its executive power. They preside over the Grand and General Council, the *Arengo,* the Congress of State and the Council of XII, none of which bodies may meet except by their convocation. They may not be reelected until three years following the end of their mandate.

The *Arengo,* once the holder of sovereignty, the Assembly of the Heads of Families, has now the functions of presenting petitions in the public interest twice a year for discussion in the Grand and General Council.

JUDICIAL DEPARTMENT

The judicial power is confided to judges who are not of San Marino nationality, in order to ensure impartiality. One judge must reside in San Marino. The Council of XII has appellate jurisdiction in certain civil matters.

AREA, POPULATION, ETC.

The area of San Marino is 60,57 square kilometres, the population (1964) 17,000.

ELECTORAL LAW of SAN MARINO[1]

December 29, 1958

CHAPTER I

REQUIREMENTS FOR VOTERS

Art. 1. All San Marino citizens, including naturalized citizens, who have reached their majority shall be entitled to vote provided they are not excluded by any of the conditions provided in Article 2.

Art. 2. The following shall not be allowed to vote:

(a) persons forbidden or unable by reason of mental infirmity;

(b) persons condemned to permanent or temporary forfeiture of their full juridical capacity or those under criminal sentence for electoral crime or corruption;

(c) persons condemned to permanent or temporary forfeiture of their political rights.

Art. 3. The voter may exercise his right of vote only in the district assigned to him by the place where he has his residence.

If he transfers his residence to another district, he has the right to be inscribed officially in its register of voters at the time of the revision referred to in Article 4, fourth paragraph.

If he transfers his residence outside the territory of the Republic, he must be inscribed in one of the districts wholly reserved for voters residing abroad.

No more than 600 voters nor less than 50 may be assigned to each normal electoral district.

No more than 1200 voters nor less than 300 may be assigned to each district reserved to voters resident abroad.

[1] *Legge Elettorale approvata dal Consiglio Grande e Generale nella seduta del dicembre 1958 pubblicata il 29 dicembre 1958.* Published in San Marino in 1958. Supplied by the Ministry of External Affairs in July 1966. Translated by the Editor. Ed.

CHAPTER II

FORMATION OF THE ELECTORAL LISTS

Art. 4. The electoral lists, one for each district, shall be officially drawn up without distinction between men and women in alphabetical order in duplicate, and shall indicate for each voter:

(a) name and surname and, for married or widowed women, the husband's surname;
(b) father and mother;
(c) place and date of birth;
(d) academic degrees;
(e) profession or trade;
(f) place of residence, and for voters residing abroad, the country and place of residence with the address;

The electoral list must be authenticated, page by page by the signature, under the last name listed, of the President and members of the Electoral Commission.

The electoral lists shall be drawn up by a Commission composed of:
the Secretary of the Interior who shall preside;
the Head of the State Electoral Bureau;
the Officer of Civil Status;
the clerk of the Court;
five members appointed by the Grand and General Council for the duration of the legislature.

The Electoral Commission must revise and complete the lists each year and publish them not later than February 28th by deposit in the State Electoral Bureau and posting them in each electoral district.

During the course of the operation described above, those citizens who have, or will have by August 31, completed their 21st year must also be inscribed in the lists.

Art. 5. Within a time limit of fifteen days any citizen, whether or not directly concerned, may make any oral or written complaint whatsoever against the compilation of the list before the Head of the State Electoral Bureau.

When the complaint is made orally it shall be heard and recorded by the Head of the State Electoral Bureau.

The Law Commissioner shall, within the month of March, decide in final instance on such complaints.

After this the lists shall be declared definitive and may not be modified before the revision of the following year, to which the next article refers.

Those inscribed in the finally approved list shall take part in the elections at whatever time of year these occur, provided they have completed their 21st year on the date of the election.

Art. 6. After finishing the annual revision, the Electoral Commission referred to in Article 4 must proceed, at least twice a year, to eliminate from the electoral list all those who, following its revision, have died or become subject to one of the disqualifications listed in Article 2 or have lost the qualifications stipulated in Article 1.

When an election is to take place, the elimination of such voters from the list must be effected not later than fifteen days before the voting.

Art. 7. The definitive electoral list shall be open to all at the State Electoral Bureau and must be kept there.

CHAPTER III

THE ELECTORAL COLLEGE

AND CONVOCATION OF THE ELECTIONS

Art. 8. The Grand and General Council of the Republic shall consist of sixty members. It shall be wholly renewed every five years or whenever, by resignation or some other extraordinary reason, it loses one half plus one of its membership.

Art. 9. The electoral body of the Republic shall constitute a single electoral college for the election of Councillors. The election itself shall take place by list with proportional representation.

Art. 10. The elections to the Council shall be convened by the Regency by public notice issued at least sixty days before the date for convocation.

Art. 11. Within thirty days following the publication of the notice of convocation of the elections, the Head of the State Electoral Bureau shall prepare the certificates of inscription in the electoral lists for all persons inscribed in the list who have or will have by the day of voting completed their twenty first year. These certificates must be delivered to the voters concerned within forty-five days of the publication of the notice of convocation. The certificates shall indicate the electoral district to which the voter belongs, the place of meeting, the day and time of the voting and must include the coupon to be detached by the President of the District Electoral Bureau where the vote is to be exercised.

For the voters residing in the Republic the certificate shall be delivered to his domicile and notice of receipt shall be given by the voter himself or by the appropriate person of his family or his service.

When the certificate is refused or the person to whom it is delivered cannot or does not wish to acknowledge its receipt the messenger shall make an appropriate declaration.

For voters residing in Europe the certificates shall be sent by the State Electoral Bureau by registered mail.

For voters residing outside Europe the certificates shall be sent as provided in Article 40.

Art. 12. Any voter resident in the Republic or in another European country who has not received his electoral certificate at his home within the time limit mentioned in the first paragraph of the preceding article, may, from the tenth day preceding the election until the end of the voting, withdraw it in person from the State Electoral Bureau which shall remain open for this purpose every day including holidays from 9 to 19 o'clock and, on election day, for as long as the voting lasts. Any such delivery shall be noted in the appropriate register.

If a certificate has been mislaid or become unusable, the voter shall, by going in person at the end of the voting, have the right to obtain another, following annotation in the appropriate register, from the Head of the State Electoral Bureau; it must be specially countersigned and indicate that it is a duplicate.

Whenever electoral certificates are not distributed or are distributed irregularly, the Secretary of the Interior, after a summary investigation shall appeal to the direction of the State Electoral Bureau insofar as they are concerned in such distribution.

CHAPTER IV

FORMALITIES TO PRECEDE THE VOTING

Art. 13. The lists of candidates must be presented by at least sixty voters and deposited, not later than noon on the fortieth day preceding the vote at the Secretariat of the Interior which shall give a receipt therefor.

The signatures of the voters, on a single or on different documents, must be authenticated by a notary public or by the Secretary of the Interior.

For illiterate voters, the declaration of the official charged with authentication shall take the place of signature.

No voter may sign more than one list of candidates under penalty of a fine of not more than five thousand lira.

The declaration presenting the list of candidates must contain the name of the principal delegate and of a substitute with authority to receive notifications and to act on the substitutions referred to in Article 15, to participate in the operations of the Central Bureau, and to appoint, not later than the twelfth day preceding the vote, the same list's actual representative and his substitute at the Bureau of each electoral district and to the Special Electoral Bureau referred to in Article 41.

Together with the list, there must be presented the form of the symbol, printed or designed, which the voters presenting the list intend to adopt.

Parties which are known to use a particular symbol must present their lists countersigned in a manner that reproduces that symbol.

Art. 14. Each list may contain any number of candidates provided it is not more than the total of councillors to be elected nor less than ten, and must indicate the name, surname, father, mother, place and date of birth of each candidate.

No candidate may be inscribed in more than one list.

The candidatures must be accepted in a declaration signed and authenticated by a notary public or by the Secretary of the Interior and presented within the time limits fixed in the first paragraph of the preceding article.

Art. 15. Within the thirty-eight days preceding the vote, the Electoral Commission referred to in Article 4 shall verify the lists of candidates; it shall examine the symbols and reject duplicates or symbols easily confused with another symbol submitted earlier or with symbols of parties to which the presenting delegates do not belong; it shall invite the delegates referred to in Article 13 to substitute other symbols for those rejected within twenty four hours under penalty of excluding the list from the elections; it shall eliminate from the list candidates who have not furnished the prescribed acceptance; it shall eliminate lists which have not been signed by the requisite number of voters or which have not been submitted in the prescribed legal form, it shall reduce to the prescribed limit lists containing more than 60 names by deleting the last names; it shall notify the delegates involved by a notice delivered personally and immediately of the irregularities which have been found and the decisions adopted.

Art. 16. Only state ballot papers shall be used in the voting. They shall be of the same paper, of a single type, furnished by the State Electoral Bureau and shall contain the essential characteristics of the model described in Schedules A and B annexed to this law. They shall reproduce in facsimile the symbols of the accepted lists in the order of presentation. In the middle of the ballot papers two equal horizontal lines shall be placed at the number of preferential votes which the voter may make in accordance with Article 36. Any other signs or indications are forbidden.

The ballot papers must arrive at the voting bureaus of the districts duly folded.

Art. 17. The State ballot papers shall be given only to the Presidents of the Bureaus as provided in Article 24.

CHAPTER V

THE COUNCILLORS

Art. 18. Other than the general conditions required for voters in Articles 1 and 2, the following conditions must be fulfilled in order to be eligible for office:

(a) to know how to read and write;
(b) to be at least 25 years of age by the day of election;
(c) to hold no ecclesiastical office or title;
(d) to be domiciled within the Republic;
(e) to be male.

Art. 19. The following may not be Councillors:

(a) persons in diplomatic or consular posts, even honorary ones, of foreign States.
(b) members of the gendarmerie or the Corps of *Vigili Urbani.*

Art. 20. Father and son may not be councillors at the same time.

In case of both being elected the election of whomsoever receives the greater number if votes shall be considered valid.

Art. 21. The councillor or councillors whose seats fall vacant during the five year term for whatever reason shall be replaced by the candidate or candidates from the same list who received the next greatest number of votes. Should there be no candidates from the same list the post or posts shall be declared vacant and, in the event that the case foreseen in the second sentence of Article 8 has arisen, general elections shall be provided for.

CHAPTER VI

ELECTORAL PROCEDURE

Art. 22. The electoral districts, constituted in accordance with Article 3, shall be located in the following parishes: Citta, Borgo Maggiore, Serravalle, Acquaviva, Chiesanuova, Domagnano, Faetano, Fiorentino and Montegiardino.

The voters of the parish of San Giovanni shall be assigned to the Borgo Maggiore district.

The voting districts reserved to voters residing abroad shall be located in the territory of the parish of Citta.

Art. 23. The Commission referred to in Article 4 is charged with compiling each year and making public not later than February 28, by deposit at the State Electoral Bureau and by posting in all the electoral districts, a list of the citizens who will be Presidents of the voting bureaus during the year.

The Commission must choose the Presidents from the following categories of San Marino citizens, voters, domiciled or resident in the Republic:

(a) holders of academic honors or diplomas;
(b) holders of technical or secondary school diplomas;
(c) persons who have occupied the office of President of a voting bureau before at a previous election.

The following shall not be eligible: the Secretaries of the Interior and the Exterior, the Head of the State Electoral Bureau, the Official of Civil Status, the Clerk of the Court, the five elected members of the Electoral Commission.

Should there be any complaints about the composition of this list, the provisions of Article 5 on the composition of the electoral lists shall apply.

The Commission shall, before the twentieth day preceding the elections, appoint the Presidents of the voting bureaus and, in case of impediment affecting one or more such Presidents, shall provide substitutes.

The Commission shall, between the twentieth and tenth day preceding the election, appoint two scrutineers for each voting bureau from among the voters of both sexes appointed not later than the twenty first day preceding the elections, by each list of candidates; scrutineers must have finished their elementary studies; candidates and officials listed in the third paragraph of this article are not eligible.

Appointments to the presidency of voting bureaus or to the position of scrutineer must be notified to the persons concerned by messenger within forty eight hours of the meeting of the Electoral Commission.

The voter who has been appointed to the post of President of a voting bureau or of scrutineer and who abstains without justification shall be punished by a maximum fine of five thousand lira.

Art. 24. On the morning of the day fixed for the elections the President of the Voting Bureau must go to the Public Palace to receive from the Electoral Commission consignment of the material for the voting; this shall comprise a copy of the register of the district from which the Commission itself shall have cancelled the names of those who have not completed twenty one years of age by the day of the elections, the State ballot papers, an appropriate number of copying pencils, and also the list of scrutineers and of representatives appointed by each list of candidates.

The ballot papers shall be consigned in a number equal to that of the voters inscribed plus one fifth.

The ballot papers must carry the dry stamp of the Secretary of State of the Interior and be signed on the back by the Secretary of the Interior or, by his delegation, by the Head of the State Electoral Bureau.

Art. 25. At 6 o'clock the President shall constitute the District Voting Bureau by calling upon the scrutineers appointed by the Electoral Commission to form the Bureau and by inviting the representatives of the lists of candidates to attend the electoral operations if they are present.

One of the two scrutineers shall be appointed by the President as Vice-President and the other as secretary of the Bureau.

If one or both of the scrutineers is absent or has not been appointed, the President of the District Voting Bureau shall ask the voters present, provided they are not less than ten, to nominate by voice vote and simple majority the member or members of the Bureau to substitute for the absent person or persons.

If less than ten voters are present, the President shall himself make the substitution for the absent person or person by calling upon the oldest and the youngest of the voters present who fulfils the requirements set forth in Article 23, sixth paragraph.

Art. 26. The representatives of each list of candidates shall have the right to be present at all of the operations of the Voting Bureau.

The President of the Bureau may require any representative who exercises pressure or disturbs the proceedings of the election to leave.

Art. 27. Once the District Voting Bureau has been constituted, the President shall proceed, with the assistance of the scrutineers, to number consecutively the ballot papers on the attached appendix after having determined the number of voters inscribed in the section, and to sign them on the back.

During this operation noone may leave the room.

The report shall note the ballots numbered and signed by the President and, eventually, by each scrutineer.

As soon as these operations are completed the President shall declare the voting open.

Art. 28. The President of the Bureau, the scrutineers and the representatives of the lists of candidates shall vote in the section where they exercise their duties whether or not they belong to it.

Voters who follow the Presidents of the Bureaus for service reasons, such as the soldiers, may vote at the electoral district to which they have been sent by showing their electoral certificate. The President shall note in the report the name, surname, father and mother and also the electoral district in which such voters are inscribed.

Art. 29. At least two of the three members of the Voting Bureau must always be present during the voting operations .

If the President is absent his duties shall be assumed by the Vice President. If the Secretary is absent his functions shall be exercised by the Vice President.

Art. 30. It is the duty of the Bureau always to ascertain the identity of each voter, to observe the hours fixed for the voting, to report any complaints, to decide in first instance questions about the regularity of the ballot papers, to assign the votes to the candidates, to attach to the report any invalid, blank or contested ballots as well as written protests and any other relevant documents.

Art. 31. With the exception of the voters specified in Article 28 to Article 33, third paragraph and Article 35, first paragraph, noone may enter the voting booth and take part in the electoral operations unless he is provided with an electoral certificate of inscription in the list of the district.

Art. 32. Two lists must be posted in the voting booth throughout the election operations, extracted from the copy of the district register referred to in Article 24 paragraph 1: one of the voters residing within the jurisdiction of the district, and one of voters residing abroad but still inscribed in the district because of delays in ascertaining their emigration; the lists shall then be declared definitive in accordance with the last paragraph of Article 5. There must also be posted a notice indicating the number of preferential votes allowed.

In the voting booth of the district reserved for voters residing abroad there the list of such voters must be posted together with the list of voters residing in the Republic who are still inscribed in that district because of delays in ascertaining their repatriation; the lists shall then be declared definitive.

Art. 33. When the voting has been declared open the voters shall be admitted in order of arrival. They must show some identification, even an expired identity card, with a photograph, issued by the State Office of the Republic or by a government office of the foreign state in which they reside. In the latter case the provenance of such document shall be indicated in the identification column of the district register.

Voters residing in the Republic may be admitted to vote, even if not provided with a suitable identification document, provided one of the scrutineers or the President of the Bureau who knows them personally testifies to their identity with an appropriate signature in the identification column.

If none of the members of the District Voting Bureau is in a position to certify on his own responsibility the voter's identity, the latter may present two other voters inscribed in the same district and known to the bureau who will attest to his identity putting their own signatures in the identification column.

In such cases the President shall warn the voters that if they have witnessed falsely they shall be punished in accordance with the Penal Code in effect.

When the identity of the voter has been recognized, the President shall detach the coupon from the electoral certificate proving that the right to vote has been exercised, to be filed in the proper packet, and shall give a ballot paper duly folded together with the pencil, while reading aloud the number on the appendix which one of the members of the Bureau shall note on the electoral list opposite the voter's name. The latter may verify that the number noted is that of his ballot paper.

The voter must withdraw alone to a separate part of the voting booth where, after marking his vote in conformity with Article 36, he shall fold the ballot at the line drawn thereon and seal it by moistening the gummed part. The President must instruct him in this operation before the vote, abstaining from any simplification and indicating in each case the manner and the number of preferential votes which the voter may give.

When he has completed his voting, the voter shall give to the President the sealed ballot and the pencil. The President shall verify the seal of the ballot and, if it is not properly sealed shall invite the voter to seal it, making him withdraw to the separate part, shall verify the identity examining the signature and seal and checking the number written on the appendix with that in the list, shall detach the appendix at the dotted line, and shall place the ballot paper in the urn made of transparent glass placed on the table of the office and visible to all.

One of the members of the District Voting Bureau shall certify that the voter has made his vote by placing his own signature opposite the voter's name in the next column of the list above referred to.

Any ballot papers without appendices or lacking the number, stamp and signature of the Secretary of the Interior or the Head of the State Electoral Bureau which may be handed to him shall not be placed in the urn, and voters who have presented such ballots may not vote again. These shall be immediately checked by the President and one of the scrutineers and attached to the report, which shall also make special mention of any voters who received ballot papers but did not return them.

Art. 34. The President of the District Voting Bureau shall be charged with policing the voting. The police may not, except at the President's request, enter the voting booth. But they shall remain near it at the disposal of the President.

Art. 35. There may be no voting by proxy. As an exception the blind, those with a hand amputated or paralysed or afflicted with another impediment of similar gravity, may exercise the right to vote with the assistance of a voter of their own family or, lacking such, of another voter whom they have voluntarily chosen to accompany them, provided both are inscribed in the same electoral district.

No voter may accompany more than one invalid or maimed person. To ensure this the President shall make a note on the electoral certificate of the accompanying person that he has exercised this right.

The President of the Bureau shall certify, after inquiry, that the voter has freely chosen the person accompanying him and if he does not know his name and surname, shall record in the appropriate part of the report this method of voting, indicating the specific reason for the assistance, the name of the health officer who has, if such is the case, attested to the impediment, and the name and surname of the accompanying person.

The medical certificate must be issued by a health office of the Government of San Marino or, if it has been issued by another doctor exercising his profession in the territory of the Republic, it must be visaed by the Health Official.

No medical certificates issued by candidates at the election shall be accepted as valid.

The medical certificate shown shall be noted in the report.

Art. 36. Voting on the list shall be done by making a mark on the ballot paper with the pencil against the symbol corresponding to the chosen list of candidates, or in the rectangle containing it.

The voter may express his preference for a maximum of six candidates from the list he has chosen.

Preferential votes in excess of that number shall be invalid. The first ones shall remain valid.

The preferential vote shall be expressed by writing with the pencil on the lines traced in the middle part of the ballot, the name and surname, or the surname alone of the preferred candidates. If the surnames are identical both name and surname must be written and where necessary the father's name.

If a candidate has two surnames the voter may write one of them. Both must be written wherever there is the possibility of confusion among the candidates.

Any preferential votes where the candidate is not sufficiently clearly indicated to distinguish him from other candidates shall by null.

If a voter has not indicated any list symbol, but has written one or more preferential votes from one single list, it shall be understood that he intended to vote for the list to which those candidates belong.

A valid ballot shall represent a vote for a list of candidates.

The following ballots shall be null and void:

(a) those not issued by the State, not bearing the stamp of the Secretariat of the Interior (Article 24) and the signature of the Secretary of the Interior or his delegate and the signature of the President of the Voting Bureau or of one of the scrutineers appointed;

(b) those containing writing or signs made in such a fashion that they must be held to be intended to allow the voter to be identified;

(c) those which have no indication of a vote for any list or for any candidates or those which vote for several lists and offer no possibility of identifying the list preferred.

The validity of the votes contained on the ballot papers must be accepted whenever the effective wish of the voter can be discerned, except as provided in the preceding paragraphs.

Art. 37. The voting shall remain open until 20 o'clock but shall be prolonged for another hour if there is an uninterrupted succession of voters. However, at 21 o'clock, the President shall ascertain the number of voters present in the hall who have not yet voted, shall allow those only to vote, and shall then declare the voting closed.

Art. 38. When the President has declared the voting closed, the Bureau shall proceed publicly to the following operations:

(1) to count and seal in the appropriate packet the unused ballot papers;
(2) to count and seal in the appropriate packet any spoiled ballots which were replaced during the voting by ballots in good condition;
(3) to count and seal in the appropriate packet, the coupons of the certificates of the voters admitted;
(4) to count the ballots taking them one by one from the urn and verifying:
  (a) valid and invalid votes;
  (b) votes relating only to the lists of candidates;
  (c) preferential votes relating to individual candidates.
(5) make public the results of the count.

The operations described above shall be completed in the order indicated and without interruption until they are finished; each operation must be noted in the report.

The report and all other documents must be signed by the members of the Voting Bureau and all sealed in one single packet on which the members of the Voting Bureau shall place their own signatures.

The papers must be transmitted immediately after the operations described above to the Secretary of State for the Interior.

Art. 39. Voters residing in countries outside of Europe shall be permitted to vote by correspondence.

The Head of the State Electoral Bureau must, by the thirty-fifth day preceding the vote, prepare for each voter in question an envelope with his address containing the electoral certificate and an envelope for the voter's use in returning the ballot on the back of which there shall be written the address of the Electoral Commission.

The State Electoral Bureau shall compile for the voters to whom the above described envelopes are destined, a list in strict alphabetical order, in three copies, indicating the general information for each voter and the name of the district in which he is inscribed.

By the twenty-fourth day before the voting, one copy of this shall be sent to the Electoral Commission. The Commission shall make the notation "votes by correspondence" on the district lists which must be transmitted to the Presidents of the Voting Bureaus in accordance with Article 24 of this Law, next to the name of each voter residing abroad.

Two copies shall be kept in the State Electoral Bureau.

Art. 40. The State Electoral Bureau shall send, by the twenty-fifth day before the vote, to each voter residing in countries outside of Europe the envelope and documents referred to in the preceding article together with a ballot paper.

Their expedition shall be noted on one of the copies referred to in the third paragraph of the preceding article by the Post Office stamp at the moment of posting.

They must be sent by registered packet air mail.

Art. 41. A Special Voting Bureau shall be established to check and count the votes sent by voters residing in countries outside of Europe.

The rules contained in Article 23 shall apply for the appointment of the President and scrutineers for this Bureau.

This Bureau shall be constituted by its President in accordance with the rules of Article 25 at 16 o'clock of the day of the vote.

Representative of the lists of candidates may be appointed to this Voting Bureau in the manner provided in Article 13, fourth paragraph, of this Law.

Art. 42. Voters residing in countries outside of Europe, when they receive the packet referred to in Article 40, paragraph one, shall fill in the ballot paper and seal it by moistening the gummed part; they shall place it together with the electoral certificate in the return envelope provided and post the envelope.

These envelopes must reach the Post Office of San Marino not later than 16 o'clock on the election day.

Art. 43. The Post Office shall forward the envelopes referred to in the preceding article to the Electoral Commissions as they are received, except that nothing shall be forwarded later than 17 o'clock on the election day.

The Electoral Commission shall give a receipt for the packets it receives from the Post Office.

The aforesaid packets shall be kept by the Electoral Commission under the personal responsibility of the President of the Commission himself until they are transmitted to the Special Voting Bureau referred to in Article 41.

Art. 44. At 17.15 o'clock of the election day, the President of the Electoral Commission, in the presence of the members of the Commission, shall transmit to the special Voting Bureau referred to in Article 41 the packets received from voters residing in countries outside of Europe, together with a copy of the list referred to in Article 39, paragraph 3, which he has received from the State Electoral Bureau in accordance with the fourth paragraph of that article.

The President of the Special Voting Bureau shall, when he receives the packets and the list aforesaid, open each envelope and extract the electoral certificate and the ballot paper. He shall then check whether the name on the electoral certificate is contained in the list. Whenever the name is not contained in the list, the electoral certificate together with the still sealed ballot paper must be authenticated by the President of the Bureau and one scrutineer and inscribed on the original envelope which must be authenticated in the same manner and then folded to be burned together with the packets referred to in Articles 45 and 46 below.

For this purpose, at the close of the operations of the Special Voting Bureau, these folded documents shall be placed in a suitable packet apart from the others and, when sealed and countersigned by the President of the Bureau and by one scrutineer, shall be transmitted to the Electoral Commission.

When, on the other hand, the name on the certificate is contained in the list, the President, after signing the ballot paper, detaches the coupon which must not be numbered and places it unopened in the urn. The electoral certificate is kept in the appropriate packet in order to be transmitted to the Secretary of State for the Interior.

Whenever the ballot paper is not sealed, the President, before proceeding to the further operations, shall personally seal it without unfolding it.

As soon as the ballot is placed in the urn, one of the members of the Special Voting Bureau shall make a note by the name of the voter contained in the list referred to in the first paragraph of this article.

If the electoral certificate is not contained in the packet the ballot paper is considered as not received and, without being unfolded, is placed in the original return envelope and attached to the report. The ballot paper and envelope must be authenticated by the President and by one scrutineer.

When the aforesaid operations have been completed, the President of the Special Electoral Office shall start the operation of counting the ballots which must continue without interruption and, insofar as applicable, in the manner prescribed in Article 38.

The provisions of the second, third and fourth paragraphs of Article 38 shall apply to the drawing up and signing of the report, the making up of the packet and the transmission of the papers.

Art. 45. Voters residing in countries outside of Europe who return to the country before receiving the voting documents sent by the State Electoral Bureau, may vote in the district where they are inscribed.

In order to do this they must furnish themselves with the appropriate authorization of the Electoral Commission by requesting it from the Commission itself not later than 15 o'clock on the election day, and show it to the Voting Bureau in place of the electoral certificate.

The Electoral Commission shall make a note of such authorizations by the names of the voters in question on the list referred to in the third paragraph of Article 39, for the purpose of comparing the envelopes containing the votes by correspondence.

Should there be found among the packets transmitted to the Special Voting Bureau by the Electoral Commission, in accordance with Article 44, first paragraph, packets containing votes by correspondence of voters authorized to vote in the manner described in the preceding paragraph, as ascertained by checking the electoral certificate contained in each packet against the annotated list transmitted to the Special Electoral Office by the Electoral Commission, in accordance with the first paragraph of Article 44, the ballot papers shall be considered as not received and, without being unsealed, shall be authenticated together with the corresponding electoral certificate by the President of the Special Voting Bureau and by one scrutineer, placed together with the electoral certificate in the original envelope which shall be similarly authenticated and folded for burning together with the packets and documents referred to in Articles 44 and 46 of this Law.

For this purpose the aforesaid folded documents shall, at the close of the operations of the Special Voting Bureau, be placed in the same packet to which Article 44, paragraph four refers.

Art. 46. Packets arriving at the Post Office after 16 o'clock of the election day shall be transmitted to the Electoral Commission not earlier than 9 o'clock of the third following day. An appropriate list in two copies shall be made of such packets indicating the day and hour of arrival of each one. One the copies shall be signed by the President of the Electoral Commission and transmitted to the Post Office.

The President of the Electoral Commission, having taken consignment of the aforesaid packets, shall proceed to burn them together with those referred to in Articles 44 and 45.

The delegates presenting the lists of candidates shall be invited to attend the operations referred to in the preceding paragraph and they must be informed in time by the President of the Electoral Commission of the day and place where the operations will occur.

An appropriate report shall be made of the operation of burning the aforesaid packets which must be signed on the spot by the President, he members of the Electoral Commission and the delegates present.

Art. 47. Voters residing in countries outside of Europe who, having received and made use, directly or indirectly, of the envelope referred to in the first paragraph of Article 40, conceal this fact and obtain from the Electoral Commission the authorization referred to in the second paragraph of Article 45, shall be punished with the penalty prescribed in Article 479 of the penal code in force.

Should such a voter succeed in voting in the Voting Bureau where he is inscribed by use of such authorization, the penalty referred to in the preceding paragraph shall be doubled.

Art. 48. On the day following the elections, the district Voting Bureaus and the Special Voting Bureau shall, in the person of their Presidents and with the assistance of the delegate presenting each list of candidates appointed in accordance with the provisions of Article 13 by each committee—meet at 14 o'clock in the Council Hall, under the chairmanship of the Secretary of State for the Interior, in order to constitute the Central Electoral Bureau. The latter must proceed to the following operations on the basis of the reports of the district Voting Bureaus and the special Voting Bureau:

(1) Make the total count with, if desired, the assistance of one or more

experts chosen by the President, of the votes obtained by each list and each candidate in each district and the Special Voting Bureau, as shown by their reports, and proceed to the determination of:

(a) the total vote of each list;

(b) the individual total of each candidate.

The total vote of each list is arrived at by the sum of the votes obtained by the list in all the districts and in the Special Voting Bureau.

The individual total is arrived at by the sum of the votes for the list and the preferential votes which each candidate has received in all the districts and the Special Voting Bureau.

The total vote serves as a basis for determining the number of seats assigned to each list.

The individual total serves to assign the place of the candidates in each list. The order of precedence is established equally by the vote and by the order of inscription on the lists.

The assignment of seats to each list is made in the following manner:

The total of each list is divided successively by 1, 2, 3, 4 ... up to the number of councillors to be elected; of the quotients thus obtained as many of the highest quotients shall be chosen as there are councillors to be elected in accordance with a decreasing order.

To each list shall be allocated as many seats as its quotient in the graduated order. In case of equality of quotients among the lists, the seat shall belong to the list which has received the greatest number of votes.

If one list receives more seats than the total of its candidates, the extra seats are distributed among the other lists in accordance with the order of the quotients.

(2) make the official proclamation of the persons elected and of the seats assigned to each list of candidates, and also announce the order in the graduated scale of total individual votes for each list.

Art. 49. It is forbidden for the Central Bureau to consider or even to discuss the allocation of votes, complaints, protests or any incidents which may have occurred in the voting bureaus or to concern itself with anything other than what is set forth in the preceding article.

Art. 50. The Central Bureau, as soon as it has completed the operations entrusted to it, shall transmit all the papers to the Secretariat of the Interior which, in turn, shall transmit them to the Electoral Board.

Art. 51. After two days the Secretary of the Interior shall publish the results of the voting and notify each person elected of his nomination.

Art. 52. The Permanent Electoral Board, composed of five members, shall be elected from the members of the Council for the term of a legislature.

Art. 53. The Board shall have the following functions: to examine the electoral documents received, to hear any appeals formulated by the voters within five days of the election regarding all questions of eligibility or electoral procedure, to provide for the deletion of ineligible candidates where necessary and their substitution by the person on the same list coming immediately after in number of votes received, to propose expeditiously the validation of all the councillors declared elected.

For elections in which there are no protests, that is to say, in the cases where those elected fulfil all the conditions of eligibility required by the present Law and where the electoral operations have taken place regularly, the Council simply takes note of the conclusions of the Electoral Board.

In the contrary case, the Council shall vote on the conclusions of the Board for the purpose of accepting or rejecting them in each case of contested, doubtful or irregular election.

Art. 54. If it appears from the report of a District Voting Bureau or from the Special Voting Bureau that the operations have been prevented by violence or that the ballots have been scattered in such a manner as to prevent the counting, the Regency shall convoke the elections in the districts intended for the voters who have voted in accordance with Article 42, on the fifth following Sunday.

In such case the operations of the Central Bureau provided in Article 48 shall be postponed to the day following the supplementary balloting.

Art. 55. The councillors must take the oath within two months from the validation of their election.

Those who fail to comply with this requirement without just cause shall be deprived of their mandate.

Art. 56. In addition to the penalties provided in Articles 478 and 479 of the Penal Code in effect, any other infringement of the free exercise of political rights shall be punished by the penalties prescribed in the latter article regardless of whether the infringement is made in a manner other than described in the article.

TRANSITIONAL PROVISIONS

Art. 57. An extraordinary revision of the electoral list is authorized in order to eliminate all names improperly inscribed thereon and all voters residing abroad of whom the Office of Civil Status and the Register's Office have lost all trace and who might be found only by investigations undertaken by the State Electoral Bureau.

The aforesaid extraordinary revision shall be executed on the occasion of the annual revision of electoral lists of 1959.

Art. 58. At the first application of the present Law, the date specified in Article 4, last paragraph, shall be May 31st, in Article 5, third paragraph, shall be June 30, and in Article 23, first paragraph, shall be May 31.

Art. 59. The date on which the extension of the right to vote to women shall begin shall be determined in a new legislative provision to be promulgate by April 30, 1959.

CHAPTER VIII

FINAL PROVISIONS

Art. 60. A State Electoral Bureau is established for the purposes of this Law. It shall be responsible for the keeping of the electoral lists and the technical preparation of elections, which formerly was the province of the Bureau of Civil Status, in addition to the duties prescribed by this Law.

Art. 61. The provisions of Law 15 of October 1920, number 18, amended by the decrees of August 22 and September 11, 1951, together with any other provisions contrary to or incompatible with the present Law are hereby abrogated.

Art. 62. The present Law shall enter into effect on the day following its publication.

SCHEDULES A AND B

FORMS OF BALLOT PAPERS

Not reproduced

SPAIN

SUMMARY

INTERNATIONAL STATUS

Spain is a member of the United Nations (December 14, 1955). It is a member of other international organizations. It was a member of the League of Nations.

The first constitution of Spain of 1812, following the Cortes of Cadiz in 1810, limited royal power and established a regency. The King, returning after the Peninsular War, or War of Independence, refused to accept the Constitution and ruled as an absolute monarch, except for a brief period of a liberal regime, after the mutiny of the army, from 1820 until suppressed after the Congress of Verona in 1822. By 1825 all the colonies on the American continent were independent. A revolution in 1868 led to a regency. In 1873, a republic was proclaimed and followed by the second Carlist War (the first from 1834 to 1839). In 1876 the Bourbons were restored. Spain lost her last colonies in 1898. During the first two decades of the twentieth century extremist groups provoked revolutionary general strikes, there were risings of the Riff in Spanish Morocco. In 1923, a *coup d'état* established the dictatorship of Primo de Rivera which ended after the elections of 1931 when, anti-monarchic parties having won all the cities, a republic was proclaimed on April 14, 1931 and the king went into exile to avoid civil war. A constitution was promulgated on December 9, 1931. On October 4, 1931, the *Juntas de Ofensiva Nacional-Sindicalista* (JONS) were created, on October 28, 1933, the *Falange Española,* and on March 4, 1934, the two bodies were fused. Following the 1936 elections, won by the Popular Front, strikes and terrorist agitation lasted from February to July. On July 17, the military uprising against the Republic began in Morocco. On July 24, the *Junta de Defensa Nacional* was formed at Burgos and on September 29, General Franco was named Head of the government and Generalissimo. The siege of Madrid began in October 1936. The Civil War, in which took part Italy and Germany on the insurgent side and the USSR on the Republican side, lasted until April 1, 1939—Barcelona having fallen on January 26, Madrid on March 27 following internecine Communist-Republican battles, and Valencia, Almeria and Alicante on March 30th. Spain made a declaration of neutrality on September 4, 1939. In October 1965, the official press requested the formulation of a Constitution; a new Organic Law was submitted to referendum in December 1966.

FORM OF NATIONAL GOVERNMENT

The constitutional documents of Spain are the following laws which were declared to be Fundamental Laws on July 26, 1947, or (in the case of the first two listed below) at the date of promulgation:

1. Organic Law of the State of December 14, 1966.
2. Principles of the National Movement of May 17, 1958.
3. Charter of the Spanish People of July 16, 1945, amended December 14, 1966.
4. Law of the Cortes of July 17, 1942, amended March 9, 1946 and December 14, 1966.
5. Referendum Act of October 22, 1945.
6. Law of Succession to the Head of State of June 7, 1947, amended December 14, 1966.
7. Labor Charter of March 9, 1938.

Spain is a Kingdom, a traditional, Catholic, social and representative

Monarchy.[1] Sovereignty, one and indivisible, is exercised by the State.[2] The family, municipality and syndicate are the basic structures of the national community.[3] The Catholic religion is the State religion.[4] The National Movement, under its Principles, shapes the political system.[5]

RIGHTS OF THE PEOPLE

The Charter of the Spanish People provides protection without discrimination by the law, the right and duty to education, religious liberty, the right to public office, freedom of expression, liberty and inviolability of correspondence within Spain, freedom of residence, inviolability of domicile, freedom of association for lawful ends, freedom of petition, due process of law and no detention without charge; deprivation of nationality and confiscation of property are forbidden.[6] The State protects the family, workers, maintains institutions of assistance, protects private property.[7] Spaniards owe service to their country and its Armed Forces, obedience to the laws, contribution to the public charges.[8]

LEGISLATIVE DEPARTMENT

The Cortes are the superior organ through which the Spanish people participates in the tasks of the State; their principal mission is the elaboration and approval of laws, subject to the veto of the Head of State.[9] They are composed of members (*Procuradores*) *ex officio*, of representatives of the Syndicalist Organization, of the municipalities, of the family, of professional associations, and of persons appointed by the Head of State.[10] Their term of office is four years or, for *ex officio* or appointed members, the duration of their office or until revocation of their appointment.[11] Participation of the people in the legislative and other functions is accomplished through the family, municipality, syndicate and other legally recognized bodies; other political organizations are illegal.[12]

Immunities of members are provided.[13] Subjects requiring legislation by the Cortes are set out and the Government may not issue measures on such subjects.[14] There are provisions concerning the budget.[15] The approval of the Cortes is required for the choice of the King or Regent.[16]

[1] 1966 Org. Law, Art. 1; 1958 Principles, Art. VII.
[2] 1966 Org. Law, Art. 1, 2.
[3] 1958 Principles, Art. VI.
[4] 1945 Charter, Art. 6.
[5] 1966 Org. Law, Art. 3; 1958 Principles.
[6] 1945 Charter, Art. 3–6, 10–21, 32.
[7] Id., Art. 22–31; 1958 Principles, Art. IX–XII.
[8] 1945 Charter, Art. 2, 7–9.
[9] Cortes Law, Art. 1.
[10] Id., Art. 2.
[11] Id., Art. 6.
[12] 1958 Principles, Art. VIII.
[13] Cortes Law, Art. 5.
[14] Id., Art. 10, 12; 1966 Org. Law, Art. 52.
[15] 1966 Org. Law, Art. 54, 55.
[16] Succession Law, Art. 8.

EXECUTIVE DEPARTMENT

The Head of State is the Caudillo of Spain and the Crusade; should the office fall vacant its powers are exercised by a Council of the Regency.[1] The Head of State may submit the name of a person to succeed him, either as King or Regent, to the Cortes.[2] The Head of State is the supreme representative of the Nation, commands the Armed Forces, confers appointsments and honors, convenes the legislature, the Council of Ministers and the National Defense Board.[3] He is inviolable, persons countersigning his acts are responsible.[4] He is assisted by a Council of the Kingdom.[5] He directs the government of the Kingdom through the Council of Ministers composed of a President of the Government whom he appoints and Ministers.[6] There is provision for a National Council under the chairmanship of the President of the Government, as the collective representative body of the Movement, composed of councillors chosen in different ways and representing different sections of national life, which may propose laws and submit reports and move an appeal of unconstitutionality.[7] There are provisions concerning the Armed Forces,[8] the administration of the State,[9] and local administration.[10]

JUDICIAL DEPARTMENT

Justice is independent.[11] All Spaniards have free access to the courts.[12] Courts and tribunals are established by an organic law concerning justice and the President of the Supreme Court has supervisory power in judicial matters.[13] Military jurisdiction, ecclesiastical jurisdiction and labor jurisidction are provided for.[14] A chapter provides procedures for the appeal of unconstitutionality before the Council of the Kingdom.[15]

AREA, POPULATION, ETC.

The area of Spain is 504,879 square kilometres, the population (1965) 31,737,000. The capital is Madrid.

[1] Id., Art. 2, 3. [2] Id., Art. 6, 7. [3] 1966 Org. Law, Art. 6, 7.
[4] Id., Art. 8. [5] Id., Art. 10. [6] Id., Art. 13–17.
[7] Id., Art. 21–28, 60. [8] Id., Art. 37–39. [9] Id., Art. 40–44. [10] Id., Art. 45–48.
[11] Id., Art. 29. [12] Id., Art. 30; 1958 Principles, Art. IX.
[13] 1966 Org. Law, Art. 31, 33. [14] Id., Art. 32; Labor Charter Art. VII.
[15] 1966 Org. Law, Art. 59–66.

FUNDAMENTAL LAWS of SPAIN

1. Organic Law of the State[1]

December 14, 1966

CHAPTER I

THE NATIONAL STATE

Art. 1. 1. The Spanish State, constituted as a Kingdom, is the highest institution of the national community.

2. Sovereignty shall be exercised by the State through the organs appropriate to the purposes they are called upon to fulfil.

Art. 2. 1. The national sovereignty is one and indivisible; it may neither be delegated nor surrendered.

2. The institutional system of the Spanish State shall correspond to the principles of the unity of power and the co-ordination of functions.

Art. 3. The fundamental purposes of the State are the following: defense of the unity between the people and the lands of Spain; maintenance of the integrity, independence and security of the Nation; safeguarding the spiritual and material patrimony of the Spanish people; protection of the rights of the individual, the family and of society; promotion of a just social order in which every particular interest shall remain subordinate to the common good. All the above shall be inspired by and remain strictly faithful to the Principles of the National Movement promulgated by the Fundamental Law of May 17, 1958, which are by their very nature permanent and inalterable.

Art. 4. The National Movement, as a communion of all Spaniards under the Principles referred to in the preceding article, shall shape the political system; it is open to all Spaniards, and shall, for the better service of the country, further political life under a system of orderly organization of the criteria.

[1] *Ley Organica del Estado*, approved by referendum of 14 December 1966. Supplied by the Ministry of Foreign Affairs. Translated by the Editor. Ed.

Art. 5. The national flag is composed of three horizontal stripes, red, yellow and red; the yellow stripe shall be double the width of the red ones.

CHAPTER II

THE HEAD OF STATE

Art. 6. The Head of State is the supreme representative of the Nation; he personifies the national sovereignty, exercises the supreme political and administrative power, embodies the National Leadership of the Movement and supervises the exact observance of its principles and of the other Fundamental Laws of the Kingdom, guards the continuity of the State and of the National Movement, guarantees and ensures the orderly functioning of the high organs of the State and due co-ordination between them, sanctions and promulgates the laws and sees to their execution, exercises the supreme command of the Land, Sea and Air Forces, watches over the conservation of public order within the State and its security from without. Justice is administered in his name, he exercises the prerogative of pardon. He confers, in accordance with the laws, appointments, public duties and honors; he accredits and receives diplomatic representatives, and carries out other acts pertaining to his office in accordance with the Fundamental Laws of the Kingdom.

Art. 7. The following, in particular, are functions of the Head of State:

(a) To convoke the Cortes in accordance with the law, to preside over the opening session of each legislature and to present, in agreement with the Government, the inaugural address and other messages.

(b) To prorogue a legislature for the necessary period, at the request of the Cortes or of the Government and in agreement with the Council of the Kingdom, when the normal renewal of its members (*Procuradores*) is prevented by a serious reason.

(c) To submit to referendum by the Nation the bills referred to in the second paragraph of Article 10 of the Law of Succession and in Article 1 of the Referendum Act.

(d) To appoint and remove the President of the Government, the President of the Cortes and other high officials in the form provided by law.

(e) To convene the Council of Ministers and the National Defense Board and preside over their meetings when he is present.

(f) To preside, if he deems it useful, over the deliberations of the Council of the Kingdom and of the National Council, provided they do not relate to his person or to the person of the heirs to the Crown. In no case shall voting take place in the presence of the Head of State.

(g) To request rulings and advice from the Council of the Kingdom.

(h) To obtain reports from the National Council.

Art. 8. 1. The person of the Head of State is inviolable. All Spaniards owe it respect and homage.

2. All orders issued by the Head of State in the exercise of his authority must be countersigned, as the case may be, by the President of the Government or the appropriate Minister, the President of the Cortes or the President of the Council of the Kingdom, and no provision shall be valid where this formality has not been fulfilled.

3. The persons countersigning the acts of the Head of State shall be responsible therefor.

Art. 9. The Head of State requires a law or the agreement or authorization of the Cortes for the following purposes:

(a) To ratify treaties and international conventions which affect the full sovereignty or the integrity of Spanish territory.

(b) To declare war and conclude peace.

(c) To accomplish the acts referred to in Article 12 of the Law of Succession and in other rules to be determined of the Fundamental Laws of the Kingdom.

Art. 10. The Head of State shall be assisted by the Council of the Kingdom in respect of the following:

(a) Proposals to the Cortes of acts requiring a law or their agreement or authorization, in accordance with the preceding article.

(b) Returning a law drawn up by the Cortes to them for further study.

(c) Proroguing a legislature for serious reasons and for the necessary time.

(d) The adoption of exceptional measures when the external security, the independence of the Nation, the integrity of its territory or the institutional system of the Kingdom is threatened by a clear and present danger, together with a documented account to be given to the Cortes.

(e) Submitting bills of great importance to national referendum when it is not so required by law.

(f) Adopting decisions requiring a Fundamental Law to institute them.

Art. 11. During absences of the Head of State from the national territory or in case of infirmity, the heir to the Crown, if he exists and is older than thirty years of age, shall assume his functions or, failing such heir, the Council of the Regency. In all cases the President of the Government shall report to the Cortes.

Art. 12. The guardianship of royal persons succeeding to the Throne while still minors, or of a King who is incapacitated, shall be approved by the Cortes on the proposal of the Council of the Kingdom. The person appointed must be of Spanish nationality and must profess the Catholic religion, and tho office is incompatible with the exercise of the Regency, the Presidency of the Government or the Presidency of the Cortes.

CHAPTER III

THE GOVERNMENT OF THE NATION

Art. 13. 1. The Head of State shall direct the government of the Kingdom through the Council of Ministers.

2. The Council of Ministers, composed of the President of the Government, the Vice President or Vice Presidents if they exist, and the Ministers, is the organ which determines national policy, ensures the application of the laws, exercises the regulatory power and permanently assists the Head of State in political and administrative matters.

3. Agreements of the Government shall always be countersigned by the President or by the appropriate Minister.

Art. 14. 1. The President of the Government must be Spanish and shall be appointed by the Head of State from a list of three names proposed by the Council of the Kingdom.

2. His term shall be for five years. Fifteen days before the expiration thereof, the Council of the Kingdom shall submit the proposal referred to in the preceding paragraph.

3. The laws shall stipulate the activities incompatible with the office of President of the Government.

4. The President of the Government shall represent the Government of the Nation, direct general policy and ensure the co-ordination of all the organs of government and administration.

5. The President of the Government, in the name of the Head of State, exercises the national Leadership of the Movement, assisted by the National Council and the Secretary General.

Art. 15. The President of the Government shall relinquish his office:

(a) at the expiration of his term.

(b) At his own request once his resignation has been accepted by the Head of State in the Council of the Kingdom.

(c) By decision of the Head of State with the agreement of the Council of the Kingdom.

(d) At the proposal of the Council of the Kingdom for incapacity attested by two thirds of its members.

Art. 16. 1. In the case of the death of the President of the Government, or in any of the cases provided in paragraphs (b), (c) and (d) of the preceding article, his functions shall be temporarily assumed by the Vice President or by one of the Vice Presidents in the order of their appointment, or, if there are no Vice Presidents, by the Minister appointed by the Head of State.

2. A new President shall be appointed in the manner stipulated in Article 14 within a time limit of ten days.

Art. 17. 1. The other members of the Government shall be Spanish and their appointment and dismissal shall be effected by the Head of State on the proposal of the President of the Government.

2. The laws shall specify the activities incompatible with their office.

Art. 18. The members of the Government shall relinquish their office:

(a) When the President of the Government changes.

(b) At the request of the President of the Government, accepted by the Head of State.

(c) At their own request when their resignation has been accepted by the Head of State at the proposal of the President of the Government.

Art. 19. The President and other members of the Government, before taking office, shall, before the Head of State, take an oath of fidelity to him, to the Principles of the National Movement and the other Fundamental Laws of the Kingdom, and also shall swear to keep secret their deliberations.

Art. 20. 1. The President and other members of the Government shall be collectively responsible for the agreements reached in the Council of Ministers. Each member shall be responsible for the acts which he performs or authorizes within his own Department.

2. The President and other members of the Government shall be criminally responsible before the Supreme Court of Justice in plenary session and civilly responsible for acts committed in the exercise of their functions before the same court.

CHAPTER IV

THE NATIONAL COUNCIL

Art. 21. The National Council, as the collective representative body of the Movement, shall have the following purposes:

(a) To strengthen the unity between the people and the lands of Spain.

(b) To defend the integrity of the Principles of the National Movement and ensure that the transformation and development of the economic, social and cultural structures be adjusted to the requirements of social justice.

(c) To watch over the development and exercise of the rights and liberties recognized by the Fundamental Laws and to stimulate the real and effective participation of natural groups and of public opinion in political tasks.

(d) To contribute to the formation of Spanish youth in faithfulness to the Principles of the National Movement and to incorporate the new generations in the collective task.

(e) To channel differences of opinion on political action within the Principles of the Movement.

(f) To watch over the permanence and improvement of the National Movement itself.

Art. 22. The National Council shall be composed of the following Councillors.

(a) One Councillor elected for each province in the manner stipulated by the corresponding organic law.

(b) Forty Councillors appointed by the Caudillo from among persons who have given recognized service. When the provisions concerning the succession have been carried out, these forty Councillors shall acquire permanent tenure until the age of seventy five years; vacancies in the succession among the Councillors shall be filled by election from a list of three names presented by this group of Councillors to the plenary session of the Council.

(c) Twelve Councillors representing the basic structures of the national community:

- Four elected from among their members by the members (*Procuradores*) of the Cortes representing the Family;
- Four elected from among their members the by members of the Cortes representing local Corporations;
- Four elected from among their members by the members of the Cortes representing the Syndicalist Organization.

(d) Six Councillors appointed by the President of the Council from among persons who have contributed notably to the purposes enumerated in the preceding article.

(e) The Secretary General who shall exercise the functions of Vice-President.

Art. 23. In order to accomplish the purposes listed in Article 21, the National Council shall have the following powers:

(a) To promote the adaptation of laws and general provisions to the Principles of the National Movement and to the other Fundamental Laws of the Kingdom, and shall exercise, for this purpose, the appeal of unconstitutionality provided in Chapter X of this Law.

(b) To propose to the Government the adoption of whatever measures it deems appropriate to increase the effectiveness of the Principles of the Movement and of the other Fundamental Laws of the Kingdom and in every case to consider and report upon any proposal or modification of a Fundamental Law before its transmission to the Cortes.

(c) To transmit to the Government advice or reports that it considers appropriate and to deliberate matters which the Government may submit to it, for which purpose it may request such background information as it considers necessary.

Art. 24. The National Council shall function in plenary session and in permanent commission in accordance with its organic law.

Art. 25. The President of the Government, in his capacity as National

Head of the Movement by delegation of the Head of State, shall exercise the Chairmanship of the National Council and of its permanent commission, assisted by the Secretary General to whom he may delegate such powers as he deems appropriate.

Art. 26. The Secretary General shall be appointed by the Head of State on the proposal of the President of the Government. The laws shall stipulate the activities incompatible with the office of Secretary General.

Art. 27. 1. The Chairman of the National Council shall relinquish his office when he ceases to be President of the Government.

2. The Secretary General shall relinquish his office:

(a) When the President of the Government changes.

(b) At the request of the President of the Government accepted by the Head of State.

(c) At his own request when his resignation has been accepted by the Head of State upon a proposal of the President of the Government.

3. National Councillors shall relinquish office:

(a) Those in groups (a) and (c) at the end of their term of office; those in group (b) at the age of seventy five; and those in group (d) by decision of the President of the Council.

(b) At their own request when their resignations have been accepted by the Head of State upon a proposal of the President of the Government.

(c) For incapacity attested by the Council.

(d) For other reasons which cause them to lose their seat as a member of the Cortes.

Art. 28. An organic law shall establish the rules regulating the National Council.

CHAPTER V

JUSTICE

Art. 29. Justice shall be completely independent. It shall be administered in the name of the Head of State, in accordance with the laws, by independent judges and magistrates, having permanent tenure and responsible in accordance with the law.

Art. 30. All Spaniards shall have free access to the courts. Justice shall be free for those who lack economic means.

Art. 31. Only the courts and tribunals established by the organic law concerning justice shall, in accordance with their different powers, have jurisdictional authority, the right to hand down and execute verdicts, in all civil, criminal, administrative litigation, labor and other matters established by law.

Art. 32. 1. Military jurisdiction shall be subject to the laws and provisions which apply only to it.

2. The sphere of ecclesiastical jurisdiction shall be established by the Concordat with the Holy See.

Art. 33. The President of the Supreme Court shall have supervisory power in judicial matters; he shall be appointed from among Spanish jurists of recognized standing.

Art. 34. Judges and magistrates may not be dismissed, suspended, transferred or retired except for the reasons and subject to the guarantees prescribed by law.

Art. 35. 1. The Ministry of Justice which is the organ of communication between the government and the courts of justice, shall have the duty of furthering judicial action in the defense of public interests protected by law and of acting before the courts and tribunals for the maintenance of the judicial order and the satisfaction of social interests.

2. The functions entrusted to the Ministry of Justice shall be exercised through its organs in accordance with the principles of unity and seniority.

Art. 36. Both public and private authorities and organizations are required to give the necessary assistance to the courts and tribunals for the exercise of the judicial authority.

CHAPTER VI

THE ARMED FORCES

Art. 37. The Armed Forces of the Nation, constituted by the Armies of the Land, Sea and Air and the forces of public order, guarantee the unity and independence of the Nation, the integrity of its territories, national security and the defense of the institutional order.

Art. 38. A National Defense Board, composed by the President of the Government, the Ministers of the military departments, the Chief of the High General Staff and the chiefs of the general staff of the Armies of the Land, Sea and Air, shall propose to the Government the general lines for national security and defense. The National Defense Board may also include Ministers and high officials who are considered useful because of the subjects under discussion.

Art. 39. A High General Staff, subordinate to the President of the Government, shall be the technical organ of national defense and shall be charged with co-ordinating the action of the general staffs of the three Armies.

CHAPTER VII

THE ADMINISTRATION OF THE STATE

Art. 40. 1. The Administration, constituted by organs in order of seniority, shall be charged with the accomplishment of the purposes of the State for the rapid and efficient satisfaction of the general interest.

2. A law shall determine the higher organs of the Administration, their respective jurisdiction and the basic principles regulating their officers.

3. The Administration shall be advised by the consultative organs established by law.

4. The Council of State is the highest consultative body of the Administration and its jurisdiction and functions shall be settled in accordance with the law.

5. The Council of National Economy is the consultative, advising and technical organ for important matters affecting the national economy.

Art. 41. 1. The Administration may not issue orders contrary to the laws nor may it regulate, except with the express authorization of a law, matters which fall within the exclusive jurisdiction of the Cortes.

2. Any administrative orders which infringe the stipulations of the preceding paragraph shall be null and void.

Art. 42. 1. Resolutions and agreements shall be issued by the Administration in accordance with the standards regulating administrative procedure.

2. Suits and appeals may be made against acts and agreements terminating administrative proceedings before the competent jurisdictions in accordance with the laws.

3. The responsiblity of the Administration and of its authorities, officials and agents may be invoked for the reasons and in the manner determined by law.

Art. 43. All public authorities and officials owe fidelity to the Principles of the National Movement and to the other Fundamental Laws of the Kingdom and shall take the appropriate oath before taking office.

Art. 44. The Court of Accounts of the Kingdom shall examine and approve, in full independence, the accounts for acts carried out in accordance with the Budget Laws and others of a fiscal character, and also the accounts of all official organs receiving assistance or a subsidy from the General Budgets of the State and of its autonomous organs; it shall carry out other functions assigned to it by its organic law.

CHAPTER VIII

LOCAL ADMINISTRATION

Art. 45. 1. The municipalities are natural entities and constitute the basic structures of the national community; they are grouped territorially in provinces.

2. The province is a unit determined by the grouping of the municipalities and it is also a territorial division of the State Administration. Other territorial divisions than the provinces may also be established.

Art. 46. 1. The municipalities and provinces have full legal status and competence for the accomplishment of their particular purposes within the limits established by law, without prejudice to their functions in co-operation with the services of the State.

2. The municipal and provincial corporations, as representative and administrative organs of the municipality and the province respectively, shall be elected by suffrage expressed through the representative group, indicated in Article 10 of the Charter of the Spanish People.

Art. 47. The State shall promote the development of municipal and provincial life, shall protect and encourage the patrimony of the local corporations and shall ensure them the necessary economic means for the accomplishment of their purposes.

Art. 48. The system of local administration and of the local corporations shall be determined by law in conformity with the provisions of the preceding articles and the guarantees required for the common good in this domain.

CHAPTER IX

RELATIONS

BETWEEN THE OTHER ORGANS OF THE STATE

Art. 49. The Spanish *Cortes* shall be informed immediately of the appointment of a new Government and of the substitution of any of the members of the Government.

Art. 50. The Cortes, in addition to their participation in the legislative tasks, shall have the following functions in relation to the Head of State:

(a) To receive the oath of office of the Head of State and of the heir to the Throne when he has reached thirty years of age, swearing fidelity to the Principles of the Movement and to the other Fundamental Laws of the Kingdom.

(b) To resolve any questions that may arise in connection with the succession to the Head of State in accordance with the Law of Succession.

(c) To authorize the Head of State to carry out the acts that require, according to a fundamental law, the intervention of the Cortes.

(d) Any other functions conferred upon them by the fundamental laws.

Art. 51. The Government may submit for approval by the Head of State measure having the force of law in accordance with the express authorization of the Cortes.

Art. 52. With the exception of the case provided in the preceding article and those stipulated in paragraph (d) of Article 10 of this Law and Article 13 of the Law of the Cortes, the Government may not issue measures which, according to Articles 10 and 12 of the Law of the Cortes, must take the form of laws.

Art. 53. The President of the Government and the Ministers shall inform the Cortes concerning the administration of the Government and its respective departments and shall reply to inquiries, questions and interpellations that are properly addressed.

Art. 54. 1. The Government shall have the duty of drawing up the bill for the general budget of the State and the Cortes shall have the duty of approving, amending or returning it. If the Budget Law is not approved before the first day of the following financial year, the budget of the preceding financial year shall be considered automatically prorogued until the approval of the new budget.

2. Once the general Budget of the State has been approved, only the Government may propose bills involving the increase of public expenditure or the decrease of revenue; any bill or any amendment to a bill which would result in the increase of expenditure or the diminution of revenue shall require the agreement of the Government before it can be proceeded with.

3. The Government shall submit to the approval of the Cortes the general accounts of the State after they have been examined and approved by the Court of Accounts of the Kingdom.

Art. 55. The Court of Accounts of the Kingdom, in the exercise of its duties in the fiscal domain, must inform the Government and the Cortes, by means of the appropriate statements and reports, of its opinion concerning the manner in which the Budget Law and other laws of a fiscal character have been executed, in accordance with the provisions of the law regulating this obligation of the Court; it shall do likewise in all other cases in relation to which because of their exceptional importance, it considers it should make use of this power.

Art. 56. Only the Head of State may request the opinion of the Council of the Kingdom.

Art. 57. The Head of State shall decide, in accordance with the laws, upon questions of competence between the Administration and the ordinary and special judges and courts, and upon questions of competence arising between the Court of Accounts and the Administration or between the Court of Accounts and the other ordinary and special courts.

Art. 58. 1. The Presidents of the Supreme Court of Justice, of the Council of State, of the Court of Accounts of the Kingdom and of the Council of National Economy shall be appointed by the Head of State upon the proposal of the Council of the Kingdom.

2. Their term of office shall be six years and activities incompatible with their office shall be as stipulated by law.

3. They shall cease from office:

(a) at the expiration of their term;

(b) at their own request after their resignation has been accepted by the Head of State in the Council of the Kingdom;

(c) by decision of the Head of State in agreement with the Council of the Kingdom;

(d) at the proposal of the Council of the Kingdom for incapacity attested by two thirds of its members.

CHAPTER X

THE APPEAL OF UNCONSTITUTIONALITY

Art. 59. 1. Any legislative act or general measure of the Government which violates the Principles of the National Movement or the other Fundamental Laws of the Kingdom is unconstitutional.

2. Appeal to the Head of State is established to guarantee the principles and standards infringed by unconstitutional acts.

Art. 60. The appeal of unconstitutionality may be moved by:

(a) The National Council, by agreement of two thirds of the Councillors, in respect of all matters.

(b) The Permanent Commission of the Cortes, by agreement of a majority of two thirds of its members, in respect of Government measures of a general character.

Art. 61. The appeal of unconstitutionality shall be tabled before the Council of the Kingdom within a time limit of two months from the publication in the "Official Bulletin of the State" of the law or general measure concerned.

2. The President of the Council of the Kingdom shall immediately inform the Head of State of the intervention of the appeal of unconstitutionality and shall advise the Permanent Commission of the Cortes or the President of the Government, whichever is concerned, who shall, if he deems it necessary, appoint a representative to defend the legality of the law or general measure in question before the Council of the Kingdom.

3. If the Council of the Kingdom agrees that there are good reasons, it may propose to the Head of State that the law or general measure in question or, as the case may be, the disposition or dispositions contained therein to which the appeal refers, be suspended during the procedure of the appeal.

Art. 62. 1. The Council of the Kingdom shall request an opinion on the question raised by the appeal of unconstitutionality from a Committee presided over by a President of a Chamber of the Supreme Court of Justice and composed of a National Councillor, a Permanent Councillor of State, a Judge of the Supreme Court of Justice and an attorney at law, appointed by the Permanent Commission of the respective institutions and, in the case of the Supreme Court, by its Governing Chamber. This opinion shall be transmitted to the Council of the Kingdom with an account of the individual views where such have been expressed.

2. The Council of the Kingdom, presided over by the President of the Supreme Court of Justice, shall propose to the Head of State the resolution arrived at.

Art. 63. Should the Permanent Commission of the Cortes observe infringement of the Principles of the Movement or of the other Fundamental Laws in any bill passed by the corresponding Committee of the Cortes, it shall express its opinion in writing with the reasons therefor to the President of the Cortes within eight days following the publication of the passage by the Committee of the bill in the "Official Journal" of the Cortes; the President of the Cortes shall transmit this opinion to the Committee concerned so that it may subject the bill in question to further study. The inclusion of the bill on the agenda of the plenary session shall be suspended in the meantime or, as the case may be, withdrawn.

Art. 64. A resolution of annulment for unconstitutionality of a legislative act or general Government measure which has been appealed against, shall require the immediate publication in the "Official Bulletin of the State" of the annulment granted, together with the report of the proceedings.

Art. 65. 1. The Head of State, before submitting a bill drawn up by the Cortes to referendum, shall inform the National Council which shall, within fifteen days, advise whether there exists, in its opinion, any reason to invoke the appeal of unconstitutionality.

2. If the National Council agrees that such reason does exist, it shall table the appeal in the form provided in Article 61. If not, or if such appeal is rejected, the law may be submitted to referendum and may not, after its promulgation, be the object of an appeal of unconstitutionality.

Art. 66. A special law shall establish the conditions, forms and terms according to which the procedure arising out of an appeal of unconstitutionality shall be conducted and substantiated.

ADDITIONAL PROVISIONS

This section contains amendments to the other Fundamental Laws which are incorporated in the text of the Laws reproduced on the following pages.

TRANSITIONAL PROVISIONS

First. 1. When the provisions of the Law of Succession are fulfilled, the person called to exercise the position of Head of State, whether as King or as Regent, shall assume the functions and duties of the Head of State as set forth in this Law.

2. The attributes granted to the Head of State by the Laws of January 30, 1938 and August 8, 1939, as well as the prerogatives authorized by Articles 6 and 13 of the Law of Succession shall remain and continue in force until the succession to which the previous paragraph refers takes place.

3. The National Leadership of the Movement shall belong for life to Francisco Franco, Caudillo of Spain. When the provisions concerning the succession are fulfilled this shall pass to the Head of State and, by his delegation, to the President of the Government.

Second. The amendments introduced by the third Additional Provision of this Law to Articles 2, 6 and 7, paragraph 5, of the Law of the Cortes shall enter into effect when the next legislature of the Cortes is constituted; following this, the amendments concerning the Council of the Kingdom provided by the new wording of Article 4 of the Law of Succession contained in the fourth Additional Provision shall become effective.

Third. Excepting the reservations stipulated in the preceding Transitional Provision, this Law shall enter into effect on the day following its promulgation.

Fourth. New texts of the Fundamental Laws containing the modifications referred to in the Additional Provisions of this Law shall be published within four months from the promulgation of this Law, subject to the judgment of the Council of the Kingdom and following deliberation in the Council of Ministers.

Fifth. The Government shall, within the shortest possible time, present to the Cortes the bills or issue the decrees necessary to the due execution of the present Law.

FINAL PROVISIONS

First. From the date of entry into force of this Law any provisions contrary to it shall be abrogated.

Second. This Law shall have the status of a Fundamental Law as defined in Article 10 of the Law of Succession to the Chief of State.

2. Principles of the National Movement[1]

May 17, 1958

I. Spain is a unity of destiny within the universal. The service of the unity, grandeur and freedom of the Country is the sacred duty and collective task of all Spaniards.

II. The Spanish Nation considers as a mark of honor obedience to the Law of God according to the doctrine of the Holy Apostolic and Roman Catholic Church, the only true faith, inseparable from the national conscience and inspiring its legislation.

II. Spain, the root of a great family of peoples with whom she feels herself indissolubly linked, aspires to the renewal of justice and peace among nations.

IV. The unity between the people and lands of Spain is untouchable. The integrity and independence of the Country are the supreme requirements of the national community. The armies of Spain, guarantee of its security and expression of the heroic virtues of our people, must have the necessary fortitude for the best service of the Country.

V. The national community is based on man as bearer of the eternal values and on the family as the basis of social life. Individual and collective interest must, however, be always subordinate to the general good of the Nation as constituted by the generations past, present and future. The laws shall protect equally the rights of all Spaniards.

VI. The natural units of social life, the family, the municipality and the syndicate, are the basic structures of the national community.Institution s and corporations of another character which satisfy social requirements of general interest must be protected in order to participate effectively in the perfectioning of the purposes of the national community.

VII. The Spanish people, united under one order of Law, informed by the postulates of authority, liberty and service, constitutes the National State. Its political form, within the immutable principles of the National Movement and of those contained in the Law of Succession and the other basic laws, shall be that of a traditional, Catholic, social and representative Monarchy.

VIII. The representative character of the political order is the basic principle of our public institutions. The participation of the people in legislative tasks and in other functions of general interest shall be accom-

[1] *Principios del Movimiento Nacional.* In *Leyes Fundamentales. Coleccion de Textos Legales. Boletin Oficial del Estado.* Marid 1964. Supplied by the Ministry of Foreign Affairs in August 1966. Translations included in Second Edition provided by the Spanish Embassy in Washington of all except *Principles of the National Movement,* 1958. The latter translated by and other texts checked against latest Spanish edition by the Editor. Ed.

plished through the family, the municipality, the syndicate and other bodies of organic representation recognized by the law for this purpose. Political organizations of whatever kind outside this representative system shall be considered illegal.

All Spaniards shall have access to public office and duties in accordance with their merits and capacities.

IX. All Spaniards have the right to the following: an independent justice which shall be given free to whomsoever lacks the economic means; a general and professional education that shall not be dependent on material means; the benefits of social assistance and security and an equitable distribution of the national income and of the fiscal burden. The Christian ideal of social justice, reflected in the Labor Charter, shall inspire both policy and the laws.

X. Work is recognized as the origin of rank, duties and honor for Spaniards; private property in all its forms is recognized as a right conditioned by its social function. Private initiative, as the basis of economic activity, must be stimulated, prosecuted and where necessary supplemented by State action.

XI. Enterprise, as an association of men and the means of production, constitutes a community of interests and a unity of purpose. The relations between its elements must be based on justice and reciprocal loyalty; the economic values shall be subordinated to human and social values.

XII. The State shall endeavor by all the means in its reach to perfect the physical and moral heath of Spaniards and to ensure the most fitting conditions of work; to encourage the economic progress of the Nation by improving agriculture, increasing irrigation and by a social reform of the countryside; to achieve the most just use and distribution of public assets; to safeguard and encourage prospecting and the exploitation of mineral wealth; to intensify the process of industrialization, patronize scientific investigation and favor maritime activities corresponding to the expansion of our maritime population and our naval forces.

3. Charter of the Spanish People[1]

July 16, 1945, amended December 15, 1966

Art. 1. The Spanish State proclaims as a guiding principle of its acts, respect for the dignity, integrity, and liberty of the human person, recognizing man, as bearer of eternal values and member of the national community, to be holder of titles of duties and rights, the exercise of which it guarantees for the common good.

1 *Fuero de los Españoles.* Amendments contained in *Organic Law of the State.* See notes on pages 810 and 824.

TITLE I

DUTIES AND RIGHTS OF THE SPANISH PEOPLE

CHAPTER I

Art. 2. Spaniards owe faithful service to their country, loyalty to the Head of State and obedience to its laws.

Art. 3. The law protects equally the rights of all Spaniards without class preference or discrimination of persons.

Art. 4. Spaniards have a right to the respect of their personal and family honor. He who should offend it, whatever be his condition, will be made responsible.

Art. 5. All Spaniards have a right to receive education and instruction and the duty of acquiring them either in the family circle or in private or public centers of their own free election. The State will see that no talent is wasted because of lack of economic means.

Art. 6. The profession and practice of the Catholic religion, which is that of the Spanish State, will enjoy official protection.

The State will protect religious liberty, which shall be guaranteed by efficient juridical protection which shall, at the same time, safeguard morality and public order.

Art. 7. It is a title of honor for Spaniards to serve in the Armed Forces of their country.

All Spaniards are obliged to this service when they are called to it according to law.

Art. 8. Such personal services as are necessary for the national interest or the public need may be made obligatory by laws of a general character.

Art. 9. Spaniards will contribute to meeting public expenditure according to their economic capacity. Nobody will be obliged to pay tributes that have not been established by laws voted by the Cortes.

Art. 10. All Spaniards have a right to participate in public office of a representative character, through the family, the municipality, and the syndicate without prejudice to other representation that the laws may establish.

Art. 11. All Spaniards may hold office and public functions according to their merits and capacity.

Art. 12. All Spaniards may freely express their ideas as long as they do not threaten the fundamental principles of government.

Art. 13. Inside national territory, the State guarantees the liberty and inviolability of correspondence.

Art. 14. Spaniards are at liberty to fix their residence inside national territory.

Art. 15. Nobody may enter the home of a Spaniard or effect a search in it without his permission, unless with a warrant from the competent authority and in the case and form established by law.

Art. 16. Spaniards may unite and associate themselves freely for lawful ends and according to what is established by law.

The State may create and maintain such agencies as are deemed necessary for the accomplishment of its service. Fundamental rulings which will have the character of law, will co-ordinate the exercise of this right with that recognized in the preceding paragraph.

Art. 17. Spaniards have a right to legal security. All organs of the State will act according to a hierarchical order of pre-established rulings, that may not be interpreted arbitrarily nor altered.

Art. 18. No Spaniard may be arrested except in the cases and in the form prescribed by law. Within a period of seventy-two hours all arrested persons will be set free or turned over to the judicial authorities.

Art. 19. Nobody may be condemned except under a law prior to the act, by sentence by a competent tribunal, and after hearing and defense of the interested party.

Art. 20. No Spaniard may be deprived of his nationality except for treason, as defined in the penal laws, or for entering the Armed Services or exercising public office in a foreign country against the expressed prohibition of the Chief of State.

Art. 21. Spaniards may address individual petitions to the Chief of State, to the Cortes, and to public authorities.

Corporations, public officers, and members of the armed forces and institutions may only exercise this right according to the laws by which they are ruled.

Chapter II

Art. 22. The State recognizes and protects the family as a natural and fundamental institution of society with rights and duties prior and superior to all human positive law.

Matrimony is one and indissoluble.

The State will specially protect families with numerous children.

Art. 23. Parents are obliged to provide for, educate, and instruct their children. The State will suspend or annul the exercise of his *patria potestad* for whomsoever does not exercise it properly, and will transfer the custody and education of minors to those to whom it corresponds by law.

Chapter III

Art. 24. All Spaniards have a right to work and the duty to occupy themselves in some socially useful activity.

Art. 25. Work, because of its essentially human character, cannot be relegated to a material concept of merchandise, nor be the object of any transaction incompatible with personal dignity. It constitutes in itself an attribute of honor and a sufficient title to demand protection and assistance from the State.

Art. 26. The State recognizes in an enterprise a community of efforts of technique, labor, and capital in their different forms, and consequently proclaims the right of these elements to participate in gains.

The State will see that relations between them shall be maintained in the strictest equity and in an order that subordinates economic values to human values, to the interests of the nation and the requirements of the common good.

Art. 27. All workers will be protected by the State in their right to a just and sufficient return, which will as a minimum provide them and their families with well-being sufficient for a moral and dignified existence.

Art. 28. The Spanish State guarantees the workers security in distress, and recognizes their rights to assistance in the cases of old age, death, sickness, maternity, accidents, invalidity, unemployment, and other hazards that are the objects of social insurance.

Art. 29. The State will maintain institutions of assistance and will protect and foster those created by the Church, the corporations, and private enterprise.

Art. 30. The Spanish State recognizes and protects private property as a natural means for the fulfilment of individual, family and social purposes.

All forms of property remain subordinated to the necessities of the nation and to the common good.

No source of wealth will be allowed to remain unproductive, unduly destroyed, or applied to illicit ends.

Art. 31. The State will make available to all Spaniards the access to those forms of property more intimately connected with the human person, the home, inheritance, implements of work, and goods of daily use.

Art. 32. In no case will a sentence of confiscation of property be passed.

Nobody may be expropriated except in the interest of public and/or social welfare, after corresponding indemnity and according to what the law disposes.

TITLE II

THE EXERCISE AND GUARANTEES OF THE RIGHTS

Art. 33. The exercise of the rights that are recognized in this Charter may not prejudice the spiritual, national, and social unity of the community.

Art. 34. The Cortes will vote the necessary laws for the exercise of the rights recognized by this Charter.

Art. 35. The enforcement of Articles 12, 13, 14, 15, 16 and 18 may temporarily be suspended in part or in whole by the government by means of a decree which must define and limit the scope and duration of this measure.

Art. 36. Any violation of any of the rights proclaimed in this Charter will be punishable by laws which will determine, in each case, the actions that may be taken in its defense before the competent jurisdictions.

4. Law of the Cortes[1]

July 17, 1942, as amended March 9, 1946 and December 14, 1966

Art. 1. The Cortes are the superior organ through which the Spanish people participate in the tasks of the State. The principal mission of the Cortes consists in the elaboration and approval of the laws without prejudice to the right of veto of the Head of State.

Art. 2. 1. The Cortes are composed of the members (*procuradores*) comprised in the following categories:

(a) The members of the Government.

(b) The National Councillors.

(c) The Presidents of the Supreme Court of Justice, the Council of State, the Supreme Council of Military Justice, the Court of Accounts of the Kingdom and the Council of National Economy.

(d) One hundred and fifty representatives of the Syndicalist Organization.

(e) One representative of the municipalities of each of the provinces elected by the municipal governments from among their members and an additional representative for each municipality of more than three hundred thousand inhabitants and for Ceuta and Melilla, elected by the respective municipal government from among its members; a representative for each Provincial Deputation and the Inter-Island Communal Council of the Canary Islands, elected by the respective corporations from among their members, and the representatives of the local corporations of the territories not constituted as provinces, elected in the same manner.

(f) Two representatives of the family for each province, elected by persons listed in the electoral register of heads of families and by married women, in the manner established by law.

(g) The Rectors of the Universities.

(h) The President of the Spanish Institute and two representatives elected from among the members of the Royal Academies of which it is composed; the President of the Higher Council for Scientific Research and two representatives of the same elected from among its members.

1 *Ley de Cortes.* Amendments contained in 1966 *Organic Law of the State.* See notes on page 810 and 824.

(i) The President of the Institute of Civil Engineers and one representative of the Associations of Engineers of which it is composed; two representatives of the Bar Associations; two representatives of the Medical Associations. One representative for each of the following Associations: Exchange and Stock-brokers, Architects, Economists, Pharmacists, Bachelors and Doctors of Arts and Sciences, Bachelors and Doctors of Chemical and Physical-Chemical Sciences, Notaries, Attorneys, Registrars of Property, Veterinaries, and the other professional associations based on a higher academic degree which may be recognized for this purpose in the future, elected by the respective official chambers. Three representatives of the Chambers of Commerce; one of the Chambers of Urban Property and one other to represent the Associations of Tenants, elected by their representative boards or organs.

All persons elected under this paragraph must be members of the respective associations, corporations and chambers which elect them.

The composition and distribution of the members of the Cortes covered by this paragraph may be varied by law but the total number may not be higher than thirty.

(j) Not more than twenty-five persons who because of their ecclesiastical, military or administrative rank, or of their outstanding service to Spain, are nominated by the Head of State, approved in the Council of the Kingdom.

2. All the members of the Cortes represent the Spanish people, must serve the Nation and the common good, and shall not receive any binding instructions.

Art. 3. To be a member of the Cortes, the following qualifications are required:

(1) To be a Spanish citizen and of age;

(2) To enjoy full civil rights and not to be subject to any political disqualification.

Art. 4. Members of the Cortes shall establish before its President the election, nomination, or office which entitles them to membership. The President of the Cortes shall swear them in, seat them, and issue the corresponding titles.

Art. 5. The members of the Cortes cannot be arrested without previous authorization by their President, except in cases of *flagrante delicto.* In this case, the President of the Cortes shall be notified.

Art. 6. Members *ex officio* of the Cortes shall lose their seat upon ceasing to hold office. Those nominated by the Head of State shall lose their seat by his revocation. Otherwise, the term of office shall be for four years and members may be re-elected; but if, during these four years, a representative of a deputation, municipality or corporation ceases in such office, he shall cease to be a member of the Cortes.

Art. 7. 1. The President of the Cortes shall be appointed by the Head of State from among a list of three members submitted by the Council of the Kingdom within a maximum time limit of ten days from the office being vacant. His appointment shall be countersigned by the acting President of the Council of the Kingdom.

2. His term of office shall be six years, provided he continues to be a member of the Cortes. The activities incompatible with the office of President of the Cortes shall be stipulated by law.

3. The President of the Cortes shall cease from office:

(a) At the expiration of his term of office.

(b) At his own request, when his resignation has been accepted by the Head of State in the Council of the Kingdom, meeting without his being present.

(c) By decision of the Head of State, with the agreement of the Council of the Kingdom meeting as provided in the preceding paragraph.

(d) For incapacity attested by two thirds of the members of the Cortes under the chairmanship of the first or second Vice-President, as the case may be, following a substantiated proposal of the Permanent Commission, meeting under similar charmanship, or of the Government.

4. If the office of President of the Cortes is vacant, the first or second Vice-President, as the case may be, shall preside pending the appointment of a new President within the time limit of ten days.

5. The two Vice-Presidents and the four Secretaries of the Cortes shall be elected by each legislature from among the members of the Cortes by plenary session thereof.

Art. 8. The Cortes may meet in plenary session and in committees. The committees are created and appointed by the President of the Cortes, on the proposal of the Permanent Committee and with the Government's agreement. The President also establishes, with the Government's agreement, the agenda for both plenary sessions and committees.

Art. 9. The Cortes shall meet in plenary session for the study of laws which so require, and whenever called by the President, with the Government's agreement.

Art. 10. The plenary session of the Cortes shall be required to pass upon laws bearing on any of the following matters:

(a) Ordinary and extraordinary budgets of the State;

(b) Important economic or financial bills;

(c) The creation or amendment of the system of taxation;

(d) Bank and currency regulations;

(e) The economic activity of the syndicates and legislation fundamentally affecting the national economy;

(f) Basic laws regulating the acquisition and loss of Spanish citizenship and the rights and duties of Spaniards;

(g) The political-legal organization of the institutions of government;

(h) The regulation of local government;

(i) Fundamental aspects of civil, mercantile, social, penal, and procedural law;

(j) Fundamental aspects of the judiciary and public administration;

(k) The regulation of agriculture, commerce, and industry;

(l) The laws affecting national education;

(m) Any other law which the government on its own initiative, or on that of the respective committees of the Cortes, should decide to submit to a plenary session of the Cortes.

The government may also submit to plenary session measures which do not have the character of law.

Art. 11. Bills to be submitted to the plenary session shall previously be studied and reported on by the respective committees.

Art. 12. The committees of the Cortes have jurisdiction over all measures not included in Article 10, but which must take the form of law, either because it is so provided in a law subsequent to the present law, or because it is so ordered by a Committee composed of the President of the Cortes, a Minister appointed by the Government, a Councillor of the Permanent Commission of the National Council, a member of the Cortes who is a lawyer, the President of the Council of State and the President of the Supreme Court of Justice. This Committee shall report by request of the Government or of the Permanent Commission of the Cortes.

2. If, at the time of studying any bill or independent motion, any Committee of the Cortes raises any question which is not within the competence of the Cortes, the President of the Cortes on his own initiative or at the request of the Government may request a ruling from the Committee referred to in the preceding paragraph. Should the ruling find that the question does not fall within the jurisdiction of the Cortes, the matter shall be withdrawn from the agenda of the Committee.

Art. 13. In the event of emergency, the Government may propose to the Head of State to regulate by decree-laws matters covered by Articles 10 and 12. The emergency shall be attested by the Head of State in the Committee referred to in the preceding article which may call the attention of the Permanent Commission if any question of unconstitutionality arises. The Cortes shall be informed immediately following the promulgation of a decree-law.

Art. 14. 1. The ratifications of treaties or international conventions affecting the sovereignty or territorial integrity of Spain shall require a law approved by plenary session of the Cortes.

2. The Cortes in plenary session or in committees, according to the circumstances, shall be heard for the ratification of other treaties affecting matters within the competence of the Cortes as specified in Articles 10 and 12.

Art. 15. The legislative committees, apart from passing on Government bills, may propose laws to the President of the Cortes, who, by agreement with the Government, may include them in the agenda.

The legislative committees may be empowered by the President of the Cortes to study special subjects, carry out investigations, and draft petitions or suggestions. For this purpose, they may establish special committees as distinct from legislative committees.

Art. 16. The President of the Cortes shall submit laws approved by the same to the Head of State for his approval and such laws must be promulgated within a time limit of one month from their receipt by the Head of State.

Art. 17. The Head of State, by a subtantiated message and following a favorable ruling by the Council of the Kingdom, may return a law to the Cortes for further study.

ADDITIONAL ARTICLES

1. The Cortes shall establish with government agreement their rules of procedure.
2. Elections for those members who hold elective seats shall be announced during the first fifteen days of October.

5. Referendum Act[1]

October 22, 1945

All Spaniards are entitled to co-operate in the tasks of the State through the natural institutions constituted by the family, the municipal corporations, and the syndicates, and the Basic Laws; these, which are to give new life and greater spontaneity to these institutions within a system of Christian life in common, having been published with the object of protecting the Nation against the errors observed in the political history of peoples which cause the will of the Nation to be supplanted by the subjective judgment of its rulers in matters of major importance. The Head of the State, invoking the faculties conferred upon him by the Acts of the thirtieth of January, 1938 (R. 1938, 91) and the eighth of August, 1939 (R. 1939, 970), has thought fit to institute a direct consultation of the nation by public referendum when he considers such consultation opportune and advisable owing to the exceptional importance of the laws or the uncertainty of public opinion.

In virtue of which, I declare:

Art. 1. When the exceptional importance of any law makes it advisable or the public interest so demands, the Head of the State shall be em-

[1] *Ley de Referendum.* See note on page 824.

powered, in order to serve the nation more faithfully, to submit to referendum a bill drafted by the Cortes.

Art. 2. The referendum shall be carried out by all men and women of the Nation who have reached their majority of twenty-one years of age.

Art. 3. The government is hereby authorized to issue complementary orders for the compiling of the register of voters and the execution of the present act.

6. Law of Succession to the Head of State[1]

June 7, 1947, amended December 14, 1966

Art. 1. Spain, as a political unit, is a Catholic, social, and representative State which, in accordance with its traditions, declares itself to be a Kingdom.

Art. 2. The office of Head of State is held by the Caudillo of Spain and of the Crusade, Generalissimo of the Spanish Armies, Don Francisco Franco Bahamonde.

Art. 3. Should the Office of Head of State fall vacant, its powers shall be exercised by a Council of Regency composed of (1) the President of the Cortes, (2) the highest and most senior prelate of the Church, Councillor of the Kingdom, and (3) the Captain-General of the Land, Sea, and Air Forces or the highest ranking Lieutenant-General, in that order, or their respective substitutes appointed in accordance with the following article. The President of the Council shall be the President of the Cortes and its decisions, to be legal, must be passed upon by two of its three members and always by the President or the Vice President of the Council of the Kingdom.

Art. 4. 1. A Council of the Kingdom, which shall take precedence over all the Consultative Bodies of the Nation, shall assist the Head of State in all matters and resolutions of great importance which fall within his exclusive jurisdiction. Its President shall be the President of the Cortes and it shall be composed of the following members:

– The highest ranking and most senior Prelate among those who are members of the Cortes.

– The Captain General of the Land, Sea and Air Forces, or the highest ranking Lieutenant-General on the active list, in that order.

– The General who is Chief of the High General Staff or, in his absence, the most senior of the three Generals who are Chiefs of the General Staffs of the Land, Sea and Air Forces.

– The President of the Supreme Court of Justice.

[1] *Ley de Sucesion a la Jefatura del Estado.* Amendments contained in *Organic Law of the State.* See notes on page 810 and 824.

- The President of the Council of State.
- The President of the Spanish Institute.
- Two Councillors elected by the vote of each of the following groups of members of the Cortes:

(a) The National Councillors;
(b) The Syndicalist Organization;
(c) The local administration;
(d) The family representatives.

- One Councillor elected by the vote of each of the following groups of members of the Cortes:

(a) The Rectors of the Universities;
(b) The Professional Associations.

2. Membership of the Council shall be predicated on the tenure of the office to which the Councillor was elected or appointed.

3. The Head of State shall appoint, upon the proposal of the Council of the Kingdom and from among its members, a Vice-President and alternates for each of the Councillors members of the Council of Regency.

4. In cases of incapacity of the President or the acting President of the Cortes and, in the latter case, pending the filling of the office of President, his duties shall be exercised by the Vice-President of the Council of the Kingdom.

5. The agreements, rulings and proposals of the Council of the Kingdom shall be passed by a majority of votes of the Councillors present which may not be less than half plus one of the total membership, except where the Fundamental Laws require a specified majority. In case of tie the President shall have the casting vote.

Art. 5. The Head of State must consult the Council of the Kingdom in the cases required by this Law or the other Fundamental Laws.

Art. 6. At any moment the Head of State may submit to the Cortes the name of the person he believes should succeed him, either as King or as Regent, and according to the conditions stipulated by this law; he may also, likewise, submit to the Cortes the repeal of any previous proposal of succession, although this last may have already been accepted by the Cortes.

Art. 7. Should the office of Head of State be vacant and the successor have been appointed in accordance with the previous article, the Council of the Regency shall assume the powers of this office to call a joint session of the Cortes and the Council of the Kingdom to take the successor's oath of office as prescribed in this law and to name him King or Regent.

Art. 8. 1. Should the Head of State die or be declared incapable of exercising office without a successor having been named, the Council of the Regency shall assume full powers save that of revoking the appointment of any of its own members who shall in all cases retain their positions; within a period of three days, it shall call a meeting of the members of the

Government and of the Council of the Kingdom who, in an uninterrupted and secret session, shall decide, by two thirds of those present forming at least an absolute majority, on the person of royal blood whom, possessing the conditions stipulated by this law, and in consideration of the superior interests of the nation, they shall propose to the Cortes as King. If the proposal is not accepted, the Government and the Council of the Kingdom may draw up, according to the same procedure, a second proposal in favor of another person of royal blood who also fulfils the conditions stipulated by law.

2. If in the judgment of this session, there exists no person of royal blood fulfilling the necessary requirements, or if their proposals are not accepted by the Cortes, they shall propose to the Cortes, under the same conditions, as Regent the person who should occupy this position in view of his prestige, capacity and potential services to the Nation. On making this proposal, the session may fix a time limit and other conditions to the duration of the Regency, and the Cortes shall pass on each of these. If the person proposed as Regent is not accepted by the Cortes, the Government and the Council of the Kingdom must make new proposals, following the same procedures, until the acceptance of the Cortes is obtained.

3. In the cases referred to in the preceding paragraphs when the two-thirds majority is not achieved at the first voting, a second and, if necessary, a third voting shall follow. At the third voting an agreement securing a three-fifths majority, provided that it comprises an absolute majority, shall be valid.

4. A plenary session of the Cortes shall be held within eight days at most of each proposal, and the successor, having obtained the approval of the Cortes in accordance with the provisions of Article 15, shall take the oath of office stipulated by this Law, in virtue of which the Council of Regency shall immediately cede its powers to the successor.

5. Insofar as the conditions stipulated in Article 11 of this Law are not fulfilled, the successor the the Head of State shall be appointed in accordance with the stipulations of this article.

Art. 9. To exercise the office of Head of State as King or Regent, it shall be necessary to be male, Spanish, to be thirty years of age, to profess the Catholic religion, to possess those qualities necessary to fulfil the high office, to pledge respect of the Fundamental Laws and to swear to uphold the principles of the national movement. The Heir to the Throne shall take the same oath when he has reached thirty years of age.

Art. 10. The Fundamental Laws of the nation are: The Charter of the Spanish People, the Labor Charter, the Constituent Law of the Cortes, the present Law of Succession, the Law of National Referendum, and whatever other law shall be latterly promulgated as fundamental.

To repeal or modify these laws, a national referendum shall be required, as well as the approval of the Cortes.

Art. 11. 1. Once the Crown has been restored in the person of a King, the regular order of succession shall be that of primogeniture, with preference to the older over the younger line; within the same line, to the closer over the more distant grade of relationship; within the same grade to the male over the female who may not reign but who shall, in such cases, transmit her rights to her male heirs; and within the same sex, the older over the younger; all without prejudice to those exceptions and requisites set forth in the preceding articles.

2. If the heir to the Throne according to the order set forth in the preceding paragraph, has not reached the age of thirty years at the time the throne is vacant, a Regent appointed in accordance with Article 8 of this Law shall exercise his public functions until he reaches the legal age.

3. The same rule shall apply if the Cortes, because of the incapacity of the King attested in the manner prescribed in Article 14 of this Law, declare the beginning of the Regency and the heir has not reached thirty years of age.

4. Pursuant to the meaning of the preceding paragraphs, the Regency shall cease as soon as the reasons for it cease or disappear.

Art. 12. All delegation of rights before assuming the throne, abdication once the successor has been named, renunciation in any case, royal marriage of the immediate successor, must be approved by the Cortes after report from the Council of the Kingdom.

Art. 13. On the advice of the Council of the Kingdom, the Head of State may submit to the Cortes the exclusion from succession of those persons of royal blood who lack the necessary capacity to govern or, because of their noted indifference to the basic principles of the State or because of their actions, have forfeited their rights to succession as established by this law.

Art. 14. The incapacity of the Head of State, attested by two thirds of the members of the Government, shall be communicated by report to the Council of the Kingdom. Should the Council agree to this report, by a two-thirds majority, its President shall submit it to the Cortes which, meeting within eight days, shall adopt the necessary measures.

Art. 15. 1. Any act taken under this law by the Cortes must be approved by a majority of two thirds of the members present who must form an absolute majority of the total membership of the Cortes.

2. Nevertheless, if in the matters referred to in Articles 6 and 8 a majority vote of two thirds is not achieved at the first voting, a second and if necessary a third vote shall follow. At the third voting, a majority of three fifths, providing it constitutes at least an absolute majority, shall be sufficient for the result to be valid.

7. Labor Charter[1]

Declaration of March 9, 1938, converted into basic law of the nation by the referendum of July 6, 1947, amended December 14, 1966

Renewing the Catholic tradition of social justice and human feeling which inspired the laws of our glorious past, the State undertakes the task of guaranteeing to Spaniards country, bread, and justice.

To achieve this end—and laboring for the unity, freedom, and greatness of Spain—the State shall enter the social sphere with the resolve to place wealth at the service of the Spanish people and to subordinate its economy to the dignity of the human person, taking account of his material needs and the requirements of his intellectual, moral, spiritual and religious life.

Basing its action upon the concept of Spain as a unit with a common destiny, it declares, herewith, its desire that the production of Spain—in the brotherly union of its elements—should also be a unit contributing to the strength of the country and to the common good of all Spaniards.

The Spanish State makes these declarations, which inspire its social and economic policy, for reasons of justice and to express the desires and the demands of all those who having worked for their country, because of their honor, courage, and work, are the aristocracy of this national age.

Before all Spaniards, irrevocably united in sacrifice and hope, WE DECLARE:

I

1. Work is man's share in production through the voluntary contribution of his intellectual and manual faculties, according to personal vocation, with a view to decency and ease in his own life and the greater development of the nation's economy.

2. Because it is essentially personal and human, work cannot be debased to a material concept of merchandise, nor can it be the object of transactions incompatible with the personal dignity of man.

3. The right to work is consequent to the duty imposed by God upon man to achieve his individual end and the prosperity and greatness of the country.

4. The State values and esteems the performance of work as the fruitful expression of man's creative spirit, it shall protect it by virtue of the law, concede it every consideration and make it compatible with the fulfilment of man's other individual ends in the family and society.

[1] *Fuero del Trabajo.* Amendments contained in *Organic Law of the State.* See notes on pages 810 and 824.

5. The performance of work in any form, as a social duty, shall be required from all able-bodied Spaniards, as an obligatory contribution to the nation's wealth.

6. Work constitutes one of the noblest attributes of rank and honor and constitutes sufficient title to help and protection from the State.

7. Service is work performed with heroism, disinterestedness and abnegation, because of a desire to contribute to that higher good represented by Spain.

8. All Spaniards have a right to work. The satisfaction of this right is the State's first mission.

II

1. The State undertakes to exert constant and effective action on behalf of workers, their life, and their work. It shall limit the duration of the working day so that it may not be excessive, and shall grant labor every kind of defensive and humanitarian guarantee. It shall expressly forbid night work for women and children, regulate work at home, and free married women from the need to work in shops and factories.

2. The State shall maintain Sunday rest as a condition sacred to work.

3. The law shall require that the religious feasts and civic holidays ordered by the State be respected, without loss of pay but providing for the technical needs of industry and trade.

4. The eighteenth of July, the anniversary of the Glorious Uprising, having been declared a national feast, it shall be considered the Feast of "the Exaltation of Labor."

5. Every worker shall be entitled to a yearly holiday with full pay to enable him to take a well earned rest, and institutions to ensure the fulfillment of this clause shall be established for that purpose.

6. The necessary institutions shall be set up to give workers access, during their spare time and hours of recreation, to the enjoyment of all the benefits of culture, military service, health, and games.

III

1. Remuneration for work shall be sufficient, as a minimum, to enable the worker and his family to live a moral and dignified life.

2. Family allowances shall be established by means of special agencies.

3. Gradually and inflexibly, the standard of living of workers shall be raised in a measure compatible with the higher interests of the nation.

4. The State shall fix the minimum bases for the regulation of work and the relations between workers and management shall be ruled by these. The performance of work and its remuneration, the basic organization of

management, based on justice, reciprocal loyalty and the subordination of economic values to human and social ones shall be the matter of these regulations.

5. Through the syndicates, the State shall seek information as to whether the financial and other conditions of work are those to which workers are justly entitled.

6. The security and permanence of workers in their employment shall be of concern to the State.

7. As stipulated by the law, employers shall be obliged to keep their staffs informed of the progress of production and thus strengthen the workers' sense of responsibility.

IV

1. Craftsmanship—a living legacy of the old guilds—shall be encouraged and effectively protected, for it is the projection of the human person in work and represents a form of production equally distant from capitalist concentration and Marxism.

V

1. The regulations for work on the land shall be adjusted to the special circumstances of such work and to the seasonal changes imposed by nature.

2. The State shall provide specially for the technical training of agricultural producers, fitting them to perform all the jobs required by their specialty.

3. The prices of main products shall be controlled and reassessed in order to ensure employers on the land a minimum profit in normal circumstances and, as a consequence of this, to make it possible to exact wages that shall enable workers to improve their living conditions.

4. An aim shall be to endow every peasant family with a small holding, or family garden, so that its members may provide their elementary needs and be occupied in their spare time.

5. The embellishment of rural life shall be achieved by perfecting rural dwellings and improving the hygienic conditions of the villages and hamlets of Spain.

6. The State shall guarantee the tenant-farmers security in the cultivation of the land by means of long-term contracts ensuring them against unjustified eviction and enabling them to recover the money spent in improving their farms. The State desires to invervene in order to make the land pass, on just terms, into the ownership of those who work it directly.

VI

1. The State shall attend with special care to those who earn their living on the sea, providing them with institutions capable of preventing the depreciation of their goods and making it easier for them to attain to the ownership of the necessary implements for the plying of their trade.

VII

1. A new labor judiciary shall be created, governed by the principle that this function of justice belongs to the State.

VIII

1. Capital is an instrument of production.
2. The company, as a producing unit, shall regulate its elements in such a way as to give precedence to the human over the instrumental, and subordinating them all to the common good.
3. The head of the company shall be responsible for its contribution to the common good of the national economy.
4. The company's profits, after payment of a just interest on capital, shall be applied to building up reserves needed to ensure its stability, perfect its production, and improve the working and living conditions of its employees.

IX

1. Credit shall be regulated in such a way that, in addition to performing its function of developing the nation's wealth, it shall contribute to the creation and maintenance of small agricultural, fishing, industrial, and commercial holdings.
2. Honor and trust, founded on competence and work, shall constitute effective guarantees for the granting of loans.

The State shall prosecute all forms of usury.

X

1. Provident foresight shall give workers the certainty of help in misfortune.
2. Social insurance providing for old age, incapacity, maternity, industrial accidents, occupational diseases, tuberculosis, and forced unemployment shall be provided and the aim shall be total insurance. The first objective shall be the providing of adequate pensions to aged workers.

XI

1. National production constitutes an economic unit at the service of the country. It is the duty of all Spaniards to defend, improve, and increase it. All factors concerned in production shall be subordinated to the higher interest of the nation.

2. All illegal individual or collective acts that seriously disturb production or militate against it shall be sanctioned in accordance with law.

3. Any wilful lowering of output at work shall be penalized.

4. As a general rule, the State shall not enter the business field except where private enterprise is lacking or when the interests of the nation so demand.

5. The State, either through its agencies or through syndicates, shall prevent all unfair competition in the fields of production, as well as all such activities as may prejudice the normal development of the national economy, and, on the other hand, it shall encourage all such activities as may lead to the perfection of this economy.

6. The State recognizes private initiative as the well-spring of the economic life of the nation.

XII

1. The State recognizes and protects private enterprise as a natural means for the performance of individual, family, and social functions. All forms of property shall be subordinated to the interest of the nation, whose interpreter is the State.

2. The State assumes the task of multiplying the forms of ownership vitally bound to the human person and making them accessible to all Spaniards; i.e., the home, small land holdings, and the working instruments or goods of daily use.

3. It recognizes the family as the primary natural unit, the basis of society, and as a moral institution endowed with rights that are inalienable and above all positive law. In order better to guarantee its preservation and continuity, family heritages are not subject to seizure.

XIII

1. All Spaniards insofar as they participate in work and production constitute the Syndicalist Organization.

2. The Syndicalist Organization shall be constituted in a group of industrial, agricultural and service syndicates, by branches of activities on a territorial and national scale which shall include all the factors of production.

3. The syndicates shall have the status of corporations of public law with a representative basis; they shall enjoy legal status and the full right to act within their respective spheres of competence. There shall be constituted, within the syndicates in the form to be determined by law, the respective associations of employers, technicians and workers, organized for the defense of their particular interests and as a means of free and representative participation in syndicalist activities and, through the syndicates in the community tasks of political, economic and social life.

4. The syndicates are the instruments and representatives of professional and economic interests for the accomplishment of the purposes of the national community.

5. The syndicates shall collaborate in the study of the problems of production and may propose solutions and intervene in the regulation, supervision and enforcement of working conditions.

6. The syndicates may set up and maintain organizations for research, moral, cultural and professional training, for charity, assistance and other social matters of concern to those participating in production.

XIV

1. The State shall issue the necessary orders to protect national labor within our territory and, by means of labor treaties with other powers, it shall take steps to ensure the status of Spanish workers residing abroad.

XV

1. At the time when this Charter is published, Spain is engaged in a heroic military task in which she is preserving the values of the spirit and of world culture at the expense of a great part of her own material wealth.

National production must correspond in all its phases to the generosity of our fighting youth and to that of Spain itself.

Therefore, in this Charter of rights and duties, we hereby declares as urgent and inevitable that the elements of production should resolutely contribute their fair share to the remaking of Spain and the bases of its strength.

XVI

1. The State undertakes to place its fighting youth in positions of work, honor, and command, to which they are entitled as Spaniards and which they have won as heroes.

SWEDEN

SUMMARY

INTERNATIONAL STATUS

Sweden is a member of the United Nations (November 19, 1946).[1] It is a member of the Nordic Council, the European Free Trade Association and other international organizations. It was a member of the League of Nations.

The Riksdag of 1435 was the first Parliament on the European continent. In 1617, the first organic law determining parliamentary forms was

[1] It has accepted the compulsory jurisdiction of the International Court under Article 36 of its Statute.

promulgated. The period of Swedish dominion in Germany and the Baltic ended in the early eighteenth century. The Instruments of Government of 1719 and 1720, Europe's first written Constitution, instituted legislative rule and "The Era of Liberty," following a forty year period of absolute monarchy. In 1766 a Freedom of the Press Act was passed as a fundamental law. Absolute monarchy returned from 1772 to 1809. Defeat in the war with Russia in 1809 lost Finland to Russia after a union which had lasted since the twelfth century, and resulted in the deposition of the King. A Constituent Assembly drew up the Constitution of 1809 and elected Marshal Bernadotte King; in 1810, the law of Royal Succession was promulgated. In 1814, Norway was united to the Swedish crown in personal union with an independent government. The medieval Riksdag was made into a modern Parliament by the Parliament Act of 1866 which abolished the old four estates; government by Parliament through a responsible Cabinet was established in 1917. The existing Freedom of the Press Act of 1949 replaces those of 1810 and 1812. Sweden pursues a policy of neutrality.

FORM OF NATIONAL GOVERNMENT

The constitutional documents of Sweden are the Instrument of Government of June 6, 1809, as amended to 1965, the Riksdag Act of June 22, 1866 as amended to 1953, the Act of Succession of September 26, 1810 as amended to 1953 and the Freedom of the Press Act of April 5, 1949 amended to 1953.[1] Sweden is a hereditary monarchy, the Sovereign must be of the Evangelical faith and male.[2] No part of the Realm may be severed therefrom.[3]

RIGHTS OF THE PEOPLE

Article 16 of the Instrument of Government provides that the King must maintain and further justice and truth, prevent and forbid iniquity and injustice; noone may be deprived of life, honor, liberty or well being without legal trial and sentence, of property except in accordance with the law, the home is inviolable, banishment forbidden, conscience and religion are free and everyone must be tried by his legal judge. The Freedom of the Press Act provides freedom of the press and of public documents.[4] The ancient privileges, advantages, rights and liberties of the Estates of the Realm shall remain in force.[5]

[1] IG, Art. 85.
[2] Id., Art. 1, 2; A. Suc. Art. 3, 4.
[3] IG, Art. 78.
[4] Id., Art. 86.
[5] Id., Art. 114.

LEGISLATIVE DEPARTMENT

The bicameral Riksdag represents the Swedish people.[1] It has the legislative power together with the King.[2] It convenes in one or two annual sessions.[3] The one hundred and fifty members of the Upper House are elected by the county and city councils for a term of eight years.[4] The two hundred and thirty members of the Lower House are elected from constituencies for a term of four years by universal suffrage.[5] The terms of both Houses are subject to dissolution.[6] Immunities of Riksdagmen are provided.[7] The Riksdag alone has the power to tax and there are provisions concerning finances.[8] The Riksdag Act stipulates the rules and procedure of the Houses, the division into Committees, the method of work, etc.

EXECUTIVE DEPARTMENT

The King governs the realm; his person is sacred and inviolable.[9] He is assisted by a Council of State composed of Ministers and the Prime Minister and all matters of Government are decided there.[10] Persons related to each other may not be members concurrently of the Council of State.[11] The King is the Commander-in-Chief of the Armed Forces, has the power of pardon, the power of appointment including the appointment of Archbishops and bishops, is the fount of honor.[12] The succession is regulated by the Act of Succession.

JUDICIAL DEPARTMENT

A Supreme Court is provided composed of twelve justices.[13] There is provision for a Supreme Administrative Court and for a King's Law Council, composed of three members of the Supreme Court and one of the Supreme Administrative Court, to give its opinion on laws and statutes referred to it.[14] An Attorney General is provided.[15] The Riksdag appoints, as its representatives, two Ombudsmen to supervise the observance of the laws and statutes as applied by public officials and employees.[16]

AREA, POPULATION, ETC.

The area of Sweden is 449,793 square kilometres, its population (1965) 7,773,000. The capital is Stockholm and the language Swedish.

[1] Id., Art. 49. [2] Id., Art. 87. [3] RA, Art. 2. [4] Id., Art. 6.
[5] Id., Art. 13–16. [6] Id., Art. 3, 5. [7] IG, Art. 110, 111.
[8] Id., Art. 57–77, RA, Art. 39–41, 65, 70–73. [9] IG, Art. 3, 4.
[10] Id., Art. 6, 7. [11] Id., Art. 4. [12] Id., Art. 14, 26, 28, 29, 37.
[13] Id., Art. 17. [14] Id., Art. 18, 21. [15] Id., Art. 27 [16] Id., Art. 96–102.

CONSTITUTIONAL DOCUMENTS of SWEDEN[1]

The Instrument of Government

June 6, 1809, as amended up to and including the year 1965

We, Carl, by the Grace of God King of Sweden, the Goths, and the Wends, &c., &c., &c., Heir to Norway, Duke of Sleswig-Holstein, Stormarn, and Ditmarsen, Count of Oldenburg and Delmenhorst, &c., &c., hereby make known that we, having with unlimited confidence unconditionally entrusted the Estates of the Realm with the provision of a new Instrument of Government, to form in perpetuity the basis of the happiness and independence of a common fatherland, do carry out a duty coveted and dear to our heart when we hereby publicly promulgate the fundamental law which has, after the most careful consideration, been unanimously enacted and accepted by the Estates of the Realm now assembled and delivered to us in the Hall of State this day, in conjunction with their voluntary and unanimous offer of Sweden's crown and government. As we, with deepest emotion and loving participation in the fortunes of the people who have given us such an unforgettable proof of confidence and affection, have acceded to this their desire, we have attached a much more certain hope for the success of our unremitting endeavors to serve the welfare of the fatherland, inasmuch as our and our subjects' mutual rights and obligations are so clearly laid down in the new Instrument of Government that they incorporate the liberty of the people of Sweden as by law established while maintaining the sanctity of the crown and its capacity of action. We are, consequently, pleased to adopt, accept and confirm this Instrument of Government approved by the Estates of the Realm, exactly as follows word for word:

We, the undersigned Estates of the Realm of Sweden, counts, barons, bishops, nobles, clergy, burghers, and peasants who are now, on our own

[1] *The Constitution of Sweden*. Translated by Sarah V. Thorelli. *Documents, Published by the Royal Ministry for Foreign Affairs. New Series II: 4.* Stockholm 1953. Supplied by the Ministry of Foreign Affairs in August 1966. Further amendments to 1965 supplied by them in Swedish and translated by P. Ryberg. Ed.

behalf and on behalf of our brethern at home, convened at a general national assembly, hereby make known that, in consequence of the recent change of rule, to which we have given our unanimous ratification, we, delegates of the Swedish people, have acquired the right, by drawing up an amended State constitution, ourselves to ameliorate the condition of the fatherland in the future; we have, therefore, in repealing the fundamental laws more or less in operation prior to the present, namely. The Instrument of Government of the 21st of August, 1772, the Act of Union and Security of the 21st of February and the 3rd of April, 1789, The Riksdag Act of the 24th of January, 1617, as well as all such other ancient and modern laws, acts, decrees, enactments and decisions as have been comprised under the name of fundamental laws, agreed and confirmed that there be enacted for the realm of Sweden and lands subject thereto the following Instrument of Government, which shall be in operation from this day onwards as the principal fundamental law of the realm; we reserve, moreover, the right to enact before the close of this national assembly, in the manner prescribed in Article 85 of this Instrument of Government, the remaining fundamental laws there specified.

Art. 1. The realm of Sweden shall be governed by a King and shall be a hereditary monarchy with the order of succession which is established by The Act of Succession.

Art. 2. The King shall always profess the pure evangelical faith, as adopted and explained in the unaltered Augsburg Confession and in the Resolution of the Uppsala Meeting of the year 1593.

Art. 3. The person of the King shall be held sacred and reverenced; he shall not be subject to any prosecution for his actions.

Art. 4. The King alone shall govern the realm in accordance with the provisions of this Instrument of Government; he shall, however, in the instances hereafter specified, seek the information and advice of a Council of State, to which the King shall call and appoint capable, experienced, honorable and generally respected native Swedish subjects. Persons related by direct ascending or descending kinship, siblings and spouses, may not be members of the Council of State at the same time.

Art. 5. There shall be ministries of State for the various branches of the government of the realm, in the number determined by law enacted jointly by the King and the Riksdag.

The names of the ministries and the distribution of duties among them shall be determined by the King in a special order, publicly promulgated.

For each ministry the King shall select a head and spokesman from among the members of the Council of State, provided that the King may appoint another member of the Council than the head of the ministry to present in the Council those matters specified by the King. The head of the ministry to which foreign affairs appertain shall be the Minister for Foreign Affairs. Article 28 specifies when a member of the Council of

State, who does not belong to the Church of Sweden, is prevented from presenting certain matters.

Art. 6. The Council of State shall be composed of the heads of the ministries, and not less than three Council members without portfolio, as determined by law enacted jointly by the King and the Riksdag. Of the Council members without portfolio at least two must have held civil office.

The King shall appoint one member of the Council of State to be Prime Minister and principal member of the Council.

The members of the Council of State have the right to be present at the consideration of all business in the Council.

Art. 7. All matters of government, except those mentioned in Article 15 shall be submitted to the King in Council of State and be decided there.

Art. 8. The King shall not make a decision upon a matter upon which the Council of State must be consulted, unless at least three Councillors of State are present in addition to the one submitting the matter. Unless they have a legitimate excuse, all members of the Council shall be present for the consideration of all matters of special importance and magnitude, which, according to the agenda previously circulated, are brought before the Council and affect the general administration of the realm. Such matters are: questions and proposals regarding the adoption of new general laws, the repeal or amendment of those hitherto in force, new general establishments within the various branches of administration, and other questions of a similar character.

Art. 9. Minutes shall be kept of all matters which are submitted to the King in Council. When the security of the realm or other extremely important reasons demand secrecy in a matter concerning the relations of the realm with foreign powers, separate minutes on the matter shall be kept.

Such members of the Council of State as are present, being held responsible for their advice, with the consequences specified in Articles 106 and 107, are positively obliged to express and explain their opinions, which shall be entered in the minutes; nevertheless, it is reserved to the King alone to decide. Should at any time the unexpected event occur that the King's decision would be manifestly in conflict with fundamental or general law of the realm, it shall be the duty of the members of the Council of State to make vigorous representations against such decision. Any member who does not separately enter his opinion in the minutes shall be held responsible for the decision as if he had counseled the King to make it.

Art. 10. Before matters are submitted to the King in Council, they shall be prepared by the member submitting them, who shall collect for this purpose the necessary information from the competent administrative offices.

Art. 11. In matters which concern the relations of the State with foreign powers, all communications to such powers or to the King's envoys abroad, without regard to the nature of the business, shall be made through the Minister for Foreign Affairs.

Art. 12. The King shall have the power to enter into agreements with foreign powers after the Council of State has been heard upon the subject. When such agreements deal with matters which are required under this Instrument of Government to be decided by the Riksdag, either alone or jointly with the King, or when, though not dealing with such matters, they are of major importance, they shall be laid before the Riksdag for approval; and such agreements shall contain a reservation making their validity dependent upon the sanction of the Riksdag.

Should an occasion arise when the interests of the realm require that an agreement, which is of great importance but does not deal with a matter which the Riksdag is entitled to decide, be concluded without the confirmation of the Riksdag, this may be done, but in such a case the Advisory Council on Foreign Affairs, or the Committee on Foreign Affairs, shall be given an opportunity to express its opinion before the agreement is concluded.

Art. 13. If the King wishes to declare war or to conclude peace, he shall convene all the members of the Council of State in extraordinary Council, lay before them the causes and circumstances to be considered, and ask for their opinions concerning the matter; each of them shall separately enter his opinion in the minutes, with the responsibility specified in Article 107. The King may then make and execute such decision as he considers in the best interest of the realm.

Art. 14. The King shall be Commander-in-Chief of the Armed Forces of the realm.

Art. 15. Matters of military command, that is, those in which the King acts directly in his capacity as Commander-in-Chief of the Armed Forces, may be decided by the King in the presence of the head of the ministry under whose authority the matter falls whenever the King is himself exercising the royal power. The head of the ministry is bound, under the responsibility of Councillors of State, to express his opinion upon the measures adopted by the King at the time when such measures are under consideration; when his opinion is not in conformity with the King's decision, he shall enter his objection and advice in the minutes which the King shall authenticate with his royal signature.

The matters of government which are to be considered matters of military command shall be determined by a law enacted jointly by the King and the Riksdag.

Art. 16. The King shall maintain and further justice and truth, prevent and forbid iniquity and injustice; he shall not deprive anyone or allow anyone to be deprived of life, honor, personal liberty or well-being, without legal trial and sentence; he shall not deprive anyone or permit anyone to be deprived of any real or personal property without due trial and judgment in accordance with the provisions of the Swedish law and statutes; he shall not disturb or allow to be disturbed the peace of any person in his home; he shall not banish any person from one place to another; he shall not constrain or allow to be contrained the conscience of any person, but shall protect everyone in the free exercise of his religion, provided that he does not thereby disturb public order or occasion general offense. The King shall cause everyone to be tried by the court to the jurisdiction of which he is legally subject.

Art. 17. The judicial power of the King shall be vested in at least twelve experienced and honorable persons, learned in the law, who shall be appointed by him; they must have fulfilled the conditions required by law for the exercise of judicial functions. They shall be called justices and shall constitute the King's Supreme Court.

Further provisions as to the composition, sessions and duties of the Supreme Court shall be prescribed by a separate law, enacted jointly by the King and the Riksdag, in the manner provided by Article 87, Section 1.

Art. 18. The King's right to examine and decide appeals which, according to the laws, may be brought before him in the ministries of State shall be delegated, to the extent prescribed by a separate law enacted jointly by the King and the Riksdag, as provided in Article 87, Section 1, to not less than seven persons appointed by the King, who shall have held civil office and manifested insight, experience and honesty. They shall be called justices and constitute the King's Supreme Administrative Court. At least two thirds of the total number of justices shall have fulfilled the conditions required by law for the exercise of judicial functions.

Further provisions as to the composition, sessions and duties of the Supreme Administrative Court shall be prescribed by the law mentioned above.

Art. 19. It also devolves upon the Supreme Administrative Court, in matters which may be submitted to it or the Cameral Court for final decision, to receive and decide all petitions asking that the King set aside judgments that have acquired legal force, or that he grant relief from forfeiture of rights resulting from the expiration of a legal term. All other petitions of this kind shall be decided by the Supreme Court.

Art. 20. Should inquiries be made to the King by courts or officials regarding the true meaning of the law in cases appertaining to the judiciary, the Supreme Court shall furnish the interpretations required.

Art. 21. The King's Law Council shall give its opinion on proposals for the enactment, repeal, amendment or interpretation of the laws or statutes which are, for this purpose, referred to them by the King.

Three members of the Supreme Court and one of the legally trained members of the Supreme Administrative Court shall together constitute the King's Law Council. In the place of one of the members of the Supreme Court another legally trained, honest and well known person may be appointed by decision of the King. The four King's Councillors shall participate in the consideration of all matters referred to the King's Law Council. Whenever it should prove necessary for certain business, the King may appoint one additional person known to possess insight, experience and honesty to be a member of the Law Council. If the Law Council is divided into sections, the same provisions as are applicable to the Law Council shall apply to each section.

Further provisions as to the service on the Law Council shall be prescribed by a separate law enacted jointly by the King and the Riksdag, as provided by Article 87, Section 1.

Art. 22. 1. Cases may be heard and decided in the Supreme Court by five justices. No more than seven members shall, at the same time, take part in the trial of any case, except in such instances as may be otherwise provided for in the manner prescribed by Article 87, Section 1. In the same manner it shall be determined how many justices shall take part in deciding whether cases, in which appeal is made to the Supreme Court, may be considered by it, when such special permission is required by law, and also in considering petitions submitted to the Court according to Article 26.

2. In the Supreme Administrative Court, five members may hear and decide cases, and four members may do so when three are in agreement as to the outcome of the case. It shall be determined in the manner prescribed by Article 87, Section 1, how many justices shall take part in cases in which appeal is made to the Supreme Administrative Court.

Art. 23. All decisions of the Supreme Court and of the Supreme Administrative Court are issued in the name of the King and under his signature or seal.

Art. 24. Business for trial and decision by the Supreme Court shall be prepared by the subordinate body for the examination of laws.

Art. 25. Matters for consideration and decision by the Supreme Administrative Court shall be prepared by the respective ministries under the jurisdiction of which the matters fall, according to the distribution mentioned in Article 5.

Art. 26. The King shall have the power to grant pardons in criminal cases, to commute death penalties, to restore honors, and to return property forfeited to the crown. However, in applications for pardons where it is not clear that there is reason to grant such pardon, the King shall consult the Supreme Administrative Court in those cases which, by their nature, may come before it or before the Cameral Court for final decision, and in other cases the Supreme Court shall be consulted; and the King's decision shall be taken in Council of State. The offender shall then have the right to accept the pardon granted by the King or to suffer the punishment to which he has been sentenced.

Art. 27. The King shall appoint as Attorney General an able, impartial person, versed in the law, who has had experience as a judge. It shall be the principal duty of the Attorney General, as the highest legal officer of the King, to prosecute or cause prosecution to be brought, in the name of the King, in cases which affect the rights of the crown and also, on behalf of the King, to exercise supervision over the administration of justice, and in this capacity to prosecute for offences committed by judges and officials.

Art. 28. The King in Council of State shall have the power to appoint and promote Swedish citizens to all positions and offices, high and low, for which royal letters of appointment are issued; the proper authority shall, however, first submit nominations when such a practice has heretofore been customary. Foreigners of both sexes may be appointed to teaching positions in the universities, excepting however, to the theological faculties, to teaching positions and other positions in other institutions for science, crafts or fine arts, as well as to positions where it is necessary to have special education in the natural sciences, medicine or technology.

In all promotions the King shall take into consideration only merit and ability of the candidates, but not their birth. No person other than one who professes the faith of the Church may be appointed to clerical office within the Church of Sweden. For other offices involving the obligation to give instruction in the Christian religion or in theology the King shall take such consideration to the candidates' faith as may be required. Holders of official positions who do not belong to the Church of Sweden may not participate in decisions of cases or matters relating to the divine worship or religious instruction of the Church, the exercise of clerical functions, promotion and official responsibility within the Church. Concerning members of the Council of State, however, such ground for disqualification shall not apply to other than the member submitting the matter in Council.

No woman may be appointed to a clerical office unless otherwise provided in accordance with Article 87, Section 2.

Each head of a ministry shall submit all matters relative to the promotion, appointment, leave of absence and discharge of all officials and employees in the offices and establishments under the ministry to the King in Council and execute the decision.

Art. 29. The King shall appoint the archbishop and bishops from a list of three candidates presented to him in the manner provided by the ecclesiastical law.

Art. 30. The appointment of clergymen to parishes, and the rights which appertain to the King and to the parishes in this connection, shall be governed by a special law enacted in accordance with Article 87, Section 2.

Art. 31. Repealed.

Art. 32. Whenever appointments are to be made by the King to offices, for which candidates have been nominated, the members of the Council of State shall express their views as to the competence and merits of the applicants. They shall also have the right to make humble representations against the King's appointments to other offices and positions.

Art. 33. Foreign men and women can, by means of naturalization, in the manner and on the conditions determined by a separate law enacted in accordance with Article 87, Section 1 obtain Swedish citizenship. A foreigner thus naturalized shall enjoy the same rights and privileges as a native Swedish citizen, except that he may not be appointed a member of the Council of State.

All matters concerning naturalization may be examined by the King if it is not otherwise provided in the above-mentioned law.

Art. 34. The Prime Minister and the Minister for Foreign Affairs shall have the highest rank in the realm, and members of the Council of State shall rank next. Members of the Council of State may not perform the duties of, or receive income from, any other office. A justice of the Supreme Court or the Supreme Administrative Court may not hold any other office or perform other duties.

Art. 35. If the King's Councillors hold posts of confidence the King may remove them whenever he considers that the interest of the realm demands such action. Such a decision shall be taken in the Council of State.

Art. 36. Persons holding judicial office, and all public officials or employees other than those mentioned in the preceding Article, may be removed from their posts by the King only after a court decision or a decision in connection with the payment of a pension. If, however, it is found preferable for organizational reasons, they can be transferred to other posts corresponding to their previous one.

All other regulations concerning the legal position of employees of the State shall be set forth in a law to be drawn up in accordance with Article 87, section 1.

Transitional Note: Until the above mentioned law enters into force, Articles 35 and 36 before amendment shall be taken into account.

Art. 37. The King shall have the power to ennoble persons who by fidelity, courage, virtue, learning and zealous performance, have rendered the King and realm outstanding service. The King may also, as a reward for great and distinguished services, confer upon a noble the rank of baron, or upon a baron the rank of count. The noble rank and the dignities of baron and count hereafter granted shall be borne only by the person ennobled or elevated in rank, and, after his death, in direct line of descent, by the eldest male heir of the oldest branch of his family and, after its extinction, by the nearest male heir of the ancestor in the oldest branch in existence, and so forth. If noble rank should pass by inheritance to a person who has already been ennobled or has received a title by previous inheritance, his own rank shall lapse, unless it is of a higher grade, in which case the ancestor's rank shall go to the nearest branch of the family; if no such branch is in existence, the title shall become extinct. If anyone should forfeit his noble rank, the title shall go to the person most nearly entitled thereto, in accordance with the rules herein established.

An ordinance regarding the nobility, to be adopted jointly by the King and the nobles, shall prescribe the manner in which members of the nobility may assemble to decide upon matters which they have in common.

Art. 38. The King's written messages and propositions [1] to the Riksdag or to the Synod of the Church, public laws, the King's letters of appointment for public offices and other documents and orders issued by the King and specified by him shall, in order to be valid, be signed by the King and bear the countersignature of the competent Councillor who shall be responsible that the action taken is in agreement with the Council minutes concerning it. All other decisions by the King shall be issued over the signature of the competent Councillor, who also may issue directions and instructions regarding the execution of orders given directly to the proper parties. Should the Councillor find any decision of the King to be in conflict with this Instrument of Government, he shall make representations in the Council of State against it; should the King notwithstanding insist upon promulgating the order, it shall be the Councillor's right and duty to refuse his countersignature or signature thereto and, as a consequence, to resign his office, which he shall not resume until the Riksdag has examined and approved his conduct. In the meantime his salary and other emoluments of his office shall continue.

Art. 39. If the King desires to travel abroad, he shall inform a full meeting of the Council of State and obtain its opinion, as provided by Article 9. Should the King then decide to make such a journey and carry his decision into execution, he shall not take part in the administration of the realm or exercise the royal power as long as he is outside the realm, but during his absence the government shall be carried on in the King's name by the heir apparent to the throne, if he has attained twenty-five years of age. This prince shall govern as regent with all the royal power and authority, in accordance with this Instrument of Government; he shall not, however, confer the rank and title of nobility, raise persons to the rank of count or baron, or confer knighthood; and likewise all vacant posts of confidence shall only be held until further notice by persons appointed by the regent.

If the prince who is heir apparent to the throne has not reached twenty-five years of age, or is prevented by illness or absence abroad from exercising the royal power, then the prince who is next entitled to succeed to the throne and who has reached such age and for whom there is no such obstacle, shall govern as regent in the King's name, with the above-mentioned authority.

[1] The nearest English equivalent to the Swedish term "propositioner" is "government bills." Similarly, the English expression corresponding most closely to the Swedish term "motioner" is "private members' bills." (Cf. Article 55 of The Riksdag Act, et al.) One of the reasons for using "propositions" and "private members' motions," respectively, in this translation is that in Sweden it is not necessary to introduce "bills" in the form of draft laws. "Motion" is used here only in the phrase "private members' motion," hence in a more restricted sense than in Anglo-American constitutional law.

If there is no prince entitled to govern under these conditions, the Council of State shall conduct the government with the same powers as a regent.

Article 91 contains the measures to be taken in case the King remains out of the realm for more than twelve months.

Art. 40. Should the King become too ill to perform his functions, the government of the realm shall be carried on as determined in the preceding Article.

Art. 41. Should the King die before the heir apparent has reached twenty-five years of age, the government shall be carried on in conformity with Article 39, until the Riksdag assembles and the regency established by it has assumed the government; the regent or the Council of State shall conform strictly to this Instrument of Government.

Art. 42. If unfortunately the entire royal house, in which the succession is vested, becomes extinct in the male line, the Council of State shall similarly carry on the government, with the powers determined by Article 39, until the Riksdag is able to assemble and choose a new royal house and the King elected assumes the government.

In all cases when the government of the realm, in accordance with the present and the three preceding Articles, is being conducted by the Council of State, all the members thereof shall be present and vote, unless they have a legitimate excuse.

Art. 43. When the King goes on a military expedition, or visits distant parts of the realm, he shall designate at least three members of the Council of State, under a chairman whom he shall specially appoint, either from among the princes of his house or from among the members of the Council of State, to conduct such matters of government as the King may prescribe. Matters in which the King himself acts shall be dealt with in accordance with Article 8.

The above provisions regarding the King shall also apply to the regent when the latter is exercising the royal power.

Art. 44. No prince of the royal house, whether crown prince, hereditary prince or other prince, may marry unless the King, having obtained the opinion of the Council of State, has given his consent thereto. Should a prince nevertheless do so, he shall have forfeited all hereditary rights to the crown for himself, his children and their descendants.

Art. 45. Neither the crown prince of Sweden, the hereditary prince, nor the princes of the royal house shall have any appanage or civil office; there may be conferred on them, however, according to ancient custom, titles of duchies and principalities, without any rights over the territory, the name of which they bear.

Art. 46. The country shall remain divided into counties under the customary county government. No governor-general shall hereafter be appointed within the realm.

Art. 47. The Courts of Appeal of the realm and all other courts shall decide cases in accordance with the laws and statutes; the administrative boards of the realm, the county governments, and all other administrative agencies, as well as all officials, superior or inferior, shall perform their duties and functions in accordance with the instructions, rules and regulations and orders already issued or which may hereafter be issued; they shall obey the King's orders and commands and assist one another in the execution of such orders and commands and in the performance of everything which the service of the realm may require of them, being responsible to the King, in accordance with the law, for any omission, negligence or illegal action.

Art. 48. The court of the King shall be under his own direction and subject to such arrangements as he finds appropriate. He may appoint to or dismiss from all posts at his court at his own pleasure.

Art. 49. 1. The Riksdag represents the Swedish people. The rights and obligations now vested by laws in force in the Estates of the Realm shall hereafter be vested in the Riksdag. It shall be divided into two houses, the members of which shall be elected in the manner prescribed by The Riksdag Act and other legislation enacted jointly by the King and the Riksdag. The houses shall have equal competence and authority in all matters. The Riksdag shall, by virtue of this Instrument of Government assemble annually on the 10th of January, or, if that day be a holiday, on the following day.

Article 2 of The Riksdag Act contains the provisions governing the sessions of the Riksdag and the right of the King or a specified number of members of each house to bring about the summoning of the Riksdag during the time when the Riksdag is not in session. Articles 91, 92, 93, 94 and 108 contain further provisions governing the summoning of the Riksdag on certain special occasions.

2. Should it be deemed necessary in view of the particular importance or character of some measure, to ascertain the opinion of the people before the decision, the King and the Riksdag may, by a law enacted jointly, provide that a referendum shall be held. This law shall determine the question or questions to be answered by the referendum, as well as the date and manner of holding the same. The right to take part in the voting shall be vested in those who are entitled to vote in elections to the Lower House of the Riksdag. After the referendum the measure shall be dealt with in conformity with the fundamental law.

Art. 50. The Riksdag shall meet in the capital city of the realm, unless hostile invasion, pestilence, or other equally grave circumstances makes it impossible or dangerous to the liberty and security of the Riksdag. In such cases it devolves on the King, after conferring with the persons elected by the Riksdag as Commissioners of the Bank of Sweden and of the National Debt Office to designate and announce another place for the Riksdag meeting.

If the country enters a war and the conditions of war require such a measure, the Delegation for War of the Riksdag shall act in the place of the Riksdag. Such a measure shall be decided either by the Conference of Chairmen mentioned in paragraph 50 of the Rules of Procedure of the Riksdag which may meet after consultation with the Prime Minister, or if the Conference of Chairmen cannot meet because of the conditions of war, by the King. Such a decision shall be valid until a cease-fire or, failing a cease-fire, until the King or Delegation for War decides that the Riksdag shall resume its powers.

If, because of the country's involvement in a war, the administration of the country cannot be carried out according to this Constitution, either the Riksdag or the Delegation of War where the latter has replaced the Riksdag, is authorized to decide how the administration of the country should be carried on for the protection of the country and the bringing to an end of the war.

If, because of the country's involvement in a war, neither the Riksdag nor its Delegation of War are able to fulfil their obligations, all measures to protect the country and to end the war which are the duty of the King and Riksdag together or of the Riksdag alone, shall be taken in pursuance of the general policy set forth by the Government. The King may not, however, draw up, amend, interpret or revoke the Constitution or the Law concerning elections to the Riksdag.

Art. 51. Whenever the Riksdag is convened by the King, the regent, or the Council of State, the time for its meeting shall be fixed for not earlier than the first day after the summons is published in the public gazette and not later than twenty days after said date.

Art. 52. Each house of the Riksdag shall select its own Speaker as well as a First and Second Deputy Speaker according to the procedure laid down in the Riksdag Act.

Art. 53. Each Riksdag shall select the following committees for the preparation of business: one Committee on Foreign Affairs, one Committee on the Constitution, one Committee of Supply, one Committee of Ways and Means, one Committee on Banking, three Committees on Laws, one Committee on Agriculture, and one Committee on Miscellaneous Affairs, the composition and the duties of which shall be determined by the Riksdag Act.

No more committees shall be selected than are necessary at a Riksdag convening after a dissolution, as provided for in Article 108.

Art. 54. The members of the Committee on Foreign Affairs mentioned in the preceding Article shall also be members of an Advisory Council to confer with the King concerning the relations of the realm with foreign powers. Conference with this Advisory Council should take place before all matters of major importance relating to foreign affairs are decided. When a matter comes up for consideration all available documents and information shall be communicated. The decisions made by the King in matters which have been the subject of a conference with the Council shall be communicated to its members not later than at their next meeting.

At the beginning of each session of the Riksdag, and afterwards as often as circumstances may require, the Minister for Foreign Affairs shall present to the Advisory Council a statement of the general state of foreign affairs which may become of importance to the realm.

The members of the Council shall observe the utmost caution with regard to communicating to others information concerning what occurs at meetings of the Council. Should the King, or whoever may be conducting the conference in his absence, deem it necessary that absolute secrecy be observed, the members shall be bound to such secrecy.

Art. 55. Neither the Riksdag, the houses, nor any of the committees of the Riksdag may deliberate or decide upon any matter in the presence of the King.

Art. 56. The Riksdag Act shall determine the order in which propositions of the King and matters raised by members in the houses shall be considered.

Art. 57. The ancient right of the Swedish people to tax themselves shall be exercised by the Riksdag alone.

The manner in which separate communities shall tax themselves for their own needs shall be determined by local government laws to be enacted jointly by the King and the Riksdag.

Art. 58. The King shall cause a statement of the financial condition of the administration in all its branches, both income and expenditures, assets and liabilities, to be presented annually to the Riksdag. Should the realm receive any revenue because of treaties with foreign powers, it shall be accounted for in the same manner.

Art. 59. In connection with the statement of the condition and requirements of the administration, the King shall cause to be presented to the Riksdag a proposal as to the manner of providing by taxation for the needs of the budget in excess of the standing revenues.

Art. 60. The customs and excise taxes, postal charges, stamp duties, taxes on domestic distillation, and all such other taxes as each Riksdag may vote shall be reckoned as taxation. No general tax or duty of whatever name or character may be increased without the consent of the Riksdag, the duties on imported and exported grain alone excepted; nor shall the revenues of the State be leased, nor shall any monopoly for the benefit of the crown or of private individuals and corporations be established, otherwise than by law, enacted jointly by the King and the Riksdag in the manner provided by Article 87.

Art. 61. All taxes and duties voted by the Riksdag under the headings mentioned in the preceding Article shall be valid until the beginning of the fiscal year, for which new taxes shall be voted by the Riksdag.

Art. 62. After consideration by the Riksdag of the requirements of the administration it is the responsibility of the Riksdag to vote supplies to meet such needs, and also to prescribe the special purposes for which the separate items of appropriation may be used, and to grant these items under definite budgetary headings.

The Committee for Salaries of the Riksdag is authorized, if the Riksdag has not decided otherwise, to consult with the Council of State in all negotiations concerning conditions of employment of employees of the State or of offices approved by the Riksdag. In all such questions, the Committee shall consult with a King's Council specially appointed by the King and on behalf of the Riksdag shall approve agreements reached in such matters.

Art. 63. 1. Every year the Riksdag, on a proposal from the King and in the manner applicable to appropriations in general, shall adopt an emergency budget for the Armed Forces, containing the extraordinary appropriations necessary to maintain the peace and independence of the realm in danger of ar or war. The Riksdag may make the condition that these appropriations may not be used before the Riksdag has been called into session.

When the Riksdag is not in session or within ten days from the beginning of the session, the King may, after conference with the Advisory Council on Foreign Affairs, authorize an advance budget, containing appropriations included in the emergency budget for the armed forces.

The advance budget shall remain in force for thirty days after the beginning of the session if the Riksdag does not otherwise decide.

2. The Riksdag may, in the manner prescribed in Section 1, pass a general emergency budget containing the appropriations which may be necessary in an economic crisis or another emergency; and the Riksdag may at the same time regulate the manner in which the King may use the appropriations included in such an emergency budget.

Art. 64. The regular public funds and standing revenues, as well as the supplies voted by the Riksdag for the finances of the State as extraordinary advances or otherwise, in the manner above mentioned, shall be at the disposal of the King to meet the needs recognized by the Riksdag in accordance with the budget.

Art. 65. Such funds may not be applied to other purposes than those authorized; the members of the Council of State shall be responsible if they permit any deviation from this rule without entering their representations in the minutes of the Council and calling attention to what the Riksdag has prescribed in the matter.

Art. 66. The National Debt Office shall remain under the direction, control and administration of the Riksdag; and, as the Riksdag is responsible for the public debt administered by that Office, it shall, after the condition and needs of that Office have been duly examined, provide by special taxation the funds which are found to be indispensable for the payment of the interest and capital of this debt, in order that the credit of the realm may be maintained and preserved.

Art. 67. The delegate of the King in the National Debt Office shall not attend the meetings of the Commissioners of that Office except when they desire to consult with him.

Art. 68. The funds belonging to, or appropriated, for the National Debt Office may not, under any pretext or condition, be withdrawn or applied to other purposes than those specified by the Riksdag. All orders in conflict with this provision shall be void.

Art. 69. When the proposals of the competent committee with reference to the establishment of the budget, or the entire amount necessary according to the budget by means of taxation, or matters concerning the expenses and income of the National Debt Office, or the principles of direction and administration of the National Debt Office, come before the Riksdag for deliberation, the provisions of the Riksdag Act regarding the consideration of proposals submitted by the committees shall apply. Should the houses reach conflicting decisions which can not be reconciled, each house shall vote separately on the different decisions previously reached by each of them. The opinion then receiving the majority of the aggregate number of votes of both houses shall constitute the decision of the Riksdag.

Art. 70. Whenever the houses disagree with regard to regulations for the Bank of Sweden, as to its income and expenditures, or as to discharging the Commissioners of the Bank from their responsibility, each house shall vote separately as provided in the preceding Article.

Art. 71. The same procedure shall also be followed when the houses do not agree upon the grounds for any tax, the manner of its application or repartition.

Art. 72. The Bank of Sweden shall remain under the guarantee of the Riksdag, and shall be administered by the Commissioners appointed for that purpose, in accordance with a law enacted jointly by the King and the Riksdag.

The Commissioners of the Bank of Sweden shall be seven in number, of whom the King shall appoint one for periods of three years and also a substitute; the other six Commissioners and six substitutes shall be chosen by the Riksdag for the term and in the manner prescribed by The Riksdag Act. The regular member appointed by the King shall preside over the Commissioners, but shall hold no other position in the administration of the Bank. A Commisioner whom the Riksdag refuses to discharge from responsibility shall retire from his position. The appointment by the King of a Commissioner or substitute may be revoked when the King deems such action advisable.

The Commissioners shall elect one of their number to be governor of the

Bank of Sweden, and also, from or outside their number, a substitute to take the governor's place with full power and responsibility when the latter is unavoidably absent.

The Bank of Sweden alone shall have the right to issue bank notes which shall be accepted as legal tender in the realm. These notes shall be redeemed by the Bank, upon demand, in gold at their face value; provided that when, by reason of war, the danger of war, or a severe financial crisis it is considered absolutely necessary to suspend such redemption, the King and the Riksdag jointly or, if the Riksdag is not in session, the King on the initiative of the Commissioners of the Bank of Sweden and after consultation with the Commissioners of the National Debt Office, may permit such suspension for a certain period of time. Such permission when given by the King between sessions of the Riksdag, shall after the lapse of that period cease to have effect, if not confirmed by the Riksdag within twenty days from the beginning of its next session.

Art. 73. No new taxes, levies of troops, money or goods shall hereafter be imposed, collected or demanded without the free will and consent of the Riksdag, in the manner provided above.

Art. 74. From the day when, by decision of the King in Council of State, and after the Riksdag, if not in session, has been summoned, the forces of the realm or part thereof are placed upon a war footing, either for the preservation of the neutrality of the realm when, in a war between foreign powers, such neutrality is threatened or violated by any of the belligerents or to ward off an apprehended or actual attack, until the return of the forces to a peace-time footing, the King shall have power, in the forms and manner, and under the conditions, and with the obligation of the State to indemnify, prescribed by special legislation enacted jointly by the King and the Riksdag to make requisitions upon local authorities or private individuals for such necessities and services as may be available locally and are required to meet such indispensable needs of the armed forces as can not be otherwise met with sufficient expedition.

Art. 75. The annual table of market rates shall be prepared by persons chosen in the manner specially provided by the Riksdag; the rates thus determined shall be in force until their modification is sought and obtained in the proper manner.

Art. 76. The King can not, without the consent of the Riksdag, contract loans at home or abroad or burden the realm with new debts.

Art. 77. The King may not, without the consent of the Riksdag, alienate from the crown by sale, mortgage, grant or otherwise, royal demesnes and farms with the houses and appurtenances thereof, royal forests, parks and preserves, the royal grazing meadows, and the salmon or other fisheries belonging to the crown or other crown lands. Such property shall be administered in accordance with principles established by the Riksdag; but persons and communities that, according to the law hitherto in force, are now in possession or enjoyment of such crown property may retain their legal rights therein, and cultivated or cultivable land in the royal forests may be sold in the traditional manner to private individuals subject to taxes in accordance with the laws now in force or hereafter to be enacted.

Art. 78. No part of the realm may be severed therefrom by sale, mortgage, grant or in any similar manner.

Art. 79. 1. No change shall be made in the arms or flag of the realm without the consent of the Riksdag.

2. Nor shall any change be made in the standard of the money of the realm, either by way of increase or decrease, without the consent of the Riksdag; the King's right to coin money shall, however, remain unaffected.

Art. 80. The cavalry and infantry and the naval forces shall continue under the system of recruitment and service based on the contracts and military tenure arrangements made with the rural districts and towns; this system shall not be altered in its fundamental principles until the King and the Riksdag jointly agree upon the necessity of some change; no new or increased conscription can be imposed except by common decision of the King and the Riksdag.

Should a special law abolish the military tenure system and establish some other principle for organization of the ground and naval forces, no change may be made in such law except by agreement between the King and the Riksdag.

Art. 81. This Instrument of Government and the other fundamental laws of the realm can not be altered or repealed except by decision of the King and two Riksdags.

When the Riksdag announces its decision to the King with reference to a fundamental law, the King shall, if the decision includes consent to a proposal made by him, cause such constitutional amendment to be publicly proclaimed before the Riksdag adjourns; and the King's decision on the subject shall be communicated to the Riksdag by means of an open letter which shall be read in each house simultaneously by the member of the Council of State designated by the King for that purpose. If the Riksdag adopts a proposal relating to a fundamental law which is initiated in the Riksdag itself, the King shall consult the entire Council of State on the matter and, if he concurs in the proposal, shall cause that fact to be announced by proclamation and open letter in the time and manner above stated. If the King does not give his consent he shall, before the Riksdag adjourns, notify the Riksdag in a written message of his reasons for not approving the decision of the Riksdag.

The right to make decisions which, according to this Constitution belongs to the King and Riksdag either separately or together, or to another organ of the State, when such decisions do not relate to the drawing up, amendment, interpretation or revocation of the Constitution, may, in a limited sphere, be handed over to an internal oral organization for peaceful co-existence of which the country is or is becoming a member. Such a question shall be decided either according to the rules for amending the Constitution or, where delay might be prejudicial to the country, by a decision of both the King and the Riksdag. In the latter case, the decision must be approved by a majority of at least five sixths of the votes in each House which shall include at least three fourths of the members of the Council of State having the right to vote.

Art. 82. Amendments to the fundamental laws adopted by the Riksdag and approved by the King, or proposed by the King and adopted by the Riksdag, in the prescribed manner, shall have force as fundamental law after the reading in the houses of the Riksdag of the open letter mentioned in the preceding Article.

Art. 83. No interpretation of the fundamental laws shall be binding for the future unless adopted in the manner provided for amending such laws.

Art. 84. The fundamental laws shall be applied literally in each particular case.

Art. 85. The following shall be considered fundamental laws: this Instrument of Government, The Riksdag Act, The Act of Succession and The Freedom of the Press Act, all of which shall be adopted by the King and the Riksdag jointly in accordance with the principles laid down in this Instrument of Government.

Art. 86. By freedom of the press is understood the right of every Swedish citizen to publish his writings without any previous interference on the part of public authorities, to be prosecuted afterwards on account of the contents of his publication before a regular court only, and to be punished only if such contents are in conflict with a law enacted to preserve public peace without restricting public enlightenment. All public documents may be published without any restriction whatever, unless otherwise provided by the Freedom of the Press Act.

Art. 87. 1. The Riksdag shall have the power together with the King to enact general civil and criminal laws, and criminal laws for the Armed Forces, and to amend or repeal any such laws previously enacted. Neither the King without the approval of the Riksdag, nor the Riksdag without the consent of the King, shall have the power to make new laws or to repeal existing laws. Proposals on these matters may be introduced in the houses and, after the competent committee has been consulted, a decision shall be made by the Riksdag. If the Riksdag decides, on its own initiative, to adopt a new law or to repeal or amend an existing law, its proposal in the matter shall bo submitted to the King, who shall consult the Council of State and the Law Council regarding it and, after having reached his decision, shall inform the Riksdag of his consent to its request or of his reasons for refusing it. Should the King not be able to make and announce his decision before the adjournment of the Riksdag, he shall be at liberty, before the opening of the next Riksdag, or if the following Riksdag is opened within ten days of the adjournment of the previous Riksdag not later than ten days after its opening, to approve the measure unaltered and cause it to be published. If this does not take place, the proposal shall be regarded as rejected, and the King shall inform the Riksdag at its next meeting of the reasons which prevented the adoption of the measure. If the King considers it appropriate to submit a proposal to the Riksdag, he shall obtain the opinions of the Council of State and the Law Council regarding the matter, and shall communicate his proposition, together with such opinions, to the Riksdag; the latter shall then proceed with the proposition according to the provisions of the Riksdag Act.

2. The Riksdag shall likewise have the power together with the King to enact, amend or repeal ecclesiastical laws, but in such matters the consent of the Synod of the Church shall also be necessary. The views of the Council of State and the Law Council regarding such laws shall be obtained, as in Section 1, and these, together with the King's proposition, when such is made, shall be communicated to the Riksdag. If the proposal in question has not been promulgated as a law before the opening of the Riksdag following next to the one in which the proposal was presented or adopted, or if that following Riksdag is opened within ten days of the adjournment of the preceding Riksdag, not later than ten days after its opening, it shall lapse, and the King shall inform the Riksdag of the reasons which prevented the acceptance of the proposal.

Art. 88. The interpretation of civil, criminal, and ecclesiastical laws shall be dealt with in the same manner as the enactment of such laws. The interpretations which the King gives through the Supreme Court when the Riksdag is not in session, in answer to questions regarding the true meaning of the law, may be overruled at the latest by the Riksdag which meets the following year; if the interpretation relates to an ecclesiastical law, it may also be overruled by the first meeting of the Synod of the Church after its publication. Such interpretations as have thus been overruled shall no longer be valid and shall not be observed or invoked by the courts.

Art. 89. Matters regarding the amendment, interpretation or repeal of law and statutes relating to the general economy of the realm, new laws of this character, and the principles underlying public institutions of all kinds, may be introduced in the houses of the Riksdag. In such matters, however, the Riksdag has no power to make any other decision or do more than submit its representations and wishes to the King; the latter, after consulting the Council of State, shall take such action as he considers appropriate in the interest of the realm. If the King wishes to entrust to the Riksdag, together with himself, the solution of any matter relating to the general administration of the realm, the procedure shall be the same as that prescribed in Article 87, Section 1, regarding questions relating to general civil and criminal laws.

Art. 90. Matters relating to the appointment and removal of officials, the decisions, resolutions and judgments of the executive or judicial authorities, the affairs of private citizens and corporations, or the execution of any law, statute, or regulations, shall in no case or manner be subject to consideration or investigation by the Riksdag, its houses, or committees, except as literally prescribed by the fundamental laws.

Art. 91. Should the King, in the event referred to in Article 39, after leaving the realm, remain out of the realm for more than twelve months, the regent, or the Council of State, if the latter is charged with the government, shall summon the Riksdag by public proclamation, such summons to be published in the public gazette within fifteen days after the expiration of the said period. If the King, duly notified of this action, does not return to the realm, the Riksdag shall take such measures regarding the government of the realm as it finds in the best interest of the realm.

Art. 92. The same procedure shall be followed if the King's illness is of such a nature that he has been unable to perform the duties of his office for more than twelve months.

Art. 93. Should the King die when the heir apparent has not yet reached twenty-five years of ages, the regent or the Council of State, if the latter is charged with the government, shall summon the Riksdag, such summons to be published in the public gazette within fifteen days from the death of the King. The Riksdag shall have the power, without regard to anything in the deceased King's will regarding the administration of the realm, to appoint one regent to exercise the government in the King's name, in accordance with this Instrument of Government, until the King attains twenty-five years of age.

Art. 94. Should it unfortunately occur that the royal dynasty in which is vested the right of succession to the throne becomes extinct in the male line, the Council of State, after the last King's death, within the period prescribed by the preceding Article, shall summon the Riksdag, which shall choose a new royal house; this Instrument of Government being maintained.

Art. 95. If, contrary to expectation, the regent or the Council of State should fail to summon the Riksdag immediately in the cases mentioned in the four preceding Articles, it shall prevail unconditionally on the Courts of Appeal of the realm publicly to proclaim the fact, in order that the Riksdag may assemble to observe and protect its own rights and those of the realm. In such a case the Riksdag shall assemble on the twentieth day after the day the regent or the Council of State should at the latest have issued the summons.

Art. 96. The Riksdag shall appoint at least two citizens of known legal ability and outstanding integrity to act as Ombudsmen to supervise in the capacity of representatives of the Riksdag, according to instructions issued by the Riksdag, the observance of the laws and statutes as applied in all matters by all public officials and employees; and they shall institute proceedings before the competent courts against those who, in the execution of their official duties, have through partiality, favoritism or other cause committed any unlawful act or neglected to perform their official duties properly. The Ombudsmen shall be subject in all respects to the same responsibility and obligation as are prescribed for public prosecutors by general civil and criminal laws and the laws of procedure.

Art. 97. The Ombudsmen of the Riksdag shall be elected by the Riksdag for the time and in the manner provided by the Riksdag Act; and at the same time a deputy for each of them shall also be appointed. The deputy shall possess the same qualifications as the Ombudsman and exercise the office in his stead in the cases provided for by the instructions for the office of Ombudsman.

If a Ombudsman or his deputy no longer enjoys the confidence of the Riksdag, the Riksdag may, on request by the committee examining his conduct in office, discharge him before the end of the time for which he has been elected.

Art. 98. In the event of an Ombudsman resigning the trust confided in him or of an Ombudsman's office otherwise becoming vacant, the deputy shall immediately take over the office; and election of a new Ombudsman shall be undertaken by the Riksdag as soon as possible. In the event of a deputy resigning the trust confided in him or being installed in the office of Ombudsman, or of his office otherwise becoming vacant, a new election of a deputy shall be undertaken. Should an election be necessary while the Riksdag is not in session, the powers of that body with regard to this matter shall be exercised by those Commissioners of the Bank of Sweden and the National Debt Office who are elected by the Riksdag.

Art. 99. The Ombudsmen may, whenever they consider it necessary in the exercise of their duties, attend the deliberations and decisions of all courts and authorities but shall have no right to express their views on such occasions; they shall also have access to the minutes and records of all courts and authorities. The King's officials in general are bound to afford the Ombudsmen lawful assistance, and all public prosecutors shall aid them in the bringing of actions when requested to do so.

Art. 100. It shall be the duty of the each Ombudsman to present to the Riksdag, in accordance with their instructions, an annual report on the administration of his office, in which each shall give an account of the administration of justice throughout the realm, to call attention to defects in the laws and statutes and make suggestions for their improvement.

Art. 101. Should it happen, contrary to expectation, that either the entire Supreme Court, or one or more of its members, is found to have rendered, by reason of self-interest, iniquity or negligence, such a wrongful judgment, in conflict with clear law and evidence of facts duly established, that it causes or might have caused someone loss of life, personal liberty, honor or property; or if the Supreme Administrative Court or one or more of its members, is found to have been guilty of such conduct in the hearing of administrative cases on appeal, it shall be the duty of the Ombudsmen, as it shall be within the power of the King's Attorney General, to institute proceedings against the offender before the court of the realm hereinafter provided and to call him to responsibility in accordance with the law of the realm.

Art. 102. This Court, to be known as the Court of Impeachment, shall in such cases be composed of the President of the *Svea* Court of Appeal, who shall preside, the presidents of all the administrative boards of the realm; and, in actions against the Supreme Court, the four senior justices of the Supreme Administrative Court or, if the Supreme Administrative Court is arraigned, the four senior justices of the Supreme Court; and in both cases, the commandant of the troops on duty in the capital city; the highest officer present of the units of the fleet stationed at the capital city; the two senior members of the *Svea* Court of Appeal; and the senior member of each of the administrative boards of the realm. When the Attorney General or either of the Ombudsmen considers himself justified in prosecuting the Supreme Court, or the Supreme Administrative Court as a whole or individual members thereof, he shall request the President of the *Svea* Court of Appeal, as President of the Court of Impeachment, to issue a summons in legal form to the person or persons to be prosecuted. The President of the Court of Appeal shall then make arrangements for the meeting of the Court of Impeachment in order that the summons may be issued and the matter dealt with further according to law. Should he, contrary to expectation, fail to do this, or should any of the above mentioned officials refuse to participate in the Court of Impeachment, they shall be legally responsible for such intentional neglect of their official duty. If one or more members of the Court of Impeachment has a legitimate excuse, or if there is legal ground for disqualification of any of them, a quorum shall nevertheless exist if the Court consits of twelve persons. If the President of the Court of Appeal is prevented from acting by a legitimate excuse or legal ground of disqualification, the senior of the presidents in service shall take his place. After the trial has been terminated and the sentence pronounced in accordance with law, the Court shall hand down the judgment in open session. No one shall have the power to modify this judgment; the King, however, may grant pardon, which shall not extend to a reinstatement of the convicted person in the service of the realm.

Art. 103. Every fourth year the Riksdag shall, in the manner provided by the Riksdag Act, appoint a delegation whose duty it shall be to decide whether all the members of the Supreme Court and of the Supreme Administrative Court deserve to be retained in their important office, or if, without any of them having demonstrably committed the offences or crimes referred to in the preceding Article, it might yet be deemed that they ought to be deprived of their offices. Should this delegation, after voting in the manner prescribed by the Riksdag Act, decide that one or more of the members of the Supreme Court or the Supreme Administrative Court shall be considered to be excluded from the confidence of the Riksdag, the person or persons in question shall be graciously discharged from their offices by the King, to whom the Riksdag shall report its decision. The King shall, however, grant to each person an annual pension amounting to one half of his salary.

Art. 104. The Riksdag shall not enter into any special examination of decisions of the Supreme Court or of the Supreme Administrative Court, nor shall any general consideration of such matters take place in the delegation.

Art. 105. It is incumbent on the Committee on the Constitution to ask for the minutes kept by the Council of State. The separate minutes referred to in Article 9 may only be demanded, however, with reference to a particular matter specified by the Committee. In such case the King shall consider whether, in the light of the security of the realm or of other particularly important reasons determined by relations with foreign powers, he finds any objection to the delivery of the minutes to the Committee. They shall not be refused until the Advisory Council on Foreign Affairs has had an opportunity to express its views on the subject.

Minutes relating to matters of military command may be demanded only with reference to matters already generally known and specified by the Committee.

Art. 106. If the Committee discovers from these minutes that any member of the Council of State has manifestly acted in violation of the fundamental or general laws of the realm, or has supported such violation or neglected to make representations against it, or has occasioned or encouraged it by wilful concealment of any information, or that the Councillor of State submitting a matter to the King has failed to refuse his countersignature or signature to a decision of the King in the cases contemplated in Article 38 of this Instrument of Government, the Committee on the Constitution shall cause an action to be brought against such person by the Ombudsmen before the Court of Impeachment, and the proceedings shall be instituted in accordance with the provisions of Articles 101 and 102 regarding proceedings against the Supreme Administrative Court. Whenever members of the Council of State are found guilty in the manner mentioned above, the Court of Impeachment shall sentence them in accordance with general civil and criminal law and with the special statute defining their responsibility to be enacted by the King and the Riksdag.

Art. 107. Should the Committee on the Constitution observe that the members of the Council of State collectively or one or more of them, in their advice upon public measures, have not paid due regard to the true welfare of the State, or that any Councillor of State has failed to perform his duties with impartiality, zeal, ability and energy, it shall bring the matter to the knowledge of the Riksdag, which, if it finds that the welfare of the realm so requires, may inform the King in writing of its desire that he remove from the Council of State and from office the person or persons critized.

Questions of this character may be introduced in the houses of the Riksdag and may be presented to the houses by committees other than the Committee on the Constitution, but no decision shall be made by the Riksdag until the latter Committee has been heard on the subject. In the consideration of such matters by the Riksdag, decisions of the King with reference to the rights and affairs of private individuals or corporations may not even be mentioned, much less made the subject of any consideration by the Riksdag.

Everything that the Riksdag, after examination, has approved or left without comment shall be considered to have won acceptance as regards the points examined, and no further examination of the same matter shall be undertaken by another Riksdag for the purpose of fixing responsibility; nevertheless, notwithstanding the general inspection of the expenditure of public funds made by committees or auditors of the Riksdag, it shall be incumbent on the proper officials to make such special audits as pertain to their official duties.

Art. 108. The King has the right to dissolve the Riksdag provided that, in accordance with the provisions of the Riksdag Act, he orders new elections to one or both houses. If the Riksdag has been dissolved, it shall convene within three months of the dissolution upon a date set by the King, and it may not be dissolved again by the King until four months from the beginning of the last meeting have elapsed.

Art. 109. If, contrary to expectation, the Riksdag has not passed the budget or voted new taxes before the beginning of the new fiscal year, the former budget and taxes shall remain in force until the new budget is passed and new taxes voted.

Art. 110. No member of the Riksdag shall be prosecuted or deprived of his liberty on account of his actions or utterances in that capacity unless the house to which he belongs has authorized such action by an explicit decision, adopted by at least fives sixths of those voting. No member of the Riksdag shall be banished from the place where the Riksdag meets. Should any private individual or body, military or civil, or any group of people of whatever name, either on its own initiative or under under orders, do violence to the Riksdag, its houses or committees, or any one of its members, or disturb the freedom of its discussions and decisions, such action, whenever it does not amount to treason, shall be regarded as rebellion; all provisions regarding attempt, preparation or conspiracy to rebellion and neglect to reveal such crimes shall also be applicable. It shall appertain to the Riksdag to cause such crimes to be prosecuted in accordance with law.

If a member of the Riksdag, during a session or when proceeding to or from a session, when the nature of his travel is known, is molested by word or action, the provisions of the general criminal law regarding assaults upon or insults to the King's officers in, or because of, the exercise of their duties shall apply. The same law shall apply to assaults upon or insults to the Riksdag's Commissioners, Auditors, Ombudsmen, the secretaries or employees of either house, or any of their committees, in, or because of, the exercise of their duties.

Art. 111. If a member of the Riksdag is accused of a gross misdemeanor he may not, unless he was caught in the act, be committed to custody until the judge, after investigation, considers such action justifiable; nevertheless, if he does not appear on the summons of the court, the provisions of the general civil and criminal laws relating to such cases shall apply. No member of the Riksdag shall be deprived of his liberty in any other cases than those mentioned in this and the preceding Article.

The Commissioners of the Bank of Sweden and of the National Debt Office and the auditors of the Riksdag may not, in, or for the exercise of, their duties, receive orders from anyone except the Riksdag, and in accordance with its instructions, nor may they be called to account or responsibility except by decision of the Riksdag.

Art. 112. No public official or employee may make an improper use of his authority in the election of members of the Riksdag. Should he do so he shall be deprived of his post.

Art. 113. Assessors whose duty it is, on behalf of the Riksdag, to apply the provisions of the laws on taxation can not be held liable on account on the charges or assessments they make.

Art. 114. The ancient privileges, advantages, rights and liberties of the Estates of the Realm shall remain in force, except those intrinsically connected with the right of representation formerly appertaining to the Estates, and ceasing to exist with that right. They shall not be altered or abolished except by joint decision of the King and the Riksdag, and with the consent of the nobility if their privileges, advantages, rights and liberties are in question, or of the Synod of the Church if those of the clergy are concerned.

In witness hereof we have put our names and seals to attest, confirm and endorse the same, in Stockholm on the sixth day of June, in the year of our Lord 1809.

Everything as herein provided we not only accept for ourselves as the established fundamental law, but also direct and graciously command all who are united in loyalty, fealty, and obedience to us, our successors and the realm, to acknowledge, observe, follow and obey this Instrument of

Government. In witness whereof we have with our own hand signed and confirmed it, and duly affixed our royal seal below, in Stockholm, our city of residence, on the sixth day of June in the year of our Lord and Savior Jesus Christ 1809.

The Riksdag Act

June 22, 1866, as amended up to and including the year 1953

We, CARL, by the Grace of God, King of Sweden, Norway, the Goths and the Wends, hereby make known that as the Estates of the Realm in the manner conforming to the fundamental law have adopted the proposal brought forward by us regarding a new Riksdag Act, this Riksdag Act in accordance with Article 82 of the Instrument of Government shall have the force of a fundamental law exactly as follows word for word:

We, the undersigned Estates of the Realm of Sweden, counts, barons, bishops, nobles, clergy, burghers and peasants, who are now, on our own behalf and on behalf of our brethren at home, assembled at a general Riksdag, hereby make known that as the King in Council by means of a gracious proposition of January 5, 1863, has delivered for our consideration a proposal for a new Riksdag Act, in accordance with Article 81 of the Instrument of Government, we have, following the procedure prescribed by the fundamental law for such important business, adopted the aforementioned graciously presented proposal as follows:

GENERAL PRINCIPLES

Art. 1. 1. The Swedish people are represented by the Riksdag, divided into two houses, the Upper House and the Lower House, which in all matters shall have equal competence and authority.

In the exercise of their duties members of the Riksdag (Riksdagmen) can not be bound by other instructions than the fundamental laws of the realm.

2. Should it be deemed necessary in view of the particular importance or character of some measure to ascertain the opinion of the people before the decision, the King and the Riksdag may, by a law enacted jointly, provide that a referendum shall be held, in accordance with the provisions of Article 49, Section 2, of the Instrument of Government.

Art. 2. By virtue of the Instrument of Government and without special summons the Riksdag shall convene annually on the 10th of January, or, if that be a holiday, on the following day. Nothing shall prevent the King, however, if he considers it necessary, to summon the Riksdag at an earlier date.

The Spring session of the Riksdag shall adjourn not later than May 31; however, if it is considered that the business pending can be finished by not later than June 15, the Riskdag may, after consultation with the Speakers' Conference referred to in Article 50, decide that the session shall continue up until the last named date. If the Riksdag according to Article 58 has postponed the consideration of business pending to the autumn session, the Speakers shall summon the Riksdag to an autumn session beginning on the first suitable day after October 15; the session shall continue thereafter as long as it is necessary. The Riksdag shall adjourn not later than December 31; however, the King may, when particular reasons warrant, decide to postpone the adjournment of the Riksdag, with a corresponding extension of expiring terms of office. The adjournment shall take place not later than the day before the beginning of the spring session of the next Riksdag.

During the time when the Riksdag is not in session, the King may also, if he deems it necessary, summon the Riksdag to an extra session.

If the Riksdag is not in session, sixty-five members of the Upper House or one hundred members of the Lower House may request the summoning of the Riksdag to an extra session, in which case special reasons prompting the action shall be given and the summons issued not later than twenty days after the request has been presented.

Provisions for the summoning of the Riksdag on certain special occasions are contained in Articles 91, 92, 93, 94 and 108 of the Instrument of Government.

Art. 3. Riksdagmen are elected to both houses for a definite period of time. The King has the right, however, to order new elections throughout the entire realm to one or both houses before the expiration of this period.

Art. 4. No one shall prevent a Riksdagman from exercising his duties as a representative; however, in wartime an exception may be made for military personnel, when they are ordered by the King into the service of the realm.

Art. 5. The King has the right to dissolve the Riksdag, provided he orders new elections to one or both houses. If the Riksdag has been dissolved, it shall convene within three months of the dissolution on a date set by the King and it may not be dissolved again until four months from the beginning of the last meeting have elapsed.

THE COMPOSITION OF THE HOUSES

A. Upper House

Art. 6. 1. The members of the Upper House, one hundred and fifty in number, shall be elected by the county councils and the city councils in cities not represented on a county council. Election is for eight years from the beginning of January of the year following the election.

2. For election to the Upper House the realm is divided into constituencies. The cities of Stockholm and Gothenburg each form a separate constituency. Any other city not represented on a county council belongs to the same constituency as the county council area in which the city formerly was included. Several county council areas can be included in one constituency; but no such area shall be divided into separate constituencies. The division into constituencies is set forth in the Electoral Law.

3. Each constituency shall elect one Riksdagman for every full number of its population corresponding to one one hundred and fiftieth part of the population of the realm.

4. For the purpose of attaining a number of Riksdagmen of one hundred and fifty, where the number of Riksdagmen to be elected after the application of the provisions in Section 3 does not reach that figure, those constituencies whose population most exceeds the number which according to the same Section governs the distribution of Riksdagmen among the constituencies, shall be entitled to elect an additional Riksdagman.

5. The number of Riksdagmen to be elected from each constituency according to the above mentioned principles, is established every tenth year by the King; the number of Riksdagmen for a constituency shall not, however, on account of what is thus established, be reduced during the current election period.

6. If, when the provisions of Section 5 are to be applied, there are not so many vacancies within the house that all the constituencies for which an increase in the number of Riksdagmen ought to occur, can at the same time be entitled to the right to elect the full number of Riksdagmen, the following principles shall be applied in establishing the order in which these constituencies shall be entitled to this right: constituencies for which the increase in the number of Riksdagmen is based on the provisions in Section 3 shall have priority over those for which the increase is derived from the provisions in Section 4; among constituencies which on account of provisions in Section 3 shall choose an increased number of Riksdagmen, priority is given to the constituency for which the number is the largest, or, if the number is equal for two or more constituencies, the one among them whose population most exceeds the number which according to the same Section governs the distribution of Riksdagmen among the constituencies; among constituencies which pursuant to Section 4 have the right to choose an increased number of Riksdagmen priority shall be given the one in which the excess defined in the same Section is largest; and in those cases where this excess, equally large in two or more constituencies, can not serve as a basis for the determination of priority among them, priority shall be established by lot before the head of the Ministry of Justice, in

the presence of three of the Commissioners of the Bank of Sweden and three of the Commissioners of the National Debt Office.

7. If several county council areas belong to the same constituency, and if in any of the areas the number of council members is larger than the number which would have been chosen provided the rules governing the election to the county council of another area within the constituency had been applied, then no more councilmen in the first named area shall participate in the election of Riksdagmen than the number corresponding to the rules just mentioned; and therefore the county council in the area, when election to the Riksdag is to be held in the constituency, shall select such a number of its members as should take part in the election to the Riksdag.

If one or several cities which are not represented on a county council belong to the same constituency as the county council area, then no more city council members in such a city, or cities, shall take part in the election of Riksdagmen than the number which according to the population in the city, or cities, corresponds to the general rules concerning elections to county councils; and therefore when election to the Riksdag for the constituency is to be held, the city council, or councils, shall select such a number of its members as should take part in the election to the Riksdag; the city council, or councils, when selecting such electors shall also select, from among council members, substitutes for the electors.

Election provided for in this Section shall be proportional and in accordance with specifications set forth in legislation enacted jointly by the King and the Riksdag.

Where a county councilman who has been selected an elector is unable to perform his duties a substitute shall be called in the order generally applicable in cases of unavoidable absence on the part of councilmen. If a city councilman who has been selected an elector is similarly incapacitated he shall without delay inform the court in the city which shall call the proper substitute to participate in the election.

8. If a constituency for election of members of the Upper House comprises several counties, or parts of several counties, it shall be incumbent upon the County Governor in the one of those counties named by the King to attend to all those matters connected with the election, which, according to what is provided concerning such matters, devolves upon the County Governor.

Art. 7. 1. Constituencies shall be divided into eight groups. This division is set forth in the Electoral Law.

2. Each year during the month of October an election shall be held within one of the groups mentioned in Section 1 for the eight year period following that year. The order to be observed among the groups in holding elections is prescribed in the Electoral Law.

3. If the King has ordered new elections throughout the entire realm,

an election shall be held in each constituency for the time not yet expired of the eight year period for which elections last were held within the group to which the constituency belongs.

4. If a Riksdagman in one constituency has retired before the expiration of the eight year period, or if the seat, when the eight year period for a constituency has expired, shall be transferred from that constituency to a constituency in another group, the seat shall be filled in the manner provided in the Electoral Law for the time until the expiration of the eight year period for which election last was held in the constituency entitled to the seat; provided that when the seat is already filled for the time after the current year, the seat shall be held only for the time until the end of the year.

Art. 8. Elections to the Upper House shall be proportional in all cases where two or more Riksdagmen are to be elected.

Further provisions regarding these elections are given in the Electoral Law.

Art. 9. Only men and women who are entitled to vote in local affairs and who have attained the age of twenty-three years can be elected as members of the Upper House. If a Riksdagman, after he has been elected, ceases to be eligible to be a member of the house, he shall reliquish his position.

Art. 10. For each person who has been elected as a member of the Upper House a certificate of election in two copies shall be issued without delay and in the manner set forth in detail by the Electoral Law, one copy to be delivered to the person elected and the other to be sent to the Ministry of Justice.

Art. 11. Whoever has objections to raise over the election of a Riksdagman to the Upper House may humbly file a complaint with the King. For such a purpose the complainant shall request from the proper recorder an appropriate extract from the records which is to be delivered to the complainant within two days; and in order to preserve his right to proceed he shall file his complaint, which shall be addressed to the King, with the County Governor within a month of the completion of the election. By proclamation to be published in the official gazette the Governor shall set a certain brief period in which a humble demurrer may be lodged with him against the complaint. After the lapse of that time the County Governor shall send the documents concerning the complaint together with whatever demurrer that may have been made without delay to the King so that the matter may be pleaded and decided promptly by the Supreme Administrativo Court.

Art. 12. If a member of the Upper House wishes to resign he may do so at the time of the election, or later, when the Riksdag is not in session, by notifying the County Governor.

B. Lower House

Art. 13. The members of the Lower House shall be two hundred and thirty in number or that larger number which may be occasioned by the application of Article 15, Section 3. They shall be elected for a period of four years, from the beginning of January of the year following election.

Art. 14. The division of the realm into constituencies is set forth in the Electoral Law.

Art. 15. 1. Each constituency shall elect one Riksdagman for every full number of its population at the beginning of the year immediately preceding the four year period for which the election is held corresponding to one two hundred and thirtieth part of the population of the realm.

2. For the purpose of attaining the number of Riksdagmen of two hundred and thirty, in case the number of Riksdagmen to be elected after the application of the provisions in Section 1 does not reach that figure, those constituencies whose population most exceeds the number which according to the same Section governs the distribution of Riksdagmen among the constituencies, each in the order determined by the size of the excess shall be entitled to elect an additional Riksdagman. If the excess number is equal for two or more constituencies priority shall be established when necessary by lot in the manner provided by Article 6, Section 6.

3. If the number of Riksdagmen which according to Section 1 and 2 shall be elected in a constituency is either less than three or at least three but not five the number shall be increased in the former instance to three and in the latter to five.

4. The number of Riksdagmen to be elected from each constituency according to the above designated principles shall be established for each four year period by the King.

Art. 16. Each man and woman who is a Swedish subject and has attained the age of twenty-one years not later than during the calendar year preceding the election year, shall have the right to vote at elections.

The right to vote at elections shall not be exercised, however, by anyone who is under guardianship.

There shall be a record of persons entitled to vote for use at elections; and, in the manner set forth in the Electoral Law, the right to vote at elections shall be based on circumstances existing at te time this record is compiled, changes occurring before the election notwithstanding.

Art. 17. 1. Election of Riksdagmen to the Lower House shall be held the year immediately preceding the four year period for which the election is held, on the day during the month of September designated in the Electoral Law.

2. If the King orders new elections they shall be held without delay for the remainder of the four year period.

3. If a Riksdagman retires before the period for which he was elected

has expired, the seat shall be filled in the manner provided for in the Electoral Law. If the seat is to be filled by new election, such election shall be held without delay for the remaining period.

Art. 18. Elections to the Lower House shall be direct and when two or more Riksdagmen are to be elected, proportional. At these elections each voter shall have an equal vote.

Further provisions concerning the elections are given in the Electoral Law.

Art. 19. Only men and women who have attained the age of twenty-three years and have the right to vote within the constituency or, in a city consisting of several constituencies, in one of them, can be elected as members of the Lower House.

Art. 20. For each person who has been elected a member of the Lower House a certificate of election in two copies shall be issued without delay in the manner set forth in detail by the Electoral Law, one copy to be delivered to the person elected and the other to be sent to the Ministry of Justice.

Art. 21. If a member of the Lower House wishes to resign he may do so at the time of the election, or later, when the Riksdag is not in session, by notifying the County Governor.

Art. 22. Whoever has objections to raise over the election of a Riksdagman to the Lower House may humbly file a complaint with the King. For such a purpose the complainant shall request of the County Governor an appropriate extract from the records which is to be delivered to the complainant within three days; and in order to preserve his right to proceed he shall file his complaint, which shall be addressed to the King, with the County Governor within ten days after completion of the election. In the manner prescribed in Article 11 the Governor shall allow those concerned the opportunity to demur. After the time set for making demurrers has expired the County Governor shall send the complaint together with all other documents in the case without delay to the King, whereupon the case shall be disposed of in the manner set forth in Article 11.

C. Provisions Applicable to Both Houses

Art. 23. Members of the Riksdag are entitled to a salary and traveling expenses out of public funds. Further provisions concerning this matter are prescribed in an act jointly adopted by the King and the Riksdag.

Art. 24. The right to vote may not be exercised by anyone entitled to vote unless he appears personally at the place of election in the manner prescribed in the Electoral Law; provided that citizens entitled to vote, who are prevented from appearing in person as a consequence of an absence from the realm or on account of duties relating to their occupations or professions may, to the extent and under the conditions provided for in the aforementioned law, vote before the election, and provided that a spouse may, in the manner prescribed in the same law, submit a completed ballot through the other spouse if the latter is also entitled to vote.

Art. 25. Election of Riksdagmen is carried out by secret ballot. If more than half the number of ballots are invalid a new election shall be held.

Art. 26. Membership of the Riksdag can be held only by Swedish citizens.

No one shall be accepted as a Riksdagman

(a) who is under guardianship,

(b) who is a bankrupt,

(c) who has been convicted of having tried to solicit votes at an election to the Riksdag by money or gifts, or who has given his vote in return for recompense, or who has interfered with the freedom of election by means of violence or threat.

The provisions in general or special laws according to which a person who is sentenced to punishment in certain cases shall also be sentenced to be deprived of such public office as he may have held, or be disqualified from taking up such office, shall also be applied with regard to membership of the Riksdag.

Art. 27. In anyone is elected for the same time a member of both houses, or a member of one house from two or more constituencies, he shall have the right to decide in which house he is to sit or for which constituency he wants to regard himself as elected Riksdagman. It is his duty, however, to notify promptly the County Governor in the area for which he does not accept the position of Riksdagman.

Art. 28. 1. While the Riksdag is in session the Speakers of each house shall notify the King of the vacant seats within their respective houses which shall be filled during the same Riksdag or before the next, whereupon the King shall enjoin his county governors to make arrangements for the selection of new Riksdagmen to take the place of the retired members.

2. If a vacancy in either house occurs owing to the retirement of a member during the time when the Riksdag is not in session, it is incumbent upon the County Governor to proceed in the manner set forth in Section 1.

Art. 29. A Riksdagman may not resign while the Riksdag is in session unless he shows such cause preventing him from carrying out the duties of a Riksdagman as will be accepted by the house to which he belongs, provided that by this provision no change is made in what is stated above concerning the right to resign at the time of election.

Art. 30. If the realm is at war or in danger of war the King and the Riksdag jointly may decide, if it is found absolutely necessary, that election to the Riksdag shall be postponed for one year at the most from the time the election would normally have been held, and that the election period which would have expired shall be extended by one year. At the same time it may be decided that the term of the election that takes place for the election postponed shall be reduced by one year. Decisions taken by authority of this paragraph may be repeated.

For a valid decision of the Riksdag according to the first paragraph it is necessary that a division be taken and that at least three fourths of those voting in each house concur in the decision.

The extension of the period of election does not curtail the right of the King to order new elections.

THE BEGINNING AND DISSOLUTION OF THE RIKSDAG

Art. 31. The Riksdag shall meet in the capital city of the realm unless hostile invasion, pestilence or other equally grave circumstances make it impossible or dangerous to the liberty or security of the Riksdag. It devolves upon the King in such instances to designate and announce another place of meeting in the manner specified in Article 50 of the Instrument of Government.

Art. 32. 1. Before the Riksdag convenes, the certificates of election, issued for the members of the Riksdag and received by the Ministry of Justice, shall be examined before the head of the Ministry, or before the person designated by the King to act in his stead, in the presence of three of the Commissioners of the Bank of Sweden chosen by the Riksdag, and three of the Commissioners of the National Debt Office. This examination, the purpose of which is to investigate whether the certificates of election have been issued in the prescribed form, shall be completed not later than the day before the beginning of the Riksdag. If certificates of election arrive after the beginning of the Riksdag such examination shall take place immediately.

2. It devolves upon each house, however, to pass on the competence to exercise the duties of Riksdagmen not only for those members whose certificates of election have not been approved but also for those against whom objections based on this fundamental law have otherwise been raised. The member whose right to exercise the duties of a Riksdagman is being questioned in the house shall nevertheless retain his position as a member of the Riksdag until he has been declared imcompetent by the house.

Art. 33. 1. As soon as the Riksdag is convened and the report made by the head of the Ministry of Justice, or the person designated to act in his stead on the examination prescribed in Section 1 of the preceding Article has been communicated to each of the houses as far as its members are concerned, each house shall elect from among its members a Speaker and a First and a Second Deputy Speaker.

At the election of Speakers and Deputy Speakers the candidate who has received more than half of the votes cast shall be considered elected. Further provisions concerning such elections are given in the Riksdag Regulations, mentioned in Article 78.

2. Before the election mentioned in the first Section takes place, the member present who has attended the greatest number of Riksdags, or, if there are two or more members who have attended an equal number, the one of them who is the oldest in years, shall preside.

3. If a Speaker or Deputy dies or resigns his position during a Riksdag, the house shall elect as soon as possible a new Speaker or Deputy Speaker.

4. If both the Speaker and the Deputy Speakers of a house are unavoidably absent at the same time another member shall be elected by the house, under the chairmanship as provided in Section 2, to act as Speaker until one of them again resumes his duties.

Art. 34. The King shall cause the time designated by him for the opening of the Riksdag to be publicly proclaimed. This time may not be fixed for a later date than the second weekday after the beginning of the Riksdag. At that time the Riksdagmen, after a religious service has been held, shall assemble in the Hall of State where the King, or if he finds it suitable, the Prime Minister or another member of the Council of State shall preside. On this occasion the King will cause to be delivered to the Riksdag in two copies, of which one shall be given to each house, the proposition as to the state and requirements of the administration, containing also a proposal relating to the manner of providing by taxation for the needs of the State in excess of the standing revenues, as well as the report on what has occurred in the government of the realm since the beginning of the preceding Riksdag. If, however, in accordance with Article 2, the King has summoned the Riksdag to convene on a day before January 10, the proposition and the report mentioned may be presented to the houses in a different manner although not later than at the first meeting after the 11th of January.

At a Riksdag convening after dissolution according to Article 5, the report just mentioned shall not be delivered, and the proposition concerning the state and requirements of the administration shall be presented only if the budget has not been passed.

When the King, in the manner here provided for, has opened the Riksdag, the Speakers of the houses on the same occasion shall convey to the King in the name of the houses their loyal respect.

Art. 35. If, when the Riksdag is in session, the King desires to order new general elections to one or both houses, the King, after he has caused the Riksdag to be called to the Hall of State, shall communicate this decision to the Riksdag. The decision may also, if the King deems it appropriate, be announced to the Riksdag by open letter, which shall be read simultaneously in both houses by the member of the Council of State designated by the King. The Riksdag shall be dissolved immediately after the reading.

THE PREPARATION OF BUSINESS

Art. 36. 1. At each Riksdag, within six days after the opening of the Riksdag, the following committees shall be constituted: one Committee on Foreign Affairs, one Committee on the Constitution, one Committee, of Supply, one Committee of Ways and Means, one Committee on Banking, three Committees on Laws, one Committee on Agriculture and one Committee on Miscellaneous Affairs. These standing committees of the Riksdag shall consist of the following number of members, half the number always to be chosen by each house from among its own members; the Committee on Foreign Affairs 16, the Committee on the Constitution 20, the Committee of Supply 30, the Committee of Ways and Means 20, the Committee on Banking 16, the Committees on Laws 16 each, the Committee on Agriculture 20 and the Committee on Miscellaneous Affairs 24. By joint decision the houses, whenever it is considered necessary, may resolve to constitute a special committee to take up questions belonging to the jurisdiction of a standing committee, and also, whenever a committee other than the Committee on Foreign Affairs reports a need for an increase in the number of committee members, to provide for such enlargement.

If a question is closely associated with a subject matter under the jurisdiction of a certain standing committee the question may be referred to that committee, notwithstanding that the matter according to regulations in Articles 37–44 ought to have been dealt with by another standing committee.

2. If a question is raised in a house which concerns that house only, a Committee on House Internal Matters may be constituted within the house, consisting of as many members as the house deems necessary.

3. Each house shall also choose from among its members substitutes to take the place of committee members who resign or are temporarily unable to fulfil their duties. The number of substitutes for members of the Committee on Foreign Affairs shall be eight from each house.

4. At a Riksdag convening after dissolution, provided for in Article 5, no more committees than necessary shall be constituted.

5. Elections to committees shall be governed by the provisions in Article 75 below as well as the Riksdag Regulations, mentioned in Article 78.

6. Members of the Council of State may not participate in elections to the Committee on the Constitution; nor may a former Council of State member participate in the first election to the Committee on the Constitution following the termination of his service.

Neither members of the Council of State nor justices of the Supreme Court or the Supreme Administrative Court may participate in committees, with the exception indicated in Article 37, Section 2, for the Committee on Foreign Affairs.

No one whom the Riksdag can call to account may be elected to a committee in which his own official action might be reviewed, provided that former members of the Council of State shall not be excluded from being elected to the Committee of Supply, in which, however, such a member shall not have the right to participate in the consideration of business defined in Article 39, Section 2.

Art. 37. 1. The Committee on Foreign Affairs shall make reports and submit proposals with regard to matters referred to it which concern the relations of the realm with foreign powers and are not subject to the jurisdiction of another committee.

2. When a matter submitted by the King to the Riksdag is on the agenda of the Committee all available documents shall be communicated to the Committee.

The Prime Minister, the Minister for Foreign Affairs, as well as, when the nature of the matter under consideration so warrants, any other member of the Council of State, may personally or through a public official communicate verbal or written information to the Committee.

3. If in the opinion of the King or the Committee information submitted on a certain matter is of such a character that it should be kept secret for reasons of the security of the realm or for other extremely important reasons based on the relations with foreign powers the members of the Committee shall be committed to secrecy. The first time a member, or a substitute, is present at a meeting of the Committee he shall vow to observe such commitments.

Art. 38. 1. It devolves upon the Committee on the Constitution to examine the fundamental laws, the law restricting the right of access to public documents, the Electoral Law, the statute on emoluments for the performance of the duties of Riksdagmen, as well as the Riksdag Regulations adopted pursuant to Article 78, and to propose to the Riksdag those amendments thereto which the Committee considers most necessary or useful and possible to effect, and, also, to report on matters referred to the Committee from the houses concerning these enactments.

2. The Committee shall further make reports and submit proposals with regard to matters referred to it which concern the enactment, amendment, interpretation or repeal of laws relating to local government and the laws and statutes on the responsibility of the Council of State, on the number of ministries and Council members without portfolio, on matters of military command, on the arms and flag of the realm, on the Synod of the Church, and on general referendum in questions not subject to the jurisdiction of another committee.

3. It is incumbent upon the Committee to ask for the minutes kept in the Council of State, provided that what is prescribed in Article 105 of the

Instrument of Government shall obtain with regard to certain minutes. The provisions of the Instrument of Government govern the right and duty of the Committee, after inspection of the minutes, to report criticisms to the Riksdag arising from this inspection or to take such other action as may be necessary with reference to reported censure, and, also, when a question has been raised by a Riksdagman or a committee other than the Committee on the Constitution that the Council of State or one of its members has exercised his office in an unauthorized manner, to report on the matter before it is decided upon by the Riksdag.

4. It devolves upon the Committee likewise to render a decision when differences arise between the houses as to which committee a matter under discussion ought to be referred, and also to render a decision when a difference arises between a house and its Speaker concerning a refusal of the latter to put a matter to a vote.

5. If in the opinion of the Committee information submitted on a certain matter is of such a character that it should be kept secret for reasons of the security of the realm or for other extremely important reasons based on the relations with foreign powers the members of the Committee shall be committed to secrecy. The first time a member or a substitute is present at a meeting of the Committee he shall vow to observe such commitments.

Art. 39. 1. It is incumbent upon the Committee of Supply to which shall be communicated the proposition issued to the Riksdag by the King concerning the state and requirements of the administration and which Committee shall also have access to all governmental accounts and documents, to inspect, investigate and give account of the state and administration of the government insofar as it does not concern agricultural matters, the cost of the Riksdag, the activities of its auditors or the expenses for the Riksdag building, or the offices and agencies of the Riksdag, and to propose what is necessary to meet the needs of government with due consideration for the reductions and saving that ought to be effected. It is likewise incumbent upon the Committee either jointly, in the manner prescribed by Article 47, or otherwise, after consultation with the other committees handling budgetary matters, to estimate the standing revenue, to report the need of taxation, and to draw up a proposed budget.

2. It devolves upon the Committee, furthermore, to examine and inspect whether completed or authorized disbursements from public funds have not exceeded the total of the main headings which were set by the Riksdag in the final budget, and whether disbursements have been based on duly established budget accounts, or the King's directions for payment issued in the prescribed manner, and verified by the receipt required from those persons who have received the funds. If, contrary to the decisions of the Riksdag, the sums appropriated to any main heading are found to have been used for other purposes than those covered by that same main heading, or if any appropriation voted by the Riksdag has been exceeded,

the Committee shall submit a report to the houses on the official who has countersigned or signed such a direction to pay, whereupon the provisions in Articles 106 and 107 of the Instrument of Government shall be applied. The Committee may not, however, in contravention of Article 90 of the Instrument of Government, enter upon any criticism of the King's directions to pay, nor hold those government officials in charge of the state accounts personally responsible to the Committee or the Riksdag; but the Riksdag, when it is found necessary, shall report to the King the grounds that have been brought to its attention for legal action against any such official.

Art. 40. 1. It is incumbent upon the Committee of Ways and Means to prepare all questions concerning taxation referred to the Committee from the houses. The Committee, furthermore, either jointly, in the manner prescribed by Article 47, or otherwise after consultation with the other committees handling budgetary matters, shall estimate the income of each of the several taxes and, after the needs of the administration have been investigated and determined, recommend the manner in which the budget may be balanced by means of taxation. The Committee may also recommend such measures relating to matters of taxation as it considers just, reasonable and useful.

2. It devolves upon the Committee, moreover, to make reports and present proposals in matters referred to it by the houses concerning the enactment, amendment, interpretation or repeal of laws and statutes relating to taxation by local government and relating to products containing alcohol, including cases not covered by Section 1.

Art. 41. 1. It is incumbent upon the Committee on Banking to investigate and inquire into the management and state of the Bank of Sweden and the National Debt Office and to propose, and, wherever the Riksdag has delegated such power to the Committee, to make regulations on the management of the Bank of Sweden and the National Debt Office. The Committee shall propose what is necessary to meet the needs of the National Debt Office. The Committee, furthermore, shall make reports and present proposals with reference to those matters referred to the Committee from the houses which concern the use of loan funds administered by the National Debt Office.

2. It devolves upon the Committee, moreover, to make reports and present proposals with regard to matters referred to the Committee from the houses concerning the enactment, amendment, interpretation or repeal of laws and statutes relating to the Bank of Sweden as well as other banking establishments and the currency of the realm, and also such matters concerning the organization and condition of the general economy or particular branches of economic life as are not of the nature to be handled in another committee.

3. The proposition presented by the King concerning the state and

requirements of the administration shall also be communicated to the Committee insofar as the proposition pertains to the expenses of the Riksdag and the activities of its auditors or the expenses for the Riksdag building and the offices and agencies of the Riksdag, and submit reports and proposals occasioned by those parts of the proposition or by matters concerning the subjects mentioned referred to the Committee from the houses.

Art. 42. 1. The Committees on Laws shall make reports and present proposals with regard to matters which, not being subject to the jurisdiction of another committee, are referred to them from the houses concerning the enactment, amendment, interpretation or repeal of civil, criminal or ecclesiastical law or other laws and statutes, which are enacted jointly by the King and the Riksdag.

2. It devolves upon a Committee on Laws moreover to inspect the reports of the Procurators General of Civil and Military Affairs and likewise their official diaries, minutes and registers, and to submit a report on the inspection to the Riksdag. If the Committee finds from the inspection that a Procurator General or his deputy does not deserve the confidence of the Riksdag and that on this account he should be relieved of his duties before the end of the time for which he has been elected, the Committee shall make a recommendation on the matter to the Riksdag in its report.

3. The division among the Committees on Laws of the work under their jurisdiction shall be executed in the manner decided by the Riksdag.

Art. 43. It is incumbent upon the Committee on Agriculture to which shall be communicated the proposition presented by the King to the Riksdag on the state and requirements of the administration insofar as it pertains to agricultural matters, to inspect and, with due consideration to necessary reductions and savings, investigate and give an account of the needs of the administration with reference to that branch of government, and furthermore, to submit reports and proposals concerning agricultural matters referred to the Committee from the houses.

Art. 44. The Committee on Miscellaneous Affairs shall make reports and present proposals on those matters, not under the jurisdiction of another committee and referred to it from the houses, which are of such a nature as to require a committee opinion.

Art. 45. 1. All committees shall meet within two days from the time they are constituted.

2. The committees shall elect, each from among its members, a chairman and a vice-chairman. Until this election has been held, the member who has attended the greatest number of Riksdag, or if there are two or more members who have attended an equal number, the one of them who is the oldest in years, shall preside.

3. The committees shall, as soon as possible, submit such reports as are incumbent upon them.

Art. 46. If a committee needs verbal or written information from any government official or agency, the committee through its chairman may request the King's order, through the member of the Council of State whom the King shall designate for this purpose at each Riksdag, to the proper person or agency to submit the information requested; provided that the Office of the Paymaster General, the Bank of Sweden and the National Debt Office shall submit directly all information requested concerning the accounting of public moneys.

Art. 47. When a standing committee considers it necessary to meet with another standing committee to consider a matter, a meeting shall be held, comprising representatives of the committees, in the manner agreed upon by the committees. Such a combined committee has the right to present reports on questions with which it has dealt without the participation of the other members of the two standing committees.

Art. 48. Open voting shall be used in the committees. If the votes are evenly divided, the chairman shall place in an urn used exclusively for this purpose a yes-ballot and a no-ballot, both exactly alike in size and appearance, printed and unmarked and each closed and rolled up, and the result of the voting is determined by the ballot which one of the members of the committee draws from the voting urn at the request of the chairman.

Elections which occur within committees are governed by the provisions of Article 75, Section 2.

A member who does not concur in the decision of a committee shall retain the right to submit to the houses, along with the report of the committee, his dissenting opinion which in that case is to be presented in writing to the committee. The committee report must not thereby be delayed.

Art. 49. The members and substitutes elected to the Committee on Foreign Affairs provided for in Article 36 also constitute the members and substitutes of the Advisory Council on Foreign Affairs referred to in Article 54 of the Instrument of Government. A member of this Council retains his membership until new elections to the Committee on Foreign Affairs take place. A member of the Advisory Council who ceases to be a member of the Riksdag before the termination of the period for which he was elected to the Riksdag, or who is appointed a member of the Council of State, shall, however, no longer be recognized as a member of the Advisory Council. If the King orders new elections to one or both houses, the members of the Advisory Council retain their membership on the Council notwithstanding.

If a vacancy on the Council arises, it shall be filled by a substitute. If a member is unavoidably absent from a meeting a substitute shall be called upon to serve in his stead. The regulations concerning the order of priority to be observed in calling upon substitutes to the committees of the Riksdag shall also have validity with regard to the Council. A substitute although not called upon to serve as a member on the Council shall nevertheless be given the opportunity to attend the meetings of the Council.

The King convenes the Council as often as business demands, and is chairman of the Council when he is present. In the King's absence, the Prime Minister, or in the latter's absence, the Minister for Foreign Affairs, takes the chair. The King may summon other members of the Council of State, as well as special experts to the meetings. The King appoints the secretary of the Council.

The Council shall be convened if at least six members propose to the Minister for Foreign Affairs that a certain stated question be considered.

The first time a member a substitute is present at a meeting of the Council, he shall vow to observe the rules of secrecy specified in Article 54 of the Instrument of Government.

THE CONSIDERATION

OF BUSINESS IN THE HOUSES

Art. 50. The Speaker shall ensure that the work of the Riksdag is pursued with due promptness and as systematically as possible.

Each house shall choose four members to confer with the Speakers and Deputy Speakers on what should be observed with respect to the consideration of business in the committees and houses in order to attain that end (Speakers' Conference). Further provisions on the Speakers' Conference are given in the Riksdag Regulations mentioned in Article 78.

Art. 51. It is incumbent upon the Speakers or, in case they are unavoidably absent, the Deputy Speakers, each for his house, to summon meetings, to state the business at the meeting, to take notice of, clarify and present the expressed opinions, to put the questions for final decision and maintain order at the meetings, according to the provisions of this fundamental law. However, the member who exercises the functions of the Speaker may not participate in the debates or voting, nor propose anything other than that which is required for the execution of the fundamental laws, of the several decisions of the Riksdag or the houses, or in general of the rules and regulations which have been adopted for the consideration of the business of the Riksdag.

A Speaker does not have the power to adjourn a meeting of a house without its approval.

Art. 52. At a meeting of a house each member has the right, with those exceptions embodied in this Riksdag Act, or in regulations adopted by the house, based on the same Act, to speak freely for the minutes and to elaborate on all matters under consideration and on the lawfulness of everything which occurs within the house.

Each member may speak in the order in which he has registered himself for that purpose and is called by the Speaker. However, in the manner especially prescribed by the house a member may speak in a different order for the purpose of making a reply to another member.

A Riksdagman may, in the manner especially prescribed by the house, pose an interrogation to a member of the Council of State on a subject not appearing on the agenda. Such interrogations are either interpellations or simple questions to elicit information. The house may prescribe limitations on the right of a member to speak in connection with the presentation of interpellations or replies to simple questions.

No one shall have the right to speak without his remarks being recorded in the minutes.

No one shall indulge in personally insulting remarks or otherwise conduct himself in a manner inconsistent with good order. Should this happen and the offender not mend his ways on the Speaker's admonition, the Speaker shall have the right to deprive him of his right to speak. If that has taken place, the offender may not speak again for the remainder of that meeting. If a proposal is presented that the Speaker also issue a warning to the member who has thus misconducted himself or that the matter be referred to the competent court, such a decision shall be taken by the house at the next meeting without previous deliberation.

Art. 53. Neither the Riksdag nor the houses may deliberate or decide on any subject in the presence of the King, nor may regents acting on behalf of a King who is under age be present at the deliberations or decisions of the houses.

The members of the Council of State shall have the right to be present in each house with the right to participate in the debates but not in the decisions if they are not themselves members of the house.

In matters which concern any member of a house personally he may be present at the debates but not at the decision.

Art. 54. The King's written messages and propositions shall be presented to both houses and shall always be accompanied by reports of the Council of State and, when the Law Council has also submitted a report, by that report.

Propositions which refer to the income and expenditure of the State for the next fiscal year shall be presented to the Riksdag within seventy days from its opening, and, with the exception of propositions concerning the final settlement of the budget, such a proposition may not be presented later unless the King considers that delay in presenting it would cause serious detriment to the public interest.

Other propositions are to be presented to the Riksdag within ninety days from its opening, and such a proposition may not be presented later unless the King considers that delay in presenting it would cause detriment to the public interest or otherwise finds that special reasons call for its presentation.

Art. 55. 1. Private members' motions may be introduced by a Riksdagman in the house of which he is a member within fifteen days from the day the proposition concerning the state and requirements of the administration was delivered to the house.

Private members' motions occasioned by a proposition which has been presented after the opening of the Riksdag may, however, be introduced not later than at the first meeting occurring ten days after the proposition was presented to the house, provided that the house in such cases may grant an extension of this time if that is considered necessary owing to intervening holidays or the extraordinary magnitude of the matter concerned. However, the time may not be extended beyond the first meeting occurring fifteen days after the proposition was presented to the house, and the question of extension may not be raised later than at the second meeting after the one at which the proposition was thus presented.

If consideration of a proposition has been postponed to the autumn session, private members' motions occasioned by the proposition may be introduced not later than the day after the beginning of the autumn session.

What is provided in the second paragraph shall be applied similarly to private members' motions occasioned by requests from any of the offices and agencies of the Riksdag. In such cases the time for the introduction of private members' motions shall be calculated from the day when the house was notified in the manner prescribed by the Riksdag of the filing of such a request.

On questions which concern one house only and on questions which have already been decided by one house or are immediately related to some other development occurring during the Riksdag, private members' motions may be presented as long as the Riksdag is in session.

Private members' motions shall always be delivered in writing for the minutes. Several matters of a different nature may not be combined in one and the same proposal.

2. Propositions from the King, and also private members' motions on subjects under the jurisdiction of a standing committee, can not be decided by the house before they have been reported on by a committee. Questions which concern one house only may be decided immediately.

Art. 56. Whenever the King deems it desirable that information be communicated orally to the Riksdag on any matter concerning the relations of the realm with foreign powers, or on any other matter of major interest, it devolves upon the member of the Council of State named by the King for this purpose to deliver the message in each house. No member of the house shall be denied the right to express himself concerning the information communicated.

The King may decide, in such cases, that the meetings of the houses shall take place behind closed doors.

Art. 57. Whenever a question is raised in the houses by a Riksdagman or by any committee other than the Committee on the Constitution, that the Council of State or any one of its members have exercised their office in an unauthorized manner the following wording only shall be used: "There is cause for censure of the Council of State or of such and such a member, on which matter reference to the Committee on the Constitution is requested, before which Committee the cause will be stated." Such reference must not be refused but shall take place immediately. The deliberations in a house on such a question shall be governed, as regards the King's decisions in matters concerning the rights and affairs of private persons or corporations, by the provisions in Article 107 of the Instrument of Government.

Art. 58. When a proposition or private member's motion is presented for the first time in a house it shall, provided that the house does not refer it to a committee immediately, lie on the table until the next meeting when such reference shall be made, unless the proposal is withdrawn, or, if it concerns one house only, otherwise acted upon. Each member has the right to state his opinion on the matter, such opinion likewise to be delivered to the committee, but the reference to the committee must not thereby be delayed.

If the question is raised in a house of extending the time for private members' motions in the manner prescribed in the second paragraph of Section 1, Article 55, or if a question arises as to which committee a matter should be referred, such a question may be tabled, but shall absolutely be decided at the next meeting.

The houses may by joint decision postpone the consideration of propositions and private members' motions which do not concern the budget to another session or to the following Riksdag. Further postponements may be agreed to, provided that the matter shall be decided at the latest during the following Riksdag. Consideration of a matter may not be postponed to the following Riksdag if new general elections to the Lower House are to be held before that time. If the King orders new elections to one or both houses, the decision on postponement shall cease to have effect.

Postponement of a matter referred to a committee may be decided on the request of the committee, which has to secure the opinion of the Speakers' Conference on the question; the houses are entitled, however, at the consideration of the report of the committee in the matter to decide on postponement in accordance with the preceding paragraph.

By joint decision the houses, after conferring with the Speakers' Conference mentioned in Article 50, may decide that a postponed question shall be taken up at an extra session.

Proposals to enact, amend, interpret or repeal a fundamental law adopted as pending by the Riksdag may only be postponed to such an extent as is compatible with the provisions of Article 64.

Art. 59. Reports made by a standing committee or a committee especially constituted in its stead shall be read, as far as possible, at the same time in both houses for the purpose of deciding on the matter. After the first reading of the report it shall lie on the table. At the next reading whether debate then takes place or not, it shall again lie on the table, provided the house does not otherwise decide on the basis of a request of the proper committee. When the matter comes up for the third time it must be taken up for decision.

Preliminary requests and inquiries from a committee may be decided immediately unless a member of the house requests that they be tabled.

Art. 60. 1. No matter which has been subject to debate may be taken up for final decision until the house, on the Speaker's proposal, has declared the debate concluded.

2. Except in those cases mentioned in Section 3 the question shall then be put in the manner prescribed below in this Section.

If the question is of such a character that it can be assented to or rejected, the Speaker's first question shall relate to the affirmative alternative. If that is answered by "no," and amendments have been offered in the matter during the debate, the next question shall be put in accordance with them. If a proposal is composed of several parts, which can not appropriately be decided upon in one and the same connection, a separate question relating to each part shall be put in the order just prescribed.

A question shall always be answered only by "yes" or "no," and the Speaker shall make known his finding of the answer which was given, which shall stand unless a division is requested. In such a case a division shall not be denied. Whether a division is taken or not each member shall be entitled to have his individual opinion recorded in the minutes. No member may try to rescind a decision by opening a fresh debate.

When a division shall be taken the proposal and a succinct counter-proposal which are to be voted upon shall be drawn up, approved and read without delay, and the vote taken immediately thereafter; but no quest on may be put and no vote be taken on a request for a division. The division shall be taken openly. If the votes are evenly divided, the Speaker shall place in a special voting urn one "yes" and ' no" ballot, both exactly alike in size and appearance, printed and unmarked and each one closed and rolled up, and the result of the division is decided by the ballot which one of the members of the house draws from the urn at the request of the Speaker.

3. A question on matters referred to in the first clause of Article 110 in

the Instrument of Government or Article 32, Section 2, or the last paragraph of Article 52 of this Riksdag Act, shall always be decided by a division. In such cases the provisions in the preceding Section concerning the proposal and the counter-proposal to be voted upon shall be adhered to; provided that approved proposals shall be posted and the vote taken immediately thereafter. Such a division shall always be taken with printed and unmarked ballots, separate, closed and rolled up, and in order to avoid an equal number of votes for "yes" and "no," in matters where only a simple majority is necessary, the Speaker at each division before the counting of the ballots shall take out one of them and immediately lay it aside sealed. If at the counting of the other ballots the votes are evenly divided, the sealed ballot shall be opened and determine the decision. If majority has already been obtained the ballot laid aside shall be destroyed immediately without being opened.

Art. 61. The Speaker may not refuse to put the question, except when he finds the question raised in violation of the wording of the fundamental laws; and in such cases he shall always state the reasons for his refusal. If the house nevertheless demands that the question be put, the Speaker shall have the right to declare the deliberations temporarily closed, and the matter is then referred to the Committee on the Constitution, upon which it is incumbent without delay to submit a reasoned and definitive opinion as to whether the question is in violation of or in conformity with the fundamental laws. The Speaker can not refuse to put the question on any matter the Committee declares is not in violation of the fundamental laws.

Art. 62. Decisions of a house which do not concern that house only shall be communicated to the other house by extracts from the minutes. If the matter has been considered by a standing committee or a committee especially constituted in its stead, the committee shall also be informed of the decision in the identical manner. Should a member who did not concur in the decision of the house wish to communicate his dissenting opinion to the other house he may do so; in such a case he shall deliver his dissenting opinion in written form to the minutes, after which it is communicated to the other house by extract from the minutes; but this may not in any case delay the dispatch of the decision.

Art. 63. When a question on which a committee has reported comes up for decision the house may either immediately assent to the report, or make its decision without respect to what the committee has proposed, or recommit the matter if it is considered to require further investigation.

If the houses reach decisions on a matter which in the main or in certain respects are not identical, and if the matter is one on which a standing committee or a committee especially constituted in its stead has reported, then the committee shall try to reconcile the different opinions, provided that that is possible, and present a proposal on the matter to the houses.

What the houses jointly decide shall be the decision of the Riksdag. If the houses, having followed the procedure prescribed above, are not in agreement on the decision, the matter shall be considered dropped for that session, except in those cases which are mentioned in Article 65.

Art. 64. A proposal to enact, amend, interpret or repeal a fundamental law can be rejected by the Riksdag at which the proposal was presented, but it can not be finally adopted or assented to at that Riksdag as more than a proposal which shall be pending, to be considered again by the first Riksdag meeting after the next general election to the Lower House. If the poposal is then accepted by both houses it shall constitute the decision of the Riksdag. The houses shall not have the right to make changes in a pending proposal. The decision on such a proposal may not be postponed to any other Riksdag than that mentioned above, unless the King and both houses jointly agree.

Art. 65. When, in matters concerning State expenditure or taxation, or regulations for the Bank of Sweden, or the income and expenditure of the Bank, or discharge from responsibility for the Commissioners of the Bank of Sweden, or the management and administration of the National Debt Office, or the income and expenditure of the Office, the houses reach different decisions, which are not reconciled on the proposal of the competent committee, both houses shall vote separately on the different decisions reached by each of them. The opinion then receiving a majority of the aggregate number of votes of both houses shall constitute the decision of the Riksdag. If the aggregate number of votes is found to be evenly divided, the Speaker of the Lower House shall deposit in a special voting urn a "yes" and a "no" ballot, both exactly alike in size and appearance, printed and unmarked and each one closed and rolled up, and the result of the voting is decided by the ballot which one of the members of the Lower House draws from the urn at the request of the Speaker.

Art. 66. When election of a King or heir apparent is to take place a delegation shall be constituted, consisting of sixty-four persons, of which each house shall select thirty-two from among its members, with the duty of performing the election in case of a disagreement between the houses. The day after the selection of the delegation the houses shall proceed to the election of a King or heir apparent. If the houses are agreed on one and the same person he is to be regarded as chosen. In other cases the delegation shall decide. No other persons may be voted upon by the delegation, however, than those who received the greatest number of votes in each house. Neither house may present more than one candidate. The members of the delegation who shall not, by reason of this commission, be excluded from their rights as Riksdagmen in the houses, shall convene the day after the election has taken place in the houses, and shall not adjourn until the election procedure is completed. The one of the two persons voted upon receiving the greatest number of votes in the delegation is duly elected. In the event mentioned in Article 94 of the Instrument of Government the delegation shall be selected within ten days of the day which is designated in the summons to the Riksdag as the date for the meeting of the Riksdag.

Art. 67. If regents are to be appointed for a King who is under age a delegation shall be selected by the houses, not later than the day after the Riksdag has convened, in the manner and comprising the number of persons determined by the preceding Article. This delegation shall vote for regents, the number of which shall be one, three or five, as determined by the Riksdag. Each member of the delegation shall record by secret ballot a number of persons whom he considers worthy of this confidence, which shall exceed by one the number decided upon by the Riksdag. Of those who are named, the person receiving the greatest number of votes shall then be subject to new voting, the majority of the delegation determining the outcome. In the same manner the delegation proceeds with the person who next has been named by the greatest number of delegation members, etc., until the designated number of regents has been filled. The delegation may not adjourn before the election is completed, and this election constitutes the decision of the Riksdag.

If it should happen that the houses do not agree on the number of regents within three days of the assembling of the Riksdag, a special delegation shall be appointed in the manner, and comprising the number of persons prescribed concerning the delegation referred to in the previous paragraph, to decide the question within two days by voting, with the same force and effect as a decision of the Riksdag. The delegation selected shall thereafter, likewise within two days, elect the regents, so that in all events the election of the regents shall be executed within the course of seven days from the day the Riksdag convened.

Art. 68. In accordance with Article 96 of the Instrument of Government the Riksdag shall appoint an Ombudsman of Civil Affairs and an Ombudsman of Military Affairs of the qualifications stated in that Article. These Ombudsmen of the Riksdag shall be elected to serve from the election until such an election four years thence has again taken place.

The Ombudsman of Civil Affairs and the Ombudsman of Military Affairs shall be elected by forty-eight electors named for that purpose, of which each house selects twenty-four from among its members. These electors shall meet for the election not later than ten days after the one on which they were selected. The rules applicable to the election of the Speakers of the houses shall also govern this election.

On the occasion when an Ombudsman is elected the electors shall also, in the identical manner, elect a deputy for him. The deputy shall be elected to serve until a new election for the procurator takes place.

In the event that the Ombudsman of Civil Affairs or the Ombudsman of Military Affairs resigns from his position of confidence or the office of Ombudsman otherwise becomes vacant, the deputy shall take over the office immediately; and the Riksdag thereafter shall provide for the election of a new Ombudsman as soon as possible for the time and in the manner prescribed scribed above. If the deputy resigns from his position of confidence, or if he has taken over the office of Ombudsman, or his position otherwise becomes vacant, the election of a new deputy shall take place for the time and in the manner prescribed above; provided that if such an election is necessary during the time when the Riksdag is not in session, the rights of the Riksdag in this matter shall be exercised by those Commissioners of the Bank of Sweden who are selected by the Riksdag and the Commissioners of the National Debt Office.

Art. 69. The Riksdag shall every fourth year select a delegation of forty-eight persons of which each house shall choose twenty-four from among its members, and which delegation in the manner prescribed in Articles 103 and 104 of the Instrument of Government has the duty to decide whether all members of the Supreme Court and the Supreme Administrative Court deserve to be retained in their important office, or if without any of them having demonstrably committed the offenses or crimes referred to in Article 102 of the Instrument of Government it might yet be deemed that they ought to be deprived of their offices. This delegation shall meet the same day it is elected.

The members of the delegation, each separately, shall first vote on the question: Shall a vote be taken to exclude any member of the Supreme Court? If this question is answered unanimously, or by the majority of votes, with "no," all of the members of the Supreme Court shall be retained. If it is answered, on the other hand, with "yes," each member of the delegation shall compile a closed list of these members of the Supreme Court, many or few, who in his opinion should be dismissed. Of those listed, the three against whom the largest number of votes was cast shall then, one after the other, be subject to new voting; provided that a two-thirds majority of the votes shall be required for a member to be considered excluded from the confidence of the Riksdag; and thereafter what is further prescribed in Article 103 of the Instrument of Government shall be followed.

In the identical manner voting shall take place concerning the members of the Supreme Administrative Court.

Art. 70. 1. The six Commissioners of the Bank of Sweden, who shall be appointed by the Riksdag according to Article 72 of the Instrument of Government, shall be elected to serve from the election until such an election three years thence has again taken place. Two of the Commissioners appointed by the Riksdag shall retire every year. If a Commissioner appointed by the Riksdag retires before the end of his term of office, or if he is refused discharge from responsibility, a new election shall take place for the time which remains of his term of office.

2. The Riksdag shall also elect Commissioners who shall administer, according to special regulations, the funds and property of the National Debt Office. These Commissioners shall be seven in number and shall be elected to serve from the election until such an election three years thence has again taken place. The chairman of the Commissioners shall be elected separately. Of the other six Commissioners two shall retire annually. If a Commissioner retires before the end of his term of office, or if he is refused discharge from responsibility, a new election shall take place for the time which remains of his term. When election of a chairman takes place, he shall be elected before the other Commissioners are elected.

3. The Commissioners of the Bank of Sweden and the National Debt Office shall be elected by forty-eight electors, of which each house shall select twenty-four from among its own members. The election shall take place by secret ballot. Election for longer terms of office shall take place before election for shorter terms. Retiring Commissioners may be re-elected.

4. The Commissioners shall select a vice-chairman from among their own members. The Commissioner presiding shall possess the casting vote when in questions which come up for voting among the Commissioners, the votes are evenly divided on two divergent opinions.

Art. 71. At the same time as the Commissioners are appointed according to Article 70 and in a similar manner, a substitute for each Commissioner appointed by the Riksdag shall be appointed to take his place in case of unavoidable absence, provided that the substitute thus selected for the Commissioner appointed to be head of the Bank of Sweden shall act for that Commissioner only in cases when the substitute appointed for the head of the Bank of Sweden by the Commissioners in accordance with Article 72 of the Instrument of Government is also unavoidably absent. If a Commissioner and his substitute elected by the Riksdag are both absent the Commissioners shall call in another substitute.

Art. 72. The Riksdag annually within six days of its opening shall appoint auditors, twelve in number, six of whom shall be elected by each house, to inspect the government, management and condition of the administration, the Bank of Sweden and the National Debt Office in accordance with the Instrument of Government and special instructions. The auditors shall exercise their duties until new elections of auditors are held.

The auditors shall elect from among themselves a chairman who shall have the casting vote when in voting the votes are evenly divided on any matter.

The critical remarks, which the auditors consider themselves justified to make, shall, after explanations have been given thereto, be delivered to the proper committee for inspection and further consideration.

Art. 73. For each auditor elected according to Article 72 a substitute shall be elected to act in his place in case of unavoidable absence. If both the auditor and his substitute are unavoidably absent, another substitute is to be called in according to the order in which the substitutes were elected.

Art. 74. The electors and delegations of the Riksdag, with the exception of the Advisory Council on Foreign Affairs, select their chairmen from among their own members.

Art. 75. 1. If a common list is presented at an election which shall take place in a house, and the list contains the names of as many persons as shall be elected, and if the list has been approved by those members of the house elected by it to the Speakers' Conference, the Speaker shall put the question to approve the list, and declare the listed persons elected, unless election by secret ballot is requested by at least as many members as corresponds to the number which is obtained if the number of all the members entitled to vote is divided by the number of the persons to be elected, increased by one. If such a request is made the election shall take place by secret ballot at a later meeting.

All elections, except the election of the members of the house to the Speakers' Conference, shall be proportional, if two or more persons are to be selected. Further provisions concerning the elections are given in the Riksdag Regulations mentioned in Article 78.

2. Elections which are held by the committees, delegations and electors of the Riksdag shall be held by secret ballot when that is requested by a member or by an elector; and it shall be observed in such cases that to be valid the ballots shall be separate, rolled up, unmarked and free from all ambiguities relative to the names of persons listed as well as from incorrectness relative to their number. When persons receive an equal number of votes the decision shall be made by lot if necessary.

If special provisions are contained in the fundamental laws concerning an election referred to in this Section the provisions of the preceding paragraph shall not apply.

Art. 76. A decision may not be changed at the approval of the minutes, but such amendments may be made as do not cause any change in the decision. A statement by a member, and also the debate to which it may have given rise, may be excluded from the minutes at their approval with the consent of the house and the concordance of the member; provided that no utterances may be excluded on which the decision is clearly based.

Art. 77. A Riksdagman who is absent when a decision is made by the house of which he is a member, shall have the right to have recorded in the minutes that he did not take part in that decision, but he shall not be allowed to comment on the decisions of those who were present.

Art. 78. The Riksdag shall prescribe rules and regulations for the transaction of business in the Riksdag, for the preservation of order in its houses and committees and for the elections to be held within the Riksdag, and shall also adopt such other provisions as are considered necessary for the observance of the fundamental laws (The Riksdag Regulations). Each house may also establish regulations on matters which concern that house only (Standing Orders). Nothing may be introduced into these provisions which is in violation of fundamental or other general laws.

COMMUNICATION

OF THE DECISIONS OF THE RIKSDAG

Art. 79. The requests which the Riksdag decides to submit to the King, and also the replies to the proposals presented to the Riksdag by the King, shall be delivered by written message to the King.

Art. 80. In matters which have been considered by a standing committee or a committee especially constituted in its stead the messages emanating from the Riksdag shall be drafted and issued by the secretariat of the committee which prepared the matter.

Other messages common to both houses shall be drafted and issued by a special Secretariat of the Riksdag under the supervision of two members of the Upper House and two members of the Lower House, these members to be selected from among the members of the respective houses (Supervisory Committee of the Secretariat).

No message concerning a decision of the Riksdag shall be dispatched before it has been approved by the houses. Messages emanating from the Riksdag shall be signed by the Speakers.

Art. 81. The general laws and statutes upon which the King and the Riksdag jointly decide shall be issued only in the King's name and with his signature.

Art. 82. The minutes kept in the houses and other documents of the Riksdag shall be published as soon as possible at the expense of the State, the minutes to be published to the extent prescribed by each house, and the other documents in full.

In witness whereof we have put our names and our seal to attest, confirm and endorse the same in Stockholm on the twenty-second day of June, in the year of our Lord 1866.

Everything as herein provided we not only accept for ourselves as the established fundamental law, but also direct and graciously command all who are united in loyalty, fealty and obedience to us, our successors and the realm, to acknowledge, observe and obey this Riksdag Act. In witness whereof we have with our own hand signed and confirmed it, and duly affixed our royal seal below, in Stockholm, our city of residence, on the twenty-second day of June in the year of our Lord 1866.

The Act of Succession

according to which the male heirs begotten by His Noble-Born Highness, the chosen Crown Prince of the realm of Sweden, HRH Prince Johan Baptist Julius of Ponte-Corvo, shall have the right to the Royal Swedish throne and to accede to the government of Sweden.

Örebro, September 26, 1810, as amended up to and including the year 1953

We, CARL, by the Grace of God King of Sweden, the Goths, and the Wends, &c., &c., &c., Heir to Norway, Duke of Sleswig-Holstein, Stormarn and Ditmarsen, Count of Oldenburg and Delmenhorst, &c., &c., hereby make known that we, after the unanimous acceptance and confirmation by the Estates of the Realm of the Act of Succession according to which the male heirs begotten by His Noble-Born Highness, the chosen Crown Prince of Sweden, HRH Prince JOHAN BAPTIST JULIUS shall have the right to the Swedish throne and to accede to the government of Sweden, and after the submission of this fundamental law for our gracious approval, by virtue of the right accruing to us according to Article 85 of the Instrument of Government, adopt, accept and confirm this Act of Succession approved by the Estates of the Realm exactly as follows word for word:

ACT OF SUCCESSION,

according to which the male heirs begotten by His Noble-Born Highness, the chosen Crown Prince of Sweden, HRH Prince JOHAN BAPTIST JULIUS of Ponte-Corvo, shall have the right to the Royal Swedish throne and to accede to the government of Sweden; adopted and confirmed by the King and the Estates of the Realm at the extradorinary session of the Riksdag in Örebro on September 26, 1810.

We, the undersigned Estates of the Realm of Sweden, counts, barons, bishops, nobles, clergy, burghers and peasants, who are now convened at a general extraordinary session of the Riksdag here in Örebro, hereby make known that, with the decease, without male heirs begotten by him, of His Noble-Born Highness, the chosen Crown Prince of Sweden, HRH Prince CARL AUGUST, and by our choice, as evidenced by the Act of Agreement and Election of August 21, 1810, of His Noble-Born Highness, Prince JOHAN BAPTIST JULIUS of Ponte-Corvo, as Crown Prince of Sweden, to succeed to the government of Sweden and its subordinate provinces His Royal Majesty, our present most gracious King and Lord, Carl XIII, after his death (be it long deferred by the Grace of God the Almighty) to be crowned and hailed as King of Sweden, and to govern the realm, on the conditions specified in the Act of Agreement and Election above mentioned as well as in the royal oath to be made, as required by us, by His Noble-Born Highness, we have this day determined and confirmed for the legitimate direct male heirs of HRH JOHAN BAPTIST JULIUS, Prince of Ponte-Corvo, the following order of succession to the crown and government of Sweden, applicable in the manner and on the conditions expressedly set forth below.

Art. 1. Since the marriage of HRH Crown Prince JOHAN BAPTIST JULIUS is already blessed with a male heir begotten by him, and since it may yet be blessed by other such heirs, the rule shall apply that the eldest son of His Royal Highness shall succeed His Royal Highness in the government, and after the eldest son his male descendants in the order of nearness of kin, in direct line of descent, in relation to the head of the family. If there are no male heirs in the oldest branch of the family the next oldest son of His Royal Highness shall accede to the government, and after the next oldest son his male descendants in the order prescribed above with regard to the oldest branch of the family, that is, according to nearness of kin, in direct line of descent, in relation to the head of the family. If there are no male heirs in the next oldest branch of the family the third son and his branch of the family shall have the right of succession, thereafter the fourth and so forth in the same order, and in direct line of descent in accordance with the principle of primogeniture, as prescribed above with regard to the oldest branch of the family.

Art. 2. If at the death of a King in Sweden there is no male heir begotten by him, but the Queen is in a blessed state, the regent or the Council of State shall conduct the government with royal power and authority, in the manner and on the conditions prescribed in Article 41 and 93 of the Instrument of Government, until the time when the Riksdag shall convene in accordance with the Instrument of Government, at which time the Riksdag shall make necessary provisions concerning the government. If the Queen's issue is of male sex, the Riksdag shall appoint a regency as provided in Article 93 of the Instrument of Government. If the Queen's issue is of female sex, that member of the family who according to Article I is next in the order of succession shall be King and accede to the government.

Art. 3. Female members of the royal family, and their descendants, male or female, shall have no right to the crown and government of Sweden.

Art. 4. In accordance with the express provision of Article 2 of the Instrument of Government that the King shall always profess the pure evangelical faith, as adopted and explained in the unaltered Augsburg Confession and in the Resolution of the Uppsala Meeting of the year 1593, princes of the royal family shall be brought up in that same faith and within the realm. Any member of the royal family not professing this faith shall be excluded from all rights of succession.

Art. 5. A prince of the royal family may not marry unless the King, having obtained the opinion of the Council of State, has given his consent thereto. Should a prince marry without such consent, or if he, with or without consent, marries the daughter of a private Swedish citizen, he shall have forfeited the right of succession for himself, his children and their descendants.

Art. 6. Princesses of the royal family may not marry without the King's knowledge and consent.

Art. 7. The heir apparent may not embark upon a journey to any foreign country without the King's knowledge and consent.

Art. 8. A prince of the Swedish royal family may not become the ruling prince of a foreign state without the consent of the King and the Riksdag, be it by election, succession or marriage. Should he do so he and his descendants shall not be entitled to succeed to the Swedish throne.

Art. 9. Should it unfortunately occur that the royal house in which is vested the right of succession to the throne either becomes extinct in the male line or loses the right of succession by failure to comply with the express provisions of this Act of Succession, the throne shall be vacant until the Riksdag shall elect a new royal house.

In witness of the fact that all that has been thus prescribed is identical with our intent and decision we, representing all the Estates of the Realm of Sweden, have attached our names and seals, in Örebro on the twenty-sixth day of September, in the year of our Lord 1810.

Everything as herein provided we not only accept for ourselves as the established fundamental law, but also direct and graciously command all who are united in loyalty, fealty and obedience to us, our successors and the realm, to acknowledge, observe, follow and obey this Act of Succession. In witness whereof we have with our own hand signed and confirmed it, and duly affixed our royal seal below, in Örebro, on the twenty-sixth day of September, in the year of our Lord and Saviour Jesus Christ 1810.

The Freedom of the Press Act

April 5, 1949, as amended up to and including the year 1953

We, Gustaf, by the Grace of God King of Sweden, the Goths and the Wends, hereby make known that we, together with the Riksdag, in conformity with the constitution, have adopted a new Freedom of the Press Act as follows:

CHAPTER 1

ON FREEDOM OF THE PRESS

Art. 1. In accordance with the principles laid down in the Instrument of Government concerning freedom of the press for all, and in order to ensure free interchange of opinion and general enlightenment, every Swedish citizen shall have the right to express his thoughts and opinions in print, to publish official documents and to make statements and communicate information on any subject whatever, subject to the regulations set forth in this Act for the protection of individual rights and public security.

Every person shall also have the right in all cases not otherwise provided for in this Act to make statements and communicate information on any subject whatever to the author or editor or to the editorial office, if any, of a publication with a view to have the matter published therein.

Art. 2. No publication shall be subject to censorship before being printed nor shall the printing thereof be prohibited.

Furthermore, no authority or other public body may, by reason of the contents of a publication, take any action not authorized by this Act to prevent the printing or publication of the written matter or the circulation of the publication among the general public.

Art. 3. Except in the manner and in the cases provided in this Act, a person shall not on grounds of abuse of the freedom of the press, or complicity in such abuse, be prosecuted or declared liable or responsible for damages and the publication shall not be confiscated or seized.

Art. 4. A person whose duty it is to pass judgment on abuses of the freedom of the press or otherwise to ensure compliance with this Act shall constantly bear in mind that freedom of the press is the foundation of a free society and should always pay more attention to illegality in the subject-matter and thought than in the form of expression, in the aim rather than in the manner of presentation, and in doubtful cases, should acquit rather than convict.

In determining the consequences attendant upon abuses of the freedom of the press under this Act, particular attention, in the case of statements requiring correction, shall be given to whether such correction was brought to the notice of the public in an appropriate manner.

Art. 5. This Act shall apply only to matter produced by means of a printing press. The term "printed matter" includes maps, drawings or pictures, even if there is no accompanying text.

Art. 6. Printed matter shall not be considered as such unless it is published. Printed matter shall be deemed to have been published when it has been delivered for sale or for circulation in some other manner; nevertheless, this definition shall not apply to such documents printed for a public authority as are to be kept secret.

Art. 7. The term "periodical printed matter" refers to a newspaper, magazine or other similar printed matter, as well as accompanying posters and supplements, provided that the intention is according to the publishing schedule to issue at least four separate numbers or sections of the publication under a fixed title at different periods during the year. Printed matter shall be deemed to be a periodical from the time of issue of a publishing license until such license is revoked.

Art. 8. No exclusive privileges to publish may be granted, provided that such privileges for the support of public institutions as have already been granted may be renewed by the King, each time for not more than twenty years.

The exclusive right of the author of literary and musical works or other works of art to reproduce printed copies of such works shall be governed by special legislation.

CHAPTER 2

ON THE PUBLIC CHARACTER OF OFFICIAL DOCUMENTS

Art. 1. To further free interchange of opinion and general enlightenment, every Swedish citizen shall have free access to official documents in the manner specified below. This right shall be subject only to such restrictions as are demanded out of consideration for the security of the realm and its relations with foreign powers, or in connection with official activities for inspection, control or other supervision, or for the prevention and prosecution of crime, or to protect the legitimate economic interest of the State, communities and individuals, or out of consideration for the maintenance of privacy, security of the person, decency and morality.

The specific cases in which official documents are to be kept secret, according to the aforementioned principles, shall be closely defined in special legislation enacted jointly by the King and the Riksdag.

Art. 2. The term "official documents" refers to all documents kept by a State or local governmental authority, whether received or prepared by such authority.

The provisions of this Chapter concerning documents shall also apply to maps, drawings and pictures.

Art. 3. In this Chapter "State authority "refers to the ministries of State, the Office of the Defense Command, the Riksdag, and the Synod of the Church, and their divisions, committees, delegations, commissioners, deputies and auditors, the courts and the administrative boards and all other authorities and establishments, councils, commissions and committees which constitute integral parts of the State administration.

In this Chapter "local authority" refers to all assemblies and representative bodies as well as authorities, boards, corporations, agencies, councils, commissions, auditors, committees and delegations and all their subsidiary departments and establishments, which constitute integral parts of local selfgovernment.

Art. 4. A memorandum or other note drawn by an authority solely to present or prepare a case or matter for decision shall not be deemed to be an official document in the hands of such authority unless, after the case or matter has been settled by the authority, the note is placed on permanent record.

Art. 5. A document shall be deemed to have arrived at an authority when it has been delivered to the authority or official who has the duty to receive the document or is otherwise concerned with the case or matter to which the document is related.

Diaries, journals, registers and other similar lists shall be deemed to be prepared when they have been made ready for entry or posting. Minutes and other similar records shall be deemed to be prepared when they have been revised and approved by the authority or have otherwise been made ready. Other documents relating to a certain case or matter shall be deemed to be prepared when they have been issued or, if they are not issued, when the case or matter has been settled by the authority.

Art. 6. Competitive entries, tenders, or other similar documents which according to announcement must be delivered in sealed envelopes, shall not be deemed to have been received before the time fixed for their opening.

A judgment or other decision of an authority which according to the relevant legislation must be pronounced or issued, and minutes and other similar records relating to such decisions, shall not be deemed to be prepared until the decision has been pronounced or issued.

Minutes kept by committees of the Riksdag or of the Synod of the Church, by the Riksdag Auditors or by Royal Commissions or by a local authority on matters dealt with by the authority solely for purposes of consideration or preparation shall not be deemed drawn up until the matter to which the minutes refer has been settled by the authority and, in the case of minutes of the Auditors of the Riksdag, until a report on the matter has been published.

Art. 7. The provisions of this Chapter concerning official documents shall not apply to copies of printed matter as referred to in Chapter 4, Article 7, or to private letters or writings delivered to public archives or libaries or otherwise to an authority for the exclusive purpose of custody and care or for research and study purposes. The making available of such documents shall be subject to such special rules as are prescribed.

Art. 8. An official document that is not secret shall upon request and without cost be made available, immediately or as soon as possible, for examination by any person who desires to read or copy it at the place where it is kept, and such person shall further be entitled to obtain a copy of the document for a fixed fee. A document need not, however, be made available at the place where it is kept if that would meet with considerable difficulties. If a document kept by a local authority can be made available at the place where it is kept, the right to obtain a copy of the document shall exist only to the extent specified by local government law or as otherwise specially provided. An authority shall not be required to make copies of maps, drawings or pictures for delivery if that would meet with difficulty and the document can be made available at the place where it is kept.

A document that is to be kept secret only in part shall, notwithstanding this fact, be made available at the place where it is kept if this can be done in such a manner that the matter contained in the secret part is not revealed. If this cannot be done, the person who wishes to examine the document shall be supplied with an extract thereof excluding the secret part.

Art. 9. A request to obtain an official document shall be made to the authority having custody of the document and shall be given due consideration by that authority.

If a specific official, under the rules and procedure of an agency or because of special commission, is entrusted with the care of a document, he himself shall decide whether the document shall be delivered, but in so doing he must conform to the instructions issued by the agency in question, and in doubtful cases he shall refer the question to the agency for decision, provided that this is possible without undue delay. If the official refuses to deliver the document, the question shall, at the request of the applicant, be referred to the agency.

The competence of an authority other than the authority specified in the first paragraph of this Article to consider the question of delivering an official document shall be governed by the provisions of the second paragraph of Article 14.

Art. 10. If an authority has refused a request to obtain an official document and the applicant considers the decision contrary to law, he shall be entitled to seek a change in the decision in the manner hereinafter described, but an appeal shall not lie from the decision of the head of a ministry.

Art. 11. Petition for a change as comtemplated in Article 10 shall be filed with the authority which is competent to entertain appeals of decisions or actions in a case or matter to which the document relates, or, if no appeal is allowed in such case or matter, or if the document does not relate to a case or matter to be dealt with by the authority, with the authority which is generally competent to entertain appeals of decisions or actions of the first-mentioned authority. The foregoing provisions shall also apply to the order in which a change shall be sought.

If no authority is competent as aforesaid, petition for a change shall be filed, in the case of a decision of a local authority, with the county government, or, in the case of a decision of an authority subject to a county government, diocese, administrative board or other superior authority, with such superior authority, or, in other cases, with the King through the competent ministry. However, in the case of a decision of an authority directly subordinate to the Riksdag or subject to its immediate supervision, the rules established by the Riksdag shall apply.

Actions carried to a ministry shall be laid before and decided by the Supreme Administrative Court.

Art. 12. The provisions of Article 11 shall apply to the bringing of an action against the decision of an authority whereby an appeal was denied, but no action shall be allowed against upholding an appeal.

Art. 13. If a person wishes to appeal the decision of an authority, he shall have the right to be informed of the procedure to be followed.

A case or matter regarding delivery of official documents shall always be dealt with promptly. Transcripts of decisions shall be supplied to the appellant free of charge. The bringing or hearing of an appeal action shall be subject to no special conditions, such as payment of an appeal fee or official authorization.

Art. 14. If an authority has an official document that is to be kept secret and if the authority considers special measures necessary to prevent its unauthorized delivery, it may place a note on such document to the effect that it is secret. The said note shall refer to the provision of law on the basis of which the document is to be kept secret and shall show the date on which the note was made and the authority that caused it to be made.

The King may order that a particular authority shall consider the question whether delivery may be made of special kinds of documents, the secrecy of which is of particular importance to the security of the realm. If such an order is made, a document which is the subject thereof shall, in addition to the particulars specified in the first paragraph, show the authority which is thus competent to consider questions of delivery. An application made to another authority to obtain a document bearing a note as aforesaid shall be referred forthwith to the competent authority at the request of the applicant.

Except as provided in this Article no document shall bear a note to the effect that it is secret.

CHAPTER 3

ON THE RIGHT TO ANONYMITY

Art. 1. The author of any printed matter shall not be bound to have his name appear thereon.

Furthermore, no printer, publisher or other person concerned with printing or publishing printed matter shall reveal in any other manner the identity of the author against his wishes, unless obliged to do so by law.

Art. 2. No question shall be raised in any action concerning the freedom of the press as to the authorship of a matter appearing in a periodical printed matter.

Art. 3. With respect to non-periodical printed matter the question of authorship may be raised in an action concerning the freedom of the press only if the author is identified by the appearance in the publication of his name, or of a pseudonym that is generally known to designate him, or if he has acknowledged himself to be the author in a written declaration, or if of his own accord he has made such an acknowledgement to the court in the action.

Art. 4. The provisions of Articles 1 and 2 on the anonymity of authors shall apply to a person who, not being an author, communicates information for publication in the manner specified in the second paragraph of Chapter 1, Article 1, and the provisions of Article 2 shall also apply to information intended for non-periodical printed matter.

The provisions of Articles 1 and 3 on the anonymity of authors shall also apply to editors of non-periodical printed matter.

Art. 5. If any person inserts the name or pseudonym of the author contrary to his wishes, or, in cases provided for under Article 4, that of the editor or informant against his wishes, such person shall be punished by *per diem* fines, or, if the offense is attended by particularly aggravating circumstances, by imprisonment for a term not to exceed one year. The same penalty shall apply if the name or pseudonym of a person who is not in fact the author, editor or informant is inserted as author, editor or informant. A fine of not less than 50 nor more than 500 crowns shall be imposed if the name of an author, editor or informant is otherwise disclosed in an unauthorized manner.

No offense referred to in this Article shall become the subject of action by a public prosecutor unless the offended person reports such offense for prosecution.

CHAPTER 4

ON PRINTERS AND PRINTING ESTABLISHMENTS

Art. 1. Every Swedish natural or legal person shall have the right alone or assisted by others to produce printed works by means of a printing press. The establishment for producing such work will be referred to in this Act as a printing establishment.

Art. 2. A guardian or trustee who operates a printing establishment on behalf of a minor or other person shall be considered under this Act to have the same responsibility as a printer.

Art. 3. If a person wishes to set up a printing establishment, he shall register the said establishment with the county government not later than two weeks before the first print is issued from it, and shall state his name or the firm name under which he intends to operate the said establishment, the place at which he intends to set it up and the kind of printing that he intends to produce. This provision on the registration of a new printing establishment shall also apply in the case of removal of an establishment to a locality other than that previously registered.

If the name of the printing establishment is changed or if the proprietor intends to produce printed matter of a kind different from that previously registered, a notice to this effect shall be made as soon as possible to the county government.

When the registration or notice referred to in the first and second paragraphs has been made, it shall be incumbent upon the county government forthwith to inform the head of the Ministry of Justice and the local police authority thereof.

The provisions of this Article on the obligation of a printer to make a registration shall not apply in the case of a printing establishment which does picture or job printing solely for the use of the proprietor.

Art. 4. All printed matter produced in the realm and intended to be published here shall bear the name or firm name of the printing establishment and the place and year of printing.

This provision shall not apply, however, to printed matter classifiable as picture or job printing.

Art. 5. If printed matter is produced for a certain printer entirely or in part at another establishment and the whole edition is delivered to him, the said printed matter may at the request of such printer bear the imprint of his printing establishment. If this is done, he shall be deemed to be the printer of such printed matter.

Art. 6. One copy of all printed matter issued by a printing establishment shall be kept for one year by the printer and be made available by him for inspection at the request of the police authority.

Art. 7. A copy (to be known as an inspection copy) of all printed matter produced in a printing establishment in the realm shall at the time of publication of the matter be delivered by the printer for inspection in Stockholm to the head of the Ministry of Justice and in other localities to his appointed representatives. Nevertheless, subject to the approval of the head of the said Ministry, delivery of the matter may be deferred for a certain time after publication.

An inspection copy shall be complete and undamaged and otherwise in the same condition as the copies intended for circulation.

The provisions of the first paragraph shall not apply to picture or job printing nor to communications from a public authority. The King may also grant exemptions from provisions of the first paragraph in other cases.

The obligation of a printer to deliver library copies of printed matter shall governed be by the provisions of law.

Art. 8. Failure to comply with the obligation to register as provided in Article 3 shall be punished by fines of not less than 50 nor more than 500 crowns.

A printer who violates the provisions of Articles 4 or 6, or neglects his obligation to deliver inspection copies under Article 7, shall be punished by *per diem* fines, provided that if the matter has been declared criminal, or if other particularly aggravating circumstances are present, he may be sentenced to imprisonment for a term not to exceed one year.

Art. 9. In this Act the term "picture or job printing" refers to picture postcards and picture albums, calling cards and formal announcements, address cards, labels, forms, advertising matter and printed wrappers and other commercial printing and similar printed matter, provided always that no abuse of the freedom of the press can be considered possible by reason of the text or other matter produced.

CHAPTER 5

ON THE PUBLICATION OF PERIODICAL PRINTED MATTER

Art. 1. The owner of a periodical printed matter shall be a Swedish natural or legal person.

A guardian or trustee who administers the property of the owner shall be deemed to have the responsibility accruing to an owner under this Act.

Art. 2. A printed periodical shall have an editor.

The editor must be a Swedish subject and be domiciled within the realm. A person under guardianship or a bankrupt shall not be an editor.

Art. 3. The editor of a printed periodical shall be appointed by the owner.

The duties of an editor shall include the power to supervise the publication of the periodical and to determine the contents thereof in such a manner that nothing may be inserted therein contrary to the wishes of the editor. Any restriction on the powers which thus by this Act belong to the editor shall be without effect.

Art. 4. The owner shall be bound to register the appointment of an editor with the head of the Ministry of Justice. The registration shall comprise the name and domicile of the editor. The registration shall be accompanied by evidence that the editor meets the qualifications prescribed in Article 2 and by a statement by the editor that he has assumed the duties of editor.

Art. 5. A printed periodical shall not be published until a license has been issued stating that no obstacle exists under this Act to the publication of the periodical. A publishing license shall be issued by the head of the Ministry of Justice on application by the owner. The application shall state the title of the periodical, the place of printing, and the publishing schedule.

No publishing license shall be issued until the registration of the editor specified in Article 4 has been made.

If the title of any periodical resembles the title of a periodical for which a publishing license has been previously issued to such an extent that confusion may easily occur, the application may be rejected.

Art. 6. The head of the Ministry of Justice shall be entitled to revoke a publishing license previously issued:

1. if the owner has given notice that publication of the periodical has ceased;

2. if the ownership of the periodical has been transferred to a person other than a Swedish natural or legal person;

3. if there is no editor, or if the editor does not meet the qualifications prescribed in Article 2, and a qualified editor is not immediately appointed;

4. if six months have lapsed from the date on which the publishing license was issued and the periodical has not appeared;

5. if during neither of the two last calendar years at least four issues or numbers of the periodical specified in the license have appreared;

6. if within six months after the first issue has appeared it becomes evident that under the provisions of the last paragraph of Article 5 the license should not have been issued;

7. if the title of a periodical has been given a typographical appearance resembling the title of another periodical for which a publishing license has been previously issued to such an extent that confusion may easily occur and this condition is not immediately corrected.

In the matters referred to in sub-paragraphs 2–7 of the first paragraph the owner and editor shall, if possible, be given an opportunity to express their views.

Art. 7. If owing to provisions of sub-paragraphs 2, 3, 5 or 7 of the first paragraph of Article 6 a publishing license has been revoked, the consent of the owner of the periodical in question shall nevertheless be required for the issue, within two years from the date of the decision to revoke the license, of a publishing license for another periodical with a title so similar to that of the aforementioned periodical that confusion might easily occur.

Art. 8. If under the provisions of Article 2 an editor is no longer qualified, or if he otherwise ceases to function as editor, the owner is required forthwith to provide for the appointment of a new editor and to notify the head of the Ministry of Justice thereof. The provisions of Article 4 shall apply to such notification, which shall be accompanied, if possible, by evidence to the effect that the previous editor has been informed of the notice.

Art. 9. The editor of a printed periodical may have one or more deputies who shall be appointed by the editor. The appointment of such a deputy shall be registered with the head of the Ministry of Justice. Such registration shall be accompanied by evidence that the deputy meets the qualifications prescribed for editors in Article 2 and by a statement by the deputy that he has assumed the duties of a deputy as well as a statement by the owner that he has approved the deputy.

The provisions of the second paragraph of Article 2 shall also apply to deputies. If the employment of an editor is terminated, deputy appointments shall also come to an end.

Art. 10. After the registration of a deputy, the editor may authorize such a deputy or any of several such deputies, if there are more than one, to exercise in his place the powers vested in the editor according to Article 3.

If it can be assumed that by reason of illness or some other temporary cause an editor shall for at least one month continuously be unable to exercise his powers as editor, he shall as soon as possible delegate such power to a deputy. If there is no deputy, or if the appointment of the person or persons named as deputy will come to an end, the editor shall forthwith provide for the appointment of a deputy and for the registration of the appointment as provided in Article 9.

Art. 11. Every separate issue or number of a printed periodical shall bear the name of the editor.

If the powers of the editor have been delegated to a deputy, every issue of the periodical in question shall state that the deputy is acting as editor, and if this is done, the name of the editor shall not be required in addition.

Art. 12. If the owner of a printed periodical publishes the periodical without a publishing license or without being qualified for that purpose,

or an owner fails to provide in the manner specified in Article 8 for the appointment of a new editor or to register such appointment,

or an editor in the cases specified in the second paragraph of Article 10 fails to delegate his functions to a deputy, or any person publishes a periodical the publication of which has been prohibited under this Act or which periodical obviously is a continuation of such a periodical,

or any person causes his name to appear in a periodical as editor or deputy without being qualified,

he shall be punished by *per diem* fines; if the periodical has been declared criminal or if other particularly aggravating circumstances are present, the penalty may be imprisonment for a term not to exceed one year.

Art. 13. The penalties specified in Article 12 shall also apply to any person who knowingly submits false imformation in an application or registration referred to in this Chapter, or in a statement attached to such application or registration.

Art. 14. If an editor violates the provisions of Article 11, he shall be punished by a fine of not less than 50 nor more than 500 crowns. This provision shall also apply to a deputy who acts as editor.

CHAPTER 6

ON THE CIRCULATION OF PRINTED MATTER

Art. 1. Every Swedish natural or legal person shall have the right alone or with the assistance of others to sell, dispatch or otherwise circulate printed matter.

Art. 2. Notwithstanding the provisions of this Act, the circulation among children and young persons of printed matter, the contents of which may have a brutalizing effect, or may otherwise involve serious danger to the moral upbringing of young persons, shall be governed by special legislation.

The circulation of such maps of Sweden or parts thereof as contain information of importance with respect to the defense of the realm, and the circulation of drawings or pictures of a similar character, shall be governed by special legislation.

Art. 3. If printed matter lacks the prescribed statement concerning the printer or place or year of printing, or if such statement to the knowledge of the distributor is incorrect, the distributor shall be punished by a fine of not less than 50 nor more than 500 crowns.

The penalty for the circulation of printed matter which to the knowledge of the distributor has been seized, or declared confiscated, or has been published in violation of a publishing ban issued on authority of this Act, or obviously is a continuation of printed matter the publication of which has thus been banned, shall be *per diem* fines or, if particularly aggravating circumstances are present, imprisonment not to exceed one year.

Art. 4. The dispatch of printed matter by mail or common carrier shall not owing to the contents of the matter be subject to special restrictions or conditions. This provision shall not apply, however, to a dispatch constituting a violation of the provisions of Article 3.

A common carrier which has received printed matter for transportation shall not be considered a distributor.

CHAPTER 7

ON OFFENSES

AGAINST THE FREEDOM OF THE PRESS

Art. 1. In this Act the term "offense against the freedom of the press" refers to an offense consisting of an unlawful statement in printed matter or an unlawful publication by means of printed matter.

Art. 2. No announcement by advertisement or other similar communication shall be considered an offense against the freedom of the press if from the contents of the communication it is not immediately apparent that liability for such offense may be involved. If a communication is punishable owing to circumstances that are not immediately apparent from the contents of the communication, the relevant provisions of law shall apply. The foregoing provisions shall have similar application to communications in cipher or in any other manner which is not understandable to the public.

Art. 3. If a communication constitutes defamation of a private person and has been delivered for publication in printed matter as mentioned in the second paragraph of Chapter 1, Article 1, but has not been printed, the relevant provisions of law shall apply to the liability for such defamation.

If a person makes known what he has learned while in public office or in the exercise of national service concerning matters the disclosure of which would constitute an offense against the security of the realm, or concerning which he is required by law to observe silence, he may, even though the commmunication was made for publication, be prosecuted and punished under the relevant special legislation.

The provisions of the special law referred to in Chapter 2, Article 1, shall apply to liability for the delivery of secret official documents.

Art. 4. Having due regard for the purpose of freedom of the press as stated in Chapter 1, statements in printed matter shall be considered unlawful when they include representations generally punishable according to law as amounting to:

1. high treason, committed with the intention of making the realm, or a part thereof, by violence or other unlawful means, or with foreign assistance, subject to a foreign power or dependent upon such power, or of thus

detaching a part of the realm or of compelling or obstructing with foreign assistance actions or decisions of the King, the Riksdag or the supreme judicial authority, provided that the act involves a danger that the intention may be carried out;

an attempt or preparation with a view to such high treason;

2. insurrection, committed with the intention of overthrowing the government by armed force or other violent means or of thus compelling or obstructing actions or decisions of the King, the Riksdag, or the supreme judicial authority, provided that the act involves a danger that the intention may be carried out;

an attempt or preparation with a view to such insurrection;

3. war treason, whereby, when the realm is at war or the laws respecting war treason are otherwise in force, a person induces members of the armed forces of the realm or of a State allied with the realm to become discouraged or mutinous, or by false statements spreads such despair among the people as may be of considerable detriment to the national defense or to resistance activities within an occupied part of the realm;

4. an act of the nature specified in 3 when committed as the result of negligence;

5. libel or other defamatory act against the King or any other member of the royal family, affronting a regency governing the realm in place of the King, or the Riksdag, its divisions or committees, or the flag or arms of Sweden, or any other symbol of the sovereignty of the realm;

6. libel or other defamatory act against a person who holds, or has held, an official position, or other position of official responsibility or a person who by order of the King enjoys protection as an official, provided that the defamation is committed with respect to his office;

7. affronting the flag or arms of a foreign power, or any other symbol of its sovereignty, or libel or other defamatory act against the head of a foreign power or a representative of such a power here in the realm;

8. incitement to criminal acts, neglect of civic duties, or disobedience to authority;

9. dissemination of false rumors or other false statements which are apt to endanger the security of the realm, the provision of supplies for the public, or public order and security, or to undermine respect for public authorities or other bodies with the right to make decisions in public matters;

10. threats, slander or libel against groups of people because of their origin or religion;

11. the defamation of anything held sacred by the Church of Sweden or any other religious body active within the realm;

12. actions offensive to decency;

13. defamation of a private person by accusing him of criminal or other acts detrimental to his honor, good name and reputation as a citizen or to

his occupation, trade or advancement, or by libelous statements or other defamatory act.

Art. 5. An official document which is to be kept secret may not be published in print.

Nor shall any information be published in print the disclosure of which according to law would constitute an offense against the security of the realm, irrespective of whether the said information was obtained from public documents or in some other manner.

Whenever the disclosure of any matter has been prohibited by the order of a court, or by the order of the chief investigator in a criminal case, or owing to reservations made by an authority in delivering documents specified in the first paragraph, the publication of such matter shall also be prohibited.

Art. 6. The provisions of law concerning punishment for offenses specified in Articles 4 and 5 shall also apply where the offense is considered an offense against the freedom of the press.

Provisions concerning individual claims owing to offenses against the freedom of the press are set forth in Chapter 11. If the accused has been convicted of an offense specified in sub-paragraphs 6 or 13 of Article 4 and the printed matter is a periodical, an order may in addition be issued, if demanded, that the judgment be inserted in the periodical.

Art. 7. Printed matter that contains an offense against the freedom of the press may be confiscated.

When confiscation of printed matter shall take place all copies intended for circulation shall be destroyed, and such action shall be taken with respect to moulds, lithographic stones, stereotypes, plates and other similar materials adapted exclusively for the printing of that matter as will make abuse of them impossible.

Art. 8. In the case of an unlawful statement as mentioned in sub-paragraphs 1–3 of Article 4, or in the case of the publication of any matter the publication of which under the provisions of the second paragraph of Article 5 is unlawful and which constitutes espionage, the court may, in addition to ordering confiscation, prohibit the publication of a periodical printed matter for a certain period which shall not exceed six months from the date on which the judgment in the action concerning the freedom of the press shall acquire legal force. Such a prohibition may, however, be issued only when the realm is at war.

The provisions of law generally applicable to forfeiture owing to a crime shall apply to the confiscation of a periodical printed matter circulated in violation of a publishing ban or manifestly constituting a continuation of a periodical specified in such ban.

CHAPTER 8

REGULATIONS CONCERNING RESPONSIBILITY

On Responsibility for Periodical Printed Matter

Art. 1. Liability for offenses against the freedom of the press committed in a periodical printed matter shall lie with the person who was registered with the head of the Ministry of Justice as the editor when the periodical was published.

If a deputy was so registered and acted as editor, the deputy shall be liable.

Art. 2. If a publishing license did not exist when the periodical was published, or if the editor responsible under the provisions of the first paragraph of Article 1, was no longer qualified according to Chapter 5, Article 2, or if he had otherwise ceased to function as editor, the owner shall be liable.

The owner shall also be liable where the editor was appointed merely for the sake of appearances or was otherwise at the time of publication of the periodical obviously not in due possession of the powers accruing to him according to Chapter 5, Article 3.

If a deputy acting as editor was no longer qualified at the time of publication of the periodical, or if his commission had otherwise expired, or if the circumstances specified in the second paragraph were applicable to the deputy, the editor shall be liable.

Art. 3. If the identity of the owner, at the time of the publication of the periodical, cannot be established, the printer shall be liable in place of the owner.

Art. 4. If a person circulates a periodical printed matter which does not bear a statement concerning the printing establishment, or if such a statement is known to the distributor to be incorrect, such distributor shall be liable in place of the printer if the printing establishment which issued the periodical cannot be determined.

On Responsibility for Non-Periodical Printed Matter

Art. 5. When an offense is committed against the freedom of the press by means of non-periodical printed matter the author shall be liable, provided that he has been named as the author of the publication as laid down in Chapter 3, Article 3. The author shall not, however, be liable if the matter was published without his consent, or if his name or pseudonym appeared thereon contrary to his wishes.

Art. 6. If under Article 5 an author is not liable for matter which includes or is intended to include contributions by several authors, and if a special editor of the printed matter has been named, as provided in Chapter 3, Article 3, such editor shall be liable.

For printed matter other than that contemplated in the first paragraph the editor shall be liable only if the author was dead at the time of publication.

The editor shall not be liable if his name or pseudonym has appeared contrary to his wishes.

The editor óf non-periodical printed matter is taken to be that person who, although not the author, delivers it to a printer or publisher for printing or publication.

Art. 7. If under Articles 5 or 6 neither the author nor the editor is liable, or if he was dead when the matter was published, the publisher shall be liable.

The publisher of non-periodical printed matter is taken to be that person who has taken charge of the printing and publication of the writing of another person.

Art. 8. If there was no publisher or if his identity can not be established, the printer shall be liable in place of the publisher.

Art. 9. The provisions of Article 4 shall also apply with respect to the liability of a distributor of non-periodical printed matter.

Provisions Applicable to All Printed Matter

Art. 10. If the person who according to Articles 2, 5, 6 or 7 would have been liable at the publication of the printed matter has no known domicile within the realm, and if in the course of the action his present where abouts in the realm can not be ascertained, liability shall pass to the person next liable in his place, provided that liability shall not pass to the editor of non-periodical printed matter in cases other than those specified in the first paragraph of Article 6, or to a distributor.

Liability shall also pass as aforesaid if there existed circumstances which according to law exclude from punishment the person who would have been liable under Articles 1, 2, 5, 6 or 7, and such circumstances were known, or should have been known, to the person next to him in the line of liability.

Art. 11. Circumstances which under this Chapter would involve liability for a person other than the accused shall be taken into consideration only if the relevant evidence is produced prior to the main court proceedings.

Art. 12. In determining the liability of a person who under this Chapter is liable for printed matter, the contents of the matter shall be deemed to have inserted with the knowledge and consent of the said person.

CHAPTER 9

ON SUPERVISION AND LEGAL PROCEEDINGS

Art. 1. The head of the Ministry of Justice himself or through representatives appointed by him shall supervise the observance of this Act.

Instructions for the representatives shall be issued by the head of the Ministry of Justice.

Art. 2. If the head of the Ministry of Justice considers that public proceedings should be instituted concerning an offense against the freedom of the press, he shall deliver the printed matter to the Attorney General with a notification to that effect. Even without being notified as aforesaid the Attorney General may bring action concerning such offenses against the freedom of the press as may be the subject of public proceedings.

The Attorney General shall be the prosecutor of other violations of the provisions of this Act.

Art. 3. Unless public proceedings concerning an offense against the freedom of the press have been instituted within six months from the date of publication and delivery of an inspection copy as provided in Chapter 4, Article 7, such proceedings shall not be allowed. If, however, public proceedings have been instituted within the said period, new proceedings may be instituted, notwithstanding the foregoing provisions, against another person who is responsible for the offense.

The statutory provisions regarding the time within which an offense must be prosecuted if punishment is to follow shall also apply to offenses against the freedom of the press.

Art. 4. The provisions of law shall apply to the right of a private plaintiff to report offenses against the freedom of the press or to plead with respect to such offenses.

Art. 5. If, according to the provisions of Chapter 8, no person may be charged as liable for the offense, or if no summons can be served here in the realm on the person liable, the prosecutor or plaintiff may, in lieu of instituting legal proceedings, petition for the confiscation of the printed matter.

CHAPTER 10

ON SPECIAL COERCIVE MEASURES

Art. 1. If there is reason to believe that a printed matter may be subject to confiscation owing to an offense against the freedom of the press, the publication may be seized pending a decision on the question.

Furthermore, pending decision of the court, a publishing ban may be issued with respect to a periodical in the cases contemplated in Chapter 7, Article 8.

Art. 2. If an offense against the freedom of the press may be made the subject of public prosecution, a seizure order under Article 1 and a publishing ban may be issued by the head of the Ministry of Justice before prosecution proceedings have been instituted or petition has been made to the court for the confiscation of the printed matter. The head of the Ministry of Justice may also commission one of his representatives to issue of seizure order.

Art. 3. The order provided for in Article 2 shall not be issued later than one week after publication or delivery of an inspection copy under the provisions of Chapter 4, Article 7.

When a representative of the head of the Ministry of Justice has ordered a seizure, a notice to that effect shall be forwarded without delay together with a copy of the publication to the head of the Ministry of Justice, who shall forthwith determine whether the seizure shall be upheld. If, under the provisions set forth below, the printed matter has been impounded, the head of the Ministry of Justice shall determine, as soon as possible, whether it shall be seized, and a decision to this effect may be given notwithstanding the provisions of the first paragraph.

Art. 4. When the head of the Ministry of Justice has ordered a seizure or confirmed a seizure order issued by a representative, the printed matter and information concerning the seizure shall be submitted forthwith to the Attorney General. If criminal proceedings have not been initiated, nor petition for confiscation been made, within two weeks from the date on which the Attorney General received the information, the seizure and any publishing ban attending it shall become void.

Art. 5. After the institution of proceedings concerning an offense against the freedom of the press or after a petition has been made to the court for confiscation, the court may order a seizure and issue a publishing ban or repeal an order of seizure or ban previously issued.

When a decision is given in an action, the court shall determine whether an order issued shall continue in force. If a case is dismissed because the court is not competent, or if the court otherwise dismisses a case without deciding whether the printed matter is of a criminal nature, and there is reason to believe that confiscation will be demanded in another action, the court may confirm the order for a limited period to be determined by the court. If no action has been brought within that period, the order shall become void.

Art. 6. A seizure order shall contain a statement as to the passage or passages in the publication that have occasioned the seizure and shall apply only to the volume, part, issue or number wherein such passages occur.

Art. 7. A seizure order shall be executed forthwith by the police authority, provided that a seizure order issued in a locality by a representative of the head of the Ministry of Justice may be executed only in that locality until it has been confirmed by the head of the Ministry of Justice.

The circulation of printed matter which has been seized is subject to the prohibition embodied in Chapter 6, Article 3.

Art. 8. Seizure of a publication shall be carried out only with regard to those copies which were intended for circulation.

Official evidence of the seizure shall be furnished without cost to the person on whose premises the seizure takes place and to the printing establishment at which the publication was printed. Such evidence shall contain information concerning the passage or passages in the publication which caused the seizure.

Art. 9. Whenever a seizure order has been repealed or has become void, the seizure shall forthwith cease to have effect.

Art. 10. Printed matter which manifestly constitutes an offense against decency punishable according to Chapter 7, Article 4, may, pending a seizure order, be impounded by a decision of the police authority. If there is danger in delay, action as aforesaid may also be taken by a police officer without such decision, but this action shall be reported without delay to the police authority, which must forthwith consider whether the publication shall remain impounded.

Art. 11. If in a detachment of the armed forces, printed matter is discovered which manifestly constitutes such incitement, punishable under the provisions of Chapter 7, Article 4, as may induce members of the armed forces to neglect their duties, such matter, by decision of the officer who according to law has the right to impose punishment with regard to personnel in the detachment, may be impounded pending a seizure order. If there is danger in delay, action as aforesaid may also be taken without such decision by another official of the rank of officer or non-commissioned officer. However, such action shall be reported without delay to the first-mentioned officer, who shall forthwith consider whether the publication shall remain impounded.

Art. 12. When under the provisions of Articles 10 or 11 a decision has been made on the impounding of printed matter, a notice to that effect together with a copy of the publication shall, as soon as possible, be submitted to the head of the Ministry of Justice.

Art. 13. The provisions of law generally applicable to the seizure of objects that may be declared forfeited shall apply to the seizure of a periodical printed matter circulated in violation of a publishing ban or manifestly constituting a continuation of a periodical specified in such ban.

CHAPTER 11

ON PRIVATE CLAIMS

Art. 1. A private claim based on abuse of the freedom of the press may be entered solely on the ground that the printed matter specified in the claim contains an offense against the freedom of the press. Unless otherwise provided below, such claim may be made only against the person who is liable for the offense in accordance with Chapter 8. If by reason of the circumstances contemplated in Chapter 8, Article 10, liability has devolved on such person, the claim may also be made against the person liable immediately before him, provided that, and to such an extent as, the said claim may otherwise be made according to law.

The provisions of Chapter 8, Article 12, concerning liability shall also apply to private claims.

Art. 2. A private claim that may be made against the editor of a periodical printed matter or his deputy may also be made against the owner. For other printed matter, a claim that may be made against the author or editor may also be made against the publisher.

Art. 3. If any person as legal representative of a legal person, or as guardian or trustee, is answerable for a private claim owing to an offense against the freedom of the press, such claim may also be made against the legal person, or against the person for whom the guardian or trustee was appointed, provided that, and to such extent as, the said claim may otherwise be made according to law.

Art. 4. If a person under this Chapter is answerable together with another person for a private claim, both such persons shall be jointly and severally answerable. Determination of the respective liability of the two parties shall be governed by the relevant provisions of law.

Art. 5. A private claim based on an offense against the freedom of the press may be made even though criminal liability for the offense has ceased or no action in the matter may otherwise be brought.

CHAPTER 12

ON TRIAL OF ACTIONS

IN FREEDOM OF THE PRESS CASES

Art. 1. Actions concerning the freedom of the press shall be brought before the city court in the city which is the seat of the county government or, if no city court exists in that city, before such city court within the county as by order of the King is designated to hear such cases arising within the county. If there is any reason prompting the designation of another city court within the county to hear actions concerning the freedom of the press, the King may issue orders to that effect.

If no city court exists within the county the King may designate a city court outside the county to adjudge freedom of the press actions arising within the county.

Actions concerning the freedom of the press include actions arising out of liability and private claims resulting from offenses against the freedom of the press, as well as petition cases as specified in Chapter 9, Article 5.

Art. 2. In a case concerning the freedom of the press involving a liability action the question whether the printed matter is criminal shall be tried by a jury of nine members, unless both parties declare themselves willing to refer the case to the court for decision without a jury. Whenever the criminal nature of printed matter is tried by a jury, the matter shall be considered criminal if at least six members of the jury concur in that opinion.

If the jury finds that the matter is not criminal, the accused shall be acquitted. If the jury considers it criminal, the court shall also consider whether the matter is criminal. If the opinion of the court differs from that of the jury, the court shall have the right to acquit the accused or to apply a penal provision less severe than that contemplated by the jury.

Art. 3. Jurors shall be selected in each county and shall be divided into two groups with sixteen jurors in the first group and eight in the second group. The jurors in the second group must be or have been lay members on an ordinary court of first instance. In the city and county of Stockholm the jurors shall be selected jointly.

Art. 4. Jurors shall be selected for a term of four calendar years.

In the city and county of Stockholm the jurors shall be elected by the city council of Stockholm and the county council of the county of Stockholm, and in other counties by the county council or, where there is more than one council in the county or a city that is not represented on a county council, by such county councils, or by the county council and the city council of the said city. If, as aforesaid, jurors are to be elected by more than one electoral body, the number of jurors in each group shall be divided between the electoral bodies in proportion to the population, in the case of the city and county of Stockholm, by the King, and in all other cases by the county government.

Elections shall be executed during the year immediately preceding the election term, by the county councils in ordinary session and by the city councils after the county councils have completed their elections.

When jurors are to be elected it shall be incumbent upon the city court to give notice to this effect to the authority responsible for arranging the election.

Art. 5. Jurors shall be chosen from among Swedish citizens resident in the county who have attained the age of twenty-five years. They shall be known for soundness of judgment, independence and fair-mindedness. The different social groups and currents of opinion, and various parts of the county, shall be represented among the jurors.

A person under guardianship or a bankrupt shall not be a juror.

Art. 6. Jurors who have attained the age of sixty years shall be entitled to withdraw from their duties. If a juror otherwise wishes to retire, the city court shall examine whether valid reasons exist which prevent him from fulfilling his duties. If a juror ceases to be eligible, his commission shall no longer be valid.

Art. 7. If a juror retires or ceases to be eligible, the electoral body shall select another person from the group to which the retired member belonged to replace him for the remainder of the election period. Such a juror may be elected by the executive committee of the county council on behalf of the county council, but such election shall be valid only until the next ordinary session of the county council.

Art. 8. Complaints concerning the election of jurors shall be lodged with the city court. Even though no complaint has been lodged, the court shall examine the qualifications of the persons elected.

The provisions of law concerning appeal of the decision of a court of first instance in a trial shall also apply to an appeal of the decision of a city court on a question specified in the first paragraph. An appeal shall not lie from the decision of a court of appeal.

Even if a complaint is lodged, the election shall be valid unless the court decides otherwise.

Art. 9. Persons chosen as jurors shall be entered on a jurors' list on which each group shall be included separately.

Art. 10. When a case in which a jury is to participate comes before the court, the court shall present the jurors' list and shall raise the question whether any challenge lies before the court to a person included on the list. The provisions of law on judges shall apply to such a challenge.

The jury shall then be composed of unchallengeable jurors in the following manner: each party shall have the right to exclude three jurors in the first group and one in the second, and the court shall then by lot select substitutes from among those who remain until six jurors remain in the first group and three in the second.

Art. 11. If there are several parties on one side and only one of them wishes to make use of his right of exclusion, the exclusion made by him shall be deemed also to be made by the others. If joint parties wish to exclude different jurors, and are unable to reach an agreement, the court shall make the exclusion by lot.

Art. 12. No person shall be excused from jury duty without a legitimate excuse.

If because of challenges or legitimate excuses the number of members required in a group cannot be obtained, the court shall name for each juror required, three persons eligible to be jurors in that group. Each party shall have the right to exclude one of the persons so named. No person shall be named as juror who was previously excluded in the same case.

Art. 13. If several cases in which a jury is to take part come before the court at the same time, the court may, with the consent of the parties, provide that the same jury shall serve in all the cases. If a jury is to be selected jointly for several cases, the provisions of Article 11 shall apply concerning the exclusion of jurors in a case in which there are several parties on one side.

Art. 14. If in a case concerning liability an action involving a private claim is also brought against a person other than the accused, the steps to be taken by the defendant as specified in the first paragraph of Article 2, the second paragraph of Article 10, and the second paragraph of Article 12 shall be incumbent upon the accused.

If an action not involving prosecution is brought concerning the confiscation of printed matter or a private claim, the provisions of Article 2 and of Articles 10–13 shall apply to the trial, but if the criminal nature of the matter has been previously considered in a case involving liability for an offense against the freedom of the press, the criminal nature of such matter shall not again be considered. In a petition case the exclusion of jurors which is otherwise the right of the parties, shall be made by the court by lot.

Art. 15. Further regulations concerning the trial of freedom of the press cases shall be given in a special law passed in the manner prescribed in Article 87 of the Instrument of Government.

If within one county there are several city courts before which an action concerning the freedom of the press may be brought, the duties specified in Articles 4, 6, 8 and 9 shall be performed by that city court which the King shall designate.

CHAPTER 13

ON MATTERS PRINTED IN FOREIGN COUNTRIES

Art. 1. Matter printed outside the realm shall be deemed to have been published here when in the manner set forth in Chapter 1, Article 6, it has been delivered for circulation within the realm.

Art. 2. If a periodical that is printed outside the realm is intended principally for circulation within the realm, the provisions of Chapter 5 shall apply where relevant, but what is said therein regarding the qualifications of owners shall not be applicable.

Publication in the realm of any other periodical that is printed outside the realm shall not require a publishing license, provided, however, that if such a license exists, the provisions of the first paragraph shall apply to the publication.

Art. 3. With regard to matter printed outside the realm, the provisions of this Act concerning the responsibility of printers shall refer to the person who caused the matter to be delivered for circulation in the realm, or if the identity of such person can not be established or, if at the time it was published here he was not domiciled in the realm, to the person who is to be considered as the distributor according to the provisions of Chapter 6.

Art. 4. Inspection copies of a periodical printed matter for which a publishing license is required, or has nevertheless been issued, shall be delivered as provided in Chapter 4, Article 7. This shall also apply to non-periodical printed matter, if such matter is entirely or partially in the Swedish language and has been imported otherwise than in the form of a few copies.

The obligation specified in the first paragraph shall be incumbent, in the case of periodicals, upon the editor, and with respect to other printed matter, upon the publisher or, if there is no publisher, upon the person who caused it to be delivered for circulation in the realm. If the obligation is not complied with, the provisions of Chapter 4, Article 8, shall be applicable.

The obligation to deliver library copies of matter that has been printed outside the realm shall be regulated by law.

Art. 5. The provisions of the second paragraph of Chapter 1, Article 1, concerning the making of statements and the communication of information with a view to publication shall also apply to communications for publication in matter printed outside the realm, provided that the communication does not refer to conditions the disclosure of which would constitute an offense against the security of the realm, or concerning which the informant is otherwise obliged by law to observe silence. If the communication in this respect is punishable as a crime special legislation is applicable. If the communication constitutes defamation of a private person but has not been printed, the provisions of law concerning responsibility for such defamation shall apply.

The relevant provisions of Chapters 1, 3, 4 (Article 9), 6, 7, 8 (Articles 1, 2, 5–7 and 10–12) and Chapters 9–12 shall also apply to matter that is printed outside the realm and published herein.

CHAPTER 14

GENERAL PROVISIONS

Art. 1. The provisions of law concerning the retrial of cases in general shall also apply to actions concerning the freedom of the press, even if the criminal nature of the printed matter has been considered by a jury.

If a case in which a jury has considered the criminal nature of printed matter becomes subject to retrial owing to circumstances that may be presumed to have influenced the jury's deliberations, the Supreme Court shall order such case again to be presented to a jury before the court which first pronounced judgment, provided that where a retrial has been granted for the benefit of the accused, and the facts are obvious, the Supreme Court may change the judgment directly.

Art. 2. The provisions of Chapter 12, Articles 10–14, shall apply to the appointment of a jury when on the decision of a higher court an action concerning the freedom of the press, in which a jury had participated, is again to be presented to a jury before the court that first pronounced judgment.

Art. 3. Actions concerning the freedom of the press and other actions concerning offenses against the provisions of this Act shall always be dealt with promptly.

Art. 4. Fines and penalties imposed under this Act shall accrue to the crown.

Art. 5. In all matters not dealt with by this Act or by special legislation authorized by this Act, the provisions of laws or statutes in general shall apply.

Except as otherwise provided in this Act or in other laws or statutes, foreign nationals shall be treated on a basis of equality with Swedish citizens.

Art. 6. In this Act the terms "laws" and "legislation" refer to enactments passed by joint decision of the King and the Riksdag as provided in each case by fundamental law.

Whereunto all whom it may concern shall be required to conform. In witness whereof we have with our own hand signed and with our royal seal confirmed this Act.

The Royal Palace in Stockholm, April 5, 1949.

SWITZERLAND

SUMMARY

INTERNATIONAL STATUS

Switzerland is not a member of the United Nations. It is a party to the Statute of the International Court of Justice (1948)[1] and a member of other international organizations. It was a member of the League of Nations.

The ancient alliances which, since the original Eternal Alliance of the three cantons of Uri, Schwyz and Nidwalden in 1291, had developed into

[1] It accepts the compulsory jurisdiction of the International Court under Article 36 of its Statute.

a complex network of treaties, collapsed under the influence of the French Revolution. On April 12, 1798, the Constitution of the Helvetic Republic, drawn up in Paris, established a unitary system. On February 19, 1802, this was replaced by the Act of Mediation based on the principle of a federal state. On August 7, 1815, after months of negotiation between the cantons and under the pressure of the Congress of Vienna, the Federal Pact between the twenty-two cantons was sworn in Zurich. It created a common confederal link between the cantons instead of the numerous and disparate pre-1798 treaties, without instituting a central authority, and thus established cohesion in external affairs while leaving complete internal autonomy to the cantons. A period of reconstruction followed.

In 1830, the "Regeneration" movement led to reforms in the cantonal constitutions and discussions concerning reinforcing of the federal power. A commission meeting from October 29 to December 15, 1832, drew up a proposed Federal Pact for the Swiss Confederation. The vote by the cantons on the revision was not favorable, divergences between the cantons grew wider in the succeeding years, and only after the war of the Sonderbund in November 1847, won after a brief campaign by the federal army, was a new Revision Commission able to meet and prepare the constitution which was adopted on September 12, 1848. A movement to amend the constitution began in 1864, in order to take account of the extension of political rights in the cantonal constitutions and the unifying movements in Germany and Italy. After the 1870 war between France and Germany it became clear that an entirely revised constitution was necessary and a proposal submitted in 1872 with strongly centralist tendencies was narrowly defeated in the referendum, to be accepted after revision and moderation by the referendum of April 19, 1874.

FORM OF NATIONAL GOVERNMENT

The Constitution of May 29, 1874, as amended and revised to December 31, 1964, provides that the peoples of the twenty-two sovereign cantons form together the Swiss Confederation. The cantons are sovereign insofar as their sovereignty is not limited by the Federal Constitution.[1] The Confederation must guarantee the constitutions of the cantons.[2] The Confederation may not maintain a standing army.[3] The Constitution describes matters falling within federal or cantonal jurisdiction.[4]

RIGHTS OF THE PEOPLE

All Swiss are equal before the law.[5] The Constitution provides freedom of conscience and belief, the right to marry without impediment of religion,

[1] Const., Art. 3. [2] Id., Art. 6. [3] Id., Art. 13.
[4] Id., Art. 7–10, 20–41B, 64–69B. [5] Id., Art. 4.

poverty or any "considerations of a police nature", freedom of the press, of association, the right of petition, no extraordinary tribunals, no ecclesiastical jurisdiction, no imprisonment for debt.[1] It guarantees freedom of domicile and secrecy of correspondence.[2] Swiss nationals may not be expelled from the Confederation or from their canton of origin.[3] There are provisions concerning social legislation to be enacted by the Confederation.[4]

LEGISLATIVE DEPARTMENT

The legislature is the bicameral Federal Assembly which exercises the supreme authority of the Confederation and is composed of the National Council and the Council of States.[5] The National Council is composed of 200 deputies apportioned among the cantons in proportion to population, directly elected by proportional representation for a term of four years.[6] The Council of State is composed of two deputies appointed by and from each canton.[7] The Legislature meets once a year in ordinary session.[8] There are provisions relating to finance.[9] Provision is made for submitting laws and decrees to and amending the Constitution by popular referendum.[10]

EXECUTIVE DEPARTMENT

The supreme directing and executive authority of the Confederation is exercised by the Federal Council composed of seven members appointed by the Legislature in joint session, no more than one member of which may be chosen in the same canton, for a term of four years.[11] It is presided over by the President of the Confederation, nominated by the Federal Assembly for one year among from the members of the Council.[12]

JUDICIAL DEPARTMENT

The Constitution provides for a Federal Tribunal for the administration of justice in federal matters whose members are appointed by the Federal Assembly.[13] There is provision also for a Federal administrative court.[14]

[1] Id., Art. 49, 54–59. [2] Id., Art. 45, 36. [3] Id., Art. 44.
[4] Id., Art. 34–34D. [5] Id., Art. 71. [6] Id., Art. 72–76. [7] Id., Art. 80–82.
[8] Id., Art. 86. [9] Id., Art. 41A, 41B, 42, 42A–C. [10] Id., Act. 89, 121.
[11] Id., Art. 95–102. [12] Id., Art. 98. [13] Id., Art. 106, 107. [14] Id., Art. 114A.

AREA, POPULATION, ETC.

The area of Switzerland is 41,288 square kilometres, the population (1960) 5,429,061. The capital is Berne. The national languages are German, French, Italian and Romanche, the official ones are German, French and Italian.[1]

[1] Id., Art. 116.

FEDERAL CONSTITUTION of the SWISS CONFEDERATION [1]

May 29, 1874, as amended and revised to December 31, 1964

In the name of Almighty God! The Swiss Confederation, resolved to consolidate the alliance of the confederated members and to maintain and increase the unity, strength, and honor of the Swiss nation, has adopted the following Federal Constitution:

CHAPTER I

GENERAL PROVISIONS

Art. 1. The peoples of the twenty-two sovereign cantons of Switzerland united in the present alliance, namely: Zurich, Bern, Lucerne, Uri, Schwyz, Unterwalden (Upper and Lower), Glaris, Zug, Freiburg, Solothurn, Basel (City and Country), Schaffhausen, Appenzell (the two Rhodes), St. Gall, Grisons, Aargau, Thurgau, Ticino, Vaud, Valais, Neuchâtel, and Geneva, form together the Swiss Confederation.

Art. 2. The object of the Confederation is to ensure the independence of the country against the foreigner, to maintain tranquillity and order within its borders, to protect the liberties and rights of its members, and to promote their common prosperity.

Art. 3. The cantons are sovereign so far as their sovereignty is not limited by the federal Constitution, and as such they exercise all the rights which are not delegated to the federal power.

Art. 4. All Swiss are equal before the law. In Switzerland there are no subjects nor any privileges of rank, birth, person, or family.

Art. 5. The Confederation guarantees to the cantons their territory, their sovereignty within the limits fixed by Article 3, their constitutions,

[1] *Constitution Fédérale de la Confédération Suisse du 29 Mai 1874 avec les modifications intervenues jusqu'au 1 janvier 1960.* Published by the Chancellerie Fédérale, Berne. English translation reproduced in second edition from *131 British and Foreign State Papers 713*, revised by Editor to bring it to date and conform to French text, including further amendments of 1960 and 1964. Texts supplied by Chancellerie Fédérale, Berne, in November 1965. Ed.

the liberty and rights of their people, the constitutional rights of the citizens, and the rights and power conferred by the people on the authorities.

Art. 6. The cantons are required to demand from the Confederation its guarantee of their constitutions.

This guarantee shall be accorded, provided that:

(a) The constitutions contains nothing contrary to the provisions of the federal Constitution.

(b) They ensure the exercise of political rights according to republican forms—representative or democratic.

(c) They have been accepted by the people and can be revised when an absolute majority of citizens so demand.

Art. 7. All separate alliances and treaties of a political character between cantons are forbidden.

The cantons, however, have the right to make agreement with one another on matters of legislation, administration, or justice; they must, nevertheless, communicate such agreement to the federal authority, which may prohibit their execution if they contain anything prejudicial to the Confederation or the rights of the other cantons. In the absence of such prohibition, the cantons making the agreement are authorized to require the co-operation of the federal authorities in their execution.

Art. 8. The Confederation has the sole right to declare war and conclude peace, and to make alliances and treaties, particularly customs and commercial treaties, with foreign States.

Art. 9. Exceptionally, the cantons retain the right to conclude treaties with foreign States in respect of matters of public economy and police and border relations; but such treaties must not contain anything prejudicial to the Confederation or the rights of other cantons.

Art. 10. Official intercourse between the cantons and foreign governments or their representatives shall take place through the Federal Council.

In regard to the matters mentioned in the preceding article, however, the cantons may correspond directly with the subordinate authorities and officers of a foreign state.

Art. 11. Military "capitulations" [1] may not be concluded.

Art. 12.[2] Members of the federal authorities, civil and military officials, and federal representatives or commissioners, as also members of the cantonal governments and legislative assemblies, may not accept from a foreign government any pension, salary, title, gift, or decoration. Contravention of this prohibition involves loss of the mandate or office.

[1] Agreements for the supply of mercenary troops to foreign countries.

[2] As amended February 8, 1931. A transitory provision adopted at the same time reads: Anyone who, before the the revised Article 12 became effective, has received in a legal manner a decoration or title, may be elected or appointed a member of a federal authority, civil or military functionary of the Confederation, federal representative er commissioner, member of the government or legislative asembly of a canton if he agrees to renounce, for the term of his mandate or function, usage of his title or decoration. Contravention of this agreement will result in the loss of the mandate or function."

No one who is in possession of such a pension, title, or decoration may be elected or appointed member of a federal authority, civil or military official or the Confederation, federal representative or commissioner, or member of a cantonal government or legislative assembly unless, before exercising the mandate or office, he expressly renounces the enjoyment of his pension or the bearing of his title, or returns his decoration.

In the Federal army decorations and titles awarded by any foreign government are prohibited.

No officer, non-commissioned officer, or soldier may accept any such distinction.

Art. 13. The Confederation may not maintain a standing army.

No canton or half-canton may maintain more than 300 men as a permanent military force (excluding police) without permission of the Federal authority.

Art. 14. The cantons must abstain, in the event of differences arising between them, from any attack or resort to arms. They must submit to the settlement of such differences in the manner prescribed by the Confederation.

Art. 15. In case of sudden danger from without, the government of the canton threatened must invoke the assistance of the Confederated States and immediately notify the Federal Authority, the measures which may subsequently be taken by the latter not being prejudiced thereby. The cantons so called upon are bound to give their assistance. The cost shall be borne by the Confederation.

Art. 16. In case of internal disorder or of danger being threatened from another canton, the Government of the canton threatened must immediately notify the Federal Council, in order that that body may take the necessary measures within the limits of its competence (Article 102, Nos. 3, 10 and 11) or convene the Federal Assembly. In case of urgency the cantonal Government, while immediately notifying the Federal Council, may call for the assistance of the other Confederated States, which the latter are bound to render.

When the cantonal Government is not in a position to summon assistance, the competent Federal Authority may intervene on its own initiative, and is bound to do so if the disorders endanger the safety of Switzerland.

When the Federal Authorities intervene, they must ensure the observance of the provisions of Article 5.

The costs shall be borne by the canton by which assistance was invoked or intervention necessitated, unless the Federal Assembly on consideration of the special circumstances should otherwise decide.

Art. 17. Every canton must give free passage to troops in the cases mentioned in Articles 15 and 16.

The troops are placed immediately under Federal command.

Art. 18. Every Swiss male is liable for military service. Soldiers who lose their lives or suffer permanent injury to their health in the Federal service are entitled to assistance from the Confederation for themselves or their families, if in need.

Every soldier shall be supplied, free of charge, with his first outfit of arms, equipment and clothing. Arms remain in the possession of the soldier upon conditions to be determined by Federal legislation.

The tax on exemption from military service shall be collected by the cantons for the account of the Confederation according to the provisions of federal legislation.

Art. 19. The Federal army consists of:

(a) the cantonal corps;

(b) all Swiss who, not being members of these corps, are nevertheless liable for military service.

The control of the Federal army and of war material provided in accordance with the law is vested in the Confederation.

In case of danger, the Confederation has also the right of exclusive and immediate control over all men not incorporated in the Federal army and of all other military resources of the cantons.

The cantons exercise control over the military forces of their territory save insofar as this right is limited by the Constitution or by Federal legislation.

Art. 20. Laws as to the organization of the army are enacted by the Confederation. The execution of military laws within the cantons is undertaken by the Cantonal authorities within the limits prescribed by Federal legislation and under the supervision of the Confederation.

Military instruction and the arming of troops are under the exclusive control of the Confederation.

The supply and renewal of clothing and equipment are within the competence of the cantons, but the cost thereof shall be reimbursed to the cantons in manner to be prescribed by Federal law.

Art. 21. So far as military considerations permit, each corps shall consist of troops from the same canton.

The composition of such corps, the obligation of maintaining their strength, and the appointment and promotion of their officers rests with the cantons, subject to general regulations communicated to them by the Confederation.

Art. 22. In return for reasonable compensation, the Confederation has the right to make use of or to acquire drill grounds and buildings used for military purposes, together with all accessories, in the cantons.

The conditions governing compensation shall be regulated by Federal legislation.

Art. 22A. Legislation regarding civil protection of persons or goods against the consequences of acts of war fall within the competence of the Confederation.

The cantons shall be consulted at the time such laws are drawn up and are obliged to apply them under the supervision of the Confederation.

A law shall establish the subsidies to be granted by the Confederation to cover the expenses arising out of civilian protection.

The Confederation is authorized to institute obligatory service for men. Women may take part voluntarily in civilian protection under conditions to be stipulated by law.

Compensation, insurance and allocations for loss of livelihood by persons in the service of civilian protection shall be regulated by law.

A law shall regulate the use of organizations of civilian protection in cases of emergency help.

Art. 23. The Confederation may construct at its own expense, or encourage by subsidies the construction of, public works of utility to Switzerland as a whole, or to any considerable part of the country.

For this purpose it may order expropriations on payment of just compensation. Federal legislation will make the necessary provision in this respect.

The Federal Assembly may prohibit public works which endanger the military interests of the Confederation.

Art. 23A. The Confederation shall maintain the wheat reserves which are necessary to ensure the provisioning of the country. It may oblige millers to stock wheat or acquire reserves of wheat in order to facilitate the renewal of supplies.

The Confederation shall encourage the cultivation of wheat in the country, shall facilitate the selection and acquisition of native seed of good quality, and shall grant assistance to producers cultivating wheat for this own needs, special consideration being given to mountanous regions. It shall buy native wheat of good quality suitable for grinding at a price which allows the cultivation. Millers may be compelled to purchase such wheat at its market value.

The Confederation shall ensure the maintenance of the national milling industry; it shall also safeguard the interests of consumers of flour and bread. It shall supervise within the limits of its powers trade in and the prices of wheat, bread flour and bread. The Confederation shall take the necessary measures to regulate the importation of bread-flour and may reserve to itself the exclusive right of importing this product. In case of need, the Confederation shall grant the mills facilities to enable them to reduce costs of transport to the interior of the country. It shall take appropriate measures in favor of mountainous districts to equalize the prices of flour.

The statistical duty charged on all merchandise passing the Swiss customs shall be raised. The proceeds of this duty shall contribute to covering the expenses arising out of supplying the country with wheat.

Art. 24. The Confederation has the right of supreme control of the policing of embankments and forests.

It will assist in the control and embanking of rivers and the reafforestation of the districts in which they rise, and will decree the measures necessary for the maintenance of such works and the preservation of the existing forests.

Art. 24A. The utilization of water-power is under the supreme control of the Confederation.

Federal legislation will make the necessary provision for safeguarding the public interest and ensuring the rational utilization of water-power, taking into account, as far as possible, the interests of internal navigation.

Subject to such Federal legislation, the cantons regulate the utilization of water-power.

Concessions shall, notwithstanding, be granted by the Confederation in any case where the utilization of a watercourse under the jurisdiction of more than one canton is sought for the production of hydraulic power and the cantons have failed to come to any agreement as to the granting of a concession. The Confederation shall likewise have power to grant concessions, after hearing the views of the cantons concerned, in respect of watercourses forming the frontier of the country.

Fees and royalties payable in respect of the utilization of water-power are the property of the cantons or of those entitled to them under cantonal law.

Fees and royalties payable in respect of concessions made by the Confederation shall be determined by the Confederation, after consideration of the views of the cantons concerned and having due regard to their legislation. Fees and royalties payable in respect of other concessions shall be determined by the cantons, subject to the limitations imposed by Federal legislation.

The diversion abroad of energy produced from water-power may not take place without authority from the Confederation.

Upon the coming into force of this Article all new water-power concessions shall be subject to future Federal legislation.

The Confederation has the right to legislate upon the transmission and distribution of electrical energy.

Art. 24B. Legislation affecting navigation is within the province of the Confederation.

Art. 24C. The Confederation has the right to legislate in order to protect surface and subterranean waters against pollution. The implementation of such measures is reserved to the cantons under the supervision of the Confederation.

Art. 24D. Legislation on atomic energy falls within the domain of the Confederation. The Confederation shall issue regulations concerning protection against ionizing rays.

Art. 24E. The protection of nature and the countryside falls within the domain of cantonal law.

In carrying out its tasks, the Confederation must respect the characteristic aspects of the countryside and localities, sites reminiscent of the past, natural curiosities and monuments, and conserve them intact wherever there is a preponderant general interest.

The Confederation may subsidize efforts for the protection of nature and the countryside and may acquire or preserve, by contract or appropriation, nature reservations, sites evocative of the past and monuments of national importance.

The Confederation may legislate for the protection of fauna and flora.

Art. 25. The Confederation may make laws for the regulating of fishing and hunting, particularly with a view to the preservation of forest animals in the mountains and the protection of birds useful to agriculture and sylviculture.

Art. 25A. The bleeding of animals for slaughter which have not been previously stunned is expressly forbidden. This provision applies to all methods of slaughter and to all kinds of animals.

Art. 26. Legislation on the construction and working of railways is within the province of the Confederation.

Art. 26A. Legislation on transport installations by pipe lines of fuel or liquid or gas carburants falls within the domain of the Confederation.

Art. 27. The Confederation may establish, in addition to the existing Federal Polytechnic, a Federal University and other institutions for higher education, or may subsidise establishments of this kind.

The cantons provide for primary education, which must be adequate and exclusively under the control of the civil authorities. Primary education is compulsory and, in the public schools, free.

Public schools must be open for the attendance of members of all religions faiths without prejudice to them in any way in respect of their conscience or belief.

The Confederation will take any necessary measures against cantons which fail to fulfil these obligations.

Art. 27. Subventions shall be granted to the cantons to aid them in carrying out their obligations in respect of primary education. Effect will be given to this provision by legislation. The organization, direction and supervision of primary schools remains within the competence of the cantons, subject to the provisions of Article 27.

Art. 27B. The Confederation has the right to legislate in the form of laws or general decrees in order to:

(a) encourage Swiss cinematographic production and other cultural activities in the realm of the cinema;

(b) regulate the importation and distribution of films, and the opening and transformation of film projection enterprises; it may where necessary in the general interest of culture or of the State depart from the principles of freedom of commerce and industry.

The cantons shall be consulted in the elaboration of implementing legislation, as well as the cultural and economic associations concerned.

Wherever federal legislation makes the opening or transformation of film projection enterprises subject to authorization, it shall be the duty of the cantons to grant such authorizations according to procedure which they shall determine.

In all other matters, the drawing up and implementation of legislation relating to the cinema shall fall within the competence of the cantons.

Art. 27C. The Confederation may grant subventions to the cantons for their expenses for scholarships and other financial aids to eduction.

It may itself take or support measures, additional to cantonal regulations, designed to assist education by scholarships or other financial assistance.

In all cases, cantonal autonomy in educational matters shall be respected.

Implementing provisions shall be issued in the form of federal laws or general decrees. The cantons shall be consulted before they are taken.

Art. 28. Customs duties are within the province of the Confederation, which may impose import and export taxes.

Art. 29. The collection of Federal customs must be regulated in accordance with the following principles:

1. Import taxes.

   (a) Materials necessary to the industry and agriculture of the country must be taxed as lightly as possible.

   (b) The same principle applies to commodities necessary for the maintenance of life.

   (c) Articles of luxury must be subject to the heaviest taxes. Except where circumstances render it impossible, these principles must be observed in the conclusion of commercial treaties with foreign countries.

2. Export taxes must be as moderate as possible.

3. Legislation on customs will contain suitable provisions for the continuance of commercial and market intercourse across the frontier.

The foregoing provisions do not preclude the Confederation from taking exceptional measures temporarily to meet abnormal circumstances.

Art. 30. Revenue from customs duties belongs to the Confederation.

Art. 31. The freedom of trade and commerce is guaranteed throughout the Confederation, insofar as it is not limited by the Federal Constitution and laws based on constitutional provisions.

Cantonal regulations concerning the exercise of commercial and industrial occupations, and taxes in connection therewith, remain unaffected. Such regulations may not contain any provisions contravening the principle of freedom of trade and commerce unless permitted by the Federal Constitution. Cantonal monopolies are also excepted.

Art. 31A. The Confederation takes the necessary measures within its constitutional authority for the welfare of the people and the economic security of the citizens.

With due regard for the general interest of the Swiss economy as a whole, the Confederation may enact regulations concerning the exercise of trades and industries and may take measures for the development of certain branches or professions. The Confederation is bound (excluding the exceptions contained in paragraph 3 of this Article) to the observance of the principle of freedom of trade and commerce.

If justified in the national interest, the Confederation is authorized to enact regulations in the following matters which may, if necessary, deviate from the principle of freedom of trade and commerce:

(a) Measures for the maintenance of important branches and professions whose existence is jeopardized; as well as measures for the professional furtherance of self-employed persons in these branches or professions.

(b) Measures for the maintenance of a healthy and productive agriculture; as well as measures for the protection of land ownership by farmers.

(c) Measures for the protection of distressed areas.

(d) Measures against economically and socially dangerous effects of cartels and similar groups.

(e) Measures to insure preparedness in time of war.

Measures in accordance with (a) and (b) may be taken only if the branches or professions to be protected have exhausted all ordinary means of self-help.

The federal legislation adopted in accordance with paragraph 3, (a) and (b), must guarantee the development of economic organizations based on mutual assistance.

Art. 31B. The cantons are authorized to enact legislation with regard to the requirements for the management of hotels and restaurants. The cantons may limit the number of such enterprises if they exceed the public need and if the existence of the industry is threatened by excessive competition. These regulations must take into account the relative importance of the different types of hostelries for the public welfare.

The Confederation, within its own legislative powers, may furthermore authorize the cantons to issue regulations in fields which do not require general regulation by the Confederation itself and which actually do not fall under the jurisdiction of the cantons.

Art. 31C. The Confederation is authorized to regulate banks.

These regulations must take into account the special function and position of the cantonal banks.

Art. 31D. The Confederation, in connection with the cantons and private business, takes measures to prevent economic crises and, if necessary, to relieve existing unemployment. The Confederation may act with regard to the creation of employment opportunities.

Art. 32. The measures provided for in Article 31A, 31B, paragraph 2, 31C and 31D may be introduced only in the form of federal laws or federal decrees subject to the referendum. For cases of an urgent character, in times of economic stress, Article 89, paragraph 3,[1] may be invoked.

The cantons must be consulted before the enactment of laws providing for the execution of these measures. As a rule, the execution of the federal regulations must be entrusted to the cantons.

The competent business organizations should also be consulted before the enactment of the laws of execution. They may be asked to co-operate in the execution of these measures.

Art. 32A. The Confederation has the right to legislate regarding the manufacture, importation, purification, sale, and taxation of distilled beverages.

Such legislation shall conduce to diminish the consumption and consequently the importation and production of spirits. It shall encourage the production of table fruit and the use of native distillable matters for food or fodder. The Confederation will reduce the number of distilling plants by means of private purchases.

The concession for the industrial production of distilled beverages is granted to co-operative societies and other private undertakings. The concessions granted must permit of the utilization of the waste matter and residues of fruit, vine, and sugar-beet cultivation and the surplus crops of fruit and potatoes, as far as these raw materials are incapable of being rationally used otherwise than in distillation.

The non-industrial production of spirits from fruit and fruit waste, of cider, wine, grape and wine dregs, gentian roots and other similar materials is permitted in domestic distilleries already existing or in itinerant distilleries, provided that such materials originate exclusively from the individual crop of the producer or have been gathered in a wild state in the country. The spirit thus obtained, which is necessary in the household or agricultural business of the producer, is exempt from taxation. Domestic distilleries which are still in existence after the expiration of a period of fifteen years dating from the acceptance of the present article must, in order to continue working, apply for a concession, which will be granted without payment on conditions to be fixed by law.

Specialties obtained by the distillation of kernel fruit, wine, grape and wine dregs, gentian roots and other similar materials are subjected to the payment of a tax. The producer must, however, be able to get a fair price for his raw materials of native origin.

[1] Article 89, paragraph 3, has been repealed and replaced by Article 89A.

With the exception of the quantities necessary to the producer, which are exempt from taxation, and specialties, spirits manufactured in the country shall be handed over to the Confederation. The latter shall take them over at fair prices.

Products exported or in transit or adulterated are exempt from tax.

The receipts accruing from duties upon the sale and retail trade within the limits of the cantonal territory remain the property of the cantons. Licences for intercantonal and international trade issued by the Confederation; the receipts therefrom shall be distributed among the cantons in proportion to their populations ordinarily resident.

Half of the net receipts accruing to the Confederation from the taxation of distilled beverages shall be distributed among the cantons in proportion to their populations ordinarily resident; each canton is bound to expend at least ten per cent of its share in combating the causes and effects of alcoholism. The other half of the receipts remains the property of the Confederation; it shall be set apart for old age and dependents' insurance, and shall be paid into the funds established for the same until the time such insurance is introduced.

Art. 32B. The manufacture, importation, transport, sale and keeping for sale of the liquor called absinthe are prohibited throughout the Confederation. This prohibition extends to all beverages, by whatever names called, which constitute imitations of absinthe. The transport in transit of absinthe and its use for pharmaceutical purposes are excepted.

The foregoing prohibition will come into operation two years after its adoption. Federal legislation will enact the necessary provisions consequent on this prohibition.

The Confederation has the right to impose by law the same prohibition on all other beverages containing absinthe which might constitute a public danger.

Art. 32C. Cantons have the right to subject, by means of legislation, the exercise of the calling of publican and the retail trade in spirituous beverages to the restrictions required by the public welfare. Trade in quantities of less than two liters is deemed to be retail trade in non-distilled spirituous beverages.

Trade in non-distilled spirituous beverages in quantities from two to ten liters may, within the limits of Article 31, paragraph 2, and by means of legislation, be made conditional by the cantons on the payment of a small fee and subjected to the supervision of the authorities.

The sale of non-distilled spirituous beverages may not be subjected by the cantons to special taxation other than license duties.

Juridical persons must not be treated less favorably than physical persons. Producers of wine and cider may, without permission and without paying any duty, sell the product of their own crop in quantities of two liters or over.

The Confederation has the right to legislate on trade in non-distilled spirituous beverages in quantities of two liters or over. The regulations which it may issue must not contain anything which contravenes the principle of freedom of commerce and industry.

Colportage and other means of itinerant sale of spirituous beverages are prohibited.

Art. 33. The cantons may require evidence of capacity from persons desiring to practice the liberal professions.

Federal legislation shall make provision that such persons may be able to obtain certificates of qualification valid throughout the Confederation.

Art. 34. The Confederation has the right to make uniform regulations concerning child labor in factories, the hours of work of adults therein, and the protection of workers in unhealthy and dangerous industries.

The operations of emigration agencies and insurance undertakings not established by the State are subject to federal supervision and legislation.

Art. 34A. The Confederation will introduce, by means of legislation, accident and sickness insurance, regard being had to assistance funds in existence.

It may declare participation in such insurance to be compulsory in general or as regards certain specified categories of citizens.

Art. 34B. The Confederation is authorized to enact regulations with regard to the following matters:

(a) Protection of employees or workers.

(b) Relations between employers and employees or workers; in particular, mutual regulation of professional and business matters of common concern.

(c) General compulsory effect of collective contracts and of other common measures of employers', employees' and workers' organizations intended to insure labor peace.

(d) Fair compensation for loss of salary during military service.

(e) Employment placement.

(f) Unemployment compensation and relief.

(g) Professional training in industry, trade, commerce, agriculture, and domestic work.

The declaration of a general compulsory effect according to (c) may apply only to matters concerning the conditions of employment and is permissible only if minority interests and regional differences are given due consideration and if there is no infringement of the principles of equality before the law and freedom of association.

Unemployment insurance will be carried out by public and private funds made up of bilateral or unilateral contributions. The establishment of public unemployment insurance funds and of a compulsory unemployment insurance system is left to the decision of the individual canton.

The provisions of Article 32 will be applied in this sense.

Art. 34C. The Confederation shall, by means of legislation, institute a system of old age and surviving dependents' insurance; it may later introduce invalidity insurance.

It may declare such insurance to be obligatory in general or as regards certain categories of citizens.

The insurance plan shall be carried into effect with the co-operation of the cantons; application may be made to the public or private insurance societies for their collaboration.

The first two branches of insurance shall be introduced simultaneously.

The financial contributions of the Confederation and the cantons shall not exceed, altogether, one-half of the total sum necessary for the insurance.

From January first, 1926, the Confederation shall set apart for old age and surviving dependents' insurance, the total yield of the tobacco tax.

The Confederation's share of the net receipts accruing from the taxation of spirits shall be set apart for old age and surviving dependents' insurance.

Art. 34D. The Confederation, in the exercise of the powers conferred on it and within the limits of the Constitution, is concerned with the needs of the family.

The Confederation is authorized to legislate regarding family compensation funds. It may declare participation therein to be obligatory in general or for certain groups of the population. It is concerned with the existing funds, supports the efforts of cantons and professional associations for the establishment of new funds, and may create a central compensation fund. It may make its financial advances contingent upon equitable participation of the cantons.

The Confederation is authorized, in the matter of housing and internal colonization, to support the efforts in favor of the family. A federal law shall indicate the conditions which the Confederation may attach to its financial participation, subject to the cantonal police provisions with respect to buildings.

The Confederation shall, by means of legislation, establish maternity insurance. It may declare participation therein to be obligatory in general or for certain groups of the population and may require contributions to be made even by persons not qualified to benefit by insurance payments. It may make its financial advantages contingent upon equitable participation of the cantons.

The laws issued by virtue of the present article shall be executed with the co-operation of the cantons; the collaboration of associations of public or private law may be requested.

Art. 35. It is forbidden to open and run gaming houses.

The cantonal governments may, on certain conditions dictated by public interest, permit gambling for pleasure as in vogue in kursaals up to the spring of 1925, provided that the competent authorities are of the opinion that such play is necessary for the maintenance or development of the tourist industry and that its organization is assured by an enterprise running a kursaal for that purpose. The cantons may likewise forbid such play.

An ordinance of the Federal Council shall determine the conditions dictated by public interest.

Cantonal authorizations shall be submitted to the Federal Council for approval.

One-quarter of the gross receipts from the play shall be paid over to the Confederation, which shall set the same apart, without taking into accounts its own contributions, for victims of natural catastrophes and works of public utility.

The Confederation may also take the necessary measures in regard to lotteries.

Art. 36. Throughout Switzerland posts and telegraphs are within the domain of the Confederation.

The revenues from posts and telegraphs belong to the federal treasury.

The charges shall be fixed according to the same principles and as equitably as possible in every part of Switzerland.

The inviolable secrecy of letters and telegrams is guaranteed.

Art. 36A. The Confederation shall ensure by means of legislation the establishment and utilization of a network of national roads. The most important roads which are of concern to Switzerland as a whole may be declared national roads.

The cantons shall construct and maintain the national roads in accordance with the provisions decreed by the Confederation and under its supervision. The Confederation may itself undertake the task of the canton if the latter so requests or if the importance of the work so requires.

As far as possible productive land shall be spared. Difficulties arising from the fact that the construction of a road detracts from the exploitation or use of lands must be compensated by appropriate measures the expense of which shall be charged to the construction of the road.

The expenses of construction of national roads shall be shared between the Confederation and the cantons, taking into account the expenses to the various cantons of the national roads, their interests and their financial capacity.

In special cases, the Confederation may contribute to the expenses of exploitation and maintenance of the national roads, basing its action on the considerations mentioned in paragraph 4.

With the exception of the powers assigned to the Confederation, the national roads are placed under the sovereignty of the cantons.

Art. 36B. The Confederation shall assign, in accordance with legislation, three fifths of the revenue from the duty on motor fuel for the following purposes:

(a) Contributions to the expenses of national roads;

(b) Contributions to the expenses of construction of other principal roads forming part of the network to be established by the Federal Council in response to precise technical requirements;

(c) General contributions to the expenses of roads open to motor vehicles;

(d) Supplementary contributions to the road charges of cantons requiring financial equalization;

(e) Annual subsidies to the cantons of Uri, Grisons, Ticino and the Valais because of their alpine routes serving international traffic. The figures shall be as follows:

Uri	240,000 Fr.
Grisons	600,000 ,,
Ticino	600,000 ,,
Valais	150,000 ,,

If it appears from the finance plans that the resources available do not suffice to cover the Confederation's share in the expenses of the national roads, the Federal Assembly shall decide by a general decree to what extent the deficits must be covered by the levy of a supplementary tax on motor fuel or by the general resources of the Confederation.

Art. 37. The Confederation exercises supreme control over the roads and bridges in the maintenance of which it is concerned.

The sums due to the cantons specified in Article 30 on account of their international Alpine highways shall be withheld by the federal authorities if these highways are not properly maintained by the cantons.

Art. 37A. The Confederation may make regulations concerning motor cars and cycles.

The cantons retain the right to restrict or prohibit motor and cycle traffic. The Confederation may, nevertheless, declare open or partially open to traffic certain highways necessary for through traffic. The use of highways for the business of the Confederation remains reserved.

Art. 37B. Legislation concerning aerial navigation is within the sphere of the Confederation.

Art. 38. The Confederation shall exercise all the rights comprised in the coinage monopoly.

It has the sole right of coining money.

It shall determine the monetary system and may, if necessary, regulate the rate of exchange of foreign money.

Art. 39. The right of issuing bank-notes and any other fiduciary money is vested exclusively in the Confederation.

The Confederation may exercise its monopoly of note issue through a state bank under a special administration, or may concede its exercise, subject to the right of redemption, to a central joint-stock bank administered with the assistance and under the control of the Confederation.

The principal function of the bank holding the monopoly of bank notes is to regulate the money market in Switzerland and to facilitate payments and to practice a credit and monetary policy serving the general interests of the country.

At least two thirds of the net profits of the bank, after payment of interest or reasonable dividend on the endowment or share capital, and deductions of payments to the reserve funds, shall go to the cantons.

The bank and its branches shall be exempt from all cantonal taxation.

The Confederation may not suspend the obligation to reimburse bank notes and any other fiduciary money nor decree their compulsory acceptance except in time of war or of disturbance of the monetary situation.

The bank notes issued must be covered by gold and by short term credits.

Federal legislation makes provision as to the carrying into effect of this Article.

Art. 40. The system of weights and measures shall be determined by the Confederation.

The laws relating thereto shall be carried out by the cantons under federal supervision.

Art. 41. The Confederation has the exclusive monopoly of the manufacture and sale of gunpowder.

The manufacture, purchase, trade and distribution of arms, munitions, explosives and other materials of war and of pieces of ordinance shall be subject to authorization by the Confederation. Authorization shall be granted only to persons and companies presenting, from the point of view of national interest, the necessary guarantees. The rights of establishments under state control of the Confederation are reserved.

The importation and exportation of arms, munitions and war materials within the meaning of the present constitutional provisions can take place only with the authorization of the Confederation. Their transit may also be made subject to prior authorization by the Confederation.

The Federal Council shall establish by ordinance, subject to federal legislation, the necessary provisions for the implementation of the second and third paragraphs. It shall, in particular, establish detailed provisions regarding the granting, duration and withdrawal of authorizations and the supervision of those receiving such concessions. Furthermore, it shall determine to which arms, munitions, explosives, other war materials and pieces of ordinance this article applies.

Art. 41A. The Confederation may impose the following taxes:

(a) Stamp duties on deeds, including the coupons, on bills of exchange and similar instruments, on receipts for insurance premiums and on other documents relating to commercial operations; such duties may not be imposed on documents concerning transactions in landed property and mortgages. One fifth of the net yield of such stamp duties shall be paid to the cantons;

(b) An anticipatory tax on the income from transferable securities, lottery winnings and insurance payments;

(c) Taxes on raw and manufactured tobacco;

(d) Special taxes on persons residing abroad in order to provide against fiscal measures taken by foreign States.

The items which federal legislation makes subject to any of the federal taxes mentioned in the first paragraph, sub-paragraphs (a), (b) and (c), or which it declares exempt therefrom, may not be made subject to any cantonal or communal tax of the same kind.

Federal legislation shall regulate the implementation of this article.

Art. 41B. During the years 1959 to 1974, the Confederation may impose, in addition to the taxes within its competence under Article 41A, a turnover tax, a national defense tax and a tax on beer.

The turnover tax shall be established in accordance with the following rules:

(a) The tax shall affect merchandise transactions on Swiss territory, the importation of merchandise, professional work carried out on movable property, buildings and land with the exception of cultivation of the soil for purposes of natural production. The turnover taxed or declared exempt from tax by the Confederation may not be subjected by the cantons or the communes to any similar tax;

(b) The tax may be no more, in the case of retail deliveries, than 3.6% and, in the case of wholesale deliveries, 5.4% of the receipts;

(c) The list of merchandise the transactions in which are free of tax may be neither restricted nor enlarged from its content as of 1 January 1959;

The national defense tax shall be drawn up in accordance with the following rules:

(a) The tax shall affect the income of natural persons and the net income, capital and reserves of juridical persons;

(b) The tax on personal income is calculated in accordance with a progressive scale and may not exceed 8% of the total taxable income. Incomes of less than 6000 francs for single persons or 7500 for married persons shall not be subject to this tax;

(c) Juridical persons, whatever their legal form, shall be subject to tax according to their economic capacity in as equal a manner as possible. The tax on net income may not exceed 5% if calculated proportionally or 8% if calculated progressively, and the tax on capital and reserves may not exceed 0.75 per thousand;

(d) The tax shall be imposed by the cantons for the account of the Confederation. Three tenths of the gross yield of the tax shall be paid to the cantons; one sixth of the amount due to the cantons must be attributed to inter-cantonal financial equalization.

The total amount charged upon beer in proportion to its price and including the tax on beer, the supplementary customs duties on the primary materials for beer and brewing and the turnover tax, may be neither increased nor diminished from what it was on 31 December 1958.

Federal legislation shall regulate the implementation of this article.

Art. 42. The expenses of the Confederation shall be defrayed by:

(a) The revenue from federal property;

(b) The revenue from the administration of posts, telegraphs, and telephones (Article 36) and from the powder monopoly (Article 41);

(c) The net revenue from the tax on exemption from military service (Article 18, 4th paragraph);

(d) The revenue (Article 30) from customs duties;

(e) The federal part of the net revenue from the tax on distilled liquors (Article 32A and 34C, 7th paragraph) as well as the federal portion of the gross gambling receipts (Article 35, fifth paragraph);

(f) The federal portion of the net profits of the bank holding the monopoly of bank notes (Article 39 fourth paragraph);

(g) The revenue from federal taxes (Article 41A and ff.);

(h) The revenue from emoluments and other receipts provided for by legislation.

Art. 42A. The Confederation must amortize the deficit in its budget, taking into account the economic situation.

Art. 42B. The Confederation shall encourage financial equalization among the cantons. When federal subventions are accorded, in particular, the financial capacity of the cantons and the situation of the mountainous regions must be given appropriate consideration.

Art. 42C. The Confederation may, by legislation, enact provisions against arrangements concluded with taxpayers for the purpose of giving them unjustifiable fiscal advantages.

Art. 43. Every citizen of a canton is a Swiss citizen. As such he may, after having duly proved his qualification as a voter, take part at his place of domicile in all federal elections and referenda.

No person may exercise political rights in more than one canton.

A Swiss who has settled anywhere shall enjoy at his place of domicile all the rights of citizens of the canton, together with all the rights of a burgess of the commune. Participation in the property of commonalties and corporations, and the right to vote in matters exclusively connected therewith, are excluded from these rights, unless cantonal legislation otherwise decides.

In cantonal and communal matters he shall become an elector after settlement for 3 months.

Cantonal laws concerning settlement and on electoral rights in communal affairs possessed by citizens who have settled anywhere shall be submitted to the Federal Council for approval.

Art. 44. No Swiss national may be expelled from the territory of the Confederation or from his canton of origin.

Federal legislation shall determine the rules applicable to the acquisition or loss of Swiss nationality.

It may enact that a child born of foreign parents is a Swiss national from birth when the mother was of Swiss origin by filiation and if the parents are domiciled in Switzerland at the moment of the child's birth. The child acquires civic rights in the mother's commune of origin.

Federal legislation shall lay down the principles governing the establishment of civic rights.

Persons incorporated in virtue of the present provisions enjoy the same rights as other nationals; they have, however, no right to property which is exclusively communal and corporative unless cantonal legislation provide otherwise. The Confederation shall defray at least one half of the expenditure for assistance which persons incorporated on birth occasion to cantons and communes up to the completion of their eighteenth year. The same applies in the case of establishment of civic rights during the ten years which follow such.

Federal legislation shall determine the cases in which the Confederation shall participate in the expenditure incurred by cantons and communes in assisting naturalized *heimatlos* persons.

Art. 45. Every Swiss citizen has the right to settle at any place in Swiss territory, subject to the production of a certificate of origin or similar document.

The right of settlement may, by way of exception, be refused or withdrawn in the case of persons who have been deprived of their civic rights as a result of a penal conviction.

The right of settlement may further be withdrawn from persons who have been repeatedly sentenced for grave misdemeanors and from persons who become a permanent burden upon public charity and whose commune, or canton of origin, refuses adequate help to them after having been officially requested to provide the same.

In cantons in which domiciliary relief exists, permission to settle may be made conditional, in the case of citizens of the canton, upon the persons being capable of work and not having been a permanent burden upon public charity at their former domicile in the canton of origin.

Every expulsion on account of poverty must be approved by the government of the canton of domicile and notified in advance to the government of the canton of origin.

The canton in which a Swiss citizen establishes his domicile may not require from him any security or impose on him any special charge in respect of such settlement. Similarly, communes may not impose on Swiss citizens domiciled in their territory any taxes other than those imposed upon their own citizens.

The maximum fee chargeable in respect of permits for settlement shall be fixed by federal law.

Art. 46. Persons settled in Switzerland shall normally be subject in matters of civil law to the jurisdiction and legislation of their place of domicile.

Federal legislation will make the necessary provisions for the application of this principle and for preventing the double taxation of a citizen.

Art. 47. Federal legislation shall define the difference between establishment and sojourn, and shall at the same time prescribe the regulations governing the political and civil rights of Swiss citizens during temporary residence.

Art. 48. A federal law shall make the necessary provisions as to the expenses of the illness and burial of poor citizens of one canton who fall ill or die in another.

Art. 49. Liberty of conscience and belief is inviolable.

No person may be compelled to become a member of any religious body, submit to any religious instruction, perform any religious act or incur any penalties, of whatsoever kind, by reason of religious opinions.

Persons exercising the authority of parent or guardian are entitled, in conformity with the foregoing principles, to determine the religious education of children up to the age of sixteen years.

The exercise of civil or political rights may not be limited by ecclesiastical or religious requirements or conditions of any kind whatsoever.

No person may secure exemption, on the ground of religious opinion, from the fulfilment of any civic obligation.

No person may be compelled to pay taxes the proceeds of which are specifically appropriated in payment of the purely religious expenses of any religious community of which he is not a member. The exact execution of this principle is reserved to federal legislation.

Art. 50. The free exercise of forms of worship is guaranteed within the limits compatible with public order and morality.

The cantons and the Confederation may take the measures necessary to maintain public order and peace between the members of the various religious communities and to prevent encroachments by ecclesiastical authorities upon the rights of citizens and of the State.

Disputes within the sphere of public or private law arising out of the formation of religious communities, or the division of existing religious communities, may be submitted to the competent federal authorities.

No bishopric may be established within Swiss territory without the approval of the Confederation.

Art. 51. The Order of Jesuits and societies affiliated with it, may not be admitted in any part of Switzerland and all activities in church and school are forbidden to their members.

This prohibition may be extended, by federal decree, to other religious orders whose activity is dangerous to the State or disturbs the peace between the various religious bodies.

Art. 52. The founding of new religious orders, and the re-establishment of those which have been suppressed, are forbidden.

Art. 53. Civil status and registration in connection therewith are within the sphere of the civil authorities. Federal legislation will enact further provision on this matter.

The control of burial places is vested in the civil authorities, which must provide that every deceased person may receive decent burial.

Art. 54. The right to marry is placed under the protection of the Confederation.

No impediment to marriage may be based upon grounds of religious belief, the poverty of either party, their conduct, or any other considerations whatever of a police nature.

Marriages celebrated in any canton or abroad, in accordance with the law there prevailing, shall be recognized as valid throughout the Confederation.

A wife acquires by marriage the civic and burgher rights of her husband.

Children born before marriage are legitimized by the subsequent marriage of their parents.

No marriage fee or similar tax may be levied on either spouse.

Art. 55. The liberty of the press is guaranteed.

Art. 56. Citizens have the right to form associations, provided that the objects and methods of such associations are not unlawful or dangerous to the State. Cantonal laws will make the necessary provisions for the prevention of abuses.

Art. 57. The right of petition is guaranteed.

Art. 58. No person may be withdrawn from his natural judge. Accordingly, no extraordinary tribunals may be established.

Ecclesiastical jurisdiction is abolished.

Art. 59. Suits for personal claims against a solvent debtor domiciled in Switzerland must be brought before the judge of his place of domicile; consequently the property of such a person may not be seized or sequestrated outside the canton in which he is domiciled by reason of personal claims.

These provisions are, in respect of foreigners, without prejudice to the provisions of international treaties.

Imprisonment for debt is abolished.

Art. 60. Every canton is bound to accord to citizens of the other confederated states the same treatment as to its own citizens in regard to legislation and all that concerns judicial proceedings.

Art. 61. Final civil judgments delivered in one canton may be enforced throughout Switzerland.

Art. 62. Internal taxes on the transfer of property from one canton to another (*traite foraine*) are abolished throughout Switzerland, together with all rights of pre-emption possessed by citizens of one canton against those of other confederated states.

Art. 63. Taxes on the transfer of property to foreign countries are abolished, subject to reciprocity.

Art. 64. Legislation in regard to the following matters falls within the domain of the Confederation:

Civil capacity;

All matters of law relating to commerce and transactions affecting movable property (law of obligation, including commercial law and the law on bills of exchange);

Literary and artistic property;

The protection of inventions applicable to industry, including designs and models;

Suits for debt and bankruptcy;

The Confederation has the right to legislate upon other matters of civil law.

The organization of the judiciary, legal procedure, and the administration of justice remain vested in the cantons to the same extent as hitherto.

Art. 64A. The Confederation has power to legislate in regard to penal law.

The organization of the judiciary, legal procedure, and the administration of justice remain vested in the cantons to the same extent as hitherto.

The Confederation has power to grant subventions to the cantons for the construction of penitentiaries, labor establishments, and houses of correction, and for the carrying out of reforms in the execution of punishments. It has likewise power to give assistance to institutions for the care of deserted children.

Art. 65. Sentence of death may not be pronounced for any political offense.

Corporal punishment is forbidden .

Art. 66. Federal legislation shall prescribe the limits within which a Swiss citizen may be deprived of his political rights.

Art. 67. Federal legislation shall deal with the extradition of accused persons from one canton to another; extradition, may not, however, be made obligatory for political or press offenses.

Art. 68. The measures to be taken to incorporate persons without nationality, and for preventing the occurrence of such cases in future, shall be prescribed by federal law.

Art. 69. The Confederation may take legislative measures to deal with infectious, widespread, and exceptionally dangerous diseases of human beings and animals.

Art. 69A. The Confederation has the right to legislate regarding trade in:

(a) Foodstuffs;

(b) Other household commodities and articles of general use, in so far as they may be prejudicial to health or life.

Laws passed in such spheres shall be executed by the cantons under the supervision and with the financial assistance of the Confederation.

The control of importation at the national frontiers is vested in the Confederation.

Art. 69B. The Confederation has the right to legislate regarding the entry, exit, residence, and establishment of foreigners.

The cantons decide, in accordance with federal law, regarding residence and establishment. The Confederation has, however, the right to give rulings in the last resort regarding:

(a) Permission granted by cantons for residence over prolonged periods and for establishment, as also cases in which indulgent treatment is given;

(b) The violation of establishment treaties;

(c) Cantonal expulsions producing effects in federal territory;

(d) Refusals to grant asylum.

Art. 70. The Confederation has power to expel from its territory foreigners who compromise the internal or external security of Switzerland.

CHAPTER II

THE FEDERAL AUTHORITIES

I. The Federal Assembly

Art. 71. Subject to the rights reserved to the people and the cantons (Articles 89 and 123), the supreme authority of the Confederation is exercised by the Federal Assembly, composed of two divisions or Councils, viz.:

(A) The National Council;

(B) The Council of States.

(A) The National Council

Art. 72. The National Council is composed of two hundred deputies of the Swiss people. Seats shall be apportioned among the cantons and half-cantons in proportion to their resident population, each canton and half-canton having, however, the right to at least one seat.

Detailed provisions regarding the above shall be established by federal legislation.

Art. 73. Elections to the National Council are direct. They are conducted on the principle of proportional representation, each canton or half-canton forming an electoral constituency.

Federal legislation shall enact detailed provisions to give effect to this principle.

Art. 74. Every Swiss who has reached the age of twenty years, and who is not excluded from the rights of active citizenship by the legislation of the canton in which he is domiciled, has the right to take part in elections and referenda.

Federal legislation may nevertheless pass uniform regulations regarding the exercise of this law.

Art. 75. Every lay Swiss citizen entitled to vote is eligible for membership of the National Council.

Art. 76. The National Council is elected for four years, and shall be completely renewed at each election.

Art. 77. Deputies to the Council of States, members of the Federal Council, and officials appointed by the latter council, may not at the same time be members of the National Council.

Art. 78. The National Council shall select a President and Vice-President from amongst its members for each ordinary or extraordinary session.

A member who has been President during an ordinary session may not in the following ordinary session hold this office or that of Vice-President.

The same member may not be Vice-President during two consecutive ordinary sessions.

In case of an equality of opinions, the President shall have a casting vote; in elections, he shall vote in the same way as other members.

Art. 79. The members of the National Council receive an allowance from the federal treasury.

(*B*) *The Council of States*

Art. 80. The Council of States is composed of forty-four deputies from the cantons. Each canton appoints two deputies; in divided cantons, each half-canton elects one.

Art. 81. Members of the National Council and those of the Federal Council may not be deputies to the Council of States.

Art. 82. The Council of States selects a President and Vice-President from among its members for each ordinary or extraordinary session.

Neither the President nor the Vice-President may be elected from amongst the deputies of the canton from which the President was chosen for the ordinary session immediately preceding.

Deputies from the same canton may not occupy the office of Vice-President during two consecutive ordinary sessions.

In case of an equality of opinions, the President has a casting vote; in elections, he shall vote in the same manner as other members.

Art. 83. The deputies to the Council of States receive an allowance from the cantons.

(*C*) *Powers of the Federal Assembly*

Art. 84. The National Council and the Council of States deliberate on all matters which the present Constitution places within the competence of the Confederation, and which are not assigned to any other federal authority.

Art. 85. The following matters in particular are within the competence of the two councils:

(1) Laws dealing with the organization and mode of election of the federal authorities;

(2) Laws and ordinances dealing with matters which the Constitution places within the competence of the federal authorities;

(3) Salaries and allowances of members of the authorities of the Confederation and of the federal chancery; the creation of permanent federal offices and the determination of their remuneration;

(4) The election of the Federal Council, the Federal Tribunal, the Chancellor, and the Commander in Chief of the federal army.

Other rights of election or confirmation may be vested in the Federal Assembly by federal legislation;

(5) Alliances and treaties with foreign states, as also the approval of treaties made by the cantons between themselves or with foreign states; nevertheless, treaties between cantons shall only be brought before the Federal Assembly when the Federal Council or another canton raises objection;

(6) Measures to ensure external safety and the preservation of the independence and neutrality of Switzerland; the declaration of war and the conclusion of peace;

(7) The guarantee of the constitutions and territory of the cantons; intervention in consequence of this guarantee; measures for the internal security of Switzerland and for the maintenance of peace and order; amnesties and pardons;

(8) Measures necessary to ensure the observance of the federal Constitution and the guarantee of cantonal constitutions, and those whose object is to secure the fulfilment of federal obligations;

(9) The control of the federal army;

(10) The enactment of the annual budget, the approval of the state accounts, and decrees authorizing loans;

(11) The general supervision of federal administration and justice;

(12) Appeals against decisions of the Federal Council relating to administrative disputes (Article 113);

(13) Conflicts of jurisdiction between federal authorities;

(14) The revision of the federal Constitution.

Art. 86. Both councils meet once a year in ordinary session on a day fixed by standing orders.

Extraordinary meetings are summoned by the Federal Council, or on the demand of one quarter of the members of the National Council, or on that of five cantons.

Art. 87. A council may not deliberate unless the deputies present form an absolute majority of the total number of its members.

Art. 88. In the National Council and the Council of States, decisions shall be taken by an absolute majority of persons voting.

Art. 89. Federal laws and decrees may be issued only with the consent of the two councils.

Federal laws and decrees of general import shall be submitted for adoption or rejection by the people when such a demand is made by thirty thousand active citizens or by eight cantons.

International treaties concluded for a period of indeterminate duration, or for more than fifteen years, shall likewise be submitted for acceptance or rejection by the people if a demand to this effect be made by thirty thousand active citizens or by eight cantons.

Art. 89bis. Federal decrees of general import whose entry into force permits of no delay can be put into effect immediately by a decision of the majority of all the members of each of the two councils; the length of their application must be limited.

When popular voting is demanded by thirty thousand active citizens or by eight cantons, the urgent federal decrees become invalid one year following their adoption by the Federal Assembly, unless they have been approved by the people within the period; in such a case they may be renewed.

Urgent federal decrees which derogate from the Constitution must be ratified by the people and the cantons within the year following their adoption by the Federal Assembly; failing this, they become invalid upon the expiration of this period and cannot be renewed.

Art. 90. Federal legislation shall determine the forms and waiting periods to be observed in referenda.

Art. 91. The members of the two councils vote without instructions.

Art. 92. Each council shall deliberate separately. Nevertheless, in the cases of the elections mentioned in Article 85: 4,the exercise of the right of pardon or a decision on a conflict of jurisdiction (Article 85:13,) the two councils shall meet in joint session under the chairmanship of the President of the National Council, decisions being reached by a majority of all the members of the two councils voting.

Art. 93. The initiative appertains to each of the two councils and each of their members.

The cantons may exercise the same right by correspondence.

Art. 94. Meeting of the councils shall normally be public.

II. The Federal Council

Art. 95. The supreme directing and executive authority of the Confederation is exercised by a Federal Council composed of seven members.

Art. 96. Members of the Federal Council are appointed for four years by the councils in joint session, and are chosen from among all Swiss citizens eligible for the National Council. No more than one member of the Federal Council may, however, be chosen in the same canton.

The Federal Council is completely renewed after every renewal of the National Council.

Vacancies arising during the period of four years are filled at the next meeting of the Federal Assembly, for the remainder of the period of office.

Art. 97. The members of the Federal Council may not, during their term of office, occupy any other position, either in the service of the Confederation or of a canton, or engage in any other calling or profession.

Art. 98. The President of the Confederation shall preside over the Federal Council. A Vice-President shall be appointed.

The President of the Confederation and the Vice-President of the Federal Council are nominated by the Federal Assembly for one year from amongst members of the council.

An outgoing President cannot be elected President or Vice-President for the following year.

The same member cannot occupy the position of Vice-President for two consecutive years.

Art. 99. The President of the Confederation and the other members of the Federal Council shall receive an annual salary from the federal treasury.

Art. 100. The Federal Council may not deliberate unless at least four members are present.

Art. 101. Members of the Council have the right to speak, but not to vote, in both divisions of the Assembly, as well as the right of proposing motions on subjects under discussion.

Art. 102. The powers and duties of the Federal Council, within the limits of the present Constitution, are more particularly the following:

(1) It directs all federal business in accordance with the laws and ordinances of the Confederation.

(2) It ensures the observance of the Constitution, the laws and ordi-

nances of the Confederation and the provisions of federal concordats. It takes the necessary measures to this end, of its own accord or upon complaint, in such cases as are not included among those which have to be submitted to the Federal Tribunal in accordance with Article 113.

(3) It enforces the guarantee of the cantonal constitutions.

(4) It submits drafts of laws and ordinances to the Federal Assembly and reports upon proposals submitted to it by the councils or the cantons.

(5) It provides for the execution of the laws and ordinances of the Confederation, the judgments of the Federal Tribunal, and the compromises or arbitral awards upon disputes between cantons.

(6) It makes such appointments as are not assigned to the Federal Assembly, the Federal Tribunal, or other authority.

(7) It examines treaties of the cantons between themselves or with foreign countries, and gives its approval thereto if it thinks fit. (Article 85:5.

(8) It watches over the interests of the Confederation abroad, paying particular notice to its international relations, and has general charge of foreign affairs.

(9) It ensures the external security of Switzerland and the maintenance of its independence and neutrality.

(10) It ensures the internal security of Switzerland and the maintenance of tranquillity and order.

(11) In case of urgency arising when the Federal Assembly is not in session, the Federal Council has authority to raise the necessary troops and dispose of them, provided that it convene the councils immediately if the number of troops raised exceeds two thousand, or if they remain mobilized for more than three weeks.

(12) It has charge of federal army affairs and of all the other branches of administration which are vested in the Confederation.

(13) It examines the laws and ordinances of the cantons which are required to be submitted for its approval; it supervises the branches of cantonal administration which are placed under its control.

(14) It administers the finances of the Confederation, prepares the budget, and renders accounts of receipts and expenditure.

(15) It supervises the conduct of business by all officials and servants of the federal administration.

(16) It gives account of its work to the Federal Assembly in each ordinary session, submits to it a report upon the internal condition and foreign relations of the Confederation, and recommends for consideration such measures as it thinks appropriate for promoting the general welfare. In addition, it makes special reports whenever the Federal Assembly or either division thereof so requests.

Art. 103. The business of the Federal Council is distributed among its members by departments. Decisions emanate from the Federal Council as a single authority.

Federal legislation may authorize departments, or services in connection therewith, to settle certain affairs themselves, subject to a right of appeal.

The cases in which such appeal may be made to a federal administrative court shall be determined by federal legislation.

Art. 104. The Federal Council and its departments are authorized to call in experts for special purposes.

III. The Federal Chancery

Art. 105. A Federal Chancery, at the head of which is the Chancellor of the Confederation, acts as the secretariat of the Federal Assembly and the Federal Council.

The Chancellor is elected for the period of four years by the Federal Assembly, at the same time as the Federal Council.

The chancery is under the special supervision of the Federal Council.

The organization of the Chancery is determined by a federal law.

IV. The Federal Tribunal

Art. 106. There is a Federal Tribunal for the administration of justice in federal matters.

In penal cases there exists, in addition, trial by jury (Article 112).

Art. 107. Members of the Federal Tribunal and their substitutes are appointed by the Federal Assembly, who shall pay regard to the representation of the three official languages.

The organization of the Federal Tribunal and its divisions, the number of its members and their substitutes, their term of office and emoluments shall be determined by law.

Art. 108. Any Swiss citizen eligible for the National Council may be appointed to the Federal Tribunal.

Members of the Federal Assembly and the Federal Council, and officials appointed by them, may simultaneously form part of the Federal Tribunal.

Members of the Federal Tribunal may not, during their term of office, occupy any other position, either in the service of the Confederation or in a canton, or follow any other calling or profession.

Art. 109. The Federal Tribunal shall organize its secretariat and appoint the staff thereof.

Art. 110. The Federal Tribunal shall have civil cognizance of disputes:

(1) Between the Confederation and the cantons;

(2) Between the Confederation of the one part, and corporations or private individuals of the other part, when the latter are plaintiffs and

the dispute reaches the degree of importance to be prescribed by federal legislation;

(3) Between cantons;

(4) Between cantons of the one part, and corporations or private individuals of the other part, where either party so demands and the dispute reaches the degree of importance to be prescribed by federal legislation.

The Federal Tribunal shall further take cognizance of differences in regard to loss of nationality and disputes between communes of different cantons concerning civic rights.

Art. 111. The Federal Tribunal is bound to judge other cases when the parties agree to appeal to it and the matter in dispute is of the degree of importance to be prescribed by federal legislation.

Art. 112. The Federal Tribunal, with the assistance of a jury to decide the facts, has penal jurisdiction as to:

(1) Cases of high treason against the Confederation, and revolt and violence against the federal authorities;

(2) Crimes and offenses against the law of nations;

(3) Crimes and political offenses which are the cause or consequence of disorders necessitating armed federal intervention;

(4) Charges against officials appointed by a federal authority, when brought before the tribunal by that authority.

Art. 113. The Federal Tribunal has also jurisdiction in regard to:

(1) Conflicts of competence between federal authorities of the one part, and cantonal authorities of the other part;

(2) Disputes between cantons, when in the sphere of public law;

(3) Complaints in respect of violation of constitutional rights of citizens, and complaints by individuals in respect of violation of concordats or treaties.

Administrative disputes to be determined by federal legislation are excluded.

In all the cases above mentioned, the Federal Tribunal shall administer the laws passed by the Federal Assembly, and such ordinances of that Assembly as are of general application. It shall likewise act in accordance with treaties ratified by the Federal Assembly.

Art. 114. In addition to the matters mentioned in Articles 110, 112, and 113, other matters may be placed by federal legislation within the competence of the Federal Tribunal; in particular, powers may be conferred on the tribunal for the purpose of ensuring the uniform application of the laws contempated in Article 64.

IVa. Federal Administrative and Disciplinary Jurisdiction

Art. 114A. The Federal Administrative Court has cognizance of administrative disputes in federal matters referred to it by federal legislation.

It has also jurisdiction in the disciplinary cases of the federal administration which are referred to it by federal legislation, insofar as such cases have not been referred to a special jurisdiction.

The Administrative Court shall apply the federal legislation and treaties approved by the Federal Assembly.

Subject to the approval of the Federal Assembly, the cantons have the right to give the Federal Administrative Court jurisdiction in administrative disputes regarding cantonal affairs.

The organization of federal administrative and disciplinary jurisdiction, and its procedure, are regulated by law.

V. Various Provisions

Art. 115. Everything which concerns the authorities of the Confederation shall be the subject of federal legislation.

Art. 116. German, French, Italian, and Romanche are the national languages of Switzerland.

The official languages of the Confederation shall be: German, French, and Italian.

Art. 117. Officials of the Confederation are responsible for their conduct in office. A federal law shall determine what such responsibility involves.

CHAPTER III

THE REVISION OF THE FEDERAL CONSTITUTION

Art. 118. The federal Constitution may at any time be wholly or partially revised.

Art. 119. Total revision shall be effected in the forms laid down in respect of federal legislation.

Art. 120. When either division of the Federal Assembly decides in favor of a total revision of the federal Constitution, and the other division does not agree, or when fifty thousand Swiss voters demand a total revision, the question whether the federal Constitution ought to be revised is in either case submitted to the Swiss nation, which votes in the affirmative or negative.

If in either case a majority of the Swiss nation who vote pronounce in the affirmative, the two councils shall be renewed for the purpose of undertaking the revision.

Art. 121. A partial revision may be effected either by means of the popular initiative, or in the forms laid down in respect of federal legislation.

The popular initiative consists of a demand by fifty thousand Swiss voters for the adoption of a new constitutional article or for the repeal or modification of certain articles of the Constitution already in force.

If by means of the initiative several different provisions are submitted for revision of or for addition to the federal Constitution, each of them must form the subject of a separate initiative demand.

The initiative demand may take the form of a proposal couched in general terms, or of a bill complete in all details.

When the demand is couched in general terms, the federal chambers, if they approve thereof, will proceed to undertake the partial revision in the sense indicated, and will submit and draft acceptance or rejection by the people and the cantons. If, on the contrary, they do not approve the demand, the question of partial revision shall be submitted to the vote of the people; if a majority of the Swiss citizens taking part in the vote pronounce in the affirmative, the Federal Assembly will proceed to undertake the revision in conformity with the popular decision.

When a demand is presented in the form of a bill complete in all details, and the Federal Assembly approves thereof, the bill shall be submitted for acceptance or rejection by the people and the cantons. If the Federal Assembly is not in agreement, it may draw up a separate bill or recommend to the people the rejection of the bill proposed, and submit to the vote its counter-draft or its proposal for rejection at the same time as the bill presented by popular initiative.

Art. 122. Federal legislation shall determine the formalities to be observed in regard to popular initiative and to referenda concerning the revision of the federal Constitution.

Art. 123. The revised federal Constitution, or the revised part thereof, shall enter into force when it has been accepted by the majority of the Swiss citizens taking part in the vote thereon and by the majority of the states.

In reckoning a majority of the states, the vote of a half-canton shall be counted as half a vote.

The result of the popular vote in each canton shall be regarded as the vote of the State.

TRANSITIONAL PROVISIONS

(Not reproduced)

TEMPORARY ARTICLES

1. Temporary maintenance of controlled lower prices.
2. Supplying the country with bread cereals.
3. Temporary maintenance of measures of price control.

UKRAINIAN SOVIET SOCIALIST REPUBLIC

SUMMARY

INTERNATIONAL STATUS

The Ukrainian Soviet Socialist Republic is a member of the United Nations (October 24, 1945). It is a member of other international organizations.

The Ukraine placed itself under Russian protection in 1654, and its autonomy was gradually diminished thereafter. The Ukrainian Soviet

Socialist Republic was proclaimed on December 27, 1917 and the First All-Ukrainian Congress of Soviets declared the Ukrainian S.S.R. a federative part of the Russian Republic. During the two years following the Ukraine suffered from the Civil War and foreign intervention. On January 22, 1918, the Assembly (*Rada*) declared the Ukraine an independent republic. A Provisional Workers' and Peasants' Governmentissued a manifesto on November 29, 1918, on the need to unite the Soviet republics in the face of foreign intervention and counter-revolution..On March 10, 1919, the All-Ukrainian Congress of Soviets adopted the constitution of the Ukrainian S.S.R. and on May 20, 1920, the Fourth All Ukrainian-Conference announced that the Ukrainian S.S.R. was a member of the Russian Socialist Federative Soviet Republic, while retaining its independent constitution, a federation that was established by treaty between the R.S.F.S.R. and the Ukrainian S.S.R. of December 28, 1920. On December 29, 1922, the formation of the U.S.S.R. was sanctioned by a Conference of delegates of the R.S.F.S.R., the Ukrainian S.S.R., the Byelorussian S.S.R. and Trans-Caucasia. The Ukraine was invaded and devastated by Germany during the war. At the San Francisco Conference in 1945, at the request of the U.S.S.R., it was accorded separate representation and separate membership in the United Nations.

FORM OF NATIONAL GOVERNMENT

The Constitution of January 30, 1937, as amended to 1965, states that the Ukrainian Soviet Socialist Republic is a socialist state of workers and peasants.[1] Its political foundation is the Soviets of Working People's Deputies and all power is vested in the working people of town and country as represented therein.[2] The socialist system of economy and socialist ownership of the instruments and means of production are described.[3] The Constitution states that the Uk.S.S.R. has voluntarily united with other equal Soviet Socialist Republics, which are named, and has delegated to the U.S.S.R. the rights set forth in Article 14 of the latter's Constitution; beyond those provisions, the Uk.S.S.R. preserves fully its sovereign rights, including the right to secede.[4] The provinces are listed.[5] The Uk.S.S.R. has the right to enter into direct relations with foreign states.[6]

RIGHTS OF THE PEOPLE

The Constitution guarantees the right to work, rest and leisure, social security, education, equal rights of women and equality of all citizens, freedom of consciences, freedom of speech, press, assembly, demonstration, association.[7] Inviolability of the person, domicile, the right of asylum are

[1] Const., Art. 1. [2] Id., Art. 2, 3. [3] Id., Art. 4–11. [4] Id., Art. 13, 14.
[5] Id., Art. 18. [6] Id., Art. 15B. [7] Id., Art. 98–106.

guaranteed.[1] Citizens must abide by the Constitution and the laws, maintain labor discipline, safeguard socialist property, perform military service and defend the country.[2] The right to own and inherit specified personal property is protected by law.[3]Work is a duty and honor for all able-bodied citizens, and the socialist principle "from each according to his ability, to each according to his work" applies.[4]

LEGISLATIVE DEPARTMENT

The highest organ of state power and sole legislative organ is the Supreme Soviet of the Uk.S.S.R. whose members are elected in constituencies for a term of four years by universal, equal and direct suffrage by secret ballot.[5] It meets in two regular sessions a year. [6]Immunities of members are provided.[7] The local organs of state power are described.[8] There are provisions for the state budget.[9]

EXECUTIVE DEPARTMENT

The Supreme Soviet of the Uk.S.S.R. elects the Presidium of the Supreme Soviet composed of a President, two Vice-Presidents, a Secretary and fifteen members, which exercises the functions of Head of State; it convenes sessions of the Supreme Soviet, issues decrees and interprets the laws, awards honors, grants pardons, appoints representatives to foreign states.[10]

The highest executive and administrative organ is the Council of Ministers appointed by the Supreme Soviet of the Uk.S.S.R. and accountable to it.[11] The Ministers are listed and the Constitution states that they issue orders and instructions on the basis and in pursuance of laws, decisions and orders of the U.S.S.R. and the Uk.S.S.R.[12] Union-Republican Ministries are subordinate to the Council of Ministers of the Uk.S.S.R. and to the corresponding Union-Republic Ministry of the U.S.S.R.[13] There are also Republic Ministries subordinate to the Council of Ministers of the Uk. S.S.R.[14]

JUDICIAL DEPARTMENT

Justice is administered by the Supreme Court of the Uk.S.S.R., the provincial and People's Courts and the special courts of the U.S.S.R.[15] The Supreme Court is elected by the Supreme Soviet of the Uk.S.S.R. for a

[1] Id., Art. 107–109 [2] Id., Art. 110–113. [3] Id., Art. 10. [4] Id., Art. 12
[5] Id., Art. 20, 21, 114–122. [6] Id., Art. 31. [7] Id., Art. 34.
[8] Id., Art. 54–79. [9] Id., Art. 80–83.
[10] Id., Art. 28–30. [11] Id., Art. 39, 40. [12] Id., Art. 41, 45–49.
[13] Id., Art. 51. [14] Id., Art. 49, 52. [15] Id., Art. 84.

term of five years.[1] Judges are independent and subject only to the law.[2] There is provision for people's assessors to participate in all court cases,[3] and for a Procuraror's Office.[4]

AREA, POPULATION, ETC.

The area of the Uk.S.S.R. is 601,000 square kilometres, its population (1965) 45,100,000. Judicial proceedings are conducted in Ukrainian, persons not knowing that language being guaranteed the right to interpretation and to the use of their own.[5] The capital is Kiev.[6]

[1] Id., Art. 87.
[2] Id., Art. 92.
[3] Id., Art. 85, 89.
[4] Id., Art. 93–97.
[5] Id., Art. 90.
[6] Id., Art. 126.

CONSTITUTION of the UKRAINIAN SOVIET SOCIALIST REPUBLIC[1]

January 30, 1937, as amended to 1965

CHAPTER I

THE SOCIAL STRUCTURE

Art. 1. The Ukrainian Soviet Socialist Republic is a socialist state of workers and peasants.

Art. 2. The political foundation of the Uk.S.S.R. is the Soviets of the Working People's Deputies, which grew and became strong as a result of the overthrow of the power of the landlords and capitalists, the attainment of the dictatorship of the proletariat, the freeing of the Ukrainian people from the chauvinist yoke of czarism and the Russian imperialist bourgeoisie, and the destruction of chauvinist counter-revolution.

Art. 3. All power in the Uk.S.S.R. is vested in the working people of town and country as represented by the Soviets of Working People's Deputies.

Art. 4. The economic foundation of the Uk.S.S.R. is the socialist system of economy and the socialist ownership of the instruments and means of production, firmly established as a result of the abolition of the capitalist system of economy, private ownership of the instruments and means of production, and the exploitation of man by man.

Art. 5. Socialist property in the Uk.S.S.R. exists either in the form of state property (belonging to the whole people) or in the form of co-operative and collective-farm property (the property of collective farms or co-operative societies).

Art. 6. The land, its mineral wealth, waters, forests, the factories and mines, rail, water and air transport facilities, the banks, means of com-

[1] Constitution (Basic Law) of the Ukrainian Soviet Socialist Republic, published in Russian in Kiev 1965, supplied by the Ministry of Foreign Affairs, Kiev, in February 1966. Translation contained in second edition revised by L. Kipourides and the Editor. Ed.

munication, large state-organized agricultural enterprises (state farms, machine and tractor stations, etc.) as well as municipal enterprises and the bulk of the dwelling-houses in the cities and industrial localities, are state property, that is, belong to the whole people.

Art. 7. The enterprises of the collective farms and co-operative organizations, with their livestock, buildings, implements, and output, are the common, socialist property of the collective farms and co-operative organizations.

Every collective-farm household, in addition to its basic income from the collective farms, has for its own use a small plot of land attached to the house and, as its own property, a dwelling-house, livestock, poultry and minor agricultural implements—in conformity—with the rules of the Agricultural Artel.

Art. 8. The land occupied by the collective farms is made over to them for their free use for an unlimited time, that is, in perpetuity.

Art. 9. In addition to the socialist system of economy, which is the predominant form of economy in the Uk.S.S.R., the law permits the small private undertakings of individual peasants and handicraftsmen based on their own labor and precluding the exploitation of the labor of others.

Art. 10. The right of citizens to own, as their personal property, income and savings derived from work, to own a dwelling-house and a supplementary husbandry, articles of household and articles of personal use and convenience, is protected by law, as is also the right of citizens to inherit personal property.

Art. 11. The economic life of the Uk.S.S.R. is determined and guided by the state economic plan for the purpose of increasing the wealth of society as a whole, steadily raising the material and cultural standards of the working people and strengthening the independence of the Uk.S.S.R. and its capacity for defense.

Art. 12. Work in the Uk.S.S.R. is a duty and a matter of honor for every able-bodied citizen, in accordance with the principle: "He who does not work, neither shall he eat".

The principle applied in the Uk.S.S.R. is that of socialism: "From each according to his ability, to each according to his work".

CHAPTER II

THE STATE STRUCTURE

Art. 13. For the purpose of reciprocal assistance in economic and political matters. as well as in questions of defense, the Uk.S.S.R. has voluntarily united with the other equal Soviet Socialist Republics, namely:

The Russian Soviet Federative Socialist Republic,

The Byelorussian Soviet Socialist Republic,

The Uzbek Soviet Socialist Republic,
The Kazakh Soviet Socialist Republic,
The Georgian Soviet Socialist Republic,
The Azerbaijan Soviet Socialist Republic,
The Lithuanian Soviet Socialist Republic,
The Moldavian Soviet Socialist Republic,
The Latvian Soviet Socialist Republic,
The Kirghiz Soviet Socialist Republic,
The Tajik Soviet Socialist Republic,
The Armenian Soviet Socialist Republic,
The Turkmen Soviet Socialist Republic,
The Estonian Soviet Socialist Republic.

In accordance with the above, the Uk.S.S.R. delegates to the U.S.S.R. in the person of its higher organs of government authority and administration, the rights set forth in Article 14 of the Constitution of the U.S.S.R.

Art. 14. The Uk.S.S.R. reserves the right freely to secede from the U.S.S.R.

Art. 15. The territory of the Uk.S.S.R. may not be altered without its own consent.

Art. 15A. The Uk.S.S.R. has its own Republican military formations.

Art. 15B. The Uk.S.S.R. has the right to enter into direct relations with foreign states and to conclude agreements and exchange diplomatic and consular representatives with them.

Art. 16. The laws of the U.S.S.R. are binding within the territory of the Uk.S.S.R.

Art. 17. Every citizen of the Uk.S.S.R. is a citizen of the U.S.S.R.

Citizens of all the other Union Republics have equal rights with the citizens of the Uk.S.S.R. in the territory of the Uk.S.S.R.

Art. 18. The Uk.S.S.R. includes the following provinces: Vinnitsa, Volhynia, Dniepropetrovsk, Donets, Zhitomir, Transcarpathia, Zaporozhye, Ivano-Frankov, Kiev, Kirovograd, Crimea, Lugansk, Lvov, Nikolayev, Odessa, Poltava, Rovno, Sumi, Ternopol, Kharkov, Kherson, Khmelnits, Cherkassy, Chernigov, Chernovits.

Art. 19. The highest executive and administrative organs of the Uk.S.S.R. have the following functions:

(a) To adopt the Constitution of the Uk.S.S.R. and supervise its execution;

(b) To create new provinces within the Uk.S.S.R.;

(c) To define the boundaries and regional divisions of provinces of the Uk.S.S.R.;

(d) To legislate for the Uk.S.S.R.;

(e) To preserve order in the state and the rights of citizens;

(f) To approve the economic plan of the Uk.S.S.R.;

(g) To draw up and supervise the execution of the budget of the Uk.S.S.R.;
(h) To establish, in accordance with the laws of the U.S.S.R. state and local taxes, their collection, and non-tax income;
(i) To supervise the local provincial budgets;
(j) To supervise insurance and savings;
(k) To supervise industries and constructions subordinate to the Republic, banking, industrial, farming and trading enterprises, and to supervise local industries;
(l) To control and supervise the conditions and management of all-Republic enterprises;
(m) To establish management methods for land, mines, forests and waters;
(n) To supervise housing and communal enterprises, building and the general welfare of cities and other inhabited places;
(o) To supervise road construction, Republic and local transportation and communication;
(p) To draw up labor legislation;
(q) To supervise social security;
(r) To supervise primary, secondary and higher education;
(s) To supervise cultural, educational and scientific organizations and foundations in the Uk.S.S.R. and to administer those of an all-Republic character;
(t) To supervise public health and administer public health foundations of an all-Republic character;
(u) To supervise and create organizations for sport and physical culture;
(v) To legislate concerning the organization and functioning of the courts, to approve the civil and criminal Codes of the Uk.S.S.R.;
(w) To confer Uk.S.S.R. citizenship;
(x) To legislate concerning marriage and the family;
(y) To exercise the right of amnesty and pardon of citizens sentenced by the judicial organs of the Uk.S.S.R.;
(z) To determine the manner of organizing the Uk.S.S.R.'s military formations;
(zz) To decide questions of representation of the Uk.S.S.R. in its international relations.

CHAPTER III

THE HIGHER ORGANS OF STATE POWER IN THE Uk.S.S.R.

Art. 20. The highest organ of state power in the Uk.S.S.R. is the Supreme Soviet of the Uk.S.S.R.

Art. 21. The members of the Supreme Soviet of the Uk.S.S.R. are elected by the citizens of the Uk.S.S.R. for a term of four years on the basis of one deputy for each one hundred thousand of the population.

Art. 22. The Supreme Soviet of the Uk.S.S.R. exercises all the rights vested in the Republic according to Articles 13 and 19 of its Constitution, insofar as they do not fall within the constitutionally defined jurisdiction of bodies of the Republic which are subordinate to the Supreme Soviet of the Republic, namely, the Presidium of the Supreme Soviet of the Uk.S.S.R., the Council of Ministers and the Ministries of the Uk.S.S.R.

Art. 23. The Supreme Soviet of the Uk.S.S.R. is the sole legislative organ of the Republic.

Art. 24. A law is considered adopted if passed by a simple majority vote of the Supreme Soviet.

Art. 25. Laws passed by the Supreme Soviet of the Uk.S.S.R. are published over the signatures of the President and Secretary of the Presidium of the Supreme Soviet of the Uk.S.S.R.

Art. 26. The Supreme Soviet of the Uk.S.S.R. elects a Chairman of the Soviet and four Vice-Chairmen.

Art. 27. The Chairman of the Supreme Soviet of the Uk.S.S.R. presides at the sittings of the Supreme Soviet and has charge of the conduct of its business and proceedings.

Art. 28. The Supreme Soviet of the Uk.S.S.R. elects the Presidium of the Supreme Soviet consisting of a President of the Presidium, two Vice-Presidents, a Secretary of the Presidium and nineteen members of the Presidium of the Supreme Soviet.

Art. 29. The Presidium of the Supreme Soviet of the Uk.S.S.R. is accountable to the Supreme Soviet of the Uk.S.S.R. for all its activities.

Art. 30. The Presidium of the Supreme Soviet of the Uk.S.S.R.:

(a) Convenes the sessions of the Supreme Soviet of the Uk.S.S.R.;

(b) Issues decrees;

(c) Interprets the laws of the Uk.S.S.R. in operation;

(d) Conducts national referendums;

(e) Annuls decisions and orders of the Council of Ministers and of the Provincial Soviets of Working People's Deputies if they do not conform to law;

(f) In the intervals between sessions of the Supreme Soviet of the Uk.S.S.R., releases and appoints Ministers of the Uk.S.S.R. on the recommendation of the Chairman of the Council of Ministers of the Uk.S.S.R., subject to subsequent confirmation by the Supreme Soviet of the Uk.S.S.R.;

(g) Confers citizenship of the Uk.S.S.R.;

(h) Awards titles of honor of the Uk.S.S.R. and rewards;

(i) Exercises the right of pardon of citizens sentenced by the judicial organs of the Uk.S.S.R.;

(j) Appoints and recalls plenipotentiary representatives of the Uk.S.S.R. to foreign states;

(k) Receives letters of credence and recall of diplomatic representatives accredited to it by foreign states;

Art. 31. Sessions of the Supreme Soviet of the Uk.S.S.R. are convened by the Presidium of the Supreme Soviet of the Uk.S.S.R. twice a year.

Extraordinary sessions are convened by the Presidium of the Uk.S.S.R. at its discretion or on the demand of at least one third of the deputies of the Supreme Soviet.

Art. 32. The Supreme Soviet of the Uk.S.S.R. elects a Credentials Committee to verify the credentials of the deputies.

On the report of the Credentials Committee, the Supreme Soviet decides whether to recognize the credentials of deputies or to annul their election.

Art. 33. The Supreme Soviet of the Uk.S.S.R., when it deems necessary, appoints commissions of investigation and audit on any matter. It is the duty of all institutions and officials to comply with the demands of such commissions and to submit to them all necessary materials and documents.

Art. 34. A member of the Supreme Soviet of the Uk.S.S.R. may not be prosecuted or arrested without the consent of the Supreme Soviet of the Uk.S.S.R. or, when the Supreme Soviet is not in session, without the consent of the Presidium of the Supreme Soviet.

Art. 35. On the expiration of the term of office of the Supreme Soviet of the Uk.S.S.R. the Presidium of the Supreme Soviet orders new elections to be held within a period not exceeding two months from the date of expiration of the term of office.

Art. 36. On the expiration of the term of office of the Supreme Soviet of the Uk.S.S.R., the Presidium of the Supreme Soviet retains its powers until the newly-elected Supreme Soviet of the Uk.S.S.R. shall have formed a new Presidium.

Art. 37. The newly elected Supreme Soviet of the Uk.S.S.R. is convened by the out-going Presidium of the Supreme Soviet not later than three months after the elections.

Art. 38. The Supreme Soviet of the Uk.S.S.R. appoints the Government of the Uk.S.S.R. namely the Council of Ministers of the Uk.S.S.R.

CHAPTER IV

THE ORGANS OF STATE ADMINISTRATION OF THE Uk.S.S.R.

Art. 39. The highest executive and administrative organ of the state power of the Uk.S.S.R. is the Council of Ministers of the Uk.S.S.R.

Art. 40. The Council of Ministers is responsible and accountable to the Supreme Soviet of the Uk.S.S.R. or, in the intervals between sessions of the Supreme Soviet to the Presidium of the Supreme Soviet of the Uk.S.S.R.

Art. 41. The Council of Ministers of the Uk.S.S.R. issues decisions and orders on the basis and in pursuance of the laws in operation of the U.S.S.R. and of the Uk.S.S.R., and of the decisions and orders of the Council of Ministers of the U.S.S.R., and verifies their execution.

Art. 42. Decisions and orders of the Council of Ministers of the Uk.S.S.R. are binding throughout the territory of the U.S.S.R.

Art. 43. The Council of Ministers of the Uk.S.S.R.:

(a) Co-ordinates and directs the work of the Union-Republican and Republican Ministries of the Uk.S.S.R. and of other institutions under its jurisdiction;

(b) Adopts measures to carry out the economic plan;

(c) Adopts measures to carry out the state and local budget of the Uk.S.S.R.;

(d) Adopts measures for the maintenance of law and order, for the protection of the interests of the state, and for the safeguarding of the rights of citizens;

(e) Directs and supervises the work of the provincial Executive Committees of the Soviets of Working People's Deputies;

(f) Sets up, whenever necessary, special Committees and Central Boards under the Council of Ministers of the Uk.S.S.R. for economic and cultural affairs;

(g) Directs the general organization of the Armed Forces of the Uk.S.S.R.;

(h) Directs the relations of the Uk.S.S.R. with foreign states in accordance with the general procedure established by the U.S.S.R. concerning the relations of the Union Republics with foreign states.

Art. 44. The Council of Ministers of the Uk.S.S.R. has the right to suspend decisions and orders of the provincial Councils of Ministers and to annul decisions and orders of the Executive Committees of the provincial Soviets of Working People's Deputies.

Art. 45. The Council of Ministers of the Uk.S.S.R. is appointed by the Supreme Soviet of the Uk.S.S.R. and consists of:

The Chairman of the Council of Ministers of the Uk.S.S.R.;

The First Vice-Chairman of the Council of Ministers;

The Vice-Chairmen of the Council of Ministers;

The Chairman of the State Planning Committee of the Council of Ministers;

The Chairman of the State Committee for Reconstruction of the Council of Ministers;

The Chairman of the Commission of Party and State Control of the

Central Committee of the Communist Party of the Ukraine and of the Council of Ministers;

The Chairman of the State Committee on Radio and Television of the Council of Ministers;

The Chairman of the State Committee on the cinematograph of the Council of Ministers;

The Chairman of the State Committee on the Press of the Council of Ministers;

The Chairman of the State Committee on Wheat Production and Food Industries of the Council of Ministers;

The Chairman of the State Committee on Industrial Safety and Inspection of Mines of the Council of Ministers;

The Chairman of the State Security Committee under the Council of Ministers;

The Chairman of the State Board for the Sale of Agricultural Machinery, Spare Parts, Mineral Fertilizer and Other Production and Technical Supplies, Organization of Machinery Maintenance and Service on State and Collective Farms;

The Chief of the State Board of the Council of Ministers on Technical and Material Supplies;

The Chief of the Central Statistical Board under the Council Statistical Board under the Council of Ministers.

Art. 46. The Ministers of the Uk.S.S.R. direct the branches of the State administration which come within the jurisdiction of the Uk.S.S.R.

Art. 47. The Ministries of the Uk.S.S.R. are either Union-Republican or Republican Ministries.

Art. 48. The following Ministries of the Uk.S.S.R. are Union-Republican Ministries:

Higher and Secondary Special Education
Coal
Geological Survey
Electricity and Electrification
Foreign Affairs
Co-ordination
Culture
Light Industry
Forestry, wood-pulp, and woodworking industries
Land improvement and Irrigation
Assembly and construction of Factories
Meat and Dairy Industries
Defense
Health
Building Materials Industry
Farm Implements Industry

Agricultural Economy
Commerce
Economic Affairs
Food Industry
Chemical Industry
Metallurgy

Art. 49. The following Ministries are Republican Ministries:
Automobile transport and country roads
Construction
Communal Economy
Local Industry
Instruction
Public Order
Social Insurance.

Art. 50. The Ministers of the Uk.S.S.R., within the limits of the jurisdiction of their respective Ministries, issue orders and instructions on the basis and in pursuance of the laws in operation in the U.S.S.R. and the Uk.S.S.R., and also of decisions and orders of the Council of Ministers of the U.S.S.R.and the Uk.S.S.R., and of the Union-Republican Ministries of the U.S.S.R. and verify their execution.

Art. 51. Each Union-Republican Ministry of the Uk.S.S.R. directs the branch of state administration entrusted to it, and is subordinate both to the Council of ministers of the Uk.S.S.R. and to the corresponding Union-Republican Ministry of the U.S.S.R.

Art. 52. Each Republican Ministry directs the branch of state administration entrusted to it, and is directly subordinate to the Council of Ministers of the Uk.S.S.R.

Art. 53. The Government of the Uk.S.S.R. or a Minister of the Uk.S.S.R. to whom a question of a member of the Supreme Soviet of the Uk.S.S.R. is addressed must give a verbal or written reply in the Supreme Soviet within a period not exceeding three days.

CHAPTER V

THE LOCAL ORGANS OF STATE POWER

Art. 54. The organs of state power in provinces, regions, districts, cities and rural localities of the Uk.S.S.R. are the Soviets of Working People's Deputies.

Art. 55. The Soviets of Working People's Deputies of provinces, regions, districts, cities and rural localities are elected by the working people of the respective provinces, regions, districts, cities and rural localities for a term of two years.

Art. 56. The Soviet of Working People's Deputies (of a province, region, district, city or rural locality) directs local economic and cultural affairs, determines the local budget, directs the work of subordinate organs of administration, ensures the maintenance of law and order, cooperates in the defense and improvement of the land, and protects the rights of citizens.

Art. 57. The Soviets of Working People's Deputies adopt decisions and issue orders within the limits of the powers vested in them by the laws of the U.S.S.R. and the Uk.S.S.R.

Art. 58. The executive and administrative organ of the Soviet of Working People's Deputies of a province, district, city or rural locality is the Executive Committee elected by it, consisting of a Chairman, Vice-Chairmen, a Secretary and members.

Art. 59. The executive and administrative organ of the Soviet of Working People's Deputies in a small locality, is the Chairman, the Vice-Chairman and the Secretary elected by the Soviet of Working People's Deputies.

Art. 60. The executive organs of the Soviets of Working People's Deputies direct local economic and cultural affairs on the basis of decisions of their respective Soviets of Working People's Deputies and of higher organs of state power.

Art. 61. Sessions of the provincial Soviets of Working People's Deputies are convened by their Executive Committees at least four times a year.

Art. 62. Sessions of the regional and district Soviets of Working People's Deputies are convened by their Executive Committees at least six times a year.

Art. 63. Sessions of the city, city district and rural Soviets of Working People's Deputies are convened by their executive organs at least six times a year; in the case of Soviets of Working People's Deputies of cities comprising districts, at least four times a year.

Art. 64. The Soviets of Working People's Deputies of provinces, regions, districts and cities elect a Chairman and Vice-Chairman to conduct their sittings.

Art. 65. The Chairman of a rural Soviet convenes and conducts its sittings.

Art. 66. The executive organs of the Soviets of Working People's Deputies are directly accountable both to the Soviets of Working People's Deputies which elected them and to the executive organ of the superior Soviet of Working People's Deputies.

Art. 67. The Executive Committees of the superior Soviets of Working People's Deputies have the right to annul decisions and orders of the lower executive organs and to suspend decisions and orders of the lower Soviets of Working People's Deputies.

Art. 68. The superior Soviets of Working People's Deputies have the right to annul decisions and orders of the lower Soviets of Working People's Deputies and of their executive organs.

Art. 69. The Soviets of Working People's Deputies of provinces and cities within the Republic may create departments or boards of the Executive Committees, subject to the approval of the Presidium of the Supreme Soviet of the Uk.S.S.R.

Art. 70. In conformity with the conditions in a province and with the laws of the U.S.S.R. and the Uk.S.S.R., the Republican Ministries, the Ministry of Co-ordination of the Uk.S.S.R. and the State Security Committee of the Council of Ministers of the Uk.S.S.R. may establish their administrative organs in the provincial Soviets of Working People's Deputies.

Art. 71. The departments and administrative organs of a provincial Soviet of Working People's Deputies are directly accountable for their activities both to the provincial Soviet of Working People's Deputies and its Executive Committee and to the corresponding Ministry of the Uk.S.S.R.

Art. 72. Repealed.

Art. 73. The district Soviets of Working People's Deputies may create departments of the executive organs subject to the approval of the Provincial Soviet of Working People's Deputies.

Art. 74. Repealed.

Art. 75. The departments of a district Soviet of Working People's Deputies are directly accountable for their activities both to the district Soviet of Working People's Deputies and its Executive Committee and to the corresponding department of the provincial Soviet of Working People's Deputies.

Art. 76. The city Soviets of Working People's Deputies may create departments of the executive organs subject to the approval of the provincial Soviet of Working People's Deputies.

Art. 77. The departments of a city Soviet of Working People's Deputies are directly accountable for their activities both to the city Soviet of Working People's Deputies and its Executive Committee and to the corresponding department of the provincial Soviet of working People's Deputies.

Art. 78. The departments of a city Soviet of Working People's Deputies are subordinate to the Soviets of Working People's and their Executive Committees of the cities within the Republic, and directly accountable to the corresponding Ministry of the Uk.S.S.R.

Art. 79. On the expiration of the term of office of the provincial, district, city or rural Soviet of Working People's Deputies, their executive and administrative organs retain their power until the newly-elected Soviets of Working People's Deputies shall have formed new executive and administrative organs.

CHAPTER VI

BUDGET OF THE UKRAINIAN S.S.R.

Art. 80. The state budget of the Uk.S.S.R. is drawn up by the Council of Ministers of the Uk.S.S.R. and is submitted by it to the Supreme Soviet of the Uk.S.S.R. for approval.

After approval of the state budget by the Supreme Soviet of the Uk.S.S.R. it is published for general information.

Art. 81. The Supreme Soviet of the Uk.S.S.R. elects the budgetary commission which reports to the Supreme Soviet its conclusions in regard to the state budget of the Uk.S.S.R.

Art. 82. A report on the performance of the state budget of the Uk.S.S.R. is approved by the Supreme Soviet of the Uk.S.S.R. and is then published for general information.

Art. 83. The budgets of the provincial, regional, district, city, and village Soviets include the income from the local economy and a share of the state income received on their territory, and must also include the income from local taxes and levies in amounts established by the laws of the U.S.S.R. and of the Uk.S.S.R.

CHAPTER VII

THE COURTS AND THE PROCURATOR'S OFFICE

Art. 84. In the Uk.S.S.R. justice is administered by the Supreme Court of the Uk.S.S.R., the Provincial Courts, the People's Courts and the Special Courts of the U.S.S.R. established by decision of the Supreme Soviet of the U.S.S.R.

Art. 85. In all Courts cases are tried with the participation of people's assessors, except in cases specially provided for by law.

Art. 86. The Supreme Court of the Uk.S.S.R. is the highest judicial organ of the Uk.S.S.R. The Supreme Court of the Uk.S.S.R. is charged with the supervision of the judicial activities of all the judicial organs of the Uk.S.S.R.

Art. 87. The Supreme Court of the Uk.S.S.R. is elected by the Supreme Soviet of the Uk.S.S.R. for a term of five years.

Art. 88. The Provincial Courts are elected by the provincial Soviets of Working People's Deputies for a term of five years.

Art. 89. People's judges of District (City) People's Courts are elected by the citizens of the districts (cities) on the basis of universal, direct and equal suffrage by secret ballot for a term of five years.

People's Assessors of District (City) People's Courts are elected at general meetings of industrial, office and professional workers, and peasants in the place of work or residence, and of servicemen in military units, for a term of two years.

Art. 90. Judicial proceedings in the Uk.S.S.R. are conducted in the Ukrainian language, persons not knowing this language being guaranteed the opportunity of fully acquainting themselves with the material of the case through an interpreter and likewise the right to use their own language in court.

Art. 91. In all courts of the Uk.S.S.R. cases are heard in public, unless otherwise provided for by law, and the accused is guaranteed the right to defense.

Art. 92. Judges are independent and subject only to the law.

Art. 93. Supreme supervisory power to ensure the strict observance of the law by all Ministries and institutions subordinate to them, as well as by people in office and citizens of the Uk.S.S.R. generally, is vested in the Procurator-General of the Uk.S.S.R.

Art. 94. The Procurator-General of the Uk.S.S.R. is appointed by the Procurator-General of the U.S.S.R. for a term of five years.

Art. 95. The provincial Procurator-General are appointed by the Procurator-General of the U.S.S.R. for a term of five years.

Art. 96. The procurators-general of the regions, districts and cities are appointed by the Procurator-General of the Uk.S.S.R., subject to the approval of the Procurator-General of the U.S.S.R., for a term of five years.

Art. 97. The organs of the Procurator's Office perform their functions independently of any local organs whatsoever, being subordinate solely to the Procurator-General of the U.S.S.R.

CHAPTER VIII

FUNDAMENTAL RIGHTS AND DUTIES OF CITIZENS

Art. 98. Citizens of the Uk.S.S.R. have the right to work, that is the right to guaranteed employment and payment for their work in accordance with its quantity and quality.

The right to work is ensured by the socialist organization of the national economy, the steady growth of the productive forces of Soviet society, the elimination of the possibility of economic crises, and the abolition of unemployment.

Art. 99. Citizens of the Uk.S.S.R. have the right to rest and leisure.

The right to rest and leisure is ensured by the establishment of a seven-hour day for industrial, office and professional workers, the reduction of the working day to six hours for arduous trades and to four hours in shops where conditions of work are particularly arduous; by the institution of annual vacations with full pay for industrial, office and professional workers, and by the provision of a wide network of sanatoriums, holiday homes and clubs for the accomodation of the working people.

Art. 100. Citizens of the Uk.S.S.R. have the right to maintenance in old age and also in case of sickness or disability.

This right is ensured by the extensive development of social insurance of industrial, office and professional workers at state expense, free medical service for the working people, and the provision of a wide network of health resorts for the use of the working people.

Art. 101. Citizens of the Uk.S.S.R. have the right to education.

This right is ensured by universal compulsory eight-year education; by extensive development of secondary polytechnical education, vocational-technical education, and secondary special and higher education based on close ties between the school, real life and production activities; by the utmost development of evening and extramural education; by free education in all schools; by a system of state grants; by instruction in schools in the native language, and by the organization of free vocational, technical and agronomic training for the working people in the factories, state farms, and collective farms.

Art. 102. Women in the Uk.S.S.R. are accorded all rights on an equal footing with men in all spheres of economic, government, cultural, political, and other social activity.

The possibility of exercising these rights is ensured by women being accorded the same rights as men to work, payment for work, rest and leisure, social insurance and education, and also by state protection of the interests of mother and child, state aid to mothers of large families and to unmarried mothers, maternity leave with full pay, and the provision of a wide network of maternity homes, nurseries and kindergartens.

Art. 103. Equality of rights of citizens of the Uk.S.S.R., irrespective of their nationality or race, in all spheres of economic, government, cultural, political and other social activity, is an indefeasible law.

Any direct or indirect restriction of the rights of, or conversely, the establishment of any direct or indirect privileges for, citizens on account of their race or nationality, as well as any advocacy of racial or national exclusiveness or hatred and contempt, are punishable by law.

Art. 104. In order to ensure to citizens freedom of conscience, the church in the Uk.S.S.R. is separated from the state, and the school from the church. Freedom of religious worship and freedom of anti-religious propaganda is recognized for all citizens.

Art. 105. In conformity with the interests of the working people, and in order to strengthen the socialist system, the citizens of the Uk.S.S.R. are guaranteed by law:

(a) freedom of speech;
(b) freedom of the press;
(c) freedom of assembly, including the holding of mass meetings;

(d) freedom of street processions and demonstrations.

These civil rights are ensured by placing at the disposal of the working people and their organizations printing presses, stocks of paper, public buildings, the streets, communications facilities and other material requisites for the exercise of these rights.

Art. 106. In conformity with the interests of the working people, and in order to develop the organizational initiative and political activity of the masses of the people, citizens of the Uk.S.S.R. are guaranteed the right to unite in public organizations: trade unions, co-operative societies, youth organizations, sport and defense organizations, cultural, technical and scientific societies; and the most active and politically-conscious citizens in the ranks of the working class, working peasants and working intelligentsia voluntarily unite in the Communist Party of the Soviet Union, which is the vanguard of the working people in their struggle to build communist society and is the leading core of all organizations of the working people, both public and state.

Art. 107. Citizens of the Uk.S.S.R. are guaranteed inviolability of the person. No person may be placed under arrest except by decision of a court or with the sanction of a procurator.

Art. 108. The inviolability of the homes of citizens and privacy of correspondence are protected by law.

Art. 109. The Uk.S.S.R. affords the right of asylum to foreign citizens persecuted for defending the interests of the working people, or for scientific activities, or for struggling for national liberation.

Art. 110. It is the duty of every citizen of the Uk.S.S.R. to abide by the Constitution of the Uk.S.S.R., to observe the laws, to maintain labor discipline, honestly to perform public duties, and to respect the rules of socialist society.

Art. 111. It is the duty of every citizen of the Uk.S.S.R. to safeguard and fortify public, socialist property as the sacred and inviolable foundation of the Soviet system, as the source of the wealth and might of the country, as the source of the prosperity and culture of all the working people.

Persons committing offences against public, socialist property are enemies of the people.

Art. 112. Universal military service is law.

Military service in the Armed Forces of the U.S.S.R. is the honorable duty of citizens of the Uk.S.S.R.

Art. 113. To defend the country is the sacred duty of every citizen of the Uk.S.S.R. Treason to the Motherland—violation of the oath of allegiance, desertion to the enemy, impairing the military power of the state, espionage—is punishable with all the severity of the law as the most heinous of crimes.

CHAPTER XI

THE ELECTORAL SYSTEM

Art. 114. Members of all Soviets of Working People's Deputies—of the Supreme Soviet of the Uk.S.S.R., the Soviets of Working People's Deputies of the regions, districts, cities and rural areas—are chosen by electors on the basis of universal, equal, and direct suffrage by secret ballot.

Art. 115. Elections of deputies are universal: all citizens of the Uk.S.S.R. who have reached the age of eighteen, irrespective of race or nationality, sex, religion, education, domicile, social origin, property status or past activities, have the right to vote in the election of deputies, with the exception of persons who have been legally certified insane.

Every citizen of the Uk.S.S.R. who has reached the age of twenty-one is eligible for election to the Supreme Soviet of the Uk.S.S.R., irrespective of race or nationality, sex, religion, education, domicile, social origin, property status or past activities.

Art. 116. Elections of deputies are equal: each citizen has one vote; all citizens participate in elections on an equal footing.

Art. 117. Women have the right to elect and be elected on equal terms with men.

Art. 118. Citizens serving in the Armed Forces of the U.S.S.R. have the right to elect and be elected on equal terms with all other citizens.

Art. 119. Elections of deputies are direct: all Soviets of WorkingPeople's Deputies, from rural and city Soviets of Working People's Deputies to the Supreme Soviet of the Uk.S.S.R., are elected by the citizens by direct vote.

Art. 120. The voting for election of the deputies is secret.

Art. 121. Elections to the Soviets of Working People's Deputies of the Uk.S.S.R. are conducted in constituencies. The electoral norms for each region, district, city and rural area Soviet of Working People's Deputies are established by the Electoral Law for provincial, district, city and rural area Soviets of Working People's Deputies of the Uk.S.S.R.

Art. 122. Candidates are nominated for each constituency.

The right to nominate candidates is secured to public organizations and societies of the working people: Communist Party organizations, trade unions, co-operatives, youth organizations and cultural societies.

Art. 123. It is the duty of every deputy to report to his electors on his work and on the work of his Soviet of Working People's Deputies, and he may be recalled at any time upon decision of a majority of the electors in the manner established by law.

CHAPTER X

ARMS, FLAG, CAPITAL

Art. 124. The arms of the Ukrainian Soviet Socialist Republic are a golden sickle and hammer against a red background of sun's rays surrounded by a wreath of wheat, with the inscription on a red band at the bottom of the wreath "Ukrainian Soviet Socialist Republic", on the right side the inscription "Workers of All Countries, Unite!" in the Russian language, and on the left side the same inscription in the Ukrainian language. At the top of the arms is a five-pointed star.

Art. 125. The state flag of the Uk.S.S.R. is of rectangular cloth composed of two horizontal colored stripes. The top stripe, forming two thirds of the width of the flag is red, the bottom stripe forming one third of the width is blue. In the upper stripe, one third of the length from the staff, are depicted the sickle and hammer in gold and above them a five pointed red star bordered in gold. The ratio of the width to the length is 1:2.

Art. 126. The capital of the Ukrainian Soviet Socialist Republic is the city of Kiev.

CHAPTER XI

PROCEDURE FOR AMENDING THE CONSTITUTION

Art. 127. The Constitution of the Uk.S.S.R. may be amended only by decision of the Supreme Soviet of the Uk.S.S.R. adopted by a majority of not less than two thirds of the votes of the members of the Supreme Soviet.

UNION OF SOVIET SOCIALIST REPUBLICS

SUMMARY

INTERNATIONAL STATUS

The Union of Soviet Socialist Republics is a member of the United Nations (October 24, 1945). It is a member of the Warsaw Treaty Organization, the Comecon and other international organizations. It was a member of the League of Nations.

The first planned attempt to replace autocracy with a constitutional regime was the revolt of the Decembrists in December 1825. It was dispersed and followed by severe repression. In 1898, the Russian Socialist Democratic Party was founded. The 1905 uprising was followed by the October Manifesto granting a constitution and Duma with limited legislative powers. In 1917, the March Revolution brought about the abdication of the Czar and the installation of a Provisional Government of Mensheviks and Socialist Revolutionaries which, on September 14, 1917, proclaimed a republic. The October revolution brought Lenin and the Bolsheviks to power. The Provisional Government was arrested and power transferred to the Second All-Russian Congress of Soviets. By January 1918, the new socialist state apparatus had been created and the government named the Workers' and Peasants' Government of the Russian Soviet Republic. On July 10, 1918, the constitution of the Russian Socialist Federative Soviet Republic was approved, based on the principles of voluntary union and equality of the territories forming part. It served as a model for other soviet socialist republics. The outbreak of civil war accompanied by foreign intervention led to increasing centralization. A Decree was issued on June 1, 1919, for the unification of the Soviet Republics of Russia, the Ukraine, Latvia, Lithuania and Byelorussia for the purpose of fighting world imperialism. In December 1919, the Presidium of the All-Russian Central Executive Committee was formed with centralizing powers which were further extended a year later. Federative relationship was established with the Ukrainian S.S.R. in December 1920 and with the Byelorussian S.S.R. in January 1921. By the autumn of 1920 the Civil War and foreign intervention were virtually ended. The preparations for the unification of Republic in a single union state were begun in 1922 under the direction of the Communist Party, for the purpose of rebuilding the devastated national economy and creating a single system of planned economy, to carry out industrialization, the collectivization of agriculture, etc; it was further required by the international situation. On December 29, 1922, a conference of delegates of the R.S.F.S.R., the Ukrainian S.S.R., the Byelorussian S.S.R. and the Trans-Caucasian (Azerbaijan, Armenia, Georgia) S.S.R. adopted a draft declaration and draft treaty on the form of the Union of Soviet Socialist Republics and submitted it to the First Congress of Soviets of the U.S.S.R. which, on December 30, 1922, approved them and thus legislatively sanctioned the formation of the U.S.S.R.

On January 31, 1924, the Constitution of the U.S.S.R. was promulgated. In the years following, the constitutions of the Union Republics were amended to conform, other autonomous republics and regions were formed —by 1936 the number of autonomous republics had reached 22—the constitution was variously amended to reflect this and the administrative-territorial reorganizations, the development of national and state organizations, etc. On December 5, 1936, a new Constitution was promulgated. It has been since amended for the admission of new Union Republics and the extension of the rights of Union Republics in the field of defence, foreign relations, economic activity, judicial functions, the reorganization of management, certain fundamental rights, etc.

After the Second World War when the U.S.S.R. was invaded and large areas devastated by Germany, the U.S.S.R. received a number of territorial additions.

FORM OF NATIONAL GOVERNMENT

The Constitution of December 5, 1936, as amended to 1965, replaces the Constitution of 1924. It states that the U.S.S.R. is a socialist state of workers and peasants, the political foundation of which is the Soviets of Working People's Deputies.[1] All power is vested in the working people of town and country as represented by the Soviets of Working People's Deputies.[2] The socialist system of economy and socialist ownership of the instruments and means of production are described.[3] The Republics forming the Union are named, the jurisdiction of the U.S.S.R. described, their sovereign rights are protected and their right freely to secede is set forth.[4]

RIGHTS OF THE PEOPLE

The Constitution guarantees the right to work, rest and leisure, social security, education, equal rights of women and equality of all citizens, freedom of conscience, freedom of speech, press, assembly, demonstrations, association.[5] Inviolability of the person, domicile, the right of asylum are provided.[6] Citizens must abide by the Constitution and the laws, maintain labor discipline, safeguard socialist property, perform military service and defend the country.[7] The right to own and inherit specified personal property is protected by law.[8] Work is a duty and honor for all able bodied citizens, and the socialist principle "from each according to his ability, to each according to his work" applies.[9]

LEGISLATIVE DEPARTMENT

The highest organ of state power is the bicameral Supreme Soviet which exercises exclusively the legislative power.[10] The Soviet of the Union is elected by the citizens by election districts on the basis of one deputy for every 300,000 of population, by universal, equal and direct suffrage by secret ballot.[11]

The Soviet of Nationalities is elected by the citizens voting by republics, regions and areas for a specified number of deputies from each.[12] The term of the Supreme Soviet is for four years subject to dissolution.[13] It meets in two regular sessions a year.[14] Immunities of deputies are provided.[15]

[1] Const., Art. 1, 2. [2] Id., Art. 3. [3] Id., Art. 4–12. [4] Id., Art. 13–28.
[5] Id., Art. 118–126. [6] Id., Art. 127–129. [7] Id., Atr. 130–133. [8] Id., Art. 10.
[9] Id., Art. 12. [10] Id., Art. 30, 32. [11] Id., Art. 34, 134. [12] Id., Art. 35.
[13] Id., Art. 36, 47. [14] Id., Art. 46. [15] Id., Art. 52.

The higher organs of state power in the Union Republics are described, as are the local organs, the Soviets of Working People's Deputies in the territories, regions, autonomous regions, areas, districts, cities and rural localities.[1]

EXECUTIVE DEPARTMENT

The Supreme Soviet elects, at a joint sitting, the Presidium of the Supreme Soviet composed of a President, fifteen Vice-Presidents (one from each Union Republic), a Secretary and sixteen members.[2] This exercises the function of Head of State, convenes and dissolves the Supreme Soviet, promulgates and interprets laws, awards honors and titles, has the power of appointment, conducts foreign policy.[3]

The highest executive and administrative organ is the Council of Ministers which is responsible to the Supreme Soviet or to its Presidium in intervals between sessions.[4] The Council of Ministers is appointed by the Supreme Soviet and the titles of the Ministers are set forth.[5] Union Ministers, directing branches of state administration throughout the territory of the U.S.S.R. are listed,[6] as are the Union-Republican Ministers directing branches of state administration largely through the relevant Ministers of the Union Republics.[7]

There are provisions concerning the organs of state administration in the Union republics[8] and the Autonomous Republics.[9]

JUDICIAL DEPARTMENT

Justice is administered by the Supreme Court of the U.S.S.R., the Supreme Courts of the Union Republics, the Courts of the other regional divisions and special courts.[10] Judges are independent and subject only to the law.[11] The Supreme Court is elected by the Supreme Soviet for a term of five years.[12] There are provisions for a Procurator General, elected by the Supreme Soviet for a term of seven years.[13]

AREA, POPULATION, ETC.

The area of the U.S.S.R. is 22,400,000 square kilometres, its population (1965) 229,100,000. Judicial proceedings are conducted in the language of the Union or Autonomous Republic or Region and persons not knowing this language are guaranteed the opportunity to acquaint themselves with the subject through an interpreter and to use their own language in court.[14] The capital is Moscow.[15]

[1] Id., Art. 57–63, 94, 101.
[2] Id., Art. 48.
[3] Id., Art. 49.
[4] Id., Art. 64, 65.
[5] Id., Art 70.
[6] Id., Art. 75, 77.
[7] Id., Art. 76, 78.
[8] Id., Art. 79–88.
[9] Id., Art. 89–93.
[10] Id., Art. 102.
[11] Id., Art. 112.
[12] Id., Art. 105.
[13] Id., Art. 114.
[14] Id., Art. 110.
[15] Id., Art. 145.

CONSTITUTION of THE UNION OF SOVIET SOCIALIST REPUBLICS[1]

December 5, 1936, amended to 1965

CHAPTER I

THE SOCIAL STRUCTURE

Art. 1. The Union of Soviet Socialist Republics is a socialist state of workers and peasants.

Art. 2. The political foundation of the U.S.S.R. is the Soviets of Working People's Deputies, which grew and became strong as a result of the overthrow of the power of the landlords and capitalists and the attainment of the dictatorship of the proletariat.

Art. 3. All power in the U.S.S.R. is vested in the working people of town and country as represented by the Soviets of Working People's Deputies.

Art. 4. The economic foundation of the U.S.S.R. is the socialist system of economy and the socialist ownership of the instruments and means of production, firmly established as a result of abolishing the capitalist system of economy, the private ownership of the instruments and means of production, and the exploitation of man by man.

Art. 5. Socialist property in the U.S.S.R. exists either in the form of state property (belonging to the whole people) or in the form of co-operative and collective-farm property (the property of collective farms or co-operative societies).

Art. 6. The land, its mineral wealth, waters, forests, the factories and mines, rail, water and air transport facilities, the banks, means of communication, large state-organized agricultural enterprises (state farms, machine and tractor stations, etc.), as well as municipal enterprises and

[1] *Constitution (Fundamental Law) of the Union of Soviet Socialist Republics.* As amended by the Fifth Session of the Sixth Supreme Soviet of the U.S.S.R. Progress Publishers Moscow, 1965. Supplied by Ministry of Foreign Affairs in February 1966. Ed.

the bulk of the dwelling-houses in the cities and industrial localities, are state property, that is, belong to the whole people.

Art. 7. The enterprises of the collective farms and co-operative organizations, with their livestock, buildings, implements, and output, are the common, socialist property of the collective farms and co-operative organizations.

Every collective-farm household, in addition to its basic income from the collective farm, has for its own use a small plot of land attached to the house and, as its own property, a dwelling-house, livestock, poultry, and minor agricultural implements—in conformity with the Rules of the Agricultural Artel.

Art. 8. The land occupied by the collective farms is made over to them for their free use for an unlimited time, that is, in perpetuity.

Art. 9. In addition to the socialist system of economy, which is the predominant form of economy in the U.S.S.R., the law permits the small private undertakings of individual peasants and handicraftsmen based on their own labor and precluding the exploitation of the labor of others.

Art. 10. The right of citizens to own, as their personal property, income and savings derived from work, to own a dwelling-house and supplementary husbandry, articles of household and articles of personal use and convenience, is protected by law, as is also the right of citizens to inherit personal property.

Art. 11. The economic life of the U.S.S.R. is determined and guided by the state economic plan for the purpose of increasing the wealth of society, steadily raising the material and cultural standards of the working people and strengthening the independence of the U.S.S.R. and its defence potential.

Art. 12. Work in the U.S.S.R. is a duty and a matter of honor for every able-bodied citizen, in accordance with the principle: "He who does not work, neither shall he eat."

The principle applied in the U.S.S.R. is that of socialism: "From each according to his ability, to each according to his work."

CHAPTER II

THE STATE STRUCTURE

Art. 13. The Union of Soviet Socialist Republics is a federal state, formed on the basis of a voluntary union of equal Soviet Socialist Republics, namely:

Russian Soviet Federative Socialist Republic,
Ukrainian Soviet Socialist Republic,
Byelorussian Soviet Socialist Republic,
Uzbek Soviet Socialist Republic,

Kazakh Soviet Socialist Republic,
Georgian Soviet Socialist Republic,
Azerbaijan Soviet Socialist Republic,
Lithuanian Soviet Socialist Republic,
Moldavian Soviet Socialist Republic,
Latvian Soviet Socialist Republic,
Kirghiz Soviet Socialist Republic,
Tajik Soviet Socialist Republic,
Armenian Soviet Socialist Republic,
Turkmen Soviet Socialist Republic,
Estonian Soviet Socialist Republic.

Art. 14. The jurisdiction of the Union of Soviet Socialist Republics, as represented by its higher organs of state power and organs of state administration, covers:

(a) Representation of the U.S.S.R. in international relations, conclusion, ratification and denunciation of treaties of the U.S.S.R. with other states, establishment of general procedure governing the relations of the Union Republics with foreign states;

(b) Questions of war and peace;

(c) Admission of new republics into the U.S.S.R.;

(d) Control over the observance of the Constitution of the U.S.S.R. and ensuring conformity of the Constitutions of the Union Republics with the Constitution of the U.S.S.R.;

(e) Approval of changes to boundaries between Union Republics;

(f) Approval of the formation of new Autonomous Republics and Autonomous Regions within Union Republics;

(g) Organization of the defence of the U.S.S.R., direction of all the Armed Forces of the U.S.S.R., formulation of principles guiding the organization of the military formations of the Union Republics;

(h) Foreign trade on the basis of state monopoly;

(j) Approval of the economic plans of the U.S.S.R.;

(k) Approval of the consolidated state budget of the U.S.S.R. and of the report on its implementation; fixing taxes and revenues that go to the Union, Republican and local budgets;

(l) Administration of banks and industrial, agricultural and trading enterprises and institutions under Union jurisdiction; general direction of industry and building under Union-Republican jurisdiction;

(m) Administration of transport and communications of all-Union importance;

(n) Direction of the monetary and credit system;

(o) Organization of state insurance;

(p) Contracting and granting of loans;

(q) Definition of the basic principles of land tenure and of the use of mineral wealth, forests and waters;

(r) Definition of the basic principles in the spheres of education and public health;

(s) Organization of a uniform system of economic statistics;

(t) Definition of the fundamentals of labor legislation;

(u) Definition of the fundamentals of legislation on the judicial system and judicial procedure and the fundamentals of civil and criminal legislation;

(v) Legislation on Union citizenship; legislation on rights of foreigners;

(w) Definition of the fundamentals of legislation on marriage and the family;

(x) Promulgation of all-Union acts of amnesty.

Art. 15. The sovereignty of the Union Republics is limited only in the spheres defined in Article 14 of the Constitution of the U.S.S.R. Outside of these spheres each Union Republic exercises state authority independently. The U.S.S.R. protects the sovereign rights of the Union Republics.

Art. 16. Each Union Republic has its own Constitution, which takes account of the specific features of the Republic and is drawn up in full conformity with the Constitution of the U.S.S.R.

Art. 17. The right freely to secede from the U.S.S.R. is reserved to every Union Republic.

Art. 18. The territory of a Union Republic may not be altered without its consent.

Art. 18a. Each Union Republic has the right to enter into direct relations with foreign states and to conclude agreements and exchange diplomatic and consular representatives with them.

Art. 18b. Each Union Republic has its own Republican military formations.

Art. 19. The laws of the U.S.S.R. have the same force within the territory of every Union Republic.

Art. 20. In the event of divergence between a law of a Union Republic and a law of the Union, the Union law shall prevail.

Art. 21. Uniform Union citizenship is established for citizens of the U.S.S.R.

Every citizen of a Union Republic is a citizen of the U.S.S.R.

Art. 22. The Russian Soviet Federative Socialist Republic includes the Bashkirian, Buryat, Checheno-Ingush, Chuvash, Daghestan, Kabardinian-Balkar, Kalmyk, Karelian, Komi, Mari, Mordovian, North Ossetian, Tatar, Tuva, Udmurt and Yakut Autonomous Soviet Socialist Republics; and the Adygei, Gorny Altai, Jewish, Karachai-Cherkess and Khakass Autonomous Regions.

Art. 23. Repealed.

Art. 24. The Azerbaijan Soviet Socialist Republic includes the Nakhichevan Autonomous Soviet Socialist Republic and the Nagorny Karabakh Autonomous Region.

Art. 25. The Georgian Soviet Socialist Republic includes the Abkhazian and Ajarian Autonomous Soviet Socialist Republics and the South Ossetian Autonomous Region.

Art. 26. The Uzbek Soviet Socialist Republic includes the Kara-Kalpak Autonomous Soviet Socialist Republic.

Art. 27. The Tajik Soviet Socialist Republic includes the Gorny Badakhshan Autonomous Region.

Art. 28. The settlement of questions pertaining to the regional or territorial administrative division of the Union Republics comes within the jurisdiction of the Union Republics.

Art. 29. Repealed.

CHAPTER III

THE HIGHER ORGANS OF STATE POWER IN THE UNION OF SOVIET SOCIALIST REPUBLICS

Art. 30. The highest organ of state power in the U.S.S.R. is the Supreme Soviet of the U.S.S.R.

Art. 31. The Supreme Soviet of the U.S.S.R. exercises all rights vested in the Union of Soviet Socialist Republics in accordance with Article 14 of the Constitution, in so far as they do not, by virtue of the Constitution, come within the jurisdiction of organs of the U.S.S.R. that are accountable to the Supreme Soviet of the U.S.S.R., that is, the Presidium of the Supreme Soviet of the U.S.S.R., the Council of Ministers of the U.S.S.R., and the Ministries of the U.S.S.R.

Art. 32. The legislative power of the U.S.S.R. is exercised exclusively by the Supreme Soviet of the U.S.S.R.

Art. 33. The Supreme Soviet of the U.S.S.R. consists of two Chambers: the Soviet of the Union and the Soviet of Nationalities.

Art. 34. The Soviet of the Union is elected by the citizens of the U.S.S.R. voting by election districts on the basis of one deputy for every 300,000 of the population.

Art. 35. The Soviet of Nationalities is elected by the citizens of the U.S.S.R. voting by Union Republics, Autonomous Republics, Autonomous Regions, and National Areas on the basis of 25 deputies from each Union Republic, 11 deputies from each Autonomous Republic, 5 deputies from each Autonomous Region, and one deputy from each National Area.

Art. 36. The Supreme Soviet of the U.S.S.R. is elected for a term of four years.

Art. 37. The two Chambers of the Supreme Soviet of the U.S.S.R., the Soviet of the Union and the Soviet of Nationalities, have equal rights.

Art. 38. The Soviet of the Union and the Soviet of Nationalities have equal powers to initiate legislation.

Art. 39. A law is considered adopted if passed by both Chambers of the Supreme Soviet of the U.S.S.R. by a simple majority vote in each.

Art. 40. Laws passed by the Supreme Soviet of the U.S.S.R. are published in the languages of the Union Republics over the signatures of the President and Secretary of the Presidium of the Supreme Soviet of the U.S.S.R.

Art. 41. Sessions of the Soviet of the Union and of the Soviet of Nationalities begin and terminate simultaneously.

Art. 42. The Soviet of the Union elects a Chairman of the Soviet of the Union and four Vice-Chairmen.

Art. 43. The Soviet of Nationalities elects a Chairman of the Soviet of Nationalities and four Vice-Chairmen.

Art. 44. The Chairmen of the Soviet of the Union and the Soviet of Nationalities preside at the sittings of the respective Chambers and have charge of the conduct of their business and proceedings.

Art. 45. Joint sittings of the two Chambers of the Supreme Soviet of the U.S.S.R. are presided over alternately by the Chairman of the Soviet of the Union and the Chairman of the Soviet of Nationalities.

Art. 46. Sessions of the Supreme Soviet of the U.S.S.R. are convened by the Presidium of the Supreme Soviet of the U.S.S.R. twice a year.

Extraordinary sessions are convened by the Presidium of the Supreme Soviet of the U.S.S.R. at its discretion or on the demand of one of the Union Republics.

Art. 47. In the event of disagreement between the Soviet of the Union and the Soviet of Nationalities, the question is referred for settlement to a conciliation commission formed by the Chambers on a parity basis. If the conciliation commission fails to arrive at an agreement or if its decision fails to satisfy one of the Chambers, the question is considered for a second time by the Chambers. Failing agreement between the two Chambers, the Presidium of the Supreme Soviet of the U.S.S.R. dissolves the Supreme Soviet of the U.S.S.R. and orders new elections.

Art. 48. The Supreme Soviet of the U.S.S.R. at a joint sitting of the two Chambers elects the Presidium of the Supreme Soviet of the U.S.S.R., consisting of a President of the Presidium of the Supreme Soviet of the U.S.S.R., fifteen Vice-Presidents—one from each Union Republic, a Secretary of the Presidium and sixteen members of the Presidium of the Supreme Soviet of the U.S.S.R.

The Presidium of the Supreme Soviet of the U.S.S.R. is accountable to the Supreme Soviet of the U.S.S.R. for all its activities.

Art. 49. The Presidium of the Supreme Soviet of the U.S.S.R.:

(a) Convenes the sessions of the Supreme Soviet of the U.S.S.R.;

(b) Issues ordinances;

(c) Interprets the laws of the U.S.S.R. in operation;

(d) Dissolves the Supreme Soviet of the U.S.S.R. in conformity with Article 47 of the Constitution of the U.S.S.R. and orders new elections;

(e) Conducts nation-wide polls (referendums) on its own initiative or on the demand of one of the Union Republics;

(f) Annuls decisions and orders of the Council of Ministers of the U.S.S.R. and of the Councils of Ministers of the Union Republics if they do not conform to law;

(g) In the intervals between sessions of the Supreme Soviet of the U.S.S.R., appoints or removes Ministers of the U.S.S.R. on the recommendation of the Chairman of the Council of Ministers of the U.S.S.R., subject to subsequent confirmation by the Supreme Soviet of the U.S.S.R.;

(h) Institutes decorations (Orders and Medals) and titles of honor of the U.S.S.R.;

(i) Awards Orders and Medals and confers titles of honor of the U.S.S.R.;

(j) Exercises the right of pardon;

(k) Institutes military titles, diplomatic ranks and other special titles;

(l) Appoints and removes the high command of the Armed Forces of the U.S.S.R.;

(m) In the intervals between sessions of the Supreme Soviet of the U.S.S.R., proclaims a state of war in the event of an armed attack on the U.S.S.R., or when necessary to fulfil international treaty obligations providing for mutual defence against aggression;

(n) Orders general or partial mobilization;

(o) Ratifies and denounces international treaties of the U.S.S.R.;

(p) Appoints and recalls plenipotentiary representatives of the U.S.S.R. to foreign states;

(q) Receives the letters of credence and recall of diplomatic representatives accredited to it by foreign states;

(r) Proclaims martial law in separate localities or throughout the U.S.S.R. in the interests of the defence of the U.S.S.R. or of the maintenance of law and order and the security of the state.

Art. 50. The Soviet of the Union and the Soviet of Nationalities elect Credentials Committees to verify the credentials of the members of the respective Chambers.

On the report of the Credentials Committees, the Chambers decide whether to recognise the credentials of deputies or to annul their election.

Art. 51. The Supreme Soviet of the U.S.S.R., when it deems necessary, appoints commissions of inquiry and audit on any matter.

It is the duty of all institutions and officials to comply with the demands of such commissions and to submit to them all necessary materials and documents.

Art. 52. No member of the Supreme Soviet of the U.S.S.R. shall be prosecuted or arrested without the consent of the Supreme Soviet of the U.S.S.R., or, when the Supreme Soviet of the U.S.S.R. is not in session without the consent of the Presidium of the Supreme Soviet of the U.S.S.R.

Art. 53. On the expiry of the term of office of the Supreme Soviet of the U.S.S.R., or on its dissolution prior to the expiry of its term of office, the Presidium of the Supreme Soviet of the U.S.S.R. retains its powers until the newly-elected Supreme Soviet of the U.S.S.R. shall have formed a new Presidium of the Supreme Soviet of the U.S.S.R.

Art. 54. On the expiry of the term of office of the Supreme Soviet of the U.S.S.R., or in the event of its dissolution prior to the expiry of its term of office, the Presidium of the Supreme Soviet of the U.S.S.R. orders new elections to be held within a period not exceeding two months from the date of expiry of the term of office or dissolution of the Supreme Soviet of the U.S.S.R.

Art. 55. The newly-elected Supreme Soviet of the U.S.S.R. is convened by the out-going Presidium of the Supreme Soviet of the U.S.S.R. not later than three months after the elections.

Art. 56. The Supreme Soviet of the U.S.S.R., at a joint sitting of the two Chambers, appoints the Government of the U.S.S.R., namely, the Council of Ministers of the U.S.S.R.

CHAPTER IV

THE HIGHER ORGANS OF STATE POWER IN THE UNION REPUBLICS

Art. 57. The highest organ of state power in a Union Republic is the Supreme Soviet of the Union Republic.

Art. 58. The Supreme Soviet of a Union Republic is elected by the citizens of the Republic for a term of four years.

The basis of representation is established by the Constitution of the Union Republic.

Art. 59. The Supreme Soviet of a Union Republic is the sole legislative organ of the Republic.

Art. 60. The Supreme Soviet of a Union Republic:

(a) Adopts the Constitution of the Republic and amends it in conformity with Article 16 of the Constitution of the U.S.S.R.;

(b) Confirms the Constitutions of the Autonomous Republics forming part of it and defines the boundaries of their territory;

(c) Approves the economic plan and the budget of the Republic and forms economic administration areas;

(d) Exercises the right of amnesty and pardon of citizens sentenced by the judicial bodies of the Union Republic;

(e) Decides upon the representation of the Union Republic in its international relations;

(f) Determines the manner of organizing the Republic's military formations.

Art. 61. The Supreme Soviet of a Union Republic elects the Presidium of the Supreme Soviet of the Union Republic, consisting of the President of the Presidium of the Supreme Soviet of the Union Republic, Vice-Presidents, a Secretary of the Presidium and members of the Presidium of the Supreme Soviet of the Union Republic.

The powers of the Presidium of the Supreme Soviet of a Union Republic are defined by the Constitution of the Union Republic.

Art. 62. The Supreme Soviet of a Union Republic elects a Chairman and Vice-Chairmen to conduct its sittings.

Art. 63. The Supreme Soviet of a Union Republic appoints the Government of the Union Republic, namely, the Council of Ministers of the Union Republic.

CHAPTER V

THE ORGANS OF STATE ADMINISTRATION OF THE UNION OF SOVIET SOCIALIST REPUBLICS

Art. 64. The highest executive and administrative organ of the state power of the Union of Soviet Socialist Republics is the Council of Ministers of the U.S.S.R.

Art. 65. The Council of Ministers of the U S S.R. is responsible and accountable to the Supreme Soviet of the U.S.S.R., or, in the intervals between sessions of the Supreme Soviet, to the Presidium of the Supreme Soviet of the U.S.S.R.

Art. 66. The Council of Ministers of the U.S.S.R. issues decisions and orders on the basis and in pursuance of the laws in operation, and verifies their execution.

Art. 67. Decisions and orders of the Council of Ministers of the U.S.S.R. are binding throughout the territory of the U.S.S.R.

Art. 68. The Council of Ministers of the U.S.S.R.:

(a) Co-ordinates and directs the work of the Supreme Economic Council of the U.S.S.R. under the jurisdiction of the Council of Ministers of the U.S.S.R., the all-Union and Union-Republican Ministries of the U.S.S.R., the State Committees of the Council of Ministers of the U.S.S.R. and of other bodies under its jurisdiction;

(b) Adopts measures to carry out the economic plan and the state budget, and to strengthen the credit and monetary system;

(c) Adopts measures for the maintenance of law and order, for the protection of the interests of the state, and for the safeguarding of the rights of citizens;

(d) Exercises general guidance in the sphere of relations with foreign states;

(e) Fixes the annual contingent of citizens to be called up for military service and directs the general organization of the Armed Forces of the country;

(f) Sets up State Committees of the U.S.S.R., and, whenever necessary, special Committees and Central Boards under the Council of Ministers of the U.S.S.R. for economic and cultural affairs and defence.

Art. 69. The Council of Ministers of the U.S.S.R. has the right, in respect of those branches of administration and economy which come within the jurisdiction of the U.S.S.R., to suspend decisions and orders of the Councils of Ministers of the Union Republics and to annul orders and instructions of Ministers of the U.S.S.R. and also statutory acts of other bodies under its jurisdiction.

Art. 70. The Council of Ministers of the U.S.S.R. is appointed by the Supreme Soviet of the U.S.S.R. and consists of:

Chairman of the Council of Ministers of the U.S.S.R.;

First Vice-Chairmen of the Council of Ministers of the U.S.S.R.;

Vice-Chairmen of the Council of Ministers of the U.S.S.R.;

Chairman of the Supreme Economic Council of the Council of Ministers of the U.S.S.R.;

Ministers of the U.S.S.R.;

Chairman of the Economic Council of the U.S.S.R.;

Chairman of the State Building Committee of the U.S.S.R.;

Chairman of the State Planning Committee of the U.S.S.R.;

Chairman of the Party and State Control Committee of the Central Committee of the C.P.S.U. and the Council of Ministers of the U.S.S.R.;

Chairman of the State Labor and Wages Committee of the Council of Ministers of the U.S.S.R.;

Chairman of the State Committee of the U.S.S.R. for the Co-ordination of Research;

Chairman of the State Radio and Television Committee of the Council of Ministers of the U.S.S.R.;

Chairman of the State Cinematography Committee of the Council of Ministers of the U.S.S.R.;

Chairman of the State Press Committee of the Council of Ministers of the U.S.S.R.;

Chairman of the State Committee of the Council of Ministers of the U.S.S.R. on Trade;

Chairman of the State Committee of the Council of Ministers of the U.S.S.R. for Farm Produce Purchases;

Chairman of the State Foreign Economic Relations Committee of the Council of Ministers of the U.S.S.R.;

Chairman of the State Foreign Cultural Relations Committee of the Council of Ministers of the U.S.S.R.;

Chairman of the State Security Committee under the Council of Ministers of the U.S.S.R.;

Chairman of the Administrative Board of the State Bank of the U.S.S.R.;

Chief of the Central Statistical Board under the Council of Ministers of the U.S.S.R.

The Council of Ministers of the U.S.S.R. includes the Chairmen of the Councils of Ministers of the Union Republics by virtue of their office.

Art. 71. The Government of the U.S.S.R. or a Minister of the U.S.S.R. to whom a question of a member of the Supreme Soviet of the U.S.S.R. is addressed must give a verbal or written reply in the respective Chamber within a period not exceeding three days.

Art. 72. The Ministers of the U.S.S.R. direct the branches of state administration which come within the jurisdiction of the U.S.S.R.

Art. 73. The Ministers of the U.S.S.R., within the limits of the jurisdiction of their respective Ministries, issue orders and instructions on the basis and in pursuance of the laws in operation, and also of decisions and orders of the Council of Ministers of the U.S.S.R., and verify their execution.

Art. 74. The Ministries of the U.S.S.R. are either all-Union or Union-Republican Ministries.

Art. 75. The all-Union Ministries direct the branch of state administration entrusted to them throughout the territory of the U.S.S.R. either directly or through bodies appointed by them.

Art. 76. The Union-Republican Ministries, as a rule, direct the branches of state administration entrusted to them through the relevant Ministries of the Union Republics; they administer directly only a certain limited number of enterprises according to a list approved by the Presidium of the Supreme Soviet of the U.S.S.R.

Art. 77. The following are all-Union Ministries:

Ministry of Foreign Trade;

Ministry of Civil Aviation;

Ministry of the Merchant Marine;

Ministry of Railways.

Art. 78. The following are Union-Republican Ministries:

Ministry of Higher and Secondary Specialized Education;

Ministry of Public Health;

Ministry of Foreign Affairs;
Ministry of Culture;
Ministry of Defence;
Ministry of Communications;
Ministry of Agriculture;
Ministry of Finance.

CHAPTER VI

THE ORGANS OF STATE ADMINISTRATION OF THE UNION REPUBLICS

Art. 79. The highest executive and administrative organ of the state power of a Union Republic is the Council of Ministers of the Union Republic.

Art. 80. The Council of Ministers of a Union Republic is responsible and accountable to the Supreme Soviet of the Union Republic, or, in the intervals between sessions of the Supreme Soviet of the Union Republic, to the Presidium of the Supreme Soviet of the Union Republic.

Art. 81. The Council of Ministers of a Union Republic issues decisions and orders on the basis and in pursuance of the laws in operation of the U.S.S.R. and of the Union Republic, and of the decisions and orders of the Council of Ministers of the U.S.S.R., and verifies their execution.

Art. 82. The Council of Ministers of a Union Republic has the right to suspend decisions and orders of the Councils of Ministers of its Autonomous Republics, and to annul decisions and orders of the Executive Committees of the Soviets of Working People's Deputies of its Territories, Regions and Autonomous Regions, as well as decisions and orders of the Economic Councils of the Union Republic and of the economic administration areas.

Art. 83. The Council of Ministers of a Union Republic is appointed by the Supreme Soviet of the Union Republic and consists of:

The Chairman of the Council of Ministers of the Union Republic;

The Vice-Chairmen of the Council of Ministers;

The Ministers;

The Chairmen of State Committees, Commissions, and the heads of other departments of the Council of Ministers set up by the Supreme Soviet of the Union Republic in conformity with the Constitution of the Union Republic.

Art. 84. The Ministers of a Union Republic direct the branches of state administration which come within the jurisdiction of the Union Republic.

Art. 85. The Ministers of a Union Republic, within the limits of the jurisdiction of their respective Ministries, issue orders and instructions on the basis and in pursuance of the laws of the U.S.S.R. and of the Union

Republic, of the decisions and orders of the Council of Ministers of the U.S.S.R. and the Council of Ministers of the Union Republic, and of the orders and instructions of the Union-Republican Ministries of the U.S.S.R.

Art. 86. The Ministries of a Union Republic are either Union-Republican or Republican Ministries.

Art. 87. Each Union-Republican Ministry directs the branch of state administration entrusted to it, and is subordinate both to the Council of Ministers of the Union Republic and to the corresponding Union-Republican Ministry of the U.S.S.R.

Art. 88. Each Republican Ministry directs the branch of state administration entrusted to it, and is directly subordinate to the Council of Ministers of the Union Republic.

CHAPTER VII

THE HIGHER ORGANS OF STATE POWER IN THE AUTONOMOUS SOVIET SOCIALIST REPUBLICS

Art. 89. The highest organ of state power in an Autonomous Republic is the Supreme Soviet of the Autonomous Republic.

Art. 90. The Supreme Soviet of an Autonomous Republic is elected by the citizens of the Republic for a term of four years on a basis of representation established by the Constitution of the Autonomous Republic.

Art. 91. The Supreme Soviet of an Autonomous Republic is the sole legislative organ of the Autonomous Republic.

Art. 92. Each Autonomous Republic has its own Constitution, which takes account of the specific features of the Autonomous Republic and is drawn up in full conformity with the Constitution of the Union Republic.

Art. 93. The Supreme Soviet of an Autonomous Republic elects the Presidium of the Supreme Soviet of the Autonomous Republic and appoints the Council of Ministers of the Autonomous Republic, in accordance with its Constitution.

CHAPTER VIII

THE LOCAL ORGANS OF STATE POWER

Art. 94. The organs of state power in Territories, Regions, Autonomous Regions, Areas, Districts, cities and rural localities (*stanitsas*, villages, hamlets, *kishlaks, auls*) are the Soviets of Working People's Deputies.

Art. 95. The Soviets of Working People's Deputies of Territories, Regions, Autonomous Regions, Areas, Districts, cities and rural localities (*stanitsas,* villages, hamlets, *kishlaks, auls*) are elected by the working people of the respective Territories, Regions, Autonomous Regions, Areas, Districts, cities and rural localities for a term of two years.

Art. 96. The basis of representation for Soviets of Working People's Deputies is determined by the Constitutions of the Union Republics.

Art. 97. The Soviets of Working People's Deputies direct the work of the organs of administration subordinate to them, ensure the maintenance of public order, the observance of the laws, protect the rights of citizens, direct local economic and cultural affairs and draw up and approve local budgets.

Art. 98. The Soviets of Working People's Deputies adopt decisions and issue orders within the limits of the powers vested in them by the laws of the U.S.S.R. and of the Union Republic.

Art. 99. The executive and administrative organ of the Soviet of Working People's Deputies of a Territory, Region, Autonomous Region, Area, District, city or rural locality is the Executive Committee elected by it, consisting of a Chairman, Vice-Chairmen, a Secretary and members.

Art. 100. The executive and administrative organ of the Soviet of Working People's Deputies in a small locality, in accordance with the Constitution of the Union Republic, is the Chairman, the Vice-Chairman and the Secretary elected by the Soviet of Working People's Deputies.

Art. 101. The executive organs of the Soviets of Working People's Deputies are directly accountable both to the Soviets of Working People's Deputies which elected them and to the executive organ of the superior Soviet of Working People's Deputies.

CHAPTER IX

THE COURTS AND THE PROCURATOR'S OFFICE

Art. 102. In the U.S.S.R. justice is administered by the Supreme Court of the U.S.S.R., the Supreme Courts of the Union Republics, the Courts of the Territories, Regions, Autonomous Republics, Autonomous Regions and Areas, the Special Courts of the U.S.S.R., established by decision of the Supreme Soviet of the U.S.S.R., and the People's Courts.

Art. 103. In all Courts cases are tried with the participation of people's assessors, except in cases specially provided for by law.

Art. 104. The Supreme Court of the U.S.S.R. is the highest judicial organ. The Supreme Court of the U.S.S.R. is charged with the supervision of the judicial activities of all the judicial bodies of the U.S.S.R. and of the Union Republics within the limits established by law.

Art. 105. The Supreme Court of the U.S.S.R. is elected by the Supreme Soviet of the U.S.S.R. for a term of five years.

The Supreme Court of the U.S.S.R. includes the Chairmen of the Supreme Courts of the Union Republics by virtue of their office.

Art. 106. The Supreme Courts of the Union Republics are elected by the Supreme Soviets of the Union Republics for a term of five years.

Art. 107. The Supreme Courts of the Autonomous Republics are elected by the Supreme Soviets of the Autonomous Republics for a term of five years.

Art. 108. The Courts of Territories, Regions, Autonomous Regions and Areas are elected by the Soviets of Working People's Deputies of the respective Territories, Regions, Autonomous Regions or Areas for a term of five years.

Art. 109. People's judges of District (City) People's Courts are elected by the citizens of the districts (cities) on the basis of universal, equal, and direct suffrage by secret ballot for a term of five years.

People's Assessors of District (City) People's Courts are elected at general meetings of industrial, office and professional workers, and peasants in the place of their work or residence, and of service-men in military units, for a term of two years.

Art. 110. Judicial proceedings are conducted in the language of the Union Republic, Autonomous Republic or Autonomous Region, persons not knowing this language being guaranteed the opportunity of fully acquainting themselves with the material of the case through an interpreter and likewise the right to use their own language in court.

Art. 111. In all Courts of the U.S.S.R. cases are heard in public, unless otherwise provided for by law, and the accused is guaranteed the right to defence.

Art. 112. Judges are independent and subject only to the law.

Art. 113. Supreme supervisory power to ensure the strict observance of the law by all Ministries and institutions subordinated to them, as well as by people in office and citizens of the U.S.S.R. generally, is vested in the Procurator-General of the U.S.S.R.

Art. 114. The Procurator-General of the U.S.S.R. is appointed by the Supreme Soviet of the U.S.S.R. for a term of seven years.

Art. 115. Procurators of Republics, Territories, Regions, Autonomous Republics and Autonomous Regions are appointed by the Procurator-General of the U.S.S.R. for a term of five years.

Art. 116. Area, district and city procurators are appointed by the Procurators of the Union Republics, subject to the approval of the Procurator-General of the U.S.S.R., for a term of five years.

Art. 117. The organs of the Procurator's Office perform their functions independently of all local bodies, being subordinate solely to the Procurator-General of the U.S.S.R.

CHAPTER X

FUNDAMENTAL RIGHTS AND DUTIES OF CITIZENS

Art. 118. Citizens of the U.S.S.R. have the right to work, that is, the right to guaranteed employment and payment for their work in accordance with its quantity and quality.

The right to work is ensured by the socialist organization of the national economy, the steady growth of the productive forces of Soviet society, the elimination of the possibility of economic crises, and the abolition of unemployment.

Art. 119. Citizens of the U.S.S.R. have the right to rest and leisure.

The right to rest and leisure is ensured by the establishment of a seven-hour day for industrial, office, and professional workers, the reduction of the working day to six hours for arduous trades and to four hours in shops where conditions of work are particularly arduous; by the institution of annual vacations with full pay for industrial, office, and professional workers, and by placing a wide network of sanatoriums, holiday homes and clubs at the disposal of the working people.

Art. 120. Citizens of the U.S.S.R. have the right to maintenance in old age and also in case of sickness or disability.

This right is ensured by the extensive development of social insurance of industrial, office, and professional workers at state expense, free medical service for the working people, and the provision of a wide network of health resorts for the use of the working people.

Art. 121. Citizens of the U.S.S.R. have the right to education.

This right is ensured by universal compulsory eight-year education; by extensive development of secondary polytechnical education, vocational-technical education, and secondary specialised and higher education based on close ties between the school, real life and production activities; by the utmost development of evening and extramural education; by free education in all schools; by a system of state scholarship grants; by instruction in schools in the native language, and by the organization of free vocational, technical and agronomic training for the working people in the factories, state farms, and collective farms.

Art. 122. Women in the U.S.S.R. are accorded all rights on an equal footing with men in all spheres of economic, government, cultural, political, and other social activity.

The possibility of exercising these rights is ensured by women being accorded the same rights as men to work, payment for work, rest and leisure, social insurance and education, and also by state protection of the interests of mother and child, state aid to mothers of large families and to unmarried mothers, maternity leave with full pay, and the provision of a wide network of maternity homes, nurseries and kindergartens.

Art. 123. Equality of rights of citizens of the U.S.S.R., irrespective of their nationality or race, in all spheres of economic, government, cultural, political and other social activity, is an indefeasible law.

Any direct or indirect restriction of the rights of, or, conversely, the establishment of any direct or indirect privileges for, citizens on account of their race or nationality, as well as any advocacy of racial or national exclusiveness or hatred and contempt, are punishable by law.

Art. 124. In order to ensure to citizens freedom of conscience, the church in the U.S.S.R. is separated from the state, and the school from the church. Freedom of religious worship and freedom of anti-religious propaganda is recognised for all citizens.

Art. 125. In conformity with the interests of the working people, and in order to strengthen the socialist system, the citizens of the U.S.S.R. are guaranteed by law:

(a) freedom of speech;
(b) freedom of the press;
(c) freedom of assembly, including the holding of mass meetings;
(d) freedom of street processions and demonstrations.

These civil rights are ensured by placing at the disposal of the working people and their organizations printing presses, stocks of paper, public buildings, the streets, communications facilities and other material requisities for the exercise of these rights.

Art. 126. In conformity with the interests of the working people, and in order to develop the initiative and political activity of the masses of the people, citizens of the U.S.S.R. are guaranteed the right to unite in mass organizations-trade unions, co-operative societies, youth organizations, sport and defence organizations, cultural, technical and scientific societies; and the most active and politically-conscious citizens in the ranks of the working class, working peasants and working intelligentsia voluntarily unite in the Communist Party of the Soviet Union, which is the vanguard of the working people in their struggle to build communist society and is the leading core of all organizations of the working people, both government and non-government.

Art. 127. Citizens of the U.S.S.R. are guaranteed inviolability of the person. No person shall be placed under arrest except by decision of a court of law or with the sanction of a procurator.

Art. 128. The inviolability of the homes of citizens and privacy of correspondence are protected by law.

Art. 129. The U.S.S.R. affords the right of asylum to foreign citizens persecuted for defending the interests of the working people, or for scientific activities, or for struggling for national liberation.

Art. 130. It is the duty of every citizen of the U.S.S.R. to abide by the Constitution of the Union of Soviet Socialist Republics, to observe the laws, to maintain labor discipline, honestly to perform public duties, and to respect the rules of socialist society.

Art. 131. It is the duty of every citizen of the U.S.S.R. to safeguard and fortify public, socialist property as the sacred and inviolable foundation of the Soviet system, as the source of the wealth and might of the country, as the source of the prosperity and culture of all the working people.

Persons committing crimes in respect of public, socialist property are enemies of the people.

Art. 132. Universal military service is law.

Military service in the Armed Forces of the U.S.S.R. is the honorable duty of citizens of the U.S.S.R.

Art. 133. To defend the country is the sacred duty of every citizen of the U.S.S.R. Treason to the Motherland—violation of the oath of allegiance, desertion to the enemy, impairing the military power of the state, espionage—is punishable with all the severity of the law as the most heinous of crimes.

CHAPTER XI

THE ELECTORAL SYSTEM

Art. 134. Members of all Soviets of Working People's Deputies—of the Supreme Soviet of the U.S.S.R., the Supreme Soviets of the Union Republics, the Soviets of Working People's Deputies of the Territories and Regions, the Supreme Soviets of the Autonomous Republics, the Soviets of Working People's Deputies of the Autonomous Regions, and the Area, District, city and rural (*stanitsa,* village, hamlet, *kishlak, aul*) Soviets of Working People's Deputies—are elected on the basis of universal, equal and direct suffrage by secret ballot.

Art. 135. Elections of deputies are universal: all citizens of the U.S.S.R. who have reached the age of eighteen, irrespective of race or nationality, sex, religion, education, domicile, social origin, property status or past activities, have the right to vote in the election of deputies, with the exception of persons who have been legally certified insane.

Every citizen of the U.S.S.R. who has reached the age of twenty-three is eligible for election to the Supreme Soviet of the U.S.S.R., irrespective of race or nationality, sex, religion, education, domicile, social origin, property status or past activities.

Art. 136. Elections of deputies are equal: each citizen has one vote; all citizens participate in elections on an equal footing.

Art. 137. Women have the right to elect and be elected on equal terms with men.

Art. 138. Citizens serving in the Armed Forces of the U.S.S.R. have the right to elect and be elected on equal terms with all other citizens.

Art. 139. Elections of deputies are direct: all Soviets of Working People's Deputies, from rural and city Soviets of Working People's Deputies to the Supreme Soviet of the U.S.S.R., are elected by the citizens by direct vote.

Art. 140. Voting at elections of deputies is secret.

Art. 141. Candidates are nominated for each constituency.

The right to nominate candidates is secured to mass organizations and societies of the working people: Communist Party organizations, trade unions, co-operatives, youth organizations and cultural societies.

Art. 142. It is the duty of every deputy to report to his electorate on his work and on the work of his Soviet of Working People's Deputies, and he may be recalled at any time upon decision of a majority of the electors in the manner established by law.

CHAPTER XII

ARMS, FLAG, CAPITAL

Art. 143. The arms of the Union of Soviet Socialist Republics are a sickle and hammer against a globe depicted in the rays of the sun and surrounded by ears of grain, with the inscription "Workers of All Countries, Unite!" in the languages of the Union Republics. At the top of the arms is a five-pointed star.

Art. 144. The state flag of the Union of Soviet Socialist Republics is of red cloth with the sickle and hammer depicted in gold in the upper corner near the staff and above them a five-pointed red star bordered in gold. The ratio of width to length is 1:2.

Art. 145. The capital of the Union of Soviet Socialist Republics is the City of Moscow.

CHAPTER XIII

PROCEDURE FOR AMENDING THE CONSTITUTION

Art. 146. Amendments to the Constitution of the U.S.S.R. shall be adopted by a majority of not less than two thirds of the votes in each of the Chambers of the Supreme Soviet of the U.S.S.R.

THE UNITED KINGDOM OF GREAT BRITAIN AND NORTHERN IRELAND

SUMMARY

INTERNATIONAL STATUS AND FORM OF GOVERNMENT

The United Kingdom of Great Britain and Northern Ireland is a member of the United Nations (October 24, 1945).[1] It is a member of the

[1] The United Kingdom has accepted the compulsory jurisdiction of the International Court of Justice in accordance with Article 36 of its Statute.

Commonwealth of Nations and of other international organizations. It was a member of the League of Nations.

A number of statutes are considered as basic constitutional documents of Great Britain but the Constitution is not confined thereby. Dicey [1] states that the fundamental principle of the British Constitution is the rule of law and "that with us the law of the Constitution, the rules which in foreign countries naturally form part of a constitutional code, are not the source but the consequence of the rights of individuals, as defined and enforced by the courts." In addition to the constitutional laws which have accumulated since the twelfth century, many constitutional principles of prime importance are based upon precedent and convention.

The following constitutional texts are reproduced in this volume:

1. Magna Charta 1215, together with its confirmation of 1297, the Great Charter of the Liberties of England and of the Liberties of the Forest and the Confirmation of the Charters 1297.
2. Petition of Right 1627.
3. Bill of Rights 1688.
4. Act of Settlement 1700.
5. Acts of Union with Scotland Act 1706 and Union with Scotland Amendment Act 1707.
6. Parliament Act 1911.
7. Supreme Court of Judicature Act of 1925.
8. Statute of Westminster 1931.
9. Ministers of the Crown Acts 1937 and 1964.
10. Indian Independence Act 1947.
11. Representation of the People Act 1949 (extracts).
12. Peerage Act 1963.

The Magna Charta became, for the two centuries following, the authoritative expression of the rights of the Community against the Crown, and it was confirmed some forty times in those years. It received its definitive form in 1225 and by the confirmation of 1297, it became the earliest enactment of the Statute Book, insofar as not repealed still valid law. Its terms were reasserted in the Petition of Right and the Bill of Rights.

The Petition of Right, the Bill of Rights and the Act of Settlement formed stages in the struggle between Crown and Parliament to fix the limits of the prerogative of the Crown. Their result was that the Crown could no longer impose taxes nor legislate independently of Parliament, it could not carry out unconstitutional measures by force since the existence of a standing army depended on Parliament, it could not erect special courts nor issue pardons that could protect its servants against Parliament or the regular courts; the right of petition was established.

[1] Dicey, A. V. *Introduction to the study of the law of the Constitution.* 10th Ed. London 1959.

The Act of Union with Scotland united the two countries with a common parliament in London. The separate establishment of the Church of Scotland with its own Presbyterian form of government is expressly preserved.

The Parliament Act of 1911, as amended in 1949, provided that the House of Lords could have only a suspensive veto of not more than two years over legislation passed by the Commons, and removed entirely its power of veto over money bills.

The Statute of Westminster embodied the conclusions of the Imperial Conferences of 1926 and 1930, and defined the status of the dominions as equal and autonomous members of the Commonwealth with complete freedom to legislate independently, not subject to any law passed by the United Kingdom Parliament, sovereign in foreign and inter-Commonwealth relations as they had hitherto been sovereign in domestic concerns.

The Supreme Court of Judicature Act of 1925, consolidated the Judicature Acts since the first Supreme Court of Judicature Act in 1875, which united the former courts of King's Bench, Common Pleas, Exchequer, Chancery, Probate, Divorce and Matrimonial Causes, and Bankruptcy into the Supreme Court of Judicature.

The Ministers of the Crown Act of 1937, as amended 1964, established the salaries of Ministers and their distribution between Lords and Commons.

The Representation of the People Act 1949, based on the Ballot Act of 1872 and revising the Acts of 1918 and 1928, extending the vote to all adults, abolished the last relics of plural voting (university constituencies) and last surviving two-member constituencies. It guarantees free and secret elections.

The Peerage Act of 1963 provides for the disclaimer for life of hereditary peerages and certain provisions concerning Scottish and Irish peers and peeresses in their own right.

RIGHTS OF THE PEOPLE

Formal guarantees of rights are found in the ancient charters together with the restrictions on the arbitrary power of the Crown contained in the Act of Settlement. The Habeas Corpus Act of 1679 made into statute and remedied some of the defects of the writ at common law which had been in wide use since the thirteenth century and which protects the citizen from arbitrary arrest and detention. The protection of citizens lies in the ordinary law of the land, which applies equally to all; the remaining exception in the immunity of the Crown and the servants of the Crown in their official capacity from ordinary actions at law was abolished by the Crown Proceedings Act of 1947; the privilege of peers of the realm to be tried in the House of Lords for felony was discontinued in 1948. Freedom of religion was achieved by a series of acts throughout the nineteenth century the most important of which were the abolition of the test and corporation acts (concerning dissenters) in 1828 and Catholic emancipation in 1829. The Church of England is established only in England.

LEGISLATIVE DEPARTMENT

The King in Parliament constitutes the legislative power. Parliament is the supreme power in the State, the one limitation on its sovereignty being that one Parliament may not bind its successors. It is bicameral. The House of Lords is composed of hereditary peers and peeresses of England, Scotland and the United Kingdom, [1] 6 representatives of the Irish peers elected for life, [2] life peers, judicial peers and 26 spiritual peers.

The House of Commons is composed of members elected by universal suffrage from single member constituencies. The Parliament Act of 1911 fixes the duration of a legislature at five years if it has not been sooner dissolved. By convention, Parliament must be convened at least once a year. By convention, treaties and declarations of war must have the consent of Parliament. It enjoys customary privileges and immunities, renewed with each legislature. Money bills, by convention, originate in the Cabinet and the House of Lords has no power of veto, it has a suspensive veto only on other bills (Parliament Act 1911).

EXECUTIVE DEPARTMENT

The King in Council constitutes the executive. According to Forrest,[3] the Crown binds together every department of State, the prerogative of the King is the privilege of his subjects, that is, the King must exercise the prerogative for the protection of the subjects in accordance with the advice of his constitutional legal advisors. The monarchy is the oldest institution of the United Kingdom and, with the exception of the eleven years of Republic and Protectorate from 1649 to 1660, succession to the throne has been by heredity since the beginning of the ninth century. This hereditary character became statutory by the Act of Settlement of 1701. The Monarch calls and dissolves Parliament, is the fount of honor, has the right of pardon. All exercises of the royal prerogative must be approved by the Cabinet. The Crown is the symbol of the free association of the countries of the Commonwealth.

The Government is composed of the Prime Minister who, by convention, is the leader of the majority party in the House of Commons, and of

[1] See Peerage Act 1963.
[2] There has been no election since 1920.
[3] Forrest, G. A. *Constitutional Law.* 8th Ed. London 1950.

Ministers. The Ministers of the Crown Act of 1937 limits the number of Ministers members of the House of Commons and fixes a minimum number of ministers members of the House of Lords. By convention, the Cabinet is collectively responsible to Parliament, it must resign if it loses its confidence or ask for the dissolution of the House of Commons; the King must act on the advice of his Ministers. The Privy Council, composed of some 300 members including the members of the Cabinet, gives effect to decisions of the Executive by means of Orders in Council. It has certain consultative functions and a judicial function (see below).

JUDICIAL DEPARTMENT

Justice is administered by the King in his Courts. The judiciary is independent. Judges are appointed for life. Judicial neutrality is maintained by the exclusion of all wholetime salaried judges from the House of Commons;[1] Lords of Appeal are members of the House of Lords but by convention take no part in political debates.

The Supreme Court of Judicature is divided into two divisions, His Majesty's High Court of Justice and His Majesty's Court of Appeal.[2]

HM High Court of Justice is divided into the Chancery Division, comprising the Lord Chancellor as President and 6 judges; the King's Bench Division comprising the Lord Chief Justice of England as President and 19 (in 1947) judges; the Probate, Divorce and Admiralty Division comprising a President and 7 judges. Decisions of a Division Court of the High Court of Justice on appeals from inferior courts are final unless leave to appeal is given by the Division Court or the Court of Appeal. Judges sitting on Commissions of Assize are deemed to constitute a court of the High Court of Justice.

HM Court of Appeal is composed of *ex officio* judges and 5 ordinary judges who are the Lord Justices of Appeal.

The House of Lords has appellate jurisdiction from the Court of Appeal by leave of that court or of the House of Lords, not by right (Administration of Justice (Appeals) Act 1934). By convention, operative since 1844, no peer who has not held high judicial office takes part in hearing appeals.

The Judicial Committee of the Privy Council was created in 1833 by the Judicial Committee Act. The Crown may refer to it any legal issue on which it desires advice where the issue is not wholly judicial; it has done so particularly regarding colonial issues. It has certain other special and limited jurisdictions. It is the final court of appeal in certain cases for Australia, Canada and New Zealand.

There are inferior courts.

[1] Supreme Court of Judicature (Consolidated) Act, Art. 12.
[2] Id., Art. 1.

AREA, POPULATION, ETC.

The area of the United Kingdom (including Northern Ireland) is 230,609 square kilometres, its population (1965) 54,595,000. The capital is London.

Magna Charta

1215

John by the grace of God, King of England, Lord of Ireland, duke of Normandy and Aquitaine, and count of Anjou, to his archbishops, bishops, abbots, earls, barons, justiciars, foresters, sheriffs, reeves, servants, and to all his bailiffs and faithfull subjects, greeting. Know that we, having regard to God and the safety of our soul, and those of all our ancestors and heirs, to the honour of God, and the exaltation of holy church, and the betterment of our Realm, by the advice of our reverend fathers, Stephen archbishop of Canterbury, primate of all England, and cardinal of the holy Roman church, Henry, archbishop of Dublin, William of London, Peter of Winchester, Jocelin of Bath and Glastonbury, Hugh of Lincoln, Walter of Worcester, William of Coventry, and Benedict of Rochester, bishops; Master Pandulph, the Pope's subdeacon and household official; brother Aymeric, master of the Knights of the Temple in England; and of the noble persons, William Marshal, earl of Pembroke, William, earl of Salisbury, William, earl of Warenne, William, earl of Arundel; Alan de Galloway, constable of Scotland, Warin Fitz-Gerald, Peter Fitz-Herbert, Hubert de Burgh, seneschal of Poitou, Hugh de Neville, Matthew Fitz-Herbert, Thomas Basset, Alan Basset, Philip d'Aubigny, Robert de Roppelay, John Marshal, John Fitz-Hugh, and others of our faithful men,

1. Have, in the first place granted to God, and by this our present charter confirmed for us and our heirs for ever, that the English church shall be free, and enjoy her rights in their integrity and her liberties inviolate; and we will that it be so observed; and this is manifest from this, that we, of our mere and unconstrained will, before the contest between us and our barons had arisen, granted, and by our charter confirmed and procured to be confirmed by pope Innocent III, the freedom of elections which is most important and essential to the English church; and this we will observe and with to be observed in good faith by our heirs for ever. We have also granted to all the freemen of our kingdom, for us and for our heirs for ever, all the underwritten liberties, to have and to hold to them and to their heirs, of us and of our heirs.

2. If any of our earls or barons, or others who hold of us in chief by knight's service, shall die, and at the time of his death his heir shall be of full age and owe a relief, he shall have his inheritance by the old relief, namely, the heir or heirs of an earl by paying one hundred pounds for the whole barony of an earl; the heir or heirs of a baron by paying one hundred pounds for a whole barony; the heir or heirs of a knight by paying one hundred shillings at most for a whole knight's fee; and he that oweth less shall give less according to the ancient custom of fees.

3. But if the heir of any such shall be under age and in ward, he shall have his inheritance without relief or fine when he comes of age.

4. The guardian of the land of any such heir being under age, shall take therefrom only reasonable issues, customs, and services, and this without destruction or waste of men or goods; and if we commit the custody of any such lands to the sheriff, or to any other who is answerable to us for the issues thereof, and he shall make destruction and waste of his wardship, we will take amends of him, and the land shall be committed to two lawful and discreet men of that fee, who shall be answerable for the issues to us or to whomsoever we shall assign them; and if we sell or give to any one the wardship of any such lands, and he commit destruction or waste therein, he shall lose the wardship and it shall be committed to two lawful and discreet men of that fee who shall answer to us as aforesaid.

5. But the guardian, so long as he shall have the wardship of the land, shall keep up the houses, parks, fish-ponds, pools, mills and other appurtenances, from the issues of the land; and he shall restore to the heir, when he comes of age, his whole estate stocked with ploughs and tillage, as the season may require and the issues of the land can reasonably bear.

6. Heirs shall be married without disparagement, yet so that before the marriage takes place, those who are near in blood to the heir shall have notice.

7. A widow after the death of her husband shall immediately and without obstacle have her marriage-portion and her inheritance, nor shall she give anything for her dower, marriage-portion, or inheritance which she and her husband held on the day of his death; and she may remain in her husband's house for forty days after his death, within which time her dower shall be assigned to her.

8. No widow shall be distrained to marry so long as she wishes to live without a husband; provided that she gives security that she will not marry without our consent, if she holds of us, or that of the lord of whom she holds, if she holds of another.

9. Neither we nor our bailiffs shall seize any land or rent for any debt so long as the chattels of the debtor are sufficient to repay the debt; nor shall the debtor's sureties be distrained so long as the chief debtor is able to pay the debt; and if the chief debtor shall fail to pay the debt, having nothing wherewith to pay it then the sureties shall answer for it; and, if they will, they shall have the lands and rents of the debtor, until they shall be satisfied for the debt which they paid for him, unless the chief debtor can show himself to be quit thereof against them.

10. If anyone has borrowed from the Jews any sum, great or small, and shall die before the debt is paid, the debt shall not bear interest while the heir is under age, of whomsoever he may hold; and if the debt falls into our hands, we will only take the principal sum mentioned in the deed.

11. And if anyone shall die indebted to the Jews, his wife shall have her dower, and pay nothing of that debt; and if the children of the deceased be left under age, necessaries shall be provided for them according to the estate of the deceased, and out of the residue the debt shall be paid, saving the service due to the lords; in like manner it shall be done concerning debts due to others than Jews.

12. No scutage or aid shall be imposed in our kingdom, except by the common counsel of our kingdom, except for ransoming our person, knighting our eldest son, and once for marrying our eldest daughter, and for these only a reasonable aid shall be paid: likewise shall it be done concerning aids from the city of London.

13. And the city of London shall have all its ancient liberties and free customs, as well by land as by water. Further, we will and grant that all other cities, and boroughs, and towns, and ports, shall have all their liberties and free customs.

14. And for obtaining the common counsel of the realm, concerning the assessment of aids other than in the three cases aforesaid, or for assessing a scutage, we will cause to be summoned the archbishops, bishops, abbots, earls, and greater barons, singly by our letters; and further we will cause to be summoned in general, by our sheriffs and bailiffs, all those who hold of us in chief; for a fixed day, namely, forty days after their summons at least, and at a fixed place; and in all letters of such summons we will explain the cause thereof; and the summons being thus made, the business shall proceed on the appointed day according to the advice of those who are present, even if all who are summoned do not come.

15. We will not in future give leave to any one to take an aid from his free men, except for redeeming his person, or knighting his eldest son, or once marrying his eldest daughter, for which only a reasonable aid shall be levied.

16. No man shall be distrained to perform more service for a knight's fee, or other free tenement, than is due therefrom.

17. Common pleas shall not follow our court, but shall be held in some appointed place.

18. Inquests of *novel disseisin, mort d'ancestor*, and of *darrein presentment*, shall only be taken in their proper counties, and in this fashion: we, or if we should be out of the realm, our chief justiciar, will send two justices through each shire four times a year, who, with four knights of each shire, elected by the shire, shall hold the said assizes in the shire, on the day and in the place of meeting of the shire court.

19. And if the said assizes cannot be held on the days of the shire court, as many knights and free tenants shall remain of those who were present at that court, as may be required for the administration of justice, according as the business be more or less.

20. A free man shall be amerced for a small crime only according to its measure; and for a great crime he shall be amerced according to its greatness, saving his position; and a merchant likewise saving his trade, and a villein saving his tillage, if they have fallen into our mercy; and none of the said amercements shall be imposed except by the oath of honest men of the neighbourhood.

21. Earls and barons shall only be amerced by their peers, and according to the measure of their offence.

22. A clerk shall be amerced for his lay tenement only after the manner of the other persons aforesaid, and not according to the value of his ecclesiastical benefice.

23. Nor shall any *villa* or man be distrained to make bridges over rivers, except those that were of old legally bound to do so.

24. No sheriff, constable, coroners, or our other bailiffs, shall hold the pleas of the crown.

25. All shires, hundreds, wapentakes, and trithings shall be at the old farms, without any increase, except our demesne manors.

26. If any one holding a lay fief of us shall die, and our sheriff or bailiff shall show our letters patent of summons for a debt which the deceased owed to us, our sheriff or bailiff may seize and register the chattels of the deceased found on his lay fee, to the value of that debt, by the view of lawful men, so that nothing be removed therefrom until the clear debt be paid; and the residue shall be left to the executors to carry out the will of the deceased; and if nothing is due to us from him, all his chattels shall remain to the deceased, saving to his wife and children their reasonable shares.

27. If any free man shall die intestate, his chattels shall be distributed by the hands of his near kinsfolk and friends, by view of the church, saving to everyone the debts which the deceased owed to him.

28. No constable or our other bailiffs shall take the corn or other chattels of any one, without immediate payment for it, unless the seller allows him a respite.

29. No constable shall distrain any knight to give money for castle-guard, if he wishes to do the service in his own person, or by another suitable man, if for any reasonable cause he cannot do it himself; and if we lead or send him to war, he shall be free of castle-guard for the time during which he has been in the army because of us.

30. No sheriff or bailiff of ours, or any one else, shall take the horses or carts of any free man for carrying-service against the will of the said free man.

31. Neither we nor our bailiffs shall take another man's timber, for our castles, or other business of ours, except with the consent of the owner thereof.

32. We will only keep the lands of persons found guilty of felony for a year and a day, when they shall be restored to the lords of the fees.

33. All fish-weirs shall henceforth be entirely removed from the Thames and the Medway, and throughout all England, except on the sea coast.

34. The writ called *Praecipe* shall not in future be issued to anyone concerning any tenement whereby a freeman may lose his court.

35. There shall be one measure of wine throughout our kingdom, and one of ale, and one of corn, namely the London quarter, and one breadth of dyed cloth, russetts, and haberjects, namely, two ells between the selvedges; and with weights it shall be as with measures.

36. Nothing shall in future be given or taken for a writ of inquisition of life or limbs, but it shall be freely granted and not denied.

37. If any one holds of us by fee-farm, or by socage, or by burgage, and holds land of another by knight's service, we shall not have the wardship of his heir nor of the land which is of another's fee, by reason of that fee-farm, or socage, or burgage; nor shall we have the wardship of that fee-farm, socage, or burgage unless the fee-farm owers knight's service. Nor shall we have the wardship of anyone's heir or land which he holds of another by knight's service, by reason of any petty serjeanty which he holds of us by rendering us knives, arrows or the like.

38. No bailiff shall in future put any one to trial, upon his bare word, without credible witnesses to support it.

39. No free man shall be taken, or imprisoned, or disseised, or outlawed, or exiled, or in any way destroyed, nor will we go upon him, nor will we send against him, except by the lawful judgment of his peers or by the law of the land.

40. To none will we sell, to none will we deny, or delay, right or justice.

41. All merchants shall be safe and secure to leave, enter, dwell in, and travel through England, as well by land as by water, to buy and to sell, free of all evil tolls, by the ancient and right customs, except in time of war, if they are of the land which is warring against us; and if any such are found in our land at the onset of war, they shall be attached without harm to their bodies or goods, until it shall be known to us or to our chief justiciar, how the merchants of our land are treated, if they are found in the land warring against us; and if ours are safe there, the others shall be safe in our land.

42. It shall be lawful in future for anyone to leave our kingdom, and to return, safe and sound, by land and by water, saving the allegiance due to us, except for a short space in time of war, for the common good of the kingdom, except those imprisoned and outlawed according to the law of the land, and persons from a land hostile to us, and merchants who shall be dealt with as is aforesaid.

43. If anyone holding of some escheat, as of the honour of Wallingford, Nottingham, Boulogne, Lancaster, or of other escheats, which are in our hand and are baronies, shall die, his heir shall not give any relief, nor shall he do service to us other than that which he did to the baron, if that barony was in the hand of a baron; and we shall hold in the same way as the baron held it.

44. Men dwelling without the forest shall in future not come before our justices of the forest by common summonses, unless they have been impleaded, or are sureties for any person or persons impleaded for forest offences.

45. We will not appoint justices, constables, sheriffs, or bailiffs, except of such as know the law of the kindgom and are of a mind to keep it well.

46. All barons who have founded abbeys, concerning which they have charters of the kings of England, or of which they have ancient tenure, shall have the wardship of them when vacant, as they ought to have.

47. All forests made in our time shall immediately be disafforested; and so shall it be done concerning river-banks which have in our time been made by us into preserves.

48. All evil customs concerning forests and warrens, and foresters, warreners, sheriffs and their servants, river-banks and their wardens, shall be immediately inquired into in each shire by twelve sworn knights of the same shire, who are to be elected by honest men thereof, and within forty days after the making of the inquisition such customs shall be utterly and irrevocably destroyed by them, provided that we, or our justiciar if we are not in England, previously have knowledge of it.

49. We will immediately restore all hostages and charters delivered to us by Englishmen as sureties of peace or loyal service.

50. We will entirely remove from their bailiwicks the relatives of Gerard of Athée, Engelard of Cigogné, Peter, Guy, and Andrew of Chanceaux, Guy of Cigogné, Geoffrey of Martigny and his brothers, Philip Mark and his brothers, and Geoffrey his nephew, and all their followers.

51. And immediately after the restoration of peace we will expel from the kingdom all foreign knights, cross-bowmen, serjeants, and mercenary soldiers, who have come with horses and arms to the damage of the kingdom.

52. If any one has been dispossessed or removed by us without the lawful judgment of his peers, from his lands, chattels, liberties, or rights, we will immediately restore him to them; and if a dispute arise over this, then it shall be settled by the verdict of the twenty-five barons, of whom mention is made below in the clause for securing the peace; but with regard to all those things whereof anyone has been dispossessed or deprived without the lawful judgment of his peers, by king Henry our father or king Richard our brother, and which we have in our hand, or which others hold to whom we are bound to warrant them, we shall have respite until the usual term of crusaders; except those concerning which a plea has been begun or an inquisition taken by our command, before our assumption of the cross: and when we have returned from our pilgrimage, or if by chance we have remained behind from it, we will at once do full justice therein.

53. We shall have, moreover, the same respite, and in the same way, in doing justice in disafforesting or remeasuring the forests, which Henry our father or Richard our brother afforested, and concerning the wardship of lands which are of another's fee, and which we have hitherto held by reason of a fee which someone held of us by knight's service, and concerning abbeys founded on a fee other than our own, in which the lord of the fee claims the right; and when we have returned, or if we remain behind from our pilgrimage, we will do full justice to all who complain of such things.

54. No one shall be taken or imprisoned upon the appeal of a woman for the death of any other than her husband.

55. All fines made with us unjustly and against the law of the land, and all amercements levied unjustly and against the law of the land, shall be entirely pardoned, or else a verdict shall be given by the twenty-five barons, of whom mention is made below in the clause for securing the peace or by the verdict of the greater part of them, together with the said Stephen archbishop of Canterbury, if he can be present, and others whom he may wish to summon for this purpose: and if he cannot be present, the business shall nevertheless proceed without him, provided that if any one or more of the said twenty-five barons be concerned in a plaint of this kind, he or they shall be removed for this occasion, and another or others, elected and sworn by the rest of the twenty-five for this time only, shall complete the number.

56. If we have dispossessed or removed Welshmen from lands or liberties or other things, without the lawful judgment of their peers, in England or in Wales, they shall at once be restored to them; and if a dispute arises over this, then it shall be settled in the March by the judgment of their peers, according to the law of England with regard to English tenements, the law of Wales as to Welsh tenements, and the law of the March as to Marcher tenements. Welshmen shall do the same to us and ours.

57. Further, with regard to all those things of which any Welshman has been dispossessed or deprived without the lawful judgment of his peers, by king Henry our father or king Richard our brother, and which we hold in our hand, or which are held by others to whom we are bound to warrant them, we shall have a respite until the usual term of crusaders, those things excepted concerning which a plea has been begun or an inquisition made by our order before our assumption of the cross: but when we have returned, or if by chance we have remained behind from our pilgrimage, we shall at once do full justice to them therein, according to the laws of the Welsh and the said regions.

58. We will at once restore the son of Llewelyn, and all the hostages from Wales, and the charters which were delivered to us as security for the peace.

59. We will act towards Alexander king of the Scots, with regard to his sisters, and the return of hostages, and his liberties, and his right, in the manner as we shall act to our other barons of England, unless it ought to be otherwise according to the charters which we have from William his father, formerly king of the Scots; and this shall be done by the judgment of his peers in our court.

60. Moreover, all these said customs and liberties which we have granted to be observed in our realm in so far as pertains to us towards our men, as well clerk as lay, they shall themselves observe towards their own men.

61. And whereas we, for the honour of God and the betterment of our realm, and for the better allaying of the quarrel arisen between us and our barons, have granted all these things aforesaid, we, wishing that they be for ever enjoyed wholly and inviolate, establish and grant to them the following security; namely that the barons shall elect any twenty-five barons of the kingdom as they will, and these with all their power shall keep, hold, and cause to be kept the peace and liberties which we have granted to them, and by this our present charter confirmed to them, provided that if we, or our justiciar, or our bailiffs, or any of our servants, in any way fall away from them, or transgress any of the articles of peace or security, and the offence be shown to four barons of the said twenty-five, those four barons shall come before us or our justiciar if we are out of the kingdom, laying the offence before us, and asking that we cause it to be amended without delay. And if we do not amend it, or, if we are out of the kingdom and our justiciar does not amend it within forty days from the time when it was brought before us or before our justiciar if we should be out of the kingdom, the said four barons shall refer the matter to the rest of the twenty-five barons, who with the commonalty of the whole land shall distrain and grieve us in whatsoever way they can, namely by the seizure of castles, lands, possessions, and in any other way they can, until the reform is made according to their judgment, saving our person and that of our queen and children; and when it is done they shall obey us as before. And whosoever in the land wishes may take oath that he is ready, for the execution of the aforesaid matters, to obey the orders of the said twenty-five barons, and that he and his men will grieve us as best he may, and we publicly and freely allow any one to take oath who so wishes, and to none shall it ever be denied. All those, moreover, in the land who of themselves and of their own accord are unwilling to swear to the twenty-five barons, with regard to distraining and grieving us with them, we shall cause to take oath by our command, as is aforesaid. And if any of the twenty-five barons shall die, or leave the country, or in any other way be prevented from executing the aforesaid, those who remain of the said twenty-five barons shall elect another in his room, at their discretion, and he shall be sworn in like manner as the others. Further, in all things, which are referred to the said twenty-five barons to execute, if by chance all the twenty-five are present, and a dispute arises among them about anything, or some of those who are summoned are unwilling or unable to attend, the verdict of the majority of those present shall be regarded as firm and binding, as if all the twenty-five had agreed to it; and the said twenty-five shall swear that they will loyally keep the aforesaid, and cause it to be kept in so far as they can. And we will procure nothing from anyone, by ourselves or through another, by which any of these concessions and liberties might be revoked or diminished; and if any such thing has been procured let it be null and void, and we will never use it personally or by another.

62. And all ill-will, wrath, and bitterness, that has arisen between us and our men, clerk and lay, from the time of the dispute, we have fully remitted and pardoned to all. Furthermore, all trespasses made by reason of the said dispute, from Easter in the sixteenth year of our reign until the re-establishment of peace, we have fully remitted to all, clerk and lay, and completely forgiven, as far as in us lies. And further we have caused to be made for them letters patent of witness of the lord Stephen, archbishop of Canterbury, of the lord Henry, archbishop of Dublin, and of the said bishops, and of master Pandulf, concerning this security and the grants aforesaid.

63. Wherefore we wish and firmly enjoin that the English church be free and that the men in our kingdom have and hold all the aforesaid liberties, rights, and grants, well and in peace, freely and quietly, fully and wholly, to them and their heirs, of us and our heirs, in all things and places, forever as is aforesaid. This has been sworn to as well on our part as on the part of the barons, that all the aforesaid shall be kept in good faith and without malice.

Given under our hand
the above-named and many others being witnesses,
in the meadow which is called Runnymede,
between Windsor and Staines, on the fifteenth day of June,
in the seventeenth year of our reign.

The Great Charter of the Liberties of England and of the Liberties of the Forest[1]

Confirmed by King Edward in the twenty-fifth year of his reign 1297

Edward, by the grace of God, King of England, Lord of Ireland and Duke of Guyan (to all archbishops, bishops, etc.). We have seen the Great Charter of the Lord Henry sometime King of England, our father, of the liberties of England in these words.

Henry, by the grace of God, King of England, Lord of Ireland, Duke of Normandy and Guyan, and Earl of Anjou to all archbishops, bishops, abbots, priors, earls, barons, sheriffs, provosts, officers, and to all bailiffs, and other our faithful subjects, which shall see this present charter, greeting: Know ye that we, unto the honor of Almighty God, and for the salvation of the souls of our progenitors and successors (Kings of England), to the advancement of the holy church and amendment of our realm, of our meer and free will, have given and granted to all archbishops, bishops, abbots, priors, earls, barons, and to all freemen of this our realm, these liberties following to be kept in the kingdom of England forever.

CHAPTER 1

CONFIRMATION OF LIBERTIES

First, we have granted to God and by this our present charter have confirmed, for us and our heirs forever, that the church of England shall be free and shall have all her whole rights and liberties inviolable. We have granted also, and given to all the freemen of our realm, for us and our heirs forever, these liberties underwritten, to have and to hold to them and their heirs, of us and our heirs forever.

Chapters 2–6 repealed.

CHAPTER 7

WIDOW—HER MARRIAGE ESTATE—QUARANTINE—ESTOVERS—DOWER—REMARRIAGE

A widow after the death of her husband, incontinent, and without any difficulty shall have her marriage[2] and her inheritance which her husband

[1] 25 Edw. 1 (1297). As amended. *Halsbury's Statutes of England.* 2nd Ed., Vol. 4, p. 21.

[2] Marriage estate.

and she held the day of the death of her husband; and she shall tarry in the chief house of her husband by forty days after the death of her husband, within which days her dower shall be assigned her, if it were not assigned her before, or that the house be a castle, then a competent house shall be forthwith provided for her in the which she may honestly dwell, until her dower be to her assigned as it is aforesaid; and she shall have in the meantime her reasonable estovers of the common.[1] And for her dower shall be assigned unto her the third part of all the lands of her husband, which were his during coverture [2] except she were endowed of less at the church door. No widow shall be distrained to marry herself.[3] Nevertheless she shall find surety that she shall not marry without our license and assent if she hold of us, nor without the assent of the lord if she hold of another.[4]

CHAPTER 8

THE KING'S DEBTOR

We, or our bailiffs, shall not seize any land or rent for any debt as long as the present goods and chattels of the debtor do suffice to pay the debt, and the debtor himself be ready to satifsy therefor. Neither shall the pledges of the debtor be distrained, as long as the principal debtor is sufficient for the payment of the debt; and if the principal debtor fail in payment of the debt, having nothing wherewith to pay, or will not pay where he is able, the pledges shall answer for the debt; and if they will, they shall have the lands and rents of the debtor, until they be satisfied of that which they before paid him, except that the debtor can show himself to be acquitted against the said sureties.

CHAPTER 9

LIBERTIES OF LONDON, ETC.

The city of London shall have all the old liberties and customs which it hath been used to have. Moreover we will and grant that all other cities, boroughs, towns, and the barons of the five ports and all other ports, shall have all their liberties and free customs.

[1] Out of the common estate.
[2] In his life.
[3] While she chooses to live single.
[4] *Note:* This chapter was repealed as to deaths after 1925 by the Administration of Estates Act, 1925.

CHAPTER 10

DISTRESS FOR SERVICES[1]

No man shall be distrained to do more service for a knight's fee, nor any freehold than therefore is due.

Chapters 11, 12 and 13 repealed.

CHAPTER 14

AMERCEMENTS

A freeman shall not be amerced for a small fault, but after the manner of the fault, and for a great fault, after the greatness thereof, saving to him his contenement[2]; and a merchant likewise saving him to his merchandise; and any other's villain than ours shall be likewise amerced, saving his wainage, if he fall into our mercy. And none of the said amerciements shall be assessed but by oath of honest and lawful men of the vicinage. Earls and barons shall not be amerced but by their peers, and after the manner of their offense. No man of the church shall be amerced after the quantity of his spiritual benefice, but after his lay tenement, and after the quantity of his offence.

CHAPTER 15

MAKING OF BRIDGES

No town nor freeman shall be distrained to make bridges nor banks[3] but such as of old time and of right have been accustomed to make them (in time of King Henry our grandfather).

CHAPTER 16

OBSTRUCTING OF RIVERS

No banks[4] shall be defended from henceforth, but such as were in defence in the time of King Henry our grandfather, by the same places and the same bounds, as they were wont to be in his time.

Chapters 17–21 repealed.

[1] *Note:* This chapter is obsolete.
[2] Countenance.
[3] Over rivers.
[4] Rivers.

CHAPTER 22

LANDS OF FELONS[1]

We will not hold the lands of them that be convict of felony but one year and one day and then those lands shall be delivered to the lords of the fee.

CHAPTER 23

WEIRS

All weirs from henceforth shall be utterly put down by Thames and Medway, and through all England, but only by the sea-coasts.

Chapter 24 repealed.

CHAPTER 25

MEASURES AND WEIGHTS[2]

One measure of wine shall be through our realm, and one measure of ale, and one measure of corn, that is to say, the quarter of London; and one breadth of dyed cloth, russets and haberjects, that is to say two yards within the lists. And it shall be of weights as it is of measures.

Chapters 26–28 repealed.

CHAPTER 29

IMPRISONMENT ETC. CONTRARY TO LAW

No freeman shall be taken or imprisoned, or be disseised of his freehold, or liberties, or free customs, or be outlawed, or exiled, or in any other wise destroyed; nor will we not pass upon him nor condemn him,[3] but by the lawful judgment of his peers or by the law of the land. We will sell to no man, we will not deny or defer to any man either justice or right.

CHAPTER 30

FOREIGN MERCHANTS

All merchants, if they were not openly prohibited before, shall have their safe and sure conduct to depart out of England, to tarry in, and go through

[1] *Note:* This chapter is virtually repealed.
[2] *Note:* This chapter was rendered obsolete by the Weights and Measures Act 1878.
[3] Deal with him.

England, as well by land as by water, to buy and sell without any manner of evil tolles by the old and rightful customs, except in time of war; and if they be of a land making war against us, and be found in our realm at the beginning of the wars, they shall be attached without harm to body or goods, until it be known to us, or our chief justice, how our merchants be entreated there in the land making war against us; and if our merchants be well intreated there, their shall be likewise with us.

Chapters 31–36 repealed.

CHAPTER 37

ESCUAGE

(Escuage from henceforth shall be taken like as it was wont to be in the time of King Henry our grandfather.)[1] Reserving to all archbishops, bishops, abbots, priors, templars, hospitallers, earls, barons, and all persons, as well spiritual as temporal all their free liberties and free customs, which they have had in times passed. And all these customs and liberties aforesaid, which we have granted to be holden within this our realm as much as appertaineth to us and our heirs, we shall observe; and [2] all men of this our realm, as well spiritual as temporal, as much as in them is, shall observe the same against all persons in like wise.[3] And for this our gift and grant of these liberties and of other contained in our charter of liberties of our forest, the archbishops, bishops, abbots, priors, earls, barons, knights, freeholders, and other our subjects, have given unto us the fifteenth part of all their moveables. And we have granted unto them on the other party,[4] that neither we nor our heirs shall procure or do anything whereby the liberties in this charter contained shall be infringed or broken. And if anything be procured by any person contrary to the premises, it shall be had of no force nor effect. These being witnesses:

(*A list of sixty-three names follows.*)

We ratifying and approving these gifts and grants aforesaid, confirm and make strong all the same for us and our heirs perpetually and by the tenor of these presents do renew the same; Willing and granting for us and our heirs that this charter and all and singular his articles for ever shall be steadfastly, firmly, and inviolably observed; and if any article in the same charter contained yet hitherto peradventure hath not been kept

[1] Repealed.
[2] On our part, towards our men.
[3] Shall observe on their part towards their men.
[4] For us and our heirs.

we will and by authority royal command from henceforth firmly they be observed.[1]

In witness whereof we have caused these our letters patents to be made. To Edward our son at Westminster the twenty-eight day of March in the twenty-eighth year of our reign.

Confirmation of the Charters 1297[2]

CHAPTER 1

CONFIRMATION OF THE CHARTERS

Edward, by the grace of God, King of England, Lord of Ireland, and Duke of Guyan to all those that these present letters shall hear or see, greeting. Know ye that we, to the honour of God, and of holy church, and to the profit of our realm, have granted for us and our heirs, that the Charter of Liberties, and the Charter of the Forest which were made by the common assent of all the realm, in the time of King Henry our father, shall be kept in every point without breach. And we will that the same charters shall be sent under our seal, as well to our justices of the forest as to others, and to all sheriffs of shires and to all our other officers, and to all our cities throughout the realm, together with our writs, in which it shall be contained, that they cause the aforesaid charters to be published, and to declare to the people that we have confirmed them in all points; and that our justices, sheriffs, mayors and others ministers, which under us have the laws of our land to guide, shall allow the said charters pleaded before them in judgment in all their points; [3] that is to wit, the Great Charter as the common law, and the Charter of the Forest [4] for the wealth of our realm.

CHAPTER 2

JUDGMENTS AGAINST THE CHARTERS VOID

And we will that if any judgment be given from henceforth contrary to the points of the charters aforesaid by the justices, or by any other our ministers that hold plea before them against the points of the charters, it shall be undone and holden for nought.

Chapters 3 and 4 repealed.

[1] Not in original.
[2] 25 Edw. 1 (1297). *Halsbury's Statutes of England.* 2nd Ed., Vol. 4, p. 29.
[3] That they allow the same charters in all their points, in pleas before them, and in their judgments.
[4] According the assize of the forest.

CHAPTER 5

AIDS, TASKS AND PRISES GRANTED TO THE KING SHALL NOT BE TAKEN FOR A CUSTOM

And for so much as divers people of our realm are in fear, that the aids and tasks which they have given us beforetime towards our wars and other business, of their own grant and goodwill, howsoever they were made, might turn to a bondage to them and their heirs, because they might be at another time found in the rolls, and likewise for the prises taken throughout the realm by our ministers; [1] we have granted for us and our heirs, that we shall not draw such aids, taskes, nor prises into a custom, for anything that hath been done heretofore, be it by roll or any other precedent that may be founden.[2]

CHAPTER 6

NO AIDS OR PRISES SHALL BE TAKEN BUT BY CONSENT OF THE REALM

Moreover we have granted for us and our heirs as well to archbishops, bishops, abbots, priors, and other folk of the holy church, as also to earls, barons, and to all the commonalty of the land that for no business from henceforth we shall take [3] such manner of aids, tasks, nor prises but by the common assent of the realm, and for the common profit thereof, saving the ancient aids and prises due and accustomed.

CHAPTER 7

A RELEASE OF TOLL FOR WOOL

And for so much as the more part of the commonalty of the realm find themselves sore grieved with the maletent [4] of wools, that is to wit, a toll oi forty shillings for every sack of wool, and have made petition to us to release the same; we at their requests have clearly released it, and have granted (for us and our heirs) that we shall not take such things without their common assent and good will; saving to us and our heirs the custom of wools, skins, and leather, granted before by the commonalty aforesaid.

[1] In our name.
[2] Or that may be found by roll in any other manner.
[3] Of our realm.
[4] Unjust toll.

In witness of which things we have caused these our letters to be made patents. Witness Edward our son at London the tenth day of October, the five and twentieth year of our reign.

And be it remembered that this same charter, in the same terms, word for word, was sealed in Flanders under the King's great seal, that is to say, at Ghent the fifth day of November in the twenty-fifth year of the reign of our aforesaid lord the King, and sent into England.

II. The Petition of Right 1627[1]

The Petition exhibited to His Majesty by the Lords Spiritual and Temporal and Commons in this present Parliament assembled concerning divers rights and liberties of the Subject; with the King Majesties Royal Answer thereunto in full Parliament.

To the King's most excellent Majesty.

Humbly show unto our sovereign Lord the King, the lords spiritual and temporal and commons in Parliament assembled that

1. Reciting that by (25) 34 Edw. I, st. 4. c. 1, by authority of Parliament holden 25 Edw. 3, and by other laws of this realm, the King's subjects should not be taxed but by consent of Parliament. Whereas it is declared and enacted by a Statute made in the time of the reign of King Edward the First commonly called *Statutum de Tallagio non concedendo*, that no tallage or aid should be laid or levied by the King or his heirs in this realm without the good will and assent of the archbishops, bishops, earls, barons, knights, burgesses, and other freemen of the commonalty of this realm, and by the authority of Parliament holden in the five and twentieth year of the reign of King Edward the Third, it is declared and enacted that from henceforth no person should be compelled to make any loans to the king against his will because such loans were against reason and the franchise of the land, and by other laws of this realm it is provided, that none should be charged by any charge or imposition called a benevolence nor by such like charge by which the statutes before mentioned and other the good laws and statutes of this realm your subjects have interited this freedom that they should not be compelled to contribute to any tax, tallage, aid or other like charge not set by common consent in Parliament.

2. And that commissions have of late issued on which proceedings have been contrary to law. Yet nevertheless of late divers commissions directed to sundry commissioners in several counties with instructions have issued, by means whereof your people have been in divers places assembled and required to lend certain sums of money unto your Majesty, and many of them upon their refusal so to do have had an oath administered unto

[1] 3 Car. c. 1 (1627). *Halsbury's Statutes of England*, 2nd Ed., Vol. 4, p. 129.

them not warrantable by the laws or statutes of this realm and have been constrained to become bound to make appearance and give attendance before your privy council and in other places; and other of them have been therefore imprisoned, confined, and in sundry other ways molested and disquieted and divers other charges have been laid and levied upon your people in several counties by lord lieutenants, deputy lieutenants, commissioners for musters, justices of the peace and other by command or direction from your Majesty or your privy council against the laws and free customs of the realm.

3. *Reciting 9 Hen. 3, M.C.c.29.* And whereas also by the Statute called the Great Charter of the Liberties of England, it is declared and enacted, that no freeman may be taken or imprisoned or disseised of this freehold or liberties or his free customs or be outlawed or exiled or in any manner destroyed, but by the lawful judgment of his peers or by the law of the land.

4. *Reciting 28 Edw. 3. c. 3.* And in the eight and twentieth year of the reign of King Edward the Third it was declared and enacted by authority of Parliament, that no man of what estate or condition that he be, should be put out of his land or tenements nor taken nor imprisoned nor disherited nor put to death without being brought to answer by due process of law.

5. *And that divers subjects have been imprisoned without cause shown or cause of detainer certified.* Nevertheless against the tenor of the said statutes and other the good laws and statutes of your realm to that end provided, divers of your subjects have of late been imprisoned without any cause showed: And when for their delivrance they were brought before your justices by your Majesty's writ of habeas corpus there to undergo and receive as the courts should order, and their keepers commanded to certify the causes of their detainer, no cause was certified, but that they were detained by your Majesty's special command signified by the lords of your privy council and yet were returned back to several prisons without being charged with any thing to which they might answer according to the law.

6. *And that soldiers have been dispersed in divers counties and inhabitants compelled to receive them.*[1] And whereas of late great companies of soldiers and mariners have been dispersed into divers counties of the realm, and the inhabitants against their wills have been compelled to receive them into their houses, and there to suffer them to sojourn against the laws and customs of this realm and to the great grievance and vexation of the people.

7. *Reciting 25 Edw. 3, and that commissions have issued under the great seal for proceedings according to martial law.* And whereas also by authority of Parliament in the five and twentieth year of the reign of King Edward

[1] The prohibition of billeting contained in this section is suspended by S. 102 of the Army Act and by S. 102 of the Air Force Act, insofar as billeting is authorized by those Acts.

the Third it is declared and enacted that no man should be forejudged of life and limb against the form of the Great Charter and other laws and statutes of this your realm no man ought to be adjudged to death but by the laws established in this your realm, either by the customs of the same realm or by Acts of Parliament. And whereas no offender of what kind soever is exempted from the proceedings to be used and punishments to be inflicted by the laws and statutes of this your realm, nevertheless of late time divers commissions under your Majesty's Great Seal have issued forth by which certain persons have been assigned and appointed commissioners with power and authority to proceed within the land according to the justice of martial law against such soldiers or mariners or other dissolute persons, joining with them as should commit and murder, robbery, felony, mutiny, or other outrage or misdemeanor whatsoever, and by such summary course and order as is agreeable to martial law and as is used in armies in time of war to proceed to the trial and condemnation of such offenders and them to cause to be executed and put to death according to the law martial.

By pretext whereof some of your Majesty's subjects have been by some of the said commissioners put to death, when and where, if by the same laws and statutes of the land they had deserved death, by the same laws and statutes also they might and by no other ought to have been judged and executed.

And also sundry grievous offenders by color thereof claiming an exemption have escaped the punishments due to them by the laws and statutes of this your realm, by reason that divers of your officers and ministers of justice have unjustly refused or foreborne to proceed against such offenders according to the same laws and statutes upon pretence that the said offenders were punishable only by martial law and by authority of such commissions as aforesaid. Which commissions and all other of like nature are wholly and directly contrary to the said laws and statutes of this your realm.

8. The Petition. They do therefore humbly pray your most excellent Majesty, that no man hereafter be compelled to make or yield any gift, loan, benevolence, tax, or such like charge without common consent by Act of Parliament, and that none be called to make answer or take such oath or to give attendance or be confined or otherwise molested or disquieted concerning the same or for refusal thereof. And that no freeman in any such manner as is before mentioned be imprisoned or detained. And that your Majesty would be pleased to remove the said soldiers and mariners and that your people may not be so burdened in time to come. And that the aforesaid commissions for proceeding by martial law may be revoked and annulled. And that hereafter no commissions of like nature may issue forth to any person or persons whatsoever to be executed as aforesaid, lest by colour of them any of your Majesty's subjects be destroyed or put to death contrary to the laws and franchise of the land.

All which they most humbly pray of your most excellent Majesty as their rights and liberties according to the laws and statutes of this realm and that your Majesty would also vouchsafe to declare that the awards, doings, proceedings to the prejudice of your people in any of the premises shall not be drawn hereafter into consequence or example. And that your Majesty would be also graciously pleased for the further comfort and safety of your people to declare your royal will and pleasure, that in the things aforesaid all your officers and ministers shall serve you according to the laws and statutes of this realm as they tender the honour of your Majesty and the prosperity of this kindgom.

Qua quidem Petitione lecta & plenius intellecta per dictum Dominicum Regem taliter est responsum in pleno Parliamento, viz., *soit droit fait comme est desiré.*

III. Bill of Rights 1688[1]

An Act Declaring the Rights and Liberties of the Subject and Settling the Succession of the Crown

Whereas the lords spiritual and temporal and commons assembled at Westminster fully and freely representing all the estates of the people of this realm did upon the thirteenth day of February in the year of our Lord one thousand six hundred and eighty-eight present unto their Majesties then called and known by the names and style of William and Mary, Prince and Princess of Orange, being present in their proper persons, a certain declaration in writing made by the said lords and commons in the words following ,viz.

Whereas the late King James the Second by the assistance of diverse evil councillors, judges, and ministers employed by him did endeavour to subvert and extirpate the Protestant religion and the laws and liberties of this kingdom.

By assuming and exercising a power of dispensing with and suspending of laws and the execution of laws without consent of Parliament.

By committing and prosecuting diverse worthy prelates for humbly petitioning to be excused from concurring to the said assumed power.

By issuing and causing to be executed a commission under the great seal for erecting a court called the court of commissioners for ecclesiastical causes.

By levying money for and to the use of the Crown, by pretence of prero-

[1] 1 Will. a Mar. sess. 2 c. 2 (1688). *Halsbury's Statutes of England.* 2nd Ed., vol. 4, p. 151.

gative, for other time and in other manner than the same was granted by Parliament.

By raising and keeping a standing army within this kingdom in time of peace without consent of Parliament and quartering soldiers contrary to law.

By causing several good subjects being protestants to be disarmed at the same time when papists were both armed and employed contrary to the law.

By violating the freedom of election of members to serve in Parliament

By prosecutions in the Court of Kings Bench for matters and causes cognizable only in Parliament and by diverse other arbitrary and illegal courses.

And whereas of late years partial, corrupt and unqualified persons have been returned and served on juries in trials and particularly diverse jurors in trials for high treason which were not freeholders.

And excessive bail hath been required of persons committed in criminal cases to elude the benefit of the laws made for the liberty of subjects.

And excessive fines have been imposed.

And illegal and cruel punishments inflicted.

And several grants and promises made of fines and forfeitures before any conviction or judgment against the persons upon whom the same were to be levied.

All which are utterly and directly contrary to the known laws and statutes and freedoms of this realm.

And whereas the said late King James the Second having abdicated the government and the throne being thereby vacant, his highness, the Prince of Orange (whom it hath pleased Almighty God to make the glorious instrument of delivering this kingdom from propery and arbitrary power) did (by the advice of the lords spiritual and temporal and diverse principal persons of the commons) cause letters to be written to the lords spiriual and temporal being protestants and other letters to the several counties, cities, universities, boroughs, and cinque ports for the choosing of such persons to represent them as were of right to be sent to Parliament to meet and sit at Westminster upon the two and twentieth day of January of this year one thousand six hundred and eighty-eight in order to ordain such an establishment that their religion, laws and liberties might not again be in danger of being subverted, upon which letters elections having been accordingly made.

And thereupon the said lords spiritual and temporal and commons, pursuant to their respective letters and elections, being now assembled in a full and free representative of this nation taking into their most serious consideration the best means for attaining the ends aforesaid do in the first place (as their ancestors in like cases have usually done) for the vindicating and asserting of their ancient rights and liberties, declare.

Suspending power.—That the pretended power of suspending of laws and the execution of laws by regal authority without the consent of Parliament is illegal.

Late dispending power.—That the pretended power of dispending with laws or the execution of laws by regal authority as it hath been assumed and exercised of late is illegal.

Ecclesiastical Courts illegal.—That the commission for erecting the late court of commissioners for ecclesiastical causes and all other commissions and courts of like nature are illegal and pernicious.

Levying money.—That levying money for or to the use of the crown by pretence of prerogative without grant of Parliament for longer time or in other manner than the same is or shall be granted is illegal.

Right to Petition.—That it is the right of subjects to petition the king and all commitments and prosecutions for such petitioning are illegal.

Standing Army.—That the raising or keeping a standing army within the kingdom in time of peace unless it be with the consent of Parliament is against the law.

Subjects' arms.—That the subjects which are protestants may have arms for their defence suitable to their conditions and as allowed by law.

Freedom of election.—That the election of members of Parliament ought to be free.

Freedom of speech.—That the freedom of speech and debate or proceedings in Parliament ought not to be impeached or questioned in any ocurt or place out of Parliament.

Excessive bail.—That excessive bail ought not to be required nor excessive fines imposed nor cruel and unusual punishment inflicted.

Juries.—That jurors ought to be duly impanelled and returned.

Grants of forfeiture.—That all grants and promises of fines and forfeitures of particular persons before conviction are illegal and void.

Frequent Parliaments.—And that for redress of all grievances and for the amending, strengthening and preserving of the laws Parliament ought to be held frequently.

And they do claim, demand and insist upon all and singular the premises as their undoubted rights and liberties and that no declarations, judgments, doings or proceedings to the prejudice of the people in any of the said premises ought in any wise to be drawn hereafter into consequence or example. To which demand of their rights they are particularly encouraged by the declaration of His Highness the Prince of Orange as being the only means for obtaining a full redress and remedy therein. Having therefore an entire confidence that his said Highness, the Prince of Orange, will perfect the deliverance so far advanced by him and will still preserve them from the violation of their rights which they have here asserted and from all other attempts upon their religion, rights and liberties. The said lords spiritual and temporal and commons assembled at Westminster do resolve that William and Mary, Prince and Princess of Orange, be and be declared King and Queen of England, France, and Ireland and the dominions thereunto belonging to hold the crown and royal dignity of the said kingdoms and dominions to them, the said Prince and Princess, during their lives and the life of the survivor of them. And the sole and full exercise of the regal power be onely in and executed by the said Prince of Orange in the names of the said prince and princess during their joint lives and after their deceases the said Crown and royal dignity of the said kingdoms and dominions to be to the heirs of the body of the said princess and for default of such issue to the Princess Anne of Denmark and the heirs of her body and for default of such issue to the heirs of the body of the said Prince of Orange. And the lords spiritual and temporal and commons do pray the said prince and princess to accept the same accordingly. And that the oaths hereafter mentioned be taken by all persons of whom the oaths of allegiance and supremacy might be required by law instead of them and that the said oaths of allegiance and supremacy be abrogated.

I. A.B., do sincerely promise and swear that I will be faithful and bear true allegiance to their Majesties, King William and Queen Mary.

So help me God.

I. A.B., do swear that I do from my heart abhor, detest and abjure as impious and heretical this damnable doctrine and position that princes excommunicated or deprived by the Pope or any authority of the See of Rome may be deposed or murdered by their subjects or any other whatsoever.

IV. The Act of Settlement (1700)[1]

An Act for the further Limitation of the Crown and better securing the Rights and Liberties of the Subject

Whereas in the first year of the reign of your Majesty and of our late most gracious sovereign lady Queen Mary (of blessed memory) an Act of Parliament was made intituled an Act for declaring the rights and liberties of the subject and for settling the succession of the crown wherein it was (amongst other things) enacted established and declared that the crown and regal government of the kingdoms of England, France and Ireland and the dominions thereunto belonging should be and continue to your Majesty and the said late Queen during the joint lives of your Majesty and the said Queen and to the survivor and that after the decease of your Majesty and of the said Queen the said crown and regal government

[1] 12 &, 13 Will. 3, c. 2. As amended. *Halsbury's Statutes of England.* 2nd Ed., Vol. 4, p. 158. The short title, "The Act of Settlement," was given to this Act by the Short Titles Act, 1896 (c. 14).

should be and remain to the heirs of the body of the said late Queen and for default of such issue to her royal Highness the Princess Ann of Denmark and the heirs of her body and for default of such issue to the heirs of the body of your Majesty. And it was thereby further enacted that all and every person and persons that then were or afterwards should be reconciled to or shall hold communion with the see or church of Rome or should profess the popish religion or marry a papist should be excluded and are by that Act made for ever incapable to inherit possess or enjoy the crown and government of this realm and Ireland and the dominions thereunto belonging or any part of the same or to have use or exercise any regal power authority or jurisdiction within the same and in all and every such case and cases the people of these realms shall be and are thereby absolved of their allegiance and that the said crown and government shall from time to time descend to and be enjoyed by such person or persons being protestants as should have inherited and enjoyed the same in case the said person or persons so reconciled holding communion professing or marrying as aforesaid were naturally dead. After the making of which Statute and the settlement therein contained your Majesties good subjects who were restored to the full and free possession and enjoyment of their religion rights and liberties by the providence of God giving success to your Majesties just undertakings and unwearied endeavours for that purpose had no greater temporal felicity to hope or wish for than to see a royal progeny descending from your Majesty to whom (under God) they owe their tranquillity and whose ancestors have for many years been principal assertors of the reformed religion and the liberties of Europe and from our said most gracious sovereign lady whose memory will always be precious to the subjects of these realms. And it having since pleased Almighty God to take away our said sovereign lady and also the most hopeful Prince William Duke of Gloucester (the only surviving issue of her royal Highness the Princess Ann of Denmark) to the unspeakable grief and sorrow of your Majesty and your said good subjects who under such losses being sensibly put in mind that it standeth wholly in the pleasure of Almighty God to prolong the lives of your Majesty and of her royal Highness and to grant to your Majesty or to her royal Highness such issue as may be inheritable to the crown and regal government aforesaid by the respective limitations in the said recited Act contained do constantly implore the divine mercy for those blessings. And your Majesty's said subjects having daily experience of your royal care and concern for the present and future welfare of these kingdoms and particularly recommending from your throne a further provision to be made for the succession of the crown in the protestant line for the happiness of the nation and the security of our religion and it being absolutely necessary for the safety peace and quiet of this realm to obviate all doubts and contentions in the same by reason of any pretended titles to the crown and to maintain a certainty in the succession thereof to which your subjects may safely have recourse for their protection in case the limitations in the said recited Act should determine. Therefore for a further provision of the succession of the crown in the protestant line we your Majesties most dutiful and loyal subjects the lords spiritual and temporal and commons in this present Parliament assembled do beseech your Majesty that it may be enacted and declared and be it enacted and declared by the Kings most excellent Majesty by and with the advice and consent of the lords spiritual and temporal and commons in this present Parliament assembled and by the authority of the same that

1. The Princess Sophia, Electress and Duchess dowager of Hanover, daughter of the late Queen of Bohemia, daughter of King James the First, to inherit after the King and the Princess Ann, in default of issue of the said princess and his Majesty, respectively; and the heirs of her body, being protestants.— The most excellent Princess Sophia Electress and Duchess dowager of Hanover daughter of the most excellent Princess Elizabeth late Queen of Bohemia daughter of our late sovereign lord King James the First of happy memory be and is hereby declared to be the next in succession in the protestant line to the imperial crown and dignity of the said realms of England France and Ireland with the dominions and territories thereunto belonging after his Majesty and the Princess Ann of Denmark and in default of issue of the said Princess Ann and of his Majesty respectively and that from and after the deceases of his said Majesty our now sovereign lord and of her royal Highness the Princess Ann of Denmark and for default of issue of the said Princess Ann of his Majesty respectively the crown and regal government of the said kingdoms of England France and Ireland and of the dominions thereunto belonging with the royal state and dignity of the said realms and all honours styles titles regalities prerogatives powers jurisdictions and authorities to the same belonging and appertaining shall be remain and continue to the said most excellent Princess Sophia and the heirs of her body being protestants. And thereunto the said lords spiritual and temporal and commons shall and will in the name of all the people of this realm most humbly and faithfully submit themselves their heirs and posterities and do faithfully promise that after the deceases of his Majesty and her royal Highness and the failure of the heirs of their respective bodies to stand to maintain and defend the said Princess Sophia and the heirs of her body being protestants according to the limitation and succession of the crown in this Act specified and contained to the utmost of their powers with their lives and estates against all persons whatsoever that shall attempt any thing to the contrary.

2. The persons inheritable by this Act, holding communion with the church of Rome, incapacitated as by the former Act, to take the oath at their coronation, according to Stat. 1, W. & M. c. 6.—Provided always and it is hereby enacted that all and every person and persons who shall or may take or inherit the said crown by virtue of the limitation of this present Act and is are or shall be reconciled to or shall hold communion with the see or church of Rome or shall profess the popish religion or shall marry a papist shall be subject to such incapacities as in such case or cases are by the said recited Act provided enacted and established. And that every King and Queen of this realm who shall come to and succeed in the imperial crown of this kingdom by virtue of this Act shall have the coronation oath administered to him her or them at their respective coronations according to the Act of Parliament made in the first year of the reign of his Majesty and the said late Queen Mary intituled An Act for establishing the coronation oath and shall make subscribe and repeat the declaration in the Act first above recited mentioned or referred to in the manner and form thereby prescribed.[1]

3. *Further provisions for securing the religion, laws, and liberties of these realms.*—And whereas it is requisite and necessary that some further provision be made for securing our religion laws and liberties from and after the death of his Majesty and the Princess Ann of Denmark and in default of issue of the body of the said princess and of his Majesty respectively. Be it enacted by the Kings most excellent Majesty by and with the advice and consent of the lords spiritual and temporal and commons in Parliament assembled and by the authority of the same.

That whosoever shall hereafter come to the possession of this crown shall join in communion with the Church of England as by law established.

That in case the crown and imperial dignity of this realm shall hereafter come to any person not being a native of this kingdom of England this nation be not obliged to engage in any war for the defence of any dominions or territories which do not belong to the crown of England without the consent of Parliament.

That after the said limitation shall take effect as aforesaid no person born out of the kingdoms of England Scotland of Ireland or the dominions thereunto belonging although he be made a denizen (except such as are born of English parents) shall be capable to be of the Privy Council or a member of either House of Parliament or to enjoy any office or place of trust either civil or military or to have any grant of lands tenements or hereditaments from the Crown to himself or to any other or others in trust for him.

That no pardon under the great seal of England be pleadable to an impeachment by the Commons in Parliament.

4. *The laws and statutes of the realm confirmed.*—And whereas the laws of England are the birthright of the people thereof and all the kings and queens who shall ascend the throne of this Realm ought to administer the government of the same according to the said laws and all their officers

[1] The form of declaration is now that prescribed by the Accession Declaration Act, 1910.

and ministers ought to serve them respectively according to the same. The said lords spiritual and temporal and commons do therefore further humbly pray that all the laws and statutes of this realm for securing the established religion and the rights and liberties of the people thereof and all other laws and statutes of the same now in force may be ratified and confirmed. And the same are by his Majesty by and with the advice and consent of the said lords spiritual and temporal and commons and by authority of the same ratified and confirmed accordingly.

V. The Union with Scotland Act, 1706[1]

An Act for an Union of the Two Kingdoms of England and Scotland

Most Gracious Sovereign

Whereas articles of union were agreed on the twenty-second day of July in the fifth year of your Majesties reign by the commissioners nominated on behalf of the kingdom of England under your Majesties great seal of England bearing date at Westminster the tenth day of April then last past in pursuance of an Act of Parliament made in England in the third year of your Majesties reign and the commissioners nominated on the behalf of the kingdom of Scotland under your Majesties great seal of Scotland bearing date the twenty-seventh day of February in the fourth year of your Majesties reign in pursuance of the fourth Act of the third session of the present Parliament of Scotland to treat of and concerning an union of the said kingdoms. And whereas an Act hath passed in the Parliament of Scotland at Edinburgh the sixteenth day of January in the fifth year of your Majesties reign wherein 'tis mentioned that the estates of Parliament considering the said articles of union of the two kingdoms had agreed to and approved of the said articles of union with some additions and explanations and that your Majesty with advice and consent of the estates of Parliament for establishing the Protestant religion and Presbyterian Church government within the kingdom of Scotland had passed in the same session of Parliament an Act intituled Act for securing of the Protestant religion and Presbyterian Church government which by the tenor thereof was appointed to be inserted in any Act ratifying the treaty and expressly declared to be a fundamental and essential condition of the said treaty or union in all times coming the tenor of which articles as ratified and approved of with additions and explanations by the said Act of Parliament of Scotland follows.

[1] 6 Anne, c. 11 (1706). As amended. *Halsbury's Statutes of England.* 2nd Ed., Vol. 4, p. 166. The short title was given to this Act by the Short Titles Act, 1896.

ARTICLE I

The kingdoms united; ensigns armorial.—That the two kingdoms of England and Scotland shall upon the first day of May which shall be in the year one thousand seven hundred and seven and for ever after be united into one kingdom by the name of Great Britain and that the ensigns armorial of the said United Kingdom be such as her Majesty shall appoint and the crosses of St. George and St. Andrew be conjoyned in such manner as Her Majesty shall think fit and used in all flags banners standards and ensigns both at sea and land.

ARTICLE II

Succession to the monarchy.—That the succession to the monarchy of the United Kingdom of Great Britain and of the dominions thereto belonging after her most sacred Majesty and in default of issue of her Majesty be remain and continue to the most excellent Princess Sophia Electoress and Duchess dowager of Hanover and the heirs of her body being protestants upon whom the crown of England is settled by an Act of Parliament made in England in the twelfth year of the reign of his late Majesty King William the Third intituled An Act for the further limitation of the crown and better securing the rights and liberties of the subject And that all papists and persons marrying papists shall be excluded from and for ever incapable to inherit possess or enjoy the imperial crown of Great Britain and the dominions thereunto belonging or any part thereof and in every such case the crown and government shall from time to time descend to and be enjoyed by such person being a protestant as should have inherited and enjoyed the same in case such papist or person marrying a papist was naturally dead according to the provision for the descent of the crown of England made by another Act of Parliament in England in the first year of the reign of their late Majesties King William and Queen Mary intituled An Act declaring the rights and liberties of the subject and settling the succession of the crown.

ARTICLE III

Parliament.—That the United Kingdom of Great Britain be represented by one and the same Parliament to be styled the Parliament of Great Britain.

ARTICLE IV

Trade and navigation and other rights.— That all the subjects of the United Kingdom of Great Britain shall from and after the union have full freedom and intercourse of trade and navigation to and from any port or place within the said United Kingdom and the dominions and plantations thereunto belonging and that there be a communication of all other rights privileges and advantages which do or may belong to the subjects of either kingdom except where it is otherwise expressly agreed in these articles.

ARTICLE V

Repealed.

ARTICLE VI

Regulations of trade, duties, etc.—That all parts of the United Kingdom for ever from and after the union shall have the same allowances encouragements and drawbacks and be under the same prohibitions restrictions and regulations of trade and liable to the same customs and duties on import and export and that the allowances encouragements and drawbacks prohibitions restrictions and regulations of trade and the customs and duties on import and export settled in England when the union commences shall from and after the union take place throughout the whole United Kingdom excepting and reserving the duties upon export and import of such particular commodities from which any persons the subjects of either kingdom are specially liberated and exempted by their private rights which after the union are to remain safe and entire to them in all respects as before the same. And that from and after the union no Scots cattle carried into England shall be liable to any other duties either on the public or private accompts than those duties to which the cattle of England are or shall be liable within the said kingdom

ARTICLE VII

Excise.—That all parts of the United Kingdom be for ever from and after the union liable to the same excises upon all exciseable liquors excepting only that the thirty-four gallons English barrel of beer or ale amounting to twelve gallons Scots present measure sold in Scotland by the brewer at nine shillings six pence sterling excluding all duties and retailed including duties and the retailers profit at two pence the Scots pint or eigth part of the Scots gallon be not after the union liable on accompt of the present excise upon exciseable liquors in England to any higher imposition than two shillings sterling upon the aforesaid thirty-four gallons English barrel being twelve gallons the present Scots measure and that the excise settled in England on all other liquors when the union commences take place throughout the whole United Kingdom.

ARTICLE VIII

Repealed

ARTICLE IX

Land tax.—That whensoever the sum of one million nine hundred ninety-seven thousand seven hundred and sixty-three pounds eight shillings and four pence half penny shall be enacted by the Parliament of Great Britain to be raised in that part of the United Kingdom now called England on land and other things usually charged in Acts of Parliament there for granting an aid to the crown by a land tax that part of the United Kingdom now called Scotland shall be charged by the same Act with a further sum of forty-eight thousand pounds free of all charges as the quota of Scotland to such tax and so proportionably for any greater or lesser sum raised in England by any tax on land and other things usually charged together with the land and that such quota for Scotland in the cases aforesaid be raised and collected in the same manner as the cess now is in Scotland but subject to such regulations in the manner of collecting as shall be made by the Parliament of Great Britain.

ARTICLES X–XV

Repealed.

ARTICLE XVI

Coin. That from and after the union the coin shall be of the same standard and value throughout the United Kingdom as now in England.

ARTICLE XVII

Repealed.

ARTICLE XVIII

Laws concerning public rights; private rights.—That the laws concerning regulation of trade customs and such excises to which Scotland is by virtue of this treaty to be liable be the same in Scotland from and after the union as in England and that all other laws in use within the kingdom of Scotland do after the union and notwithstanding thereof remain in the same force as before (except such as are contrary to or inconsistent with this treaty) but alterable by the Parliament of Great Britain with this difference betwixt the laws concerning public right policy and civil government and those which concern private right that the laws which concern public right policy and civil government may be made the same throughout the whole United Kingdom. But that no alteration be made in laws which concern private right except for evident utility of the subjects within Scotland.

ARTICLE XIX

Court of Session, etc.—That the Court of Session or college of justice do after the union and notwithstanding thereof remain in all time coming within Scotland as it is now constituted by the laws of that kingdom and with the same authority and privileges as before the union subject nevertheless to such regulations for the better administration of justice as shall be made by the Parliament of Great Britain and that hereafter none shall be named by Her Majesty or her royal successors to be ordinary lords of session but such who have served in the college of justice as advocates or principal clerks of session for the space of five years or as writers to the signet for the space of ten years with this provision that no writer to the signet be capable to be admitted a lord of the session unless he undergo a private and public trial on the civil law before the faculty of advocates and be found by them qualified for the said office two years before he be named to be a lord of the session yet so as the qualifications made or to be made for capacitating persons to be named ordinary lords of session may be altered by the Parliament of Great Britain. And that the Court of Justiciary do also after the union and notwithstanding thereof remain in all time coming within Scotland as it is now constituted by the laws of that kingdom and with the same authority and privileges as before the union subject nevertheless to such regulations as shall be made by the Parliament of Great Britain and without prejudice of other rights of justiciary And that all admiralty jurisdictions be under the lord high admiral or commissioners for the admiralty of Great Britain for the time being and that the Court of Admiralty now established in Scotland be continued and that all reviews reductions or suspensions of the sentences in maritime cases competent to the jurisdiction of that court remain in the same manner after the union as now in Scotland until the Parliament of Great Britain shall make such regulations and alterations as shall be judged expedient for the whole United Kingdom so as there be always continued in Scotland a Court of Admiralty such as in England for determination of all maritime cases relating to private rights in Scotland competent to the jurisdiction of the Admiralty Court subject nevertheless to such regulations and alterations as shall be thought proper to be made by the Parliament of Great Britain. And that the heritable rights of admiralty and vice admiralties in Scotland be reserved to the respective proprietors as rights of property subject nevertheless as to the manner of exercising such heritable rights to such regulations and alterations as shall be thought proper to be made by the Parliament of Great Britain. And that all other courts now being within the kingdom of Scotland do remain but subject to alterations by the Parliament of Great Britain and that all inferior courts within the said limits do remain subordinate as they are now to the supreme courts of justice within the same in all time coming. And that no causes in Scotland be cognoscible by the courts of Chancery Queen's Bench Common Pleas or any other court in Westminster Hall and that the said courts or any other of the like nature after the union shall have no power to cognosce review or alter the acts or sentences of the judicatures within Scotland or stop the execution of the same And that there be a Court of Exchequer in Scotland after the union for deciding questions concerning the revenues of customs and excises there having the same power and authority in such cases as the Court of Exchequer has in England and that the said Court of Exchequer in Scotland have power of passing signatures gifts tutories and in other things as the Court of Exchequer at present in Scotland hath and that the Court of Exchequer that now is in Scotland do remain until a new Court of Exchequer be settled by the Parliament of Great Britain in Scotland after the union.

ARTICLE XX

Heritable offices, etc.—That all heritable offices superiorities heritable jurisdictions offices for life and jurisdictions for life be reserved to the owners thereof as rights of property in the same manner as they are now enjoyed by the laws of Scotland notwithstanding this treaty.

ARTICLE XXI

Royal burghs.—That the rights and privileges of the royal burghs in Scotland as they now are do remain entire after the union and notwithstanding thereof.

ARTICLE XXII

Sixteen peers of Scotland.—That by virtue of this treaty of the peers of Scotland at the time of the union sixteen shall be the number to sit and vote in the House of Lords and forty-five the number of the representatives of Scotland in the House of Commons of the Parliament of Great Britain.

ARTICLE XXIII

Privileges of the sixteen Peers of Scotland.—That the aforesaid sixteen peers of Scotland mentioned in the last preceding article to sit in the House of Lords of the Parliament of Great Britain shall have all privileges of Parliament which the peers of England now have and which they or any peers of Great Britain shall have after the union and particularly the right of sitting upon the trials of peers. And in the case of the trial of any peer in time of adjournment or prorogation of Parliament the said sixteen peers shall be summoned in the same manner and have the same powers and privileges at such trial as any other peers of Great Britain and that in case any trials of peers shall hereafter happen when there is no Parliament in being the sixteen peers of Scotland who sat at the last preceding Parliament shall be summoned in the same manner and have the same powers and privileges at such trials as any other peers of Great Britain And that all peers of Scotland and their successors to their honours and dignities shall from and after the union be peers of Great Britain and have rank and precedency next and immediately after the peers of the like orders and degrees in England at the time of the union and before all peers of Great Britain of the like orders and decrees who may be created after the union and shall be tried as peers of Great Britain and shall enjoy all privileges of peers as fully as the peers of England do now or as they or any other peers of Great Britain may hereafter enjoy the same except the right and privilege of sitting in the House of Lords and the privileges depending thereon and particularly the right of sitting upon the trials of peers.

ARTICLE XXIV

Heraldry; great seal; privy seal; regalia.—That from and after the union there be one great seal for the United Kingdom of Great Britain which shall be different from the great seal now used in either Kingdom. And that the quartering the arms and the rank and precedency of the Lyon king of arms of the kingdom of Scotland as may best suit the union be left to her Majesty. And that in the meantime the great seal of England be used as the great seal of the United Kingdom and that the great seal of the United Kingdom be used for sealing writs to elect and summon the Parliament of Great Britain and for sealing all treaties with foreign princes and states and all public acts instruments and orders of state which concern the whole United Kingdom and in all other matters relating to England as the great seal of England is now used and that a seal in Scotland after the union be always kept and made use of in all things relating to private rights or grants which have usually passed the great seal of Scotland and which only concern offices grants commissions and private rights within that kingdom and that until such seal shall be appointed by her Majesty the present great seal of Scotland shall be used for such purposes and that the privy seal casset signet of the Justiciary Court quarter seal and seals of courts now used in Scotland be continued but that the said seals be altered and adapted to the state of the union as her Majesty shall think fit and the said seals and all of them and the keepers of them shall be subject to such regulations as the Parliament of Great Britain shall hereafter make. And that the crown scepter and sword of state the records of Parliament and all other records rolls and registers whatsoever both public and private general and particular and warrants thereof continue to be kept as they are within that part of the United Kingdom now called Scotland and that they shall so remain in all time coming notwithstanding the union.

ARTICLE XXV

Laws inconsistent with the articles, void.—That all laws and statutes in either kingdom so far as they are contrary to or inconsistent with the terms of these articles or any of them shall from and after the union cease and become void and shall be so declared to be by the respective Parliaments of the said kingdoms.

As by the said articles of union ratified and approved by the said Act of Parliament of Scotland relation being thereunto had may appear.

2. *Acts of Scotland herin mentioned, confirmed.*—And the tenor of the aforesaid Act for securing the Protestant religion and Presbyterian Church government within the kingdom of Scotland is as follows.

Our sovereign lady and the estates of Parliament considering that by the late Act of Parliament for a treaty with England for an union of both kingdoms it is provided that the commissioners for that treaty should not treat of or concerning any alteration of the worship discipline and government of the Church of this kingdom as now by law established which treaty being now reported to the Parliament and it being reasonable and necessary that the true Protestant religion as presently professed within this kingdom with the worship discipline and government of this Chirch should be effectually and unalterably secured therefore her Majesty with advice and consent of the said estates of Parliament doth hereby establish and confirm the said true Protestant religion and the worship discipline and government of this Church to continue without any alteration to the people of this land in all succeeding generations and more especially her Majesty with advice and consent aforesaid ratifies approves and for ever confirms the fifth Act of the first Parliament of King William and Queen Mary intituled Act ratifying the confession of faith and settling Presbyterian Church government with all other Acts of Parliament relating thereto in prosecution of the declaration of the estates of this kingdom containing the claim of right bearing date the eleventh of April one thousand six hundred and eighty-nine. And her Majesty with advice and consent aforesaid expressly provides and declares that the foresaid true Protestant religion contained in the above mentioned confession of faith with the form and purity of worship presently in use within this Church and its Presbyterian Church government and discipline (that is to say) the government of the Church by kirk sessions presbyteries provincial synods and general assemblies all established by the foresaid Acts of Parliament pursuant to the claim of right shall remain and continue unalterable and that the said Presbyterian government shall be the only government of the Church within the kingdom of Scotland.

Universities and colleges of Saint Andrew, Glasgow, Aberdeen and Edinburgh, to continue.—And further for the greater security of the foresaid Protestant religion and of the worship discipline and government of this Church as above established her Majesty with advice and consent foresaid statutes and ordains that the universities and colledges of Saint Andrew's Glasgow Aberdeen and Edinburgh as now established by law shall continue within this kingdom for ever and that in all time coming no professors principals regents masters or others bearing office in any university college or school within this kingdom be capable or be admitted or allowed to continue in the exercise of their said functions but such as shall own and acknowledge the civil government in manner prescribed or to be prescribed by the Acts of Parliament as also that before or at their admissions they do and shall acknowledge and profess and shall subscribe to the foresaid confession of faith as the confession of their faith and that they will practise and conform themselves to the worship presently in use in this Church and submit themselves to the government and discipline thereof and never endeavour directly or indirectly the prejudice or subversion of the same and that before the respective presbyteries of their bounds by whatsoever gift presentation or provisions they may be thereto provided.[1]

Subjects not liable to oath, test, or subscription, inconsistent with the Presbyterian Church government; successor to swear to maintain the said settlement of religion.—And further her Majesty with advice aforesaid expresly declares and statutes that none of the subjects of this kingdom shall be liable to put all and every one of them for ever free of any oath test or subscription within this kingdom contrary to or inconsistent with the foresaid true Protestant religion and Presbyterian Church government worship and discipline as above established and that the same within the bounds of this Church and kingdom shall never be imposed upon or require of them in any sort. And lastly that after the decease of her present Majesty (whom God long preserve) the sovereign succeeding to her in the royal government of the kingdom of Great Britain shall in all time coming at his or her accession to the crown swear and subscribe that they shall inviolably maintain and preserve the foresaid settlement of the true Protestant religion with the government worship discipline right and pri-

[1] A declaration of faith is no longer required or principals of, or professors in, Scottish universities.

vileges of this Church as above established by the laws of this kingdom in prosecution of the claim of right.

This Act to be held a fundamental condition of union, and to be inserted in any Act of Parliament for concluding the said union.—And it is hereby statute and ordained that this Act of Parliament with the establishment therein contained shall be held and observed in all time coming as a fundamental and essential condition of any treaty or union to be concluded betwixt the two kingdoms without any alteration thereof or derogation thereto in any sort for ever. As also that this Act of Parliament and settlement therein contained shall be insert and repeated in any Act of Parliament that shall pass for agreeing and concluding the foresaid treaty or union betwixt the two kingdoms and that the same shall be therein expressly declared to be a fundamental and essential condition of the said treaty or union in all time coming which articles of union and Act immediately above written her Majesty with advice and consent aforesaid statutes enacts and ordains to be and continued in all time coming the sure and perpetual foundation of a complete and entire union of the two kingdoms of Scotland and England under the express condition and provision that this approbation and ratification of the foresaid articles and Act shall be no ways binding on this kingdom until the said articles and Act be ratified approved and confirmed by her Majesty with and by the authority of the Parliament of England as they are now agreed to approved and confirmed by her Majesty with and by the authority of the Parliament of Scotland declaring nevertheless that the Parliament of England may provide for the security of the Church of England as they think expedient to take place within the bounds of the said kingdom of England and not derogating from the security above provided for establishing of the Church of Scotland within the bounds of this kingdom as also the said Parliament of England may extend the additions and other provisions contained in the articles of union as above insert in favours of the subjects of Scotland to and in favour of the subjects of England which shall not supend or derogate from the force and effect of this present ratification but shall be understood as herein included without the necessity of any ratification in the Parliament of Scotland.

Laws contrary to articles, void.—And lastly her Majesty enacts and declares that all laws and statutes in this kingdom so far they are contrary to or inconsistent with the terms of these articles as above mentioned shall from and after the union cease and become void.

3. Recital of 6 Ann. c. 8.—And whereas an Act hath passed in this present session of Parliament intituled An Act for securing the Church of England as by law established the tenor whereof follows.

Whereas by an Act made in the session of Parliament held in the third and fourth year of her Majesties reign whereby her Majesty was empowered to appoint commissioners under the great seal of England to treat with commissioners to be authorized by the Parliament of Scotland concerning an union of the kingdoms of England and Scotland it is provided and enacted that the commissioners to be named in pursuance of the said Act should not treat of or concerning any alteration of the liturgy rites ceremonies discipline or government of the Church as by law established within this realm. And whereas certain commissioners appointed by her Majesty in pursuance of the said Act and also other commissioners nominated by her Majesty by the authority of the Parliament of Scotland have met and agreed upon a treaty of union of the said kingdoms which treaty is now under the consideration of this present Parliament And whereas the said treaty (with some alterations therein made) is ratified and approved by Act of Parliament in Scotland and the said act of ratification is by her Majesties royal command laid before the Parliament of this kingdom And whereas it is reasonable and necessary that the true Protestant religion professed and established by law in the Church of England and the doctrine worship discipline and government thereof should be effectually and unalterably secured. Be it enacted by the Queens most excellent Majesty by and with the advice and consent of the lords spiritual and temporal and the commons in this present Parliament assembled and by authority of the same that an Act made in the thirteenth year of the reign of Queen Elizabeth of famous memory intituled An Act for the ministers of the Church to be of sound religion and also another Act made in the thirteenth year of the reign of the late King Charles the Second intituled An Act for the uniformity of the public prayers and administration of sacraments and other rites and ceremonies and for establishing the form of making ordaining and consecrating bishops priests and deacons in the Church of England (other than such clauses in the said Acts or either of them as have been repealed or altered by any subsequent Act or Acts of Parliament) and all and singular other Acts of Parliament now in force for the establishment and preservation of the Church of England and the doctrine worship discipline and government thereof shall remain and be in full force for ever.

And be it further enacted by the authority aforesaid that after the demise of her Majesty (whom God long preserve) the Sovereign next succeeding to her Majesty in the royal government of the kingdom of Great Britain and so for ever hereafter every King or Queen succeeding and coming to the royal government of the kingdom of Great Britain at his or her coronation shall in the presence of all persons who shall be attending assisting or otherwise then and there present take and subscribe an oath to maintain and preserve inviolably the said settlement of the Church of England and the doctrine worship discipline and government thereof as by law established within the kingdoms of England and Ireland the dominion of Wales and town of Berwick upon Tweed and the territories thereunto belonging.

And be it further enacted by the authority aforesaid that this Act and all and every the matters and things therein contained be and shall for ever be holden and adjudged to be a fundamental and essential part of any treaty of union to be concluded between the said two kingdoms and also that this Act shall be inserted in express terms in any Act of Parliament which shall be made for settling and ratifying any such treaty of union and shall be therein declared to be an essential and fundamental part thereof.

4. *The said articles and Act of Parliament of Scotland confirmed.*—May it therefore please your most excellent Majesty that it may be enacted and be it enacted by the Queen's most excellent Majesty by and with the advice and consent of the lords spiritual and temporal and commons in this present Parliament assembled and by authority of the same that all and every the said articles of union as ratified and approved by the said Act of Parliament of Scotland as aforesaid and herein before particularly mentioned and inserted and also the said Act of Parliament of Scotland for establishing the Protestant religion and Presbyterian Church government within that kingdom intituled Act for securing the Protestant religion and Presbyterian Church government and every clause matter and thing in the said articles and Act contained shall be and the said articles and Act are hereby for ever ratified approved and confirmed.

5. *Cap. 8, ante, and the said Act of Parliament of Scotland to be observed as fundamental conditions of the said union; and the said articles and Acts of Parliament to continue the union.*—And it is hereby further enacted by the authority aforesaid that the said Act passed in this present session of Parliament intituled An Act for securing the Church of England as by law established and all and every the matters and things therein contained and also the said Act of Parliament of Scotland intituled Act for securing the Protestant religion and Presbyterian Church government with the establishment in the said Act contained be and shall for ever be held and adjudged to be and observed as fundamental and essential conditions of the said union and shall in all times coming be taken to be and are hereby declared to be essential and fundamental parts of the said articles and union and the said articles so as aforesaid ratified approved and confirmed by Act of Parliament of Scotland and by this present Act and the said Act passed in this present session of Parliament intituled an Act for securing the Church of England as by law established and also the said Act passed in the Parliament of Scotland intituled Act for securing the Protestant religion and Presbyterian Church government are hereby enacted and ordained to be and continue in all times coming the complete and entire union of the two kingdoms of England and Scotland.

6. *Recital of Act of Parliament of Scotland for settling election of the sixteen peers and forty-five members for Scotland.*—And whereas since the passing the said Act in the Parliament of Scotland for ratifying the said articles

of union one other Act intituled Act settling the manner of electing the sixteen peers and forty-five members to represent Scotland in the Parliament of Great Britain hath likewise passed in the said Parliament of Scotland at Edinburgh the fifth day of February one thousand seven hundred and seven the tenor whereof follows.

Our sovereign lady considering that by the twenty-second article of the treaty of union as the same is ratified by an Act passed in this session of Parliament upon the sixteenth of January last it is provided that by virtue of the said treaty of the peers of Scotland at the time of the union sixteen shall be the number to sit and vote in the House of Lords and forty-five the number of the representatives of Scotland in the House of Commons of the Parliament of Great Britain and that the said sixteen peers and forty-five members in the House of Commons be named and chosen in such manner as by a subsequent Act in this present session of Parliament in Scotland should be settled which Act is thereby declared to be as valid as if it were a part of and ingrossed in the said treaty. Therefore her Majesty with advice and consent of the estates of Parliament statutes enacts and ordains that the said sixteen peers who shall have right to sit in the House of Peers in the Parliament of Great Britain on the part of Scotland by virtue of this treaty shall be named by the said peers of Scotland whom they represent their heirs or successors to their dignities and honours out of their own number and that by open election and plurality of voices of the peers present and of the proxies for such as shall be absent the said proxies being peers and producing a mandate in writing duly signed before witnesses and both the constituent and proxy being qualified according to law declaring also that such peers as are absent being qualified as aforesaid may sent to all such meetings lists of the peers whom they judge fittest validly signed by the said absent peers which shall be reckoned in the same manner as if the parties had been present and given in the said list and in case of the death or legal incapacity of any of the said sixteen peers that the aforesaid peers of Scotland shall nominate another of their own number in place of the said peer or peers in manner before and after mentioned And that of the said forty-five representatives of Scotland in the House of Commons in the Parliament of Great Britain thirty shall be chosen by the shires or steuartries and fifteen by the royal burrows as follows viz. one for every shire and steuartry excepting the shires of Bute and Cathness which shall choose one by turns Bute having the first election the shires of Nairn and Cromarty which shall also choose by turns Nairn having the first election and in like manner the shires of Clackmanan and Kinross shall choose by turns Clackmanan having the first election and in case of the death or legal incapacity of any of the said members from the respective shires or steuartries above mentioned to sit in the House of Commons it is enacted and ordained that the shire or steuartry who elected the said member shall elect another member in his place and that the said fifteen representatives for the royal burrows be chosen as follows viz. that the town of Edinburgh shall have right to elect and send one member to the Parliament of Great Britain and that each of the other burghs shall elect a commissioner in the same manner as they are now in use to elect commissioners to the Parliament of Scotland which commissioners and burghs (Edinburgh excepted) being divided into fourteen classes or districts shall meet at such time and burghs within their respective districts as her Majesty her heirs or successors shall appoint and elect one for each district viz. the burghs of Kirkwall Week Dornock Dingwall and Taine one the burghs of Fortrose Inverness Nairn and Forress one of the burghs of Elgin Cullen Banff Inverury and Kintore one the burghs of Aberdeen Inverbervy Montrose Aberbrothock and Brochine one the burghs of Forfar Perth Dundee Coupar and Saint Andrews one the burghs of Craill Kilrennie Anstruther Easter Anstruther Wester and Pittenweem one the burghs of Dysart Kirkaldie Kinghern and Bruntisland one the burghs of Innerkithen Dunfermline Queensferry Culross and Sterling one the burghs of Glasgow Renfrew Ruglen and Dumbarton one the burghs of Haddington Dunbarr North Berwick Lauder and Jedburgh one the burghs of Selkirk Peebles Linlithgow and Lanark one the burghs of Dumfries Sanquhar Annan Lockmaben and Kircudbright one the burghs of Wigtoun New Galloway Stranraver and Whitehern one and the burghs of Air Irvin Rothesay Campbletoun and Inverary one And it is hereby declared and ordained that where the votes of the commissioners for the said burghs met to choose representatives from their several districts to the Parliament of Great Britain shall be equal in that case the president of the meeting shall have a casting or decisive vote and that by and according to his vote as a commissioner from the burgh from which he is sent the commissioner from the eldest burgh presiding in the first meeting and the commissioners from the other burghs in their respective districts presiding afterwards by turns in the order as the said burghs are now called in the rolls of the Parliament of Scotland And that in case any of the said fifteen commissioners from burghs shall decease or become legally incapable to sit in the House of Commons then the town of Edinburgh or the district which chose the said member shall elect a member in his or their place It is always hereby expressly provided and declared that none shall be capable to elect or be elected for any of the said estates but such as are twenty-one years of age complete and protestant excluding all papists or such who being suspect of popery and required refuse to swear and subscribe the formula contained in the third Act made in the eighth and ninth sessions of King Williams Parliament intituled Act for preventing the growth of popery And also declaring that none shall be capable to elect or be elected to represent a shire or burgh in the Parliament of great Britain for this part of the United Kingdom except such as are now capable by the laws of this kingdom to elect or be elected as commissioners for shires or burghs to the Parliament of Scotland And further her Majesty with advice and consent aforesaid for the effectual and orderly election of the persons to be chosen to sit vote and serve in the respective Houses of the Parliament of Great Britain when her Majesty her heires and successors shall declare her or their pleasure for holding the first or any subsequent Parliament of Great Britain and when for that effect a writ shall be issued out under the great seal of the United Kingdom directed to the privy council of Scotland conform to the said twenty-second article statutes enacts and ordains that until the Parliament of Great Britain shall make further provision therein the said writ shall contain a warrant and command to the said privy council to issue out a proclamation in her Majesty's name requiring the peers of Scotland for the time to meet and assemble at such time and place within Scotland as her Majesty and royal successors shall think fit to make election of the said sixteen peers and requiring the lord clerk register or two of the clerks of session to attend all such meetings and to administer the oaths that are or shall be by law required and to ask the votes and having made up the lists in the presence of the meeting to return the names of the sixteen peers chosen (certified under the subscription of the said lord clerk register clerk or clerks of session attending) to the clerk of the privy council of Scotland and in like manner requiring and ordaining the several freeholders in the respective shires and steuartries to meet and convene at the head burghs of their several shires and steuartries to elect their commissioners conform to the order above set down and ordaining the clerks of the said meetings immediately after the said elections are over respectively to return the names of the persons elected to the clerks of the privy council and lastly ordaining the city of Edinburgh to elect their commissioner and the other royal burrows to elect each of them a commissioner as they have been in use to elect commissioners to the Parliament and to send the said respective commissioners at such times to such burghs within their respective districts as her Majesty and successors by such proclamations shall appoint requiring and ordaining the common clerk of the respective burghs where such election shall be appointed to be made to attend the said meetings and immediately after the election to return the name of the person so elected (certified under his hand) to the clerk of privy council to the end that the names of the sixteen peers thirty commissioners for shires and fifteen commissioners for burghs being so returned to the privy council may be returned to the court from whence the writ did issue under the great seal of the United Kingdom conform to the said twenty-second article. And the whereas by said twenty-second article it is agreed that if her Majesty shall on or before the first day of May next declare that it is expedient the lords and commons of the present Parliament of England should be the members of the respective Houses of the first Parliament of Great Britain for and on the part of England they shall accordingly be the members of the said respective Houses for and on the part of England Her Majesty with advice and consent aforesaid in that case only doth hereby statute and ordain that the sixteen peers and forty-five commissioners for shires and burghs who shall be chosen by the peers barons and burghs respectively in this present session of Parliament and out of the members thereof in the same manner as committees of Parliament are usually now chosen shall be the members of the respective Houses of the said first Parliament of Great Britain for and on the part of Scotland which nomination and election being certified by a writ under the lord clerk registers' hand the person so nominated and elected shall have right to sit and vote in the House of Lords and in the House of Commons of the said first Parliament of Great Britain.[1]

7. The said Act declared valid, as if it had been part of the said articles of union.—As by the said Act passed in Scotland for settling the manner of electing the sixteen peers and forty-five members to represent Scotland in the Parliament of Great Britain may appear. Be it therefore further enacted and declared by the authority aforesaid that the said last mentioned Act passed in Scotland for settling the manner of electing the sixteen peers and forty-five members to represent Scotland in the Parliament of Great Britain as aforesaid shall be and the same is hereby declared to be as valid as if the same had been part of and engrossed in the said articles of union ratified and approved by the said Act of Parliament of Scotland and by this Act as aforesaid.

The Union with Scotland (Amendment) Act, 1707[2]

An Act for rendering the Union of the Two Kingdoms more entire and complete

Whereas by her Majesty's great wisdom and goodness the union of the two kingdoms hath been happily effected and the whole island is thereby subject to one sovereignty and represented by one Parliament. To the end therefore that the said union may be rendered more complete and entire be it enacted by the Queen's most excellent Majesty by and with the advice and consent of the lords spiritual and temporal and commons in this present Parliament assembled and by the authority of the same that.

1. One privy council for Great Britain.—From and after the first day

[1] As to the representation in the House of Commons at the present time see Representation of the People Acts.

[2] 6 Anne, c. 40 (1707). (In this year was the first Parliament of Great Britain.) *Halsbury's Statutes of England.* 2nd Ed., Vol. 4, p. 179. The short title was given to this Act by the Short Titles Act, 1896.

of May in the year of our Lord one thousand seven hundred and eight the Queen's Majesty her heirs and successors shall have but one privy council in or for the kingdom of Great Britain to be sworn to her Majesty her heirs and successors as Sovereigns of Great Britain and such privy council shall have the same powers and authorities as the privy council of England lawfully had used and exercised at the time of the union and none other.

2. Appointment of justices of peace for Scotland.—And to the end the public peace may be in like manner preserved throughout the whole kingdom be it further enacted by the authority aforesaid that in every shire and stewartry within that part of Great Britain called Scotland and also in such cities boroughs liberties and precincts within Scotland as her Majesty her heirs or successors shall think fit there shall be appointed by her Majesty her heirs or successors under the great seal of Great Britain a sufficient number of good and lawful men to be justices of the peace within their respective shires stewartries cities boroughs liberties or precincts which persons so appointed over and above the several powers and authorities vested in justices of the peace by the laws of Scotland shall be further authorized to do use and exercise over all persons within their several bounds whatever doth appertain to the office and trust of a justice of peace by virtue of the laws and Acts of Parliament made in England before the union in relation to or for the preservation of the public peace. Provided nevertheless that in the sessions of the peace the methods of trial and judgment shall be according to the laws and customs of Scotland.

3. Proviso for Edinburgh, and other royal burghs.—Provided that nothing in this Act contained shall be construed to alter or infringe any rights liberties or privileges heretofore granted to the city of Edinburgh or to any other royal borough of being justices of peace within their respective bounds.

S. 4 – 6 repealed.

Parliament Act, 1911[1]

August 18, 1911, as amended December 16, 1949

Whereas it is expedient that provision should be made for regulating the relations between the two Houses of Parliament:

And Whereas it is intended to substitute for the House of Lords as it at present exists a Second Chamber constituted on a popular instead of hereditary basis, but such substitution cannot be immediately brought into operation:

And whereas provision will require hereafter to be made by Parliament in a measure effecting such substitution for limiting and defining the powers of the new Second Chamber, but it is expedient to make such provision as in this Act appears for restricting the existing powers of the House of Lords:

Be it therefore enacted by the King's most Excellent Majesty, by and with the advice and consent of the Lords Spiritual and Temporal, and Commons, in this present Parliament assembled, and by the authority of the same, as follows:

1. (1) If a Money Bill, having been passed by the House of Commons, and sent up to the House of Lords at least one month before the end of the session, is not passed by the House of Lords without amendment within one month after it is so sent up to that House, the Bill shall, unless the House of Commons direct to the contrary, be presented to His Majesty and become an Act of Parliament on the Royal Assent being signified, notwithstanding that the House of Lords have not consented to the Bill.

(2) A Money Bill means a Public Bill which in the opinion of the Speaker of the House of Commons contains only provisions dealing with all or any of the following subjects, namely, the imposition, repeal, remission, alteration, or regulation of taxation; the imposition for the payment of debt or other financial purposes of charges on the Consolidated Fund, or on money provided by Parliament, or the variation or repeal of any such charges; supply; the appropriation, receipt, custody, issue or audit of accounts of public money; the raising or guarantee of any loan or the repayment thereof; or subordinate matters incidental to those subjects or any of them. In this subsection the expressions "taxation," "public money," and "loan" respectively do not include any taxation, money, or loan raised by local authorities or bodies for local purposes.

(3) There shall be endorsed on every Money Bill when it is sent up to the House of Lords and when it is presented to His Majesty for assent the

[1] *An Act to make provision with respect to the powers of the House of Lords in relation to those of the House of Commons, and to limit the duration of Parliament.* 1 & 2 Geo. 5. Also *An Act to Amend the Parliament Act 1911,* 16 December 1949. 12, 13 & 14 Geo. 6. HMSO.

certificate of the Speaker of the House of Commons signed by him that it is a Money Bill. Before giving his certificate, the Speaker shall consult, if practicable, two members to be appointed from the Chairmen's Panel at the beginning of each Session by the Committee of Selection.

2.[1] (1) If any Public Bill (other than a Money Bill or a Bill containing any provision to extend the maximum duration of Parliament beyond five years) is passed by the House of Commons in two successive sessions (whether of the same Parliament or not), and, having been sent up to the House of Lords at least one month before the end of the session, is rejected by the House of Lords in each of those sessions, that Bill shall, on its rejection for the second time by the House of Lords, unless the House of Commons direct to the contrary, be presented to His Majesty and become an Act of Parliament on the Royal Assent being signified thereto, notwithstanding that the House of Lords have not consented to the Bill: Provided that this provision shall not take effect unless one year has elapsed between the date of the second reading in the first of those sessions of the Bill in the House of Commons and the date on which it passes the House of Commons in the second of those sessions.

(2) When a Bill is presented to His Majesty for assent in pursuance of the provisions of this section, there shall be endorsed on the Bill the certificate of the Speaker of the House of Commons signed by him that the provisions of this section have been duly complied with.

(3) A Bill shall be deemed to be rejected by the House of Lords if it is not passed by the House of Lords either without amendment or with such amendments only as may be agreed to by both Houses.

(4) A Bill shall be deemed to be the same Bill as a former Bill sent up to the House of Lords in the preceding session if, when it is sent up to the House of Lords, it is identical with the former Bill or contains only such alterations as are certified by the Speaker of the House of Commons to be necessary owing to the time which has elapsed since the date of the former Bill, or to represent any amendments which have been made by the House of Lords in the former Bill in the preceding session, and any amendments which are certified by the Speaker to have been made by the House of Lords in the second session and agreed to by the House of Commons shall be inserted in the Bill as presented for Royal Assent in pursuance of this section:

[1] Provided that, if a Bill has been rejected for the second time by the House of Lords before the signification of the Royal Assent to the Bill for this Act, whether such rejection was in the same session as that in which the Royal Assent to the Bill for this Act was signified or in an earlier session, the requirement of the said section two that a Bill is to be presented to His Majesty on its rejection for the second time by the House of Lords shall have effect in relation to the Bill rejected as a requirement that it is to be presented to His Majesty as soon as the Royal Assent to the Bill for this Act has been signified, and, notwithstanding that such rejection was in an earlier session, the Royal Assent to the Bill rejected may be signified in the session in which the Royal Assent to the Bill for this Act was signified. *Act to amend the Parliament Act* of 1949.

Provided that the House of Commons may, if they think fit, on the passage of such a Bill through the House in the second session, suggest any further amendments without inserting the amendments in the Bill, and any such suggested amendments shall be considered by the House of Lords, and, if agreed to by that House, shall be treated as amendments made by the House of Lords and agreed to by the House of Commons; but the exercise of this power by the House of Commons shall not affect the operation of this section in the event of the Bill being rejected by the House of Lords.

3. Any certificate of the Speaker of the House of Commons given under this Act shall be conclusive for all purposes, and shall not be questioned in any court of law.

4. (1) In every Bill presented to His Majesty under the preceding provisions of this Act, the words of enactment shall be as follows, that is to say:

"Be it enacted by the King's most Excellent Majesty, by and with the advice and consent of the Commons in this present Parliament assembled, in accordance with the provisions of the Parliament Act, 1911, and by authority of the same, as follows."

(2) Any alteration of a Bill necessary to give effect to this section shall not be deemed to be an amendment of the Bill.

5. In this Act the expression "Public Bill" does not include any Bill for confirming a Provisional Order.

6. Nothing in this Act shall diminish or qualify the existing rights and privileges of the House of Commons.

7. Five years shall be substituted for seven years as the time fixed for the maximum duration of Parliament under the Septennial Act, 1715.

8. This Act may be cited as the Parliament Act, 1911.

VII. Supreme Court of Judicature (Consolidation) Act, 1925[1]

July 31, 1925, as amended 1928, 1948, 1959

Be it enacted by the King's most Excellent Majesty, by and with the advice and consent of the Lords Spiritual and Temporal, and Commons, in this present Parliament assembled, and by the authority of the same, as follows:

[1] *An Act to consolidate the Judicature Acts, 1873 to 1910, and other enactments relating to the Supreme Court of Judicature in England and the administration of justice therein.* 15 & 16 Geo. 5. Printed as amended by the Administration of Justice Act, 1928, in accordance with 18 & 19 Geo. 5. c. 26. s. 20 (5) and incorporating amendments of March 24, 1948 (11 & 12 Geo. 6 c. 20) and May 14, 1959 (708 Eliz. 2 c. 39). HMSO.

PART I

CONSTITUTION OF THE SUPREME COURT

The Supreme Court

1. There shall be a Supreme Court of Judicature in England consisting of His Majesty's High Court of Justice (in this Act referred to as "the High Court") and His Majesty's Court of Appeal (in this Act referred to as "the Court of Appeal"), with such jurisdiction as is conferred on those courts respectively by this Act.

The High Court

2. (1) The High Court shall be constituted of the following judges, that is to say, the Lord Chancellor, the Lord Chief Justice, the President of the Probate Division and the puisne judges of the several Divisions.

(2) The Lord Chancellor or, in his absence, the Lord Chief Justice, shall be president of the High Court.

(3) All the judges of the High Court shall, save as is in this Act otherwise expressly provided, have in all respects equal power, authority and jurisdiction, and shall be addressed in the manner formerly customary in addressing the judges of the superior courts of common law.

(4) The puisne judges of the High Court shall be styled "Justices of the High Court."

3. (1) Subject to the provisions of this section, any judge of the Court of Appeal or any person who has held the office of a judge of the Court of Appeal or of a judge of the High Court, may, on the request of the Lord Chancellor, sit and act as a judge of the High Court or perform any other official or ministerial acts for or on behalf of any judge absent through illness or any other cause, or in the place of any other judge whose place becomes vacant, or as an additional judge of any Division:

Provided that:

(a) The Lord Chancellor shall not request any person who has held office as aforesaid to sit and act as a judge of the King's Bench Division, or of the Probate Division, except with the concurrence of the Lord Chief Justice or the President of the Probate Division respectively; and

(b) Nothing in this section shall be deemed to require any person who has held office as aforesaid to sit and act as a judge of the High Court unless he consents so to do.

(2) Every person while sitting and acting as a judge of the High Court under this section shall have all the jurisdiction, powers and privileges of, but shall not otherwise be deemed to be, a judge of that court.

4. (1) For the more convenient despatch of business in the High Court there shall be in the High Court three Divisions, namely:

(i) The Chancery Division, consisting of the Lord Chancellor, who shall be president thereof, and six puisne judges;

(ii) The King's Bench Division, consisting of the Lord Chief Justice, who shall be president thereof, and (subject to the provisions of this Act) seventeen puisne judges;

(iii) The Probate, Divorce and Admiralty Division consisting of a president and two puisne judges.

(2) Any judge of any of the said Divisions may be transferred by His Majesty, under His Royal Sign Manual, from one to another of the said Divisions.

(3) Nothing in this section shall operate to prevent a judge of any Division from sitting whenever required in a divisional court or for any judge of another Division.

(4) Without prejudice to the provisions of this Act relating to the distribution of business in the High Court, all jurisdiction vested in the High Court under this Act shall belong to all the Divisions alike.

5. (1) His Majesty in Council may from time to time, on a report or recommendation of the council of judges of the Supreme Court assembled in pursuance of the provisions of Part X. of this Act, order that any reduction or increase in the number of the Divisions or in the number of the judges of the High Court who may be attached to any Division, may pursuant to such report or recommendation be carried into effect, and may give all such further directions as may be necessary or proper for that purpose:

Provided that the total number of the judges of the Supreme Court shall not be reduced or increased by any such Order.

(2) An Order in Council under this section shall not come into operation until it has been laid before each House of Parliament for thirty days on which that House has sat, or if within that period of thirty days an address is presented to His Majesty by either House of Parliament, praying that the Order may not come into operation.

(3) An Order in Council under this section shall, on coming into operation, have effect as if it were enacted in this Act.

The Court of Appeal

6. (1) The Court of Appeal shall be constituted of *ex-officio* judges and of five ordinary judges.

(2) The *ex-officio* judges of the Court of Appeal shall be the Lord Chancellor, any person who has held the office of Lord Chancellor, any Lord of Appeal in Ordinary who at the date of his appointment would have been qualified to be appointed an ordinary judge of the Court of

Appeal, or who at that date was a judge of that court, the Lord Chief Justice, the Master of the Rolls and the President of the Probate Division:

Provided that a person who has held the office of Lord Chancellor, or a Lord of Appeal in Ordinary, shall not be required to sit and act as a judge of the Court of Appeal unless on the request of the Lord Chancellor he consents so to do.

(3) The ordinary judges of the Court of Appeal shall be styled, and are in this Act referred to as, "Lords Justices of Appeal."

(4) The Lord Chancellor shall be president of the Court of Appeal.

7. (1) The Lord Chancellor may request the attendance at any time of any judge of the High Court to sit as an additional judge at the sittings of the Court of Appeal, and any judge whose attendance is so requested shall attend accordingly.

(2) Every judge who sits as an additional judge of the Court of Appeal in pursuance of such a request shall, during the time he so sits, have all the jurisdiction and powers of a judge of the Court of Appeal, but shall not otherwise be deemed to be a judge of that court or to have ceased to be a judge of the Division to which he belongs.

(3) Any such judge shall, although the period has expired during which his attendance was requested, attend the sittings of the Court of Appeal for the purpose of giving judgment or otherwise in relation to any case which may have been heard by the Court of Appeal during his attendance on the Court of Appeal.

8. The Lord Chancellor may at any time, subject to the provisions of this section, request any person who has held the office of a judge of the Court of Appeal or of a judge of the High Court to sit and act as a judge of the Court of Appeal, and every such person so requested shall, while so sitting and acting, have all the jurisdiction, powers and privileges of, but shall not otherwise deemed to be, a judge of the Court of Appeal:

Provided that nothing in this section shall be deemed to require any such person as aforesaid to sit and act as a judge of the Court of Appeal unless he consents so to do.

Qualification of Judges, Vacancies, Tenure of Office, Salaries, &c

9. (1) Any person being a barrister of not less than ten years' standing shall be qualified for appointment as a puisne judge of the High Court.

(2) Any person being a barrister of not less than fifteen years' standing or a judge of the High Court shall be qualified for appointment as a Lord Justice of Appeal.

(3) Any person qualified for appointment as a Lord Justice of Appeal, or being a judge of the Court of Appeal, shall be qualified for appointment

as Lord Chief Justice, Master of the Rolls or President of the Probate Division.

10. (1) The office of any judge of the High Court or of the Court of Appeal may be vacated by resignation in writing under his hand addressed to the Lord Chancellor, without any deed of surrender.

(2) The office of any judge of the High Court shall be vacated by his being appointed a judge of the Court of Appeal.

(3) Each of the said courts shall be deemed to be duly constituted during and notwithstanding any vacancy in the office of any judge of that court.

11. (1) Whenever the office of a judge of the High Court (other than the Lord Chancellor) or of a Lord Justice of Appeal is vacant, a new judge may be appointed by His Majesty by Letters Patent:

Provided that:

(a) Whenever the whole number of the puisne judges attached to the King's Bench Division amounts to fifteen or upwards, a vacancy occurring among those judges shall not be filled unless and until an address is presented to His Majesty from both Houses of Parliament representing that the state of business in that Division requires that the vacancy should be filled, but where such an address has been presented, it shall be lawful for His Majesty from time to time without any further address to fill any vacancy which may arise among the said judges at any time within a period of one year next after the date of the presentation to His Majesty of that address; and

(b) The judge appointed to fill a vacancy in the High Court shall, subject to the provisions of this Act and to rules of court, become a member of the same Division as that to which the vacating judge belonged.

(2) The persons appointed to fill the offices of Lord Chief Justice and Master of the Rolls and their successors respectively shall continue to be appointed to those offices with the same respective precedence and titles and in the same manner respectively as formerly.

(3) The Letters Patent for appointing a Lord Justice of Appeal shall be passed in the same manner in which Letters Patent for appointing the judges of the High Court are passed under the Great Seal.

12. (1) All the judges of the High Court and of the Court of Appeal, with the exception of the Lord Chancellor, shall hold their offices during good behaviour subject to a power of removal by His Majesty on an address presented to His Majesty by both Houses of Parliament.

(2) No judge of either of the said courts shall be capable of being elected to or of sitting in the House of Commons.

(3) Every person appointed to be judge of either of the said courts (other than the Lord Chancellor) shall, when he enters on the execution of his office, take, in the presence of the Lord Chancellor, the oath of allegiance and judicial oath as defined by the Promissory Oaths Act, 1868.

(4) The oaths to be taken by the Lord Chancellor shall be the same as immediately before the commencement of this Act.

13. (1) There shall be paid to the several judges of the High Court and of the Court of Appeal the following salaries respectively:

To the Lord Chancellor such yearly sum as with the amount payable to him as Speaker of the House of Lords is sufficient to make up the sum of ten thousand pounds a year;

To the Lord Chief Justice the sum of eight thousand pounds a year;

To the Master of the Rolls the sum of six thousand pounds a year;

To each of the Lords Justices of Appeal, and to each of the judges of the High Court other than the Lord Chancellor and the Lord Chief Justice, the sum of five thousand pounds a year.

(2) The salary payable as aforesaid to any judge shall in each case include any pension which may have been granted to him in respect of any public office previously filled by him.

(3) Every salary payable as aforesaid shall begin from the date of appointment.

14. His Majesty may, by Letters Patent, grant to any of the judges hereinafter mentioned who has served for fifteen years as a judge in the High Court and the Court of Appeal, or either of those courts, or who is disabled by permanent infirmity from the performance of the duties of his office, a pension, by way of annuity, to be continued during his life:

In the case of the Lord Chief Justice, not exceeding four thousand pounds a year;

In the case of the Master of the Rolls, not exceeding three thousand seven hundred and fifty pounds a year;

In the case of any Lord Justice of Appeal or any judge of the High Court, other than the Lord Chancellor and the Lord Chief Justice, not exceeding three thousand five hundred pounds a year.

15. The salaries and pensions payable to the judges of the Supreme Court under this Act shall:

(a) be charged on and paid out of the Consolidated Fund or the growing produce thereof; and

(b) accrue due from day to day; and

(c) be payable on the usual quarterly days of payment or at such other periods in every year as the Treasury may from time to time determine.

16. (1) The Lord Chief Justice and the Master of the Rolls, shall, when sitting and acting in the Court of Appeal, rank in that order, and a person who has held the office of Lord Chancellor or a Lord of Appeal in Ordinary shall, when so sitting and acting, rank according to his precedence as a peer.

(2) The President of the Probate Division shall have rank and precedence next after the Master of the Rolls.

(3) The Lords Justices of Appeal, if not entitled to precedence as peers

or privy councillors, shall rank after the *ex-officio* judges and according to the priority of the dates at which they respectively became judges of the Court of Appeal.

(4) The judges of the High Court who are not also judges of the Court of Appeal shall rank next after the judges of the Court of Appeal, and among themselves according to the priority of the dates at which they respectively became judges of the High Court.

17. (1) A judge of the High Court or of the Court of Appeal shall not be incapable of acting in his judicial office in any proceeding by reason of his being as one of several ratepayers or as one of any other class of persons liable, in common with others, to contribute to or to be benefited by any rate or tax which may be increased, diminished or in any way affected by that proceeding.

(2) In this section the expression "rate or tax" means any rate, tax, duty or assessment whether public, general or local, and also any fund formed from the proceeds of any such rate, tax, duty or assessment, or applicable to the same or like purposes to which any such rate, tax, duty or assessment might be applied.

PART II

JURISDICTION AND LAW

Jurisdiction of the High Court

18. (1) The High Court shall be a superior court of record.

(2) There shall be vested in the High Court:

(a) Subject as otherwise provided in this Act, the jurisdiction which was formerly vested in, or capable of being exercised by, all or any of the courts following:

(i) The High Court of Chancery, both as a common law court and as a court of equity, including the jurisdiction of the Master of the Rolls as a judge or master of the Court of Chancery and any jurisdiction exercised by him in relation to the Court of Chancery as a common law court;

(ii) The Court of Queen's Bench;

(iii) The Court of Common Pleas at Westminster;

(iv) The Court of Exchequer, both as a court of revenue and as a common law court;

(v) The Court of Common Pleas at Lancaster;

(vi) The Court of Pleas at Durham;

(vii) The courts created by commissions of assize:

(b) All original jurisdiction which, under or by virtue of any enactment which came into force after the commencement of the Act of 1873 and is not repealed by this Act, was immediately before the commencement of this Act vested in or capable of being exercised by the High Court constituted by the Act of 1873:

(c) Such other jurisdiction, as is hereinafter in this Act conferred on the High Court.

(3) The jurisdiction vested in the High Court shall, subject as otherwise provided in this Act, include the jurisdiction which was formerly vested in, or capable of being exercised by, all or any one or more of the judges of the courts aforesaid respectively sitting in court or chambers or elsewhere, when acting as judges or a judge, in pursuance of any statute, law or custom, and all powers given to any such court or to any such judges or judge by any statute, and also all ministerial powers, duties and authorities incident to any and every part of the jurisdictions so vested.

19. Subject to the provisions of any enactment which came into force after the commencement of the Act of 1873, there shall not be vested in the High Court:

(1) Any appellate jurisdiction formerly vested in the Court of Appeal in Chancery, or in that court sitting as a court of appeal in bankruptcy:

(2) Any jurisdiction formerly vested in the Court of Appeal in Chancery of the county palatine of Lancaster:

(3) Any jurisdiction which formerly was usually vested in the Lord Chancellor or in the Lords Justices of Appeal in Chancery, or either of them, in relation to the custody of the persons and estates of idiots, lunatics and persons of unsound mind:

(4) Any jurisdiction formerly vested in the Lord Chancellor in relation to grants of Letters Patent, or the issue of commissions or other writings to be passed under the Great Seal of the United Kingdom:

(5) Any jurisdiction formerly exercised by the Lord Chancellor in right of or on behalf of Her late Majesty as visitor of any college or of any charitable or other foundation:

(6) Any jurisdiction formerly vested in the Master of the Rolls in relation to records in London or elsewhere in England.

20. Subject to the provisions of this Act the High Court shall, in relation to probates and letters of administration, have the following jurisdiction (in this Act referred to as "probate jurisdiction"), that is to say:

(a) all such voluntary and contentious jurisdiction and authority in relation to the granting or revoking of probate and administration of the effects of deceased persons as was at the commencement of the Court of Probate Act, 1857, vested in or exerciseable by any court or person in England, together with full authority to hear and determine all questions relating to testamentary causes and matters:

(b) all such powers throughout England in relation to the personal estate in England of deceased persons as the Prerogative Court of Canterbury had immediately before the commencement of the Court of Probate Act, 1857, in the Province of Canterbury or in the parts thereof within its jurisdiction in relation to those testamentary causes and matters and those effects of deceased persons which were at that date within the jurisdiction of that court:

(c) such like jurisdiction and powers with respect to the real estate of deceased persons as are hereinbefore conferred with respect to the personal estate of deceased persons:

(d) all probate jurisdiction which, under or by virtue of any enactment which came into force after the commencement of the Act of 1873 and is not repealed by this Act, was immediately before the commencement of this Act vested in or capable of being exercised by the High Court constituted by the Act of 1873:

and the court shall, in the exercise of the probate jurisdiction perform all such like duties with resepct to the estates of deceased persons as were immediately before the commencement of the Court of Probate Act, 1857, to be performed by ordinaries generally or by the Prerogative Court of Canterbury in respect of probates, administrations and testamentary causes and matters which were at that date within their respective jurisdictions.

21. The High Court shall have such jurisdiction:

(a) in relation to matrimonial causes and matters, as was immediately before the commencement of the Matrimonial Causes Act, 1857, vested in or exerciseable by any ecclesiastical court or person in England in respect of divorce *a mensa et thoro*, nullity of marriage, jactitation of marriage, or restitution of conjugal rights, and in respect of any matrimonial cause or matter except marriage licences; and

(b) with respect to declarations of legitimacy and of validity of marriage, as is hereinafter in this Act provided;

and all such jurisdiction in relation to matrimonial causes and matters as, under or by virtue of any enactment which came into force after the commencement of the Act of 1873 and is not repealed by this Act, was immediately before the commencement of this Act vested in or capable of being exercised by the High Court constituted by the Act of 1873.

22. (1) The High Court shall, in relation to admiralty matters, have the following jurisdiction (in this Act referred to as "admiralty jurisdiction") that is to say:

(a) Jurisdiction to hear and determine any of the following questions or claims:

(i) Any question as to the title to or ownership of a ship, or the proceeds of sale of a ship remaining in the admiralty registry, arising in an action of possession, salvage, damage, necessaries, wages or bottomry;

(ii) Any question arising between the co-owners of a ship registered at any port in England as to the ownership, possession, employment or earnings of that ship, or any share thereof, with power to settle any account outstanding and unsettled between the parties in relation thereto, and to direct the ship, or any share thereof, to be sold, or to make such order as the court thinks fit;

(iii) Any claim for damage received by a ship, whether received within the body of a county or on the high seas;

(iv) Any claim for damage done by a ship;

(v) Subject to the provisions of section five hundred and forty-seven of the Merchant Shipping Act, 1894, with respect to the summary determination of salvage disputes, any claim in the nature of salvage for services rendered to a ship (including, subject to the provisions of the said Act, services rendered in saving life from a ship), whether rendered on the high seas or within the body of a county, or partly on the high seas and partly within the body of a county, and whether the wreck in respect of which the salvage is claimed is found on the sea or on the land, or partly on the sea and partly on the land;

(vi) Any claim in the nature of towage, whether the services were rendered within the body of a county or on the high seas;

(vii) Any claim for necessaries supplied to a foreign ship, whether within the body of a county or on the high seas, and, unless it is shown to the court that at the time of the institution of the proceedings any owner or part owner of the ship was domiciled in England, any claim for any necessaries supplied to a ship elsewhere than in the port to which the ship belongs;

(viii) Any claim by a seaman of a ship for wages earned by him on board the ship, whether due under a special contract or otherwise, and any claim by the master of a ship for wages earned by him on board the ship and for disbursements made by him on account of the ship;

(ix) Any claim in respect of a mortgage of any ship, being a mortgage duly registered in accordance with the provisions of the Merchant Shipping Acts, 1894 to 1923, or in respect of any mortgage of a ship which is, or the proceeds whereof are, under the arrest of the court;

(x) Any claim for building, equipping or repairing a ship, if at the time of the institution of the proceedings the ship is, or the proceeds thereof are, under the arrest of the court;

(xi) Any matter concerning booty of war, or the distribution thereof, which may be referred to the court by His Majesty in Council;

(xii) Any claim:

(1) arising out of an agreement relating to the use or hire of a ship; or

(2) relating to the carriage of goods in a ship; or

(3) in tort in respect of goods carried in a ship;

unless it is shown to the court that at the time of the institution of the proceedings any owner or part owner of the ship was domiciled in England:

(b) Any other jurisdiction formerly vested in the High Court of Admiralty:

(c) All admiralty jurisdiction which, under or by virtue of any enactment which came into force after the commencement of the Act of 1873 and is not repealed by this Act, was immediately before the commencement of this Act vested in or capable of being exercised by the High Court constituted by the Act of 1873.

(2) The provisions of paragraph (a) of subsection (1) of this section which confer on the High Court admiralty jurisdiction in respect of claims for damage shall be construed as extending to claims for loss of life or personal injuries.

(3) In this Act, unless the context otherwise requires, the expression "ship" includes any description of vessel used in navigation not propelled by oars.

23. The High Court shall be a prize court within the meaning of the Naval Prize Acts, 1864 to 1916, as amended by any subsequent enactment, and shall have all such jurisdiction on the high seas and throughout His Majesty's Dominions and in every place where His Majesty has jurisdiction as, under any Act relating to naval prize or otherwise, the High Court of Admiralty possessed when acting as a prize court.

24. Subject as otherwise provided in this Act and to rules of court, the High Court shall have jurisdiction to hear and determine:

(a) any appeal from any court which might formerly have been brought to any court or judge whose jurisdiction was by the Act of 1873 transferred to the High Court constituted by that Act; and

(b) any application, or any appeal, whether by way of case stated or otherwise, which under or by virtue of any enactment which came into force after the commencement of the Act of 1873 and is not repealed by this Act, the High Court constituted by that Act had power to hear and determine immediately before the commencement of this Act.

25. (1) Every case stated by a court of quarter sessions otherwise than under the Crown Cases Act, 1848, or the Quarter Sessions Act, 1849, for the consideration of the High Court shall be deemed to be an appeal, and shall be heard and determined accordingly.

(2) On the hearing of an appeal from a court of quarter sessions the appellate court may draw any inference of fact which might have been drawn in the court of quarter sessions, and may give any judgment or make any order which ought to have been given or made by that court, or may remit the order, and in criminal matters the conviction with the order, and the case stated on it, with the opinion or direction of the appellate court, for re-hearing and determination by the court of quarter sessions, or may remit the case for re-statement.

(3) On the hearing of any such appeal the appellate court shall have full power to determine how and by whom the costs of the proceedings in the appellate court and in the court of quarter sessions are to be borne.

(4) The judgment on any such appeal or, where an appeal to a court of quarter sessions has been directed to be entered for re-hearing, then that appeal shall on motion by any party to the appeal be entered at the sessions next or next but one after the delivery of the judgment or the giving of the direction, and shall unless the appellate court otherwise directs have effect as if the judgment had been given or, in case of an appeal directed to be re-heard, the appeal had been heard and determined, by the court of quarter sessions at the time of the decision in respect of which the appeal from quarter sessions was brought, and entry and respite of any appeal to quarter sessions in respect of which a case has been stated for the consideration of the High Court shall not be necessary.

Jurisdiction of the Court of Appeal

26. (1) The Court of Appeal shall be a superior court of record.

(2) There shall be vested in the Court of Appeal:

(a) All jurisdiction and powers formerly vested in the Lord Chancellor and the Court of Appeal in Chancery when exercising appellate jurisdiction:

(b) All jurisdiction and powers formerly vested in the Court of Exchequer Chamber:

(c) Subject to the provisions of this Act, all jurisdiction formerly vested in or capable of being exercised by Her late Majesty in Council, or the Judicial Committee of the Privy Council, on appeal from any judgment or order of the High Court of Admiralty, or from any order in lunacy made by the Lord Chancellor, or any other person having jurisdiction in lunacy:

(d) All jurisdiction which, under or by virtue of any enactment which came into force after the commencement of the Act of 1873 and is not repealed by this Act, was immediately before the commencement of this Act vested in or capable of being exercised by the Court of Appeal constituted by the Act of 1873.

27. (1) Subject as otherwise provided in this Act and to rules of court, the Court of Appeal shall have jurisdiction to hear and determine appeals from any judgment or order of the High Court, and for all the purposes of and incidental to the hearing and determination of any appeal, and the amendment, execution and enforcement of any judgment or order made thereon, the Court of Appeal shall have all the power, authority and jurisdiction of the High Court:

Provided that an appeal from a judgment or order of the High Court when acting as a prize court shall not lie to the Court of Appeal, but shall lie to His Majesty in Council in accordance with the provisions of the Naval Prize Acts, 1864 to 1916.

(2) The decision of the Court of Appeal on any question arising under the provisions of this Act relating to matrimonial causes and matters and to declarations of legitimacy and of validity of marriage shall be final, except where the decision is either on the grant or refusal of a decree on a petition for dissolution or nullity of marriage or for such a declaration as aforesaid, or on a question of law on which the Court of Appeal gives leave to appeal.

28. Subject to the provisions of this Act and to rules of court, the Court of Appeal shall have jurisdiction and power to hear and determine appeals from any judgment or order of the Lancaster Chancery Court or of ths Chancellor of Durham in the same manner as the Court of Appeal hae power to hear and determine appeals from judgments and orders of the High Court or a judge thereof.

29. An appeal shall lie to the Court of Appeal from a conviction on indictment at common law in relation to the non-repair or obstruction of any highway, public bridge or navigable river, in whatever court the indictment is tried, and shall not lie under the Criminal Appeal Act, 1907.

Motions for New Trial, Restrictions on Appeals, &c

30. (1) Every motion for a new trial, or to set aside a verdict, finding or judgment, in any cause or matter in the High Court in which there has been a trial thereof or of any issue therein with a jury, shall be heard and determined by the Court of Appeal.

(2) Nothing in this section shall alter the practice in any criminal cause or matter or in bankruptcy, or in proceedings on the Crown side of the King's Bench Division.

31. (1) No appeal shall lie:

(a) except as provided by the Criminal Appeal Act, 1907, or this Act, from any judgment of the High Court in any criminal cause or matter;

(b) from an order allowing an extension of time for appealing from a judgment or order;

(c) from an order of a judge giving unconditional leave to defend an action;

(d) from the decision of the High Court or of any judge thereof where it is provided by any Act that the decision of any court or judge, the jurisdiction of which or of whom is now vested in the High Court, is to be final;

(e) from an order absolute for the dissolution or nullity of marriage in favour of any party who having had time and opportunity to appeal from the decree *nisi* on which the order was founded, has not appealed from that decree;

(f) without the leave of the divisional court or of the Court of Appeal, from the determination by a divisional court of any appeal to the High Court;

(g) subject to the provisions of this section as to appeals in matters of practice and procedure, without the leave of the judge by whom the order was made or of the Court of Appeal, from any order made by a judge of the High Court in chambers where no application to set aside or discharge the order has been made to a divisional court or the judge sitting in court, as the case may be;

(h) without the leave of the court or judge making the order, from an order of the High Court or any judge thereof made with the consent of the parties or as to costs only which by law are left to the discretion of the court;

(i) without the leave of the judge or of the Court of Appeal from any interlocutory order or interlocutory judgment made or given by a judge, except in the following cases, namely:

(i) where the liberty of the subject or the custody of infants is concerned;

(ii) where an injunction or the appointment of a receiver is granted or refused;

(iii) in the case of a decision determining the claim of any creditor or the liability of any contributory or the liability of any director or other officer under the Companies (Consolidation) Act, 1908, in respect of misfeasance or otherwise;

(iv) in the case of a decree *nisi* in a matrimonial cause or a judgment or order in an admiralty action determining liability;

(v) in the case of an order on a special case stated under the Arbitration Act, 1889;

(vi) in such other cases, to be prescribed, as are in the opinion of the authority having power to make rules of court of the nature of final decisions;

(j) without the special leave of the High Court, from the decision of the High Court on any question of law, whether on appeal or otherwise, under the Parliamentary Elections Act, 1868, or Part IV. of the Municipal Corporations Act, 1882, or any Act amending either of those Acts, and if leave to appeal is granted the decision of the Court of Appeal in the case shall be final and conclusive;

(k) from the decision of the High Court on any appeal from a county court on a point of law arising in any probate cause or matter;

(l) from an order refusing leave for the institution or continuance of legal proceedings by a person who is the subject of an order for the time being in force under section fifty-one of this Act.

(2) An order refusing unconditional leave to defend an action shall not be deemed to be an interlocutory order within the meaning of this section.

(3) In matters of practice and procedure every appeal from a judge shall be to the Court of Appeal.

32. The jurisdiction vested in the High Court and the Court of Appeal respectively shall, so far as regards procedure and practice, be exercised in the manner provided by this Act or by rules of court, and where no special provision is contained in this Act or in rules of court with reference thereto, any such jurisdiction shall be exercised as nearly as may be in the same manner as that in which it might have been exercised by the court to which it formerly appertained.

33. (1) The following provisions shall have effect in relation to the exercise by the High Court of the admiralty jurisdiction of the court:

(a) If in any claim for salvage services the plaintiff does not recover more than three hundred pounds, he shall not be entitled to recover any costs of the proceedings unless it is certified by a court or a judge that the case was a fit one to be tried otherwise than summarily in manner provided by section five hundred and forty-seven of the Merchant Shipping Act, 1894:

(b) If in any claim arising out of an agreement relating to the use or hire of a ship, or any claim relating to the carriage of goods in a ship, or any claim in tort in respect of goods carried in a ship, the plaintiff recovers a less amount than twenty pounds, he shall not be entitled to any costs of the proceedings unless it is certified by the court or a judge that there was sufficient reason for bringing the proceedings in the High Court:

(c) If in any such claim as is mentioned in paragraph (b) of this subsection, the plaintiff recovers a less amount than three hundred pounds he shall not be entitled to any more costs than those to which he would be entitled if the proceedings had been brought in the county court unless it is certified by the court or a judge that there was sufficient reason for bringing the proceedings in the High Court:

(d) In any matter concerning booty of war the procedure of the court shall be the same as in cases of prize:

(e) Disputes relating to salvage may be determined on the application either of the salvor or of the owner of the property saved, or of their respective agents.

(2) The admiralty jurisdiction of the High Court may be exercised either in proceedings *in rem* or in proceedings *in personam*.

(3) Where, on an appeal from an admiralty action which has been heard in the county court with the assistance of nautical assessors, any party makes application to the High Court in that behalf, the court shall summon Trinity Masters to assist on the hearing of the appeal if the court is of opinion that such assistance is necessary or desirable.

34. (1) If in any case not expressly provided for by this Act any duty or any authority or power, not incident to the administration of justice in any court the jurisdiction of which is now vested in the High Court, has been imposed or conferred by any statute, law or custom on any judge of that court, every judge of the High Court shall, save as in this Act mentioned, be liable to perform that duty and empowered to exercise that authority or power, as if he had been duly appointed the successor of a judge formerly subject to that duty or possessing that authority or power and the Act of 1873 had not passed.

(2) Any such duty, authority or power imposed or conferred by any statute, law or custom in any such case as aforesaid on the Lord Chancellor, the Lord Chief Justice or the Master of the Rolls, shall continue to be performed and exercised by them respectively, and by their respective successors, in the same manner as formerly.

35. (1) Where by any statute any power was given to or any act was required or authorised to be done by the Lord Chief Justice of the Common Pleas and the Lord Chief Baron of the Exchequer, or either of them, either solely or jointly with the Lord Chief Justice of the Queen's Bench or the Lord Chief Justice, and either with or without the Lord Chancellor or any judge, officer or person, that power may be exercised and that act done by the Lord Chief Justice.

(2) Where by any statute the concurrence of the Lord Chief Justice of the Common Pleas and the Lord Chief Baron of the Exchequer, or either of them, is required for the exercise of any power or the performance of any act, the concurrence of the Lord Chief Justice shall be sufficient.

Law and Equity

36. Subject to the express provisions of any other Act, in every civil cause or matter commenced in the High Court law and equity shall be administered by the High Court and the Court of Appeal, as the case may be, according to the provisions of the seven sections of this Act next following.

37. If a plaintiff or petitioner claims to be entitled to any equitable estate or right, or to relief on any equitable ground against any deed, instrument or contract, or against any right, title or claim whatsoever asserted by any defendant or respondent in the cause or matter, or to any relief founded upon a legal right, which formerly could only have been given by a court of equity, the court or judge shall give to the plaintiff or petitioner the same relief as ought formerly to have been given by the Court of Chancery in a suit or proceeding for the like purpose properly instituted.

38. If a defendant claims to be entitled to any equitable estate or right, or to relief on any equitable ground against any deed, instrument or contract, or against any right, title or claim asserted by any plaintiff or petitioner in the cause or matter, or alleges any ground of equitable defence to any such claim of the plaintiff or petitioner, the court or judge shall give to every equitable estate, right or ground of relief so claimed, and to every equitable defence so alleged, the same effect by way of defence against the claim of the plaintiff or petitioner, as the Court of Chancery ought formerly to have given if the like matters had been relied on by way of defence in any suit or proceeding instituted in that court for the like purpose.

39. (1) The court or judge shall have power to grant to any defendant in respect of any equitable estate or right or other matter or equity, and also in respect of any legal estate, right or title claimed or asserted by him:

(a) all such relief against any plaintiff or petitioner as the defendant has properly claimed by his pleading, and as the court or judge might have granted in any suit instituted for that purpose by that defendant against the same plaintiff or petitioner; and

(b) all such relief relating to or connected with the original subject of the cause or matter, claimed in like manner against any other person, whether already a party to the cause or matter or not, who has been duly served with notice in writing of the claim pursuant to rules of court or any order of the court, as might properly have been granted against that person if he had been made a defendant to a cause duly instituted by the same defendant for the like purpose.

(2) Every person served with any such notice as aforesaid shall thenceforth be deemed a party to the cause or matter with the same rights in respect of his defence against the claim as if he had been duly sued in the ordinary way by the defendant.

40. The court or judge shall take notice of all equitable estates, titles and rights, and all equitable duties and liabilities appearing incidentally in the course of any cause or matter, in the same manner in which the Court of Chancery would formerly have taken notice of those matters in any suit or proceeding duly instituted therein.

41. No cause or proceeding at any time pending in the High Court or the Court of Appeal shall be restrained by prohibition or injunction, but every matter of equity on which an injunction against the prosecution of any such cause or proceeding might formerly have been obtained, whether unconditionally or on any terms or conditions, may be relied on by way of defence thereto:

Provided that:

(a) Nothing in this Act shall disable either of the said courts, if it thinks fit so to do, from directing a stay of proceedings in any cause or matter pending before it; and

(b) Any person, whether a party or not to any such cause or matter, who would formerly have been entitled to apply to any court to restrain the prosecution thereof, or who may be entitled to enforce, by attachment or otherwise, any judgment, decree, rule or order, in contravention of which all or any part of the proceedings in the cause or matter have been taken, may apply to the High Court or the Court of Appeal, as the case may be, by motion in a summary way, for a stay of proceedings in the cause or matter, either generally, or so far as may be necessary for the purposes of justice, and the court shall thereupon make such order as shall be just.

42. Subject to the provisions of this Act for giving effect to equitable rights and other matters of equity, the court or judge shall give effect to all legal claims and demands, and all estates, titles, rights, duties, obligations and liabilities existing by the common law or by any custom, or created by any statute, in the same manner as those matters would formerly have been given effect to by any of the courts the jurisdiction of which was vested in the High Court constituted by the Act of 1873.

43. The High Court and the Court of Appeal respectively, in the exercise of the jurisdiction vested in them by this Act, shall, in every cause or matter pending before the court, grant, either absolutely or on such terms and conditions as the court thinks just, all such remedies whatsoever as any of the parties thereto may appear to be entitled to in respect of any legal or equitable claim properly brought forward by them in the cause or matter, so that, as far as possible, all matters in controversy between the parties may be completely and finally determined, and all multiplicity of legal proceedings concerning any of those matters avoided.

44. Subject to the express provisions of any other Act, in questions relating to the custody and education of infants and generally in all matters not particularly mentioned in this Act, in which there was formerly or is any conflict or variance between the rules of equity and the rules of the common law with reference to the same matter, the rules of equity shall prevail in all courts whatsoever in England so far as the matters to which those rules relate are cognizable by those courts.

Miscellaneous

45. (1) The High Court may grant a *mandamus* or an injunction or appoint a receiver by an interlocutory order in all cases in which it appears to the court to be just or convenient so to do.

(2) Any such order may be made either unconditionally or on such terms and conditions as the court thinks just.

(3) If, whether before, or at, or after the hearing of any cause or matter, an application is made for an injunction to prevent any threatened or apprehended waste or trespass, the injunction may be granted, if the court thinks fit, whether the person against whom the injunction is sought is or is not in possession under any claim of title or otherwise, or (if out of possession) does or does not claim a right to do the act sought to be restrained under any colour of title, and whether the estates claimed by both or by either of the parties are legal or equitable.

46. In the case of any action for a forfeiture brought for non-payment of rent, the High Court or a judge thereof shall have power to give relief in a summary manner, and subject to the same terms and conditions in all respects as to payment of rent, costs and otherwise as could formerly have been imposed in the Court of Chancery, and if the lessee, his executors, administrators or assigns are so relieved they shall hold the demised premises according to the terms of the lease and without the necessity of any new lease.

47. Where any person neglects or refuses to comply with a judgment or order directing him to execute any conveyance, contract or other document, or to indorse any negotiable instrument, the High Court may, on such terms and conditions, if any, as may be just, order that the conveyance, contract or other document shall be executed or that the negotiable instrument shall be indorsed by such person as the court may nominate for that purpose, and a conveyance, contract, document or instrument so executed or indorsed shall operate and be for all purposes available as if it had been executed or indorsed by the person originally directed to execute or indorse it.

48. Proceedings in *quo warranto* shall be deemed to be civil proceedings whether for purposes of appeal or otherwise.

49. (1) If in any cause or matter in the High Court (including a cause or matter referred to an official or special referee or arbitrator under the provisions of this Act relating to inquiries and trials by referees) it appears to the court or a judge that it is proper to compel the personal attendance at any trial of a witness who may not be within the jurisdiction of the court, it shall be lawful for the court or a judge, if in the discretion of the court or a judge it seems fit so to do, to order that a writ of subpoena *ad testificandum* or writ of subpoena *duces tecum* shall issue in special form commanding the witness to attend the trial wherever he shall be within the United Kingdom, and the service of any such writ in any part of the United Kingdom, shall be as valid and effectual to all intents and purposes as if it had been served within the jurisdiction of the High Court.

(2) Every such writ shall have at its foot a statement to the effect that it is issued by the special order of the court or a judge as the case may be, and no such writ shall issue without such a special order.

(3) If any person served with a writ issued under this section does not appear as required by the writ, the High Court, on proof to the satisfaction of the court of the service of the writ and of the default, may transmit a certificate of the default under the seal of the court or under the hand of a judge of the court, in case the service was in Scotland to the Court of Session at Edinburgh, and in case the service was in Northern Ireland to the High Court of Justice of Northern Ireland at Belfast, and the court to which the certificate is so sent shall thereupon proceed against and punish the person so having made the default in like manner as if that

person had neglected or refused to appear in obedience to process issued out of that court.

(4) No court shall in any case proceed against or punish any person for having made such default as aforesaid unless it is shown to the court that a reasonable and sufficient sum of money to defray the expenses of coming and attending to give evidence and of returning from giving evidence was tendered to that person at the time when the writ was served upon him.

(5) Nothing herein contained shall alter or affect:

(a) the power of the High Court to issue a commission for the examination of witnesses out of the jurisdiction of the court in any case in which, notwithstanding this section, the court thinks fit to issue such a commission; or

(b) the admissibility of any evidence at any trial where such evidence is now by law receivable on the ground of any witness being beyond the jurisdiction of the court, and the admissibility of any such evidence shall be determined as if this section and any enactment reproduced by this section had not passed.

50. (1) Subject to the provisions of this Act and to rules of court and to the express provisions of any other Act, the costs of and incidental to all proceedings in the Supreme Court, including the administration of estates and trusts, shall be in the discretion of the court or judge, and the court or judge shall have full power to determine by whom and to what extent the costs are to be paid.

(2) Nothing in this section shall alter the practice in any criminal cause or matter, in bankruptcy or in proceedings on the Crown side of the King's Bench Division.

51. (1) If, on an application made by the Attorney-General under this section, the High Court is satisfied that any person has habitually and persistently and without any reasonable ground instituted vexatious legal proceedings, whether in the High Court or in any inferior court, and whether against the same person or against different persons, the court may, after hearing that person or giving him an opportunity of being heard, order that no legal proceedings shall without the leave of the High Court or a judge thereof be instituted by him in any court, and that any legal proceedings instituted by him in any court before the making of the order shall not be continued by him without such leave, and such leave shall not be given unless the court or judge is satisfied that the proceedings are not an abuse of the process of the court and that there is *prima facie* ground for the proceedings.

(2) If the person against whom an order is sought under this section is unable on account of poverty to retain counsel, the High Court shall assign counsel to him.

(3) A copy of any order made under this section shall be published in the London Gazette.

PART III

SITTINGS,

DISTRIBUTION OF BUSINESS, AND ASSIZES

Sittings and Vacations

52. Subject to rules of court, such number of judges of the High Court as may be requisite having regard to the business to be disposed of shall, so far as reasonably practicable and subject to vacations, sit continuously at the Royal Courts of Justice for the trial of causes in the King's Bench Division.

53. (1) His Majesty may from time to time by Order in Council, on a report or recommendation made, with the concurrence of the Lord Chancellor, by the council of judges of the Supreme Court assembled in pursuance of the provisions of Part X. of this Act, make, revoke or modify orders regulating the vacations to be observed by the High Court and the Court of Appeal and in the offices of the said courts respectively.

(2) Any Order in Council made in pursuance of this section shall, so long as it continues in force, have effect as if enacted in this Act, and rules of court may be made accordingly for carrying the Order into effect.

54. Provision shall be made by rules of court for the hearing during vacation by judges of the High Court and the Court of Appeal respectively of all such applications as may require to be immediately or promptly heard.

Distribution of Business

55. Without prejudice to any other provision of this Act, all causes and matters in the High Court shall, subject to the power of transfer, be distributed among the several Divisions and judges of the High Court, in such manner as may be directed by rules of court, and subject thereto all such causes and matters shall be assigned to the said Divisions respectively in the manner hereinafter provided.

56. Without prejudice to any other provision of this Act, there shall be assigned:

(1) To the Chancery Division:

(a) All causes and matters in respect of which exclusive jurisdiction was under any Act given to the Court of Chancery or to any judge thereof:

(b) All causes and matters for any of the following purposes:

The administration of the estates of deceased persons;

The dissolution of partnerships or the taking of partnership or other accounts;

The redemption or foreclosure of mortgages;
The raising of portions or other charges on land;
The sale and distribution of the proceeds of property subject to any lien or charge;
The execution of trusts, charitable or private;
The rectification or setting aside, or cancellation of deeds or other written instruments;
The specific performance of contracts between vendors and purchasers of real estates, including contracts for leases;
The partition or sale of real estates;
The wardship of infants and the care of infants' estates:

(c) All causes and matters which under, by virtue of or in pursuance of any enactment for the time being in force are assigned to that Division.

(2) To the King's Bench Division:

(a) All causes and matters, civil and criminal, which if the Act of 1873 had not passed, would have been within the exclusive cognizance of the Court of Queen's Bench in the exercise of its original jurisdiction, or of the Court of Common Pleas at Westminster, or of the Court of Exchequer, either as a court of revenue or as a common law court:

(b) All causes and matters which under, by virtue of or in pursuance of any enactment for the time being in force are assigned to that Division.

(3) To the Probate Division:

(a) All causes and matters which, if the Act of 1873 had not passed, would have been within the exclusive cognizance of the Court of Probate, or the Court for Divorce and Matrimonial Causes, or of the High Court of Admiralty:

(b) All causes and matters within the jurisdiction of the High Court as a prize court:

(c) All causes and matters which under, by virtue of or in pursuance of any enactment for the time being in force are assigned to that Division.

57. (1) The Lord Chancellor may, if at any time it appears to him desirable so to do with a view to the more convenient administration of justice, by order direct that any jurisdiction vested in the High Court in respect of any proceeding which by any enactment (including this Act) or any rule or order made under any enactment (including this Act) is assigned to any Division shall, notwithstanding that enactment, rule or order, be assigned to such other Division as may be specified in the order and shall be exercised either by any special judge or judges or by all the judges of that order Division:

Provided that an order shall not be made under this subsection except with the concurrence both of the president of the Division to which the jurisdiction is at the time assigned and of the president of the Division to which the jurisdiction is to be transferred.

(2) Where under any enactment a right of appeal to the High Court or to any Division is given from decisions given by county courts in pursuance of the jurisdiction vested in county courts in respect of any matter, the Lord Chancellor may, notwithstanding anything in any enactment, by order direct to which Division the appeal shall lie.

(3) Any order made under this section may at any time be revoked, varied or amended by a subsequent order so made.

58. Subject to rules of court and to the provisions of this Act, every person by whom any cause or matter is commenced in the High Court shall assign the cause or matter to such Division as he thinks fit by marking the document by which the cause or matter is commenced with the name of that Division and giving notice thereof to the proper officer:

Provided that:

(1) All interlocutory and other steps and proceedings in or before the High Court in any cause or matter subsequent to the commencement thereof, shall, subject to rules of court and to the power of transfer, be taken in the Division to which the cause or matter is for the time being attached; and

(2) If any plaintiff or petitioner assigns his cause or matter to any Division to which, according to rules of court or the provisions of this Act, it ought not to be assigned, the court or any judge of that Division, on being informed thereof, may, on a summary application at any stage of the cause or matter, direct the cause or matter to be transferred to the Division to which, according to those rules or provisions, it ought to have been assigned, or may retain it in the Division in which it was commenced; and

(3) All steps and proceedings taken by the plaintiff or petitioner or by any other party in any cause or matter and all orders made therein by the court or any judge thereof before any transfer shall be valid and effectual to all intents and purposes in the same manner as if the steps and proceedings had been taken and the orders had been made in the Division to which the cause or matter ought to have been assigned; and

(4) Subject to rules of court, a person commencing any cause or matter shall not assign it to the Probate Division, unless he would have formerly been entitled to commence that cause or matter in the Court of Probate or the Court for Divorce and Matrimonial Causes, or unless the cause or matter is within the admiralty jurisdiction of the High Court.

59. Any cause or matter may at any time and at any stage thereof, and either with or without application from any of the parties thereto, be transferred by such authority and in such manner as rules of court may direct from one Division or judge of the High Court to any other Division or judge thereof, or may by the like authority be retained in the Division in which it was commenced, although not the Division to which it ought in the first instance to have been assigned.

60. Every proceeding in the High Court and all business arising thereout shall, so far as is practicable and convenient and subject to the provisions of this Act relating to divisional courts, be heard and disposed of before a single judge, and all proceedings in an action subsequent to the hearing or trial, down to and including the final judgment or order, shall, so far as is practicable and convenient, be taken before the judge before whom the trial or hearing took place.

60A. (1) Where by any enactment, rule or order any proceedings are directed to be transacted or disposed of by or under the direction of a special judge or judges of the High Court, the Lord Chancellor may, if at any time it appears to him desirable so to do, with a view to the more convenient administration of justice, by order direct that notwithstanding any such enactment, rule or order such proceedings may be transacted and disposed of by or under the direction of any one or more of the judges of the High Court:

Provided that an order shall not be made under this subsection except with the concurrence of the President of the Division to which the jurisdiction with respect to the proceedings is at the time assigned.

(2) Any order made under this section may at any time be revoked, varied or amended by a subsequent order so made.

61. (1) A judge of the High Court may, subject to rules of court, exercise in court or in chambers all or any part of the jurisdiction vested in the High Court, in all such causes and matters and in all such proceedings in any causes or matters as might formerly have been heard in court or in chambers respectively by a single judge of any of the courts whose jurisdiction is vested in the High Court, or as may be directed or authorised to be so heard by rules of court, or by or in pursuance of any Act passed after the commencement of the Act of 1873, and for the time being in force.

(2) A judge of the High Court sitting in court shall be deemed to constitute a court of the High Court.

62. Subject to the provisions of this Act with respect to appeals in matters of practice and procedure, every order made by a judge of the High Court in chambers, except orders as to costs only which by law are left to the discretion of the court, may be set aside or discharged upon notice by any divisional court, or by the judge sitting in court, according to the practice of the Division to which the cause or matter in which the order was made is assigned.

63. (1) Divisional courts may be held for the transaction of any business in the High Court which may be ordered by rules of court to be heard by a divisional court, and in all cases where there is a right of appeal to the High Court from any court or person the appeal shall be heard and determined by a divisional court.

(2) Divisional courts shall, for the purpose of the causes and matters which are to be heard by such courts, exercise all or any part of the jurisdiction of the High Court.

(3) Any number of divisional courts may sit at the same time.

(4) Every judge of the High Court shall be qualified to sit in any divisional court.

(5) The judge who is according to the order of precedence under this Act the senior of the judges constituting a divisional court shall be the president of the court.

(6) A divisional court shall be constituted of two judges and no more: Provided that:

(a) The decisions of a divisional court shall not be invalidated by reason of the court being constituted of a greater number than two judges; and

(b) If the president of the Division to which the divisional court belongs, with the concurrence of the other judges of the Division or a majority thereof, or in the case of the King's Bench Division with the concurrence of not less than two other judges of the Division, is of opinion that the divisional court should be constituted of a greater number of judges than two, the court may be constituted of such number of judges as the president, with such concurrence as aforesaid, thinks expedient; and

(c) A divisional court for hearing such an appeal as aforesaid shall be constituted in accordance with rules of court.

64. (1) Subject to rules of court, it shall be the duty of every judge of the High Court who is not for the time being occupied in the transaction of any business specially assigned to him or in the business of any other divisional court, to take part, if required, in the sittings of such divisional courts as may from time to time be necessary for the transaction of the business assigned to the King's Bench Division.

(2) All such arrangements as may be necessary or proper for that purpose or for constituting or holding divisional courts for any other purpose authorised by this Act, and also for the proper transaction of that part of the business of the King's Bench Division which is not to be transacted by a divisional court, shall be made from time to time under the direction and superintendence of the judges of the High Court, and in case of difference among them, in such manner as the majority of the judges, with the concurrence of the Lord Chief Justice, shall determine.

65. Every cause or matter which is commenced in the Chancery Division shall be assigned in accordance with rules of court to one of the judges of that Division.

66. (1) Any judge of any Division who may consent so to do may, on the request of the Lord Chancellor, sit and act for or on behalf of any other judge of the High Court absent from illness or any other cause, or in the place of any judge whose office has become vacant, or as an additional judge of any Division, for the purpose of hearing any causes or matters which may be assigned to him by the Lord Chancellor, or any applications therein:

Provided that no judge shall sit and act as an additional judge of any Division, except with the concurrence of the president of the Division to which he belongs and of the president of the Division in which he is requested so to sit and act, and the assignment to him of any causes or matters depending in the Division in which he so sits and acts shall not be made except with the concurrence of the president of that last-mentioned Division.

(2) Any proceeding in any cause or matter assigned to any judge of the High Court may, on the request and on behalf of that judge, at any time and without any transfer, be heard and disposed of by any other judge of the same Division, who may be willing to hear and dispose of the same:

Provided that if any party to the proceeding objects to the proceeding being so heard and disposed of it shall not be so heard and disposed of without the concurrence of the Lord Chancellor, to be signified by an order in writing under his hand.

(3) In any case of urgency arising during the absence from illness or any other cause of any judge of the High Court to whom any cause or matter has been assigned, or during any vacancy in the office of any such judge, any other judge of the High Court, who consents so to do, may hear and dispose of any application for an injunction or other interlocutory order for or on behalf of the absent judge, or in the place of the judge whose office is vacant.

(4) A judge shall, while sitting and acting under this section for another judge or as an additional judge of another Division, have all such power and authority as that other judge would have had or as ordinarily belongs to a judge of that other Division, as the case may be.

67. (1) The judges to be placed on the rota for the trial of election petitions in England in each year, under the provisions of the Parliamentary Elections Act, 1868, or any Act amending that Act, shall be selected out of the judges of the King's Bench Division in such manner as may be provided by rules of court, and, subject thereto, shall be selected as follows, that is to say, the judges of the King's Bench Division shall, on or before the fourth day of November in every year select by a majority of votes three of the puisne judges of that Division (none of whom shall be a member of the House of Lords) to be placed on the rota for the trial of election petitions during the ensuing year.

(2) If in any case the judges present at the time of their meeting to make such selection are equally divided in their choice of any judge to be placed on the rota, the Lord Chief Justice, or in case of his absence the senior judge then present, shall have a second or casting vote.

(3) The choice of a judge to fill any occasional vacancy on the rota or to assist the judge on the rota as an additional judge, shall be made in like manner.

(4) If at the end of the year for which a judge has been appointed under this section, any trial or other matter is pending before him, either alone or together with any other judge, or if after the conclusion of any trial or hearing judgment has not been given thereon, it shall be lawful for the judge to proceed with and to conclude that pending trial or other matter and to give judgment thereon after the end of that year, in the same manner in all respects as if the year for which he was appointed had not expired.

68. (1) Subject to the provisions of this Act every appeal to the Court of Appeal which is an appeal against a final order or judgment, or is by way of motion for a new trial or to set aside a verdict, finding or judgment in any cause or matter in the High Court in which there has been a trial thereof or of any issue therein with a jury, shall be heard before not less than three judges of the Court of Appeal, and every such appeal shall, when it is an appeal against an interlocutory order or judgment, be heard before not less than two judges of that court.

(2) Any doubt which may arise as to what orders or judgments are final, and what are interlocutory, shall be determined by the Court of Appeal.

(3) Subject to the provisions of this section the Court of Appeal may sit in four divisions at the same time.

(4) No judge of the Court of Appeal shall sit as a judge on the hearing of an appeal from a judgment or order made in any case by himself or by any divisional court of the High Court of which he was a member.

(5) Notwithstanding anything in the foregoing provisions of this section, if all parties to an appeal or motion before the hearing file a consent to the appeal or motion being heard and determined before two judges of the Court of Appeal, the appeal or motion may be heard and determined accordingly, subject nevertheless to the same right, if any, of appeal to the House of Lords as if the hearing and determination had been before three judges:

Provided that:

(a) In all causes or matters to which any infant or person of unsound mind, whether so found by inquisition or not, or person under any other disability, is a party, no such consent shall be given by the next friend, guardian, committee or other person acting on behalf of the person under disability, so as to have the same force and effect as if that party were under no disability and had given such consent, unless with the previous consent of a court or a judge, nor so as to make such consent valid as between any committee of a lunatic and the lunatic, unless with the previous sanction of the Lord Chancellor or Lords Justices sitting in lunacy; and

(b) If two judges having heard an appeal or motion differ in opinion, the case shall, on the application of any party to the appeal, be re-argued and determined by three judges before appeal to the House of Lords.

69. (1) In any cause or matter pending before the Court of Appeal, any direction incidental thereto not involving the decision of the appeal may be given by a single judge of that court, and a single judge of that court may at any time during vacation make any interim order to prevent prejudice to the claims of any parties pending an appeal, as he may think fit.

(2) Every order made by a single judge of the Court of Appeal in pursuance of this section may be discharged or varied by any judges of that court having power to hear and determine the appeal.

Circuits and Assizes

70. (1) His Majesty may, by commission of assize or any other commission, either general or special, assign to such judges of the High Court or other persons as are named therein, the duty of trying and determining within any place or district specially fixed for that purpose by the commission, any causes or matters, or any questions or issues of fact or of law or partly of fact and partly of law in any cause or matter, depending in the High Court, or the exercise of any civil or criminal jurisdiction capable of being exercised by the High Court, and any commission so granted by His Majesty shall have effect as if enacted in this Act.

(2) Commissioners of assize shall be appointed by His Majesty by Letters Patent.

(3) The judges of the High Court to be named in commissions of assize shall be judges of the King's Bench Division, but every judge of the Probate Division shall, so far as the state of business in that Division will admit, share with the other judges the duty of holding sittings under commissions of assize, and His Majesty may include in any such commission the Master of the Rolls, any Lord Justice of Appeal, any judge of the Chancery Division, any judge of county courts, any of His Majesty's counsel learned in the law, and, if he consents to act, any person who has held the office of a judge of the Court of Appeal or of a judge of the High Court, and any person included in a commission of assize shall for the purposes of the commission have all the power, authority and jurisdiction of a judge of the High Court.

(4) A commissioner appointed in pursuance of this section shall when engaged in the exercise of any jurisdiction assigned to him in pursuance of this Act be deemed to constitute a court of the High Court.

(5) A commissioner acting under a commission of assize or any other commission issued under this section, shall, subject to rules of court, have power to try and determine matrimonial causes of any prescribed class and any matters arising out of or connected with any such causes, and shall for that purpose have all such powers and duties as are vested in the Probate Division under the enactments (including this Act) relating to matrimonial causes and matters.

For the purpose of the foregoing provision, the expression "prescribed" means prescribed by the Lord Chancellor by order made with the concurrence of the Lord Chief Justice and the President of the Probate Division.

(6) The counties palatine of Lancaster and Durham respectively shall not, so far as respects any commission issued under this section, be counties palatine, and a commission under this section may be issued for the trial of all causes and matters within those counties respectively in the same manner in all respects as in any other county.

71. All commissioners of assize shall have power and authority on their respective circuits to try revenue causes and proceedings and to proceed thereon in like manner as they may do in respect of other civil causes, and it shall not be necessary to issue any special commission to enable revenue causes to be tried.

72. (1) His Majesty may from time to time, by Order in Council, provide in such manner and subject to such regulations as to His Majesty may seem meet, for all or any of the following matters:

(a) For the discontinuance, either temporarily or permanently and either wholly or partially, of any former circuit, and the formation of any new circuit by the union of any counties or parts of counties, or partly in one way and partly in the other, or by the constitution of any county or part of a county to be a circuit by itself:

(b) For the appointment of the place or places at which assizes are to be held on any circuit, and for directing that assizes or any special commissions shall be held at more than one place in the same county on the same circuit, and for the holding of assizes for the despatch of criminal business for a whole county at one place, and for the despatch of civil business at one or more place or places in the same county on the same circuit:

(c) Where any Order is made under this section directing that assizes or any special commission shall be held at more than one place in any one county, for dividing the county for the purposes of the Order:

(d) For altering by such authority and in such manner as may be specified in the Order the day appointed for holding the assizes at any place on a circuit in any case, where by reason of the pressure of business or other unforeseen cause it is expedient to alter the day so appointed:

(e) Where it appears to His Majesty that by reason of the small number of prisoners or otherwise it is usually inexpedient to hold separate winter or spring assizes in a county, for uniting the county for the purpose of winter or spring assizes to any neighbouring county or counties, for appointing the place or places at which winter or spring assizes are to be held for the united counties, and for directing that winter or spring assizes to be held for the united counties shall be held at different places in different years:

(f) For the jurisdiction of the court and the attendance, jurisdiction, authority and duty of sheriffs, gaolers, officers, jurors and persons, the use of any prison, the removal of prisoners, the alteration of any commission, writ, precept, indictment, recognizance, proceeding or document, the transmission of recognizances, inquisitions and documents, and the costs of the prosecution and defence, and of maintaining and removing prisoners, so far as may seem to His Majesty necessary for carrying into effect any Order made under this section:

(g) For the regulation, so far as may be necessary for carrying into effect any Order made under this section, of the venue in all cases, civil and criminal, triable on any circuit or elsewhere:

(h) For any matters which appear to His Majesty to be necessary or proper for carrying into effect any Order made under this section.

(2) Where by Order in Council counties are united for the purpose of winter or spring assizes, the counties united shall, subject to the provisions of the Order, be deemed to be one county, and the winter and spring assizes held in and for the united county shall be deemed also to be held in and for each of the constituent counties.

(3) His Majesty may from time to time by Order in Council revoke, amend or vary any Order made in pursuance of this section.

(4) Every Order in Council made under this section shall be laid before Parliament, and notice of the Order having been made and of the place where copies thereof may be purchased shall be published in the London Gazette.

(5) Every Order in Council purporting to be made in pursuance of this section shall, while in force, have effect as if enacted in this Act.

73. (1) His Majesty may, by Order in Council, direct that, subject to any exceptions contained in the Order, the jurisdiction of the justices and judges of the Central Criminal Court at any session of oyer and terminer and gaol delivery held for the district within the jurisdiction of the Central Criminal Court in September, October, November, December, January, March, April or May, shall extend to any adjoining county or part of a county mentioned in the Order as if that county or part were included within the limits of the said district, and may apply, with such modifications and exceptions, if any, as to His Majesty seem fit, the Central Criminal Court Acts, 1834 and 1881, to the said county or part of a county and offences committed therein, as if that county or part were a county or part of a county mentioned in those Acts.

(2) Every Order in Council made under this section shall be laid before Parliament, and notice of the Order having been made and of the place where copies thereof may be purchased shall be published in the London Gazette.

(3) Every Order in Council purporting to be made in pursuance of this section shall, while in force, have effect as if enacted in this Act.

74. The power of making general orders for fixing the times of holding sessions of the Central Criminal Court under section fifteen of the Central Criminal Court Act, 1834, may be exercised by any four or more of the judges of the High Court.

75. (1) A court of assize may be held in any building, whether in or belonging to the county, city, town, borough or other area of jurisdiction, for which the court is held.

(2) A commissioner of assize may, by proclamation in open court, adjourn the court from the building in which he is then holding the assizes to such other building as he may deem convenient, whether within the same area of jurisdiction or not, and all persons required to attend at the assizes shall attend wherever the court is so held, and shall do all things which they might have been required to do if the court had not been adjourned, and shall be subject to the like penalties in default thereof, and all evidence given and all things done at any such court shall be deemed, and in all indictments, pleadings, rules and entries shall be alleged, to have been given and done respectively within the area of jurisdiction within which the court would have been held if there had been no adjournment.

(3) Nothing in this section shall authorise the holding of a court of assize in any place more than three miles distant from the area of jurisdiction for which the court is held.

76. Where a commission of assize is not opened at any place on the day appointed, all records and other proceedings relating to the commission of assize shall be drawn out, entered and made up under the same date and in the same form in all respects as if the commission of assize had been opened on the day originally appointed for that purpose.

77. (1) If at any time it appears to the Lord Chief Justice that there is no business, or no substantial amount of business, to be transacted at the assizes then about to be held at any place on a circuit and that having regard to all the circumstances of the case it is desirable that an order should be made under this section, he may, with the concurrence of the Lord Chancellor, by order direct that assizes shall not on the occasion of that circuit be held at that place, and where any such order is made then, notwithstanding any enactment or custom to the contrary, assizes shall not on that occasion be held at the place specified in the order.

(2) There may be included in an order made under this section provision for any matters (including any of the matters mentioned in paragraph (f) of subsection (1) of section seventy-two of this Act) for which it appears to the Lord Chief Justice to be necessary or proper to make provision with a view to giving full effect to the order.

(3) Any order made under this section may at any time be revoked, varied or amended by a subsequent order so made.

78. (1) If, not more than five days before the day appointed by Order in Council for the holding of assizes in any place (in this section referred to as "the commission day"), it appears to the clerk of assize that the attendance of any jurors summoned to attend at the assizes will not be required by reason of there being no business to be transacted for which those jurors are required, he may, in manner provided by this section, cause notice to be sent by post to those jurors by or on behalf of the person who has summoned them dispensing with their attendance in pursuance of the summons, and any person so summoned as juror to whom such a notice is sent shall not be liable to any fine or penalty for failing to attend in pursuance of the summons.

(2) For the purpose of causing notice to be sent under this section, the clerk of assize may direct the sheriff, under-sheriff or other officer who has summoned the jurors to send the required notice, and that officer shall send the notice as so directed.

(3) Where the clerk of assize causes notices to be sent to jurors dispensing with their attendance, he shall at the same time send information thereof to all clerks to justices in the area for which the assizes are to be held, and those justices shall, after the receipt of that information, in committing any person for trial, act as if the assizes were not to be held:

Provided that the justices may, if they think fit, for the purpose of enabling any person who would have been committeed for trial at any such assizes to have an early trial in case he is not admitted to bail, commit him for trial at any other assizes or quarter sessions about to be held at any place or town convenient for the trial, and His Majesty may by Order in Council make such provisions as to the jurisdiction of the court, and the attendance, jurisdiction, authority and duty of sheriffs, gaolers, officers, jurors and persons, the use of any prison, the removal of prisoners, the alteration of any commissions, writs, precepts, indictments, recognizances, proceedings and documents, the transmission of recognizances, inquisitions and documents, and the costs of the prosecution and defence and the expenses of maintaining and removing prisoners, as seem necessary or expedient to carry into effect this provision, but:

(a) the costs and expenses of any prosecutors and witnesses shall be paid by the council of the county or borough who would have been liable to pay those costs and expenses if the person had been committed for trial in the ordinary course; and

(b) the council of the county or borough who would have paid the costs of the trial of the person, if he had been committed in the ordinary course, shall pay to the council of the county or borough by whom the costs of the assizes or quarter sessions to which he is committed under this provision are paid, such sum on account of his trial as may be agreed upon between the councils, or, in default of agreement determined by the Secretary of State.

If the justices have already committed any person for trial at the assizes in respect of which notices have been sent under this section, they shall have power to alter the committal, and to make any alteration or extension of any recognizances which may appear necessary under the circumstances.

(4) Any warrant for arresting or detaining any person, and any recognizance to appear and give evidence, or to appear for trial, issued or taken in the case of a person charged with murder or manslaughter on a coroner's inquisition, shall, if the trial of the person charged cannot take place in the ordinary course owing to assizes to which the warrant or recognizances relate not being held by virtue of the provisions of this section, continue in operation until the next assizes, or, if the person charged is committed to any other assizes by justices, such other assizes.

(5) Any person having by law a right to present a bill of indictment to a grand jury in a case where no person has been committed for trial, and proposing to do so at any assizes shall give notice of his intention to do so to the clerk of assize more than five days before the commission day.

(6) Where notices have been given in pursuance of this section dispensing with the attendance of all jurors at any assizes it shall not be necessary to hold the assizes in respect of which the notices have been given unless there is any business not requiring the attendance of jurors to be transacted by the court.

79. (1) Whenever any vacancy occurs in the office of clerk of assize the Treasury may, having regard to the nature of the duties and responsibility of the office, revise the salary attached to the office.

(2) A person shall not be appointed a clerk of assize unless he has, during a period of not less than three years, been either:

(a) a barrister-at-law in actual practice; or

(b) a solicitor of the Supreme Court in actual practice; or

(c) a subordinate officer of a clerk of assize on circuit;

and any appointment made in contravention of this subsection shall be void.

(3) Where any enactment authorises a clerk of assize to take any fee for any duty performed by him, he shall take the fee by stamps or otherwise and account for it and pay it over in such manner as the Treasury may direct, and a clerk of assize shall not take any fee for his own use.

(4) A clerk of assize shall not be entitled to any compensation in respect of the emoluments of his office in case any alteration is made in the duties thereof or his office is abolished by the authority of Parliament.

(5) A person who is employed by a clerk of assize and is paid any salary or allowance out of moneys provided by Parliament shall not be removed from his office or employment without the sanction of the Treasury.

(6) If any clerk of assize practises as a barrister at any assize within the circuit of which he is clerk of assize he shall be liable to forfeit ten pounds for each offence, one half to be paid to His Majesty and the other half to the party aggrieved.

80. The power of appointment to such offices connected with the circuits of the judges under commissions of assize, or otherwise, as formerly were in the appointment of the senior judge going on any circuit, and also the power of appointment to all subordinate offices, the salaries of which are paid out of moneys provided by Parliament and which are held under any circuit officer, shall be vested in the senior judge going on that circuit for the winter and summer assizes respectively:

Provided that the provisions contained in this Act with respect to the abolition, reduction of salary or alteration of the designation or duties of offices in the Supreme Court, and as to giving notice of any vacancy in any such office, shall apply to all offices, whether principal or subordinate, mentioned in this section.

81. A commission of assize shall not be determined by the demise of the Crown, and shall, unless superseded or otherwise determined, continue in force for six months after such demise.

82. No proceeding, either civil or criminal, in any court of assize shall be discontinued by reason of the issue of any new commission of assize or of the altering of the names of or of the promotion to any dignity of any of the commissioners of assize, and the new commissioners may proceed in every behalf as if the old commission and commissioners had continued without alteration, and in particular where judgment against a person found guilty at the former assize has been respited, may pronounce judgment against that person.

83. Except as otherwise expressly provided in this Part of this Act, nothing in this Act shall affect the custom of holding separate assizes in and for each county twice a year.

PART IV

GENERAL PROVISIONS

AS TO TRIAL AND PROCEDURE

District Registries

84. (1) His Majesty may by Order in Council from time to time direct that there shall be in such places as are specified in the Order district registries for districts to be defined in the Order, from which writs of summons for the commencement of actions in the High Court may be issued, and in which the proceedings herein-after mentioned may be taken and recorded.

(2) Any person being the registrar of a county court or being a solicitor of not less than seven years' standing shall be qualified for appointment as district registrar of the High Court.

(3) The Lord Chancellor may, if he thinks fit, appoint two persons to

execute jointly the office of district registrar in any district registry, and may in any case where joint district registrars are appointed give directions with respect to the division between them of the duties of the office and may, as he thinks fit, on the death, resignation or removal of a joint district registrar, either appoint another person to be joint district registrar in the place of the person so dying, resigning or removed, or give directions that the continuing registrar shall act as sole registrar.

(4) On a vacancy occurring in the office of a district registrar, any person being a person qualified for appointment as district registrar may be appointed to act as provisional district registrar for such period not exceeding six months from the date on which the vacancy occurs as the Lord Chancellor may direct.

(5) The power to make appointments to the office of district registrar and provisional district registrar shall be vested in the Lord Chancellor.

(6) All acts authorised or required to be done by, to or before a district registrar may be done by, to or before a provisional district registrar appointed under this section, and a provisional district registrar shall receive in respect of the period during which he so acts remuneration on a scale not higher than the scale applicable in the case of the registrar of the district for which he is appointed to act.

(7) Every district registrar and provisional district registrar shall be an officer of the Supreme Court, and no person who is, or is acting as, the district registrar or the provisional district registrar of any district shall, either by himself or his partner, be directly or indirectly engaged as a solicitor or agent for a party to any proceeding whatsoever in the registry of that district.

85. (1) In every district registry there shall be used such seal as the Lord Chancellor from time to time directs.

(2) The seal of the district registry shall be impressed on every writ and other document issued out of or filed in that registry, and all writs and documents, and all exemplifications and copies thereof, purporting to be sealed with the seal of a district registry, shall be received in evidence in all parts of the United Kingdom without further proof.

86. District registrars shall have power to administer oaths and perform such other duties with respect to any proceedings in the High Court or in the Court of Appeal as may be prescribed by rules of court or by any special order of the court.

87. Any party to an action commenced by the issue of a writ out of a district registry may at any time apply, in the prescribed manner, to the High Court or to a judge in chambers of the Division to which the action is assigned, to remove the proceedings from the district registry into the proper office of the High Court, and the court or judge may, if it seems fit, make an order granting the application, and the proceedings and such original documents, if any, as have been filed therein shall upon receipt of the order be transmitted by the district registrar to the proper office of the High Court, and the action shall thenceforth proceed in the same manner as if it had been originally commenced by a writ of summons issued out of the proper office in London.

Inquiries and Trials by Referees

88. (1) Subjects to rules of court and to any right to have particular cases tried with a jury, the Court or a judge may refer to an official or special referee for inquiry or report any question arising in any cause or matter, other than a criminal proceeding by the Crown.

(2) The report of an official or special referee may be adopted wholly or partially by the Court or a judge, and if so adopted may be enforced as a judgment or order to the same effect.

89. In any cause or matter, other than a criminal proceeding by the Crown,

(a) If all the parties interested who are not under disability consent; or

(b) If the cause or matter requires any prolonged examination of documents or any scientific or local investigation which cannot in the opinion of the Court or a judge conveniently be made before a jury or conducted by the Court through its other ordinary officers; or

(c) If the question in dispute consists wholly or in part of matters of account;

the Court or a judge may at any time order the whole cause or matter, or any question or issue of fact arising therein, to be tried before a special referee or arbitrator respectively agreed on by the parties, or before an official referee or officer of the Court.

90. (1) In all cases of reference to an official or special referee or arbitrator, the official or special referee or arbitrator shall be deemed to be an officer of the Court, and subject to rules of court shall have such authority, and conduct the reference in such manner, as the Court or a judge may direct.

(2) The report or award of an official or special referee or arbitrator on any reference shall, unless set aside by the Court or a judge, be equivalent to the verdict of a jury.

(3) The remuneration to be paid to a special referee or arbitrator to whom any matter is referred under an order of the Court or a judge shall be determined by the Court or a judge.

91. The Court or a judge shall, in relation to references, have all such powers as are conferred by the Arbitration Act, 1889, on the Court or a judge in relation to references by consent out of court.

92. The Court of Appeal shall have all such powers as are conferred by the provisions of this Part of this Act on the Court or a judge in relation to references.

93. The Court or a judge may order that a writ of *habeas corpus ad* *testificandum* shall issue to bring up a prisoner for examination before an official or special referee or arbitrator.

94. A referee or arbitrator may at any stage of the proceedings under a reference, and shall, if so directed by the Court or a judge, state in the form of a special case for the opinion of the Court any question of law arising in the course of the reference.

95. An order made under the provisions of this Part of this Act relating to inquiries and trials by referees may be made on such terms as to costs or otherwise as the Court or a judge thinks fit.

96. Nothing in the provisions of this Part of this Act relating to inquiries and trials by referees shall empower the Court or a judge to order any proceedings to which His Majesty or the Duke of Cornwall is a party, or any question or issue in any such proceedings, to be tried before any referee, arbitrator or officer without the consent of His Majesty or the Duke of Cornwall, as the case may be, or shall affect the law as to costs payable by the Crown.

97. In the provisions of this Part of this Act relating to inquiries and trials by referees, unless the context otherwise requires:

The expression "the Court" means the High Court;

The expression "reference" means a reference under an order made by the Court or a judge under the said provisions.

Assessors

98. (1) In any cause or matter before the High Court or the Court of Appeal, other than a criminal proceeding by the Crown, the court may, if it thinks it expedient so to do, call in the aid of one or more assessors specially qualified, and try and hear the cause or matter wholly or partially with their assistance.

(2) The remuneration, if any, to be paid to an assessor shall be determined by the court.

Rules of Court

99. (1) Rules of court may be made under this Act for the following purposes:

(a) For regulating and prescribing the procedure (including the method of pleading) and the practice to be followed in the Court of Appeal and the High Court respectively in all causes and matters whatsoever in or with respect to which those courts respectively have for the time being jurisdiction (including the procedure and practice to be followed in the offices of the Supreme Court and in district registries), and any matters incidental to or relating to any such procedure or practice, including (but without prejudice to the generality of the foregoing provision) the manner in which, and the time within which, any applications which under this or any other Act are to be made to the Court or Appeal or to the High Court shall be made:

(b) For regulating and prescribing the procedure on appeals from any court or person to the Court of Appeal or the High Court, and the procedure in connection with the transfer of proceedings from any inferior court to the High Court or from the High Court to an inferior court:

(c) For regulating the sittings of the Court of Appeal and the High Court, of the divisional courts of the High Court, and of the judges of the High Court whether sitting in court or in chambers:

(d) For prescribing what part of the business which may be transacted and of the jurisdiction which may be exercised by judges of the High Court in chambers may be transacted or exercised by masters of the Supreme Court, registrars of the Probate Division, or other officers of the Supreme Court, and for providing that any interlocutory application to be made in connection with or for the purpose of any appeal or proposed appeal to be heard by a divisional court shall be heard and disposed of before a single judge:

(e) For regulating any matters relating to the costs of proceedings in the Court of Appeal or the High Court:

(f) For regulating and prescribing the procedure and practice to be followed in the Court of Appeal or the High Court and the procedure on appeals from any court or person to the Court of Appeal or the High Court, and the procedure in connection with the transfer of proceedings from any inferior court to the High Court or from the High Court to an inferior court in cases in which the procedure or practice is regulated by enactments in force immediately before the commencement of this Act or by any provisions of this Act re-enacting any such enactments (including so much of any of the Acts set out in the First Schedule to this Act as is specified in the third column of that Schedule):

(g) For repealing any enactments which relate to matters with respect to which rules are made under this section:

(h) For prescribing in what cases trials in the High Court are to be with a jury and in what cases they are to be without a jury:

(i) For regulating the means by which particular facts may be proved, and the mode in which evidence thereof may be given, in any proceedings or on any application in connection with or at any stage of any proceedings:

(j) For regulating or making provision with respect to any other matters which were regulated or with respect to which provision was made by the rules of the Supreme Court in force on the thirtieth day of September, nineteen hundred and twenty-five, or by any rules or regulations so in force with respect to practice and procedure in matrimonial causes and matters or with respect to applications and proceedings relating to legitimacy declarations.

(2) No rule of the Supreme Court which may involve an increase of expenditure out of public funds shall be made except with the concurrence of the Treasury, but the validity of a rule of the Supreme Court shall not in any proceedings in any court be called in question either by the court or by any party to the proceedings on the ground only that it was a rule to which the concurrence of the Treasury was necessary and that the Treasury did not concur or are not expressed to have concurred in the making thereof.

(3) Rules of court made under this section shall apply to all proceedings by or against the Crown.

(4) Rules of court may be made by the Lord Chancellor together with any four or more of the following persons, namely, the Lord Chief Justice, the Master of the Rolls, the President of the Probate Division, and four other judges of the Supreme Court, two practising barristers being members of the General Council of the Bar, and two practising solicitors of whom one shall be a member of the Council of the Law Society and the other a member of the Law Society and also of a provincial Law Society.

The four other judges and the barristers and solicitors to act as aforesaid shall be appointed by the Lord Chancellor in writing under his hand and shall hold office for the time specified in the appointment.

(5) Rules of court made under this section shall be laid before Parliament, but section one of the Rules Publication Act, 1893 (which requires notice to be given of a proposal to make statutory rules), shall not apply to rules so made.

(6) Nothing in this section shall affect the power conferred by section two hundred and thirty-seven of the Companies (Consolidation) Act, 1908, or by section one hundred and thirty-two of the Bankruptcy Act, 1914, of making general rules for carrying into effect the objects of those Acts respectively, or the power conferred on the President of the Probate Division by the next following section of this Act of making probate rules and orders, and the power to make rules of court under this section shall not extend to the matters with respect to which rules or orders may be made by virtue of the enactments mentioned in this subsection.

100. (1) The President of the Probate Division may, with the concurrence of the Lord Chancellor and the Lord Chief Justice or any judge of the High Court named by the Lord Chief Justice on his behalf, make rules and orders (in this Act referred to as "probate rules and orders") for regulating the procedure and practice of the High Court with respect to non-contentious or common form probate business.

(2) Every rule or order made under this section shall be laid before Parliament.

Evidence, Juries, Foreign Law, and Saving

101. Nothing in this Act and, subject as hereinafter in this section expressly provided, nothing in rules of court made under this Act, shall affect the mode of giving evidence by the oral examination of witnesses in trials with a jury, or the rules of evidence, or the law relating to jurymen or juries:

Provided that nothing in this section shall:

(a) prejudice the operation of any rules of court made in pursuance of the express power conferred by this Act to make rules of court for regulating the means by which particular facts may be proved and the mode in which evidence thereof may be given; or

(b) affect the power of the court for special reasons to allow depositions or affidavits to be read.

102. Where for the purpose of disposing of any action or other matter which is being tried in the High Court by a judge with a jury it is necessary to ascertain the law of any other country which is applicable to the facts of the case, any question as to the effect of the evidence given with respect to that law shall, instead of being submitted to the jury, be decided by the judge alone.

103. (1) Save as is otherwise provided by this Act or by rules of court, all forms and methods of procedure which, under or by virtue of any law, custom, general order or rules whatsoever, were formerly in force in any of the courts the jurisdiction of which is vested in the High Court or the Court of Appeal respectively, and which are not inconsistent with this Act or with rules of court, may continue to be used in the High Court and the Court of Appeal respectively in the like cases and for the like purposes as those in and for which they would have been applicable in the former respective courts.

(2) Subject to rules of court, the practice and procedure in all criminal causes and matters whatsoever in the High Court shall be the same as the practice and procedure in force at the commencement of this Act in relation to similar causes and matters.

PART V

OFFICERS AND OFFICES

Central Office

104. (1) There shall be a central office of the Supreme Court comprising such offices as were immediately before the commencement of this Act comprised in, and such officers and persons (including the officers and persons employed in the Court of Criminal Appeal) as then were officers of, the central office of the Supreme Court constituted under the Act of 1873, together with such other offices of the Supreme Court and such other officers and persons employed in the Supreme Court, or any offices thereof, as may from time to time be amalgamated with or transferred to the central office by rules of court.

(2) The central office shall be under the control and superintendence of the masters of the Supreme Court (King's Bench Division).

105. (1) The business to be performed in the central office shall, subject to any order of the Lord Chancellor, comprise all such business as was immediately before the commencement of this Act performed in the central office then existing, together with such other business as is performed in any offices which are at any time after the commencement of this Act amalgamated with or transferred to the central office, and shall be distributed among the several officers of the central office in the prescribed manner.

(2) The several officers of the central office shall be interchangeable one with another, and shall be capable of performing and liable to perform the duties of each other in any department of the office, and generally shall perform such duties and have such powers in relation to the business of the Supreme Court as the Lord Chancellor may by order direct.

(3) Any order made under this section may at any time be revoked, varied or amended by a subsequent order so made.

106. (1) The right of filling any vacancy in the office of masters of the Supreme Court (King's Bench Division) or in any clerkship in the central office, shall (subject as provided in the next following subsection) be vested in the Lord Chancellor, the Lord Chief Justice and the Master of the Rolls, in rotation, or in such order or manner as they by agreement among themselves may determine.

(2) The right of filling any vacancy in the office of King's coroner and attorney and master in the Crown Office shall be vested in the Lord Chief Justice, and the person appointed to that office shall by virtue of his appointment be a master of the Supreme Court (King's Bench Division).

(3) Subject as aforesaid, the right of filling any vacancy in, and of making any new appointment in or for the purposes of, the central office shall be vested in the Lord Chancellor subject to the concurrence of the Treasury.

Principal Probate Registry and District Probate Registries

107. The principal registry of the High Court for the purpose of the exercise of the probate jurisdiction (in this Act referred to as "the principal probate registry") shall be at such place in the County of London as His Majesty may by Order in Council from time to time appoint.

108. (1) For the purposes of this Act there shall be district probate registries which shall be attached to and under the control of the High Court.

(2) Subject as hereinafter provided, district probate registries shall be

established at the places mentioned in, and otherwise in accordance with, the Scheme set out in the Second Schedule to this Act:

Provided that a district probate registry to be established at a place at which no such registry was established by the Court of Probate Act, 1857, shall be established at such date as the President of the Probate Division may, with the concurrence of the Lord Chancellor, determine, and no district probate registry which was established by the said Act and is in existence at the commencement of this Act shall be discontinued until such date as may be so determined.

(3) The President of the Probate Division may from time to time, with the concurrence of the Lord Chancellor and the Treasury, by order modify or vary the said Second Schedule:

Provided that before any order is made under this subsection a draft thereof shall be laid before both Houses of Parliament, and the order shall not be made unless both Houses by resolution approve the draft either without modification or addition or with modifications or additions to which both Houses agree, and on the draft being so approved the order may be made in the form of the draft as approved.

(4) His Majesty may by Order in Council make such adaptations of any enactments as may appear to Him to be rendered necessary or expedient by reason of the passing of section seventeen of the Administration of Justice Act, 1925, or of anything done under the provisions of this section.

(5) Any order made by the Lord Chancellor or the President of the Probate Division under the foregoing provisions of this section may be revoked, varied or amended by a subsequent order so made.

109. (1) The President of the Probate Division may from time to time:

(a) with the sanction of the Treasury give directions as to the number of clerks to be employed in the several district probate registries and as to the amounts of their respective salaries; and

(b) prescribe the qualifications to be possessed by any person appointed a clerk in a district probate registry; and

(c) regulate the establishment of the district probate registries with respect to the duties to be performed therein.

(2) The clerks in a district probate registry shall be appointed by, and shall be removable by, the President of the Probate Division, and shall accordingly be deemed (subject always to the provisions of this Act) to be officers of the Supreme Court:

Provided that the provisions as to officers of the Supreme Court contained in subsection (1) of section one hundred and ten, section one hundred and eleven and subsection (1) of section one hundred and eighteen of this Act shall not have effect in relation to such clerks, and notwithstanding anything in section one hundred and nineteen of this Act any such clerk shall, if the President with the approval of the Treasury so directs, be entitled to a salary under this Part of this Act notwithstanding that he has been admitted to his office without a certificate from the Civil Service Commissioners.

109A. (1) Subject to the provisions of this section, employment as a clerk in a district probate registry shall, on whatever date the employment commenced, be deemed to be for all purposes employment in the civil service of the State, and if a certificate has been issued to him by the Civil Service Commissioners allowances may be granted in his case accordingly under the Superannuation Acts, 1834 to 1919:

Provided that, except in so far as the Treasury may direct, no account shall be taken for the purposes of this section of service before the issue of the certificate.

(2) Where a person who was immediately before the first day of October, nineteen hundred and twenty-eight, employed as a clerk in a district probate registry is required by reason only of his having attained any age to retire from service as such a clerk, the Treasury may, if he has been required to devote his whole time to employment as such a clerk and if he had attained the age of fifty-five years before the eighteenth day of January, nineteen hundred and twenty-seven, grant to him by way of compensation such gratuity, not exceeding twice the amount of the salary received by him during his last year of employment, as may seem to them just.

(3) Where any person to whom by virtue of this section any allowance or gratuity may be granted has during the whole or any part of the three years immediately preceding his retirement been in receipt of agency fees, his annual salary for those three years or that part of those three years shall, for the purposes of this section, be deemed, if the Treasury so direct, to include an amount not exceeding the average annual amount of any agency fees received by him during the three years ending on the thirty-first day of December, nineteen hundred and twenty-five, or, in the case of a clerk whose grade was changed at any time between the dirst day of January, nineteen hundred and twenty-three, and the eighteenth day of January, nineteen hundred and twenty-seven, during a period of three years ending on such later date as the Treasury may think proper to fix, and any amount so included shall be deemed to have been wholly paid out of moneys provided by Parliament.

(4) The decision of the Treasury on any question which arises as to the application of this section to any person or as to the amount of any superannuation allowance or gratuity thereunder shall be final.

General provisions as to Officers of the Supreme Court

110. (1) Such of the officers attached to the Supreme Court as may be thought necessary or proper for the performance of any special duties in connection either with the Supreme Court generally, or with the High

Court or the Court of Appeal, or any one of the Divisions, or any particular judge of either of the said courts, may by the Lord Chancellor, with the concurrence of the Lord Chief Justice and with the sanction of the Treasury, be attached to the said respective courts, Divisions and judges accordingly.

(2) The authority of the Supreme Court over its officers may be exercised in and by the High Court and the Court of Appeal respectively, and also in the case if officers attached to any Division by the president of that Division with respect to any duties to be discharged by them respectively.

111. The Lord Chancellor may, with the concurrence of the Treasury, from time to time determine as respects any class of officers in the Supreme Court the number of persons who may be appointed to be officers of that class.

112. (1) The clerks employed in the offices of the Supreme Court shall be classified in such manner as the Lord Chancellor, with the concurrence of the Treasury, may by order direct, and shall be employed in such capacities, as the Lord Chancellor may by order direct.

For the purposes of this subsection, the expression "the offices of the Supreme Court" shall include the department of the official solicitor to the Supreme Court, the bankruptcy department and the companies (winding-up) department, but shall not include the principal or a district probate registry.

(2) Any order made under this section may at any time be revoked, varied or amended by a subsequent order so made.

113. The Lord Chancellor may, with the approval of the Lord Chief Justice, the Master of the Rolls and the President of the Probate Division, as respects offices to which they have respectively a power of appointment, abolish any office in the Supreme Court which appears to him to be unnecessary.

114. (1) All officers assigned to perform duties with respect to the Supreme Court generally, or attached to the High Court or the Court of Appeal, shall be appointed by the Lord Chancellor.

(2) All officers attached to the Chancery Division who were formerly appointed by the Master of the Rolls, shall continue, while so attached, to be appointed by the Master of the Rolls.

(3) All other officers attached to any Division shall be appointed by the president of that Division.

(4) All officers attached to any judge shall be appointed by the judge to whom they are attached.

(5) The provisions of this section shall have effect subject to any provisions contained in this Part of this Act with respect to the appointing of any particular officers or the filling of vacancies in any particular offices.

115. (1) Any officer of the Supreme Court who by virtue of the provisions of subsection (1) of section one hundred and twenty-seven of this

Act is required to vacate office at the end of the completed year of service in the course of which he attains the age of seventy-two years shall, subject to the provisions of the said subsection and subject as hereinafter provided, hold office during good behaviour:

Provided that the power to remove any such person from his office on account of misbehaviour shall be exercisable by the Lord Chancellor, and the Lord Chancellor shall have power to remove any such person from his office on account of inability to perform the duties of his office.

(2) Every officer of the Supreme Court, not being an officer to whom subsection (1) of this section applies, shall hold office during His Majesty's pleasure:

Provided that nothing in this subsection shall affect the tenure of any officer appointed before the commencement of the Administration of Justice Act, 1925.

(3) In the application of this section to registrars of the Probate Division, the President of the Probate Division shall be substituted for the Lord Chancellor.

116. (1) Subject to the provisions of this section, where an officer of the Supreme Court is absent from illness or other reasonable cause, he may, with the approval of the Lord Chancellor, appoint a deputy, and if being so absent he fails to make such an appointment, the Lord Chancellor may appoint a deputy.

(2) Every deputy appointed under the foregoing provisions of this section shall have all the powers and authorities of the officer for whom he is appointed to act.

(3) A person shall not be qualified to be appointed under the foregoing provisions of this section to act as a deputy in any office unless he is qualified for appointment to that office.

(4) If any officer holding any office a vacancy in which is to be filled under the provisions of this Act by the President of the Probate Division becomes by reason of illness or other infirmity temporarily incapable of performing the duties of his office, the President of the Probate Division may appoint some other fit person to discharge his duties for any period not exceeding six months at one time, and the person so appointed shall, during that period, have the same powers as the officer in whose place he is appointed, and shall be paid by that officer such sum by way of salary or allowance as may be agreed on between them or be fixed by the President.

The President may in his discretion grant to any officer appointed under the said Acts or under the said provisions of this Act, leave of absence for any period not exceeding two months in any year, and may make provision for the discharge of the duties of that officer during his absence.

117. On the occurrence of any vacancy in the office of any officer of the Supreme Court, notice thereof shall be forthwith given to the Lord

Chancellor and also to the Treasury by the senior continuing or surviving officer of the department in which the vacancy occurs, and no appointment shall be made to fill the vacancy within the period of one month next after the date of the notice without the assent of the Lord Chancellor, given with the concurrence of the Treasury, and the Lord Chancellor may, if it be necessary, make provision in such manner as he thinks fit for the temporary discharge in the meantime of the duties of the office.

118. (1) The salaries of the several officers of the Supreme Court shall be of such amounts as the Lord Chancellor, with the concurrence of the Treasury, from time to time determines, and (without prejudice to the provisions contained in this Part of this Act with respect to the pensions of persons holding any of the offices specified in Part I. of the Third Schedule to this Act or with respect to officers employed in district probate registries) every such officer shall be deemed, for the purposes of salary and pension, to be a permanent civil servant of the State.

(2) All salaries, pensions and allowances payable to officers of the Supreme Court shall be paid out of moneys provided by Parliament, and shall be deemed to accrue from day to day but shall be payable on such days as the Treasury may from time to time appoint.

119. (1) An officer of the Supreme Court shall not, if appointed since the commencement of the Supreme Court of Judicature (Officers) Act, 1879, be entitled to a pension under this Part of this Act, or if appointed since the commencement of the Supreme Court of Judicature Act, 1884, be entitled to a salary under this Part of this Act, unless he has been admitted to his office with a certificate from the Civil Service Commissioners:

Provided that:

(a) The provisions of this section shall not apply in the case of a person appointed to any of the offices specified in Part I. of the Third Schedule to this Act; and

(b) The Lord Chancellor may from time to time, with the concurrence of the Treasury, make, revoke and alter orders declaring that this section shall not apply to any office or class of offices specified in the order, and if any such order is made the application of this section shall be limited accordingly.

(2) Before any person is appointed to any of the offices specified in Part I. of the Third Schedule to this Act the person making the appointment shall take steps to satisfy himself that the state of health of the person proposed to be appointed is satisfactory.

(3) This section shall in relation to a district probate registrar have effect as if for the words "if appointed since the commencement of the Supreme Court of Judicature Act, 1884," there were substituted the words "if appointed on or after the first day of October, nineteen hundred and twenty-eight."

120. An officer of the Supreme Court shall not either directly or indirectly practise as a barrister or solicitor or as an agent of a solicitor in any court in the United Kingdom:

Provided that this section shall not apply to district registrars of the High Court or any part-time district probate registrars, or to the official solicitor to the Supreme Court acting in his capacity as such.

Provisions as to particular Officers

121. (1) There shall be attached to the Lord Chief Justice and the Master of the Rolls respectively, a secretary, whose salary shall be five hundred pounds per annum, and a clerk, whose salary shall be four hundred pounds per annum, and to each of the other judges of the High Court and to each of the Lords Justices of Appeal, a clerk, whose salary shall be four hundred pounds per annum.

(2) An officer so attached shall:

(a) be attached to the person of the judge as such and shall be appointed and removable by him at his pleasure; and

(b) be liable, if required, while in attendance on the judge, to discharge without further remuneration the duties of crier in court or on circuit, or of usher or train bearer.

122. The senior master of the Supreme Court (King's Bench Division) shall hold and perform the duties of the offices of the King's Remembrancer, registrar of certificates of acknowledgments of deeds by married women and registrar of judgments, with such additional salary in respect of the office of King's Remembrancer as the Lord Chancellor, with the concurrence of the Treasury, amy determine.

123. (1) The registrars of the Chancery Division (in this section referred to as "the registrars") and the clerks to the registrars shall be appointed by the Lord Chancellor, and the number of the registrars and of the clerks respectively shall be such as the Lord Chancellor, with the approval of the Treasury, may fix.

(2) The Lord Chancellor shall appoint one of the registrars to be chief registrar, and the chief registrar shall exercise as respects the other registrars and the clerks to the registrars such duties and functions as the Lord Chancellor may from time to time assign to him.

(3) The clerks to the registrars shall retire from office at such age as the Lord Chancellor, with the consent of the Treasury, may fix.

(4) Any person who was on the nineteenth day of August, nineteen hundred and twenty-one, exercising functions as a registrar or as a clerk to the registrars shall be deemed to have been duly appointed in accordance with the provisions of this section to the office of registrar or clerk, as the case may be, but shall be entitled to reckon as a period of service for the purpose of the Superannuation Acts, 1834 to 1919, any period before that date during which he exercised such functions.

124. The power to appoint a person to be a clerk in the office of the master in lunacy shall be vested in and exercisable by the Lord Chancellor, and that office shall be included among the offices of the Supreme Court.

125. (1) There shall be attached to the Supreme Court permanent officers, to be called official referees, who shall report on such questions and try such causes, matters, questions and issues as may be referred to them for report or trial respectively under the provisions of Part IV. of this Act.

(2) The number of the official referees, and the tenure of their office, shall be determined by the Lord Chancellor, with the concurrence of the Lord Chief Justice and the President of the Probate Division, and with the sanction of the Treasury.

(3) The official referees shall perform the duties entrusted to them in such places, whether in London or in the country, as may from time to time be directed or authorised by any order of the High Court or of the Court of Appeal.

(4) All proper and reasonable travelling expenses incurred by the official referees in the discharge of their duties shall be defrayed out of moneys provided by Parliament.

126. (1) A person shall not be qualified for appointment to any of the offices in the Supreme Court specified in the first column of the Fourth Schedule to this Act unless he is a person of the description specified in the second column of that Schedule in respect of that office:

Provided that notwithstanding anything in this section any person who held any office in the Supreme Court at the commencement of the Administration of Justice Act, 1925, shall be qualified for appointment to any office to which he might have been appointed if that Act had not passed.

(2) The registrars of the Chancery Division shall be appointed from among the persons who at the time of the appointment are clerks to the registrars, and a person shall not be qualified to be appointed as clerk to the registrars unless he is a solicitor of the Supreme Court of not less than two years' standing.

(3) A person shall not:

(a) be qualified to be appointed a probate registrar, unless he is a practising barrister or solicitor of not less than ten years' standing, or a district probate registrar of not less than five years' standing, or has served not less than ten years as a clerk in the principal probate registry:

(b) be qualified to be appointed a district probate registrar unless he is a practising barrister or solicitor of not less than five years' standing, or a probate registrar, or has served not less than ten years as a clerk in the principal probate registry or a district probate registry.

(4) A person shall not be qualified to be appointed an admiralty

registrar or assistant registrar unless he is a barrister or solicitor of ten years' standing.

127. (1) A person holding any of the offices in the Supreme Court specified in Part I. or Part II. of the Third Schedule to this Act shall vacate his office at the end of the completed year of service in the course of which he attains the age of seventy-two years:

Provided that, where the Lord Chancellor considers it desirable in the public interest to retain any such person in the public service after he attains the age of seventy-two years, he may, with the approval of the Treasury, authorise his continuance in the service up to such later age, not exceeding seventy-five years, as he thinks fit.

(2) The provisions of this section shall not apply to a person holding any of the offices specified in Part I. of the said Third Schedule if he was appointed to that office before the first day of July, nineteen hundred and fifteen, and did not give notice in accordance with the provisions of section three of the Supreme Court Officers (Retirement, Pensions, &c.) Act, 1921, of his desire to accept the provisions contained in that Act in respect of the pensions of the persons holding the offices aforesaid in lieu of the provisions in respect of pensions which would have applied if that Act had not passed, or to a person holding either of the offices specified in Part II. of the said Third Schedule if he was appointed to that office before the date aforesaid.

128. (1) The provisions of the Superannuation Acts, 1834 to 1919, shall apply to persons holding any of the offices specified in Part I. of the Third Schedule to this Act, subject to the following modifications:

(a) On the retirement of a person from any of the offices aforesaid there may be granted to him a superannuation allowance calculated in accordance with the provisions of Part III. of the said Third Schedule instead of a superannuation allowance calculated in accordance with the provisions of the Superannuation Acts, 1834 to 1919:

(b) Section two of the Superannuation Act, 1909 (which authorises the grant of a gratuity in case of death), section three of that Act (which provides for the application of the Act to existing male civil servants), and subsection (2) of section six of that Act (which relates to compensation for abolition of office), and section two of the Superannuation Act, 1914 (which amends subsection (1) of section two of the Superannuation Act, 1909), shall not apply:

(c) Section ten of the Superannuation Act, 1859 (which prohibits the grant of superannuation allowance to a person under the age of sixty years except upon evidence of infirmity) shall not apply, but it shall not be lawful to grant any superannuation allowance under the provisions of this section to any person who is under the age of seventy-two years, unless upon a medical certificate to the satisfaction of the Treasury to the effect that he is incapable from infirmity of mind or body of discharging the duties of his office and that the infirmity is likely to be permanent, or unless he has served fifteen years in one or more of the offices specified in Part I. of the said Third Schedule and has attained the age of sixty-five years:

Provided that:

(i) The foregoing provisions of this section shall not apply to any person to whom, if the Supreme Court Officers (Retirement, Pensions, &c.) Act, 1921, had not been repealed by this Act, section two of that Act would not have applied or to any person who, having been appointed to one of the offices aforesaid was at the time of his appointment a civil servant within the meaning of the Superannuation Act, 1887, unless he gives notice in such form and within such period as may be prescribed by the Lord Chancellor, of his desire to accept those provisions in lieu of the general provisions of the Superannuation Acts, 1834 to 1919:

(ii) In the case of any person who in pursuance of the provisions of proviso (ii) to subsection (1) of section two of the Supreme Court Officers (Retirement, Pensions, &c.) Act, 1921, gave notice that he desired to accept the provisions of that section with the substitution for the allowances under the Second Schedule to that Act of the allowances and other benefits set out in the Third Schedule to that Act, this section shall have effect as if references to Part IV. of the Third Schedule to this Act were substituted for references to Part III. of that Schedule.

(2) For the purpose of computing any allowance or benefit under Part III. or Part IV. of the Third Schedule to this Act, no account shall be taken of any years of service in any office other than an office specified in Part I. of that Schedule.

(3) The provisions of this section shall not apply to a person holding any of the offices specified in Part I. of the said Third Schedule if he was appointed to that office before the first day of July, nineteen hundred and fifteen, and did not give notice in accordance with the provisions of section three of the Supreme Court Officers (Retirement, Pensions, &c.) Act, 1921, of his desire to accept those provisions in lieu of the provisions in respect of pensions which would have applied to him if that Act had not passed.

128A. (1) A district probate registrar shall be an officer of the Supreme Court, and (except in the case of a part-time or provisional registrar) shall be deemed for all purposes to be a permanent civil servant of the State.

(2) If in any case it appears to the President of the Probate Division that the business to be performed in any district probate registry is not such as to require the services of a whole-time registrar, he may, notwithstanding anything in this Act, appoint a person to act as part-time registrar, and a person so appointed shall be entitled to a salary under this Part of this Act, notwithstanding that he has been admitted to his office without a certificate from the Civil Service Commissioners.

(3) On a vacancy occurring in the office of a district probate registrar,

any person, being a person qualified for appointment as district probate registrar, may be appointed to act as provisional district probate registrar for such period, not exceeding six months from the date on which the vacancy occurs, as the President of the Probate Division may direct and with such remuneration as the President, with the concurrence of the Treasury, may determine.

129. (1) Where under or by virtue of any order, grant or appointment, any powers and duties have been or are hereafter conferred or imposed on the official solicitor to the Supreme Court, then, unless and until the Supreme Court or a judge thereof, or in matters and proceedings in lunacy a judge or master in lunacy, otherwise directs in any particular case, those powers may be exercised and those duties shall be performed by the holder of the office for the time being, and no further order or appointment shall be necessary by reason only of the person on whom the powers and duties were conferred or imposed dying or ceasing to hold office.

(2) Any bond entered into by the official solicitor as such in connection with any grant of administration shall be binding on the holder of the office for the time being, and any property vested in the official solicitor as such shall, on his dying or ceasing to hold office, without any conveyance, assignment or transfer, become vested in his successor in like manner as it was vested in him.

130. (1) The Lord Chancellor may from time to time, with the concurrence of the Treasury, make regulations with respect to:

(a) the appointment, removal, payment and duties of persons to keep order in the Royal Courts of Justice;

(b) the appointment, removal, payment and duties of persons charged with the care and cleaning of the Royal Courts of Justice; and

(c) any other matters necessary or incidental to the use or management of the Royal Courts of Justice.

(2) Any remuneration payable under this section shall be paid out of moneys provided by Parliament.

Miscellaneous

131. Subject to the provisions of this Act, any rights of patronage and other rights or powers incident to any court or to the office of any judge of any court whose jurisdiction is now vested in the High Court or the Court of Appeal, in respect of which rights of patronage or other rights or powers no provision is made by this Act, shall be exercised in such manner as His Majesty may by Sign Manual direct.

132. Any enactment or document referring to an officer or office abolished by the Supreme Court of Judicature (Officers) Act, 1879, shall, as far as it continues applicable, be construed as referring to the officer or office substituted by that Act, and rules of court may determine what officer or office is so substituted.

PART VI

FUNDS IN COURT

133. (1) There shall be an Accountant-General of, and an accounting department for, the Supreme Court.

(2) The Clerk of the Crown shall be the Accountant-General of the Supreme Court (in this Part of this Act referred to as "the Accountant-General").

(3) The office of the Accountant-General shall be an office of the Supreme Court.

(4) All funds transferred or paid into or deposited in court, to the credit of any cause, matter or account in any Division, shall be vested in the Accountant-General on behalf of the Supreme Court, and shall be subject to the provisions of this Part of this Act and to any rules made under this Part of this Act (in this Part of this Act referred to as "the rules").

(5) The Accountant-General may do any act, sign or execute any instrument, and exercise any authority required or authorised to be done, signed, executed or exercised by him for the purposes of this Part of this Act or of the rules, by a deputy appointed by him in writing under his hand.

(6) References to the Paymaster-General in any rules made under or for the purposes of the Court of Chancery (Funds) Act, 1872, or any Act amending that Act, before the commencement of this Act shall be construed as references to the Accountant-General.

134. (1) The Consolidated Fund shall be liable to make good to the suitors of the High Court all funds in court.

(2) If the Lord Chancellor, whether on a representation made to him by any suitor or without any such representation, certifies to the Treasury in writing that the Accountant-General has failed to pay any money in court, or transfer or deliver any securities in court, required by any order of the court to be paid, transferred or delivered from his account, or has been guilty of any default with respect to any such money or securities, the Treasury shall cause to be paid out of the Consolidated Fund or the growing produce thereof into the Bank to the credit of the Accountant-General for and on behalf of the Supreme Court, such sum as may be certified by the Lord Chancellor in writing to be required for the purpose of paying the money so required to be paid, or of replacing the securities so required to be transferred or delivered or of making good such default.

135. All Acts, all rules and orders made in pursuance of any Act, all orders of the Court of Chancery, and all instruments and proceedings of every description referring to the Accountant-General of the Court of Chancery or Court of Exchequer, shall, subject to the provisions of this Part of this Act and of the rules, be construed and have effect as if the Accountant-General were therein referred to in place of the Accountant-General of the Court of Chancery or Court of Exchequer, so however that all money and securities shall be paid, transferred or deposited to the credit or account of the Accountant-General for and on behalf of the Supreme Court:

Provided that nothing in this section shall affect the King's Remembrancer, or the performance by him of any duties formerly performed by the Accountant-General of the Court of Exchequer, or apply to any Act, rule, order, instrument or proceeding relating to any such duties.

136. The Treasury shall cause the Accountant-General to keep in or near the Royal Courts of Justice an office for the purpose of carrying on the business of the Accountant-General under this Part of this Act.

137. All funds in court in pursuance of this Part of this Act shall vest in the Accountant-General for and on behalf of the Supreme Court without any conveyance, assignment or transfer, notwithstanding the death or removal from office of the person who is Accountant-General, and shall be held by him in trust to attend the orders of the court and subject to the rules, and all acts done by the Accountant-General with reference to any such funds in pursuance of an order of the court shall be valid and effectual.

138. (1) All securities transferred, standing or deposited into, in or to the account of the Accountant-General in pursuance of this Part of this Act, shall be held by him in trust in the several causes and matters in which those securities are transferred, standing or deposited respectively, and shall not be transferred, sold or delivered out except in pursuance of an order of the court.

(2) The rules may determine what evidence of an order of the court and of the directions contained in the order shall be necessary and sufficient for authorising the Bank or any other person to transfer on sale or otherwise or deliver out any securities or other things standing in the books of or deposited with the Bank or that person to the credit or account of the Accountant-General, and the securities or things so directed to be transferred or delivered out shall be transferred or delivered out accordingly on behalf of the Accountant-General by some officer of the Bank or that person.

(3) The Bank shall, by one of their cashiers or some other proper officer, receive all dividends accruing due on all securities standing to the account of the Accountant-General for and on behalf of the Supreme Court of which a certificate has been sent to them by him, and shall also receive any principal money payable in respect of any such securities, and the said certificate shall be a sufficient authority to the Bank to receive the dividends and principal money.

(4) Any receipt given by the Bank or by any cashier or other proper officer of the Bank for any dividends on any securities standing to the account of the Accountant-General under this Part of this Act, or any principal money payable in respect of any such securities, shall be a good discharge for those dividends or that money.

(5) The Bank shall place all money received by them in pursuance of this section to the credit of the Accountant-General for and on behalf of the Supreme Court.

139. Section sixty of the Bills of Exchange Act, 1882 (which relates to the indorsement of drafts or orders drawn upon bankers for the payment of money), shall extend to any document issued by the Accountant-General in pursuance of this Part of this Act which authorises the payment of money.

140. Nothing in this Part of this Act shall be deemed to require the Bank to keep the account of the Accountant-General for and on behalf of the Supreme Court causewise, and the Bank are hereby indemnified for all acts and things done or permitted to be done in pursuance of this Part of this Act or of the rules, or of any order of the court made or purporting to be made in pursuance of this Part of this Act or of any such rule, or done or permitted to be done in pursuance of any certificate signed and countersigned as directed by this Part of this Act or the rules, and no such acts or things respectively shall be questioned in any court to the detriment of the Bank.

141. (1) Save as otherwise provided by the rules, all money in court shall, subject to the provisions of this Part of this Act and of the rules, be placed on deposit without, in the case of money paid into court after the commencement of the Court of Chancery (Funds) Act, 1872, any application or request for that purpose, and when so placed on deposit shall bear interest at the rate of two per cent per annum together with any income tax chargeable thereon.

(2) Any money which may at any time be standing to the credit of the Accountant-General for and on behalf of the Supreme Court beyond the amount which the Accountant-General considers to be required for meeting current demands shall be placed in the hands of the National Debt Commissioners, who shall pay to the credit of the Accountant-General for and on behalf of the Supreme Court such sum as, with such money as is at the time standing to his credit, may be certified by him to be required to meet current demands, and the Consolidated Fund shall be liable to make good all money so placed in the hands of the Commissioners and the interest payable on sums placed on deposit, in like manner as it is liable to make good money in court.

142. Any money in court which under the rules or under rules of court or under an order of the court is required to be laid out in any particular investment shall, subject to the rules, be so laid out notwithstanding anything in this Part of this Act.

143. All acts done by the Accountant-General with reference to funds in court pursuant to and in accordance with rules of court shall be as valid and effectual as if they had been done in pursuance of an order of the court.

144. Where by the rules or any regulations of the Treasury the Accountant-General is authorised to make payments of money to persons entitled thereto upon their request by transmitting to them by post crossed cheques or other documents intended to enable them to obtain payment of the sums expressed therein, the posting of a letter containing the cheque or document and addressed to the person entitled thereto at the address given by him in his request shall, as respects the liability of the Accountant-General and of the Consolidated Fund respectively, be equivalent to the delivery of the cheque or document to that person himself.

145. (1) The National Debt Commissioners shall, subject to the directions of the Treasury, from time to time invest all money placed in their hands in pursuance of this Part of this Act in Government securities, and shall out of the dividends on the securities purchased with that money and on the securities, if any, purchased with the accumulation of those dividends, pay the sums payable by them under this Part of this Act, and invest any residue thereof in Government securities, and may from time to time change any such securities into Government securities of another description of equivalent value.

(2) If at any time the money in the hands of the National Debt Commissioners under this Part of this Act is unsufficient to pay the amount payable by them in pursuance of this Part of this Act, the Treasury shall either direct the Commissioners to realise a sufficient portion of the securities so purchased as aforesaid and apply the proceeds of such realisation in paying the amount so payable by them, or cause the required sum to be issued to the Commissioners out of any money applicable to the sinking fund, or out of the Consolidated Fund or the growing produce thereof.

146. (1) The Lord Chancellor, with the concurrence of the Treasury, may make rules for carrying this Part of this Act into effect, and regulating the deposit, payment, delivery and transfer in, into and out of court of money and securities which belong to suitors, or are otherwise capable of being deposited in or paid or transferred into court, or in or into the Bank with the privity of the Accountant-General, or are under the custody of the court, and the evidence of such deposit, payment, delivery or transfer, and the investment of and other dealing with money and securities in court in pursuance of the orders of the court, and the execution of the orders of the court, and the powers and duties of the Accountant-General with reference to such money and securities, and in particular for:

(a) Regulating the mode in which the Accountant-General is to deal with money and securities in pursuance of the orders of the court, and the mode in which effect is to be given to an order of the court which is to be executed by or through the office of the Accountant-General, and generally the arrangements between that office and the court and the officers thereof, and the certificates and information to be given by the Accountant-General with reference to the business of the court:

(b) Regulating the deposit, payment, sale, transfer and delivery with, to and by the Accountant-General of the funds, and the proceedings, evidence and duties of persons in relation thereto:

(c) Determining the mode of ascertaining the value of Government securities transferred to the National Debt Commissioners, or otherwise ordered to be dealt with by the Accountant-General:

(d) Regulating the investment in securities of money in court and the conversion into money of securities in court, and the transfer to the National Debt Commissioners of Government securities ordered by the court to be sold or converted into cash, and the transfer by the Commissioners to the Accountant-General for and on behalf of the Supreme Court of Government securities ordered by the court to be purchased:

(e) Regulating the placing on and withdrawal from deposit of money in court, and the payment or crediting of interest on money placed on deposit:

(f) Determining the smallest amount which is to be invested in securities, unless directed to be so invested notwithstanding the smallness of the amount, and determining the smallest amount which is to be placed or remain on deposit, and the smallest amount of money on deposit on which interest in pursuance of this Part of this Act is to be credited to an account to which money placed on deposit belongs:

(g) Determining the smallest amount which shall, notwithstanding any order of the court, be paid by the Accountant-General:

Provided that:

(i) No rules made in pursuance of this paragraph shall apply to any periodical payments of annuities, or of dividends or interest on funds in court;

(ii) The amount determined under this paragraph shall not exceed one shilling; and

(iii) Any sums retained by the Accountant-General in accordance with any rule made under this paragraph shall, in such manner as the Treasury may direct, be either paid into the Exchequer or applied as an appropriation in aid of the moneys granted by Parliament for the expenses of the Supreme Court:

(h) Determining the time at which money in court is to be placed on deposit, and at which interest on money so placed on deposit is to begin and cease, and the mode of computing any such interest:

(i) Determining the cases in which interest on money placed on deposit, and the dividends on any securities standing to the account of the

Accountant-General for and on behalf of the Supreme Court, is or are to be placed on deposit:

(k) Dealing with:

(a) accounts on which the balance of money and securities together amounts to less than five pounds;

(b) accounts on which that balance amounts to five pounds or more, but less than fifty pounds, and which have not been dealt with for a period of five years;

(c) accounts on which that balance amounts to fifty pounds or more and which have not been dealt with for a period of fifteen years;

and providing for the publication of lists of all or any of such last-mentioned accounts:

(l) Regulating the mode of framing and expressing orders of the court and instruments and proceedings of the Accountant-General with reference to the business of the court:

(m) Abrogating any general orders of the Court of Chancery relating to the matters aforesaid.

(2) Every rule made in pursuance of this section shall be laid before Parliament and every rule purporting to be so made shall be deemed to have been duly made and to have been within the powers of this Act.

147. The Treasury may make regulations with respect to the stockbroker to be employed in transacting the business relating to the funds vested in the Accountant-General for and on behalf of the Supreme Court, and the amount of commission to be received by him, or his payment by salary or otherwise.

148. (1) Accounts in such form as the Treasury may direct, including all such accounts as may be necessary for carrying into effect the orders of the High Court, shall be kept for the purposes of this Part of this Act, and separate accounts shall be kept for the transactions under this Part of this Act of the Accountant-General and of the National Debt Commissioners and of the liability of the Consolidated Fund under this Part of this Act.

(2) The accounts to be kept under this section shall be examined by the Comptroller and Auditor-General, and the Treasury shall cause copies of the accounts certified by the Comptroller and Auditor-General, together with his report thereon, to be sent to the Lord Chancellor and to be laid before both Houses of Parliament.

149. In this Part of this Act, unless the context otherwise requires, the following expressions have the meanings hereby assigned to them respectively, that is to say,

"Supreme Court," "High Court" and "court" include the Lord Chancellor and any person exercising the powers of the judge in lunacy:

"Order of the court" means any such order, decree, report, certificate or direction of the court, or any judge or officer thereof, as may be prescribed by the rules:

"Dividends" includes interest or other periodical produce:

"Government securities" means any annuities, exchequer bonds or other parliamentary securities of the Government of the United Kingdom:

"Securities" includes Government securities, and any security of any foreign state, of any part of His Majesty's Dominions outside the United Kingdom, or of any body corporate or company, or any securities standing in books kept by any person in the United Kingdom:

"Securities in court" means any securities standing or deposited in the name or to the credit or account of the Accountant-General for and on behalf of the Supreme Court, or placed to the credit of a cause, matter or account in court:

"Money in court" means any sum of money paid into the Bank with the privity of the Accountant-General for and on behalf of the Supreme Court or placed to the credit of any cause, matter or account in court, and includes dividends on securities in court and interest on money on deposit:

"Funds" and "funds in court" mean any money, securities or effects or any part thereof, standing or to be placed to the account or credit of the Accountant-General for and on behalf of the Supreme Court in the books of the Bank:

"The Bank" means the Bank of England.

PART VII

PROBATE CAUSES AND MATTERS

Grants of Probate and Administration

150. An application for the grant or revocation of probate or administration may be made through the principal probate registry:

Provided that:

(a) Where, in any contentious matter arising out of the application, the court is satisfied that the state of the property and the place of abode of the deceased were such as to give jurisdiction in the matter to a county court the court may remit the matter to that county court and the judge thereof shall proceed in the matter as if the application had been made to the county court in the first instance:

(b) Where a registrar of the principal probate registry is satisfied by affidavit that the personal estate of the person in respect of whose estate the application for the grant or revocation is made exclusive of what he was possessed of or entitled to as a trustee and not beneficially, but without any deduction on account of his debts, was at the time of his death under the value of two hundred pounds, and that at that time he was not seised or entitled beneficially of or to any real estate of the value of three hundred pounds or upwards, the judge of the county court having jurisdiction in the place of abode of the deceased shall have the jurisdiction of the High Court in respect of any contentious matter arising in connection with the said grant or revocation.

151. (1) Grants may be made in common form by district probate registrars in the name of the High Court and under the seal of the registry, and any such grant shall have effect over the personal estate of the deceased, and, subject to the provisions of this Part of this Act, over the real estate of the deceased, in all parts of England.

(2) No grant shall be made by a district probate registrar in any case in which there is contention until the contention is disposed of, or in any case in which it appears to him that a grant ought not to be made without the direction of the court.

(3) In any case where it appears doubtful to a district probate registrar whether an application for a grant of probate or administration should or should not be granted, or where any question arises in relation to a grant, or an application for a grant, the district probate registrar shall send a statement of the matter in question to the principal probate registry for the directions of the court, and the court may direct the district probate registrar to proceed with the matter in accordance with such instructions as the court may think necessary, or may forbid any further proceedings by the district probate registrar in relation to the matter, leaving the party applying for the grant to apply to the High Court through the principal probate registry or, if the case is within the jurisdiction of a county court, to the county court.

152. (1) A district probate registrar shall send to the principal probate registry a notice in the prescribed form of every application made in the registry for a grant as soon as may be after the application has been made, and no grant shall be made by him until he has received from the principal probate registry a certificate that no other application appears to have been made in respect of the estate of the testator or intestate.

(2) The certificate aforesaid shall be forwarded as soon as may be to the district probate registrar, and may be issued from the principal probate registry under a stamp provided for that purpose and approved by the President of the Probate Division.

(3) All notices so transmitted to the principal probate registry shall be filed and kept in that registry.

(4) Where any such notice is received from any district probate registry the registrars of the principal probate registry shall examine all notices of applications for grants received from the several other district probate registries and all applications for grants made at the principal probate registry, so far as may be necessary for the purpose of ascertaining whether application for a grant in respect of the estate of the same deceased person

has been made in more than one registry, and shall communicate with the district probate registrar as occasion may require in relation thereto.

(5) A district probate registrar shall, once in every month, or oftener if required by probate rules or orders, transmit to the principal probate registry a list in the prescribed form of the grants made by him and not included in a previous return, and also copies of the wills to which the grants relate, certified by him to be correct under a stamp provided by the district probate registrar for that purpose and approved by the President of the Probate Division.

(6) A district probate registrar shall file and preserve all original wills of which probate or administration with the will annexed has been granted by him, subject to such regulations with respect to the preservation and inspection of the wills as may from time to time be made by the President of the Probate Division.

153. Second and subsequent grants shall be made in the principal probate registry or in the district probate registry where the original will is registered or the original grant was made, or to which the original will or a registered copy thereof or the record of the original grant has been transmitted in pursuance of section eighty-nine of the Court of Probate Act, 1857, or of this Part of this Act.

154. (1) A caveat against a grant of probate or administration may be entered in the principal probate registry or in any district probate registry.

(2) On a caveat being entered in a district registry, the district probate registrar shall immediately send a copy thereof to the principal probate registry to be entered among the caveats in that registry.

155. (1) Probate or administration in respect of the real estate of a deceased person, or any part thereof, may be granted either separately or together with probate or administration of his personal estate, and may also be granted in respect of real estate only where there is no personal estate, or in respect of a trust estate only, and a grant of administration to real estate may be limited in any way the court thinks proper:

Provided that where the estate of the deceased is known to be insolvent, the grant of representation to the estate shall not be severed except as regards a trust estate.

(2) Provision may be made by probate rules and orders for adapting to the case of real estate the procedure and practice on the grant of administration.

156. (1) The President of the Probate Division shall cause to be prepared and printed from time to time in the principal probate registry calendars of the grants made in that registry and in the several district probate registries for such periods as the President of the Probate Division may direct.

(2) Every such calendar shall contain a note of every probate or administration with the will annexed and of every other administration

granted within the period specified in the calendar, setting forth the date of the grant, the registry in which it was made, the name and the place and time of death of the testator or intestate, the names and descriptions of the executors or administrators, and the value of the estate.

(3) A printed copy of every calendar so prepared shall be sent by post or otherwise to every district probate registry, to the probate registry in Belfast, to the office of the commissary clerk of Edinburgh, and to such other offices as the President shall from time to time direct, and every copy so transmitted shall be kept in the registry or office to which it is transmitted, and may be inspected by any person on payment of a fee of one shilling for each search, without reference to the number of calendars inspected.

157. Subject to any arrangements which may from time to time be made between the President of the Probate Division and the Commissioners of Inland Revenue, every probate registry shall, within such period after a grant as the President may direct, deliver to the Commissioners of Inland Revenue or their proper officer the following documents:

(a) In the case of a probate or of letters of administration with a will annexed, the Inland Revenue affidavit and a copy of the will:

(b) In the case of letters of administration without a will annexed, the Inland Revenue affidavit:

(c) In every case of letters of administration a copy or extract of the letters of administration:

(d) In every case such certificate or note of the grant as the said Commissioners may require.

158. The foregoing provisions of this Part of this Act shall have effect subject to the temporary provisions set out in Part I. of the Fifth Schedule to this Act, and the extension of the power to make grants in district probate registries which will come into operation when the temporary provisions cease to have effect shall be subject to probate rules and orders.

Provisions as to Executors and Administrators

159. The High Court shall have power to summon any person named as executor in a will to prove or renounce probate of the will, and to do such other things concerning the will as were customary before the commencement of this Act.

160. (1) Probate or administration shall not be granted to more than four persons in respect of the same property, and administration shall, if there is a minority or if a life interest arises under the will or intestacy, be granted either to a trust corporation, with or without an individual, or to not less than two individuals:

Provided that the court in granting administration may act on such *prima facie* evidence, furnished by the applicant or any other person, as to whether or not there is a minority or life interest, as may be prescribed by probate rules and orders.

(2) If there is only one personal representative (not being a trust corporation) then, during the minority of a beneficiary or the subsistence of a life interest and until the estate is fully administered, the court may, on the application of any person interested or of the guardian, committee or receiver of any such person, appoint one or more personal representatives in addition to the original personal representative in accordance with probate rules and orders.

(3) This section shall apply to grants made after the date of the commencement of this Act, whether the testator or intestate died before or after that date.

161. (1) The High Court may:

(a) where a trust corporation is named in a will as executor, whether alone or jointly with another person, grant probate to the corporation either solely or jointly with another person, as the case may require; and

(b) grant administration to a trust corporation, either solely or jointly with another person,

and the corporation may act accordingly as executor or administrator, as the case may be.

(2) Probate or administration shall not be granted to a syndic or nominee on behalf of a trust corporation.

(3) Any officer authorised for the purpose by a trust corporation or the directors or governing body thereof may, on behalf of the corporation, swear affidavits, give security and do any other act or thing which the court may require with a view to the grant to the corporation of probate or administration, and the acts of an officer so authorised shall be binding on the corporation.

(4) Where, at the commencement of this Act, any interest in any estate is vested in a syndic on behalf of a trust corporation acting as the personal representatives of a deceased person, the said interest shall, by virtue of this Act, vest in the corporation, and the syndic shall be kept indemnified by the corporation in respect of the said interest.

This subsection shall not apply to securities registered or inscribed in the name of a syndic or to land or a charge registered under the Land Registration Act, 1925, in the name of a syndic, but any such securities, land or charge, shall be transferred by the syndic to the corporation or as the corporation may direct.

(5) This section shall have effect whether the testator or the intestate died before or after the commencement of this Act, and no such vesting or transfer as aforesaid shall operate as a breach of a covenant or condition against alienation or give rise to a forfeiture.

162. (1) In granting administration the High Court shall have regard to the rights of all persons interested in the estate of the deceased person or the proceeds of sale thereof, and, in particular, administration with the will annexed may be granted to a devisee or legatee, and in regard to land settled previously to the death of the deceased and not by his will, may be granted to the trustees of the settlement, and any such administration may be limited in any way the court thinks fit:

Provided that:

(a) where the deceased died wholly intestate as to his estate, administration shall be granted to some one or more persons interested in the residuary estate of the deceased, if they make an application for the purpose, and as regards lands settled previously to the death of the deceased, be granted to the trustees, if any, of the settlement, if willing to act; and

(b) if, by reason of the insolvency of the estate of the deceased or of any other special circumstances, it appears to the court to be necessary or expedient to appoint as administrator some person other than the person who, but for this provision, would by law have been entitled to the grant of administration, the court may in its discretion, notwithstanding anything in this Act, appoint as administrator such person as it thinks expedient, and any administration granted under this provision may be limited in any way the court thinks fit.

(2) This section shall apply only in the case of persons dying after the date of the commencement of this Act, and the High Court in granting administration in the case of persons dying at any time before that date shall act in accordance with the principles and rules in accordance with which it would have acted if this Act had not passed.

163. (1) Where any legal proceedings touching the validity of the will of a deceased person, or for obtaining, recalling or revoking any grant, are pending, the High Court may grant administration of the estate of the deceased to an administrator, who shall have all the rights and powers of a general administrator, other than the right of distributing the residue of the estate, and every such administrator shall be subject to the immediate control of the court and act under its direction.

(2) The court may, out of the estate of the deceased, assign to an administrator appointed under this section such reasonable remuneration as the court thinks fit.

164. (1) If at the expiration of twelve months from the death of a person any personal representative of the deceased to whom a grant has been made is residing out of the jurisdiction of High Court, the court may, on the application of any creditor or person interested in the estate of the deceased, grant to him in the prescribed form special administration of the estate of the deceased.

(2) The court may, for the purpose of any legal proceedings to which the administrator under the special administration is a party, order the trans-

fer into court of any money or securities belonging to the estate of the deceased person, and all persons shall obey any such order.

(3) If the personal representative capable of acting as such returns to and resides within the jurisdiction of the High Court while any legal proceedings to which a special administrator is a party are pending, that personal representative shall be made a party to the legal proceedings, and the costs of and incidental to the special administration and the legal proceedings shall be paid by such person and out of such fund as the court in which the proceedings are pending may direct.

165. (1) Where an infant is sole executor of a will, administration with the will annexed shall be granted to his guardian, or to such other person as the court thinks fit, until the infant attains the age of twenty-one years, and on his attaining that age, and not before, probate of the will may be granted to him.

(2) Where a testator by his will appoints an infant to be an executor, the appointment shall not operate to transfer any interest in the property of the deceased to the infant or to constitute him a personal representative for any purpose unless and until probate is granted to him under this section.

166. Subject to the provisions of any enactment relating to special executors in the case of settled land, administration with the will annexed shall continue to be granted in every case where such a grant was customary before the commencement of this Act, and in such case the will of the deceased shall be performed and observed in like manner as if probate thereof had been granted to an executor.

167. (1) Every person to whom a grant of administration is made shall give a bond (in this section referred to as "an administration bond") to the senior registrar of the Probate Division by the name of "the principal probate registrar," and, subject to the provisions of this section, if the principal probate registrar, or, where the grant was made in a district registry, the district probate registrar, so requires, with one or more sureties conditioned for duly collecting, getting in, and administering the real and personal estate of the deceased.

(2) The principal probate registrar for the time being shall have power to enforce any administration bond or to assign it in accordance with the provisions of this section to some other person.

(3) An administration bond shall be in such form as may be directed by probate rules and orders.

(4) Where it appears to the satisfaction of the court or a judge that the condition of an administration bond has been broken, the court or judge may, on an application in that behalf, order that the bond shall be assigned to such person as may be specified in the order, and the person to whom the bond ordered to be assigned shall be entitled by virtue of the order to sue thereon in his own name as if it had been originally given to him in-

stead of to the principal probate registrar, and to recover thereon as trustee for all persons interested the full amount recoverable in respect of the breach of the condition thereof.

(5) Without prejudice to any proceedings instituted before the first day of October, nineteen hundred and twenty-five, any admininistration bond given before that date under any enactment repealed by the Administration of Justice Act, 1925, or which is to be enforceable as if it had been given under any such enactment, may be enforced or assigned as if it had been given to the principal probate registrar under this section.

(6) Nothing in this section shall require the Solicitor for the affairs of His Majesty's Treasury or the Solicitor for the affairs of the Duchy of Lancaster, when applying for or obtaining administration for the use or benefit of His Majesty, to give an administration bond.

(7) Probate rules and orders may be made for providing that sureties to administration bonds shall not be required when the grant is made to a trust corporation or to two or more individuals, or in any other proper case.

Resealing of Grants made in other Countries

168. (1) If a confirmation of the executor of a person who died domiciled in Scotland, which includes besides the estate situate in Scotland also personal estate situate in England, is produced to the High Court, and a copy thereof deposited in the principal probate registry, the confirmation shall, if there is inserted therein or noted thereon a statement signed by the sheriff clerk to the effect that the deceased died domiciled in Scotland, be sealed with the seal of the principal probate registry and returned to the person producing it, and shall on being so sealed have the like effect in England as if it were a grant made by the High Court.

(2) The foregoing provisions of this section shall apply:

(a) to an additional confirmation granted in a sheriff court in Scotland of estate situate in England of a person who died domiciled in Scotland, whether the original confirmation has been sealed with the seal of the principal probate registry or not, and notwithstanding that the additional inventory confirmed does not contain any estate of the deceased situate in Scotland; and

(b) to a confirmation or additional confirmation of personal estate situate in Scotland which contains or has appended thereto and signed by the sheriff clerk a note or a statement of funds in England held by the deceased in trust, being a note or statement which has been set forth in any inventory recorded in the books of the court of which the sheriff clerk is clerk;

as they apply with respect to confirmations which include personal estate situate in England.

(3) Where a confirmation granted under the Intestates Widows and Children (Scotland) Act, 1875, or the Small Testate Estates (Scotland) Act, 1876, contains estate in England, the principal probate registrar shall, on the confirmation being sent to him for the purpose by the commissary clerk or sheriff clerk together with a fee of two shillings and sixpence, affix thereto the seal of the principal probate registry.

169. (1) If probate or letters of administration granted by the High Court of Justice in Northern Ireland in respect of the personal estate of a person who died domiciled in Northern Ireland is or are produced to the High Court and a copy thereof is deposited with the principal probate registry, the grant shall, subject to the provisions of this section, be sealed with the seal of the principal probate registry, and shall have the like effect in England as if it had been originally made by the High Court.

(2) Where a grant has been made under section sixteen of the Finance Act, 1894, by the High Court of Justice in Northern Ireland in respect of the estate of any person and there is estate of that person in England, the principal probate registrar, if the case is one in which a grant might have been made under the said section sixteen in England, shall, subject to the provisions of this section, on the grant being sent to him for the purpose together with a fee of two shillings and sixpence, affix thereto the seal of the principal probate registry.

(3) No grant shall be resealed under the provisions of this section unless and until there is delivered to the principal probate registry, together with the grant:

(a) a certificate under the hand of the proper officer of the High Court of Justice in Northern Ireland that a bond has been given to that Court in a sum sufficient to cover the property in England as well as in Northern Ireland in respect of the grant to be resealed; and

(b) an Inland Revenue affidavit accounting, as on an application for an original grant, for the estate duty, if any, payable in Great Britain in respect of the personal estate of which the deceased was competent to dispose at his death, except that if the estate duty has previously been paid on a prior certification in Scotland of the grant in question, the Inland Revenue affidavit shall be endorsed to that effect by the Commissioners of Inland Revenue.

(4) Notwithstanding the provisions of section forty-eight of the Finance (No. 2) Act, 1915, a grant made by the High Court of Justice in Northern Ireland shall not have effect with respect to Government stock in England unless it is resealed under the provisions of this section.

(5) This section shall apply to grants in respect of the estates of persons dying on or after the first day of April, nineteen hundred and twenty-three.

Miscellaneous

170. All original wills and other documents which are under the control of the High Court either in the principal probate registry or in any district probate registry, shall be deposited and preserved in such places as the President of the Probate Division, with the consent of the Lord Chancellor, may direct, and any wills or other documents so deposited shall, subject to the control of the High Court and the provisions of probate rules and orders, be open to inspection.

171. An official copy of the whole or any part of a will or an official certificate of any grant of administration may, on payment of the prescribed fee, be obtained:

(a) from the registry in which the will or documents relating to the grant are preserved; or

(b) where the will or other document is preserved in some place other than a registry; from the principal probate registry; or

(c) subject to the approval of the principal probate registrar, from the principal probate registry in any case in which the will was proved in or the grant was issued from a district probate registry.

172. There shall, under the control and direction of the High Court, be provided safe and convenient depositories for the custody of the wills of living persons, and any person may deposit his will therein on payment of such fees and subject to such regulations as may from time to time be prescribed by the President of the Probate Division.

173. (1) Every person having the custody of documents which belonged to any court or person who had jurisdiction, immediately before the commencement of the Court of Probate Act, 1857, to grant probate or administration shall, upon receiving a requisition from any probate registrar under the seal of the principal probate registry transmit to the principal probate registry or to any other place mentioned in the requisition, at the time and in the manner therein mentioned, any one or more of any documents relating exclusively or principally to testamentary causes or matters which may be in his possession or control, and any document so requisitioned shall be deposited and arranged in the principal probate registry or the district probate registry, as the case may be, under the control and direction of the High Court so as to be easy of reference.

(2) If any person refuses or neglects to comply with a requisition made under this section he shall be liable to a penalty of one hundred pounds, which (together with the costs of the proceedings) shall be recoverable in the High Court by a probate registrar.

(3) The Treasury may, out of moneys provided by Parliament, pay such expenses of arranging, classifying, indexing, transmitting or otherwise connected with the removal of documents in consequence of any requisition under this section as the President of the Probate Division

may from time to time certify to the Treasury to be proper and necessary.

(4) Notwithstanding anything in this section, it shall be lawful for the University of Oxford to retain the custody of any such documents belonging to the court of the Chancellor of Oxford University as are included in the index of which a copy has been transmitted to the principal probate registrar under section two of the Oxford University Act, 1860:

Provided that any person shall at all convenient times, under the authority of a registrar of the principal probate registry or of the district probate registrar at Oxford, be entitled to inspect and to take extracts or copies therefrom on payment of the same fees as would be payable if the documents had been deposited in the principal probate registry or in the district probate registry at Oxford, and all such fees shall be payable to the persons who would in that event be entitled to receive them, and no officer of the University or of the said court shall be entitled to receive any such fees.

174. (1) In the principal probate registry and in every district probate registry there shall be used such seal as the President of the Probate Division may from time to time direct.

(2) All probates, letters of administration, orders and other instruments and copies thereof and all exemplifications purporting to be sealed with any such seal as aforesaid shall be received in evidence in all parts of the United Kingdom without further proof.

175. (1) In this Part of this Act, and in the other provisions of this Act relating to probate causes and matters, unless the context otherwise requires, the following expressions shall have the meaning hereby assigned to them respectively, that is to say:

"Administration" includes all letters of administration of the effects of deceased persons, whether with or without a will annexed, and whether granted for general, special or limited purposes:

"The court" means the High Court or a judge:

"Estate" means real and personal estate, and the expression "real estate" includes:

(a) chattels real and land in possession, remainder or reversion and every interest in or over land to which the deceased person was entitled at the time of his death; and

(b) real estate held on trust or by way of mortgage, whether by demise or sub-demise, or of security, but not money to arise under a trust for sale of land, nor money secured or charged on land:

"Grant" means a grant of probate or of administration:

"Inland Revenue affidavit" has the same meaning as in Part I. of the Finance Act, 1894:

"Non-contentious or common form probate business" means the business of obtaining probate and administration where there is no contention as to the right thereto, including the passing of probates and administrations through the High Court in contentious cases where the contest has been terminated, and all business of a non-contentious nature in matters of testacy and intestacy not being proceedings in any action, and also the business of lodging caveats against the grant of probate or administration:

"Prescribed" means prescribed by probate rules and orders:

"Settled land" and trustees of the settlement" have the same meaning as in the Settled Land Act, 1925:

"Testamentary cause or matter" includes all cases or matters relating to the grant or revocation of probate or administration:

"Trust corporation" means the public trustee or a corporation either appointed by the court in any particular case to be a trustee or authorised by rules made under subsection (3) of section four of the Public Trustee Act, 1906, to act as custodian trustee:

"Will" includes any testamentary instrument of which probate may be granted.

(2) Nothing in this Act shall operate to extend to any real estate to which any person dying before the first day of January, eighteen hundred and ninety-eight, or any person dying on or after that day and before the commencement of this Act was entitled, any enactments or rules of law which did not immediately before the said first day of January or the commencement of this Act, as the case may be, extend to the real estate of such a person or to confer on the High Court with respect to any such real estate any probate jurisdiction which was not immediately before the said first day of January or immediately before the commencement of this Act, as the case may be, vested in the High Court constituted under the Act of 1873.

(3) The provisions set out in Part II. of the Fifth Schedule to this Act shall, subject in the case of a person dying on or after the first day of January, eighteen hundred and ninety-eight, and before the commencement of this Act to the provisions of the Land Transfer Act, 1897, have effect with respect to the probate or revocation of the probate of the will of any person dying as is mentioned in subsection (2) of this section which affects real estate and with respect to the evidentiary effect in actions concerning real estate of probate or administration granted in respect of the estate of a person so dying.

PART VIII

MATRIMONIAL CAUSES AND MATTERS

Divorce and Nullity of Marriage

176. A petition for divorce may be presented to the High Court (in this Part of this Act referred to as "the court"):

(a) by a husband on the ground that his wife has since the celebration of the marriage been guilty of adultery; and

(b) by a wife on the ground that her husband has since the celebration of the marriage been guilty of rape, or of sodomy or bestiality, or that he has since the celebration of the marriage and since the seventeenth day of July, nineteen hundred and twenty-three, been guilty of adultery:

Provided that nothing in this Act shall affect the right of a wife to present a petition for divorce on any ground on which she might, if the Matrimonial Causes Act, 1923, had not passed, have presented such a petition, and on any petition presented by a wife for divorce on the ground of the adultery and cruelty, or adultery and desertion, of her husband, the husband and wife shall be competent and compellable to give evidence with respect to the cruelty or desertion.

177. (1) On a petition for divorce presented by the husband or in the answer of a husband praying for divorce the petitioner or respondent, as the case may be, shall make the alleged adulterer a co-respondent unless he is excused by the court on special grounds from so doing.

(2) On a petition for divorce presented by the wife the court may, if it thinks fit, direct that the person with whom the husband is alleged to have committed adultery be made a respondent.

178. (1) On a petition for divorce it shall be the duty of the court to satisfy itself so far as it reasonably can both as to the facts alleged and also as to whether the petitioner has been accessory to or has connived at or condoned the adultery or not, and also to enquire into any counter-charge which is made against the petitioner.

(2) If on the evidence the court is not satisfied that the alleged adultery has been committed or finds that the petitioner has during the marriage been accessory to or has connived at or condoned the adultery complained of, or that the petition is presented or prosecuted in collusion with either of the respondents, the court shall dismiss the petition.

(3) If the court is satisfied on the evidence that the case for the petition has been proved and does not find that the petitioner has in any manner been accessory to or connived at or condoned the adultery or that the petition is presented or prosecuted in collusion with either of the respondents, the court shall pronounce a decree of divorce:

Provided that the court shall not be bound to pronounce a decree of divorce if it finds that the petitioner has during the marriage been guilty of adultery, or if in the opinion of the court he has been guilty:

(a) of unreasonable delay in presenting or prosecuting the petition; or

(b) of cruelty towards the other party to the marriage; or

(c) of having without reasonable excuse deserted, or of having without reasonable excuse wilfully separated himself or herself from, the other party before the adultery complained of; or

(d) of such wilful neglect or misconduct as has conduced to the adultery.

179. In any case in which, on the petition of a husband for divorce, the alleged adulterer is made a co-respondent or in which, on the petition of a wife for divorce, the person with whom the husband is alleged to have committed adultery is made a respondent, the court may, after the close of the evidence on the part of the petitioner, direct the co-respondent or the respondent, as the case may be, to be dismissed from the proceedings if the court is of opinion that there is not sufficient evidence against him or her.

180. If in any proceedings for divorce the respondent opposes the relief sought, in the case of proceedings instituted by the husband, on the ground of his adultery, cruelty or desertion, or, in the case of proceedings instituted by the wife, on the ground of her adultery, cruelty or desertion, the court may give to the respondent the same relief to which he or she would have been entitled if he or she had presented a petition seeking such relief.

181. In the case of any petition for divorce or for nullity of marriage:

(1) The court may, if it thinks fit, direct all necessary papers in the matter to be sent to His Majesty's Proctor, who shall under the directions of the Attorney-General instruct counsel to argue before the court any question in relation to the matter which the court deems to be necessary or expedient to have fully argued, and His Majesty's Proctor shall be entitled to charge the costs of the proceedings as part of the expenses of his office:

(2) Any person may at any time during the progress of the proceedings or before the decree *nisi* is made absolute give information to His Majesty's Proctor of any matter material to the due decision of the case, and His Majesty's Proctor may thereupon take such steps as the Attorney-General considers necessary or expedient:

(3) If in consequence of any such information or otherwise His Majesty's Proctor suspects that any parties to the petition are or have been acting in collusion for the purpose of obtaining a decree contrary to the justice of the case, he may, under the direction of the Attorney-General, after obtaining the leave of the court, intervene and retain counsel and subpoena witnesses to prove the alleged collusion.

182. (1) Where His Majesty's Proctor intervenes or shows cause against a decree *nisi* in any proceedings for divorce or for nullity of marriage, the court may make such order as to the payment by other parties to the proceedings of the costs incurred by him in so doing or as to the payment by him of any costs incurred by any of the said parties by reason of his so doing, as may seem just.

(2) So far as the reasonable costs incurred by His Majesty's Proctor in so intervening or showing cause are not fully satisfied by any order made under this section for the payment of his costs, he shall be entitled to charge the difference as part of the expenses of his office, and the Treasury may, if they think fit, order that any costs which under any order made by

the court under this section His Majesty's Proctor pays to any parties shall be deemed to be part of the expenses of his office.

183. (1) Every decree for a divorce or for nullity of marriage shall, in the first instance, be a decree *nisi* not to be made absolute until after the expiration of six months from the pronouncing thereof, unless the court by general or special order from time to time fixes a shorter time.

(2) After the pronouncing of the decree *nisi* and before the decree is made absolute, any person may, in the prescribed manner, show cause why the decree should not be made absolute by reason of the decree having been obtained by collusion or by reason of material facts not having been brought before the court, and in any such case the court may make the decree absolute, reverse the decree *nisi*, require further inquiry or otherwise deal with the case as the court thinks fit.

184. (1) As soon as any decree for divorce is made absolute, either of the parties to the marriage may, if there is no right of appeal against the decree absolute, marry again as if the prior marriage had been dissolved by death or, if there is such a right of appeal, may so marry again, if no appeal is presented against the decree, as soon as the time for appealing has expired, or, if an appeal is so presented, as soon as the appeal has been dismissed:

Provided that it shall not be lawful for a man to marry the sister or half-sister of his divorced wife or of his wife by whom he has been divorced during the lifetime of the wife, or the divorced wife of his brother or half-brother or the wife of his brother or half-brother who has divorced his brother during the lifetime of the brother or half-brother.

(2) No clergyman of the Church of England shall be compelled to solemnise the marriage of any person whose former marriage has been dissolved on the ground of his or her adultery, or shall be liable to any proceedings, penalty or censure for solemnising or refusing to solemnise the marriage of any such person.

(3) If any minister of any church or chapel of the Church of England refuses to perform the marriage service between any persons who but for his refusal would be entitled to have the service performed in that church or chapel, he shall permit any other minister of the Church of England entitled to officiate within the diocese in which the church or chapel is situate to perform the marriage service in that church or chapel.

Judicial Separation and Restitution of Conjugal Rights

185. (1) A petition for judicial separation may be presented to the court either by the husband or the wife on the ground of adultery or cruelty, desertion without cause for not less than two years, failure to comply with a decree for restitution of conjugal rights, or on any ground on which a decree for divorce *a mensa et thoro* might have been pronounced immediately before the commencement of the Matrimonial Causes Act, 1857.

(2) The court may, on being satisfied that the allegations contained in the petition are true and that there is no legal ground why the petition should not be granted, make a decree for judicial separation, and any such decree shall have the same force and effect as a decree for divorce *a mensa et thoro* had immediately before the commencement of the Matrimonial Causes Act, 1857.

(3) The court may, on the application by petition of the husband or wife against whom a decree for judicial separation has been made, and on being satisfied that the allegations contained in the petition are true, reverse the decree at any time after the making thereof, on the ground that it was obtained in the absence of the person making the application, or if desertion was the ground of the decree, that there was reasonable cause for the alleged desertion.

(4) The reversal of a decree for judicial separation shall not affect the rights or remedies which any other person would have had if the decree had not been reversed in respect of any debts, contracts or acts of the wife incurred, entered into or done between the date of the decree and of the reversal thereof.

186. A petition for restitution of conjugal rights may be presented to the court either by the husband or the wife, and the court, on being satisfied that the allegations contained in the petition are true, and that there is no legal ground why a decree for restitution of conjugal rights should not be granted, may make the decree accordingly.

187. (1) A decree for restitution of conjugal rights shall not be enforced by attachment, but where the application is by the wife the court, at the time of making the decree or at any time afterwards, may, in the event of the decree not being complied with within any time in that behalf limited by the court, order the respondent to make to the petitioner such periodical payments as may be just, and the order may be enforced in the same manner as an order for alimony in proceedings for judicial separation.

(2) The court may, if it thinks fit, order that the husband shall, to the satisfaction of the court, secure to the wife the periodical payments, and for that purpose may direct that it shall be referred to one of the conveyancing counsel of the court to settle and approve a proper deed or instrument to be executed by all necessary parties.

Legitimacy Declarations

188. (1) Any person who is a natural-born subject of His Majesty, or whose right to be deemed a natural-born subject of His Majesty depends wholly or in part on his legitimacy or on the validity of any marriage, may, if he is domiciled in England or Northern Ireland or claims any real or personal estate situate in England, apply by petition to the court for a decree declaring that the petitioner is the legitimate child of his parents, and that the marriage of his father and mother or of his grandfather and grandmother was a valid marriage or that his own marriage was a valid marriage.

(2) Any person who is so domiciled or claims as aforesaid, may apply to the court for a decree declaring his right to be deemed a natural-born subject of His Majesty.

(3) Applications under subsections (1) and (2) of this section may be included in the same petition and on any such application the court shall make such decree as the court thinks just, and the decree shall be binding on His Majesty and all other persons whatsoever:

Provided that the decree of the court shall not prejudice any person:

(i) if it is subsequently proved to have been obtained by fraud or collusion; or

(ii) unless that person has been cited or made a party to the proceedings or is the heir-at-law, next of kin, or other real or personal representative of, or derives title under or through a person so cited or made a party.

(4) A copy of every petition under this section and of any affidavit accompanying the petition shall be delivered to the Attorney-General at least one month before the petition is presented or filed, and the Attorney-General shall be a respondent on the hearing of the petition and on any subsequent proceedings relating thereto.

(5) In any application under this section such persons shall, subject to rules of court, be cited to see proceedings or otherwise summoned as the court shall think fit, and any such persons may be permitted to become parties to the proceedings and to oppose the application.

(6) The provisions of this Act relating to matrimonial causes shall, so far as applicable, extend to any proceedings under this section.

(7) No proceedings under this section shall affect any final judgment or decree already pronounced or made by any court of competent jurisdiction.

Miscellaneous

189. (1) A husband may on a petition for divorce or for judicial separation or for damages only, claim damages from any person on the ground of adultery with the wife of the petitioner.

(2) A claim for damages on the ground of adultery shall, subject to the provisions of any enactment relating to trial by jury in the court, be tried on the same principles and in the same manner as actions for criminal conversation were tried immediately before the commencement of the Matrimonial Causes Act, 1857, and the provisions of this Act with reference to the hearing and decision of petitions shall so far as may be necessary

apply to the hearing and decision of petitions on which damages are claimed.

(3) The court may direct in what manner the damages recovered on any such petition are to be paid or applied, and may direct the whole or any part of the damages to be settled for the benefit of the children, if any, of the marriage, or as a provision for the maintenance of the wife.

190. (1) The court may, if it thinks fit, on any decree for divorce or nullity of marriage, order that the husband shall, to the satisfaction of the court, secure to the wife such gross sum of money or annual sum of money for any term, not exceeding her life, as having regard to her fortune, if any, to the ability of her husband and to the conduct of the parties, the court may deem to be reasonable, and the court may for that purpose order that it shall be referred to one of the conveyancing counsel of the court to settle and approve a proper deed or instrument, to be executed by all the necessary parties, and may, if it thinks fit, suspend the pronouncing of the decree until the deed or instrument has been duly executed.

(2) In any such case as aforesaid the court may, if it thinks fit, by order, either in addition to or instead of an order under subsection (1) of this section, direct the husband to pay to the wife during the joint lives of the husband and wife such monthly or weekly sum for her maintenance and support as the court may think reasonable:

Provided that:

(a) if the husband, after any such order has been made, becomes from any cause unable to make the payments, the court may discharge or modify the order, or temporarily suspend the order as to the whole or any part of the money ordered to be paid, and subsequently revive it wholly or in part as the court thinks fit; and

(b) where the court has made any such order as is mentioned in this subsection and the court is satisfied that the means of the husband have increased, the court may, if it thinks fit, increase the amount payable under the order.

(3) On any petition for divorce or nullity of marriage the court shall have the same power to make interim orders for the payment of money by way of alimony or otherwise to the wife as the court has in proceedings for judicial separation.

(4) Where any decree for restitution of conjugal rights or judicial separation is made on the application of the wife, the court may make such order for alimony as the court thinks just.

(5) In all cases where the court makes an order for alimony, the court may direct the alimony to be paid either to the wife or to a trustee approved by the court on her behalf, and may impose such terms or restrictions as the court thinks expedient, and may from time to time appoint a new trustee if for any reason it appears to the court expedient so to do.

191. (1) If it appears to the court in any case in which the court pronounces a decree for divorce or for judicial separation by reason of the adultery of the wife that the wife is entitled to any property either in possession or reversion, the court may, if it thinks fit, order such settlement as it thinks reasonable to be made of the property, or any part thereof, for the benefit of the innocent party, and of the children of the marriage or any or either of them.

Any instrument made under any order of the court made under this section shall be valid and effectual, notwithstanding the existence of coverture at the time of the execution thereof.

(2) Where the application for restitution of conjugal rights is by the husband, and it appears to the court that the wife is entitled to any property, either in possession or reversion, or is in receipt of any profits of trade or earnings, the court may, if it thinks fit, order a settlement to be made to the satisfaction of the court of the property or any part thereof for the benefit of the petitioner and of the children of the marriage or either or any of them or may order such part of the profits of trade or earnings, as the court thinks reasonable, to be periodically paid by the respondent to the petitioner for his own benefit, or to the petitioner or any other person for the benefit of the children of the marriage, or either or any of them.

192. The court may after pronouncing a decree for divorce or for nullity of marriage enquire into the existence of ante-nuptial or post-nuptial settlements made on the parties whose marriage is the subject of the decree, and may make such orders with reference to the application of the whole or any part of the property settled either for the benefit of the children of the marriage or of the parties to the marriage, as the court thinks fit, and the court may exercise the powers conferred by this subsection notwithstanding that there are no children of the marriage.

193. (1) In any proceedings for divorce or nullity of marriage or judicial separation, the court may from time to time, either before or by or after the final decree, make such provision as appears just with respect to the custody, maintenance and education of the children, the marriage of whose parents is the subject of the proceedings, or, if it thinks fit, direct proper proceedings to be taken for placing the children under the protection of the court.

(2) On an application made in that behalf the court may, at any time before final decree, in any proceedings for restitution of conjugal rights, or, if the respondent fails to comply therewith, after final decree, make from time to time all such orders and provisions with respect to the custody, maintenance and education of the children of the petitioner and respondent as might have been made by interim orders if proceedings for judicial separation had been pending between the same parties.

194. (1) In every case of judicial separation:

(a) the wife shall, as from the date of the decree and so long as the separation continues, be considered as a *feme sole* with respect to any property which she may acquire or which may devolve upon her, and any such property may be disposed of by her in all respects as a *feme sole* and if she dies intestate shall devolve as if her husband had been then dead; and

(b) the wife shall, during the separation, be considered as a *feme sole* for the purpose of contract and wrongs and injuries, and of suing and being sued, and the husband shall not be liable in respect of her contracts or for any wrongful act or omission by her or for any costs she incurs as plaintiff or defendant:

Provided that:

(i) where on any judicial separation alimony has been ordered to be paid and has not been duly paid by the husband, he shall be liable for necessaries supplied for the use of the wife:

(ii) if the wife returns to cohabitation with her husband, any property to which she is entitled at the date of her return shall, subject to any agreement in writing made between herself and her husband while separate, be her separate property:

(iii) nothing in this section shall prevent the wife from joining at any time during the separation in the exercise of any joint power given to herself and her husband.

(2) In any case where the decree for judicial separation is obtained by the wife, any property to which she is entitled for an estate in remainder or reversion at the date of the decree, and any property to which she becomes entitled as executrix, administratrix or trustee after the date of the decree, shall be deemed to be property to which this section applies, and for the purpose aforesaid the death of the testator or intestate shall be deemed to be the date when the wife became entitled as executrix or administratrix.

195. (1) Where a wife obtains a decree for judicial separation, the decree shall, so far as may be necessary for the protection of any person dealing with the wife, be valid and effectual until discharged, and the discharge or variation of the decree shall not affect any rights or remedies which any person would have had, if the decree had not been discharged or varied, in respect of any debts, contracts or acts of the wife incurred, entered into or done during the period between the date of the decree and the discharge or variation thereof.

(2) Any person who, in reliance on any such decree as aforesaid, makes any payment to or permits any transfer or act to be made or done by the wife, shall, notwithstanding the subsequent discharge or variation of the decree, or the fact that the separation has ceased or has been discontinued, be protected and indemnified in the same way in all respects as if at the time of the payment, transfer or other act the decree were valid and still subsisting without variation in full force and effect, or the separation had not ceased or been discontinued, as the case may be, unless at that time

that person had notice of the discharge or variation of the decree or that the separation had ceased or been discontinued.

196. The court may from time to time vary or modify any order for the periodical payment of money made under the provisions of this Act relating to matrimonial causes and matters either by altering the times of payment or by increasing or diminishing the amount, or may temporarily suspend the order as to the whole or any part of the money ordered to be paid, and subsequently revive it wholly or in part, as the court thinks just.

197. In every case in which any person is charged with adultery with any party to a suit or in which the court may consider, in the interest of any person not already a party to the suit, that that person should be made a party to the suit, the court may, if it thinks fit, allow that person to intervene upon such terms, if any, as the court thinks just.

198. The parties to any proceedings instituted in consequence of adultery and the husbands and wives of the parties shall be competent to give evidence in the proceedings, but no witness in any such proceedings, whether a party thereto or not, shall be liable to be asked or be bound to answer any question tending to show that he or she has been guilty of adultery unless he or she has already given evidence in the same proceedings in disproof of the alleged adultery.

199. (1) A Secretary of State may order any judge, registrar or other officer of any ecclesiastical court in England or the Isle of Man, or any other person having the public custody or control of any records, books, documents or other instruments relating to matrimonial causes and matters, to transmit the same at such times, and in such manner, and to such places in London or Westminster, and subject to such regulations, as the Secretary of State may appoint.

(2) If any person wilfully disobeys an order made under this section he shall for the first offence forfeit the sum of one hundred pounds to be recoverable as a debt in the court by any registrar of the principal probate registry, and for a second or any subsequent offence the court may, by a warrant of committal countersigned by a Secretary of State, commit the person so offending to prison for any period not exceeding three months.

200. (1) The seal of the court to be used in respect of its jurisdiction in matrimonial causes and matters shall be such as the Lord Chancellor may from time to time direct.

(2) All decrees and orders of the court, or copies thereof, made in pursuance of the said jurisdiction shall, if purporting to be sealed with the said seal, be received in evidence in all parts of the United Kingdom without further proof.

PART IX

JURISDICTION OF INFERIOR COURTS

201. His Majesty may from time to time by Order in Council confer on any inferior court of civil jurisdiction the same jurisdiction in equity and in admiralty respectively as any county court has, and that jurisdiction, if and when conferred, shall be exercised in manner directed by this Act.

202. Every inferior court which has jurisdiction in equity, or at law and in equity, and in admiralty respectively, shall, as regards all causes of action within its jurisdiction for the time being, grant in any proceeding before it such relief, redress or remedy, or combination of remedies, either absolute or conditional, and shall in every such proceeding give such and the like effect to every ground of defence or counter-claim, equitable or legal (subject to the provisions of the next following section), as ought to be granted or given in the like case by the High Court and in as full and ample a manner.

203. Where in any proceeding before any such inferior court any defence or counter-claim of the defendant involves matter beyond the jurisdiction of the court, the defence or counter-claim shall not affect the competence or the duty of the court to dispose of the whole matter in controversy so far as relates to the demand of the plaintiff and the defence thereto, but no relief exceeding that which the court has jurisdiction to administer shall be given to the defendant upon any such counter-claim:

Provided that:

(1) It shall be lawful for the High Court, or any Division or judge thereof, if it be thought fit, on the application of any party to the proceeding, to order that the whole proceeding be transferred from the inferior court to the High Court or to any Division, and in such case the record in the proceeding shall be transmitted by the registrar or other proper officer of the inferior court to the High Court, and the proceeding shall thenceforth be continued and prosecuted in the High Court as if it had been originally commenced therein:

(2) The jurisdiction of an inferior court in cases of counter-claim shall not be excluded:

(a) by reason that the counter-claim involves matter not within the local jurisdiction of that court, but within the jurisdiction of any other inferior court in England; or

(b) where the counter-claim involves two or more causes of action as to each of which the defendant might have maintained a separate action and each of which is within the jurisdiction of the court, by reason that the aggregate amount of the counter-claim exceeds the jurisdiction of the court; or

(c) by reason that the counter-claim is for an amount of money exceeding the jurisdiction of the court, unless the plaintiff, within the prescribed time, objects in writing to relief being given by the court in excess of the relief which the court would before the twenty-fourth day of October, eighteen hundred and eighty-four, have had jurisdiction to administer:

(3) In any case where the counter-claim involves matter beyond the jurisdiction of the court, the court, notwithstanding the provisions of this section, may, on such terms, if any, as the court thinks just, either adjourn the hearing of the case or stay execution on the judgment for such time as may be necessary to enable any party to apply to remove the proceedings into the High Court or to enable the defendant to take proceedings in a court of competent jurisdiction for the purpose of establishing his counterclaim, and in default of any such application being made or any such action being brought, the court shall, after the expiration of the time limited, have jurisdiction to hear and determine the whole matter in controversy to the same extent as if all parties had consented thereto.

204. If it appears to the court or a judge that any proceeding in the High Court by way of interpleader, in which the amount or value of the matter in dispute does not exceed the sum of five hundred pounds, may be more conveniently tried and determined in a county court, the court or judge may at any time order the transfer thereof to any county court in which an action or proceeding might have been brought by any party to the interpleader against any other party thereto if there had been a trust to be executed concerning the matter in question, and every such order shall have the same effect as if it had been for the transfer of an action or matter under section sixty-nine of the County Courts Act, 1888, as amended by section four of the County Courts Act, 1919, and the county court shall have jurisdiction and authority to proceed therein, as may be prescribed by county court rules.

205. (1) Where in any cause or matter in the King's Bench Division or in an admiralty action in the Probate Division money is in any manner recovered by or on behalf of, or adjudged or ordered to be paid to or for the benefit of, a person who is an infant or of unsound mind, the High Court or a judge may order the money or any part thereof to be paid into or transferred to the county court of the district in which that person resides or such other county court as the High Court or judge may order, and the money or the part thereof to which the order relates shall thereupon be paid or transferred accordingly, and shall, subject to any special order or direction of the High Court or a judge and to county court rules, be invested, applied or otherwise dealt with for the benefit of that person in such manner as the county court in its discretion thinks fit.

(2) The provisions of this section shall apply to money which in proceedings under the Fatal Accidents Acts, 1846 to 1908, is recovered by or

adjudged or ordered to be paid to the widow of the person killed as they apply to money recovered by or adjudged or ordered to be paid to an infant.

(3) The Lord Chancellor may, with the concurrence of the Treasury, by order prescribe the fees to be charged in respect of the payment and investment of money or the application thereof or dealing therewith under this section.

(4) Where before the first day of October, nineteen hundred and twenty-five, money recovered in any cause or matter in the King's Bench Division by or on behalf of a person who is an infant or of unsound mind has been paid to the Public Trustee, it shall be lawful for the Public Trustee to pay that money, or so much of it as remains in his possession into the county court of the district in which that person resides, and money so transferred shall be invested, applied or dealt with in the same manner as if it had been paid into the county court under subsection (1) of this section.

(5) County court rules may be made for the purpose of carrying into effect the provisions of this section so far as they relate to the receipt of money into county courts and the investment thereof or application thereof or dealing therewith and the duties of registrars of county courts, and any such rules may provide for the transfer of money paid into a county court under this section or the investment representing any such money from one county court to another.

(6) Any order made by the Lord Chancellor under this section may be revoked, varied or amended by a subsequent order so made.

206. Where by virtue of any statute or charter or otherwise powers of making rules and orders for regulating the procedure or practice of or the costs or fees in any inferior court of civil jurisdiction are given to or have been exercised by the judge of any such court or any other person, either solely or jointly with any other person, and either with or without the concurrence of any judge of the Supreme Court or any other person, any rules or orders made by virtue of any of those powers shall be subject to the concurrence of the authority for the time being empowered to make rules of court under this Act:

Provided that the same authority may alter or annul any rule or order made before the twenty-fourth day of October, eighteen hundred and eighty-four, as to the matters aforesaid in any such court.

207. His Majesty may from time to time by Order in Council extend to any inferior court of civil jurisdiction any of the provisions of this Act relating to practice or procedure or of the rules of the Supreme Court with such modifications as may be necessary or desirable.

208. His Majesty may from time to time by Order in Council direct that the enactments relating to appeals from county courts shall apply to any other inferior court of record, and those enactments, subject to any exceptions, conditions and limitations contained in the Order, shall apply accordingly as from the date mentioned in the Order.

209. If and in so far as any enactment repealed by the Statute Law Revision and Civil Procedure Act, 1883, applies, or may have been applied by Order in Council, to the Court of the County Palatine of Lancaster, or to any inferior court of civil jurisdiction, that enactment shall be construed as if it were contained in a local and personal Act specially relating to that court, and shall have effect accordingly.

PART X

MISCELLANEOUS PROVISIONS

210. (1) A council of the judges of the Supreme Court, of which due notice shall be given to all the said judges, shall assemble once at least in every year, on such day or days as shall be fixed by the Lord Chancellor with the concurrence of the Lord Chief Justice, for the purpose of considering the operation of this Act and of any rules of court, and also the working of the several offices and the arrangements relative to the duties of the officers of the Supreme Court, and of enquiring and examining into any defects which may appear to exist in the system of procedure or the administration of the law in the High Court or the Court of Appeal, or in any other court from which any appeal lies to the High Court or any judge thereof or to the Court of Appeal.

(2) The said council shall report annually to a Secretary of State what amendments or alterations, if any, it would in their judgment be expedient to make in this Act, or otherwise relating to the administration of justice, and what other provisions, if any, which cannot be carried into effect without the authority of Parliament it would be expedient to make for the better administration of justice.

(3) The Lord Chancellor may convene at any time an extraordinary council of the judges.

211. When the Great Seal is in commission, the Lords Commissioners shall represent the Lord Chancellor for the purposes of this Act:

Provided that the powers vested in the Lord Chancellor by this Act in relation to:

(a) the presidency of the Court of Appeal;

(b) the appointment or approval of officers;

(c) the approval of any order for the removal of officers;

(d) any other act to which the concurrence or presence of the Lord Chancellor is by this Act made necessary;

may be exercised by the senior Lord Commissioner for the time being.

212. Every Order in Council, (other than an Order in Council altering the number of the Divisions or of the judges attached to any Division), rule (other than a rule made in pursuance of the provisions of this Act for facilitating the production of documents filed in or in the custody of the central office) or regulation made under this Act and by this Act required to be laid before Parliament shall be laid before each House of Parliament within one month after it is made, if Parliament is then sitting, or, if Parliament is not then sitting, within one month after the commencement of the next session of Parliament, and if either House before the expiration of forty days on which that House has sat next after the Order in Council, rule or regulation is laid before it presents an address to His Majesty praying that the Order in Council, rule or regulation may be annulled, His Majesty may by Order in Council annul it, and it shall thenceforth be void, but without prejudice to the validity of anything previously done thereunder.

213. (1) Subject to the provisions of this Act, the Lord Chancellor, with the advice and consent of the judges of the Supreme Court or any three of them, and with the concurrence of the Treasury, may by order fix the fees and percentages to be taken in the High Court or in the Court of Appeal or in any court created by any commission or in any office which is connected with any of those courts, or in which any business connected with any of those courts is conducted, or by any officer paid wholly or partly out of public moneys who is attached to any of those courts or the Supreme Court or any judge of those courts, and may from time to time by order increase, reduce or abolish all or any of such fees and percentages, and appoint new fees and percentages to be taken in the said courts or offices or any of them, or by any such officer as aforesaid.

(2) Provision for imposing or fixing the amount of any fees to be taken in connection with proceedings in the Supreme Court which might before the commencement of the Administration of Justice Act, 1925, have been imposed or fixed by rules of court may be imposed or fixed by means of orders under this section.

(3) Any order made in pursuance of this section shall have effect as if enacted in this Act.

(4) The Treasury, with the concurrence of the Lord Chancellor, may make such rules as they may think fit for publishing the amount of the fees.

(5) An order under this section may abolish any former fees and percentages which may be taken in the said courts or offices, or any of them, or by the said officers or any of them, but, subject to the provisions of any order made in pursuance of this section, the former fees and percentages shall continue to be taken, applied and accounted for in the same manner as formerly.

214. (1) The Lord Chancellor shall cause to be prepared annually an account for the year ending the thirty-first day of March, showing the receipts and expenditure during the preceding year in respect of the High

Court and the Court of Appeal, and of any court, office or officer, the fees taken in which or by whom can be fixed in pursuance of this Act.

(2) The account shall be made out in such form and contain such particulars as the Treasury, with the concurrence of the Lord Chancellor, may from time to time direct.

(3) Every officer by whom or in whose office fees are taken which can be fixed in pursuance of this Act shall make such returns and give such information as the Lord Chancellor may from time to time require for the purpose of enabling him to make out the said account.

(4) The said account shall be laid before both Houses of Parliament within one month after the thirty-first day of March in each year, if Parliament is then sitting, or if Parliament is not then sitting, within one month after the next meeting of Parliament.

215. (1) Any person duly admitted as a solicitor of the Supreme Court shall be an officer of the Court, and the High Court and the Court of Appeal respectively, or any Division or judge thereof, may exercise the same jurisdiction in respect of solicitors as any one of Her late Majesty's superior courts of law or equity might formerly have exercised in respect of any solicitor, attorney or proctor admitted to practice therein.

(2) References in any enactment to solicitors, attorneys or proctors, shall be construed as references to solicitors of the Supreme Court, and the officer formerly known as the registrar of attorneys and solicitors shall be called the registrar of solicitors.

(3) The powers relating to solicitors vested in the Master of the Rolls jointly with any other judge by the Solicitors Act, 1843, the Solicitors Act, 1860, and the Solicitors Act, 1877, and any Act amending those Acts, shall be vested in the Master of the Rolls, with the concurrence of the Lord Chancellor and the Lord Chief Justice, or (in case of difference) of one of them, and anything required by those Acts to be done to or before any judge jointly with the Master of the Rolls, may be done to or before the Master of the Rolls, the Lord Chancellor and the Lord Chief Justice.

216. (1) Such fees shall be chargeable:

(a) by commissioners for oaths in respect of the administration of an oath or the taking of an affidavit; and

(b) by the registrar of solicitors in respect of the registration under section thirty of the Solicitors Act, 1860, of any authority or appointment;

as may be prescribed by the Lord Chancellor by order made with the concurrence of the Lord Chief Justice and the Master of the Rolls.

(2) Any order made under this section may be revoked or varied by a sybsequent order so made.

(3) In this section the expression "affidavit" has the same meaning as in the Commissioners for Oaths Act, 1889.

217. (1) The conveyancing counsel of the court shall be conveyancing counsel in actual practice who have practised as such for ten years at least.

(2) The conveyancing counsel of the court shall not be less than six in number and shall be appointed by the Lord Chancellor.

(3) Business shall be distributed among the conveyancing counsel in such order and manner as the Lord Chancellor thinks fit.

218. (1) The Master of the Rolls may, subject to the provisions of this section, make regulations:

(a) for authorising and regulating the enrolment or filing of deeds in the Supreme Court and for prescribing the form in which certificates of enrolment or filing are to be granted; and

(b) prescribing the fees to be paid on the enrolment or filing of any deed, including any additional fees payable on the enrolment or filing of any deed out-of-time:

Provided that regulations shall not be made under paragraph (a) of this subsection so as to affect or prejudice in any manner the operation of any enactment requiring or authorising the enrolment in the Supreme Court of any deed or prescribing the manner in which any deed is to be so enrolled, and shall not be made under paragraph (b) of this subsection without the concurrence of the Treasury.

(2) Any instrument which is required or authorised under or in pursuance of the provision of any enactment to be enrolled or engrossed or enrolled and engrossed in any manner in the Supreme Court shall be deemed to have been duly enrolled, engrossed, or enrolled and engrossed in accordance with those provisions if it is written on such material and has been filed or otherwise preserved in such manner as the Master of the Rolls may by order direct.

(3) Every regulation made under this section shall be laid before Parliament.

(4) In this section the expression "deeds" includes assurances and other instruments.

219. (1) An instrument creating a power of attorney, the execution of which has been verified by affidavit, statutory declaration or other sufficient evidence, may, with the affidavit or declaration, if any, be deposited in the central office.

(2) A separate file of instruments so deposited shall be kept, and any person may search that file, and inspect every instrument so deposited, and an office copy thereof shall be delivered out to him on request.

(3) A copy of an instrument so deposited may be presented at the office, and may be stamped or marked as, and when so stamped and marked shall become, an office copy.

(4) An office copy of an instrument so deposited shall without further proof be sufficient evidence of the contents of the instrument and of the deposit thereof in the central office.

(5) Rules of court may be made for the purposes of this section regula-

ting the practice of the central office and prescribing, with the concurrence of the Treasury, the fees to be taken therein.

219A. (1) A bond to be given by any person under or for the purposes of any order of the Court of Appeal or the High Court shall be given, except where otherwise expressly provided in this Act, in such form and to such officer of the court, and by such official name, as may be prescribed, with, if the court so requires, one or more sureties, and that officer shall as such have power to enforce any such bond or to assign it, in accordance with the provisions of this section to some other person.

(2) Where by rules of court made for the purposes of this section an officer is at any time substituted for the officer theretofore prescribed as the officer to whom bonds of any class are to be given, such rules may provide that bonds of that class given before the rules come into operation shall have effect as if the official name of the substituted officer were therein inserted in lieu of that of the officer theretofore prescribed.

(3) Where it appears to the satisfaction of the court that the condition of a bond given in accordance with the provisions of this section has been broken, the court may, on an application in that behalf, order that the bond shall be assigned to such person as may be specified in the order and the person to whom the bond is ordered to be assigned shall be entitled by virtue of the order to sue thereon in his own name as if it had been originally given to him, and to recover thereon as trustee for all persons interested the full amount recoverable in respect of the breach of the condition thereof.

220. (1) Rules may be made under this section for providing that, in any case where a document filed in or in the custody of any department of the central office is required to be produced to any court or tribunal (including an umpire or arbitrator) sitting elsewhere than at the Royal Courts of Justice, it shall not be necessary for an officer of the department, whether served with a subpoena in that behalf or not, to attend for the purpose of producing the document, and that the document may be produced to the court or tribunal by sending it by registered post, together with a certificate in the form prescribed by the rules to the effect that the document has been filed in, or is in the custody of, the department, to such judge or officer of the court as may be so prescribed, and any such certificate shall be *prima facie* evidence of the facts stated therein.

(2) Rules made under this section may contain provisions for securing the safe custody and return to the proper department of the central office of any document sent to a court or tribunal in pursuance of the rules, and such other provisions as appear to the rule-making authority necessary or expedient for carrying this section into effect.

(3) Rules for the purposes of this section may be made by the Lord Chancellor, the Lord Chief Justice and the senior master of the Supreme

Court (King's Bench Division), and all such rules shall be laid before Parliament.

221. Any master of the Supreme Court (Chancery Division), or any person appointed in that behalf by any such master, may, without any licence as an auctioneer and without being liable to the duty imposed by the Auctioneers Act, 1845, or any other Act in force at the commencement of this Act, sell under the order of the High Court any goods or chattels, lands, tenements or hereditaments, or any interests therein.

222. The buildings erected under the Courts of Justice Building Act, 1865, and the Courts of Justice Concentration (Site) Act, 1865, together with all additions thereto, shall be styled "The Royal Courts of Justice."

223. The presentation and swearing of the Lord Mayor of the City of London shall take place in the King's Bench Division, or before the judges of that Division, on the ninth day of November in every year, or, if that day is a Sunday, on the day following, and in the same manner as was formerly accustomed in the Court of Exchequer.

224. (1) All Acts relating to the several courts and judges whose jurisdiction is vested in the High Court and the Court of Appeal respectively, or wherein any of those courts or judges are referred to, shall be construed and have effect as if the High Court or the Court of Appeal and the judges thereof respectively, as the case may be, had been referred to therein instead of the first-mentioned courts or judges, and all statutes, charters and other instruments in which Westminster is described or referred to as the locality of the said courts shall be construed as if the Royal Courts of Justice had been so described or referred to.

(2) In all cases not hereby expressly provided for in which under any such Act as aforesaid the concurrence or the advice or consent of the judge, or of any of the judges, of any one or more of the courts whose jurisdiction is vested in the High Court is required for the exercise of any power or authority, that power or authority may be exercised by and with the concurrence, advice or consent of the same or a like number of judges of the High Court.

225. In this Act, unless the context otherwise requires the following expressions have the meanings hereby assigned to them respectively, that is to say:

"Action" means a civil proceeding commenced by writ or in such other manner as may be prescribed by rules of court, but does not include a criminal proceeding by the Crown:

"The Act of 1873" means the Supreme Court of Judicature Act, 1873:

"Cause" includes any action, suit or other original proceeding between a plaintiff and defendant, and any criminal proceeding by the Crown:

"Clerk of assize" includes the clerk of the Crown and associate on circuit and any other office the duties of which may be performed by the clerk of assize:

"Commission of assize" includes a commission of assize a commission of oyer and terminer and a commission of gaol delivery, and any commission in lieu thereof issued under this Act:

"County" includes a county of a city or county of a town and any division of any county constituted by any Order in Council made under the provisions of this Act relating to assizes, and the sheriff for a county so divided shall, for the purpose of those provisions be deemed to be the sheriff for the division of the county:

"Defendant" includes any person served with any writ of summons or process, or served with notice of, or entitled to attend, any proceedings:

"Division" means Division of the High Court:

"Formerly" means immediately before the date of the commencement of the Act of 1873, that is to say, the first day of November, eighteen hundred and seventy-five, and the expression "former" shall be construed accordingly:

"Inferior court" includes a county court as well as any other inferior court:

"Judgment" includes decree:

"Lord Chief Justice" means Lord Chief Justice of England:

"Matrimonial cause" means any action for divorce, nullity of marriage, judicial separation, jactitation of marriage or restitution of conjugal rights:

"Matter" includes every proceeding in court not in a cause:

"Officer of the Supreme Court" in the provisions of this Act relating to the salaries and pensions of officers includes officer in lunacy:

"Party" includes every person served with notice of or attending any proceeding, although not named on the record:

"Petitioner" includes every person making any application to the court, either by petition, motion or summons, otherwise than as against any defendant:

"Plaintiff" includes every person asking any relief (otherwise than by way of counter-claim as a defendant) against any other person by any form of proceeding, whether the proceeding is by action, suit, petition, motion, summons or otherwise:

"Pleading" includes any petition or summons, and also includes the statements in writing of the claim or demand of any plaintiff, and of the defence of any defendant thereto, and of the reply of the plaintiff to any counter-claim of a defendant:

"Prescribed" means prescribed by rules of court:

"Probate Division" means the Probate, Divorce and Admiralty Division:

"Rules of court" includes forms:

"Solicitor" means solicitor of the Supreme Court:

"Spring assizes" means any court of assize held in March, April or May:

"Suit" includes action:

"United Kingdom" means, in relation to anything done before the date of the constitution of the Irish Free State, Great Britain and Ireland, and in relation to anything done or to be done after that date, Great Britain and Northern Ireland:

"Winter assizes" means any court of assize held in September, October, November, December or January.

226. (1) The enactments set out in the Sixth Schedule to this Act are hereby repealed to the extent specified in the third column of that Schedule:

Provided that, subject as in this Act otherwise expressly provided and without prejudice to the provisions of section thirty-eight of the Interpretation Act, 1889:

(a) Nothing in this repeal shall affect any Order in Council, rule, order or regulation made, commission issued, direction given, or thing done, under any enactment repealed by this Act, or deemed to have been made, issued, given or done respectively under any such enactment, and every such Order, rule, order, regulation, commission or direction shall continue in force, and, so far as it could have been made, issued or given under this Act, shall have effect as if made, issued or given under this Act:

(b) Nothing in this repeal shall affect any right of appointment vested in any judge or circuit officer or in the Master of the Rolls as Keeper of the Records:

(c) Any document referring to any Act or enactment repealed by this Act shall be construed as referring to this Act or to the corresponding enactment in this Act.

(2) Any person holding office or serving, or deemed to be serving, under any enactment repealed by this Act, shall continue in office or service as if he had been appointed under this Act, and nothing in this repeal shall affect the terms and conditions on and subject to which any person held office immediately before the commencement of this Act or prejudice or affect any right to pension, compensation or allowance which a person would otherwise have had on the abolition of, or on retirement from, his office or otherwise, or the amount thereof.

(3) References in any enactment or document to the Supreme Court, Court of Appeal or High Court constituted under the Judicature Acts, 1873 to 1910, or to the Divisions or offices thereof, shall be construed respectively as references to the Supreme Court, Court of Appeal, or High Court constituted under this Act, or the Divisions or offices thereof, and any act done or proceedings taken in respect of any cause or matter whatsoever before the commencement of this Act in the Supreme Court consti-

tuted under the Judicature Acts, 1873 to 1910, shall be deemed to have been done or taken in the Supreme Court constituted under this Act.

(4) Nothing in this Act shall affect the office of marshal attending any commissioner of assize.

(5) Save as therein otherwise expressly provided, nothing in this Act shall affect the operation of any enactment which is in force at the commencement of this Act and is not expressly repealed by this Act.

227. (1) This Act may be cited as the Supreme Court of Judicature (Consolidation) Act, 1925.

(2) This Act shall come into force on the first day of January, nineteen hundred and twenty-six.

SCHEDULES

(Not reproduced)

First Schedule. Enactments containing and regulating matters with respect to which rules of court may be made.

Second Schedule. Scheme for establishment of district probate registers.

Third Schedule. Offices in the case of which special provisions as to appointment, retirement and pension apply. Offices in case of which special provisions as to retirement apply. Scale of superannuation allowances in the case of the officers mentioned in Part i. Allowances &c. in the case of officers to whom the Superannuation Act 1909 applies.

Fourth Schedule. Qualifications for certain offices in the Supreme Court.

Fifth Schedule. Temporary Provisions with respect to grants in district probate registries. Provisions to apply in the case of persons dying before the commencement of the act with respect to the probate of wills affecting real estate and with respect to the evidentiary effect of probate and letters of administration.

Sixth Schedule. Enactments repealed.

VIII. Statute of Westminster 1931[1]

December 11, 1931

Whereas the delegates of His Majesty's Governments in the United Kingdom, the Dominion of Canada, the Commonwealth of Australia, the Dominion of New Zealand, the Union of South Africa, the Irish Free State and Newfoundland, at Imperial Conferences holden at Westminster in the years of our Lord nineteen hundred and twenty-six and nineteen

[1] An Act to give effect to certain resolutions passed by Imperial Conferences held in the years 1926 and 1930. 22 Geo. 5. HMSO.

hundred and thirty did concur in making the declarations and resolutions set forth in the Reports of the said Conferences:

And whereas it is meet and proper to set out by way of preamble to this Act that, inasmuch as the Crown is the symbol of the free association of the members of the British Commonwealth of Nations, and as they are united by a common allegiance to the Crown, it would be in accord with the established constitutional position of all the members of the Commonwealth in relation to one another that any alteration in the law touching the Succession to the Throne or the Royal Style and Titles shall hereafter require the assent as well of the Parliaments of all the Dominions as of the Parliament of the United Kingdom:

And whereas it is in accord with the established constitutional position that no law hereafter made by the Parliament of the United Kingdom shall extend to any of the said Dominions as part of the law of that Dominion otherwise than at the request and with the consent of that Dominion:

And whereas it is necessary for the ratifying, confirming and establishing of certain of the said declarations and resolutions of the said Conferences that a law be made and enacted in due form by authority of the Parliament of the United Kingdom:

And whereas the Dominion of Canada, the Commonwealth of Australia, the Dominion of New Zealand, the Union of South Africa, the Irish Free State and Newfoundland have severally requested and consented to the submission of a measure to the Parliament of the United Kingdom for making such provision with regard to the matters aforesaid as is hereafter in this Act contained:

Now, therefore, be it enacted by the King's most Excellent Majesty by and with the advice and consent of the Lords Spiritual and Temporal, and Commons, in this present Parliament assembled, and by the authority of the same, as follows:

1. In this Act the expression "Dominion" means any of the following Dominions, that is to say, the Dominion of Canada, the Commonwealth of Australia, the Dominion of New Zealand, the Union of South Africa, the Irish Free State and Newfoundland.

2. (1) The Colonial Laws Validity Act, 1865, shall not apply to any law made after the commencement of this Act by the Parliament of a Dominion.

(2) No law and no provision of any law made after the commencement of this Act by the Parliament of a Dominion shall be void or inoperative on the ground that it is repugnant to the law of England, or to the provisions of any existing or future Act of Parliament of the United Kingdom, or to any order, rule or regulation made under any such Act, and the powers of the Parliament of a Dominion shall include the power to repeal or amend any such Act, order, rule or regulation in so far as the same is part of the law of the Dominion.

3. It is hereby declared and enacted that the Parliament of a Dominion has full power to make laws having extra-territorial operation.

4. No Act of Parliament of the United Kingdom passed after the commencement of this Act shall extend, or be deemed to extend, to a Dominion as part of the law of that Dominion, unless it is expressly declared in that Act that that Dominion has requested, and consented to, the enactment thereof.

5. Without prejudice to the generality of the foregoing provisions of this Act, sections seven hundred and thirty-five and seven hundred and thirty-six of the Merchant Shipping Act, 1894, shall be construed as though reference therein to the Legislature of a British possession did not include reference to the Parliament of a Dominion.

6. Without prejudice to the generality of the foregoing provisions of this Act, section four of the Colonial Courts of Admiralty Act, 1890 (which requires certain laws to be reserved for the signification of His Majesty's pleasure or to contain a suspending clause), and so much of section seven of that Act as requires the approval of His Majesty in Council to any rules of Court for regulating the practice and procedure of a Colonial Court of Admiralty, shall cease to have effect in any Dominion as from the commencement of this Act.

7. (1) Nothing in this Act shall be deemed to apply to the repeal, amendment or alteration of the British North America Acts, 1867 to 1930, or any order, rule or regulation made thereunder.

(2) The provisions of section two of this Act shall extend to laws made by any of the Provinces of Canada and to the powers of the legislatures of such Provinces.

(3) The powers conferred by this Act upon the Parliament of Canada or upon the legislatures of the Provinces shall be restricted to the enactment of laws in relation to matters within the competence of the Parliament of Canada or of any of the legislatures of the Provinces respectively.

8. Nothing in this Act shall be deemed to confer any power to repeal or alter the Constitution or the Constitution Act of the Commonwealth of Australia or the Constitution Act of the Dominion of New Zealand otherwise than in accordance with the law existing before the commencement of this Act.

9. (1) Nothing in this Act shall be deemed to authorise the Parliament of the Commonwealth of Australia to make laws on any matter within the authority of the States of Australia, not being a matter within the authority of the Parliament or Government of the Commonwealth of Australia.

(2) Nothing in this Act shall be deemed to require the concurrence of the Parliament or Government of the Commonwealth of Australia in any law made by the Parliament of the United Kingdom with respect to any matter within the authority of the States of Australia, not being a matter within the authority of the Parliament or Government of the Common-

wealth of Australia, in any case where it would have been in accordance with the constitutional practice existing before the commencement of this Act that the Parliament of the United Kingdom should make that law without such concurrence.

(3) In the application of this Act to the Commonwealth of Australia the request and consent referred to in section four shall mean the request and consent of the Parliament and Government of the Commonwealth.

10. (1) None of the following sections of this Act, that is to say, sections two, three, four, five and six, shall extend to a Dominion to which this section applies as part of the law of that Dominion unless that section is adopted by the Parliament of the Dominion, and any Act of that Parliament adopting any section of this Act may provide that the adoption shall have effect either from the commencement of this Act or from such later date as is specified in the adopting Act.

(2) The Parliament of any such Dominion as aforesaid may at any time revoke the adoption of any section referred to in subsection (1) of this section.

(3) The Dominions to which this section applies are the Commonwealth of Australia, the Dominion of New Zealand and Newfoundland.

11. Notwithstanding anything in the Interpretation Act, 1889, the expression "Colony" shall not, in any Act of the Parliament of the United Kingdom passed after the commencement of this Act, include a Dominion or any Province or State forming part of a Dominion.

12. This Act may be cited as the Statute of Westminster, 1931.

IX. Ministers of the Crown Act, 1937[1]

July 1, 1937

Be it enacted by the King's most Excellent Majesty, by and with the advice and consent of the Lords Spiritual and Temporal, and Commons, in this present Parliament assembled, and by the authority of the same, as follows:

[1] *An Act to regulate the salaries payable in respect of certain Administrative Offices of State; to provide for the payment of additional salaries to members of the Cabinet holding offices at salaries less than five thousand pounds a year, of a salary to any person being Prime Minister, of pensions to persons who have been Prime Minister, and of a salary to any person being Leader of the Opposition; to simplify the law as to the capacity of persons holding offices of profit to sit and vote in Parliament; and for purposes connected with the matters aforesaid.* 1 EDW. 8 & 1 GEO. 6. Amended by ELIZ II 1964 c. 98, HMSO, see below.

PART I

SALARIES AND PENSION

1. (1) The annual salaries payable:

(a) to each of the Ministers of the Crown named in Part I of the First Schedule to this Act, shall, subject to the provisions of this Act as to number, be five thousand pounds;

(b) to each of the Ministers of the Crown named in Part II of the said Schedule, shall be three thousand pounds;

(c) to the Minister of the Crown named in Part III of the said Schedule, shall be two thousand pounds.

(2)[1] Subject to the provisions of this Act as to number, the annual salaries payable to the Parliamentary Under-Secretaries to the Departments of State shall:

(a) in the case of the Parliamentary Secretary to the Treasury, be three thousand pounds, and in the case of the Financial Secretary to the Treasury, be two thousand pounds;

(b) in the case of the Secretary for Mines and of the Secretary of the Department of Overseas Trade, be two thousand pounds each;

(c) in the case of each of the Parliamentary Under-Secretaries to the Departments of State specified in the Second Schedule to this Act, other than the Parliamentary Secretaries mentioned in the last foregoing paragraph, be fifteen hundred pounds;

(d) in the case of the Assistant Postmaster-General, be twelve hundred pounds:

Provided that, if and so long as there are two Parliamentary Under-Secretaries to the Foreign Office, to the Admiralty, or to the War Office, the annual salary payable to each of the two Parliamentary Under-Secretaries may be of such amount as may be determined by the Treasury, but so that the aggregate of the annual salaries payable to both of them does not exceed three thousand pounds.

(3) Subject to the provisions of this Act as to number, the annual salaries payable to each of the Junior Lords of the Treasury shall be one thousand pounds.

2.[1] (1) The number of persons holding office as Secretary of State to whom salaries may be paid under this Act shall not exceed eight.

(2) The number of Parliamentary Under-Secretaries to the Departments of State to whom salaries may be paid under this Act shall:

(a) in the case of the Treasury, not exceed two;

(b) in the case of the Board of Trade, not exceed three, including the Secretary for Mines and the Secretary of the Department of Overseas Trade;

[1] See amendment p. 1156 ff.

(c) in the case of the Foreign Office, of the War Office, and of the Admiralty, not exceed two;

(d) in the case of any other Department of State mentioned in the Second Schedule to this Act, and in the case of the Post Office, not exceed one.

(3) The number of the Junior Lords of the Treasury to whom salaries may be paid under this Act shall not exceed five.

3. (1) If and so long as any Minister of the Crown to whom this section applies is a member of the Cabinet, there shall be paid to him an additional salary of such amount as together with the salary payable to him in respect of the office held by him will amount to five thousand pounds a year.

(2) The date upon which any Minister of the Crown to whom this section applies becomes or ceases to be a member of the Cabinet shall be published in the London Gazette, and any such notification shall be conclusive evidence for the purposes of this section.

(3) This section applies to any Minister of the Crown named in Part II of the First Schedule to this Act, and to the Chancellor of the Duchy of Lancaster, if, in any case, his salary as such is less than five thousand pounds a year.

4. (1) There shall be paid to the person who is Prime Minister and First Lord of the Treasury an annual salary of ten thousand pounds.

(2) Any person who, whether before or after the passing of this Act, has been Prime Minister and has as First Lord of the Treasury taken the official oath prescribed by section five of the Promissory Oaths Act, 1868, shall be entitled to a pension of two thousand pounds a year:

Provided that no pension shall be payable under this subsection to any person so long as he is in receipt of any pension under the Political Offices Pension Act, 1869, or any salary payable out of moneys provided by Parliament, the revenues of the Duchy of Lancaster or the Consolidated Fund of the United Kingdom.

5. There shall be paid to the Leader of the Opposition an annual salary of two thousand pounds:

Provided that, if the Leader of the Opposition is in receipt of a pension payable to him under this Act, no salary shall be payable to him under this section, and if he is in receipt of a pension under the Political Offices Pension Act, 1869, the salary payable to him under this section shall be reduced by an amount equal to the amount of that pension.

6. (1) Subject to the provisions of this Act as to the payment of additional salaries to certain Cabinet Ministers, a person to whom any salary is payable under this Act, shall be entitled to receive only one such salary, but if he is the holder of two or more offices in respect of which a salary is so payable and there is a difference in the salaries payable in respect of those offices, the office in respect of which salary is payable to him shall be that in respect of which the highest salary is payable.

(2) No person in receipt of a salary or pension under this Act shall be entitled to receive any sum out of moneys provided by Parliament by way of salary or allowance in respect of his membership of the House of Commons.

7. (1) The salaries payable under this Act, except that payable to the Leader of the Opposition, shall be paid out of moneys provided by Parliament.

(2) The salary payable under this Act to the Leader of the Opposition, and any pension payable under this Act to a person who has been Prime Minister and First Lord of the Treasury, shall be charged on and payable out of the Consolidated Fund of the United Kingdom or the growing produce thereof.

8. The amount specified in this Act as being the amount of any salary payable thereunder out of moneys provided by Parliament shall be taken to be the maximum amount so payable, and accordingly, notwithstanding the provisions of this Act as to any such amount, the salary so payable in any year in respect of any office may be of a less amount than that so specified.

PART II

CAPACITY TO SIT IN THE HOUSE OF COMMONS

9. (1) Subject as hereinafter provided no person to whom a salary is payable under this Act shall by reason of his being the holder of the office or place in respect of which such a salary is payable, be rendered incapable of being elected, or of sitting and voting, as a member of the House of Commons:

Provided that:

(a) the number of persons entitled to sit and vote in that House while they are Ministers of the Crown named in Part I of the First Schedule to this Act shall not exceed fifteen;

(b) the number of persons entitled to sit and vote in that House while they are Ministers of the Crown named in Part II of the said Schedule shall not exceed three; and

(c) the number of persons entitled to sit and vote in that House while they are Parliamentary Under-Secretaries shall not exceed twenty.

(2) If at any time the number of persons who are members of the House of Commons while they are Ministers of the Crown named in Part I or in Part II of the First Schedule to this Act, or while they are Parliamentary Under-Secretaries, exceeds the number respectively entitled under this section to sit and vote in that House, the election of those members shall not be invalidated by reason of the excess, but of the number none except any who held his office and was a member of that House before the excess

occurred, shall sit or vote therein until the number of Ministers of the Crown named in the said Part I or in the said Part II or of Parliamentary Under-Secretaries, as the case may be, who are members of the House of Commons has been reduced, by death, resignation or otherwise, to the number entitled under this section to sit and vote in that House.

(3) If any Minister of the Crown named in Part I or in Part II of the First Schedule to this Act or any Parliamentary Under-Secretary sits or votes in the House of Commons at a time when he is not entitled to do so by virtue of this section he shall be liable to a penalty not exceeding five hundred pounds for each day on which he so sits or votes.

PART III

SUPPLEMENTARY

10. (1) In this Act unless the context otherwise requires the following expressions have the meanings hereby respectively assigned to them, that is to say:

"Junior Lords of the Treasury" means the Lords Commissioners of the Treasury other than the First Lord and the Chancellor of the Exchequer;

"Leader of the Opposition" means that member of the House of Commons who is for the time being the Leader in that House of the party in opposition to His Majesty's Government having the greatest numerical strength in that House;

"Parliamentary Under-Secretary" means the Parliamentary Secretary and the Financial Secretary to the Treasury, and Parliamentary Under-Secretary of State, the Parliamentary and Financial Secretary to the Admiralty, the Financial Secretary of the War Office, the Civil Lord of the Admiralty, the Parliamentary Secretaries to the Departments of State specified in the Second Schedule to this Act, and the Assistant Postmaster-General; but does not include any Parliamentary Secretary to whom no salary is payable.

(2) For the purposes of this Act, the Secretary of the Department of Overseas Trade shall be deemed to be a Parliamentary Secretary to the Board of Trade, but without prejudice to the provisions of the Overseas Trade Department (Secretary) Act, 1918, relating to the method of his appointment and the functions to be discharged by him.

(3) If any doubt arises as to which is or was at any material time the party in opposition to His Majesty's Government having the greatest numerical strength in the House of Commons, or as to who is or was at any material time the leader in that House of such a party, the question shall be decided for the purposes of this Act by the Speaker of the House of

Commons, and his decision, certified in writing under his hand, shall be final and conclusive.

11. (1) The enactments specified in the first column of the Third Schedule to this Act shall have effect subject to the amendments specified in the second column of that Schedule.

(2) The enactments specified in the first column of the Fourth Schedule to this Act are hereby repealed to the extent specified in the third column of that Schedule.

12. This Act may be cited as the Ministers of the Crown Act, 1937.

SCHEDULES

(*Not reproduced*)

First Schedule. Ministers of the Crown to whom Salaries are payable under this Act.

Second Schedule. Departments of State referred to in paragraph (c) of subsection (2) of Section 1 of this Act.

Third Schedule. Consequential amendment of enactments.

Fourth Schedule. Enactments repealed.

Ministers of the Crown Act 1964[1]

December, 23, 1964

Be it enacted by the Queen's most Excellent Majesty, by and with the advice and consent of the Lords Spiritual and Temporal, and Commons, in this present Parliament assembled, and by the authority of the same, as follows:

1. The provisions of Schedule 1 to this Act shall apply to the Minister of Land and Natural Resources, the Minister of Overseas Development and the Minister of Technology; and references in that Schedule to the Minister and the Ministry shall be construed accordingly.

2. (1) There shall be paid under and subject to the provisions of the Ministers of the Crown Act 1937:

(a) to any Minister to whom Schedule 1 to this Act applies, an annual salary of five thousand pounds;

(b) to the Chief Secretary to the Treasury and to any Minister of State,

[1] *An Act to make provision with respect to the departments and salaries of certain Ministers; to amend the provisions of the House of Commons Disqualification Act 1957 relating to Ministerial offices; to extend existing powers to transfer functions of Ministers; and for purposes connected with the matters aforesaid.* Eliz. II 1964 c. 98. HMSO.

an annual salary of such amount as the First Lord of the Treasury may determine, not exceeding in any case five thousand pounds;

(c) to any Parliamentary Under-Secretary of State to the Department of Economic Affairs or to the Welsh Office, and to any Parliamentary Secretary to the Ministry of a Minister to whom Schedule 1 to this Act applies, an annual salary two of thousand five hundred pounds;

(d) to any Assistant Government Whip in the House of Commons an annual salary of two thousand pounds.

(2) So much of section 1(2)(a) of the Ministers of the Crown Act 1937 as provides for the salary of the Economic Secretary to the Treasury and section 1(2)(b) of that Act (salary of the Secretary for Overseas Trade) shall cease to have effect.

(3) The number of persons to whom salaries may be paid at any time as the holders of Ministerial offices mentioned in this subsection shall be as follows, that is to say:

(a) in the case of Secretaries of State, not more than nine;

(b) in the case of Ministers of State, not more than nineteen;

(c) in the case of Treasury Secretaries, not more than two;

(d) in the case of Parliamentary Secretaries other than Treasury secretaries, not more than thirty-six;

(e) in the case of Assistant Government Whips, not more than six.

(4) In this section "Minister of State" has the same meaning as in the House of Commons Disqualification Act 1957; "Treasury Secretaries" means the Parliamentary Secretary and the Financial Secretary to the Treasury; and "Parliamentary Secretary" includes any Parliamentary Under-Secretary of State and the Assistant Postmaster General.

3. (1) There shall be included among the offices specified in Schedule 2 to the House of Commons Disqualification Act 1957 (Ministerial offices subject to the limits of numbers prescribed by section 2 of that Act) each office not already described therein in respect of which salary is payable by virtue of section 2 of this Act.

(2) So much of section 2 of the said Act of 1957 as prescribes a limit of twenty-seven upon the number of holders of Ministerial offices specified in Part I of the said Schedule 2 who may sit and vote in the House of Commons at any one time shall cease to have effect; and the limit of seventy prescribed by that section upon the number of holders of all Ministerial offices specified in that Schedule who may so sit and vote shall be raised to ninety-one.

4. The powers exercisable by Order in Council under section 1 of the Ministers of the Crown (Transfer of Functions) Act 1946 (transfer of functions from one Minister of the Crown to another) shall include power to direct that functions of any Minister of the Crown within the meaning of that Act shall be exercisable concurrently with another such Minister, or shall cease to be so exercisable; and references in that Act to the transfer of functions or to functions transferred shall be construed accordingly.

5. (1) Section 2 of the House of Commons Disqualification Act 1957, and Schedule 2 to that Act, shall be amended as provided by Part I of Schedule 2 to this Act, and accordingly shall have effect as set out in Part II of that Schedule.

(2) Subsection (2) of section 5 of the House of Commons Disqualification Act 1957 (reprinting of Schedule 1 as from time to time amended) shall apply to provisions of that Act other than Schedule 1 as it applies to that Schedule.

(3) In section 13(1) of the said Act, in the definition of "Minister of State," the words "appointed at a salary" shall be omitted, and at the end there shall be added the words "or any office in respect of which a salary is payable out of moneys provided by Parliament under section 2 of the Ministerial Salaries Act 1946."

(4) The enactments described in Schedule 3 to this Act are hereby repealed to the extent specified in column 3 of that Schedule.

6. (1) Any reference in this Act to any enactment is a reference thereto as amended by or under any other enactment including this Act.

(2) This Act may be cited as the Ministers of the Crown Act 1964.

SCHEDULES

(Not reproduced)

Schedule 1. Provisions as to new Ministers and their Departments.
Schedule 2. The House of Commons Disqualification Act 1957.
Schedule 3. Enactments repealed.

X. Indian Independence Act, 1947 [1]

July 18, 1947

Be it enacted by the King's most Excellent Majesty, by and with the advice and consent of the Lords Spiritual and Temporal, and Commons, in this present Parliament assembled, and by the authority of the same, as follows:

1. (1) As from the fifteenth day of August, nineteen hundred and forty-seven, two independent Dominions shall be set up in India, to be known respectively as India and Pakistan.

[1] *An Act to make provision for the setting up in India of two independent Dominions, to substitute other provisions for certain provisions of the Government of India Act, 1935, which apply outside those Dominions, and to provide for other matters consequential on or connected with the setting up of those Dominions.* 10 & 11 Geo. 6. HMSO.

(2) The said Dominions are hereafter in this Act referred to as "the new Dominions," and the said fifteenth day of August is hereafter in this Act referred to as "the appointed day."

2. (1) Subject to the provisions of subsections (3) and (4) of this section, the territories of India shall be the territories under the sovereignty of His Majesty which, immediately before the appointed day, were included in British India except the territories which, under subsection (2) of this section, are to be the territories of Pakistan.

(2) Subject to the provisions of subsections (3) and (4) of this section, the territories of Pakistan shall be:

(a) the territories which, on the appointed day, are included in the Provinces of East Bengal and West Punjab, as constituted under the two following sections;

(b) the territories which, at the date of the passing of this Act, are included in the Province of Sind and the Chief Commissioner's Province of British Baluchistan; and

(c) if, whether before or after the passing of this Act but before the appointed day, the Governor-General declares that the majority of the valid votes cast in the referendum which, at the date of the passing of this Act, is being or has recently been held in that behalf under his authority in the North West Frontier Province are in favour of representatives of that Province taking part in the Constituent Assembly of Pakistan, the territories which, at the date of the passing of this Act, are included in that Province.

(3) Nothing in this section shall prevent any area being at any time included in or excluded from either of the new Dominions, so, however, that:

(a) no area not forming part of the territories specified in subsection (1) or, as the case may be, subsection (2), of this section shall be included in either Dominion without the consent of that Dominion; and

(b) no area which forms part of the territories specified in the said subsection (1) or, as the case may be, the said subsection (2), or which has after the appointed day been included in either Dominion, shall be excluded from that Dominion without the consent of that Dominion.

(4) Without prejudice to the generality of the provisions of subsection (3) of this section, nothing in this section shall be construed as preventing the accession of Indian States to either of the new Dominions.

3. (1) As from the appointed day:

(a) the Province of Bengal, as constituted under the Government of India Act, 1935, shall cease to exist; and

(b) there shall be constituted in lieu thereof two new Provinces, to be known respectively as East Bengal and West Bengal.

(2) If, whether before or after the passing of this Act, but before the appointed day, the Governor-General declares that the majority of the

valid votes cast in the referendum which, at the date of the passing of this Act, is being or has recently been held in that behalf under his authority in the District of Sylhet are in favour of that District forming part of the new Province of East Bengal, then, as from that day, a part of the Province of Assam shall, in accordance with the provisions of subsection (3) of this section, form part of the new Province of East Bengal.

(3) The boundaries of the new Provinces aforesaid and, in the event mentioned in subsection (2) of this section, the boundaries after the appointed day of the Province of Assam, shall be such as may be determined, whether before or after the appointed day, by the award of a boundary commission appointed or to be appointed by the Governor-General in that behalf, but until the boundaries are so determined:

(a) the Bengal Districts specified in the First Schedule to this Act, together with, in the event mentioned in subsection (2) of this section, the Assam District of Sylhet, shall be treated as the territories which are to be comprised in the new Province of East Bengal;

(b) the remainder of the territories comprised at the date of the passing of this Act in the Province of Bengal shall be treated as the territories which are to be comprised in the new Province of West Bengal; and

(c) in the event mentioned in subsection (2) of this section, the District of Sylhet shall be excluded from the Province of Assam.

(4) In this section, the expression "award" means, in relation to a boundary commission, the decisions of the chairman of that commission contained in his report to the Governor-General at the conclusion of the commission's proceedings.

4. (1) As from the appointed day:

(a) the Province of the Punjab, as constituted under the Government of India Act, 1935, shall cease to exist; and

(b) there shall be constituted two new Provinces, to be known respectively as West Punjab and East Punjab.

(2) The boundaries of the said new Provinces shall be such as may be determined, whether before or after the appointed day, by the award of a boundary commission appointed or to be appointed by the Governor-General in that behalf, but until the boundaries are so determined:

(a) the Districts specified in the Second Schedule to this Act shall be treated as the territories to be comprised in the new Province of West Punjab; and

(b) the remainder of the territories comprised at the date of the passing of this Act in the Province of the Punjab shall be treated as the territories which are to be comprised in the new Province of East Punjab.

(3) In this section, the expression "award," means, in relation to a boundary commission, the decisions of the chairman of that commission contained in his report to the Governor-General at the conclusion of the commission's proceedings.

5. For each of the new Dominions, there shall be a Governor-General who shall be appointed by His Majesty and shall represent His Majesty for the purposes of the government of the Dominion:

Provided that, unless and until provision to the contrary is made by a law of the Legislature of either of the new Dominions, the same person may be Governor-General of both the new Dominions.

6. (1) The Legislature of each of the new Dominions shall have full power to make laws for that Dominion, including laws having extra-territorial operation.

(2) No law and no provision of any law made by the Legislature of either of the new Dominions shall be void or inoperative on the ground that it is repugnant to the law of England, or to the provisions of this or any existing or future Act of Parliament of the United Kingdom, or to any order, rule or regulation made under any such Act, and the powers of the Legislature of each Dominion include the power to repeal or amend any such Act, order, rule or regulation in so far as it is part of the law of the Dominion.

(3) The Governor-General of each of the new Dominions shall have full power to assent in His Majesty's name to any law of the Legislature of that Dominion and so much of any Act as relates to the disallowance of laws by His Majesty or the reservation of laws for the signification of His Majesty's pleasure thereon or the suspension of the operation of laws until the signification of His Majesty's pleasure thereon shall not apply to laws of the Legislature of either of the new Dominions.

(4) No Act of Parliament of the United Kingdom passed on or after the appointed day shall extend, or be deemed to extend, to either of the new Dominions as part of the law of that Dominion unless it is extended thereto by a law of the Legislature of the Dominion.

(5) No Order in Council made on or after the appointed day under any Act passed before the appointed day, and no order, rule or other instrument made on or after the appointed day under any such Act by any United Kingdom Minister or other authority, shall extend, or be deemed to extend, to either of the new Dominions as part of the law of that Dominion.

(6) The power referred to in subsection (1) of this section extends to the making of laws limiting for the future the powers of the Legislature of the Dominion.

7. (1) As from the appointed day:

(a) His Majesty's Government in the United Kingdom have no responsibility as respects the government of any of the territories which, immediately before that day, were included in British India;

(b) the suzerainty of His Majesty over the Indian States lapses, and with it, all treaties and agreements in force at the date of the passing of this Act between His Majesty and the rulers of Indian States, all functions exercisable by His Majesty at that date with respect to Indian States, all obligations of His Majesty existing at that date towards Indian States or the rulers thereof, and all powers, rights, authority or jurisdiction exercisable by His Majesty at that date in or in relation to Indian States by treaty, grant, usage, sufferance or otherwise; and

(c) there lapse also any treaties or agreements in force at the date of the passing of this Act between His Majesty and any persons having authority in the tribal areas, any obligations of His Majesty existing at that date to any such persons or with respect to the tribal areas, and all powers, rights, authority or jurisdiction exercisable at that date by His Majesty in or in relation to the tribal areas by treaty, grant, usage, sufferance or otherwise:

Provided that, notwithstanding anything in paragraph (b) or paragraph (c) of this subsection, effect shall, as nearly as may be, continue to be given to the provisions of any such agreement as is therein referred to which relate to customs, transit and communications, posts and telegraphs, or other like matters, until the provisions in question are denounced by the Ruler of the Indian State or person having authority in the tribal areas on the one hand, or by the Dominion or Province or other part thereof concerned on the other hand, or are superseded by subsequent agreeements.

(2) The assent of the Parliament of the United Kingdom is hereby given to the omission from the Royal Style and Titles of the words "Indiae Imperator" and the words "Emperor of India" and to the issue by His Majesty for that purpose of His Royal Proclamation under the Great Seal of the Realm.

8. (1) In the case of each of the new Dominions, the powers of the Legislature of the Dominion shall, for the purpose of making provision as to the constitution of the Dominion, be exercisable in the first instance by the Constituent Assembly of that Dominion, and references in this Act to the Legislature of the Dominion shall be construed accordingly.

(2) Except in so far as other provision is made by or in accordance with a law made by the Constituent Assembly of the Dominion under subsection (1) of this section, each of the new Dominions and all Provinces and other parts thereof shall be governed as nearly as may be in accordance with the Government of India Act, 1935; and the provisions of that Act, and of the Orders in Council, rules and other instruments made thereunder, shall, so far as applicable, and subject to any express provisions of this Act, and with such omissions, additions, adaptations and modifications as may be specified in orders of the Governor-General under the next succeeding section, have effect accordingly:

Provided that:

(a) the said provisions shall apply separately in relation to each of the new Dominions and nothing in this subsection shall be construed as continuing on or after the appointed day any Central Government or Legislature common to both the new Dominions;

(b) nothing in this subsection shall be construed as continuing in force on or after the appointed day any form of control by His Majesty's Government in the United Kingdom over the affairs of the new Dominions or of any Province or other part thereof;

(c) so much of the said provisions as requires the Governor-General or any Governor to act in his discretion or exercise his individual judgment as respects any matter shall cease to have effect as from the appointed day;

(d) as from the appointed day, no Provincial Bill shall be reserved under the Government of India Act, 1935, for the signification of His Majesty's pleasure, and no Provincial Act shall be disallowed by His Majesty thereunder; and

(e) the powers of the Federal Legislature or Indian Legislature under that Act, as in force in relation to each Dominion, shall, in the first instance, be exercisable by the Constituent Assembly of the Dominion in addition to the powers exercisable by that Assembly under subsection (1) of this section.

(3) Any provision of the Government of India Act, 1935, which, as applied to either of the new Dominions by subsection (2) of this section and the orders therein referred to, operates to limit the power of the legislature of that Dominion shall, unless and until other provision is made by or in accordance with a law made by the Constituent Assembly of the Dominion in accordance with the provisions of subsection (1) of this section, have the like effect as a law of the Legislature of the Dominion limiting for the future the powers of that Legislature.

9. (1) The Governor-General shall by order make such provision as appears to him to be necessary or expedient:

(a) for bringing the provisions of this Act into effective operation;

(b) for dividing between the new Dominions, and between the new Provinces to be constituted under this Act, the powers, rights, property, duties and liabilities of the Governor-General in Council or, as the case may be, of the relevant Provinces which, under this Act, are to cease to exist;

(c) for making omissions from, additions to, and adaptations and modifications of, the Government of India Act, 1935, and the Orders in Council, rules and other instruments made thereunder, in their application to the separate new Dominions;

(d) for removing difficulties arising in connection with the transition to the provisions of this Act;

(e) for authorising the carrying on of the business of the Governor-General in Council between the passing of this Act and the appointed day otherwise than in accordance with the provisions in that behalf of the Ninth Schedule to the Government of India Act, 1935;

(f) for enabling agreements to be entered into, and other acts done, on behalf of either of the new Dominions before the appointed day;

(g) for authorising the continued carrying on for the time being on behalf of the new Dominions, or on behalf of any two or more of the said new Provinces, of services and activities previously carried on on behalf of British India as a whole or on behalf of the former Provinces which those new Provinces represent;

(h) for regulating the monetary system and any matters pertaining to the Reserve Bank of India; and

(i) so far as it appears necessary or expedient in connection with any of the matters aforesaid, for varying the constitution, powers or jurisdiction of any legislature, court or other authority in the new Dominions and creating new legislatures, courts or other authorities therein.

(2) The powers conferred by this section on the Governor-General shall, in relation to their respective Provinces, be exercisable also by the Governors of the Provinces which, under this Act, are to cease to exist; and those powers shall, for the purposes of the Government of India Act, 1935, be deemed to be matters as respects which the Governors are, under that Act, to exercise their individual judgment.

(3) This section shall be deemed to have had effect as from the third day of June, nineteen hundred and forty-seven, and any order of the Governor-General or any Governor made on or after that date as to any matter shall have effect accordingly, and any order made under this section may be made so as to be retrospective to any date not earlier than the said third day of June:

Provided that no person shall be deemed to be guilty of an offence by reason of so much of any such order as makes any provision thereof retrospective to any date before the making thereof.

(4) Any orders made under this section, whether before or after the appointed day, shall have effect:

(a) up to the appointed day, in British India;

(b) on and after the appointed day, in the new Dominion or Dominions concerned; and

(c) outside British India, or, as the case may be, outside the new Dominion or Dominions concerned, to such extent, whether before, on or after the appointed day, as a law of the Legislature of the Dominion or Dominions concerned would have on or after the appointed day,

but shall, in the case of each of the Dominions, be subject to the same powers of repeal and amendment as laws of the Legislature of that Dominion.

(5) No order shall be made under this section, by the Governor of any Province, after the appointed day, or, by the Governor-General, after the thirty-first day of March, nineteen hundred and forty-eight, or such earlier

date as may be determined, in the case of either Dominion, by any law of the Legislature of that Dominion.

(6) If it appears that a part of the Province of Assam is, on the appointed day, to become part of the new Province of East Bengal, the preceding provisions of this section shall have effect as if, under this Act, the Province of Assam was to cease to exist on the appointed day and be reconstituted on that day as a new Province.

10. (1) The provisions of this Act keeping in force provisions of the Government of India Act, 1935, shall not continue in force the provisions of that Act relating to appointments to the civil services of, and civil posts under, the Crown in India by the Secretary of State, or the provisions of that Act relating to the reservation of posts.

(2) Every person who:

(a) having been appointed by the Secretary of State, or Secretary of State in Council, to a civil service of the Crown in India continues on and after the appointed day to serve under the Government of either of the new Dominions or of any Province or part thereof; or

(b) having been appointed by His Majesty before the appointed day to be a judge of the Federal Court or of any court which is a High Court within the meaning of the Government of India Act, 1935, continues on and after the appointed day to serve as a judge in either of the new Dominions,

shall be entitled to receive from the Governments of the Dominions and Provinces or parts which he is from time to time serving or, as the case may be, which are served by the courts in which he is from time to time a judge, the same conditions of service as respects remuneration, leave and pension, and the same rights as respects disciplinary matters or, as the case may be, as respects the tenure of his office, or rights as similar thereto as changed circumstances may permit, as that person was entitled to immediately before the appointed day.

(3) Nothing in this Act shall be construed as enabling the rights and liabilities of any person with respect to the family pension funds vested in Commissioners under section two hundred and seventy-three of the Government of India Act, 1935, to be governed otherwise than by Orders in Council made (whether before or after the passing of this Act or the appointed day) by His Majesty in Council and rules made (whether before or after the passing of this Act or the appointed day) by a Secretary of State or such other Minister of the Crown as may be designated in that behalf by Order in Council under the Ministers of the Crown (Transfer of Functions) Act, 1946.

11. (1) The orders to be made by the Governor-General under the preceding provisions of this Act shall make provision for the division of the Indian armed forces of His Majesty between the new Dominions, and for the command and governance of those forces until the division is completed.

(2) As from the appointed day, while any member of His Majesty's forces, other than His Majesty's Indian forces, is attached to or serving with any of His Majesty's Indian forces:

(a) he shall, subject to any provision to the contrary made by a law of the Legislature of the Dominion or Dominions concerned or by any order of the Governor-General under the preceding provisions of this Act, have, in relation to the Indian forces in question, the powers of command and punishment appropriate to his rank and functions; but

(b) nothing in any enactment in force at the date of the passing of this Act shall render him subject in any way to the law governing the Indian forces in question.

12. (1) Nothing in this Act affects the jurisdiction or authority of His Majesty's Government in the United Kingdom, or of the Admiralty, the Army Council, or the Air Council or of any other United Kingdom authority, in relation to any of His Majesty's forces which may, on or after the appointed day, be in either of the new Dominions or elsewhere in the territories which, before the appointed day, were included in India, not being Indian forces.

(2) In its application in relation to His Majesty's military forces, other than Indian forces, the Army Act shall have effect on or after the appointed day:

(a) as if His Majesty's Indian forces were not included in the expressions "the forces," "His Majesty's forces" and "the regular forces"; and

(b) subject to the further modifications specified in Parts I and II of the Third Schedule to this Act.

(3) Subject to the provisions of subsection (2) of this section, and to any provisions of any law of the Legislature of the Dominion concerned, all civil authorities in the new Dominions, and, subject as aforesaid and subject also to the provisions of the last preceding section, all service authorities in the new Dominions, shall, in those Dominions and in the other territories which were included in India before the appointed day, perform in relation to His Majesty's military forces, not being Indian forces, the same functions as were, before the appointed day, performed by them, or by the authorities corresponding to them, whether by virtue of the Army Act or otherwise, and the matters for which provision is to be made by orders of the Governor-General under the preceding provisions of this Act shall include the facilitating of the withdrawal from the new Dominions and other territories aforesaid of His Majesty's military forces, not being Indian forces.

(4) The provisions of subsections (2) and (3) of this section shall apply in relation to the air forces of His Majesty, not being Indian air forces, as

they apply in relation to His Majesty's military forces, subject, however to the necessary adaptations, and, in particular, as if:

(a) for the references to the Army Act there were substituted references to the Air Force Act; and

(b) for the reference to Part II of the Third Schedule to this Act there were substituted a reference to Part III of that Schedule.

13. (1) In the application of the Naval Discipline Act to His Majesty's naval forces, other than Indian naval forces, references to His Majesty's navy and His Majesty's ships shall not, as from the appointed day, include references to His Majesty's Indian navy or the ships thereof.

(2) In the application of the Naval Discipline Act by virtue of any law made in India before the appointed day to Indian naval forces, references to His Majesty's navy and His Majesty's ships shall, as from the appointed day, be deemed to be, and to be only, references to His Majesty's Indian navy and the ships thereof.

(3) In section ninety B of the Naval Discipline Act (which, in certain cases, subjects officers and men of the Royal Navy and Royal Marines to the law and customs of the ships and naval forces of other parts of His Majesty's dominions) the words "or of India" shall be repealed as from the appointed day, wherever those words occur.

14. (1) A Secretary of State, or such other Minister of the Crown as may be designated in that behalf by Order in Council under the Ministers of the Crown (Transfer of Functions) Act, 1946, is hereby authorised to continue for the time being the performance, on behalf of whatever government or governments may be concerned, of functions as to the making of payments and other matters similar to the functions which, up to the appointed day, the Secretary of State was performing on behalf of governments constituted or continued under the Government of India Act, 1935.

(2) The functions referred to in subsection (1) of this section include functions as respects the management of, and the making of payments in respect of, government debt, and any enactments relating to such debt shall have effect accordingly:

Provided that nothing in this subsection shall be construed as continuing in force so much of any enactment as empowers the Secretary of State to contract sterling loans on behalf of any such Government as aforesaid or as applying to the Government of either of the new Dominions the prohibition imposed on the Governor-General in Council by section three hundred and fifteen of the Government of India Act, 1935, as respects the contracting of sterling loans.

(3) As from the appointed day, there shall not be any such advisers of the Secretary of State as are provided for by section two hundred and seventy-eight of the Government of India Act, 1935, and that section, and any provisions of that Act which require the Secretary of State to

obtain the concurrence of his advisers, are hereby repealed as from that day.

(4) The Auditor of Indian Home Accounts is hereby authorised to continue for the time being to exercise his functions as respects the account of the Secretary of State or any such other Minister of the Crown as is mentioned in subsection (1) of this section, both in respect of activities before, and in respect of activities after, the appointed day, in the same manner, as nearly as may be as he would have done if this Act had not passed.

15. (1) Notwithstanding anything in this Act, and, in particular, notwithstanding any of the provisions of the last preceding section, any provision of any enactment which, but for the passing of this Act, would authorise legal proceedings to be taken, in India or elsewhere, by or against the Secretary of State in respect of any right or liability of India or any part of India shall cease to have effect on the appointed day, and any legal proceedings pending by virtue of any such provision on the appointed day shall, by virtue of this Act, abate on the appointed day, so far as the Secretary of State is concerned.

(2) Subject to the provisions of this subsection, any legal proceedings which, but for the passing of this Act, could have been brought by or against the Secretary of State in respect of any right or liability of India, or any part of India, shall instead be brought:

(a) in the case of proceedings in the United Kingdom, by or against the High Commissioner;

(b) in the case of other proceedings, by or against such person as may be designated by order of the Governor-General under the preceding provisions of this Act or otherwise by the law of the new Dominion concerned,

and any legal proceedings by or against the Secretary of State in respect of any such right or liability as aforesaid which are pending immediately before the appointed day shall be continued by or against the High Commissioner or, as the case may be, the person designated as aforesaid:

Provided that, at any time after the appointed day, the right conferred by this subsection to bring or continue proceedings may, whether the proceedings are by, or are against, the High Commissioner or person designated as aforesaid, be withdrawn by a law of the Legislature of either of the new Dominions so far as that Dominion is concerned, and any such law may operate as respects proceedings pending at the date of the passing of the law.

(3) In this section, the expression "the High Commissioner" means, in relation to each of the new Dominions, any such officer as may for the time being be authorised to perform in the United Kingdom, in relation to that Dominion, functions similar to those performed before the appointed day, in relation to the Governor-General in Council, by the High Com-

missioner referred to in section three hundred and two of the Government of India Act, 1935; and any legal proceedings which, immediately before the appointed day, are the subject of an appeal to His Majesty in Council, or of a petition for special leave to appeal to His Majesty in Council, shall be treated for the purposes of this section as legal proceedings pending in the United Kingdom.

16. (1) Subsections (2) to (4) of section two hundred and eighty-eight of the Government of India Act, 1935 (which confer on His Majesty power to make by Order in Council provision for the government of Aden) shall cease to have effect and the British Settlements Acts, 1887 and 1945, (which authorise His Majesty to make laws and establish institutions for British Settlements as defined in those Acts) shall apply in relation to Aden as if it were a British Settlement as so defined.

(2) Notwithstanding the repeal of the said subsections (2) to (4), the Orders in Council in force thereunder at the date of the passing of this Act shall continue in force, but the said Orders in Council, any other Orders in Council made under the Government of India Act, 1935, in so far as they apply to Aden, and any enactments applied to Aden or amended in relation to Aden by any such Orders in Council as aforesaid, may be repealed, revoked or amended under the powers of the British Settlements Acts, 1887 and 1945.

(3) Unless and until provision to the contrary is made as respects Aden under the powers of the British Settlements Acts, 1887 and 1945, or, as respects the new Dominion in question, by a law of the Legislature of that Dominion, the provisions of the said Orders in Council and enactments relating to appeals from any courts in Aden to any courts which will, after the appointed day, be in either of the new Dominions, shall continue in force in their application both to Aden and to the Dominion in question, and the last mentioned courts shall exercise their jurisdiction accordingly.

17. (1) No court in either of the new Dominions shall, by virtue of the Indian and Colonial Divorce Jurisdiction Acts, 1926 and 1940, have jurisdiction in or in relation to any proceedings for a decree for the dissolution of a marriage, unless those proceedings were instituted before the appointed day, but, save as aforesaid and subject to any provision to the contrary which may hereafter be made by any Act of the Parliament of the United Kingdom or by any law of the Legislature of the new Dominion concerned, all courts in the new Dominions shall have the same jurisdiction under the said Acts as they would have had if this Act had not been passed.

(2) Any rules made on or after the appointed day under subsection (4) of section one of the Indian and Colonial Divorce Jurisdiction Act, 1926, for a court in either of the new Dominions shall, instead of being made by the Secretary of State with the concurrence of the Lord Chancellor, be made by such authority as may be determined by the law of the Dominion concerned, and so much of the said subsection and of any rules in force

thereunder immediately before the appointed day as require the approval of the Lord Chancellor to the nomination for any purpose of any judges of any such court shall cease to have effect.

(3) The reference in subsection (1) of this section to proceedings for a decree for the dissolution of a marriage include references to proceedings for such a decree of presumption of death and dissolution of a marriage as is authorised by section eight of the Matrimonial Causes Act, 1937.

(4) Nothing in this section affects any court outside the new Dominions, and the power conferred by section two of the Indian and Colonial Divorce Jurisdiction Act, 1926, to apply certain provisions of that Act to other parts of His Majesty's dominions as they apply to India shall be deemed to be power to apply those provisions as they would have applied to India if this Act had not passed.

18. (1) In so far as any Act of Parliament, Order in Council, order, rule, regulation or other instrument passed or made before the appointed day operates otherwise than as part of the law of British India or the new Dominions, references therein to India or British India, however worded and whether by name or not, shall, in so far as the context permits and except so far as Parliament may hereafter otherwise provide, be construed as, or as including, references to the new Dominions, taken together, or taken separately, according as the circumstances and subject matter may require:

Provided that nothing in this subsection shall be construed as continuing in operation any provision so in far as the continuance thereof as adapted by this subsection is inconsistent with any of the provisions of this Act other than this section.

(2) Subject to the provisions of subsection (1) of this section and to any other express provision of this Act, the Orders in Council made under subsection (5) of section three hundred and eleven of the Government of India Act, 1935, for adapting and modifying Acts of Parliament shall, except so far as Parliament may hereafter otherwise provide, continue in force in relation to all Acts in so far as they operate otherwise than as part of the law of British India or the new Dominions.

(3) Save as otherwise expressly provided in this Act, the law of British India and of the several parts thereof existing immediately before the appointed day shall, so far as applicable and with the necessary adaptations, continue as the law of each of the new Dominions and the several parts thereof until other provision is made by laws of the Legislature of the Dominion in question or by any other Legislature or other authority having power in that behalf.

(4) It is hereby declared that the Instruments of Instructions issued before the passing of this Act by His Majesty to the Governor-General and the Governors of Provinces lapse as from the appointed day, and nothing in this Act shall be construed as continuing in force any provision of the

Government of India Act, 1935, relating to such Instruments of Instructions.

(5) As from the appointed day, so much of any enactment as requires the approval of His Majesty in Council to any rules of court shall not apply to any court in either of the new Dominions.

19. (1) References in this Act to the Governor-General shall, in relation to any order to be made or other act done on or after the appointed day, be construed:

(a) where the order or other act concerns one only of the new Dominions, as references to the Governor-General of that Dominion;

(b) where the order or other act concerns both of the new Dominions and the same person is the Governor-General of both those Dominions, as references to that person; and

(c) in any other case, as references to the Governors-General of the new Dominions, acting jointly.

(2) References in this Act to the Governor-General shall, in relation to any order to be made or other act done before the appointed day, be construed as references to the Governor-General of India within the meaning of the Government of India Act, 1935, and so much of that or any other Act as requires references to the Governor-General to be construed as references to the Governor-General in Council shall not apply to references to the Governor-General in this Act.

(3) References in this Act to the Constituent Assembly of a Dominion shall be construed as references:

(a) in relation to India, to the Constituent Assembly, the first sitting whereof was held on the ninth day of December, nineteen hundred and forty-six, modified:

(i) by the exclusion of the members representing Bengal, the Punjab, Sind and British Baluchistan; and

(ii) should it appear that the North West Frontier Province will form part of Pakistan, by the exclusion of the members representing that Province; and

(iii) by the inclusion of members representing West Bengal and East Punjab; and

(iv) should it appear that, on the appointed day, a part of the Province of Assam is to form part of the new Province of East Bengal, by the exclusion of the members theretofore representing the Province of Assam and the inclusion of members chosen to represent the remainder of that Province;

(b) in relation to Pakistan, to the Assembly set up or about to be set up at the date of the passing of this Act under the authority of the Governor-General as the Constituent Assembly for Pakistan:

Provided that nothing in this subsection shall be construed as affecting the extent to which representatives of the Indian States take part in either of the said Assemblies, or as preventing the filling of casual vacancies in the said Assemblies, or as preventing the participation in either of the said Assemblies, in accordance with such arrangements as may be made in that behalf, of representatives of the tribal areas on the borders of the Dominion for which that Assembly sits, and the powers of the said Assemblies shall extend and be deemed always to have extended to the making of provision for the matters specified in this proviso.

(4) In this Act, except so far as the context otherwise requires:

references to the Government of India Act, 1935, include references to any enactments amending or supplementing that Act, and, in particular, references to the India (Central Government and Legislature) Act, 1946;

"India," where the reference is to a state of affairs existing before the appointed day or which would have existed but for the passing of this Act, has the meaning assigned to it by section three hundred and eleven of the Government of India Act, 1935;

"Indian forces" includes all His Majesty's Indian forces existing before the appointed day and also any forces of either of the new Dominions;

"pension" means, in relation to any person, a pension whether contributory or not, of any kind whatsoever payable to or in respect of that person, and includes retired pay so payable, a gratuity so payable and any sum or sums so payable by way of the return, with or without interest thereon or other additions thereto, of subscriptions to a provident fund;

"Province" means a Governor's Province;

"remuneration" includes leave pay, allowances and the cost of any privileges or facilities provided in kind.

(5) Any power conferred by this Act to make any order includes power to revoke or vary any order previously made in the exercise of that power

20. This Act may be cited as the Indian Independence Act, 1947.

SCHEDULES

(Not reproduced)

First Schedule. Bengal districts provisionally included in the new province of East Bengal.

Second Schedule. Districts provisionally included in the new province of West Punjab.

Third Schedule. Modifications of Army Act and Air Force Act in relation to British Forces.

XI. Representation of the People Act, 1949 [1]

(*Extracts*)
November 24, 1949

Be it enacted by the King's most Excellent Majesty, by and with the advice and consent of the Lords Spiritual and Temporal, and Commons, in this present Parliament assembled, and by the authority of the same, as follows:

PART I

PARLIAMENTARY AND

LOCAL GOVERNMENT FRANCHISE AND ITS EXERCISE

Parliamentary and local government franchise

1. (1) Subject to the provisions of subsection (2) of this section, the persons entitled to vote as electors at a parliamentary election in any constituency shall be those resident there on the qualifying date who, on that date and on the date of the poll, are of full age and not subject to any legal incapacity to vote and either British subjects or citizens of the Republic of Ireland:

Provided that a person shall not be entitled to vote as an elector in any constituency unless registered there in the register of parliamentary electors to be used at the election nor, at a general election, to vote as an elector in more than one constituency.

(2) A person shall not be entitled to vote as an elector at a parliamentary election in any constituency in Northern Ireland unless he was resident in Northern Ireland during the whole of the period of three months ending on the qualifying date for that election:

Provided that this subsection shall not have effect with respect to the autumn register published in the year nineteen hundred and forty-nine or any election for which that register is to be used.

(3) A person shall not vote as elector more than once in the same constituency at any parliamentary election.

2. (1) The persons entitled to vote as electors at a local government election in any electoral area shall be those who:

(a) on the qualifying date either:

[1] *An Act to consolidate certain enactments relating to parliamentary and local government elections, corrupt and illegal practices and election petitions.* 12 & 13 Geo. 6. HMSO.

(i) are resident in the area; or

(ii) under the provisions of section five of this Act have a non-resident qualification therein; and

(b) are in either case on that date and on the date of the poll, of full age and not subject to any legal incapacity to vote and either British subjects or citizens of the Republic of Ireland:

Provided that a person shall not be entitled to vote as an elector in any electoral area, unless registered there in the register of local government electors to be used at the election nor, at an ordinary election for any local government area which is not a single electoral area, to vote as an elector in more than one electoral area.

(2) A person shall not vote as elector more than once in the same electoral area at any local government election.

. . . .

7. (1) It shall be the duty of every registration officer to prepare and publish in the spring and autumn of each year:

(a) a register of parliamentary electors for each constituency or part of a constituency in the area for which he acts; and

(b) a register of local government electors for the local government areas or parts of local government areas included in the area for which he acts.

(2) The registers of parliamentary electors and of local government electors shall so far as practicable be combined, the names of persons registered only as local government electors being marked to indicate that fact.

(3) The elections for which any register is to be used and the date of the publication of the register shall be determined in accordance with the provisions of the First Schedule to this Act.

8. (1) Subject to any enactment imposing any disqualification for registration as a parliamentary elector, all persons who may be entitled to vote as electors at parliamentary elections for which any register is to be used shall be entitled to be registered therein:

Provided that a person who on the qualifying date has a service qualification shall not be entitled to be registered except in pursuance of a service declaration made in accordance with section ten of this Act and in force on that date.

(2) Subject to any enactment imposing any disqualification for registration as a local government elector, all persons who may be entitled to vote as electors at local government elections for which any register is to be used shall be entitled to be registered therein:

Provided that:

(a) a person shall not be entitled to be registered more than once in any local government area;

(b) a person entitled as a resident to be registered as a local government elector in any local government area shall not be entitled to be so registered as a non-resident; and

(c) a person who on the qualifying date has a service qualification shall not be entitled to be registered as redsient in any local government area, except in pursuance of a service declaration made in accordance with section ten of this Act and in force on that date.

....

12. (1) All persons voting as electors at a parliamentary election shall do so in person at the polling station allotted to them under the parliamentary elections rules except in so far as this section makes exceptions for:

(a) those registered as service voters;

(b) those unable or likely to be unable to go in person to the polling station for one of the following reasons:

(i) the general nature of the occupation, service or employment of the person in question;

(ii) that person's service as a member of any of His Majesty's reserve or auxiliary forces;

(iii) the particular circumstances of that person's employment on the date of the poll either as a constable or, for a purpose connected with the election, by the returning officer;

(iv) at a general election, the candidature in some other constituency of that person or that person's wife or husband;

(v) at a general election, the fact that that person is acting as returning officer for some other constituency;

(vi) at a general election, the particular circumstances of that person's employment on the date of the poll by the returning officer for some other constituency for a purpose connected with the election in that constituency;

(c) those unable or likely to be unable, by reason either of blindness or or any other physical incapacity, to go in person to the polling station or, if able to go, to vote unaided;

(d) those unable or likely to be unable to go in person from their qualifying address to the polling station without making a journey by air or sea;

(e) those no longer residing at their qualifying address.

(2) A person registered as a service voter may vote by proxy unless either:

(a) he is entitled in pursuance of an application made under subsection (4) of this section to vote by post; or

(b) he applies for a ballot paper to vote in person before a ballot paper has been issued for him to vote by proxy;

but (where there is in force an appointment of a proxy to vote for him) shall not be entitled to vote in person unless he does so apply.

(3) A person not registered as a service voter if unable or likely to be unable to go in person to the polling station by reason either:

(a) of the general nature of his occupation, service or employment; or

(b) of his service as a member of any of His Majesty's reserve or auxiliary forces;

may vote by proxy if he applies to be treated as an absent voter and is likely to be at sea or out of the United Kingdom on the date of the poll.

(4) Any of the persons mentioned in paragraphs (a) to (e) of subsection (1) of this section may vote by post if he applies to be treated as an absent voter and furnishes an address in the United Kingdom to which a ballot paper is to be sent for the purpose:

Provided that:

(a) a person shall not be entitled to vote by post if he is not registered as a service voter and there is in force an appointment of a proxy to vote for him; and

(b) a person shall not be entitled to vote by post on the ground that he no longer resides at his qualifying address if at the time of his application he resides at an address in the same area; and

(c) a person registered as a service voter shall not be entitled to vote by post on any ground other than his being so registered.

(5) At an election for which a person's application to be treated as an absent voter is allowed, he shall not be entitled to vote in person.

(6) A person not registered as a service voter, if he is entitled to vote in person, but unable or likely to be unable to go in person to the polling station allotted to him by reason of the particular circumstances of his employment on the date of the poll either as a constable or, for a purpose connected with the election, by the returning officer, may vote at any polling station of the constituency.

(7) For the purposes of subsection (4) of this section, two addresses shall be deemed to be in the same area if they satifsy one of the following conditions, but not otherwise, that is to say:

(a) both are within the area of the same borough or urban district;

(b) both are within the area of the same parish in England or Wales, or of the same electoral division in Scotland, or of the same rural district in Northern Ireland.

(8) Nothing in this section shall be taken as conferring a right to vote on a person not having the right apart from this section.

. . . .

Conduct of parliamentary elections

16. (1) The proceedings at a parliamentary election shall be conducted in accordance with the parliamentary elections rules in the Second Schedule to this Act.

(2) It shall be the general duty of the returning officer at a parliamentary election to do all such acts and things as may be necessary for effectually conducting the election in manner provided by the said parliamentary elections rules.

(3) No parliamentary election shall be declared invalid by reason of any act or omission by the returning officer or any other person in breach of his official duty in connection with the election of otherwise or the parliamentary elections rules if it appears to the tribunal having cognizance of the question that the election was so conducted as to be substantially in accordance with the law as to elections, and that the act or omission did not affect its result.

....

Supplemental provisions as to parliamentary and local governments elections

39. (1) The register of parliamentary electors shall for the purposes of this Part of this Act be conclusive on the following questions:

(a) whether or not a person registered therein was on the qualifying date resident at the address shown;

(b) whether or not that address is in any constituency or any particular part of a constituency;

(c) whether or not a person registered as an elector in a constituency in Northern Ireland was during the whole of the period of three months ending on the qualifying date resident in Northern Ireland;

(d) whether or not a person registered therein is registered as a service voter

(2) The register of local government electors shall for the purposes of this Part of this Act be conclusive on the following questions:

(a) whether a person registered therein is so registered as a resident or as a non-resident, and whether or not on the qualifying date he was resident at the address shown or had a non-resident qualification in respect of that address, as the case may be;

(b) whether or not that address is in any local government area or any particular part of a local government area;

(c) whether or not a person registered therein as a resident is registered as a service voter;

(d) in the case of a person registered at more than one address in the same local government area, at which of those addresses he is registered as a local government elector for that area.

(3) The relevant special lists prepared under this Act for a parliamentary or local government election shall, for the purposes of this Part of this Act, be conclusive on the following questions:

(a) whether or not a person's right to vote at the election is exercisable by post;

(b) whether or not there is in force an appointment of a proxy to vote for any person and (if so) who is appointed.

(4) A person registered as a parliamentary or local government elector, or entered in the list of proxies, shall not be excluded from voting on the ground that he is not a British subject or citizen of the Republic of Ireland or is not of full age or is otherwise subject to any legal incapacity to vote, or that on the qualifying date or the date of his appointment, as the case may be, he was not a British subject or citizen of the Republic of Ireland or was not of full age or was otherwise subject to any legal incapacity to vote; but this provision shall not prevent the rejection of the vote on a scrutiny or affect his liability to any penalty for voting.

(5) No misnomer or inaccurate description of any person or place named in the register of parliamentry electors or in the register of local government electors or in any list, record, proxy paper, nomination paper, ballot paper, notice or other document required for the purposes of this Part of this Act shall affect the full operation of the document with respect to that person or place in any case where the description of the person or place is such as to be commonly understood.

....

53. (1) The following persons, that is to say:

(a) every returning officer and every presiding officer or clerk attending at a polling station;

(b) every candidate or election agent or polling agent so attending;

shall maintain and aid in maintaining the secrecy of voting and shall not, except for some purpose authorised by law, communicate to any person before the poll is closed any information as to:

(i) the name of any elector or proxy for an elector who has or has not applied for a ballot paper or voted at a polling station;

(ii) the number on the register of electors of any elector who, or whose proxy, has or has not applied for a ballot paper or voted at a polling station; or

(iii) the official mark.

(2) Every person attending at the counting of the votes shall maintain and aid in maintaining the secrecy of voting and shall not:

(a) ascertain or attempt to ascertain at the counting of the votes the number on the back of any ballot paper;

(b) communicate any information obtained at the counting of the votes as to the candidate for whom any vote is given on any particular ballot paper.

(3) No person whosoever shall:

(a) interfere with or attempt to interfere with a voter when recording his vote;

(b) otherwise obtain or attempt to obtain in a polling station information as to the candidate for whom a voter in that station is about to vote or has voted;

(c) communicate at any time to any person any information obtained in a polling station as to the candidate for whom a voter in that station is about to vote or has voted, or as to the number on the back of the ballot paper given to a voter at that station;

(d) directly or indirectly induce a voter to display his ballot paper after he has marked it so as to make known to any person the name of the candidate for whom he has or has not voted.

(4) Every person attending the proceedings in connection with the issue or the receipt of ballot papers for persons voting by post shall maintain and aid in maintaining the secrecy of the voting and shall not:

(a) except for some purpose authorised by law, communicate, before the poll is closed, to any person any information obtained at those proceedings as to the official mark; or

(b) except for some purpose authorised by law, communicate to any person at any time any information obtained at those proceedings as to the number on the back of the ballot paper sent to any person; or

(c) except for some purpose authorised by law, attempt to ascertain at the proceedings in connection with the receipt of ballot papers the number on the back of any ballot paper; or

(d) attempt to ascertain at the proceedings in connection with the receipt of the ballot papers the candidate for whom any vote is given in any particular ballot paper or communicate any information with respect thereto obtained at those proceedings.

(5) No person having undertaken to assist a blind voter to vote shall communicate at any time to any person any information as to the candidate for whom that voter intends to vote or has voted, or as to the number on the back of the ballot paper given for the use of that voter.

(6) If any person acts in contravention of this section he shall be liable on summary conviction to imprisonment for a term not exceeding six months.

. . . .

SCHEDULES

(Not reproduced)

XII. Peerage Act 1963[1]

July 31, 1963

Be it enacted by the Queen's most Excellent Majesty, by and with the advice and consent of the Lords Spiritual and Temporal, and Commons, in this present Parliament assembled, and by the authority of the same, as follows:

Disclaimer of Peerage

1. (1) Subject to the provisions of this section, any person who, after the commencement of this Act, succeeds to a peerage in the peerage of England, Scotland, Great Britain or the United Kingdom may, by an instrument of disclaimer delivered to the Lord Chancellor within the period prescribed by this Act, disclaim that peerage for his life.

(2) Any instrument of disclaimer to be delivered under this section in respect of a peerage shall be delivered within the period of twelve months beginning with the day on which the person disclaiming succeeds to that peerage or, if he is under the age of twenty-one when he so succeeds, the period of twelve months beginning with the day on which he attains that age; and no such instrument shall be delivered in respect of a peerage by a person who has applied for a writ of summons to attend the House of Lords in right of that peerage.

(3) The foregoing provisions of this section shall apply to a person who has succeeded to a peerage before the commencement of this Act as they apply to a person who succeeds to a peerage after the commencement of this Act, but subject to the following modifications:

(a) the period within which an instrument of disclaimer may be delivered by such a person shall be twelve months beginning with the commencement of this Act or, if he is then under twenty-one years of age, twelve months beginning with the day on which he attains that age; and

(b) an instrument of disclaimer may be delivered by such a person notwithstanding that he has applied before the commencement of this Act for a writ of summons to attend the House of Lords.

(4) In reckoning any period prescribed by this section for the delivery of an instrument of disclaimer by any person no account shall be taken of any time during which that person is shown to the satisfaction of the Lord

[1] *An Act to authorise the disclaimer for life of certain hereditary peerages; to include among the peers qualified to sit in the House of Lords all peers in the peerage of Scotland and peeresses in their own right in the peerages if England, Scotland, Great Britain and the United Kingdom; to remove certain disqualifications of peers in the peerage of Ireland in relation to the House of Commons and elections thereto; and for purposes connected with the matters aforesaid.* Eliz. II 1963 c. 48. HMSO.

Chancellor to have been subject to any infirmity of body or mind rendering him incapable of exercising or determining whether to exercise his rights under this section.

(5) The provisions of Schedule 1 to this Act shall have effect with respect to the form of instruments of disclaimer under this section, and the delivery, certification and registration of such instruments.

2. (1) Where a person who succeeds to a peerage to which section 1 of this Act applies is a member of the House of Commons when he so succeeds, any instrument of disclaimer to be delivered by him under that section in respect of that peerage shall be delivered within the period of one month beginning with the date of his succession, and not later; and until the expiration of that period he shall not, by virtue of that peerage, be disqualified for membership of the House of Commons whether or not he has delivered such an instrument:

Provided that:

(a) a person who is exempt from disqualification for membership of the House of Commons by virtue only of this subsection shall not sit or vote in that House while so exempt; and

(b) if any such person applies for a writ of summons to attend the House of Lords in right of the peerage in question, this subsection shall cease to apply to him.

(2) Where a person who succeeds to such a peerage as aforesaid has been or is nominated as a candidate at a parliamentary election held in pursuance of a writ issued before his succession, he shall not (unless he applies for such a writ of summons as aforesaid) be disqualified by virtue of that peerage for election to the House of Commons at that election, and if he is so elected subsection (1) of this section shall apply to him as if he had succeeded to the peerage immediately after the declaration of the result of the election.

(3) Where an instrument of disclaimer is delivered under this Act by a person to whom this section applies, a copy of that instrument shall be delivered to the Speaker of the House of Commons.

(4) In reckoning any period prescribed by this section in relation to any person no account shall be taken:

(a) of any time during which proceedings are pending on any parliamentary election petition in which the right of that person to be elected or returned to the House of Commons is in issue;

(b) of any time during which that person is shown to the satisfaction of the Speaker of the House of Commons to have been subject to any such infirmity as is mentioned in subsection (4) of section 1 of this Act; or

(c) of any time during which Parliament is prorogued or both Houses of Parliament are adjourned for more than four days;

and if Parliament is dissolved during that period the foregoing provisions of this section shall cease to apply to that person in respect of the peerage in question.

3. (1) The disclaimer of a peerage by any person under this Act shall be irrevocable and shall operate, from the date on which the instrument of disclaimer is delivered,

(a) to divest that person (and, if he is married, his wife) of all right or interest to or in the peerage, and all titles, rights, offices, privileges and precedence attaching thereto; and

(b) to relieve him of all obligations and disabilities (including any disqualification in respect of membership of the House of Commons and elections to that House) arising therefrom,

but shall not accelerate the succession to that peerage nor affect its devolution on his death.

(2) Where a peerage is disclaimed under this Act, no other hereditary peerage shall be conferred upon the person by whom it is disclaimed, and no writ in acceleration shall be issued in respect of that peerage to the person entitled thereto on his death.

(3) The disclaimer of a peerage under this Act shall not affect any right, interest or power (whether arising before or after the disclaimer) of the person by whom the peerage is disclaimed, or of any other person, to, in or over any estates or other property limited or settled to devolve with that peerage.

(4) The reference in the foregoing subsection to estates or other property limited or settled to devolve with a peerage shall, for the purposes of the application of this Act to Scotland, be construed as including a reference to estates or other land devolving as aforesaid under an entail or special destination, or the beneficial interest in which so devolves under a trust.

Parliamentary qualifications of Scottish Peers, Irish Peers and Peeresses in own right

4. The holder of a peerage in the peerage of Scotland shall have the same right to receive writs of summons to attend the House of Lords, and to sit and vote in that House, as the holder of a peerage in the peerage of the United Kingdom; and the enactments relating to the election of Scottish representative peers shall cease to have effect.

5. The holder of a peerage in the peerage of Ireland shall not by virtue of that peerage be disqualified:

(a) for being or being elected as a member of the House of Commons for any constituency in the United Kingdom; or

(b) for voting at elections for that House whether or not he is a member of that House.

6. A woman who is the holder of a hereditary peerage in the peerage of England, Scotland, Great Britain or the United Kingdom shall (whatever the terms of the letters patent or other instrument, if any, creating that peerage) have the same right to receive writs of summons to attend the House of Lords, and to sit and vote in that House, and shall be subject to the same disqualifications in respect of membership of the House of Commons and elections to that House, as a man holding that peerage.

Supplemental

7. (1) This Act may be cited as the Peerage Act 1963.

(2) The enactments described in Schedule 2 to this Act are hereby repealed to the extent mentioned in column 3 of that Schedule.

SCHEDULES

(*Not reproduced*)

Schedule 1. Form, Delivery, Certification and Registration of Instruments of Disclaimer.

Schedule 2. Enactments repealed.

VATICAN CITY STATE

SUMMARY [1]

The Vatican City State was created by the Lateran Treaty of February 11, 1929, which settled between the Holy See and the Italian Government the "Roman Question" which dated from the occupation of Rome by Italian troops in 1870. It is a territorial State whose constitutional structure is determined by the purpose for which it exists, namely the safeguarding and guaranteeing of the independence and freedom of the Holy

[1] Source used for summary *"L'Organisation administrative du Saint-Siège et de la Cité du Vatican"* by Vittorio Bachelet, CDU 354 (456. 31) supplied by Secretariat of State, The Vatican.

See which is the governing body of the universal Catholic Church.[1] "The Holy See, so far as concerns the sovereignty belonging to it in the international domain, declares that it wishes to remain and will remain removed from the temporal competitions among other states and from international meetings convoked with such a purpose, unless the parties to a dispute make a unanimous appeal to its mission of peace, reserving to itself, however, the right to assert in every case its moral and spiritual power. In consequence the City of the Vatican shall always and in every case be considered as neutral and inviolable territory." [2] It is not a member of any international organization other than the International Postal and International Telecommunications Unions.

The constitutional documents of the Vatican City State are the Lateran Treaty of February 11, 1929, by which Italy recognizes the exclusive sovereignty and jurisdiction of the Holy See over the City of the Vatican and the sovereignty of the Holy See in the international domain,[3] the Concordat between the Holy See and Italy of the same date which regulates the conditions of religion and the Church in Italy, and the Fundamental Laws of June 7, 1929, comprising the Fundamental Law of the City of the Vatican, the Law of the Sources of the Law, the Law on the Rights of Citizenship and Sojourn, the Law on Administrative Organization, the Law of Public Security and the Ordinance provisionally controlling access to the City.

The Vatican City State is an elective monarchy and its sovereign, the Pope is the holder of all legislative, executive and judicial power, his supreme power and jurisdiction being derived from unchangeable divine laws.[4] The organ of the Sovereign (the Pope *sede plena* or the Sacred College of Cardinals *sede vacante*), the Vatican City State shares with the Holy See. Also common to both are some of the Tribunals, Offices and Sacred Congregations which together make up the Roman Curia, the organization whereof is governed by ecclesiastical laws which may be modified. The Vatican City's own organs, directly subordinate to the Sovereign Pontiff, are the Pontifical Commission for the Government of the State of Vatican City, the Governor, the General Counsellor and its own administration.

The Pope represents the Vatican City State in its relations with foreign states through the Secretariat of State.[5] The Pope has the power of pardon.[6] He delegates certain legislative and executive powers to the Governor who is appointed by and responsible to the Sovereign Pontiff.[7] The Governor's duties and powers are described in the Law on Administrative Organization. He presents the administrative budgets and accounts to the Pope.[8] The consultative organ of the Vatican City State is the General

[1] Lateran Tr., Preamble [2] Id., Art. 24. [3] Id., Art. 2, 3, 4.
[4] Fund. Law., Art. 1. [5] Id., Art. 3. [6] Id., Art. 18
[7] Id., Art. 5–7. [8] Id., Art. 4.

Counsellor of the State, appointed by and responsible to the Sovereign Pontiff.[1] The judicial power is delegated to tribunals of the first instance and exercised by the Sacred Roman Rota as a court of appeal; in extraordinary cases recourse may be had to the Supreme Tribunal of the Signature.[2] There is provision for appeals against administrative acts.[3] The sources of law are the *Codex juris* and apostolic constitutions, laws and regulations promulgated for the Vatican City by the Sovereign Pontiff or a competent authority delegated by him, and, in a supplementary manner, laws promulgated by Italy insofar as they are applicable.[4]

The area of the Vatican City State is 44 hectares (108.7 acres), its population about 900.

[1] Id., Art. 8. [2] Id., Art. 10. [3] Id., Art. 15, 16.
[4] Law on Sources of Law, Art. 1–4.

Lateran Treaty[1]

February 11, 1929

In the name of the Holy Trinity:

Inasmuch as the Holy See and Italy have recognized the necessity of setting aside all causes of difference existing between them and of arriving at a definitive settlement of their reciprocal relations which would be in accordance with justice and the dignity of the two high parties and which, while assuring to the Holy See in a stable manner a situation of fact and of law that would guarantee to it absolute independence for the accomplishment of its high mission in the world, would also permit the Holy See to recognize that the "Roman question," originating in 1870 from the annexation of Rome to the Kingdom of Italy under the dynasty of the House of Savoy, is resolved in a definitive and irrevocable manner; and

As it is necessary, in order to assure to the Holy See absolute and visible independence, to guarantee to it unquestionable sovereignty even in the international domain, and the necessity is therefore apparent of constituting the "City of the Vatican" with special characteristics by recognizing the full ownership, exclusive and absolute power, and sovereign jurisdiction of the Holy See over this territory:

His Holiness the High Pontiff Pius XI and His Majesty Victor Emmanuel III King of Italy, have resolved to draw up a Treaty and have appointed for this purpose two Plenipotentiaries, His Eminence the Most Reverend Cardinal Pietro Gasparri, His Secretary of State, representing His Holiness, and His Excellency Signor Cavaliere Benito Mussolini, Prime Minister and Head of the Government, representing His Majesty; who, their respective Full Powers having been exchanged and found to be in good and due form, have agreed to the following Articles:

Art. 1. Italy recognizes and reaffirms the principle consecrated in Article 1 of the Statute of the Kingdom dated March 4, 1848, by virtue of which the Catholic, apostolic, and Roman religion is the only religion of the State.

Art. 2. Italy recognizes the sovereignty of the Holy See in the inter-

[1] *Inter Sanctam Sedem et Italiae Regnum Conventiones. Trattato fra la Santa Sede e l'Italia. Acta Apostolicae Sedis. Commentarium officiale. Annus XXI–Vol. XXI. 7 Iunii 1929. Num. 6,* Rome. *Typis Polyglottis Vaticanis.* Supplied by the Secretariat of State, The Vatican in December 1966. Translation contained in 2nd Edition, revised by the Editor. Ed.

national domain as an attribute inherent in its nature, in accordance with its tradition and with the requirements of its mission in the world.

Art. 3. Italy recognizes that the Holy See has full ownership, exclusive and absolute power, and sovereign jurisdiction over the Vatican, as it is at present constituted with all its dependencies and endowments, creating thus the City of the Vatican for its special ends and with the characteristics set forth in the present Treaty. The limits of the said city are indicated on the plan which constitutes Annex 1 of the said Treaty of which it forms an integral part.

It is, moreover, understood that Saint Peter's Square, while it forms a part of the City of the Vatican, will continue to be normally open to the public and subject to the police powers of the Italian authorities; these will stop at the foot of the stairs of the Basilica, although that will continue to be destined for public worship, and they will abstain from mounting or entering the Basilica except in the case of being invited to intervene by the competent authority.

In case the Holy See, in view of particular ceremonies, should deem it advisable to suspend temporarily the free passage of the public, through Saint Peter's Square, the Italian authorities, unless invited to remain by the competent authority, will retire beyond the exterior lines of the colonnade of Bernini and of their extension.

Art. 4. The exclusive sovereignty and jurisdiction of the Holy See over the City of the Vatican which Italy recognizes, implies the consequence that no interference on the part of the Italian government may be there manifested, and that there will be no other authority than that of the Holy See.

Art. 5. For the execution of all that is established in the preceding Article, the territory constituting the City of the Vatican should be, through the care of the Italian government, before the present Treaty becomes effective, rendered free of all servitude and of its eventual occupants. The Holy See will watch over the closing of access, by surrounding the open parts outside Saint Peter's Square with a wall.

It is further agreed that in that which concerns the immovable and existing things belonging to the religious institutes or bodies, the Holy See will make provision directly for the regulation of its relations with them, the Italian state taking no further interest therein.

Art. 6. Italy will provide, by the necessary arrangements with interested organisms, that the City of the Vatican be assured in its own right of an adequate provision of water.

It will provide also for placing the city in communication with the railroads of the state by means of a railroad station in the City of the Vatican at the place indicated on the plan mentioned above (Annex 1) and by means of the circulation of carriages belonging to the Vatican on the Italian railroads.

It will provide, furthermore, for connections directly with the other states the telegraphic, telephonic, radiotelegraphic, radiotelephonic, and postal services of the City of the Vatican.

Finally, it will provide also for connection with the other public services.

All the above services will be provided at the cost of the Italian state and within one year from the entrance into effect of the present Treaty.

The Holy See will provide, at its own expense, for the maintenance of the existing entrances to the Vatican and those which it shall deem advisable to open hereafter.

Agreements will be made between the Holy See and the Italian state for the circulation on the territory of the latter of terrestrial vehicles and airplanes of the City of the Vatican.

Art. 7. The Italian government agrees that it will not permit, in the territory surrounding the Vatican City, new constructions which would overlook its interior, and that to this end it will proceed to the partial demolition of the structures already existing at Cavalleggeri Gate along the Via Aurelia and the Viale Vaticano.

In accordance with the rules of international law, airplanes of any kind are forbidden to fly over the territory of the Vatican.

On Rusticucci Square and in the parts adjacent to the colonnade to which the extraterritoriality mentioned in Article 15 does not extend, all changes for purposes of town planning or improvement which might interest the City of the Vatican will be made by common accord.

Art. 8. Italy, considering as sacred and inviolable the person of the Sovereign Pontiff, declares any attack upon him or provocation of an attack punishable under threat of the same penalties established for an attack or provocation of attack upon the person of the King.

Public offenses and injuries committed on Italian territory against the person of the Sovereign Pontiff by speech, acts, or writing are punished as offenses and injuries against the person of the King.

Art. 9. In accordance with the rules of international law, all persons having a permanent residence in the City of the Vatican are subject to the sovereignty of the Holy See. This residence is not lost by the simple fact of a temporary residence in another place, unless this fact is accompanied by the loss of domicile in the city itself or by other circumstances proving the abandonment of the said domicile.

When they cease to be subject to the sovereignty of the Holy See, the persons mentioned in the preceding paragraph and who, by terms of the Italian law, apart from the circumstances of fact stated above, would not be considered as possessing another citizenship, will be considered in Italy with no further formality as Italian citizens.

To these same persons, as long as they remain subject to the sovereignty of the Holy See, there shall be applicable in the territory of the Italian Kingdom, in the determination of questions governed by the law of persons (when such questions are not regulated by standards emanating from the Holy See), the provisions of the Italian law, or if the person concerned is considered as having a different citizenship, the laws of the state to which he belongs shall be applicable.

Art. 10. The dignitaries of the Church and persons belonging to the pontifical court, who shall be indicated in a table on which the high contracting parties will agree, even when they are not citizens of the Vatican, are always and in every case, in relation to Italy, exempt from military service, from jury service, and from any requirement of a personal character.

This provision applies also to career officers declared by the Holy See to be indispensable, attached permanently and with a fixed salary to the services of the Holy See, as well as to the courts and officers indicated below in Articles 13, 14, 15 and 16 which exist outside the City of the Vatican. These officers shall be indicated on another table which should be established as above by common accord and which each year shall be brought up to date by the Holy See.

The ecclesiastics who, by reason of their office, take part, outside the City of the Vatican, in the execution of the acts of the Holy See may not, by reason of their office, be the object of any accusations, inquiry, or molestation on the part of the Italian authorities.

Every foreigner invested with an ecclesiastical office in Rome enjoys the personal guaranties accorded to Italian citizens by virtue of the laws of the Kingdom.

Art. 11. The central organisms of the Catholic Church are free from all interference on the part of the Italian state (reserving the dispositions of Italian laws concerning the acquisition of legal personality) as well as from conversion of their immovable property.

Art. 12. Italy recognizes in the Holy See the power of active and passive legation according to the general rules of international law.

Envoys of foreign governments to the Holy See will continue to enjoy in the Kingdom all the prerogatives and immunities belonging to diplomatic agents according to international law, and their residences may continue to be on Italian territory; they shall enjoy the immunities due them according to international law even if their countries do not have diplomatic relations with Italy.

It is understood that Italy promises to leave free, always and in every case, the correspondence between all states, including belligerents, and the Holy See and vice versa, as well as the access of bishops of the whole world to the Apostolic See.

The high contracting parties engage to establish between themselves normal diplomatic relations by accrediting to the Holy See an Italian Ambassador and to Italy a Papal Nuncio, who will be the Head of the Diplomatic Corps under the terms of the customary law recognized by the Congress of Vienna in the Act of June 9, 1815.

As an effect of the recognition of sovereignty, and without prejudice to that provided in Article 19 below, the diplomatic agents of the Holy See and the couriers sent in the name of the Sovereign Pontiff shall enjoy in Italian territory, even in time of war, the same treatment as that due according to the rules of international law to the diplomatic agents and cabinet couriers of other foreign governments.

Art. 13. Italy recognizes that the Holy See has full ownership of the Patriarchal Basilicas of Saint John Lateran, of Saint Mary Maggiore and of Saint Paul with the annexed buildings (Annex II, 1, 2, and 3).

The state transfers to the Holy See the free management and administration of the said Basilica of Saint Paul and of the Monastery attached, turning over also to the Holy See the capital corresponding to the sums fixed annually in the budget of the Minister of Public Instruction for the said Basilica.

It is also understood that the Holy See has free ownership of the dependencies of Saint Callisto, close to Saint Mary of Trastevere (Annex II, 9).

Art. 14. Italy recognizes that the Holy See has full ownership of the Pontifical Palace of Castel Gandolfo, with all its endowments, appurtenances, and dependencies (Annex II, 4) such as are already in possession of the same Holy See, and at the same time it is obliged to grant, also in full ownership, delivery to be effected within six months from the coming into force of this Treaty, the Villa Barberini, at Castel Gandolfo, with all its endowments, appurtenances, and dependencies (Annex II, 5).

To complete the ownership of the real property situated on the north side of the Janiculum belonging to the Sacred Congregation of Propagation of the Faith and to other ecclesiastical institutes and having a view toward the Vatican palaces, the state engages to transfer to the Holy See or to the entities indicated by it the real property of the domains of the state or of individuals existing in the said zone. The real property belonging to the said Congregation and to the other institutes and those to be transferred are indicated in the annexed plan (Annex II, 12).

Italy, finally, transfers to the Holy See, in full and free ownership, the ex-conventual buildings of Rome attached to the Basilica of the Twelve Holy Apostles and to the churches of Saint Andrew della Valle and of Saint Charles ai Catinari, with all their annexes and dependencies (Annex III, 3, 4, and 5) and to deliver them free of their occupants, within the space of one year from the coming into force of the present Treaty.

Art. 15. The real property indicated in Article 13 and in paragraphs 1 and 2 of Article 14, as well as the Palaces of the Dataria, of the Cancellaria, of the Propagation of the Faith in the Piazza di Spagna, the Palace of the Holy Office and the adjacent property, that of the Convertendi (present seat of the Congregation of the Eastern Church) in the Piazza Scossacavalli, the Palace of the Cancellaria (Annex II, 6, 7, 8, 10 and 11) and the other buildings in which the Holy See shall in future deem it advisable to organize other courts, although within the territory of the Italian state, shall enjoy the immunities recognized by international law for residences of diplomatic agents of foreign states.

The same immunities apply also with regard to the other churches, even outside Rome, during the time when, even though not open to the public, ceremonies are being celebrated in the presence of the Sovereign Pontiff.

Art. 16. The real property indicated in the three preceding articles as well as the seats of the following pontifical institutes: the Gregorian University, the Biblical, Oriental, and Archaeological Institutes, the Russian Seminary, the Lombard College, the two Palaces of Saint Appollinaris and the House of Exercises for the Clergy of Saints John and Paul (Annex III, 1 *bis*, 2, 6, 7, 8) shall never be subject to servitudes or expropriations by reason of public utility unless there is a previous agreement with the Holy See, and they shall be exempt from taxes either ordinary or extraordinary, on the part of the state as well as of any other entity.

It is in the power of the Holy See to give all the real property above indicated, in the present Article and in the three preceding Articles, arrangements of its own accord, without the necessity of authorization or consent on the part of Italian governmental, provincial or communal authorities, which may rely in full security upon the noble artistic traditions which are the honor of the Catholic Church.

Art. 17. The payments of whatever nature due by the Holy See, by the other central organizations of the Catholic Church, and by the organizations managed directly by the Holy See, even outside Rome, to dignitaries, employed and salaried, whether they have permanent office or not, shall be exempt on Italian territory, beginning January 1, 1929, from all taxes whatsoever of the state or of any other administration.

Art. 18. The treasures of art and science in the City of the Vatican and the Lateran Palace shall be accessible to scholars and to visitors, the Holy See reserving to itself the full liberty of regulating the entrance of the public.

Art. 19. The diplomatic agents and envoys of the Holy See, the diplomatic agents and envoys of foreign governments to the Holy See, and the dignitaries of the Church coming from abroad to go to the City of the Vatican and provided with passports of the states from which they come visaed by the Pontifical representatives abroad, may without other formality proceed to this city across Italian territory. It will be the same for the above persons who, furnished with a pontifical passport in order, proceed abroad from the Vatican City.

Art. 20. Merchandise coming from abroad and sent to the City of the

Vatican or, outside the latter, to the institutes or offices of the Holy See shall always be admitted, from any point on the Italian frontiers or from any port in the Kingdom, to cross Italian territory with full exemption from customs and tolls.

Art. 21. All the Cardinals shall enjoy in Italy the honors due to Princes of the Blood; those who reside in Rome, even outside the City of the Vatican, are citizens of this city, with all the effects resulting therefrom.

During the vacancy of the Pontifical Seat, Italy, will see to it in a special manner that there is no obstacle to the free passage and access of Cardinals across Italian territory to the Vatican, and that no hindrance or limitation is placed on their personal liberty.

Italy will also see to it that on its territory, in the vicinity of the City of the Vatican, acts capable of troubling in any manner the meetings of the Conclave shall not be committed.

These rules are valid also for Conclaves that are held outside the City of the Vatican, as well as for the Councils presided over by the Supreme Pontiff or by his Legates, and as regards the Bishops called to participate therein.

Art. 22. Upon the demand of the Holy See, and by means of a delegation which it may establish in each case or in a permanent manner, Italy will be responsible in its territory for the punishment of crimes committed in the City of the Vatican; but, when the author of the crime has taken refuge in Italian territory, he shall be prosecuted without further formality according to the rules of Italian law.

The Holy See will return to the Italian state persons who may have taken refuge in the City of the Vatican, being accused of acts committed in Italian territory and recognized as criminal by the laws of both states.

The same procedure shall be followed as regards persons accused of crimes who may have taken refuge in the buildings which enjoy immunity according to Article 15, unless those in charge of the said buildings prefer not to invite the Italian agents to enter for the purpose of arresting the said persons.

Art. 23. For the execution within the Kingdom of sentences rendered by the tribunals of the City of the Vatican the rules of international law shall be applied.

On the other hand, the sentences and measures emanating from the ecclesiastical authorities and officially communicated to the civil authorities, on the subject of ecclesiastical or religious persons, in spiritual or disciplinary matters shall have, without other formality, full juridical effectiveness in Italy including all their civil effects.

Art. 24. The Holy See, so far as concerns the sovereignty belonging to it in the international domain, declares that it wishes to remain and will remain removed from the temporal competitions among other states and from international meetings convoked with such a purpose, unless the parties to a dispute make a unanimous appeal to its mission of peace, reserving to itself, however, the right to assert in every case its moral and spiritual power.

In consequence the City of the Vatican shall always and in every case be considered as neutral and inviolable territory.

Art. 25. By a special convention signed at the same time as the present Treaty, constituting Annex IV of the said Treaty and forming an integral part thereof, the liquidation of the debts of Italy to the Holy See is provided for.

Art. 26. The Holy See affirms that, by the agreement signed today, it possesses in an adequate manner all that is necessary to provide with due liberty and independence for the pastoral government of the Diocese of Rome and of the Catholic Church in Italy and in the world; it declares that the "Roman question" is definitively and irrevocably resolved and therefore eliminated, and it recognizes the Kingdom of Italy under the dynasty of the House of Savoy with Rome as capital of the Italian State.

On its side, Italy recognizes the State of the City of the Vatican under the sovereignty of the Sovereign Pontiff.

Law 214 of May 13, 1871, is abrogated as well as every other disposition contrary to the present Treaty.

Art. 27. The present Treaty, within a period which shall not exceed four months from the time of signature, shall be submitted to the ratification of the Sovereign Pontiff and of the King of Italy and shall become effective from the act of exchange of ratifications.

ANNEXES

(*not reproduced*)

Annex 1. Plan of the territory of the City of the Vatican.

Annex 2. Immovable property enjoying the privilege of extraterritoriality with exemption from expropriations and taxes.

Annex 3. Immovable property exempt from expropriations and taxes.

Annex 4. Financial Convention.

Concordat between the Holy See and Italy[1]

February 11, 1929

In the name of the Most Holy Trinity:

Inasmuch as, from the beginning of the negotiations between the Holy

[1] *Inter Sanctam Sede et Italiae Regnum Conventiones. Trattato fra la Santa Sede e l'Italia. Acta Apostolicae Sedis Commentarium officiale. Annus xxi–Vol. xxi. 7 Iunii.* 1929. Num. 6. Rome. *Typeis Polyglottis Vaticanis.* Supplied by Secretariat of State. The Vatican in December 1966. Translated by Editor. Ed.

See and Italy to resolve the "Roman question," the Holy See itself has proposed that the negotiations relative to this question have as a necessary complement a Concordat destined to regulate the conditions of religion and of the Church in Italy;

Inasmuch as the Treaty for the solution of the "Roman question" has been concluded and signed:

His Holiness the Sovereign Pontiff Pius XI and His Majesty Victor Emmanuel III, King of Italy, have resolved to make a Concordat and have appointed for this purpose the same Plenipotentiaries, delegated by the provisions of the Treaty, His Eminence the Most Reverend Cardinal Pietro Gasparri, His Secretary of State, representing His Holiness, and His Excellency Signor Cavaliere Benito Mussolini, Prime Minister and Head of the Government, representing His Majesty; who, their respective Full Powers having been exchanged and found to be in good and due form, have agreed to the following Articles:

Art. 1. Italy, by the terms of Article 1 of the Treaty, assures to the Catholic Church the free exercise of spiritual power, the free and public exercise of worship, as well as that of its jurisdiction in ecclesiastical matters, according to the rules established in the present Concordat; where it may be necessary, it accords to ecclesiastics, for acts of their spiritual ministry, the protection of the authorities.

In consideration of the sacred character of the Eternal City, episcopal seat of the Sovereign Pontiff, center of the Catholic world and a place of pilgrimage, the Italian Government will take care to forbid in Rome anything which might be inconsistent with this character.

Art. 2. The Holy See communicates and corresponds freely with the Bishops, with the clergy and with all the Catholic world, without any interference from the Italian Government.

Likewise, in all that relates to their pastoral ministry, the Bishops communicate and correspond freely with their clergy and with all the faithful.

Both the Holy See and the Bishops may freely publish and also post, inside and at the outer doors of buildings of worship and at the offices of their ministry, the instructions, ordinances, pastoral letters, diocesan and other bulletins concerning the spiritual government of the faithful, that they consider to be within the sphere of their jurisdiction. Such publications and notices and in general all acts and documents concerning the spiritual government of the faithful shall not be subject to taxes.

Insofar as concerns the Holy See, such publications may be made in any language; as regards the Bishops, they shall be made in the Italian or Latin language; however, the ecclesiastical authorities may accompany the Italian text with a translation into another language.

The ecclesiastical authorities may, without any interference of the civil authorities, carry out collections inside and at the entrance of churches as well as in buildings belonging to them.

Art. 3. Students of theology, those in the last two preparatory years for theology preparing for the priesthood, and novices of religious institutions may, at their own request, extend from year to year until the end of their twenty sixth year of age, their exemption from the obligations of military service.

Ordinary clergy *in sacris* and brothers who have taken their vows shall be exempt from military service except in case of general mobilization. In such a case, priests shall join the Armed Forces of the State, retaining their ecclesiastical garb, in order to exercise the holy ministry for the troops under the ecclesiastical jurisdiction of the Military Ordinary in accordance with Article 14. Other clergy and brothers shall, by preference, be assigned to the health services.

However, even if a general mobilization has been ordered, parish priests shall be exempt from presenting themselves to the call-up. The following are considered to fall within this category: Ordinaries, parish priests, officiating priests or coadjutors, vicars and priests permanently assigned to the rectory of a church open to worship.

Art. 4. Ecclesiastics and brothers are exempt from jury duty.

Art. 5. No ecclesiastic may undertake or remain in an employment or office of the Italian State or of a public body depending therefrom without the permission of the Diocesan Ordinary.

Revocation of such permission deprives the ecclesiastic of the possibility of continuing to exercise the employment or office undertaken.

Under no circumstances may apostate priests or those who have been censured be promoted or retained in education or in an office or employment where they have immediate contact with the public.

Art. 6. The stipends and other pensions enjoyed by ecclesiastics by reason of their office shall be exempt from mortgage in the same way as the stipends and pensions of State employees.

Art. 7. Ecclesiastics may not be required by magistrates or other authorities to give information on persons or matters which have come to their knowledge by reason of their holy ministry.

Art. 8. If an ecclesiastic or a brother is remanded before a magistrate of penal law for a misdemeanor, the King's Prosecutor must immediately inform the Ordinary of the diocese in the territory of which he exercises jurisdiction; the decision of the instruction or, as the case may be, the final sentence of the court both in first instance and appeal, must be immediately officially transmitted to him.

In case of arrest, the ecclesiastic or brother shall be treated with the regard due to his office and his rank.

In case of condemnation of an ecclesiastic or a brother, the penalty shall be expunged if possible in a separate place from that provided for the laity, unless the competent Ordinary has reduced the condemned man to lay status.

Art. 9. As a rule, buildings open to worship are exempt from requisition or occupation.

If a building open to worship has been occupied owing to grave public need, the authority carrying out the occupation must come to a prior agreement with the Ordinary unless reasons of extreme urgency prevent this. In such a case the authority in question must immediately inform the Ordinary.

Except in cases of urgent necessity, the public force may not enter buildings open to worship for the exercise of their duties without previous notice to the ecclesiastical authorities.

Art. 10. The demolition of buildings open to worship may not take place for any reason whatsoever without prior agreement of the competent ecclesiastical authority.

Art. 11. The State recognizes the following immovable holidays of the Church:

All Sundays;
New Year's Day;
Epiphany (6 January);
The Feast of Saint Joseph (19 March);
Ascension Day;
Corpus Christi;
The Feast of Saints Peter and Paul (29 June);
Assumption Day (15 August);
All Saints Day (1 November);
The Immaculate Conception (8 December);
Christmas Day (25 December).

Art. 12. On Sundays and the feasts listed in the preceding article, in the churches where a Chapter is officiating, the person celebrating the conventual Mass shall say a prayer, according to the rules of the holy liturgy, for the prosperity of the King of Italy and of the Italian State.

Art. 13. The Italian Government shall communicate to the Holy See the organic table of the ecclesiastical personnel registered for the service of spiritual assistance to the military forces of the State as soon as this has been approved in the form of a law.

The appointment of the ecclesiastics charged with the supreme direction of the service of spiritual assistance (Military Ordinary, vicar and inspectors) is made confidentially by the Holy See to the Italian Government. Whenever the Italian Government has reason to oppose such appointments it shall communicate with the Holy See which shall proceed to another appointment.

The Military Ordinary shall be invested with archiepiscopal rank.

The appointment of military chaplains is made by the competent authority of the Italian State from nominations of the Military Ordinary.

Art. 14. Italian Air, Land and Naval Forces enjoy, in regard to their religious duties, the privileges and exemptions allowed by canon law.

Military chaplains have parochial authority in respect to these Forces. The holy ministry is exercised under the jurisdiction of the Military Ordinary, assisted by the Curia itself.

The Military Ordinary has jurisdiction also over the religious personnel, male and female, attached to the military hospitals.

Art. 15. The Military Archbishop Ordinary is attached to the chapter of the church of the Pantheon in Rome, and together they constitute the clergy entrusted with the religious service of this Basilica.

This clergy is authorized to provide for all religious functions, including those outside of Rome, which are requested, in accordance with canon law, by the State or by the Royal Family.

The Holy See consents to confer upon all the canons composing the chapter of the Pantheon the rank of proto-notary *ad instar, durante munere.* Each appointment shall be made by the Cardinal Vicar of Rome after nomination by His Majesty the King of Italy who shall first indicate confidentially his nominees.

The Holy See reserves the right to transfer the Deaconship to another church.

Art. 16. The High Contracting Parties shall proceed to an agreement, by means of a mixed commission, for the revision of the diocesan circumscriptions for the purpose of making them correspond as far as possible with the provinces of the State.

It is understood that the Holy See will found the diocese of Zara; that no part of the territory subject to the sovereignty of the Kingdom of Italy shall come under a Bishop whose see lies in territory subject to the sovereignty of another State; and that no diocese of the Kingdom shall include any zone of territory subject to the sovereignty of another State.

This principle shall be observed for all parishes existing or to be established in territory near the borders of the State.

Any modifications to the diocesan circumscriptions which, subsequent to the original revision, are seen in the future to be necessary, shall be ordered by the Holy See after agreement with the Italian Government and in conformance with the above directives, except for small rectifications of territory requested for the good of the people.

Art. 17. The reduction of a diocese resulting from the application of the preceding article, shall be effected at the moment the diocese itself becomes vacant.

It is understood that a reduction shall not involve the suppression of the titles or the chapters of the diocese, which shall be conserved by regrouping the dioceses in such a manner that their chief towns correspond to those of the province.

The above reductions shall leave untouched all the present economic resources of the dioceses and of the other existing ecclesiastical bodies therein, including the assets now corresponding to the Italian State.

Art. 18. If, by order of the ecclesiastical authorities, several parishes are regrouped provisionally or definitively, either by confiding them to one single parish priest assisted by one or more officiating priests, or by bringing together several priests in the same house (presbytery), the State shall maintain unaltered the economic revenues due to those parishes.

Art. 19. The selection of Archbishops and bishops belongs to the Holy See.

Before proceeding to the appointment of an Archbishop or of a Diocesan Bishop or of a Coadjutor *cum jure successionis*, the Holy See shall communicate the name of the person envisaged to the Italian Government to ensure that the latter has no reason of a political character to invoke against such an appointment.

The above procedure shall be carried out with the greatest possible care and discretion in order that the name of the person envisaged shall remain secret until the nomination has been made.

Art. 20. The Bishops, before taking possession of their dioceses, shall take an oath of loyalty before the Head of State in the following terms:

"Before God and his Holy Gospels, I swear and promise insofar as is proper in a Bishop, loyalty to the Italian State. I swear and promise to respect and to ensure the respect of my clergy for the King and the Government established according to the constitutional laws of the State. I swear and promise furthermore, not to participate in any agreement nor attend any council that might cause damage to the Italian State and to the public order, and that I shall not permit such participation to my clergy. Concerned for the good and the best interests of the Italian State, I shall seek to avoid any damage that might threaten it."

Art. 21. The granting of ecclesiastical benefices belongs to the ecclesiastical authorities.

The appointments of those invested with parochial benefices are communicated provisionally to the Italian Government by the ecclesiastical authorities and may not take effect until thirty days after the date of communication.

Within this time limit the Italian Government, where there are serious reasons against the appointment, may communicate them provisionally to the ecclesiastical authorities which, if disagreement persists, shall refer the case to the Holy See.

Should grave reasons occur making an ecclesiastic's permanent tenure in a particular parochial benefice harmful, the Italian Government shall communicate those reasons to the Ordinary, who shall take within three months, in agreement with the Government, the appropriate measures. Should there be a divergence of views between the Ordinary and the Government, the Holy See will confide the solution of the question to two ecclesiastical officials which it shall choose, who, together with two delegates of the Italian Government, shall come to a definitive decision.

Art. 22. Ecclesiastics who are not Italian citizens may not be invested with benefices existing in Italy. The heads of dioceses and of parishes should also speak the Italian language. In case of need, they must have coadjutors who, in addition to Italian, understand and speak the language in local usage for the purpose of giving religious aid in the language of the faithful, according to the rules of the Church.

Art. 23. The provisions of Articles 16, 17, 19, 20, 21 and 22 do not apply to Rome and the suburban dioceses.

It is understood, however, that whenever the Holy See proceeds to a new assessment of those dioceses the revenues which at the time are due to the Italian State either from abbeys or from other ecclesiastical institutions shall remain unchanged.

Art. 24. The *exequatur* and the royal *placet* are abolished as well as all imperial or royal appointments either in the provision of benefices or to ecclesiastical offices throughout Italy, other than the exceptions provided in Article 29 (g).

Art. 25. The Italian State renounces the sovereign prerogative of royal patronage over major and minor benefices.

Royal prerogatives over major and minor benefices are abolished. The annuity of the third of the provinces of the ex-King of the two Sicilies is also abolished.

The charges involved shall cease to be a burden on the State and the dependent administrations.

Art. 26. The appointments of those invested with major and minor benefices, and of those provisionally representing the vacant see or benefice, shall take effect from the date of the ecclesiastical notification officially made to the Government. The administration and use of the revenues during a vacancy is ruled by the regulations of canon law.

In case of fraudulent administration, the Italian State, in agreement with the ecclesiastical authorities, may sequester the revenues of the benefice transferring the net return to the person invested therewith or, in the absence of such person, for the advantage of the benefice.

Art. 27. The basilicas of Santa Casa in Loreto, of San Francisco in Assisi and of Sant' Antonio in Padua with their buildings and appertaining works, except those of a purely secular character, shall be ceded to the Holy See, and their administration shall belong freely to the latter. Other bodies of whatever nature administered by the Holy See in Italy, including the Colleges of missions, shall also be free of any interference or change by the State. Italian laws concerning purchases by public corporations remain in all cases applicable.

With regard to the present assets of these sanctuaries, their distribution will be decided by a mixed commission having regard to the rights of third parties and to the endowments required for the said purely secular works.

For the other sanctuaries where civil administration exists, the free administration of the ecclesiastical authority shall be substituted except, as the case may be, for the distribution of assets in accordance with the provisions of the preceding paragraph.

Art. 28. In order to tranquillize consciences, the Holy See will grant a full pardon to all those who, in accordance with former Italian laws concerning the ecclesiastical patrimony, find themselves in possession of ecclesiastical property.

The Holy See will give the Ordinary the proper instructions for this purpose.

Art. 29. The Italian State will revise its legislation regarding ecclesiastical matters in order to reform and complete it and place it in harmony with the directives which inspire the Treaty with the Holy See and the present Concordat.

It is from the present agreed by the two High Contracting Paries as follows:

(a) The juridical personality of ecclesiastical bodies hitherto recognized by Italian law shall continue (Holy See, dioceses, chapters, seminaries, parishes, etc.), the recognition of such personality shall also be extended to public churches open to worship which do not now have it including those belonging to suppressed ecclesiastical bodies, assigning to the latter the revenues presently granted to each by the Fund for Worship.

Except insofar as is provided in Article 27 above, the councils of administration, wheresoever they exist and whatever their denomination, even if they are composed wholely or principally of laymen, must not interfere in the services of worship, and the appointment of their members shall be made by agreement with the ecclesiastical authorities.

(b) The juridical personality of religious associations with or without vows approved by the Holy See, which have their principal seat in the Kingdom and are there represented legally or in fact by persons holding Italian citizenship and resident in Italy, shall be recognized. Also shall be recognized the juridical personality of the Italian religious provinces within the limits of the territory of the State and its colonies, of associations having their principal seat abroad when the same conditions are fulfilled. The juridical personality of the households shall be recognized when the particular rules of a single order give it the power to acquire and possess such. The juridical personality shall be recognized for all time of the community houses and possessions of religious associations, including foreign ones. Religious associations and houses which already have juridical personality shall conserve it.

Acts relating to the transfer of immovable property already in the possession of the associations and of actual property willed to the associations shall be exempt from all tax.

(c) Brotherhoods exclusively or principally for religious purposes are not subject to subsequent changing of their purposes and are dependent on the ecclesiastical authority for their functioning and administration.

(d) Religious foundations of all kinds are recognized provided that it is clear that they respond to the religious requirements of the population and no financial burden devolves from them on the State. These provisions apply also to foundations already existing in fact.

(e) In the civil administrations of ecclesiastical property arising out of expired laws, the councils of administration shall be composed half of members appointed by the ecclesiastical authorities, as much as possible by the religious foundations of the new provinces.

(f) The complete acts which hitherto related to ecclesiastical or religious bodies without respect to the civil laws, may be recognized and regularized by the Italian State, at the request of the Ordinary to be presented within three years from the entry into force of this Concordat.

(g) The Italian State renounces the privileges of exemption from ecclesiastical jurisdiction of the Palatine clergy in all Italy (excepting for that applied to the church of Santa Sindone of Turin, of Superga, of the Sudario of Rome and to the chapels annexed to the palaces of residence of the Sovereign and the Royal Princes), and places all appointments and granting of benefices and offices under the rules provided in the preceding article. An appropriate commission shall provide each Palatine basilica or church with a suitable endowment according to the criteria indicated for the good of the sanctuaries in Article 27.

(h) The subsidiary facilities already existing in favor of ecclesiastical bodies under Italian law hitherto in force shall remain; the purposes of worship or monastic or life are considered for all subsidiary effects, equivalent to the purposes of beneficence and education.

The following are abolished: the extraordinary tax of thirty per cent imposed by Article 18 of the law of 15 August 1867 n. 3848; the quota of participation referred to in article 31 of the law of 7 July 1866 n. 3036 and article 20 of the law of 15 August 1867 no. 3848; also the tax on the passage of usufruct of properties constituting the gift of benefices and other ecclesiastical bodies provided by Article 1 of R.D. of 30 December 1923 n. 3270, the institution of any special tribute whatsoever charged on the property of Church to remain excluded also for the future. The tax on the professions and the patent tax instituted by R.D. 18 November 1923 no. 2538 in place of the supressed profession and retail tax, shall not be applied to ministers of worship for the exercise of the priestly ministry, nor any other tribute of the same kind.

(i) The use of the ecclesiastical or monastic habit by lay persons or by ecclesiastical or religious persons to whom it has been forbidden by a definitive ruling of the competent ecclesiastical authority, officially communicated to the Italian Government, is forbidden and shall be punished by the same sanctions and penalties with which is punished improper use of military uniform.

Art. 30. The ordinary and extraordinary administration of the property belonging to any ecclesiastical institution or religious association shall be under the vigilance and control of the competent authority of the Church, any intervention of the Italian State being excluded, and without obligation to convert immovable property.

The Italian State recognizes the right of ecclesiastical institutions and monastic bodies to acquire property subject to the provisions of civil law concerning the acquisition thereof by public corporations.

The Italian State, so long as new agreements do not provide otherwise, shall continue to supply the deficiencies in the returns of ecclesiastical benefices by corresponding income to an amount not less than the real value of that stabilized in the law presently in force; in consideration of this, the patrimonial administration of said benefices, inasmuch as concerns other than acts and contracts of simple management, shall be carried out with the participation of the Italian State and, in case of a vacancy, the assignment of the property shall be made in the presence of a representative of the Government drawing up a report upon the transaction.

The episcopal revenues of the suburban dioceses and the patrimony of the chapters and parishes of Rome and of the said dioceses shall not be subject to the participation referred to above. For the purpose of supplementing the corresponding portion, the amount of the income due to the beneficiaries of the above mentioned revenues and patrimonies shall be established by a declaration drawn up annually under the responsibility of the suburban bishopric itself, for the dioceses, and of the Cardinal Vicar for the city of Rome.

Art. 31. The erection of new ecclesiastical bodies or religious associations shall be made by the ecclesiastical authorities in accordance with canon law; their recognition for civil purposes shall be made by the civil authority.

Art. 32. The recognitions and authorizations provided in the present Concordat and Treaty shall take place according to the establish rules of civil law which must be harmonized with the provisions of the above Concordat and Treaty.

Art. 33. To the Holy See is reserved the disposition of the existing catacombs in Roman soil and in other parts of the territory of the Kingdom with the consequent obligation to guard, maintain and conserve them.

It may, thereafter, in accordance with the laws of the State and subject to the eventual rights of third parties, proceed to the appropriate excavations and transfer of holy objects.

Art. 34. The Italian State, wishing to restore to the institution of marriage which is the basis of the family, a dignity conforming to the Catholic traditions of its people, recognizes the civil effects of the sacrament of marriage regulated by canon law.

The publication of the banns shall be effected both in the parish church and in the town hall.

Immediately after the celebration of the marriage, the parish priest shall explain to the couple the civil effects of matrimony, reading the articles of the civil code regarding the rights and duties of the partners, and shall draw up the act of matrimony a full copy of which he must transmit within five days to the Commune in order that it be transcribed in the register of civil status.

Cases concerning the nullity of marriages and the dispensation of marriages ratified and not consummated are reserved to the competence of ecclesiastical tribunals and courts.

The decisions and sentences on the question, when they have become definitive, shall be referred to the Supreme Tribunal of the Signature, which will ascertain whether the rules of canon law relative to the competence of the judge, to the citation and legitimate representation, or to the contumacy of the parties have been respected.

The said definitive decisions and sentences, together with the decrees and pertinent records of the Supreme Tribunal of the Signature, shall be transmitted to the State Court of Appeal which has territorial jurisdiction which, by ordinance in Council Chamber, shall have them executed in their civil effects and order their notation on the registers of civil status in the margin of the marriage record.

In cases of legal separation, the Holy See consents to whatever may be decided by the civil judicial authority.

Art. 35. The institution of state examination remains obligatory for secondary schools kept by ecclesiastical or monastic bodies, in order that there may be effective equality between the candidates of the said schools and those of government institutes.

Art. 36. Italy considers the teaching of the Christian doctrine according to the form received from the Catholic tradition as the base and crown of public instruction. In consequence it agrees that the religious instruction now given in the elementary public schools shall proceed further in the secondary schools according to a program to be established by agreement between the Holy See and the State.

This instruction shall be given by masters or professors, priests or brothers, approved by the ecclesiastical authorities, and subsidiarily by lay masters and professors holding for this purpose a certificate of capacity to be granted by the Diocesan Ordinary.

The revocation of the said certificate by the Ordinary shall, without other formality, deprive the teacher of his capacity to teach.

Only the manuals approved by the ecclesiastical authorities shall be accepted for the said religious instruction in the public schools.

Art. 37. The directors of state associations for physical education and military preparation, of *Avanguardisti* and *Balillas*, in order to render possible religious instruction and attendance for the youth confided to their care, will regulate hours so as not to impede the performance of religious duties on Sundays and prescribed feast days.

The directors of the public schools will do the same as regards possible meetings of students on feast days.

Art. 38. The appointments of professors of the Catholic University of S. Cuore and of the subordinate Institute of Doctors (*Magistero*) Maria Immacolata are subject to the *nulla osta* of the Holy See directed to ensuring that noone objectionable from a moral and religious point of view be appointed.

Art. 39. The Universities, the major and minor Seminaries, whether diocesan, inter-diocesan or regional, the academies, colleges and other Catholic institutions for the formation and training of ecclesiastics shall continue to be subordinate solely to the Holy See without any interference of the educational authority of the Kingdom.

Art. 40. The degrees in sacred theology given by the Faculties approved by the Holy See shall be recognized by the Italian State.

The State shall also recognize the diplomas attained in the schools of paleography, archives and diplomatic documentation attached to the Library and Archives of the Vatican.

Art. 41. Italy authorizes the wearing in the Kingdom and colonies of the pontifical decorations of orders of chivalry, subject to registration of the documents of appointment and upon presentation of the said documents and the written request of the interested party.

Art. 42. Italy will recognize, by royal decree, titles of nobility confered by the Sovereign Pontiffs after 1870 and in the future.

The cases shall be established in which the said recognition shall not be subject to the payment of a tax in Italy.

Art. 43. The Italian State recognizes the organizations dependent on the Italian Catholic Action, insofar as they, pursuant to the decision of the Holy See, develop their activity outside of any political party and under the immediate authority of the hierarchy of the Church for the diffusion and effectuation of Catholic principles.

The Holy See takes the occasion of the stipulations of the present Concordat to reaffirm to all ecclesiastics and monks the prohibition against their inscription or taking part in any political party whatever.

Art. 44. If in the future any difficulty arises in the interpretation of the present Concordat, the Holy See and Italy will proceed by common accord to an amicable solution of the question.

Art. 45. The present Concordat shall enter into force upon the exchange of ratifications or the same time as the Treaty stipulated by the said High Parties eliminating the "Roman Question".

With the coming into effect of the present Concordat the provisions of the concordats which have fallen into disuse with the former Italian states shall cease to apply in Italy. The Austrian laws and the laws, regulations, ordinances and decrees of the Italian State now in effect, insofar as they are contrary to the provisions of the present Concordat, are considered as abrogated from the date of its coming into effect.

To provide for the execution of this Concordat a Commission composed of persons appointed by both the High Parties shall be appointed immediately after its signature.

Rome, eleven February one thousand nine hundred and twenty-nine.

Fundamental Laws of the City of the Vatican[1]

June 7, 1929

1. FUNDAMENTAL LAW

OF THE CITY OF THE VATICAN

1. The Sovereign Pontiff, sovereign of the City of the Vatican, has full legislative, executive, and judicial powers.

During a vacancy in the pontifical see (*la Sede vacante*) these same powers belong to the Holy College, which may promulgate legislative dispositions only in cases of urgency, these dispositions having effect only during the period of the vacancy, unless they are later confirmed by the Sovereign Pontiff elected according to the rules of the sacred constitutions.

2. Reserved to the Sovereign Pontiff is the fullness of the powers which belong to him, as regards the organs and tribunals of the Apostolic See, according to Canons 7, 230–270, 1597–1607 of the *Codex juris canonici*, and all that prescribed in Article 14 of the present law with respect to the said tribunals, and also as regards his court, including the noble, Palatine and Swiss guards, subject, as to the last mentioned, to the provisions of Article 7 of the present law.

Also depending directly on the Sovereign Pontiff are the administration of the property of the Holy See, the special administration of the Holy See, the Library and the Archives of the Vatican, the printing office, and the book shop.

[1] *Acta Apostolicae Sedis. Supplemento per la Leggi e Disposizioni dello Stato della Cittá del Vaticano. Cittá del Vaticano, Tipografia Poliglotta Vaticana 1929.* Supplied by the Secretariat of State, The Vatican, December 1966. Translation contained in 2nd Edition revised by Editor. Ed.

3. Reserved to the Sovereign Pontiff is the representation of the state of the Vatican, by the intermediary of the Secretary of State, for the conclusion of treaties and for diplomatic relations with foreign states.

4. The approval of the administrative budgets and accounts of the City of the Vatican is reserved to the Sovereign Pontiff. These shall be presented to him by the Governor upon the advice of the General Counsellor of the State.

5. The Sovereign Pontiff, in that which concerns the government of the City of the Vatican, subject to the exceptions mentioned in the preceding articles, reserves to himself the right to delegate his legislative powers in certain matters or for special objects to the Governor of the State.

Apart from express delegation, the Governor, for all that affects the government of the City of the Vatican, has likewise the right to issue regulations and ordinances for the execution of laws, without, however, being able to derogate from them or grant exemptions from them.

For the promulgation of the laws for which he is delegated, and of regulations or ordinances, the Governor, unless there are provisions to the contrary, should take the advice of the General Counsellor of the State.

6. To the Governor of the State, subject to the exceptions and limitations fixed in the preceding Articles 2, 3, and 4, is delegated the exercise of the executive power. Excepted from this delegation are the acts which are reserved to the Sovereign Pontiff and those which he may deem it advisable to reserve to himself.

7. The Governor of the State is appointed and relieved of his functions by the Sovereign Pontiff, to whom he is directly and exclusively responsible.

The corps of pontifical gendarmes is under the direct control of the Governor who may, for purposes of security and order, require also, and in the necessary measure, the assistance of the Swiss Guard.

8. The consultative organ of the City of the Vatican is the Counsellor General of the State.

He is appointed and revoked by the Sovereign Pontiff, to whom he is directly and exclusively responsible. He is obliged to give advice at all times prescribed by law and when required by the Sovereign Pontiff or the governor.

9. The judicial power is delegated to the organs indicated in the following articles, which exercise it in the name of the Sovereign Pontiff.

10. The judicial power in civil matters, in cases not coming before a single judge, and in penal matters, for the judgment of crimes, is normally exercised by a tribunal of first instance and by the Sacred Roman Rota having the function of a court of appeal; in extraordinary cases, recourse is had to the Supreme Tribunal of the Signature.

The tribunal of first instance is composed of a president, two regular judges, and an alternate.

The appointment and revocation of the judicial personnel are reserved to the Sovereign Pontiff. The disciplinary power is exercised by the Supreme Tribunal of the Signature.

11. The functions of a single judge in civil matters are usually performed by the president of the tribunal of first instance or by one of the judges, designated by him, of the sàme tribunal.

12. In penal matters, for infractions, jurisdiction is usually exercised by one or more administrative officers designated by the governor.

In cases in which the sentences, in matters of infractions, are, according to the laws above indicated, susceptible of appeal, the judge of appeal is the president of the tribunal of first instance or another judge designated by him, all further recourse being impossible.

13. In the tribunal of first instance, the president confides the functions of examining magistrate to one of the judges of the tribunal, at the beginning of each year; those of state's attorney and solicitor are, upon the designation of the Dean of the Sacred Roman Rota, performed by a consistorial advocate.

14. The Sacred Roman Rota and the Supreme Tribunal of the Signature, when they function as judicial organs of the City of the Vatican, must accomplish their acts within the limits of the territory of the city.

Representation and defense before the judicial organs of the state of the Vatican are reserved to consistorial advocates, except as prescribed on the subject of representation and defense before a single judge in a civil matter and before the judge of infractions.

15. When an administrative act injures a right, an action may be filed before the judicial authority, which, even though it deems the act unlawful, may neither annul nor modify it, but only judge its effects and, if there are grounds, decide upon the obligation of repairing the damage.

16. In any case, whoever thinks himself damaged in one of his rights or interests by an administrative act may address a petition to the Sovereign Pontiff through the General Counsellor of the State.

17. In every civil or penal case, and in all the phases of the case, the Sovereign Pontiff may refer the trial and judgment to a special commission with power to render a sentence conforming to equity and to exclude all further recourse.

18. The right to grant pardons, amnesties, dispensations, and abatements is always reserved to the Sovereign Pontiff.

Requests for pardon are transmitted through the General Counsellor of the State.

19. The flag of the City of the Vatican consists of two fields divided vertically, a yellow field on the staff side and a white field on the other side, which bears the tiara and the keys, the whole following the model A annexed to the present law.

The shield shows the tiara with the keys, according to the model B annexed to the present law.

The seal bears in the center the tiara and the keys, and on the circumference the words "State of the City of the Vatican," according to the model C annexed to the present law.

20. The standards and customs observed heretofore by the Holy See regarding titles of nobility and orders of chivalry remain effective.

21. The present law shall become effective on the day of its publication.

2. LAW OF THE SOURCES OF THE LAW

1. The principal sources of objective law in the state of the City of the Vatican are:

(a) The *Codex juris canonici* and the apostolic constitutions:

(b) The laws promulgated for the City of the Vatican by the Sovereign Pontiff or by any other authority delegated by him, as well as the regulations lawfully issued by the competent authority.

2. The laws and regulations indicated under letter (b) of the preceding Article are deposited in the archives of the government and published in a supplement of *Acta Apostolicae Sedis,* except for particular cases where a different form of publication may be prescribed in the laws or regulations themselves, and subject to the provisions of Article 24 of the present law.

The publication bears the date on which the laws and regulations have been issued and a special order number for each pontificate.

These laws and regulations become effective the seventh day after their publication, unless by the nature of their objects they should not be immediately executed, or unless a shorter or longer delay is expressly fixed in the law or regulation.

3. For matters not provided for in the sources enumerated in Article 1 and until provision concerning such matters is made by the laws of the City of the Vatican, there shall be applied, in a supplementary manner the laws promulgated by the Kingdom of Italy up to the effective date of the present law, together with the general regulations and the local regulations of the province and government of Rome, indicated in the following articles with the modifications and limitations specified in these articles, always with the reservation that these laws and regulations are not contrary to the precepts of the divine law, to the general principles of canon law, nor to the clauses of the treaty and the concordat stipulated between the Holy See and the Kingdom of Italy on the eleventh of February, 1929, and that they are applicable in the City of the Vatican with due regard to the situation there existing.

4. With the reservations expressed in the preceding Article, there shall be observed in the City of the Vatican the penal code at present in force in the Kingdom of Italy, together with the laws which have modified or completed it by pertinent regulations, up to the coming into force of the present law.

Whoever commits in the territory of the City of the Vatican an act directed against the life, integrity, and personal liberty of the king, the regent, the queen, the crown prince of any foreign state whatsoever of a monarchical form of government, against the chief of a foreign state that is not monarchical, against the chief of the government of the Kingdom of Italy or of any other state, shall be punished by the same penalty as that which would be applicable if the acts had been committed on the territory of the state to which the person against whom the attack was directed belongs.

The penalty to which the person is liable who, on the territory of the City of the Vatican, makes an attempt against the life, integrity, or personal liberty of the Sovereign Pontiff is that provided in Article 1 of Law No. 2008 of the Kingdom of Italy of November 25, 1926.

5. When the penalty fixed for any offense is simply pecuniary, the accused is always authorized to stay the course of the penal action by offering a sum of which the amount shall be fixed, within the limits between the maximum and minimum of the penalty incurred, through the consistorial lawyer in charge of the function of the public ministry or through any other authority provided for by law.

This rule is applicable to infractions even when there is an option between a pecuniary penalty and deprivation of personal liberty. The amount of the offer is fixed, in such case, by the judge of infractions or by any other functionary designated by law.

In cases where the accused is a foreigner and the penalty fixed for the offense is, at the option of the delinquent, a pecuniary penalty or deprivation of personal liberty, the judge may not apply the first of these penalties unless the accused offers, before all proceedings, appropriate guaranty for the payment of the maximum of the pecuniary sum, either by deposit of a sum equal to such guaranty or in the form of a pledge, a personal bond, a letter of exchange, or the guaranty of a Vatican citizen.

6. For offenses punished by a pecuniary penalty under the laws issued in the City of the Vatican, the commutation of the pecuniary penalty to a penalty restrictive of personal liberty, in the cases provided for by the penal code of the Kingdom of Italy, shall be calculated at the rate of one day of deprivation of personal liberty for each part of the unpaid sum equal to fifty lire or fraction of fifty lire.

7. With the reservations specified in Article 3, there shall be observed in the City of the Vatican the code of penal procedure now in effect in the Kingdom of Italy, as well as the laws which have modified or completed it and the pertinent regulations up to the coming into force of the present law. Exception is made with respect to the competence of tribunals, which is regulated by the fundamental law and the present law, and there is also reserved, according to the tenor of the treaty between the Holy See and the Kingdom of Italy of the eleventh of February, 1929, the power to delegate the exercise of penal procedure as regards offenses committed against the authorities of the same Kingdom.

8. For any offense whatsoever, and even for infractions, a foreigner accused may be arrested, even apart from cases of flagrant offense, on an order of summons, and provisional liberty may be accorded him only if he deposits a security in the forms indicated in the last paragraph of Article 5.

The security, if the penalty is pecuniary, may not be less than the maximum of the penalty.

9. Any perpetrator of an infraction taken in flagrant offense by an officer or agent of the judicial police is arrested and immediately conducted before the judge of infractions; also brought before him are the witnesses present whom the officer or agent deems it necessary to summon or whom the accused himself designates.

The judge fixes the sum which may be offered as security, and the payment of this sum ends the penal action *ipso facto.*

When no offer is made to the judge, unless the accused demands an adjournment, and the judge recognizes the merits of the reasons stated for the adjournment, the accused, if he is a foreigner, deposits security fixed according to the terms of the last paragraph of Article 5 or is subjected to preventive imprisonment; after which the proceedings continue according to the general rules following:

(a) The judge has as clerk of the court an officer of the government whom he chooses in each case;

(b) The judge appoints another officer of the government as state's attorney, and, if the accused has not the means or the time to choose a defender, appoints, of his own motion, as defender a consistorial advocate or any other person present or immediately available whom he deems capable of performing this function;

(c) The witnesses are heard under oath;

(d) An official report is drafted;

(e) The sentence is thereupon read in its entirety and immediately published with its preamble and its terms;

(f) The appeal, if it is receivable, is entered at the same hearing upon a declaration made to the clerk of the court.

The judgment of appeal before the president of the tribunal of first instance, when the judgment before the judge of infractions has occurred according to the summary procedure above indicated, must take place, with a corresponding summary procedure, within the five days which follow the sentence of the first degree.

If the judgment of appeal is not rendered within the time above indicated, the accused who has been arrested may be placed in provisional liberty even without security.

When the above mentioned summary procedure is not followed, the prescriptions of the code of penal procedure of the Kingdom of Italy, as well as the modifications of these prescriptions by communal regulations in matters of infractions, are applied as far as possible even in the judgment of infractions. The procedure by decree may be applied only to Vatican citizens.

10. The special provisions established for foreigners in the preceding articles do not apply to those whose state of origin has concluded with the City of the Vatican a treaty by which sentences to a pecuniary penalty pronounced by the Vatican tribunals are executed by means of coercive recovery or, in default of payment, by means of a commutation of a pecuniary penalty to a penalty restrictive of personal liberty in the territory of that state.

11. Under the reservations specified in Article 3, there shall be observed in the City of the Vatican the civil code of the Kingdom of Italy and the laws which have modified or completed it, as well as the pertinent regulations, up to the coming into effect of the present law, subject to the following modifications:

(a) Vatican citizenship is regulated, in conformity whith the treaty between the Holy See and the Kingdom of Italy, by Law No. 3 of this day;

(b) The capacity to accomplish a juridical act, to acquire and dispose of property by contract among the living or upon the decease of clerks and monks who are Vatican citizens is regulated by the canon law;

(c) Marriage is also exclusively regulated by the canon law;

(d) Adoption is authorized by the Sovereign Pontiff;

(e) Prescription, with respect to ecclesiastical property, remains regulated by canons 1508 to 1512 of the *Codex juris canonici*, with the further observation of the clauses of canon 63 § 2 of the same code;

(f) Gifts as well as legacies upon death in favor of pious works are regulated by canons 1513 to 1517 of the same code;

(g) The records of birth, marriage, and death are drawn up on the occasion of the baptism, marriage, or funeral ceremony and kept by the priest, who sends a copy to the governor;

(h) The registers of citizenship and of civil status are kept by the governor, through a bureau designated for this purpose;

(i) The functions of notary are performed by consistorial advocates appointed by the governor, the notarial legislation of the Kingdom of Italy being observed, subject to Article 3; the notarial archives shall be kept at the seat of the government;

(j) The functions of recorder of mortgages, in accordance with the mortgage transcriptions and inscriptions, are fulfilled by a bureau of the government, which also provides for the keeping and preservation of the register of real property, always according to Italian legislation, with the usual reservations. In appropriate cases the government arranges with competent bureaus of the Italian conserver of mortgages and register of the survey of lands to settle provisionally questions of mortgage and land transcriptions and inscriptions, and for the transfer of registers or records relating thereto.

12. Under the reservations specified in Article 3 there shall be observed in the City of the Vatican the commercial code of the Kingdom of Italy and the laws which have modified and completed it, together with the pertinent regulations up to the coming into effect of the present law; there shall accordingly be accepted, to a certain extent, the bills of exchange, bank reimbursements, and circular reimbursements issued and payable in the City of the Vatican, as well as the insurance of persons or things there situated.

In cases where, according to the tenor of the law on economic, commercial, and professional organization, the establishment and functioning of commercial agencies or enterprises are authorized in the City of the Vatican, the general and special rules regarding agency or authorized undertakings, as set forth in the Italian code of commerce and in the laws and usages of commerce effective in the City of Rome, shall be applicable in full measure unless otherwise provided in the act of authorization.

13. Under the reservations specified in Article 3, there shall be observed in the City of the Vatican the code of civil procedure of the Kingdom of Italy and the laws which have modified or completed it will be observed in the City of the Vatican, and the pertinent regulations, up to the coming into effect of the present law and, in a certain measure, the procedure of execution and the special procedures set forth in Book III, Title I (general provisions), Title III (absence), Title V (minors), Title VI (interdiction and incapacity), Title VIII (successions), Title IX (offers of payment and deposits), Title X (copy and collation of public acts), Title XII (execution of sentences rendered abroad), modified by decree Law No. 1272 of the Kingdom of Italy of June 30, 1919.

14. The powers which, in the civil code and the code of civil procedure of the Kingdom of Italy or in other laws of the same Kingdom, are conferred on the justice of the peace or on the *praetor* in matters of execution or in procedures of voluntary jurisdiction are exercised by the president of the tribunal of first instance or by a judge whom he designates.

15. Civil actions not exceeding five thousand lire and possessory actions having a declaration of new work and of possible damage, in the cases provided for in Article 82 of the code of civil procedure of the Kingdom of Italy, are within the competence of the president of the tribunal of first instance or of the judge whom he designates.

For the said actions the procedure fixed by the same code on the subject of judgments before the praetor shall be followed.

The appeal interjected against sentences pronounced in these actions is taken before the tribunal of first instance.

Before this tribunal, before the Sacred Rota and the supreme tribunal of the Signature, as regards the civil judgment of jurisdiction and other matters belonging to the civil tribunals, the rules of canons 1552 to 1998 of the *Codex juris canonici* shall be observed in the measure in which they are applicable.

16. In civil matters as well as in penal matters the functions of solicitor and advocates are fulfilled by consistorial advocates.

However, subject to the provisions of Article 9(b), the dean of the Sacred Roman Rota may draw up a list of persons having the qualities required to exercise the functions of solicitor and advocate before the single judge of civil matters and infractions.

For the tribunal of first instance the dean of the Sacred Roman Rota designates the persons charged with exercising the functions of notary and judicial officer or bailiff.

17. The following are within the territorial jurisdiction of the City of the Vatican:

(1) All actions involving a citizen having his residence in the City of the Vatican or a stranger authorized to reside in that City for an indeterminate time;

(2) Actions relative to the estates of the persons indicated in the preceding number;

(3) Actions involving a foreigner when it is a question of: (a) real or personal actions relative to movable or immovable property in the City of the Vatican; (b) actions arising from contracts concluded or events occurring in the territory of the same city, or obligations resulting therefrom and effective in the said territory.

18. The Vatican tribunals are competent to judge offenses committed by any person within the territory of the City of the Vatican, under the condition, however that the perpetrator has not taken refuge in Italian territory or has not been turned over to the tribunals of the Kingdom of Italy, all according to Article 22 of the treaty of the eleventh of February, 1929.

The competence of the Vatican tribunals exists also in regard to offenses committed in a foreign state, when, for these same offenses, it is possible to proceed within the territory of the state of the Vatican according to the provisions of the penal code of the Kingdom of Italy, subject likewise to the provisions of the above mentioned Article 22 of the Treaty.

19. In penal and civil cases, as well as in those to which the procedural provisions of the *Codex juris canonici* are not applicable, all oaths of the parties, witnesses, experts, or other persons must be taken in the forms observed before the ecclesiastical tribunals.

20. With the reservations specified in Article 3, the following shall be observed in the City of the Vatican:

(a) Law No. 2359 of the Kingdom of Italy on expropriations by reason of public utility, of the twenty-fifth of June 1855, modified by law No. 5188 of the eighteenth of December, 1879, and by the decree-law No. 691 of the eleventh of March, 1923, as well as Articles 30, 33, and 34 of the Royal Decree No. 422 on the execution of public works of the eighth of February, 1923.

If, for grave reasons, and apart from the cases provided for by the above-mentioned law on expropriation by reason of public utility, it is necessary to dispose of the use of immovable private property, to acquire proprietary rights to movable objects or to use them, or to require compulsory labor, the governor will make the decision, by executory decree on his own initiative, upon suitable indemnity fixed by him, subject to later action before a competent judge for its definitive determination.

Without prejudice to the official execution or to the civil action for the fixing of the indemnity, he who does not obey the decree of the governor in the cases above indicated is punished by a fine up to nine thousand lire or by imprisonment up to six months:

(b) The legislation of the Kingdom of Italy in effect on the date of the promulgation of the present law together with the pertinent regulations, concerning:

Antiquities and fine arts;

Panoramic sites;

The transmission of electric energy to a distance;

Public works, with the exception of matters relating to adjudications, which remain subject to successive contracts, and reserving the provisions of Article 8 of Law 5 dated this day;

(c) The legislation of the Kingdom of Italy in effect as above said, including regulations and treaties ratified by the Kingdom of Italy up to the coming into effect of the present law, as well as the prescriptions relative to the execution of these treaties, subject to subsequent adherence of the City of the Vatican to the latter, concerning:

(1) Weights and measures fo every kind;
(2) Artistic and literary property;
(3) Patents of invention, trademarks, and patents of manufacture;
(4) Railroads;
(5) Posts;
(6) Telegraphs;
(7) Telephones;
(8) Radio telegraphy and radio telephony;
(9) Aviation;
(10) Automobiles and their circulation;
(11) Prophylaxis against infectious and contagious diseases.

In the relations between the City of the Vatican and the Kingdom of Italy on the subjects above indicated, there are reserved the special conventions which will be signed and which may derogate from the above rules adopted provisionally;

(d) In a general manner, the laws of the Kingdom of Italy, with their respective general and specific regulations, as well as the regulations of the province and government of Rome, for all that concerns the public hygiene and health, the security and integrity of persons and things, the *aedile* and urban police, as well as in general for every object which, not being already regulated by the present law or by other laws of the City of the Vatican, needs to be juridically established in this city, to the exclusion, however, unless there is express indication to the contrary, of all that relates to the organization of public corporations and administrations, to the economic and juridical status of officers and employees, to the armed forces, to contributions, subsidies, and other similar measures of administration in favor of the objects just enumerated, to taxes, contributions, and fiscal charges imposed on the same objects for the benefit of the administration, to accounting, and to finances.

The government provides for medical assistance according to rules to be prescribed by the governor.

For the authorities of the Kingdom of Italy contemplated in the laws and regulations connected with the present Article, there shall be substituted the governor, the officer, or the bureau dependent upon him which he will designate for this purpose.

21. Elementary instruction is obligatory from the age of six years through fourteen for children of both sexes who, until schools are established in the City of the Vatican, must frequent those of Rome which will be designated by the governor after agreement with the local authority.

Parents or tutors who violate the above obligation shall be punished by a fine up to five hundred lire or imprisonment up to ten days, unless they can prove that they are able to give private instruction at their own expense and by appropriate methods.

The penalty may be applied twice in the course of a scholastic year.

22. In case a civil controversy is not settled, because the sources indicated in the preceding articles do not contain a precise juridical rule or because the supplemental legislation of the Kingdom of Italy is for any reason inapplicable, the judge, relying on the precepts of divine and natural law, as well as on the general principles of canon law, shall decide, applying the principles that he would follow if he were a legislator.

23. Whenever the penal provisions of the legislation of the Kingdom of Italy, used by way of supplement, seem inapplicable for any reason and no other special penal provision exists, if the act committed violates the principles of religion or of morality, public order or the security of persons or of things, the judge, always without prejudice to the provisions and spiritual penalties of the canon law, may apply to the guilty person the penalty of a fine up to nine thousand lire or imprisonment up to six months.

24. To the Governor is delegated for a period of three years the right to issue, in case of absolute necessity or urgency, and without other formality, measures having a general character and the force of law for a term not exceeding three months, in order to regulate either questions for which there is occasion, by way of supplement according to the preceding articles, to apply the legislation of the Kingdom of Italy or any other questions which have not been provided for nor made the object of any other regulation.

Such decisions of the Governor shall be published by affixing a notice to the door of the bureaus of the government and in the Saint Damasus court or in other places expressly designated in the same decisions; they shall become effective on the day of their publication.

25. The present law shall become effective on the day of its publication.

3. LAW ON THE RIGHTS OF CITIZENSHIP AND SOJOURN

CHAPTER I. THE RIGHT OF CITIZENSHIP

1. The following are citizens of the City of the Vatican:

(a) The Cardinals residing in the city or in Rome;

(b) Those who reside in the City of the Vatican in a permanent fashion because of their rank, office, service or employment, when such residence is prescribed by a law or a regulation, or when it is authorized by the Sovereign Pontiff and, in his name, by the Cardinal Secretary of State, if it concerns a person belonging in any way to the Pontifical Court or to any of the administrations indicated in Article 2 of the fundamental law of the City of the Vatican, or by the Governor when it is a question of any other person;

(c) Those who, independently of the conditions provided for in the two preceding paragraphs, are authorized by the Sovereign Pontiff, for reasons which he in his sovereign authority deems sufficient, to reside in a permanent fashion in the City of the Vatican with the concession or reservation of the right of citizenship.

2. Also Vatican citizens are the wife, children, parents, brothers, and sisters of a Vatican citizen, on the condition that they live with him and are authorized to reside in the City of the Vatican according to the rules fixed in the following articles.

3. The authorization indicated in the preceding Article is granted by the Sovereign Pontiff and in his name by the Cardinal Secretary of State, if it concerns a person attached in any way to the Pontifical Court or to any of the administrations mentioned in Article 2 of the fundamental law of the City of the Vatican, or by the Governor if it concerns any other person.

4. The authorization for the wife and children may be given on the simple statement of relationship.

The authorization ceases by law: (a) for the wife if the marriage is annulled or is the object of a dispensation, as well as if legal separation is pronounced; (b) for the children when they attain the age of twenty-five years unless they are incapable of working and are dependent on the Vatican citizen; (c) for the daughters until their marriage.

The powers of the Sovereign Pontiff indicated in Articles 1(c) and 16 and those of the Governor indicated in Article 17 are reserved and absolute.

5. The authorization indicated in Article 3 relative to parents, brothers, and sisters may not be granted except when the said relatives are dependent on the Vatican citizen for food.

The authorization ceases by law for the brothers when they attain the age of twenty-five years, unless they are incapable of working, and for the sisters at the time of their marriage.

In every case the powers mentioned in the last paragraph of the preceding article remain reserved.

6. Vatican citizenship is lost:

(a) By Cardinals when, for any reason, they cease to reside in the City of the Vatican or in Rome;

(b) By all citizens voluntarily giving up residence in the city;

(c) By the persons indicated under Article 1(b) when they leave the rank, office, service, or employment for which they were obliged or authorized to reside in the said city;

(d) By any Vatican citizen whose residence in the city depends on the authorizations indicated in the preceding articles, when the right resulting from the said authorizations by virtue of the same articles ceases, or when a revocation thereof takes place.

Always reserved, as regards residence in the City of the Vatican and, should the case arise, the resulting rights of citizenship, are the powers mentioned in the last paragraph of Article 4.

7. Since the limited extent of the City of the Vatican does not permit all the descendants and collateral relatives of Vatican citizens to reside there with their new families, the Sovereign Pontiff, desirous of encouraging the formation of new families and generations, reserves the right, for each case, by sovereign and absolute judgment, to take measures in favor of new families who are obliged to abandon the City of the Vatican and to concede to them, under favorable conditions, the use of lodgings belonging to the Holy See in the Kingdom of Italy.

8. Vatican citizenship is not lost by the simple fact of a temporary sojourn in another place unless such sojourn is accompanied by abandonment of residence in the City of the Vatican or, for Cardinals, by abandonment of residence in Rome, or by some other circumstance proving abandonment of residence.

9. The authorizations envisaged in the present Chapter are revocable at any time, with suitable advance notice, unless reasons of public order, service, morality, and discipline require immediate measures.

10. The Governor keeps a register of Vatican citizens on which are transcribed:

(a) The names of the Vatican citizens indicated under letters (a), (b), and (c) of Article 1, with mention of the title giving them this quality;

(b) The authorizations provided in the present chapter;

(c) The revocation of these authorizations;

(d) The declarations of voluntary abandonment of permanent residence;

(e) The certificates attesting the loss of Vatican citizenship for any other reason.

11. Vatican citizens must provide themselves with identity cards, which the Governor will deliver to them according to methods to be fixed by the regulations.

On presentation of such identity cards they may leave the City of the Vatican and re-enter without other formality.

Cardinals who are Vatican citizens and their suites, the Governor, and other persons to be designated by the regulations are exempt from the obligation of having identity cards.

CHAPTER II. ENTRANCE AND SOJOURN IN THE CITY OF THE VATICAN

12. Those who are not Vatican citizens, in order to enter the City of the Vatican, must provide themselves with an authorization, conforming to the model to be fixed by regulation of the Governor, which, after proof of the identity of the persons, shall be delivered by the officers or agents in charge of the maintenance of entries.

For just and grave reasons, of which the officers and agents above indicated are the only judges, the authorization may be refused.

The authorization allows remaining in the City of the Vatican only during the hours determined by regulation of the Governor.

The authorization must be kept and shown whenever asked.

13. For the entrance of societies, bands of pilgrims, and other similar groups, a collective authorization may be delivered in the name either of the leaders or of the directors of the societies or bands of pilgrims in question, with the simple indication of the number of persons accompanying them.

The Governor or official delegated by him may accord permanent authorizations of entry.

14. Those who are not Vatican citizens must, in order to remain in the City of the Vatican outside the hours indicated in Article 12 above, obtain authorization from the governor or from the officer designated for this purpose.

The authorization specifies the duration of the stay and may contain the restrictions and conditions which the governor or the said officer deems advisable.

15. Exempted from the authorization mentioned in Article 12 are foreigners furnished with passports already visaed by a diplomatic representative of the Holy See or by any other authority delegated for this purpose by the Sovereign Pontiff. This visa does not authorize remaining in the City of the Vatican outside the hours mentioned in the next to last paragraph of the Article above-mentioned.

Exempted from the authorization of entry and stay in the City of the Vatican outside the hours above indicated are the Cardinals who are not citizens of the Vatican and their suites, the members of the diplomatic corps accredited to the Holy See, the family of the Sovereign Pontiff, the dignitaries of the Pontifical Court, the ecclesiastics and other persons attached to offices or courts of the Apostolic See, the General Counsellor of the State, the employees of the Government and of other Vatican administrations, those who belong to the Armed Forces when they come for reasons of service, and the other persons who may be indicated in the regulations.

16. The Sovereign Pontiff, for such reasons as he may deem necessary in his sovereign authority, reserves the right to permit anyone to remain in the City of the Vatican for an indeterminate length of time, but without such authorization implying the acquisition of right of citizenship.

17. The Governor or office designated for this purpose may, with the same effect, grant authorizations for temporary stay:

(a) to members of the families of Vatican citizens, within the limits of relationship indicated in Article 2, even when those mentioned in Articles 4 and 5 have not existed or have ceased to exist, and also to relatives and connections of even more distant degree than those mentioned in the said articles, if their permanent residence in the City of the Vatican is necessary to a Vatican citizen for personal assistance or the management of his house. The authorization may be accorded, as a general rule, to only one person for each Vatican citizen. An authorization for several persons must be delivered by the Governor himself;

(b) to persons indicated under the preceding letter when the Vatican citizen obliged by law to furnish them with the necessities of life is able to provide them only in his own domicile;

(c) to domestics and servants of Vatican citizens or of persons who have the right to reside in the City of the Vatican;

(d) in extraordinary cases of absolute necessity.

18. No person, even though authorized to stay, may give lodging, temporary or permanent, with or without payment, without authorization of the Governor or of the office designated for this purpose.

19. The authorizations specified in this Chapter are always revocable, subject to the provisions of Article 9 relative to advance notice.

20. The granting of lodgings in the City of the Vatican to those who reside there, except in the case of lodgings in private property and subject, in that case, to the provisions relative to leases, sub-leases, and the right of requisition, is made in an absolute manner by the Sovereign Pontiff and in his name by the Governor.

The concession of lodgings is revocable, with appropriate advance notice, unless reasons of public order, service, morality, or discipline require immediate revocation.

The lodging may be changed by a decision of the authority which has granted them but subject to the rules of appropriate advance notice.

The indications concerning the capacity of lodgings assigned or assignable, as well as other particulars of the localities, must be kept up to date with a view to the concession or refusal of authorization of residence to relatives and connections in accordance with the provisions of Chapter I and of the present Chapter.

The revocation of the concession of lodgings implies by law the revocation of the authorization to reside in the City of the Vatican, unless it provides otherwise.

21. The persons who are in the City of the Vatican without the authorizations required in the preceding articles or with authorizations that have lapsed or have been revoked may be expelled by the public force.

For grave reasons, or where it is a question of persons condemned by the Vatican courts for any offense whatsoever, the expulsion may be accompanied, on order of the Governor, by permanent or temporary prohibition to enter the City of the Vatican.

22. The Governor keeps a register of civil status. Inscribed therein are: the names of the persons authorized to reside in the City of the Vatican for a limited or unlimited period according to the rules of the preceding articles; the revocations of the same authorizations; the decrees of expulsion and prohibitions of entry.

CHAPTER III. ENTRANCE INTO THE CITY OF THE VATICAN WITH VEHICLES

23. Carriages or automobiles belonging to foreigners, whether they serve for transportation of persons or things and whether they are private or for public service, may enter the City of the Vatican after delivery of special authorization: (a) when they transport persons or merchandise permitted to enter the City; (b) when, although empty, they are required by a person within the territory of the City of the Vatican for the transportation of persons or things in the interest of the person requiring them.

24–27. (Parking, registration, fueling of automobiles.)

28–31. (Penal provisions.)

32. Until the establishment of a new and special entry for the museums of the Vatican, the governor will have the right to suspend by his regulations the application of the provisions contained in Articles 12, 13, 15, 23, 24 and 25 of the present law or to issue other regulations in place of the above-mentioned provisions.

33. The present law shall become effective on the day of its publication.

4. LAW ON ADMINISTRATIVE ORGANIZATION

CHAPTER I. GENERAL RULES

1. The grants of power made by this law or others do not in any way derogate from the right of reservation possessed by the Sovereign Pontiff by virtue of Article 6 of the Fundamental Law.

2. The Sovereign Pontiff reserves to himself the right to annul, at any moment, the provisions emanating from any administrative authority which are contrary to the laws or to the general or special regulations.

He may, as well, revoke or amend at any time measures which seem inopportune or prejudicial to the public interest, subject, in case the said measures have given rights to third persons, to an equitable indemnification fixed in the decision of revocation or amendment.

3. Subject to the right of invoking at any time against an administrative measure, and by means of grace, the power of annulment, or amendment indicated in the preceding article, appeal to the Sovereign Pontiff by means of the tribunals, provided for in Article 16 of the fundamental law, must be formulated within thirty days of the publication or notification of the measure attacked, or from the day when the interested party has shown that he had knowledge thereof.

4. Action against an administrative authority to defend a right allegedly violated by it is prescribed after a period of five years. The prescription runs also as regards minors and incompetents.

CHAPTER II. ORGANIZATION OF THE GOVERNMENT

5. The governor personally exercises his powers:

(a) In matters of legislation, when they are delegated to him;

(b) In the making of regulations;

(c) In the conclusion of agreements with the communal, provincial, or local governmentral authorities residing in Rome;

(d) In relations with the said authorities or with other authorities of the Kingdom of Italy, if the occasion arises in the transaction of business within the jurisdiction of the Government;

(e) When it appears expressly from other laws or regulations that the power is strictly personal.

6. The Governor must be a Vatican citizen and reside in the Vatican.

7. In case of absence or impediment, the Governor is replaced by the chief of service whom he designates; for lack of designation, by the Secretary General and, in the absence of the latter, by the senior chief of service present, or, if there is parity in the date of nomination, by the oldest.

He who replaces the Governor may not exercise the powers reserved personally to the latter except in cases of necessity or urgency.

8. The Counsellor General of the State and the judges and officers of the judicial power are not obliged to be Vatican citizens or to reside in the Vatican; they do not belong to the category of officers and employees and receive only a simple compensation for services.

9. The distribution of offices, the number, the powers, the rights, and obligations of officers, employees, and clerks, their appointment, their discipline and their dismissal are determined by regulations to be issued by the Governor.

10. On any occasion, subject to the powers of the Sovereign Pontiff as regards the Governor and the Counsellor General of the State, and subject also to the special provisions applicable to the Armed Forces, the officers and employees dependent on the Governor may be punished, according to the gravity of their fault, by censure or by suppression of a fourth of their salary during one year or more. The faults which render an officer unworthy, unsuitable, or incapable, from the point of view of the necessary confidence, may always entail dismissal notwithstanding a contract for a period or for life.

Dismissal may also and always be pronounced in case of physical or intellectual incapacity.

11. The measures treated in the preceding Article are taken by the Governor, after hearing the interested parties and without other formality.

Recourse to the Sovereign Pontiff is admitted against these measures, to the exclusion of any other action except with respect to the civil property rights which may result from special contracts and on the subject of which it is impossible to check the reasons for the administrative measure.

12. The officers or employees who are responsible for payments or collections or who are, in any way, responsible for the handling of money, securities, or merchandise, must render account to the governor, to whose supervision they are submitted through the bureau of finances and accounting.

The Governor, when he considers a person subject to accounting to be responsible even through simple negligence, notifies such person of his reasons and gives him a period of time for his defense. If, in the opinion of the Counsellor General of the State, the responsibility is well established, the amount of reimbursement is fixed by a decision of the Governor on the basis of conservative measures, or of the inscription of a judicial mortgage, or, when the Governor deems it advisable, of a forced execution on the property of the person subject to accounting, including the property taken for security if such exists.

Against this decision the person subject to accounting may appeal to the Sacred Rota. The appeal does not have the effect of suspension.

13. The administrative officers charged with receiving pledges, ordering payments, with watching over those who handle money, securities, or commodities and also over the pledges and expenditures above indicated, are responsible for the losses which, by their fault or fraud, result to the State.

Every officer or employee who by act or omission, even though unpremeditated, causes prejudice to the State, incurs the same responsibility, unless he can show that he acted by virtue of a superior order which he was obliged to execute.

The supervision of the said responsibility is conducted according to the same procedure as that established for persons subject to accounting in the preceding Article.

The Governor of the Sacred Rota may by way of equity, however, as regards the responsible officers or employees mentioned in the present Article, charge the responsible officer or employee with only a part of the loss sustained.

14. All dignitaries, officers, and employees shall take the oath of allegiance by means of the following formula:

"I swear on the Holy Gospel to be faithful to the Sovereign Pontiff, to observe scrupulously the orders which shall be given by him, by my other superiors, and by the laws of the state, and to fulfill with zeal the obligations of my office.

The oath is taken by the Governor, the Counsellor General of the State, and the Commandants of the Armed Forces before the Sovereign Pontiff, and by other persons before the Governor.

CHAPTER III. CONTRACTS

15. All contracts entered into in the interest of the City of the Vatican for an amount greater than 5,000 lire must be first submitted for the examination of the bureau of finances and accounting, which may present on the subject the observations which seem to it legitimate, and thereafter for the approval of the Governor or his substitute.

For lack of these formalities contracts are null. The nullity may be opposed only by the public administration.

16. In all contracts for work or supplies, unless there is a contrary stipulation, the right of cancellation upon payment of ten per cent of the amount of the work or supplies to be delivered, in addition to full payment for deliveries already made, is reserved to the administration.

17. In all contracts for work or supplies, when the contractor does not execute his bargain, the administration may, by an executory decree and with the assistance of the public force, if it is necessary, occupy the shops, seize the machines, the warehouses of materials, or supplies of merchandise, and execute the contract subject to the eventual indemnities to be fixed by the judicial authority.

CHAPTER IV. GENERAL PROVISIONS

18. The present law shall become effective on the day of its publication.

5. LAW ON ECONOMIC, COMMERCIAL, AND PROFESSIONAL ORGANIZATION

1. The state of the City of the Vatican has its own currency.

The money and bank notes of the Kingdom of Italy are legal tender according to the legislation of that Kingdom until the rules concerning the currency of the City of the Vatican are formulated and that currency is issued.

2. The authorization of the Governor is necessary for the alienation of real property situated within the territory of the Vatican, for transactions between the living, whether for compensation or gratuitous, for the constitution of rights of long lease, rights to the surface of land, use, usufruct, servitude, mortgage, or any other effective right, as well as for the leases and sub-leases, even partial, of such real property, whatever may be the duration of the lease.

The same authorization is obligatory for the acquisition of the same rights over the said real property by lawful succession or by testamentary disposition, either by universal or by individual title.

Until this authorization has been granted, no one may dispose of the possession of real property or effect the operations above indicated. Infractions of this provision are punished by a fine which may amount to three thousand lire.

The absence of authorization renders null the transactions mentioned in the preceding Article. The nullity may be disregarded by the Government.

In the case where authorization is refused for entrance into possession of real property by succession, as stated above, the real property falls under the patrimony of the State in exchange for a just indemnity fixed by the Governor, but with recourse possible to the courts according to the methods and forms applicable to indemnities for expropriation. If the authorization to acquire rights with respect to real property by inheritance is refused, the heir who is authorized to receive the title to the property shall take it free of the said rights, but pecuniary compensation commensurate with the charge imposed by the said rights shall be granted and, in case of difference, fixed by the judicial authority.

3. For the real property existing in the City of the Vatican and not owned by the Holy See, no work of transformation or enlargement may be executed without the previous authorization of the Governor.

Infractions of this prohibition are punished by fines of up to five thousand lire; moreover, the Governor or the service delegated for this purpose shall have full power to require officially, without other formality and at the expense of the offender, the restoration of the property to its previous condition.

4. The purchase for resale of merchandise or commodities, of whatever nature or origin, and their sale are reserved as a monopoly to the state, according to the rules to be fixed by decree.

The State provides, further, by means of a special organization, for the pharmaceutical service.

By the sole intermediary of competent offices of the State, or following only the forms which shall be fixed by regulations, persons residing in the City of the Vatican may cause to be sent there, for their personal use or for that of their families, merchandise or commodities exempt from the customs taxes and taxes of consumption in effect in the Kingdom of Italy. Amounts exceeding the limits of this use will be confiscated with or without indemnity according to the circumstances.

5. The introduction by private persons into the City of the Vatican, for their personal use or for that of their own families, of merchandise or commodities acquired in the Kingdom of Italy and already subjected to customs taxes, as well as to taxes of consumption in effect in the said Kingdom, is free, subject, in each case, to proof by the person introducing them that the conditions above indicated exist.

It is forbidden to individuals to bring into the City of the Vatican merchandise or commodities, even when they have paid the customs taxes and taxes of consumption established by the laws of the Kingdom of Italy, if they are brought in in such abundance, and in such a manner that they are obviously intended for commerce; it is the same in regard to the storing of the said merchandise or commodities and their sale.

Infractions of the prohibition mentioned in the preceding paragraph are punished by a fine of up to five thousand lire, as well as by confiscation of the merchandise and commodities. In case of a second offense, imprisonment up to six months may be added to the fine.

It is further forbidden to individuals to bring into the City of the Vatican merchandise or commodities which have not been subjected to the customs taxes and taxes of consumption mentioned above, even when they are not brought in in such quantity or in such manner that a commercial purpose is evident; it is the same as to the holding of such merchandise or commodities and their sale.

The violation of the prohibition formulated in the preceding paragraph is punished by a fine of up to fifteen thousand lire; in every case the merchandise introduced, held, or sold in violation of this prohibition is confiscated, as well as the receptacles and means of transportation. In case of association for the accomplishment of the offense or of a second offense, the penalty of imprisonment may be also pronounced for a term which may reach three years.

6. The exportation of merchandise or commodities from the City of the Vatican to the territory of the Kingdom of Italy is forbidden. The violation or even the simple attempt to violate this prohibition is punished by a fine of the same amount as that fixed in the last paragraph of the preceding Article, and by imprisonment up to three years, in addition to the confiscation of the contraband, merchandise, or commodities and of the receptacles and means of transportation.

Exempt from the prohibition of exportation are objects of personal use in the usual quantity needed for a journey, and also the exportation of personal property in case of removal of residence from the City of the Vatican.

7. No one may open a store. a workshop, or an office, even for the purpose of simple occupations, or establish industrial or commercial enterprises of any kind, or create cabinets, offices, agencies, or fixed localities to receive the public with a view to exercising any profession whatever, without the authorization of the governor.

If the laws in effect in the City of the Vatican or the national laws of a foreigner exercising a liberal profession require for the exercise of that profession proofs of capacity, the authorization may be granted only if these proofs have been submitted in conformity with the Vatican or foreign law.

Infractions of this prohibition are punished by a fine up to three thousand lire and, as well, by the closing, as a matter of course and without other formality, of the places used.

8. Whenever, for the establishment of a business bureau or a commercial or industrial enterprise, the authorization provided for in the preceding Article has been granted, provided that other rules have not been issued by the City of the Vatican, the employer shall be subject by law to the provisions of the legislation of the Kingdom of Italy in effect upon the application of the present law, to the extent that these provisions are applicable and subject to the reservations mentioned in Article 3 of Law No. 2 of the same date on the sources of law, with respect to labor contracts, the labor of women and children, the eight hour day, rest on feast days, social insurance for accidents, maternity, illness, and old age, enforced idleness and tuberculosis; also, whenever it is not otherwise prescribed by the laws or by clauses of the act of concession, and in so far as special rules shall not have been formulated by the City of the Vatican, he shall fulfill the assurances connected with the preceding questions by means of contracts entered into with the establishments or organizations to which the legislation of the Kingdom of Italy requires him to address himself.

Also subject to the rules of the preceding paragraph are foreign entrepreneurs who, by contracts, either with the public administration or with individuals, execute enterprises or carry on any work or provisioning in the City of the Vatican.

9. The occasional and temporary work executed by representatives, even foreigners, of various professions, arts, enterprises, or occupations, for the profit of persons residing in the City of the Vatican or their property, are free, subject to the observance of the rules relative to admissions and sojourn.

However, even in the case provided for by this Article, if the Vatican law or the national law of the foreign professional requires proofs of capacity, the latter may offer his services only if he has submitted these proofs.

Infractions of the prohibitions contained in the present Articles are punished by a fine up to nine thousand lire or by imprisonment up to six months.

10. The present law shall become effective on the day of its publication.

6. LAW OF PUBLIC SECURITY

1. The Governor watches over the maintenance of public order, the security of the citizens, the integrity of their persons, the protection of their property, the safeguarding of their possessions, and the public hygiene and morality.

With this purpose, either in the execution of the laws and regulations or on the occasion of events not provided for in the general provisions, he will take the measures he deems advisable.

Whoever does not obey these measures, without committing any other graver fault, is punished by a fine up to four thousand, five hundred lire or by imprisonment up to three months.

Without prejudice to the penal action, the measures above indicated may, in such a case, be executed even immediately, with the aid of the public force, but with the obligation for the person obliged to obey, to reimburse the expenses of execution in accordance with the liquidation established by the Governor.

2. Anyone who, on the summons of the Governor or of the officers dependent on him, does not present himself on the day set, is punished, unless there are valid reasons, by a fine up to one thousand five hundred lire or by imprisonment up to one month.

Without prejudice to the penal action, the authorities indicated in the preceding paragraph may, by constraint, oblige those who have not obeyed the summons to appear.

3. The constitution of any association without the authorization of the Governor is forbidden.

The prohibition is not applicable to religious orders, to congregations and associations provided for by the *Codex juris canonici* and constituted according to the rules of the latter.

The associations constituted contrary to this prohibition are dissolved independently of measures which shall seem advisable as regards the locality and possessions.

The offenders are subject to a fine up to nine thousand lire and to imprisonment up to six months.

4. Any meeting in a public place or one open to the public is forbidden without the previous authorization of the Governor. A meeting announced by private invitation is considered as public when it appears from the place designated, the number of persons invited, and the object of the meeting that the private character of such meeting is simulated.

The provisions of the preceding Article do not apply to receptions, processions, religious ceremonies, and funeral cortèges, subject to understanding to be established with the Governor.

Unauthorized meetings are dissolved by the public force. Even authorized meetings may also be dissolved when they are disorderly or in danger of becoming so.

Anyone who takes part in an unauthorized meeting is punished by a fine from five hundred to nine thousand lire or by imprisonment from ten days to six months.

Whoever does not obey the order of dissolution of an authorized meeting is punished by a fine up to four thousand five hundred lire or by imprisonment up to three months.

5. It is forbidden to keep arms, even in one's dwelling place, or to carry them outside without the authorization of the Governor.

Sharp or cutting instruments capable of causing wounds may not be carried without just cause outside of one's dwelling.

Authorization is also necessary for collection of artistic, rare and ancient arms.

Transgressors of the prohibition to have or carry arms without authorization or to circulate without just cause with instruments capable of causing wounds are punished by a fine up to nine thousand lire or by imprisonment up to six months. The said arms or instruments are confiscated.

Those who infringe the prohibition of having collections of artistic, rare, or ancient arms without authorization are punished by a fine of three thousand lire. Confiscation is optional.

6. It is forbidden, without authorization of the Governor, to keep war weapons, deposits of arms not of war, deposits of munitions and explosive material. Whoever violates this prohibition is punished, if the act is not accompanied by a graver offense, by imprisonment from three months to three years, as well as by the confiscation of the arms, munitions and explosive matters.

7. For the observance of the two preceding Articles the Governor may order domiciliary visits or personal searches.

8. The public exercise of printing, lithography, photography, and other mechanical or chemical reproduction of characters, designs, or figures is forbidden without the authorization of the Governor.

It is forbidden to affix or offer to the public, even gratuitously, announcements, writings, printed matter, books, engraving, lithographs, photographs, statues of any kind, without the authorization of the Governor.

Infractions of the two preceding prohibitions are punished by a fine of nine thousand lire or by imprisonment up to six months.

9. The ambulatory sale of any objects whatever is absolutely prohibited. Infractions of this prohibition are punished by the penalties indicated in the preceding Article.

10. It is forbidden to exercise the profession of guide or interpreter without the authorization of the Governor which shall be subject to ascertaining the qualifications of the candidate.

Whoever violates this prohibition is punished by a fine of up to four thousand five hundred lire or by imprisonment of up to three months.

11. The authorizations and licenses referred to in the preceding articles may be given by the offices subordinate to the Governor as well as by the Governor himself, except the authorization referred to in Article 3, and may be subject to the conditions and time limits deemed opportune. They may be revoked at any time without indemnity.

12. The present law shall enter into force on the day of its publication.

No. VII. Ordinance of the Governor of the Vatican City State provisionally controlling access to the City.

June 8, 1929.

Not reproduced.

YUGOSLAVIA

SUMMARY

INTERNATIONAL STATUS

Yugoslavia is a member of the United Nations (October 24, 1945). It is a member of other international organizations. It was a member of the League of Nations.

Yugoslavia was proclaimed on December 1, 1918, as the Kingdom of the Serbs, Croats and Slovenes under the Karageorgevitch (Serbia) dynasty.

The French Revolution and the reforms imposed by Napoleon when he created the Illyrian Provinces had a profound effect upon the Croats and

Slovenes, and in 1830, the ideal of a State incorporating all the southern Slavs began to be prevalent among Croats. In the 1848–49 revolution, the Diet of Zagreb proclaimed the liberation of Croatia from Hungary and the union of all the Yugoslav provinces within a confederated Austria, then being considered by a constituent assembly in Vienna. Absolutist rule was reimposed by the Emperor in 1849 and lasted until 1860. Croatia was granted autonomous status within the Hapsburg Empire in 1868 but this autonomy was aften violated. Serbia became a principality early in the nineteenth century and a kingdom in 1862. The conflicts between the Serbs and Croats, both religious and territorial, were exploited in the succeeding period by the Empire.

In 1903, Hungarian dictatorship in Croatia ended and a constitutional parliamentary regime was installed in Serbia which acted as a pole of attraction on all the southern Slavs. The annexation of Bosnia-Herzegovina by Austria-Hungary in 1908 consolidated their desire for emancipation and union, but the second Balkan War between the other Balkan states and Bulgaria destroyed the hopes of a federation. Austria declared war on Serbia after Sarajevo. The declaration of Corfu of July 27, 1917, providing for the formation of the Kingdom as a constitutional and parliamentary monarchy, was followed by a period of conflict between those favoring federation and those favoring integration.

The first constitution of the new Kingdom of June 28, 1921, with strongly centralist tendencies and abolishing all the old provinces, was imposed by the Serbs and objected to by the majority of Croats, Slovenes and the Moslems of Bosnia-Herzegovina and Macedonia. With the assassination of the leader of the Croatian Peasant Party and principal exponent of federalism, in 1928, began the struggle for a federal state. The King, in order to prevent this, abrogated in 1929 the constitution, proclaimed his personal dictatorship, named the country Yugoslavia, forbade the use of the provincial names, and thus consolidated the great majority of the country against integration. In 1938, autonomy was granted to Croatia and a new coalition government was entrusted with preparing to reorganize the state on federalist lines. Serbian opinion was roused against Croatia and successive capitulations to Germany increased the tension and led to the *coup d'état* of March 25, 1941, followed by invasion and occupation. The Germans created a puppet state in Croatia of Oustachis and there were widespread massacres of Serbs and other minority and progressive groups. The remainder of Yugoslavia was partitioned between Germany, Italy, Hungary and Bulgaria.

The Communist party was formed in April 1919, and from 1936 supported a free, democratic and federal Yugoslavia in its program. It organized the National Liberation Movement in June 1941 on this basis, and was fully able to do so as, unlike the other parties it had no national or regional background. Its central political and administrative organ, the Anti-fascist Council of National Liberation was created on November 27, 1942, and the Committee of National Liberation, in effect the government, proclaimed a federal organization of the state on November 29, 1943, based on six federal states. In March 1945, the unified government was formed incorporating other parties, and Marshal Tito formed the government. On November 29, 1945, after the elections on a single list of Popular Front candidates, the other parties in the provisional post-war legislature refusing to participate in protest against the antidemocratic measures of the Communist Party, the monarchy was abolished and Yugoslavia was proclaimed a Popular Federal Republic. Russian objections to Yugoslav efforts towards Balkan federation led to the condemnation of Marshal Tito and other leaders by the Comintern in June 1948. The 1953 constitutional law incorporated reforms introduced following this expulsion.

FORM OF NATIONAL GOVERNMENT

The Constitution of April 7, 1963, replacing the Constitutional Law of January 13, 1953 and the Constitution of 1946, states that Yugoslavia is a federal state of voluntarily united and equal peoples and a social democracy, a community based on the powers of the working people and on self-government.[1] The socialist system and the social-economic organization in Yugoslavia are described.[2] In its international relations Yugoslavia adheres to the principles of the United Nations Charter and actively participates in the work of international organizations.[3] The working people shall be the sole holders of power and government of social affairs.[4] Self-government by the citizens in the communes is the political foundation of the unified social-political system which is described, together with the social-political communities, namely the Commune, the District, the socialist Republic and the Federation.[5] The jurisdiction of the Federation is described.[6]

RIGHTS OF THE PEOPLE

The Constitution guarantees equality before the law, the right to social self-government, the right and freedom to work, the right to a maximum working week of 42 hours and rest, safety, health and minimum income guarantees, social security, freedom of thought and determination, freedom of the press, association, speech, assembly, freedom to express nationality and culture and to use one's own language, equality of languages, education, freedom of religion, life and freedom of man, due process of

[1] Const., Art. 1. [2] Id., Basic Principles: II–VI, Art. 6–31.
[3] Id., Basic Principles: VII. [4] Id., Art. 71. [5] Id., Art. 73–131.
[6] Id., Art. 160–162.

law, no retroactive punishment, freedom of movement and abode, inviolability of domicile, privacy of communication.[1] No citizen may be deprived of citizenship, exiled or extradited.[2] The right to inheritance, protection of health, the family, mothers and children are provided.[3] Citizens must defend the country and contribute to satisfy the material requirements of the social community.[4]

LEGISLATIVE DEPARTMENT

The Federal Assembly is the supreme organ of power and the organ of social self-government.[5] It has five chambers: the Federal Chamber, the Economic Chamber, the Chamber of Education and Culture, the Chamber of Social Welfare and Health, the Organizational-Political Chamber.[6] There is also the Chamber of Nationalities whose members are members of the Federal Chamber.[7] Each Chamber is composed of 120 deputies.[8] From the point of view of function, it is in the nature of a bicameral association; the Federal Chamber, as general political body whose deputies are elected by the communal assemblies and citizens directly, takes part in the management in all the jurisdictions of the Assembly, the Chambers of the working communities whose deputies are elected by the communal assemblies, examine matters within their jurisdiction only.[9] Parliamentary immunity is provided.[10] Dissolution and elections of deputies are called by the President of the Assembly who is a member of the Federal Chamber.[11]

EXECUTIVE DEPARTMENT

The President of the Republic is the Head of State and Commander of the Armed Forces.[12] He promulgates the laws, has the power of appointment, grants decorations and pardons.[13] He is elected for four years and may be reelected once (but no limit of tenure of office applies to President Josip Broz-Tito) by the Federal Assembly.[14] The Federal Executive Council is the organ of the Federal Assembly entrusted with political executive powers.[15] It consists of the President and members elected by the Federal Chamber from among members of the Assembly and of certain members *ex officio*.[16] There are provisions regarding the federal administration [17] and the national defense and army.[18]

[1] Id., Art. 32–53. [2] Id., Art. 54. [3] Id., Art. 55–58. [4] Id., Art. 60, 62.
[5] Id., Art. 163. [6] Id., Art. 165. [7] Id., Art. 165, 190–192.
[8] Id., Art. 166. [9] Id., Art. 167, 173–185, 188–189. [10] Id., Art. 202.
[11] Id., Art. 171, 193. [12] Id., Art. 215. [13] Id., Art. 217. [14] Id., Art. 220, 221.
[15] Id., Art. 225. [16] Id., Art. 226. [17] Id., Art. 233–238. [18] Id., Art. 252–257.

JUDICIAL DEPARTMENT

Judicial power is exercised by courts as autonomous organs of the social community; protection of constitutionality is vested in constitutional courts.[1] The Constitution provides for courts of general jurisdiction and courts of special jurisdiction.[2] There is a Supreme Court and a Constitutional Court, the latter of which is composed of a President and ten judges elected for eight years by the Federal Assembly; it decides on the conformity of laws with the Constitution, on the conformity of laws of the republics with federal law, and resolves disputes on the rights and duties and conflicts of jurisdiction.[3]

AREA, POPULATION, ETC.

The area of Yugoslavia is 255,804 square kilometres, the population (1965) 19,632,000. The capital is Belgrade.[4] The languages of the peoples of Yugoslavia are stated as Serbo-Croatian and Croato-Serbian, Slovene and Macedonian; all languages used are equal; the Serbo-Croatian language is used for the army.[5]

[1] Id., Art. 74, 136, 146, 149, 150.
[2] Id., Art. 132.
[3] Id., Art. 239–251, 164.
[4] Id., Art. 5.
[5] Id., Art. 131, 42.

CONSTITUTION of YUGOSLAVIA [1]

April 17, 1963

Considering the historical fact that the working people of Yugoslavia, under the leadership of the Communist Party, overthrew the former class society based on exploitation, political oppression and national inequality by their struggle in the People's Liberation War and Socialist Revolution in order to found a community in which human labor and man will be delivered from exploitation and arbitrariness and each of the peoples of Yugoslavia and all of them together will find conditions for free and comprehensive development;

Aware that such changes have been brought about in the development of the material basis of the country and of socialist social relations as supersede the present Constitution;

Desirous of consolidating these achievements and of securing conditions for the further development of socialist and democratic relations and for comprehensive progress and freedom of the people by uniform constitutionality;

The Federal People's Assembly, as the supreme representative body of the working people and of all the peoples of Yugoslavia,

Establishes:

[1] *Constitution of the Socialist Federal Republic of Yugoslavia*. Institute of Comparative Law, Collection of Yugoslav Laws, Volume VII. Translated by Petar Mijuskovic. Belgrade 1963. Supplied by the Institute of Comparative Law in December 1965. Ed.

The Constitution of the Socialist Federal Republic of Yugoslavia

INTRODUCTORY PART
BASIC PRINCIPLES

I

The peoples of Yugoslavia, on the basis of the right of every people to self-determination, including the right to secession, on the basis of their common struggle and their will freely declared in the People's Liberation War and Socialist Revolution, and in accord with their historical aspirations, aware that the further consolidation of their brotherhood and unity is to their common interest, have united in a federal republic of free and equal peoples and nationalities and have founded a socialist federal community of working people, the Socialist Federal Republic of Yugoslavia, in which, in the interests of each people and of all of them together, they are achieving and developing:

Socialist social relations and the protection of the socialist system of society;

National freedom and independence;

Brotherhood and unity among the peoples and solidarity among the working people.

Possibilities and freedom for the comprehensive development of the human personality and for close communion of the people in accord with their interests and aspirations to create an ever richer culture and civilization in socialist society;

Unity and co-ordination of efforts to develop the material basis of the social community and the prosperity of the people;

Association of their own aspirations with the progressive strivings of mankind;

Common foundations of an economic and political system in which common interests and equality are achieved among the people.

The working people and the peoples of Yugoslavia exercise their sovereign rights in the Federation when the Constitution determines this to be in the common interest and exercise all other relations in the socialist republics.

II

The socialist system in Yugoslavia is based on relations between people acting as free and equal producers and creators, whose work serves exclusively to satisfy their personal and common needs.

Accordingly, the inviolable foundation of the position and role of man lies in:

Social ownership of the means of production, which precludes the restoration of any system of exploitation of one man by another, and which, by eliminating the separation of man from the means of production and other working conditions, provides the conditions necessary for management by the working people in production and in the distribution of the products of labor, and for social guidance of economic development;

Emancipation of work, which supersedes the historically conditioned inequality and dependence of people in work, which is assured by the abolition of wage-labor relations; by self-management of the working people, by comprehensive development of the productive forces, by the diminishing of the socially necessary labor time, by the development of science, culture, and technology, and by the continual expansion of education;

The right of man both as an individual and as a member of the working collective to enjoy the fruits of his work and of the material progress of the social community, in accordance with the principle, "From each according to his abilities; to each according to his work," along with the obligation of man to assure the development of the material foundations of his own and of socially-organized work and to contribute to the satisfaction of other social needs;

Self-management by the working people in the working organization; free association of the working people, of working and other organizations and of social-political communities in order to satisfy common needs and interests; self-government in the commune and in the other social-political communities so as to assure the direct participation of the citizens in the determination of the course of social development, in the exercise of power and in the decisions on other social affairs;

The democratic political relations that enable man to achieve his interests, to realize his right of self-government and other rights and mutual relations, and to develop his personality by direct activity in social life, especially in the organs of self-government, in the social-political organizations and associations, which he himself creates and through which he influences the development of social consciousness and expands the conditions for his activity and for the attainment of his interests and rights;

Equality of rights, duties and responsibilities of the people in conformity with uniform constitutionality and legality;

Solidarity and co-operation of the working people and working organizations, their interest and their unrestricted initiative in developing production and other social and personal activities in behalf of man and his social community;

Economic and social security of man.

It is from this position of man that the social-economic and political system derives, and it is man and his role in society that it serves.

Any form of management of production and of other social activities and any form of distribution that distort the social relations based on this position of man, whether in the form of bureaucratic arbitrariness and privileges based on monopoly position or in the form of private-ownership selfishness and particularism, is contrary to the individual and common interests of the working man and to the social-economic and political system determined by the Constitution.

III

The socially-owned means of production, being the common, inalienable basis of socially-organized work, serve to satisfy the personal and common needs and interest of the working people and to develop the material foundations of the social community and socialist social relations. The socially-owned means of production are managed directly by the working people, who work with these means on their own behalf and on behalf of the social community and are responsible to each other and to the social community.

Since no one has the right of ownership over the socially-owned means of production, neither the social-political community nor the working organization nor the working man may appropriate in any form of ownership the product of socially-organized work, or manage and dispose of socially-owned means of production and work, or arbitrarily determine the terms of distribution.

Work is the only grounds for the appropriation of the product of socially-organized work, and the foundation of management of social means.

The social product serves to restore and expand the material basis for socially-organized work, and directly to satisfy the personal and common needs of the working people, in conformity with the principle of distribution according to work.

That part of the social product which is set aside for the renewal and expansion of the material basis of socially-organized work provides the foundation for social economic growth, which the working people realize in their working organizations, and through the mutual co-operation of these organizations, as well as in the social-political communities.

A uniform system of distribution shall assure that the working organizations will employ the funds for social-economic growth in proportion to their share in creating them, subject to their ability to make the most effective use of them within the framework of the social division of labor determined by the social plans.

In order to attain self-management and to realize the individual and common interests of the working people, in order to stimulate their initiative and create the most favorable conditions for the development of the productive forces, to equalize the working conditions, to achieve distribution according to work, and to develop socialist relations, the social community plans the development of the economy and the material foundations of other social activities. Planning is done in the working organizations by the working people as the bearers of production and of socially-organized work, and by the social-political communities in the performance of their social-economic functions.

The social plan of Yugoslavia co-ordinates the basic relations in production and distribution. Within the framework of these relations and a unified economic system, the working people in the working organizations and social-political communities autonomously plan and develop the material bases for their activities.

In order to equalize the material conditions in social life and in the work of the working people, in order to achieve harmonious economic development as a whole, and in order to create the material basis for equality among the peoples of Yugoslavia, the social community, acting in the common interest, devotes special attention to the rapid development of the productive forces in those republics and areas with inadequate economic development, and to this end it provides the necessary funds and undertakes other measures.

Social ownership of the means of production is the foundation of personal ownership acquired by personal work, and serves to satisfy the personal needs and interests of man.

In order to develop socialist relations in agriculture and to promote agricultural production, conditions are assured for the development of production on the basis of socially-owned means and socially-organized work, and for association among farmers and their co-operation with the working organizations on a voluntary basis.

Having the constitutional right of ownership to arable land, the farmers have the right and obligation to utilize the land in order to promote agricultural production in their own interests and in the interests of the social community.

IV

Every form of government, including political power, is created by the working class and by all the working people for themselves in order to organize society as a free community of producers, which is assured,

By social self-government as the basis of the social-political system;

By decision of the citizens on all social matters, either directly or through delegates whom they elect to the representative bodies of the social-political communities and to other bodies of social self-government;

By the establishment and development of equal and democratic relations among the citizens, and by the attainment of human and civil freedoms and rights in accord with the strengthening of solidarity, the citizens' performance of their social duties, and the material and social development of the socialist community;

By the personal responsibility of all holders of public office, especially those with functions of power, and by the responsibility of the political-executive and administrative organs to the representative body of the social-political community and to the public;

By judicial supervision of constitutionality and legality; and by social supervision of the work of state organs, organs of social self-government, and organizations dealing with matters of public concern;

By the social and political activity of the socialist forces organized in social-political organizations.

The functions of power determined by the Constitution are vested in the representative bodies of the social-political communities as the territorial organs of social self-government. These representative bodies are constituted and removable delegations elected in the communes by all the citizens, and in the working communities by the working people.

With the exception of the functions of power and the general affairs of social self-government, which they discharge through the representative bodies and bodies accountable to them, the citizens decide on social affairs in their working and other autonomous organizations and by forms of direct determination; and they attain other common interests also in their social-political organizations and associations, which they found themselves.

In the socialist social relations and conditions of social self-government, the working people voluntarily unite in trade unions in order to co-operate as directly as possible in the development of socialist social relations and social self-government, to co-ordinate their personal and common interests with the general interests, to realize the principles of distribution according to work, and to adapt the worker for work and for management, as well as to take the initiative and undertake measures to protect their rights and interests and to improve their living and working conditions, to develop solidarity, to co-ordinate opinions and mutual relations, and to solve other questions of common interest.

The citizens are the source of initiative for social activities directly and through their social-political organizations and associations; they exercise supervision over the work of the organs of government and other holders of public office, they determine the norms for mutual relations and they lend their support to the state organs, the organs of social self-government, and organizations dealing with affairs of public concern.

In order to realize self-government and the other rights of the citizens, the public working of the state organs, organs of social self-government, organizations, and holders of public office shall be assured, and conditions shall be created so that the citizen may be fully informed and capable of discharging public affairs.

The principle of limitation of re-election and re-nomination to particular offices assures the removability of holders of government and of other public offices, in order to allow the widest possible participation of citizens in the discharge of public functions, and to consolidate and develop democratic relations in society.

V

The Socialist Alliance of the Working People of Yugoslavia, founded during the People's Liberation War and Socialist Revolution as a voluntary democratic alliance of the citizens, is the broadest base of social-political activity and social self-government of the working people.

In the Socialist Alliance of the Working People of Yugoslavia the citizens,

Discuss social-political questions from all provinces of social life, coordinate opinions and pass political resolutions dealing with the solution of these questions, the course of social development and the strengthening of self-government, the attainment of the rights and interests of man and citizen, and the promotion of socialist and democratic relations;

Give their opinions and judgments on the work of state organs, organs of social self-government, organizations, and holders of public office, and exercise social supervision over their work, especially to render their work public and themselves responsible for it;

Strive for the creation and protection of every form of social-political life stimulating socialist and democratic development; take the political initiative in every province of public life; and ensure the fullest possible realization of their voting and other rights;

Provide conditions for the comprehensive participation of youth and its organizations in social and political life;

Strive for human relations among people, for the development of socialist consciousness, and for the norms of a socialist way of life, and for the elimination of manifestations that impede the development of socialist and democratic social relations or otherwise harm them.

VI

The League of Communists of Yugoslavia, initiator and organizer of the People's Liberation War and Socialist Revolution, owing to the necessity of historical development, has become the leading organized force of the working class and working people in the development of socialism and in the attainment of solidarity among the working people and of the brotherhood and unity of the peoples.

Under the conditions of socialist democracy and social self-government, the League of Communists, with its guiding ideological and political work, is the prime mover of the political activity necessary to protect and to promote the achievements of the Socialist Revolution and socialist social relations, and especially to strengthen the socialist social and democratic consciousness of the people.

VII

Whereas peaceful co-existence and active co-operation between states and peoples, irrespective of differences in their social system, is indispensable to peace and social progress in the world, Yugoslavia bases its international relations on the principles of respect of national sovereignty and equality, non-interference in the internal affairs of other countries, peaceable settlement of international disputes, and socialist internationalism. In its international relations Yugoslavia adheres to the principles of the United Nations Charter, fulfils its international commitments and actively participates in the work of the international organizations to which it is affiliated.

In order to realise these principles, Yugoslavia strives,

For the establishment and development of every form of international co-operation that helps to consolidate peace, to strengthen mutual respect and friendship between peoples and states, and to bring about their rapprochement; for the broadest and freest exchange of material and intellectual wealth, for the freedom of mutual information, and for the development of other relations that contribute to the realization of common economic, cultural and other interests of states, nations and people, and especially to the development of democratic and socialist relations in international co-operation, and general social progress;

For the repudiation of the use or threat of force in international relations; and for general and complete disarmament;

For the right of every people to determine freely and to develop its own social and political system by ways and means of its own free choosing;

For the right of peoples to self-determination and national independence and for their right to wage liberation struggle to attain these just aims;

For international support to peoples waging a just struggle for national independence and liberation from colonialism and national oppression;

For the development of such international co-operation as assures equality in economic relations in the world, sovereign exploitation of national resources and the creation of conditions conducive to the more rapid development of the under-developed countries.

In pledging itself to comprehensive political, economic and cultural co-operation with other peoples and states, Yugoslavia, as a socialist community of peoples, holds that this co-operation should contribute to the creation of new democratic forms of association between states, nations and people which will answer to the interests of peoples and social progress, and in this respect it is an open community.

VIII

The social-political relations and the forms determined by the Constitution are aimed at broadening the conditions for the further development of socialist society, the elimination of its contradictions, and for such social progress as, on the basis of the comprehensive development of the productive forces, high productivity of labor, an abundance of products, and comprehensive development of man as an emancipated being, will bring about the development of social relations in which the communist principle, "From each according to his abilities; to each according to his needs" will be realized.

To this end all the state organs, organs of social self-government, organizations and citizens are enjoined, in all their activities,

To expand and strengthen the material basis of society and the life of the individual by developing the productive forces, raising the productivity of labor, and continually promoting socialist social relations;

To create conditions in which the social-economic differences between intellectual and physical work will be eliminated and in which human work will become an ever fuller expression of creativity and of the human personality;

To expand and develop every form of social self-government and socialist democracy, especially in those fields in which the functions of political power predominate; to limit coercion and promote the conditions for its elimination; and to establish relations among people based on awareness of common interests and on the unrestricted activity of man;

To contribute to the realization of human freedoms and rights, to the humanization of the social environment and man's personality, to the strengthening of solidarity and humanity between people, and respect for man's dignity;

To develop comprehensive co-operation and *rapprochement* with all peoples in keeping with the progressive strivings of mankind to develop a free community of all the peoples in the world.

IX

In expressing the basic principles of the socialist community and the principles for its progress, this section of the Constitution is also the basis for the interpretation of the Constitution and law and for the work of each and everyone.

PART ONE

THE SOCIAL AND POLITICAL SYSTEM

CHAPTER I. INTRODUCTORY PROVISIONS

Art. 1. The Socialist Federal Republic of Yugoslavia is a federal state of voluntarily united and equal peoples and a socialist democratic community based on the powers of the working people and on self-government.

Art. 2. The Socialist Federal Republic of Yugoslavia comprises the Socialist Republics of Bosnia and Herzegovina, Croatia, Macedonia, Montenegro, Serbia and Slovenia.

The territory of the Socialist Federal Republic of Yugoslavia is unified, consisting of the territories of the socialist republics.

Art. 3. The coat-of-arms of the Socialist Federal Republic of Yugoslavia is a field encircled with ears of wheat. At the bottom the ears of wheat are tied together with a scroll bearing the inscription 29. XI. 1943. Between the tops of the ears of wheat, there is a five-pointed red star. In the field are six torches set obliquely whose flames blend into a single flame.

Art. 4. The state flag of the Socialist Federal Republic of Yugoslavia shall consist of three colors: blue, white and red, with a red five-pointed star in the centre. The ratio of the width to the length of the flag shall be one to two. The colours of the flag shall extend horizontally; starting from the top, the order is blue, white and red. Each colour shall occupy one third of the width of the flag. The star shall have a regular five-pointed form and a golden (yellow) border. The central point of the star shall coincide with the point in which the diagonals of the flag intersect. The top point of the star shall extend as far as the middle of the blue stripe of the flag, the lower points of the star assuming equivalent places in the red stripe of the flag.

Art. 5. The capital of the Socialist Federal Republic of Yugoslavia shall be Beograd.

CHAPTER II. SOCIAL-ECONOMIC ORGANIZATION

Art. 6. The basis of the social-economic system of Yugoslavia is free, associated work with socially-owned means of labour, and self-management of the working people in production and in distribution of the social product in the working organization and social community.

Art. 7. Only work and the results of work shall determine man's material and social position.

No one may gain material or other advantage directly or indirectly by exploiting the work of others.

Art. 8. The means of production and the other means of socially-organized work, as well as mineral and other natural resources are social property.

The employment of the means of production and other socially-owned means, and all other rights over these and other means shall be regulated by law in accordance with their nature and purpose.

Art. 9. Self-management in the working organization shall include in particular the right and duty of the working people:

(1) To manage the working organization directly or through organs of management elected by themselves;

(2) To organize production or other activity, to attend to the development of the working organization, and to determine plans and programs of work and development;

(3) To decide on commerce in products and services and on other business matters of the working organization;

(4) To decide on the use of socially-owned means and their disposal, and to employ these means with economic expediency so as to gain the greatest return for the working organization and the social community;

(5) To distribute the income belonging to the working organization and to provide for the development of the material basis for their work; to distribute income among the working people; to meet the working organization's obligations to the social community;

(6) To decide on the admission of working people into the working organization, the cessation of their work, and other labor relations; to determine working hours in the working organization in accordance with general working conditions; to regulate other matters of common concern; to secure internal supervision and to render their work public;

(7) To regulate and promote their working conditions, to organize labor safety and recreation, to provide conditions for their education, and to advance their own and the general standard of living;

(8) To decide on dissociation of a part of the working organization and its establishment into a separate organization, and to decide on merger and association of the working organization with other working organizations.

In attaining self-government, the working people in the social-political communities shall decide on the course of economic and social development, on the distribution of the social product, and on other matters of common concern.

Citizens and representatives of organizations concerned and of the social community may participate in the management of a working organization in affairs of special concern to the social community.

In order to secure the uniform social-economic position of the working people, provision shall be made in law and statute determining the rights of self-management of the working people employed in the state administration, social-political organizations or associations, in accord with the nature of the work of these organs and organizations.

The working people shall exercise self-management in the unified social-economic system in accordance with the Constitution, law and statute, and shall be held accountable for their work.

Any act violating the right of self-management of the working people is unconstitutional.

Art. 10. The working people in the working organization, as members of the working community, shall establish working relations with each other and shall be equals in management.

The organization of work, and management in the working organization must enable the working people at every level and in every part of the working process which constitutes a whole to decide as directly as possible on matters of work, organization of mutual relations, distribution of income, and on other matters affecting their economic position, at the same time assuring the working organization as a whole the most favorable conditions for its work and business.

Art. 11. The product of socially-organized work, created in the working organizations, as the foundation for social economic growth and for the satisfaction of social needs and personal and common needs of the working people, shall be divided according to a uniform system of distribution and on the basis of uniform conditions and standards assuring social economic growth, distribution according to work, and social self-government.

The working organization, after providing the means to renew the value of the resources expended in work, and after allocating a part of the created value of the product for equalization of working conditions and acquisition of income, shall apportion the income of the working organization into a fund to expand the material basis work and a fund to satisfy the personal and common needs of the working people.

The working organization shall be assured a part of the created value of the product to expand the material basis of its work, proportionate to its share in producing the means of social economic growth, and in non-economic activities, a part consistent with the tasks of the working organization and in accordance with social needs. The working organization shall be entitled to a part of the created value of the product for the satisfaction of personal and common needs of the working people proportionate to the productivity of work of the working people, and subject to the business success of the working organization, and in non-economic activities, proportionate to the results of the work done to satisfy social needs.

The means of the working organization allocated for the renewal and expansion of the material basis of work, as common means of social economic growth, shall be used to expand the material basis of the working organization of the social community as a whole. The working organization shall employ these means in accordance with uniform principles of utilization of the means of social economic growth determined by federal law, and in accordance with conditions and standards determined by the regulations co-ordinating economic development and the attainment of the other basic relations envisaged by the social plans.

To expand the material basis of its work, the working organization shall be assured other social means, apart from those it has created by its own work, under equal conditions and in accordance with the uniform principles of the credit system.

Art. 12. In accordance with the principle of distribution according to work, every working man in the working organization shall be entitled to a personal income proportionate to the results of his work and to the work of his department and of the working organization as a whole.

Art. 13. Working organizations may be founded in accordance with law by social-political communities, by working and other organizations and by citizens.

The working organization shall be founded as an enterprise or other economic organization for economic activities, or as an institution or other organization for activities in the fields of education, science, culture, health, social welfare, or other social services.

The working organizations, irrespective of the founder, shall have an identical status.

The conditions under which working organizations amy amalgamate, or particular departments become independent, or separate, may be determined by law.

Art. 14. Working people who by personal work perform independent cultural, professional or other similar activities shall in principle have the same social economic status and the same fundamental rights and duties as the working people in the working organization.

Working people with occupations of this type may associate and form temporary or permanent working communities, which shall have the same fundamental status as the working organizations, and in which the working people shall have the same fundamental rights and duties as the working people in working organizations.

The conditions under which these working people and their working communities shall realize their rights and fulfil their obligations, and the conditions under which they may utilize and manage social means in the performance of their activities shall be prescribed by law.

Art. 15. The working organization is an independent and autonomous organization.

The working organization is a juristic person and possesses certain rights in relation to the socially-owned means managed by it. The working organization may not be dispossessed of these rights nor may they be restricted, unless this is required by the general interest determined by federal law and in accordance with procedure prescribed by law, and with equivalent compensation being made in return.

The working organization shall preserve undiminished the value of the social means in its possession.

The working organization shall be responsible for its obligations with the social means in its possession.

Art. 16. The general conditions under which working organizations shall discharge activities of special social concern may be prescribed by law.

The conditions under which products and services may be exchanged in internal commerce may be prescribed only on the basis of federal law.

The conditions of commerce in commodities and services and the business conditions of working organizations in their relations with other countries shall be established by federal law.

Art. 17. Co-operatives may be founded as working organizations to carry on and stimulate socially-organized work and co-operation among working people who work with their own means of labor in agriculture and in other fields of the economy, with the aim of linking these activities with the social economy and expanding socialist social relations in these provinces.

Membership in the co-operatives shall be voluntary.

Provision may be made in law and in the statute of the co-operative or other working organization according to which the working people who work with their own means of labor and permanently co-operate economically with the working organization may take part in the management of the working organization in those affairs in which they co-operate.

Provision may be made in law determining that farmers who work with their own means of labor shall associate or co-operate with a working organization in order to carry out land improvements, to further the exploitation of land so improved, to exploit water resources and to raise defences against damage by water, to protect land from erosion, and to regulate torrential streams, or whenever the social interest in the province of cultivation and exploitation of forests, or in the promotion of agricultural production on certain lands so requires.

Art. 18. Subject to the conditions and procedure provided by federal law, an economic organization may be dissolved if it is unable to renew the means of production and other means of work which it manages, or to meet other legal obligations.

An economic organization, under the conditions and in accordance with the procedure provided by federal law, may be placed under temporary emergency administration if in its work it has gravely damaged social interests.

Subject to the conditions and in accordance with the procedure provided by law, an institution may be dissolved if it no longer fulfils the conditions determined by law or if it lacks the conditions to do its work.

Art. 19. In order to bring about an efficient division of labor and to carry on activities of common concern, working organizations may form business corporations.

Working organizations may also associate in order to promote production or other activities, to co-operate with each other and to examine and solve other matters of common concern.

Management of amalgamated working organizations shall be based on the principle of self-management of the working people in the working organizations so associated.

Working organizations may pool their resources in order to promote and develop their activities, and conclude other agreements concerning joint activities and business.

In accordance with federal law, chambers and business corporations may be founded, and the conditions prescribed for the obligatory association of particular types of working organizations in chambers and business corporations.

Art. 20. Land is a resource of common concern.

All land shall be utilized in accordance with the general conditions determined by law to assure the efficient utilization of land and other general interests.

Forests and woodland shall have special protection determined by law.

Art. 21. The social community shall provide the material and other conditions for the establishment and development of agricultural working organizations based on social ownership of land and socially-organized work, and for co-operation of farmers with the co-operatives and other working organizations.

Farmers shall be guaranteed right of ownership to arable land up to a maximum area of ten hectares to the household.

The limits and conditions under which farmers may have right of ownership to other land, and the limits and conditions under which other citizens may have right of ownership to agricultural and other land shall be determined by law.

The right of ownership to forests and woodland shall be determined by law.

Art. 22. Subject to the restrictions and under the conditions provided by law, citizens may by personal work perform agricultural, handicraft and other services or similar activities in order to gain income.

The extent and the conditions under which citizens may have right of ownership to the means of work and business premises to perform agricultural, handicraft and other services or similar activities by personal work, shall be determined by law.

No one shall employ the work of others to gain income.

Subject to the restrictions and conditions determined by law, the work of other persons may be employed in agricultural production, the handicraft trades and in other services or similar activities carried on by citizens with their own means of work.

Art. 23. Citizens shall be guaranteed right of ownership to objects for personal consumption and use or for the satisfaction of cultural and other personal needs.

Citizens may have right of ownership to dwelling houses and dwellings for the satisfaction of their personal and family needs; and for occupations based on personal work in accordance with the right of citizens guaranteed by the Constitution and subject to the conditions determined by law.

The limits of the right of ownership to dwelling houses and dwellings shall be determined by federal law.

Art. 24. The conditions under which social-political organizations and associations of citizens may own real estate and other objects that serve to satisfy the common interests of their members and to perform the tasks of the organizations, and the conditions under which they may use social means for these purposes shall be determined by law.

Art. 25. If the general interest determined by federal law so requires, real estate to which citizens and juristic persons have right of ownership may be expropriated, with fair compensation being given in return, or this right may be restricted.

The right of ownership to objects of special cultural value may be restricted in accordance with law, if the general interest so requires.

Art. 26. In order to secure conditions for the most favorable economic and social development, to equalize general conditions of work and the acquisition of income, to determine general standards of distribution, to realize the principle of distribution according to work, and to develop socialist social relations, the social-political communities shall undertake, in accordance with their rights and duties, measures to develop a unified economic system, to plan economic development and the material bases of other activities, and to this end they shall adopt social plans. In order to achieve the relations determined by the social plans, the social-political communities shall pass regulations and other general decisions, set up social funds and social reserves, and undertake economic and other measures.

The social-political communities are juristic persons.

Art. 27. The means of social economic growth acquired on the territory of the social-political communities, as common means of social economic growth, shall be used in these communities in proportion to the effort made by the working people to produce them. These means shall be used in accord with the uniform principles for using the means of social economic growth and under the conditions and standards determined by the regulations co-ordinating economic development and the attainment of other relations envisaged by the social plans.

Other social means shall also be used to develop the material basis of the social-political communities in accordance with the uniform principles of the credit system.

To meet social needs on their territories, the social-political communities shall be entitled to means acquired from personal incomes and from other sources determined by federal law, in accordance with the principle of distribution according to work, and they shall autonomously determine the amount of these means and their disposal.

The social community shall provide the inadequately developed republics and regions with the material and other conditions necessary for more rapid economic development, and for the creation of the material bases of social activities.

Art. 28. The territory of Yugoslavia is a unified economic and customs area.

Commerce in goods and services shall be unrestricted on the whole territory of Yugoslavia and may be restricted only in accordance with federal law.

The working organizations may carry on economic and other activities on the whole territory of Yugoslavia under conditions of equality.

Art. 29. Money and the credit system shall be uniform. Financial transactions shall be carried on in accordance with uniform principles.

The working and other autonomous organizations, the social-political communities and their organs, and anyone else in possession of socially-owned means shall make all payments, carry out all other financial operations, and deposit money in a manner prescribed by federal law.

The working organizations and social-political communities shall be entitled to banking credits under equal conditions determined by federal law.

Banks are economic organizations whose business is of special social concern. The position, the rights and duties and the business of the banks shall be determined by federal law.

The status of the National Bank of Yugoslavia shall be determined by federal law.

Art. 30. Merger or association between working organizations, or any other activity of an organization or state organ aimed at preventing or restricting free commerce in goods and services for the purpose of material and other advantages not based on work, or violating socialist economic relations, or promoting other relations of inequality in business, or causing damage to the general interest determined by federal law shall be prohibited.

Art. 31. Control and supervision over the use of socially-owned means, as well as supervision over the meeting of obligations by the working and other autonomous organizations and social-political communities shall be performed by a unified social accounting service.

The social accounting service shall be autonomous in its work.

CHAPTER III. THE FREEDOMS, RIGHTS AND DUTIES OF MAN AND CITIZEN

Art. 32. The freedoms and rights of man and citizen are an inalienable part and expression of the socialist and democratic relations which are protected by the Constitution, and through which man is being emancipated from every exploitation and arbitrariness, and by his personal and socially-organized work is creating the conditions for comprehensive development, for the unrestricted expression and protection of his personality, and attainment of his human dignity.

The freedoms and rights shall be achieved in solidarity among the people and by the fulfilment of their duties towards each other.

Art. 33. The citizens are equal in rights and duties, regardless of differences in nationality, race, religion, sex, language, education or social position.

All shall be equal before the law.

Art. 34. The right of the citizen to social self-government shall be inviolable.

In order to achieve social self-government, the citizen shall have:

(1) the right to decide directly on social affairs at meetings of the electorate, and at meetings of the working people in the working communities, by referendum, and by other forms of direct determination;

(2) the right to decide on social affairs as a member of an organ of social self-government, as a lay judge, or in other public function;

(3) the right to elect and to stand for election to the organs of management of the working organization, the representative bodies of the social-political communities and the other organs of self-government, to nominate candidates for election to these bodies and organs, to initiate recall and to decide on the recall of elected delegates;

(4) the right to initiate the convocation of meetings of the electorate and meetings of the working people in the working communities, the right to initiate the calling of a referendum, and the right to initiate actions of social supervision;

(5) the right to be informed about the work of the representative bodies and their organs, the organs of social self-government, and organizations carrying on affairs of public concern, and in particular, in the working organization in which he works and in other organizations in which he realizes his interests, the right to be informed about material and financial conditions, the fulfilment of plans, and business, with the obligation that he keep business and other secrets;

(6) the right to examine the work of the state organs, the organs of social self-government and the organizations that discharge affairs of public concern, and to express his opinions on their work;

(7) the right to petition and present proposals to the representative

bodies and other organs, to receive an answer to them, and to undertake political and other initiatives of general concern.

Art. 35. Every citizen who is eighteen years of age shall have suffrage. In realizing this right, the citizen shall nominate candidates and elect delegates to the representative bodies and organs of social self-government and may stand for election to these bodies and organs.

Every member of a working community shall be eligible to elect the organs of management of the working organization and to stand for election to them.

Art. 36. The right to work and the freedom to work are guaranteed.

The community shall provide ever more favorable conditions towards the realization of the right to work, especially by developing the productive forces and the material basis of other socially organized activities, and by promoting concern for the interests of the working man in regard to work.

Everyone shall be free to choose an occupation and employment.

Forced labor shall be prohibited.

Every citizen shall have access, under conditions of equality, to every job and every office in the community.

Working relations may cease against the worker's will only under conditions and in a manner determined by federal law.

The right to material security during temporary unemployment shall be guaranteed under conditions determined by law.

The rights acquired on the basis of work shall be inalienable.

The social community shall create conditions to improve the capacities of citizens who are not fully capable of working, as well as conditions for their adequate employment.

The social community shall lend assistance to citizens who are incapable of working and have no means of livelihood.

Whoever will not work, though he is fit to do so, shall not enjoy the rights and the social protection that man enjoys on the basis of work.

Art. 37. The worker shall be entitled to a limited working time.

A maximum working week of 42 hours shall be guaranteed. The conditions under which the working time may be shortened may be determined by law. In exceptional cases provision may be made determining that in certain occupations or in other cases determined by law the working time may for a limited period be longer than 42 hours in the week if the particular nature of the work so requires.

The worker shall be entitled to daily and weekly rest, and, under conditions determined by law, to a paid annual vacation of not less than fourteen working days.

The working man's right to personal safety and to health and other protection at work shall be assured.

Youth, women and disabled persons shall enjoy special protection at work.

Workers shall be guaranteed a minimum personal income determined by federal law.

Art. 38. In accordance with the principle of mutualism and solidarity, the workers shall be insured within a uniform system of social security established by federal law.

On the basis of obligatory social security, workers shall be provided with health protection and other rights against illness, reduced working ability or loss of working ability and old age.

In the event of the death of the insured person, health protection and rights as well as other rights arising from social security shall be provided the members of the family of the worker, subject to conditions determined by law.

Provision shall be made in law determining security for the health protection and other rights arising from social security also for other citizens.

The social-security service shall be managed by the insured directly and through bodies which they shall elect and may recall of their own accord.

Art. 39. Freedom of thought and determination shall be guaranteed.

Art. 40. Freedom of the press and other media of information, freedom of association, freedom of speech and public expression, freedom of meeting and other public assemblage shall be guaranteed.

The citizens shall have the right to express and publish their opinions through the media of information, to inform themselves through the media of information, to publish newspapers and other publications and to disseminate information by other media of communication.

These freedoms and rights shall not be used by anyone to overthrow the foundations of the socialist democratic order determined by the Constitution, to endanger the peace, international co-operation on terms of equality, or the independence of the country, to disseminate national, racial, or religious hatred or intolerance, or to incite to crime, or in any manner that offends public decency.

The cases and conditions in which the utilization of these freedoms and rights in a manner contrary to the Constitution shall entail restriction or prohibition shall be determined by federal law.

The press, radio and television shall truthfully and objectively inform the public and publish and broadcast the opinions and information of organs, organizations, and citizens which are of interest to public information.

The right to correction of information that has violated the rights or interests of man or organization shall be guaranteed.

In order to assure the widest possible information of the public, the social community shall promote conditions conducive to the development of appropriate activities.

Art. 41. The citizen shall be guaranteed the freedom to express his nationality and culture, as well as the freedom to speak his language.

No one shall have to declare himself as to nationality or determine himself for one of the nationalities.

The dissemination or pursuance of national inequality, as well as all incitement to national, racial and religious hatred or intolerance, is unconstitutional and shall be punishable.

Art. 42. The languages of the peoples of Yugoslavia and their scripts shall be equal.

Members of the peoples of Yugoslavia on the territories of republics other than their own shall have the right to school instruction in their own languages, in conformity with republican law.

As an exception, in the Yugoslav People's Army, commands, military drill and administration shall be in the Serbo-Croatian language.

Art. 43. With the view of attaining the freedom of the citizen to express his nationality and culture, every nationality—national minority, shall have the right to use its language freely, to develop its culture, and to found organizations to this end, and it shall enjoy the other rights determined by the Constitution.

In the schools for the members of the nationalities, instruction shall be in the languages of those nationalities.

The other rights of the nationalities on the territories on which they live shall be determined by the constitutions and laws of the republics.

Art. 44. The citizens shall be entitled, under equal conditions determined by law, to acquire knowledge and training in any type of school and in any other educational institution.

Eight years of elementary education shall be obligatory. Longer obligatory education may be determined by law.

The social community shall provide the material and other conditions necessary to found and maintain schools and other educational institutions and to advance their work.

Art. 45. Scientific and artistic creativity shall be unrestricted.

The authors of scientific and artistic works, as well as of scientific discoveries and technical inventions, shall have the moral and material rights in their products. The scope, duration and protection of these rights shall be determined by federal law.

The social community shall provide conditions for the development of scientific, artistic and other cultural activities.

Art. 46. Religious confession shall not be restricted and shall be man's private affair.

The religious communities shall be detached from the State and shall be free to perform religious affairs and religious rites.

The religious communities may found religious schools in which to train their clergy.

Abuse of religion and religious work for political purposes is unconstitutional.

The social community may give material assistance to the religious communities.

The religious communities may have the right of ownership to real estate within the limits determined by federal law.

Art. 47. Life and the freedom of man shall be inviolable.

Exceptionally, capital punishment may be provided for by federal law for the gravest criminal offences, and it may be pronounced only for the most serious forms of these offences.

Arrest shall be based on law. Every unlawful arrest shall be punishable.

The inviolability of life and other privacy rights of the person shall be guaranteed.

Art. 48. During criminal proceedings, the accused may be arrested and held under arrest only if this is provided by law and it is indispensable to the criminal proceedings or for reasons of public safety.

Custody shall be reduced to the shortest necessary time.

Custody shall be determined by a court of law; only in exceptional cases prescribed by law may custody be determined by another authority empowered by law, and then for not more than three days.

Custody by decision of a court of the first instance may last not more than three months, but in exceptional cases prescribed by law, the superior court may by decision extend custody for another six months. If upon the expiration of these periods no indictment has been made, the prisoner shall be released.

A fully documented written warrant shall be brought in matters of custody, which shall be served on the person concerned at the moment of arrest or not later than twenty-four hours after arrest.

The court shall adopt a decision immediately or not later than forty-eight hours on a complaint against a warrant of arrest.

Art. 49. No one shall be punished for any act that before its commission was not defined by law or by prescript based on law as a punishable offence, or for which no penalty had been provided.

Criminal offences and punitive sanctions may be determined only by law.

Offences of an economic nature and punitive sanctions for such offences may be determined by law or by decree adopted on the basis of law.

Sanctions may be pronounced for criminal offences or offences of an economic nature only by the decision of a competent court reached in accordance with the procedure determined by law.

Organs of the administration may pronounce punitive sanctions only for misdemeanors and only within the limits and according to the procedure provided by law.

Art. 50. No one shall be deemed to have committed a criminal offence until this has been ascertained by valid conviction.

Respect of person and dignity are guaranteed in criminal and in all other proceedings as well as during enforcement of a penalty.

No one within the reach of the court or other body of authority competent to conduct proceedings shall be sentenced if he has not been heard in accordance with law or if he has not been given the opportunity to defend himself.

The right to defence is guaranteed.

During criminal proceedings, the accused shall be entitled to have defence counsel, who shall be enabled, in accordance with the law, to defend and protect the rights of the accused. Provision shall be made in law determining when the accused in criminal proceedings must have defence counsel.

Any person who has been unjustifiably sentenced for a criminal offence or who has been arrested without grounds shall be entitled to compensation from social sources for the damage that has been done to him.

Art. 51. The citizens shall enjoy freedom of movement and abode.

Limitation of the freedom of movement or abode may be prescribed by law, but only in order to assure the execution of criminal proceedings, to prevent the spread of infectious diseases, or to preserve the public order, or when the interests of the country's defence so require.

Art. 52. The dwelling shall be inviolable.

No one shall enter any dwelling or other premises or search them against the will of the owner without a warrant issued in accordance with law.

The person whose dwelling or other premises are being searched, or the members of his family or his representative shall be entitled to be present during the search.

A search may be carried out only in the presence of two witnesses.

Subject to the conditions determined by law, a person in an official capacity may enter a dwelling or premises without a warrant from the competent authority and carry out a search in the absence of witnesses if this is indispensable for the direct apprehension of a criminal offender, or for the safety of life and property, or if it is beyond doubt that evidence in criminal proceedings cannot be secured otherwise.

Illegal entry and search of a dwelling or premises are prohibited and shall be punishable.

Art. 53. The privacy of letters and of other means of communication shall be inviolable.

Provision may be made only by federal law to depart in accordance with the decision of a competent authority, from the principle of inviolability of privacy of letters and of other means of communication, if this is indispensable for the execution of criminal proceedings, or for the security of the country.

Art. 54. Every citizen of Yugoslavia shall have the protection of the Socialist Federal Republic of Yugoslavia abroad.

No citizen of Yugoslavia shall be deprived of his citizenship, exiled or extradited.

A citizen who is absent from the country may in accordance with law be deprived of Yugoslav citizenship only exceptionally, if by his work he causes harm to the international or other general interests of Yugoslavia, or if he declines to perform his basic civil duties and holds citizenship in another country.

Art. 55. The right of inheritance is guaranteed.

No one shall have real estate and means of work on grounds of inheritance in excess of the limit determined by the Constitution or law.

Art. 56. Every citizen shall be entitled to the protection of his health.

The cases in which uninsured citizens shall be entitled to the protection of their health from social means shall be determined by law.

The social community shall provide conditions for the founding of health institutions and to promote the health protection of the citizens.

The social community, particularly the commune and the working organization, shall provide conditions for the development of physical culture, and for the rest and recreation of the citizens, and shall support the initiative of the citizens and their associations in these provinces.

Art. 57. The social community shall provide special protection for the mother and child.

Minors without parental care and other persons unable to provide for themselves and to safeguard their own rights and interests shall enjoy the special protection of the social community.

Disabled war veterans shall be provided with vocational rehabilitation, disability rights and other forms of protection.

Art. 58. The family shall have the protection of the social community. Marriage and legal relations in marriage and in the family shall be regulated by law.

Marriage shall be validly contracted by persons entering into marriage in accordance with their free will before a competent authority.

It shall be the right and duty of parents to raise and to educate their children.

Children born out of marriage shall have the same rights and duties towards their parents as children born in marriage.

Art. 59. Relations among people shall be based on mutual co-operation and on respect for man and for his freedoms and rights.

It shall be the duty of every person to come to the assistance and help of any person in danger, and to participate in the elimination of general danger.

Art. 60. The defence of the country is the right and the supreme duty and honor of every citizen.

Art. 61. Every citizen shall conscientiously discharge any public or other social office vested in him, and shall be personally accountable for discharging it.

Art. 62. Every citizen shall contribute, under equal conditions determined by law, to the satisfaction of the material requirements of the social community.

Art. 63. Everyone shall abide by the Constitution and law.

Provision shall be made in law determining the conditions under which failure to discharge duties determined by the Constitution shall be punishable.

Art. 64. Aliens in Yugoslavia shall enjoy basic freedoms and human rights, and shall have other rights and duties determined by law and by international agreements.

Art. 65. Citizens of other countries and persons without citizenship who are persecuted for their defence of democratic ideas and political movements, social emancipation and national liberation, the freedom and the rights of the human personality or of the freedom of scientific or artistic creativity, shall be guaranteed right of asylum.

Art. 66. Every arbitrary act violating or restricting the rights of man by whomsoever committed is unconstitutional and punishable.

No one shall employ coercion or restrict the rights of any person, except in cases and proceedings provided by law and in accord with the Constitution.

Art. 67. Every person shall be entitled to equal protection of his rights in proceedings before a court, administrative and other state organs and organizations which decide on his rights and obligations.

The social community shall provide the conditions for legal assistance through the legal profession as an autonomous socially-organized service, and through other forms of legal assistance.

Art. 68. Everyone shall be guaranteed the right of appeal or other legal expedient against court decisions and decisions of other state organs and organizations which deliberate on his rights or his lawful interests.

Art. 69. Everyone shall be entitled to damages for the unlawful or faulty execution of an office or action by a person or officer of a state organ or organization carrying on affairs of public concern.

The damages shall be paid by the social-political community or organization in which the service or action is performed. The claimant shall be entitled, under conditions determined by law, to damages also directly from the person responsible for the damage.

Art. 70. The freedoms and rights guaranteed by the Constitution are inalienable and shall not be restricted by any act.

These freedoms and rights shall be attained on the basis of the Constitution itself. The manner of attaining particular freedoms and rights may be prescribed only by law, and only when this is envisaged by the Constitution or when it is indispensable for their attainment.

The freedoms and rights guaranteed by the Constitution shall be provided judicial protection.

CHAPTER IV. THE SOCIAL-POLITICAL SYSTEM

Art. 71. The working people shall be the sole holder of power and government of social affairs.

The citizens shall attain self-government directly at meetings of the electorate, by referendum or by other forms of direct decision in the working organization, commune and in other social-political communities, and indirectly through their delegates, whom they shall elect to the organs of management of the working and other autonomous organizations and to the representative bodies of the social-political communities.

Art. 72. No one shall exercise public powers unless they have been vested in him, in accordance with the Constitution, by the citizens or by the bodies elected by them.

Art. 73. Self-government by the citizens in the commune is the political foundation of the uniform social-political system.

The forms of social self-government from which the organs discharging the functions of power derive shall be founded and realized in the commune.

The uniformity of the social-political system shall be secured by the realization of the rights and duties of all the social-political communities, and by their mutual relations as determined by the Constitution and law.

Art. 74. The functions of power and government of social affairs shall be exercised by representative bodies, as the general organs of social self-government of the social-political communities, and by the organs responsible to them.

The judicial power shall be executed by courts as autonomous organs of the social community.

The protection of constitutionality shall be vested in constitutional courts.

Art. 75. The assembly shall be the representative body of the social-political community; it shall consist of delegates of the citizens and of the working people in the working communities.

Art. 76. The communal assembly shall comprise the communal chamber and the chamber of the working communities. The constitutions of the republics may provide for the formation of several chambers of working communities.

The members of the communal chamber shall be elected directly by the citizens; the members of the chamber of the working communities shall be elected by the working people who are engaged in working organizations, state organs, and social-political organizations and associations, by farmermembers of co-operatives or other working organizations, and by other citizens working on the territory of the commune determined by law.

Any citizen with suffrage shall be eligible for election to the communal chamber. Any working man eligible to elect the members of a chamber of working communities, any member of an organ of management of a working organization or working community, any member of an organ of management of an association of working organizations, and any trade union officer or official of a social-political organization in the commune shall be eligible for election to the chamber of the working communities.

The members of the assemblies of the district, the republic and the Federation shall be elected on the principle of communal delegation, the commune being the basic community of citizens and working people.

Art. 77. Direct elections for members of the representative bodies of the social-political communities shall be held on the basis of general and equal suffrage.

The members of all the representative bodies shall be elected and removed by secret ballot.

Art. 78. The assembly shall be the supreme organ of government and organ of social self-government within the framework of the rights and duties of the social-political community.

The assembly shall determine policy and decide on other basic matters of importance for political, economic and cultural life and social development, pass regulations, the social plan and budget and other general acts, establish the bases for the organization and the powers of its organs, elect public officials, examine the state of affairs and the general problems of the judiciary, and exercise budget supervision, supervision over the work of the political-executive and administrative authorities, and social supervision.

The assembly shall form a commission to consider matters pertaining to the election and nomination of members of the assembly bodies and other officials and to propose motions to the assembly. This commission shall also examine general personnel matters.

The commission shall comprise members of the assembly and representatives of the social-political organizations.

Matters of general interest for the social-political community may be examined by the assembly together with representatives of the social-political organizations and other associations sitting as a general convention.

Art. 79. Collegial political-executive organs of the assembly shall be formed in the social-political community in accordance with the Constitution, law and statute. The Constitution may determine that certain political-executive affairs shall also be discharged by the chambers of the representative bodies.

The political-executive organs shall attend to the execution of policy, the enforcement of law, and the fulfilment of social plans and other assembly enactments, advance proposals determining assembly policy and for the adoption of assembly decisions, pass regulations for which they are authorized, determine the general course of work of the administrative organs and perform other political-executive affairs.

The political-executive organs shall be elected and dismissed by the assembly.

The political-executive organs shall be responsible for their work to the assembly that has elected them.

Art. 80. The assembly of the social-political community shall establish administrative organs in accordance with the Constitution, law and statute.

The administrative organs shall enforce the law, carry out the social plans and other decisions of the assembly, execute the established policy, follow the state of affairs in particular fields of life, organize and discharge particular services, deliberate on administrative matters, exercise administrative supervision, and perform other administrative business, prepare acts and perform other expert services for the assemblies and their political-executive organs.

The administrative organs shall co-operate with other administrative organs and with working and other organizations in matters of common concern, inform each other about their work, and by their work enable the citizens and organizations to realize their rights and interests efficaciously.

Within the framework of their legal powers, the administrative organs shall be autonomous, and they shall be accountable for their work to the assembly and to its political-executive organs.

Art. 81. The members of the assembly shall be elected for a term of four years.

Half the members of each chamber of the assembly shall be elected every second year.

The term of the members of the assembly may be extended only by decision of the assembly in cases provided by the Constitution.

Art. 82. No one shall be twice consecutively a member of the same chamber of the same assembly or of an executive council.

No one shall at the same time be a member of the Federal Assembly and of the assembly of a republic, or a member of two chambers of the same assembly. A member of the Chamber of Nationalities of the Federal Assembly shall keep his seat in the assembly that has sent him.

A member of the Chamber of Nationalities may be returned for a further term of four years as a deputy of the republic or as a federal deputy; but during his second term he shall not again be a member of the Chamber of Nationalities.

Subject to procedure determined by the Constitution, certain members of the executive council may be returned to this office for a further consecutive term of four years.

A member of a communal assembly who has been elected member of the district assembly may be returned to the communal assembly for a further consecutive term of four years, but he shall not be returned to the district assembly for that term.

Art. 83. The federal secretaries of state, federal secretaries and officers determined by law, as well as equivalent republican officers determined by republican constitution, shall not hold office for longer than four years, nor shall they be appointed to the same office during the next four years.

Subject to special procedure determined by the Constitution, some of these officers may be nominated to one of these offices for not more than an additional consecutive four years.

Provision may be made in law introducing the principle of re-election or re-nomination after a definite period also for other holders of public functions.

A member of the assembly shall not at the same time be a nominated officer or official of an equivalent state organ responsible to the assembly. The positions of judge and member of the assembly which elects him are incompatible.

Art. 84. The assemblies, their political-executive organs and their administrative organs shall discharge their affairs on the basis of and within the restrictions of the Constitution and law.

State organs, organizations or officers vested with public powers shall perform their functions only within the limits of authorization determined by the Constitution and law.

The state organs shall have only the rights determined by the Constitution in relation to the working and other autonomous organizations.

Art. 85. The relations between the organs of various social-political communities shall be based on the rights and duties determined in accordance with the Constitution.

With respect to the supervision of execution of republican and federal regulations the rights and duties of the federal administrative organs towards the republican administrative organs, and the rights and duties of the federal and republican administrative organs towards the district and communal administrative organs may be determined by law in accordance with the rights and duties of the Federation and republics.

Art. 86. A holder of public or other social office shall be personally accountable for its execution.

The types and conditions of responsibility of all holders of public and other social offices shall be determined by law.

A holder of public office may resign from his office and may give his reason for doing so.

Art. 87. The work of the state organs, organs of social self-government and organizations carrying on affairs of public concern shall be public, and the public shall be informed about their work.

The manner in which their work will be made public shall be determined by law and statute. Provision shall be made in law determining what information must be kept secret or may not be made public.

In order to render the work of the state organs, organs of social self-government, organizations discharging affairs of public concern, and social-political communities public and responsible to the community, the representative body exercising social supervision shall examine general matters pertaining to the utilization of social funds and distribution of income and to the manner in which these organs and organizations exercise their rights and duties.

The representative bodies shall exercise social supervision in co-operation with the organs of self-government and shall develop responsibility and socialist norms in self-government, business, and utilization of social funds.

The rights of the organs, organizations and citizens determined by the Constitution and law shall not be restricted by social supervision, nor shall their rights and interests founded on law be violated.

Art. 88. At the meeting of the electorate the citizens shall examine matters of significance for the life and work of the locality and commune and other matters of social concern, initiate and submit proposals for the solution of these matters, directly decide on affairs determined by law and by the communal statute, and nominate candidates for election to the representative bodies.

At their meetings in the working communities, the working people shall nominate candidates for election to the representative bodies and carry out other affairs of management determined by law and by the statute.

Art. 89. The assembly of a social-political community may hold a referendum to obtain the preliminary views of the citizens concerning certain matters in its jurisdiction, or to sanction laws and other of its decisions.

The cases in which matters shall be decided by referendum in the working organizations shall be determined by law and by statutes of the working organizations.

The decisions brought by referendum shall be binding.

Referendum shall be regulated by law.

Art. 90. In exercising management in the working organization, the working people shall entrust, in keeping with the Constitution, law and statute, certain powers of management to the organs of the working organization: the workers' council, the managing board and the director, or other equivalent organs of management. Special supervisory, specialized and other organs of management may be established in a working organization in accordance with law and the statute.

Interested citizens and the representatives of organizations and of the social community concerned shall participate, in accordance with law, in the management of certain affairs in a working organization carrying out work or affairs of special social concern as members of the organ of management in the working organization, or in some other manner determined by law and by the statute.

The organization of work and the distribution of income in a working organization of this type shall be decided upon only by the organs of management elected by the members of the working community. Provision may be made in law determining the general conditions and standards for the distribution of income, and prescribing that a certain organ of management of the working organization, another organization or a state organ must approve certain decisions pertaining to the distribution of income or decisions pertaining to the process of work when these decisions are of special social concern.

Art. 91. In accordance with the Constitution and law, the working organization shall adopt a statute and make other general decisions regulating relations in the working organization.

The statute shall determine the internal organization, jurisdiction and responsibility of the organs of management, the position of the working departments and the rights of the working people in the management of these departments, the working and other internal relations, and the manner of doing business, as well as other matters of importance for management in the working organization and for its affairs. The statute may also grant business autonomy for certain departments of the working organization.

The statute of the working organization, before it is finally adopted, shall be presented for examination to the communal assembly. Provision may be made in law determining that the statute of certain working organizations shall be submitted for examination to the republican assembly or to the assembly of some other social-political community.

The obligation of the working organization to pass certain general decisions and the procedure for the adoption of the statute and other general acts may be established by law. Certain powers may be granted by law to the competent organ of the social-political community to confirm or approve the statute or other general decisions as a whole, or certain parts of them.

Art. 92. The workers' council shall adopt a statute and other general decisions, determine plans and a program of work and development of the working organization, and decide on other general matters.

The members of the workers' council shall be elected by the working people directly.

A working community with a small number of members shall directly carry out the functions of the workers' council.

The managing board shall decide on the affairs of the working organization.

The members of the managing board of the working organization shall be elected by the workers' council or working community. It may be provided by law or by statute that a working community with a small number of members shall directly execute the functions of the managing board also.

The members of the workers' council shall be elected for a term of two years and the members of the managing board for a term of one year.

No one shall be elected twice consecutively to the workers' council or more than twice consecutively to the managing board.

One half the members of the workers' council shall be elected every year.

Art. 93. The director of the working organization shall be in charge of the business of the working organization, execute the decisions of the workers' council and other organs of management and represent the organization. The director shall be independent in his work and shall be personally accountable to the working community and to the organs of management of the working organization, and shall also be responsible to the social-political community for the legality of the work of the working organization and for the fulfilment of its legally determined obligations.

The director shall be nominated by the workers' council on the basis of a public competition, upon the proposal of the appointments commission, subject to the conditions and procedure determined by law. The appointments commission shall be composed of a legally determined number of representatives of the working community and of the commune or other equivalent social-political community.

Some other manner of nominating the director of a working organization which performs work of special social concern may be prescribed by law.

The director of the working organization shall be nominated for a term determined by law, and he may be re-nominated in accordance with the same procedure.

The conditions under which the workers' council or other competent body may dismiss the director before the expiration of the term for which he has been nominated may be determined by law.

Art. 94. An arbitration commission shall be set up in accordance with the law to eliminate and settle collective disputes between the working people of parts of a working organization, or between the working people of a working organization and the organs of the social-political community.

Art. 95. Affairs of common concern in the management of housing, and in other fields of social life shall be discharged by the citizens directly or through bodies which they themselves elect and which shall be accountable to them for their work.

CHAPTER V. THE SOCIAL-POLITICAL COMMUNITIES

1. The Commune

Art. 96. Directly and through their organs of social self-government in the commune, being the basic social-political community, the citizens shall,

Provide the material and other conditions necessary for the work and development of the productive forces; guide and co-ordinate economic development and the development of the social services; determine and distribute the means for common communal requirements; create the conditions required to satisfy the material, social, cultural and other common needs of the citizens; co-ordinate individual and common interests with the general interests;

Exercise direct social self-government; organize the organs of government, social self-government and social services of common concern; provide conditions for the realization of the freedoms and rights of the citizens; regulate relations of direct concern to the citizens in the commune; determine the general conditions to discharge the business of the communal and similar organizations; safeguard legality and the security of the people and property; maintain public peace and order; exercise social supervision;

Execute other powers of the social community, with the exception of the powers determined by the Constitution as being the rights and duties of the republics or of the Federation.

The rights and duties of the commune shall be determined by the Constitution, by law, and by statute.

The rights and duties of the commune shall be discharged by the citizens at the meetings of the electorate and through other forms of direct decision, by the communal assembly, its organs, and the local communities. The rights and duties of the commune shall be realized by the organs of the commune and local community, with the participation of and in co-operation with other organs of social self-government in the commune.

Art. 97. The territories of the communes shall be determined by republican law in accordance with the conditions determined by republican constitution.

Art. 98. Every commune shall independently adopt a statute.

The communal statute, within the framework of the Constitution and law, shall determine the rights and duties of the commune and the manner in which they shall be exercised; the province, organization and rights of the local communities, and other forms of self-government in localities; the relations between citizens, working and other organizations in the solution of matters of common concern; the manner in which the work of the organs and organizations in the commune shall be rendered public; the organization of the communal and other services; the rights of the citizens, working organizations and other autonomous organizations in the use of funds, social and other services, resources in general use and other social means managed by the commune; the organization of the communal assembly and other communal organs and their rights, duties and powers.

Art. 99. In order to discharge its rights and duties the commune shall autonomously pass regulations, and the social plan and budget, and shall establish its own funds.

In conformity with legally determined sources and types of revenue, the commune shall autonomously determine and use its revenues.

In accordance with law, the commune shall directly discharge the functions of the social community in regard to the regulation and utilization of land resources in general use, the construction and utilization of housing and the regulation of communal housing relations.

Art. 100. Subject to conditions determined by republican constitution and law, a commune that is unable to finance its work and the work of the social services shall be allocated additional resources from republican revenues to finance social services and other services in the commune.

Art. 101. The communal authorities shall attend to the enforcement of federal and republican laws and shall directly enforce them, unless the Constitution or law has placed their enforcement in the jurisdiction of the district, republican or federal authorities.

Art. 102. In towns with more than one commune, organs of self-government may be established by town statute in accordance with republican constitution and law for affairs of general concern to the town as a whole, and these bodies may be given definite communal and district rights and duties.

Art. 103. The communes shall co-operate with each other; they may freely pool their resources to discharge particular affairs within their jurisdiction or to create the conditions to satisfy needs of common concern; found common organs, organizations and services, undertake joint actions and exchange experiences.

Art. 104. In the local community, as an autonomous community of citizens of rural and urban localities, the citizens shall directly exercise self-government in areas directly satisfying the needs of the working people and their families.

The communal statute may provide that the local community shall discharge other affairs in order to satisfy communal, social and other common needs of the citizens, and it may determine the manner in which these affairs shall be financed.

The local community is a juristic person.

2. The District

Art. 105. Districts shall be founded to discharge affairs of common concern to two or more communes.

The republican constitution may provide that only communes shall be founded in a republic.

Art. 106. The Federation and the republics, within the framework of their rights and duties, may determine by constitution and law the rights and duties of the district.

The republican constitution may provide that definite rights exercised in relation to the communal organs by the republican organs may be exercised by the district organs.

By decision of their assemblies, the communes may entrust to the district the execution of affairs of common concern to the communes, and the district may be bound by decision of the republican assemblies to discharge these affairs.

Art. 107. The members of the district assembly shall be elected by the communal assemblies from among their members.

Every district shall have a statute.

Provision shall be made in republican law determining the manner of financing districts.

3. The Socialist Republic

Art. 108. The republic is a socialist democratic state community based on the power of the working people and on self-government.

The working people in the republic shall exercise social self-government, regulate social relations, determine the course of economic development and of the development of the social services, provide for the realization of the rights of the citizens, and for constitutionality and legality, and discharge all social affairs of common concern for political, economic, and cultural life and social development in the republic, with the exception of the affairs determined by the Constitution to be the rights and the duties of the Federation.

The rights and duties of the republic shall be determined by republican constitution in accordance with the principles of this Constitution.

Art. 109. The territory of a republic shall not be altered without the consent of the republic concerned.

The boundaries between the republics may be changed only on the basis of agreement between the respective republican assemblies.

Art. 110. The republics shall co-operate with each other in affairs of common concern and develop mutual relations.

In order to attain objectives of common concern, the republics shall found common organizations, undertake common measures and promote the exchange of experiences and other forms of economic and other co-operation.

The decisions, papers and other documents issued by state organs and authorized organizations in one republic shall have equal validity in the other republics.

Art. 111. A republic may found autonomous provinces in accordance with the constitution in areas with distinctive national characteristics or in areas with other distinguishing features, on the basis of the express will of the population of these areas.

The foundation or dissolution of an autonomous province shall take effect when this is sanctioned by the Constitution of Yugoslavia.

In the Socialist Republic of Serbia there are the Autonomous Provinces of Vojvodina and Kossovo and Metohija, established in 1945 by decision of the People's Assembly of the People's Republic of Serbia in accordance with the express will of the population of these areas.

Art. 112. The autonomous provinces are social-political communities within the republic.

The autonomous rights and duties and the basic principles of organization in the autonomous provinces shall be determined by republican constitution.

4. The Federation

Art. 113. In the Socialist Federal Republic of Yugoslavia the peoples and the citizens shall realize and safeguard the sovereignty, territorial integrity, security and defence of Yugoslavia, the international relations of Yugoslavia, the unity of the social-economic and political system, the economic unity of the country, the course and co-ordination of general economic development, and the basic freedoms and rights of man and the citizen; and they shall co-ordinate their political, economic, cultural and other common interests.

In order to realize these common interests, the Constitution determines the rights and the duties of the Federation.

The citizens shall also realize their political, social-economic, cultural and other common interests by means of social-political and other organizations which are active on the whole territory of Yugoslavia.

In exercising its rights and duties the Federation shall have the co-operation of the republics and other social-political communities, and social-political and other organizations.

Art. 114. The Federation shall protect the sovereign rights and equality of the peoples and the socialist social and political organization of the republics.

Art. 115. The Federation shall be directly responsible for the sovereignty, independence, territorial integrity, security and defence of Yugoslavia and for its international relations.

In these provinces, as well as in other provinces in which the Constitution determines it to be directly responsible, the Federation shall have the exclusive right and duty to pass laws and other regulations and directly to enforce them, and it shall be responsible for their enforcement even when the execution of some of these affairs is placed in the jurisdiction of other state organs and organizations.

Within the province of the exclusive rights and duties of the Federation, the federal organs shall adopt regulations for the enforcement of federal law.

The republics may pass laws of their own in this province and in other provinces determined by the Constitution to be regulated exclusively by federal law only if the republics are authorized to do so by federal law.

Art. 116. It shall be the right and duty of the Federation to provide unity of the economic system and of the system of distribution of the social product. The Federation shall safeguard the unity of the political system, the system of social self-government and the basic freedoms and rights of man and the citizen.

Art. 117. The Federation shall provide for the unity of the monetary and credit systems, determine the policy according to which money shall be issued, and assure supervision of money circulation.

Paper money and coin shall be issued by the National Bank of Yugoslavia.

The Federation shall prescribe the obligatory bank deposits to be held by the federal banks, and the conditions and manner in which foreign currency and similar reserves and deposits shall be used.

Art. 118. The citizens of Yugoslavia shall have common Yugoslav citizenship.

Every citizen of a republic shall also be a citizen of Yugoslavia.

The citizens of one republic shall enjoy on the territory of another republic the same rights and duties as a citizen of that republic.

Art. 119. In order to exercise its rights and duties determined by the Constitution, and to provide uniform foundations for the legal system, the Federation shall enact complete, basic and general laws.

The federal laws and other general federal acts shall be binding on the whole territory of Yugoslavia unless these regulations and acts prescribe that they shall be enforced on a lesser territory.

In the provinces in which the Federation passes complete laws the republics may regulate certain matters if federal law is lacking or if they are authorized by federal law to do so.

In the provinces in which the Federation passes basic laws, the republics shall regulate relations which have not been regulated by federal law, and may fully regulate all relations in these provinces if federal law is lacking.

The provisions of republican law pertaining to matters regulated by federal law shall cease to be valid on the day on which the federal law, passed after the republican law, takes effect, unless federal law determines otherwise.

A republic may be authorized by complete and by basic federal law to regulate certain questions in a different manner in its own law.

Art. 120. The Federation, within the framework of its rights and duties, may adopt general laws in the fields of education and culture, health, and social welfare and in other provinces in which the Constitution does not provide that the Federation shall pass other federal laws.

The general laws shall determine the general principles regulating relations of concern for the basic unity of the social and political system.

General laws may also be passed in provinces in which it is provided that the Federation shall pass basic laws.

The republics shall pass laws of their own in conformity with the principles determined by the general law, and shall bring their laws into conformity with subsequently passed general laws.

The general laws shall not be directly enforceable.

Art. 121. The Federation shall determine the general course of the country's economic development and the basic relations in the distribution of the social product, co-ordinate economic development and relations between industrial branches and areas, determine the course and conditions of trade with foreign countries, equalize the general working conditions and acquisition of income so as to realize the principle of distribution according to work, and promote the most favorable general conditions for the realization of the common interests of the working people, the activities of the working organizations, and the functions of the social-political communities in the province of social-economic relations.

Art. 122. The Federation shall determine the sources and the amount of the resources required to carry out its tasks and discharge its affairs determined by the Constitution and law.

The resources of the Federation shall serve:

(1) To keep the market in full supply, and to expand trade with other countries;

(2) To intervene in the economy in order to co-ordinate relations between different occupations, to equalize working conditions and the acquisition of income, to prodive for the stability of the economy and keep the market in full supply, and to expand trade with other countries;

(3) To finance rapid economic development in the economically underdeveloped republics and areas;

(4) To take part in investments of essential importance to the co-ordination and course of Yugoslavia's economic development, and in investments determined by international agreements.

Art. 123. A special federal fund shall be established to finance the rapid economic development of the inadequately developed republics and areas.

Federal law shall provide permanent sources of finances for this fund and special credit terms, and shall determine the manner of operation of the fund.

The Federation shall provide the means for a republic that is unable to finance social and other services with funds of its own, subject to conditions determined by law.

Art. 124. The Federation may,

(1) Prescribe as obligatory that the working organizations and social-political communities shall form reserve social resources and that the working organizations shall utilize part of their freely-disposable income to develop the material bases of their work, or of economic and social development, if this is necessary for economic stability or for the attainment of the basic material relations established by the social plan of Yugoslavia;

(2) Temporarily prohibit the use of certain social resources by the working organizations and social-political communities, when this is indissable in order to prevent or eliminate major disturbances in the economy and major disproportions in the fulfilment of the social plan of Yugoslavia, or when the needs of national defence or other special needs of the country so enjoin;

(3) Prescribe obligations for the working organizations and social-political communities of concern for national defence.

These measures may be prescribed only by law.

Art. 125. The sources and types of revenue for the social-political communities shall be determined by federal law.

In order to guarantee the equal position of the working people and of working organizations in business and in the distribution of the social product, or in order to realize the basic material relations established by the social plan of Yugoslavia, the Federation may determine the limits within which the social-political communities may determine their own revenues and other resources.

Art. 126. The republics shall adopt regulations to enforce federal law if the republican organs of state are competent to enforce it, and if federal law has not provided that the regulations for the enforcement of the law shall be adopted by federal organs, or if the republic in question is authorized by federal law to pass such regulations.

The republics shall be responsible for the enforcement on their territories of the federal laws and other federal regulations.

The republic shall ensure the enforcement of federal law and other federal regulations through its organs if the competent communal organs do not enforce them.

Art. 127. In accordance with law, the Federation may found administrative organs on the territories of the republics and of other social-political communities to carry out certain administrative affairs within the province of the exclusive rights and duties of the Federation, and it may prescribe the obligation of the republics and other social-political communities to found administrative organs to discharge such affairs or affairs of concern to the whole country.

The republican, district and communal authorities shall attend to the enforcement of the laws, acts and measures of the federal authorities within these provinces, and to this end they shall co-operate with all the authorities requiring such co-operation in accordance with federal law.

Only in accordance with federal law may it be provided that in the execution of certain affairs in the province of the exclusive rights and duties of the Federation the federal administrative organs may stay the execution of general acts of the republican administrative organs which are at variance with federal law or with other federal regulations adopted in accordance with law, and hear appeals against administrative decisions of the republican administrative organs. Provisions may be made in federal law determining that in these affairs and in other affairs of concern to the country as a whole, the federal administrative organs shall have the right to issue instructions binding the republican administrative organs, to supervise their work, and to exercise other powers in order to secure the carrying out of these affairs.

Through its organs the Federation may provide for the enforcement of federal laws and other federal regulations for whose enforcement the organs of other social-political communities are competent, if these organs do not enforce the regulations in question or until they do so.

Affairs of concern to the country as a whole are those affairs designated by law whose execution shall be the responsability of the federal organs even when these affairs are discharged by the republican organs directly.

The federal authorities shall communicate with the organs of the other social-political communities in the republics through the equivalent republican authorities, and they may also communicate with them directly in affairs within the province of the exclusive rights and duties of the Federation and in other cases designated by federal law.

Art. 128. If certain matters of enforcement of federal laws within the province of the exclusive rights and duties of the Federation are transferred to the jurisdiction of the republican, district or communal authorities, the Federation shall be responsible to provide the resources or the sources of revenue necessary to discharge these relegated affairs.

Art. 129. The federal organs in charge of inspection or supervision, may perform these tasks, in accordance with federal law, on the whole territory of Yugoslavia, in order to supervise the enforcement of federal laws and to protect legality and the rights of citizens and organizations.

Art. 130. In order to realize the rights and duties of the Federation, the Constitution and federal law shall determine the jurisdiction of the federal organs and the province of the organizations in charge of affairs within the framework of the rights and duties of the Federation.

The federal organs and these organizations shall carry on the activities in their jurisdiction, within the framework of the rights and duties of the Federation established by the Constitution.

Art. 131. The federal laws and other general acts of the federal organs shall be made public in the official gazette of the Federation, in the authentic texts in the languages of the peoples of Yugoslavia: in Serbo-Croatian and Croato-Serbian, Slovene and Macedonian.

In official communication the organs of the Federation shall abide by the principle of equality of languages of the peoples of Yugoslavia.

CHAPTER VI. THE COURTS AND THE PUBLIC PROSECUTION

Art. 132. The judicial functions shall be discharged within a uniform judicial system.

The judicial system shall comprise courts of general jurisdiction and courts of special jurisdiction, wichh shall be established to hear definite cases within court jurisdiction.

The courts of general jurisdiction shall be the communal courts, the county courts, the republican supreme courts and the Supreme Court of Yugoslavia.

Economic cases and other legal matters of concern for the economy shall be heard by economic courts.

Criminal offences committed by military personnel and certain criminal offences committed by other persons, and other legal matters pertaining to cases involving service in the Yugoslav People's Army shall be heard by military courts.

The courts of special jurisdiction shall be established by law.

Art. 133. Subject to conditions determined on the basis of federal law, judicial functions may be discharged by courts of arbitration or by arbitration commissions.

Conciliation councils and other institutions to settle disputes between citizens or organizations may be founded in accordance with law.

Art. 134. The jurisdiction of the courts shall be established and altered only by law.

Art. 135. The courts shall judge basic personal, property, labor and other rights of the citizens and their obligations as well as property and other rights and obligations of organizations and social-political communities; pronounce penalties and other measures over criminal and economic offenders; judge in administrative litigation the legality of individual acts of the state organs and of organizations that discharge public powers; and decide on other relations when this is provided by law.

The courts shall follow and study social relations and manifestations of interest for the discharge of their functions, and shall advance proposals to prevent socially dangerous and harmful manifestations and to consolidate legality.

Within their jurisdiction courts shall have the right and duty to inform the assembly of the pertinent social-political community about the enforcement of law and about problems in the work of the courts.

Art. 136. The courts shall be autonomous in the performance of their judicial functions and shall hear cases in accordance with the Constitution and law.

Art. 137. Cases shall be heard by judges and lay judges.

Provision may be made in federal law determinating that only judges shall sit in certain courts and hear certain cases.

The judges and lay judges shall be chosen by the assembly of the corresponding social-political community. Provision may be made in law determining that the judges and lay judges of some courts shall be elected directly by the citizens.

The judges and lay judges may be removed from office only by the representative body that has elected them, under the conditions and in accordance with the procedure prescribed by law.

Art. 138. A judge or lay judge shall not be called to account for an opinion given in the performance of judicial functions.

A judge or lay judge may not be placed under arrest for a criminal offence committed in the performance of his judicial duty without the approval of the competent assembly.

Art. 139. Rulings in the first instance shall be passed by communal or county courts unless some other court has been given jurisdiction to hear in the first instance.

Appeals and other legal expedients against court decisions shall be heard by the competent court.

Only the competent court may amend, annul or set aside a court decision.

Art. 140. Courts shall sit in council.

Provision may be made in law determining that certain cases shall be heard by a single judge.

Art. 141. Court hearings shall be public.

The law shall designate those cases in which the public may be barred from court hearings in order to safeguard secrets, or to protect public decency, or in the interest of minors, or to safeguard other particular interests of the social community.

Art. 142. The public prosecution is an autonomous organ entrusted with criminal prosecution. The public prosecution shall also undertake measures determined by law and legal expedients to assure the uniform enforcement of law and to protect legality.

The public prosecution shall discharge its functions in accordance with law and pursuant to the policy of the Federal Assembly.

The function of public prosecution in the Yugoslav People's Army shall be exercised by the military prosecution.

Art. 143. The federal public prosecutor shall be nominated and removed by the Federal Assembly.

The public prosecutor of the republic shall be appointed and removed by the federal public prosecutor with the approval of the republican executive council. All other public prosecutors shall be appointed by the public prosecutor of the republic.

Art. 144. Superior public prosecutors shall have the right and duty to issue instructions binding subordinate public prosecutors in their work.

The superior public prosecutor may discharge certain tasks which are within the jurisdiction of a subordinate public prosecutor.

CHAPTER VII. CONSTITUTIONALITY AND LEGALITY

Art. 145. Constitutionality and legality shall be safeguarded in order to secure the constitutionally and legally established social-economic and political relations and unity of the legal order, as well as to protect the freedoms and rights of man and the citizen, the rights to self-government, and other rights of the organizations and social-political communities.

Art. 146. Constitutionality and legality shall be the concern of the courts and other state organs, the organs of self-government and everyone who discharges public or other social functions.

The constitutional courts, as the safeguard of constitutionality, shall secure legality in accordance with the Constitution.

Art. 147. Every regulation and other general act must be in conformity with the Constitution of Yugoslavia.

Every regulation and other general act enacted in the republic must also be in accord with the republican constitution.

Art. 148. The republican constitution shall not be at variance with the Constitution of Yugoslavia.

Republican law shall conform to federal law.

All other regulations and other general acts passed by the state organs shall be in conformity with law.

The statutes of the social-political communities, as well as the statutes and other general decisions adopted by the working and other autonomous organizations shall conform to the Constitution and law.

Art. 149. If the republican constitution is at variance with the Constitution of Yugoslavia, the Constitution of Yugoslavia shall be binding.

If republican law is not in accord with federal law, federal law shall be binding, pending the decision of the Constitutional Court of Yugoslavia.

Whenever a court deems that a law which it must enforce does not conform to the Constitution, it shall propose to the competent supreme court to institute proceedings to assess the conformity of such a law with the Constitution.

Art. 150. Constitutional courts shall decide on the conformity of law with the constitution and the conformity of other regulations and general acts with the constitution and law.

The constitutional courts, pursuant to law, shall also safeguard the rights of self-government and other basic freedoms and rights established by the constitution whenever these freedoms and rights have been violated by any decisions or action and other court protection has not been provided.

Art. 151. Pending the decision of the Constitutional Court of Yugoslavia, the Federal Executive Council shall have the right to stay enforcement of a regulation or other general act of the republican executive council when this regulation or act is at variance with the Constitution of Yugoslavia or federal law.

Pending the decision of the constitutional court, the republican executive council shall have the right to stay enforcement of a regulation or other general act of a communal or district assembly or of any of their organs when such regulation or act is at variance with the constitution or law. If the republican executive council does not stay enforcement of a regulation or other act which is at variance with the Constitution of Yugoslavia or federal law, the Federal Executive Council may do so.

Pending the decision of the constitutional court, the communal assembly shall have the right to stay enforcement of general decisions of an autonomous organization when these decisions are at variance with the constitution or law. Provision may be made in law determining that the enforcement of general decision of certain autonomous organizations may be stayed under the same conditions by the organ of another social-political community.

Art. 152. Laws and other regulations and general acts shall be made public before they take effect.

Federal laws and other regulations and general acts shall become effective not before the eighth day after publication.

Only with special justification may a federal law or other regulation or general act become effective within a period shorter than eight days after publication.

Art. 153. International agreements shall be applied on the day they take effect, unless the instrument of ratification, or the agreement based on the authority of the competent organ determines otherwise.

The court shall directly apply the international agreements that have been made public.

Art. 154. No regulation or other general act shall have retroactive force.

Only by the law in question may provision be made that certain of the law's provisions and the regulations passed in accordance with such provisions shall have retroactive force.

Criminal offences and economic misdemeanors and offences shall be ascertained and the penalties for these acts executed according to the law in force at the time when they were committed, unless a subsequent law is more lenient towards the offender.

Art. 155. Every decision and measure of the administrative organs and of other state organs discharging political-executive and administrative business, as well as every decision adopted by organizations in the exercise of their public functions shall be based on law or on other legally adopted regulations.

Art. 156. State organs and organizations exercising public powers may in particular matters decide on rights and duties, or, on the basis of law, apply measures of coercion or restriction only in accordance with the procedure prescribed by law, in which everyone concerned shall be able to defend his rights and interests and appeal or employ other legal expedients provided by law against the decision that has been adopted.

Administrative organs may bind particular organizations in their work only if they are explicitly authorized by law to do so and in accordance with the procedure prescribed by law.

Art. 157. Ignorance of the language in which proceedings are being conducted shall not be a hindrance for defence and the realization of the rights and justified interests of citizens and organizations.

Every person shall be entitled to speak his own language in proceedings before court or before other state organs and organizations which in exercising public powers decide on the rights and duties of citizens and during these proceedings every person shall be informed of the facts in his own language.

Art. 158. An appeal may be filed with the competent authority against the decisions and other acts passed by judicial, administrative and other state organs in the first instance, and against such decisions passed by organizations which exercise public powers.

If the protection of rights and legality has been provided for in some other manner, appeal may be ruled out in certain cases in accordance with law.

Art. 159. The legality of individual final decisions by which state organs or organizations exercising public powers decide on rights or duties shall be judged by court in administrative litigation, unless other judicial protection has been provided by law for the case in question.

Only by federal law in exceptional cases, may administrative litigation be ruled out in certain types of administrative cases.

PART TWO

ORGANIZATION OF THE FEDERATION

CHAPTER VIII. JURISDICTION OF THE FEDERAL ORGANS

Art. 160. The exclusive jurisdiction of the Federation shall comprise:

(1) Protection of the independence and territorial integrity of Yugo-

slavia, organization of the Armed Forces, and affairs pertaining to the defence of the country;

(2) Protection of the constitutional order (state security); protection of the constitutionality established by the Constitution;

(3) Representation of the Socialist Federal Republic of Yugoslavia; political, economic an dother relations with other states and inter-state organizations; international agreements; matters of war and peace;

(4) Yugoslav citizenship; security and control of the boundaries; the legal status and sojourn of aliens in Yugoslavia; organization of and supervision over foreign-trade and foreign-exchange affairs and other economic relations with other countries; customs; determination of policy for issuing money, and regulation and supervision of money circulation; supervision of security of air traffic; supervision of passenger traffic across the frontier; supervision of traffic in goods across the frontier; supervision of international transport and communications;

(5) Organization of the Federation and execution of tasks and affairs for which only the Federation is competent in accordance with the Constitution.

Art. 161. The jurisdiction of the Federation in the legislative field shall comprise:

(1) Complete laws concerning social ownership; ownership rights; obligatory and other basic property-law relations; expropriations; money and other media of payment; payment transactions; credit and banking; the social accounting service; weights and measures, standards and technical norms, patents, trade marks, samples, models and copyrights; the maritime code; the code for air traffic; the personal status of the citizen; suffrage; the manufacture of and traffic in narcotic drugs and poisons, and traffic in medicaments; the criminal code; economic offences; the enforcement of criminal sentences; public security; weapons and explosives; the organization of economic courts; the organization of the public prosecution; court procedures; general administrative procedure; administrative litigation; civil defence; protection of veterans and disabled veterans; other relations of concern for the unity of the economic area, and those relations which are to be regulated only by federal law, as determined by the Constitution;

(2) Basic laws concerning economic organizations; the association of economic organizations; business affairs; work and safety at work; the distribution of the social product; income taxes, revenues and other public dues; public loans; budgets and funds; land, forests and water resources, roads and exploitation of natural resources and other natural potential; commerce in goods and services; social planning; transport and communications and traffic safety; designs and construction; assemblage and other public gatherings; the press and other media of information; associations of the citizens; social security; marriage, the family and guardianship;

health protection of concern to the whole country; protection of livestock and vegetation of concern to the whole country; protection against elemental adversity; misdemeanors; the organization of the courts; the internal affairs service and other services whose activity is of concern to the whole country; the legal profession; public prosecution and legal representation; the legal status of religious communities; statistics, supervision and data of concern to the whole country; other relations of concern for the unity of the economic system, basic relations of concern for the political system and concerning those relations provided by the Constitution to be regulated by law;

(3) General laws.

Art. 162. The jurisdiction of the Federation shall include:

(1) Determination of policy for the enforcement of federal law and other acts of the Federal Assembly, attendance to their enforcement and execution, as well as other political-executive and administrative affairs within the framework of the rights and duties of the Federation; administrative jurisdiction in the direct execution of these regulations and other acts, when this has been provided in accordance with federal law for matters of concern to several republics or of concern to the whole country; the securing of enforcement of international agreements;

(2) Provision for the uniform enforcement of federal law and uniform punitive policy in the judicial field;

(3) Statistics and supervision of concern to the whole country;

(4) Other activities and measures to secure the realization of the rights and the discharge of the duties of the Federation;

(5) Organization of a social accounting service and supervision over its work;

(6) Other affairs determined by the Constitution.

CHAPTER IX. THE FEDERAL ASSEMBLY

1. Its Position and Jurisdiction

Art. 163. The Federal Assembly is the supreme organ of power and organ of social self-government within the framework of the rights and duties of the Federation.

The Federal Assembly shall discharge its rights and duties on the basis of and in accordance with the Constitution and law.

Art. 164. Being the basic holder of the rights and duties of the Federation, the Assembly shall directly and exclusively,

(1) Decide on a change of the Constitution of Yugoslavia;

(2) Pass federal laws, call referendums; issue authentic interpretations of federal law; grant amnesty for criminal offences determined by federal law;

(3) Adopt the social plans of Yugoslavia, the federal budget and the federal annual financial statement;

(4) Decide on political matters and determine the foundations of internal and foreign policy; determine the duties of the federal authorities and organizations in charge of those affairs of the Federation related to the enforcement of laws and other acts and policy of the assembly;

(5) Elect the President of the Republic and the Vice-President of the Republic;

(6) Elect and remove the president and the members of the Federal Executive Council; elect and remove the presidents and the judges of the Constitutional Court of Yugoslavia, the Supreme Court of Yugoslavia and the Supreme Economic Court; appoint and remove the federal secretaries of state, the federal secretaries, the secretary of the Federal Executive Council, and the deputy commander-in-chief, as well the officers and members of organs of management of organizations designated by the Constitution or federal law, or by other assembly decisions;

(7) Exercise political supervision over the work of the political-executive and administrative organs of the Federation; exercise supervision over the enforcement of the social plans of Yugoslavia, the federal budget and the financial plans of the federal funds; exercise social supervision; take positions in principle concerning the reports it may examine;

(8) Decide on alterations of the boundaries of the Socialist Federal Repulic of Yugoslavia;

(9) Decide on war and peace; ratify international agreements concerning political and military co-operation and international agreements requiring enactment of additional laws or the amendment of laws in force;

(10) Debate the reports of the federal courts and the federal public prosecution concerning the enforcement of federal law and the general problems of the judiciary; debate the reports of the autonomous organizations and other organs of the Federation designated by federal law;

(11) Discharge other affairs determined by the Constitution;

The assembly may enact declarations and resolutions and make recommendations to the state organs and autonomous organizations, giving its opinions on matters of general concern.

2. Composition and Election

Art. 165. The Federal Assembly shall comprise the Federal Chamber as a chamber of delegates of the citizens in the communes and republics, and the Economic Chamber, the Chamber of Education and Culture, the Chamber of Social Welfare and Health, and the Organizational-Political Chamber as chambers of delegates of the working people in the working communities.

The members of the Federal Chamber elected by the republican assemblies and the assemblies of the autonomous provinces shall constitute the Chamber of Nationalities, which shall have certain rights and duties under the Constitution for safeguarding the equality of the peoples of Yugoslavia and the rights of the republics, as determined by the Constitution.

Art. 166. Each chamber shall have one hundred and twenty deputies, who shall be elected in the ratio of one deputy to an equal number of inhabitants, so that one or several communes, as a constituency, shall elect one deputy to each chamber.

The republican chamber of every republican assembly shall elect ten deputies to the Federal Chamber from among its members. In a republic incorporating autonomous provinces, the provincial council of each autonomous province shall elect an additional five deputies as members of the republican delegation to the Federal Chamber, either from among its members or from among those members of the republican chamber of the republican assembly who have been elected on the territory of the autonomous province.

Art. 167. The deputies of the Federal Chamber shall be elected by the communal assemblies and citizens directly.

The deputies to the chambers of the Federal Assembly which represent working communities shall be elected by the communal assemblies.

The candidates for membership to the Federal Chamber shall be nominated by the citizens at their meetings of the electorate or by groups of citizens, and the candidates for membership to the various chambers representing the working communities shall be nominated by the working people in the working communities depending on their field of work.

Art. 168. Every citizen who enjoys suffrage shall be eligible to election to the Federal Chamber.

Every working man or member of an organ of management of a working organization or working community in the corresponding field of work, every member of an organ of management of an association of working organizations, and every trade-union officer in the corresponding field of work shall be eligible to election to the Economic Chamber, the Chamber of Education and Culture, and the Chamber of Social Welfare and Health.

Every member of an organ of management of a working organization or working community, every member of an organ of management of an association of working organizations, and every official of a social-political organization or association whose activities concern matters in the field of the social-political system shall be eligible to election to the Organizational-Political Chamber.

Any other citizen occupied in a corresponding field shall be eligible to election to any of the chambers representing the working communities, subject to the conditions determined by law.

Only a citizen who enjoys general suffrage shall be eligible to election to the chambers representing the working communities.

Art. 169. A candidate shall become a member of the Federal Chamber when he is elected in the communal assembly or communal assemblies by a legally determined majority and when after that election he receives the vote of the majority of all the voters in the constituency; and if several candidates are elected that candidate shall become a member who has received the largest number of votes in the constituency.

A candidate shall become a member of the Economic Chamber, the Chamber of Education and Culture, the Chamber of Social Welfare and Health, or the Organizational-Political Chamber when he is elected by a legally determined majority in the communal assembly or communal assemblies.

Art. 170. A federal deputy shall be deemed recalled when a majority of the electorate determined by federal law have declared themselves for his recall.

Art. 171. Elections for new deputies shall be held not later than fifteen days before the expiration of the term of the deputies whose term is expiring.

Elections for deputies shall be called by the President of the Assembly.

If an assembly chamber is dissolved, elections shall be held not later than fifteen days from the day of its dissolution.

The term of the newly elected chamber shall last until the term of the members of the dissolved chamber would have expired.

Not more than two months nor less than one month shall elapse from the day the elections are called until the day the elections are held.

The functions of the deputies whose terms are expiring shall cease on the day when the credentials of the new deputies are verified.

Art. 172. Under special circumstances the assembly may extend the term of the federal deputies for the duration of those circumstances. Elections shall be called immediately upon the cessation of the circumstances owing to which the term of the deputies has been extended.

3. Province and Work

Art. 173. Affairs within the jurisdiction of the assembly shall be discharged by the Federal Chamber acting with the other competent chamber on terms of equality.

Certain affairs in the jurisdiction of the assembly shall be discharged by each chamber independently.

The assembly shall discharge certain affairs in its jurisdiction at joint sessions of all the chambers.

The assembly shall discharge certain affairs in its jurisdiction in committees, commissions and other bodies of the chambers and assembly.

Art. 174. The Federal Chamber, acting on terms of equality with the Economic Chamber, shall,

Consider affairs of concern to the working communities in the economic sphere, as well as other matters in the fields of economy and finance;

Pass laws and other acts in these fields;

Pass the social plans of Yugoslavia.

Art. 175. The Federal Chamber, acting on terms of equality with the Chamber of Education and Culture, shall,

Consider affairs of concern to the working communities in the fields of education, science, art and other cultural fields as well as in the field of physical culture, and consider other affairs in these fields;

Pass laws and other acts in these fields.

Art. 176. The Federal Chamber, acting on terms of equality with the Chamber of Social Welfare and Health, shall,

Consider affairs of concern to the working communities in the fields of health and social security and in other fields of social welfare, and consider other affairs in these fields;

Pass laws and other acts in these fields.

Art. 177. The Federal Chamber, acting on terms of equality with the Organizational-Political Chamber, shall,

Consider affairs in the fields of the social-political system and in other fields in the jurisdiction of the assembly, with the exception of matters which in accordance with the Constitution fall equally into the jurisdiction of the other chambers or into the independent jurisdiction of one of the other chambers;

Pass laws and other acts unless they fall equally into the jurisdiction of other chambers or are the independent jurisdiction of the Federal Chamber;

Pass the federal budget and the annual financial statement.

Art. 178. The Federal Chamber shall independently,

Consider affairs in the field of foreign policy, national defence and state security and affairs of general internal policy;

Pass laws and other acts and ratify international agreements in the fields of international political relations, national defence and state security;

Elect and remove the president and the members of the Federal Executive Council; elect and remove the presidents and the judges of the Constitutional Court of Yugoslavia, the Supreme Court of Yugoslavia and the Supreme Economic Court; nominate and remove the federal secretaries of state, the federal secretaries, the secretary of the Federal Executive Council, and the deputy commander-in-chief, as well as the officials and members of the organs of management of organizations designated by the Constitution, federal law or other assembly decision; exercise the rights of the assembly with regard to the responsibilities of the political-executive organs and federal officers to the assembly;

Pass decisions concerning the compensation to be paid the federal deputies and officers whom the assembly elects or nominates;

Discharge other affairs in the jurisdiction of the assembly which do not fall equally into the jurisdiction of the other chambers or the independent jurisdiction of one of the other chambers.

Art. 179. Each of the chambers of the working communities, in its jurisdiction, may autonomously debate affairs pertaining to the enforcement of federal law and other assembly decisions, and other affairs of common concern to the working and other autonomous organizations and working communities in the corresponding field of work, in order to co-ordinate their relations and to develop mutual co-operation. The chambers shall be entitled to make recommendations concerning these affairs to the relevant autonomous organizations, working organizations and state organs.

Each of the chambers, in its jurisdiction, may require reports from the Federal Executive Council and address questions to it.

Each of the chambers, in its jurisdiction, may require reports and explanations from the federal secretaries of state, the federal secretaries and other officer, in charge of the administrative organs.

Art. 180. At a joint session of all the chambers the assembly shall elect the President of the Republic and the Vice-President of the Republic, and the president and vice-presidents of the assembly; it shall decide about extending the term of the deputies, and it shall establish when the circumstances cease owing to which the term of the deputies has been extended.

Art. 181. Each chamber shall pass valid decisions by a majority vote at sessions attended by a majority of the members of the chamber in question, unless in accordance with the Constitution a special majority shall be required to pass certain decisions.

The assembly at a joint session of all its chambers shall pass valid decisions by a majority vote unless in accordance with the Constitution a special majority shall be required. The adoption of decisions at the joint sessions shall require the presence of a majority of the members of each chamber.

Art. 182. Every deputy in his own chamber, the Federal Executive Council, and any committee of a chamber shall have the right to introduce bills and other draft acts.

Any chamber may also introduce bills and other draft acts within the jurisdiction of some other chamber.

The motion for the introduction of a bill may also come from autonomous organizations, from social-political organizations and associations, and from citizens.

Art. 183. Every chamber shall have the right to discuss a bill, the draft social plan and the budget, as well as any other affair in the jurisdiction of another chamber, and to offer its opinions to the competent chamber on the bill or affair in question, if the bill or affair in question also pertains to a province in its own jurisdiction.

The competent chamber may require an opinion from the other chambers on a bill, the draft social plan, the budget or other matters.

The competent chamber shall debate the opinions of the other chambers and take a position on them.

Art. 184. The competent chambers may resolve to place a bill before public discussion, or they may invite the representatives of autonomous organizations and social-political organizations and associations to give their opinions and proposals during the debate on a bill or draft act.

Art. 185. Each chamber shall sit and deliberate separately in its sessions; but the chambers may also decide to sit and work together.

Two chambers participating on terms of equality in the enactment of a law or other act may decide to debate the law or act or to pass it at a joint session.

Two or more chambers may resolve to debate affairs of common concern at a joint session.

If the chambers resolve to vote at a joint session, the members of each chamber shall vote separately.

Voting shall be by acclamation, unless the assembly or the chamber, in accord with the rules of procedure, determines that it shall be by ballot.

Art. 186. The assembly shall have rules of procedure, which shall be adopted at a joint session.

Each chamber shall adopt rules of procedure for its own work.

Art. 187. Each chamber shall independently verify credentials, and decide on matters relating to the credentials and parliamentary immunity of its members.

4. The Relations of the Chambers

Art. 188. A law or other act in whose enactment two chambers participate on terms of equality shall be enacted when the two chambers have passed its identical text.

If unanimity is not reached concerning the identical text of a bill or other draft act even after two consecutive discussions of the matter in dispute, the chambers shall form a joint commission composed of an equal number of members from the two chambers, and this commission shall be entrusted with the formulation of a recommendation to settle the dispute.

Should the joint commission fail to reach unanimity, or should either chamber refuse to accept the text recommended by the commission, the bill or other draft act shall be placed before a joint session of the two chambers.

Should the two chambers not reach unanimity at the joint session, the controversial bill shall be removed from the agenda of the assembly, and it may again be placed on the agenda, upon the recommendation of one of the chambers or of the Federal Executive Council, only upon the lapse of six months from the day it has been removed from the agenda. By decision of the two chambers the controversial bill may again be placed on the agenda before this term expires.

Art. 189. If owing to dispute between the Federal Chamber and another competent chamber the social plan of Yugoslavia or the federal budget has not been passed by the time when it should take effect, the two chambers shall be dissolved and the social plan or the budget shall be deemed to have been passed in the text passed by the Federal Chamber.

The newly elected chambers may pass a new social plan or budget.

If owing to dispute between the Federal Chamber and another competent chamber, a bill whose enactment is held by the President of the Republic or by the Federal Executive Council to be indispensable and urgent has not been passed even after the procedure provided for the attainment of unanimity has been followed, the two chambers shall be dissolved. The President of the Republic may decree the temporary application of the bill in the text passed by the Federal Chamber pending the decision of the newly elected chambers.

5. The Rights of the Chamber of Nationalities

Art. 190. The Chamber of Nationalities shall meet by obligation when a motion to change the Constitution of Yugoslavia is on the agenda of the Federal Chamber.

The Chamber of Nationalities may meet when a bill or other draft act, or other matters concerning the equality of the peoples and republics, or pertaining to the rights of the republics established by the Constitution are on the agenda of the Federal Chamber. The Chamber of Nationalities shall meet whenever a majority of the delegates of one republic, ten of its own members, or the president of the assembly so requires.

Art. 191. The Chamber of Nationalities may introduce an amendment to a bill or other draft act, or move that a bill or other draft act shall not be passed if it considers that the bill or other draft act violates the equality of the peoples or republics or other constitutional rights of the republics.

If the Federal Chamber does not accept the motion of the Chamber of Nationalities, the Chamber of Nationalities may again debate the matter in dispute.

If the Chamber of Nationalities stands by its original position, and again no accord is reached on the matter in dispute with the Federal Chamber, the two chambers shall form a joint commission composed of an equal number of members from each chamber, and this commission shall be entrusted with the formulation of a recommendation to settle the dispute.

If the joint commission does not reach unanimity, or if the Federal Chamber or the Chamber of Nationalities declines to accept the recommendation of the commission, further debate on the motion in dispute shall cease, and it shall not be placed on the agenda of the Federal Chamber again before the lapse of one year from the date on which the debate was closed.

The Federal Chamber shall debate and pass decisions always as a unified chamber.

Art. 192. If owing to dispute between the Federal Chamber and the Chamber of Nationalities the social plan of Yugoslavia or the federal budget has not been passed by the date when it should take effect, the Federal Chamber shall be dissolved and the social plan or the budget shall be deemed to have been passed in the text passed by the Federal Chamber.

6. The President of the Assembly and the Presidents of the Chambers

Art. 193. The assembly shall have a president and one or more vice-presidents, who shall be elected from among the members of the Federal Chamber.

Each chamber and the Chamber of Nationalities shall have a president.

The president and vice-president of the assembly and the presidents of the chambers who have been in office for four years may not be returned to the same office for a consecutive period of four years.

The assembly shall have a secretary, who shall be appointed and removed by the Federal Chamber.

Art. 194. The president of the assembly shall represent the assembly; he shall convene joint sessions of the chambers; he shall preside over them and he shall attend to the enforcement of the assembly rules of procedure.

Art. 195. The president of the assembly, with the vice-president of the assembly and the presidents of the chambers, shall interpret those provisions of the rules of procedure of the assembly and chambers related to the jurisdiction of the chambers and assembly committees, and shall resolve upon other positions pertaining to other affairs of common concern in the work of the chambers, as determined by the assembly rules of procedure.

The president of the assembly shall countersign the decree promulgating law; he shall sign decisions passed at the joint sessions of the chambers; and together with the presidents of the relevant chambers he shall sign the assembly decisions passed by the chambers.

The president of the assembly may convene all the chambers in a joint session to deliberate questions of general political importance.

The president of the assembly shall convene all the chambers in a joint session upon the motion of the President of the Republic or of not less than three chambers of the assembly, and he shall convene a joint session of two or more chambers on the motion of two chambers.

Art. 196. The president of each chamber shall convene the sessions of the chamber in accordance with the decision of the chamber concerned, or of his own accord, and he shall convene a session upon the motion of the president of the assembly or of the Federal Executive Council, and in other circumstances determined by the Constitution.

If the president of the chamber does not convene a session of the chamber when this is determined by the Constitution, the chamber shall meet when it is convened by twenty of its members or by the president of the assembly.

7. The Rights and Duties of the Deputies

Art. 197. Every deputy shall have the right to introduce bills, decisions, recommendations, declarations and resolutions, in the chamber in which he is a member, and to move other questions in jurisdiction of the chamber.

Art. 198. Every deputy shall have the right to propose to the chamber of which he is a member, the examination of matters pertaining to the policy and work of the Federal Executive Council, the enforcement of law or the work of the federal administrative organs.

A determined number of deputies shall have the right, pursuant to the rules of procedure, to move the election, nomination and removal of officers elected or nominated by the assembly, unless this is determined otherwise by the Constitution.

Every deputy shall have the right to question the Federal Executive Council or the officers in charge of the federal administrative organs on matters pertaining to their work and on matters in the jurisdiction of the organ concerned.

Art. 199. Every deputy shall have the right to require information from the federal officers in charge of autonomous federal administrative organs.

The officer in question shall give the required information.

Art. 200. Every deputy shall be accountable to his electorate and shall inform the electorate in his constituency about his work and the work of the chamber of which he is a member.

Every federal deputy shall have the right to take part in the work of the assembly of the commune in which he has been elected.

Every deputy shall inform the communal assembly, if it so requires, about his work and about the work of the chamber of which he is a member. On the request of the communal assembly he shall present the proposals or opinions of the communal assembly to the chamber of which he is a member on matters in the chamber's jurisdiction.

In order to discharge his duties, a deputy shall have the right to require information necessary for his work in the assembly from state organs and from working and other autonomous organizations in the constituency in which he has been elected.

Art. 201. No member of the Federal Chamber shall at the same time be an officer or employee of a state organ.

The conditions under which a member of the Federal Chamber shall be entitled to return to his former place of work or to some equivalent place of work, and the conditions under which he shall have the rights that are acquired on the basis of work may be determined by law.

Art. 202. Every deputy shall enjoy parliamentary immunity in the assembly and outside it.

No deputy shall be called to account, arrested or punished for an opinion expressed or vote cast in the assembly.

No deputy shall be arrested without the approval of the chamber of which he is a member, nor may criminal proceedings be instituted against him without the approval of the chamber of which he is a member if he invokes parliamentary immunity.

A deputy may be arrested without the approval of the chamber only if he has been found in the act of committing a criminal offence for which a penalty of more than five years of strict imprisonment may be pronounced. In this event the state authority that has arrested the deputy shall notify the president of the assembly, who shall bring the matter up before the relevant chamber to decide whether proceedings shall continue, i.e. whether the warrant of arrest shall remain effective.

The chamber may also grant parliamentary immunity to a deputy who has not invoked it if this is necessary for him to discharge his duties of deputy.

If the chamber is not sitting, permission to arrest and to institute or continue criminal proceedings against a deputy may be granted or the invoking of parliamentary immunity may be resolved upon by the Credentials and Privileges Commission of the relevant chamber, subject to later confirmation by the chamber.

8. The Committees and Commissions

Art. 203. Standing committees shall be set up to consider general affairs of policy and to introduce motions pertaining to these matters in the assembly, to consider bills and other assembly acts, and to consider other matters in the jurisdiction of the Federal Chamber.

These committees shall be founded and their jurisdiction determined by decision of the Federal Chamber.

Art. 204. The standing committees of the Federal Chamber, within their several jurisdictions shall,

Discuss the state of affairs in different provinces of social life, attend to the work of the federal authorities and the enforcement of law and other assembly acts, and propose policy and measures to the assembly and the Federal Executive Council for the enforcement of federal law and other assembly acts;

Study bills and other draft acts and other matters in the jurisdiction of the assembly, and present their findings and proposals to the Federal Chamber;

Determine bills and other draft acts of the assembly, and have the right to require the federal administrative organs to prepare bills and other acts of the assembly.

Art. 205. A standing committee of the Federal Chamber may require the Federal Executive Council to explain, through its spokesman, its position on certain matters on the agenda of a committee session, or forward its opinion concerning a bill or other draft act.

A committee may require federal officers to explain the state of affairs in their respective departments of administration and to present reports concerning the enforcement of federal laws and other federal regulations and concerning other matters in the jurisdiction of the pertinent administrative organs, and to answer questions either orally or in writing, and to give other information and explanations.

Art. 206. A standing committee of the Federal Chamber may hold inquiries and hearings and to this purpose may require data, files and documents from all the state organs and organizations. The committee shall have no judicial powers of inquiry.

A committee may summon the representatives of organizations in order to hear their opinions and proposals, or their advice on particular matters.

Art. 207. The Economic Chamber, the Chamber of Education and Culture, and of Social Welfare and Health, and the Organizational-Political Chamber may found committees of their own to examine bills and other draft acts and to examine other matters in their respective jurisdictions.

Art. 208. A commission for matters pertaining to elections and nominations shall be set up in the assembly.

The chairman and the majority of the members of the commission shall be elected by the Federal Chamber and other chambers, from among the federal deputies, while a certain number of the members shall be delegated by the Socialist Alliance of the Working People of Yugoslavia.

The commission shall consider all matters pertaining to elections, nominations, and dismissals in the jurisdiction of the assembly, as well as general matters pertaining to personnel.

Art. 209. The assembly and its chambers may also set up other standing and *ad hoc* commissions and other bodies to study particular matters, to prepare bills and other draft acts and to carry out inquiries. The members of these commissions shall be elected from among the deputies, although members of individual commissions may be nominated from among experts and figures prominent in public life.

The assembly may also set up specialized, advisory and similar staffs necessary for the work of the assembly.

9. The Changing of the Constitution

Art. 210. The changing of the Constitution of Yugoslavia shall be decided upon by the Federal Chamber and the Chamber of Nationalities in accordance with the procedure determined by the Constitution.

A motion to change the Constitution may be introduced by not less than thirty members of the Federal Chamber, by the Chamber of Nationalities, by the President of the Republic or by the Federal Executive Council.

The Federal Chamber and the Chamber of Nationalities shall first resolve whether or not deliberations on a change of constitution should be commenced.

If after two consecutive debates the Federal Chamber and the Chamber of Nationalities do not reach unanimity to commence deliberations on a change of constitution, a motion to change the Constitution may not be introduced before the lapse of one year from the date on which the debate was closed.

Art. 211. Before the debate is held on a motion to change the Constitution, the Federal Chamber shall forward the motion to the Economic Chamber, the Chamber of Education and Culture, the Chamber of Social Welfare and Health, and the Organizational-Political Chamber.

The chambers shall consider the motion to change the Constitution and shall give their opinions to the Federal Chamber.

Upon receiving the opinions of the other chambers, the Federal Chamber shall commence debate on the motion to change the Constitution.

Art. 212. Before the debate takes place in the Federal Chamber, the motion to change the Constitution shall be debated by the Chamber of Nationalities.

During the debate on the motion to change the Constitution, the Federal Chamber shall also form an opinion on the views held by the other assembly chambers.

The motion to change the Constitution shall be deemed to have been passed if an identical text has been passed by the Federal Chamber and the Chamber of Nationalities.

If the Federal Chamber does not accept the opinion of the Chamber of Nationalities concerning the motion to change the Constitution, the debate shall be postponed for two months.

Upon the lapse of this period, only two additional consecutive debates may be held on the matters in dispute between the Federal Chamber and the Chamber of Nationalities. If after these two consecutive debates unanimity is not reached, the Federal Chamber and the Chamber of Nationalities may decide to place the matter in dispute before a referendum. If the two chambers do not agree to place the matter in dispute before a referendum, the Federal Chamber shall be dissolved.

Art. 213. The motion to change the Constitution shall be deemed to have been passed in the Federal Chamber and in the Chamber of Nationalities if it has received the vote of two thirds of the members of the two chambers.

Art. 214. If not later than fifteen days after the adoption of the motion to change the Constitution in the Federal Chamber and the Chamber of Nationalities, at least three of the other chambers of the assembly do not agree to the accepted text of the motion to change the Constitution, the motion to change the Constitution shall be placed before a referendum.

The referendum on the motion to change the Constitution shall be called by the president of the assembly. The referendum shall be held not later than two months from the date on which the motion to change the Constitution has been passed in the Federal Chamber and the Chamber of Nationalities.

The motion to change the Constitutional shall be deemed to have been passed by referendum if a majority of the electorate on the territory of Yugoslavia has voted for the motion.

The motion to change the Constitution shall be proclaimed by the Federal Chamber.

CHAPTER X. THE PRESIDENT OF THE REPUBLIC

Art. 215. The President of the Republic shall represent the Socialist Federal Republic of Yugoslavia at home and abroad, and shall discharge other political-executive duties determined by the Constitution.

The President of the Republic shall be Commander-in-Chief of the Armed Forces of Yugoslavia.

Art. 216. The President of the Republic shall propose one of the members of the Federal Assembly to the assembly as President of the Federal Executive Council, who shall propose election of the Federal Executive Council.

The President of the Republic may convene sessions of the Federal Executive Council and place certain matters on the agenda of its sessions. The President of the Republic shall preside over sessions which he attends.

Art. 217. The President of the Republic shall,

(1) Promulgate federal laws by decree;

(2) Promulgate the decision of the Federal Assembly on the election of the Federal Executive Council; propose election of the president and judges of the Constitutional Court of Yugoslavia, propose election and

removal of the members of the Council of the Federation, propose nomination and removal of the deputy commander-in-chief;

(3) Appoint and recall by decree ambassadors and ministers of the Socialist Federal Republic of Yugoslavia, and accept the letters of credence and letters of recall of foreign diplomatic representatives accredited to him; issue instruments of ratification of international agreements;

(4) Confer decorations;

(5) Grant pardons, in accordance with federal law, for criminal offences provided by federal law;

(6) Declare a state of war if the Federal Assembly is unable to meet;

(7) Found pertinent staffs to discharge affairs in his jurisdiction;

(8) Exercise other rights and duties determined by the Constitution.

The President of the Republic, upon the proposal of the Federal Executive Council, shall during a state of war or in the event of immediate danger of war pass decrees with the force of law on matters in the jurisdiction of the Federal Assembly. The President of the Republic shall submit these decrees to the assembly for approval as soon as it is able to meet.

Particular provisions of the Constitution of Yugoslavia pertaining to the freedoms and rights of the citizens and to the rights of autonomous organizations, or to the composition of political-executive and administrative organs and their powers may in exceptional cases be suspended by decree with the force of law passed during a state of war for the duration of this emergency, if the interests of the country's defence so require.

Art. 218. The President of the Republic shall have the right to stay any decree and any other regulation of general political significance passed by the Federal Executive Council before the decree or regulation is promulgated.

If the President of the Republic stays a regulation of the Federal Executive Council, he shall immediately place the matter in dispute before the Federal Chamber for a decision.

Art. 219. The President of the Republic shall exercise his rights and duties in accordance with and within the restrictions of the Constitution and federal law.

The President of the Republic shall have Presidential immunity, and shall be accountable to the Federal Assembly in accordance with the Constitution and federal law.

The President of the Republic shall cease to be a deputy if he has been elected from among the deputies.

Art. 220. The President of the Republic shall be elected for a term of four years and may be re-elected for one further consecutive term.

No limitation of tenure of office of President of the Republic shall apply to Josip Broz-Tito.

Art. 221. The Federal Assembly shall elect the President of the Republic not later than one month before the expiration of the term of the President of the Republic then in office.

A candidate for President of the Republic may be proposed to the assembly by not less than thirty deputies, of their own accord or in accordance with a proposal made by the Federal Board of the Socialist Alliance of the Working People of Yugoslavia. Not less than five of the nominators shall be from each of the republics, and half the nominators shall be members of the Federal Chamber.

That candidate shall be elected President of the Republic who has received the vote of a majority of all the federal deputies.

Upon being elected, the President of the Republic shall make his Affirmation before the Federal Assembly.

Art. 222. The President of the Republic shall give the assembly information on the state and on problems of internal and foreign policy and may propose that the assembly discuss certain matters and pass decisions.

Art. 223. During absence of the President of the Republic, his powers shall be exercised by the Vice-President of the Republic. The President of the Republic may charge the Vice-President to represent him in certain affairs.

The Vice-President of the Republic shall be elected to a term of four years and shall not be re-elected Vice-President for a consecutive term.

The Federal Assembly shall elect the Vice-President of the Republic immediately upon electing the President of the Republic, in accordance with the same procedure.

If he has been elected from among the federal deputies, the Vice-President of the Republic shall retain his seat as deputy.

Art. 224. The President of the Republic shall convene the Council of the Federation in order to consider matters of state policy and the work of the political-executive and administrative organs.

The members of the Council of the Federation shall be elected by the Federal Chamber upon the proposal of the President of the Republic, from among federal officers and officials of the republics and from among officials of the social-political and other organizations.

CHAPTER XI. THE POLITICAL-EXECUTIVE AND ADMINISTRATIVE ORGANS OF THE FEDERAL ASSEMBLY

(a) The Federal Executive Council

Art. 225. The Federal Executive Council shall be the organ of the Federal Assembly which is entrusted with political-executive powers within the framework of the rights and duties of the Federation.

The Federal Executive Council shall be responsible for the execution of the Federation's policy, the foundations of which shall be established by the Federal Assembly.

Art. 226. The Federal Executive Council shall consist of a president and a definite number of members.

The president and the members of the Federal Executive Council shall be elected by the Federal Chamber on the proposal of a deputy whom the President of the Republic has proposed for president of the Federal Executive Council, and in accordance with the opinion of the Elections and Nominations Commission. The members of the Federal Executive Council shall be elected from among the members of the assembly, with due consideration being given to its composition in terms of nationality.

The presidents of the executive councils of the republics, the federal secretaries of state, the federal secretaries, and the secretary of the Federal Executive Council, as well as other federal officers designated by the assembly at the time of their nomination, shall be members of the Federal Executive Council by virtue of their office.

Art. 227. In exceptional cases, the Federal Chamber may elect a deputy as president or member of the Federal Executive Council who has just held this office for four years, if there are justified reasons for doing so, but he may not hold this office longer than for the next four years. With regard to the president of the Federal Executive Council a decision to this effect shall be passed by the Federal Chamber on the proposal of the President of the Republic, and with regard to a member of the Federal Executive Council, on the proposal of the president of the Federal Executive Council or the deputy who presents the proposal for the election of the Federal Executive Council.

Before the vote is taken, the Federal Chamber shall decide by a majority vote on the justifiability of the reasons for departing from the principle of limitation of re-election.

The President of the Federal Executive Council shall have the right to propose to the Federal Chamber the removal of members of the Federal Executive Council and election of new members.

The removal of the president of the Federal Executive Council or the resignation of a majority of the members of the council shall entail the resignation of the whole council.

Art. 228. The Federal Executive Council shall,

(1) Propose internal and foreign policy to the Federal Assembly and attend to the implementation of the policy determined by the assembly; attend to the enforcement of federal law, the social plan of Yugoslavia, the federal budget, and other assembly decisions; supervise the work of the federal administrative organs and give them general instructions in their work;

(2) Introduce bills and other draft acts in the assembly, and have the

right to give its opinions on bills introduced in the assembly by the assembly chambers, the committees of the chambers or the deputies;

(3) Prepare a draft of the social plan of Yugoslavia and a draft of the federal budget and the annual financial statement;

(4) Pass decrees, and decisions and directives for the enforcement of federal law and other general acts of the Federal Assembly, if it is authorized to do so by law or by these acts;

(5) Determine the general principles of internal organization and work of the federal administrative organs;

(6) Set up federal administrative organs which are not set up by law, as well as specialized staffs necessary for the council's work, and found working organizations and other organizations to discharge affairs of interest for the council and other federal organs, in conformity with the law;

(7) Set aside the regulations of the federal administrative organs when these are at variance with federal law, decree, or other regulations of the Federal Executive Council;

(8) Ratify international agreements whose ratification is not within the jurisdiction of the assembly;

(9) Propose to the Federal Chamber the election and removal of the presidents and judges of the Supreme Court of Yugoslavia and the Supreme Economic Court, and propose the nomination and dismissal of the federal public prosecutor and other federal officers designated by law;

(10) Appoint officers of the council and federal administrative organs and directors of institutions and organizations designated by law;

(11) Manage, within the provisions of the Constitution and federal law, certain funds of the Federation;

(12) Discharge other affairs provided for by federal law within the rights and duties of the Federation.

Art. 229. At its sessions the Federal Executive Council shall decide on affairs in its jurisdiction.

All the members of the council shall deliberate on general matters and matters of principle and on matters of common concern to all the administrative organs.

Other matters in the jurisdiction of the council shall be deliberated by designated members of the council and by the federal secretaries of state.

The organization of the Federal Executive Council and the manner in which it shall decide on matters in its jurisdiction shall be determined by law.

The Federal Executive Council may set up committees and other bodies to co-ordinate the work of the federal administrative organs and to consider matters of common concern to two or more administrative organs.

Federal secretaries and other officers may be nominated in the Federal Executive Council who shall independently discharge affairs.

Art. 230. The president of the Federal Executive Council shall represent the council, and shall attend to the enforcement of the decisions and to the implementation of the policy of the Federal Executive Council.

The president of the council shall convene the council on his own initiative or on the proposal of the President of the Republic, or on the proposal of no fewer than five members of the council.

The president of the council shall co-ordinate the work of the federal administrative organs in order to implement the general policy of the council.

Art. 231. The Federal Executive Council shall discharge the affairs in its jurisdiction in accordance with and within the limits of the Constitution and law.

The Federal Executive Council shall be responsible for its work to the Federal Assembly.

The assembly may rescind or cancel any regulation or other decision of the Federal Executive Council that is at variance with the Constitution or law.

Art. 232. The Federal Executive Council shall inform the Federal Assembly about its work.

The Federal Executive Council may propose to the competent assembly chambers to postpone debate on a bill or other decision, or to form a joint commission of members of the competent assembly chamber and of its own members in order to debate a certain matter, or to convene a session of the competent assembly chamber at which the Federal Executive Council shall state its position.

If the assembly passes a bill or draft act at variance with the position of the Federal Executive Council, the council may submit its collective resignation to the Federal Chamber if it considers that it is not in a position to secure the enforcement of the law or other act.

The council which has resigned shall remain in office pending election of a new federal executive council.

(b) The Federal Administration

Art. 233. Secretariats of state, federal secretariats and other federal administrative organs shall be founded to discharge the affairs of the state administration in the jurisdiction of the Federation.

Secretariats of state shall be founded only for those departments of administration which in accordance with the Constitution fall wholly within the exclusive jurisdiction of the federal organs.

Federal secretariats and other federal administrative organs shall be founded to discharge the affairs of the state administration in other provinces that are in the jurisdiction of the Federation.

Councils and other federal organs and organizations may be founded to discharge certain specialized, administrative and other affairs in the jurisdiction of the Federation.

Art. 234. The secretariats of state shall be the Secretariat of State for Foreign Affairs and the Secretariat of State for National Defence.

The province of the secretariats of state shall be determined and altered by law.

The federal secretariats and the other autonomous federal administrative organs and councils, as well as organizations discharging affairs of concern to the whole country shall be founded and dissolved, and their jurisdiction determined by law.

Art. 235. The federal administrative organs shall autonomously discharge affairs in their jurisdiction in accordance with and within the restrictions of the Constitution and federal law.

In the performance of the duties within their jurisdiction the federal administrative organs shall also abide by other federal regulations.

The federal administrative organs shall provide for the enforcement of federal law and other federal regulations, of the policy determined by the Federal Assembly and general instructions of the Federal Executive Council.

Art. 236. The federal secretaries of state, the federal secretaries, the secretary of the Federal Executive Council, and other federal officers designated by law shall be nominated and dismissed by the Federal Assembly upon the proposal of the president of the Federal Executive Council acting on behalf of the council.

An officer who has held one of the enumerated offices for four years may be appointed to that office for no more than an additional consecutive four years if justified reasons so require. Upon the proposal of the president of the Federal Executive Council, the assembly shall first determine by a majority vote whether or not the reasons given for making an exception to the principle of limitation of re-nomination are justified.

Art. 237. The federal officers who are at the head of the federal administrative organs shall be personally responsible for the work of the respective organs and for the execution of the tasks and affairs in their jurisdiction.

The federal officers at the head of the federal administrative organs may adopt regulations and issue ordinances and instructions for the enforcement of law and the regulations of the Federal Executive Council if they are authorized to do so by law or by a regulation issued by the Federal Executive Council.

Art. 238. The federal officers at the head of the federal administrative organs shall inform the Federal Assembly and the Federal Executive Council about the state of affairs in their respective fields of administration and about the work of the administrative organs in their charge.

Upon the request of the chambers, committees and commissions of the assembly, the officers shall provide information and explanations concerning matters in the jurisdiction of the organs in their charge, and give answers to questions asked by deputies.

CHARTER XII. THE SUPREME COURT OF YUGOSLAVIA

Art. 239. The Supreme Court of Yugoslavia shall,

(1) Pass basic rulings and legal judgments in matters of significance for the uniform enforcement of federal law by the courts of general jurisdiction and courts of special jurisdiction;

(2) Decide on regular legal expedients against the decisions of the republican supreme courts, when this is provided by federal law;

(3) Decide on special legal expedients against valid decisions of the courts which violate federal law, in cases provided by law;

(4) Decide on administrative litigation against administrative decisions passed by federal organs or organizations discharging public powers on the territory of Yugoslavia;

(5) Resolve conflicts of jurisdiction between courts on the territories of different republics;

(6) Discharge other business provided by federal law within the rights and duties of the Federation.

Art. 240. The jurisdiction and organization of the Supreme Court of Yugoslavia shall be determined by federal law.

CHAPTER XIII. THE CONSTITUTIONAL COURT OF YUGOSLAVIA

Art. 241. The Constitutional Court of Yugoslavia shall,

(1) Decide on the conformity of law with the Constitution of Yugoslavia;

(2) Decide on the conformity of republican law with federal law;

(3) Decide on the conformity of other regulations and other general decisions of organs and organizations with the Constitution of Yugoslavia, federal law and other federal regulations;

(4) Resolve disputes on rights and duties between the Federation and a republic, between republics, and between other social-political communities on the territories of two or more republics, if the jurisdiction of some other court has not been provided by law for the settlement of these disputes; resolve disputes concerning the boundaries between republics;

(5) Resolve conflict of jurisdiction between courts and federal organs, and between courts and other state organs on the territories of two or more republics;

(6) Discharge other business placed by the Constitution or federal law in its jurisdiction, in conformity with the constitutional rights and duties of the Federation.

The Constitutional Court of Yugoslavia shall also decide on the protection of the rights of self-government and other basic freedoms and rights established by the Constitution if these freedoms and rights have been violated by an individual decision or action of the federal organs, and in other instances determined by federal law for which other court protection has not been provided.

Art. 242. The Constitutional Court of Yugoslavia shall keep itself informed about manifestations of interest for the attainment of constitutionality and legality, and on these grounds shall offer to the Federal Assembly its opinions and proposals to pass laws and to undertake other measures to secure constitutionality and legality and to protect the rights of self-government and the other freedoms and rights of the citizens and organizations.

Art. 243. The Constitutional Court of Yugoslavia shall consist of a president and ten judges.

The president and the judges of the constitutional court shall be elected for a term of eight years, and they may be re-elected only for one more consecutive term of eight years. Half the number of judges of the constitutional court shall be elected every four years.

The president and the judges of the constitutional court shall not at the same time be members of the republican assemblies or of the Federal Assembly, or of their political-executive organs, nor officers or employees of the state administrative organs, of or any other court.

The president and the judges of the constitutional court may be dismissed from office before their terms expire, in accordance with federal law, only if they request to be relieved, or if for a criminal offence they have been sentenced to imprisonment, or if they have lost legal capability or if they have become permanently disabled physically and cannot discharge their duties.

The president and the judges of the constitutional court shall have immunity like the federal deputies.

Art. 244. The Constitutional Court of Yugoslavia shall advise the Federal Assembly as to whether the constitution of a republic is at variance with the Constitution of Yugoslavia.

Art. 245. Whenever the Constitutional Court of Yugoslavia determines that a federal law does not conform to the Constitution, the Federal Assembly shall bring the law into conformity with the Constitution not later than six months from the date of publication of the decision of the constitutional court.

If the assembly does not bring the law into conformity with the Constitution within this period, the law or those of its provisions that do not conform to the Constitution shall cease to be valid, and the Constitutional Court of Yugoslavia shall declare them invalid by its decision.

If in a case of conflict between a republican law and a federal law, the Constitutional Court of Yugoslavia finds that the federal law in question does not conform to the Constitution of Yugoslavia, it shall decide that, pending adoption of a final decision, the provisions of the federal law that do not conform to the Constitution shall be inoperative.

Art. 246. Whenever the Constitutional Court of Yugoslavia finds that a republican law does not conform to the Constitution of Yugoslavia or to federal law, the republican assembly shall bring the republican law into conformity with the Constitution or with federal law not later than six months from the date of publication of the decision of the Constitutional Court of Yugoslavia.

If the republican assembly does not bring the republican law into conformity with the Constitution or with federal law within this period, the republican law or those of its provisions that do not conform to the Constitution of Yugoslavia or to federal law shall cease to be valid, and the constitutional court shall declare them invalid by its decision.

Whenever the Constitutional Court of Yugoslavia finds that a republican law does not conform to the Constitution of Yugoslavia or to federal law, it shall decide that, pending adoption of a final decision, the provisions of the republican law that do not conform to the Constitution or to federal law shall be inoperative. The Constitutional Court of Yugoslavia may forthwith annul a republican law if it clearly violates the rights of the Federation.

Art. 247. Whenever the Constitutional Court of Yugoslavia finds that a provision other than law, or some other general act does not conform to the Constitution of Yugoslavia or to federal law, it shall annul or set aside the provision or act or regulation that does not conform to the Constitution or to federal law.

Art. 248. If a point of constitutionality or legality has been raised with regard to a provision or other general act which is at variance both with the Constitution of Yugoslavia or federal law and with the republican constitution or republican law, a ruling on constitutionality and legality shall be given on that point by the republican constitutional court, which shall judge only the conformity of the regulation or other general act in question with the republican constitution or republican law.

If the republican constitutional court decides that the regulation or general act in question conforms to the republican constitution or republican law, it shall forward the matter to the Constitutional Court of Yugoslavia to judge the conformity of the regulation or general act in question with the Constitution of Yugoslavia or federal law.

The Constitutional Court of Yugoslavia may raise a point of constitutionality or legality with regard to such a provision or other general act even before the proceedings before the republican constitutional court terminate, if the regulation or general act in question clearly violates the rights of the Federation.

Art. 249. A point of constitutionality and legality may be raised before the Constitutional Court of Yugoslavia by:

(1) The Federal Assembly and the republican assemblies;

(2) The Federal Executive Council and the republican executive councils, except when the constitutionality of laws passed by their assemblies is being judged;

(3) The Supreme Court of Yugoslavia and the other supreme courts of the Federation, as well as the republican supreme courts, if the point of constitutionality and legality ensures in court proceedings;

(4) The federal public prosecutor, if the point of constitutionality and legality ensues in the work of the public prosecution;

(5) The republican constitutional courts;

(6) The assembly of a social-political community, or a working or other autonomous organization, if any of their rights established by the Constitution of Yugoslavia have been violated.

A point of constitutionality and legality may be raised by the Constitutional Court of Yugoslavia of its own initiative.

The conditions under which other state organs, organizations and citizens may institute proceedings or move the institution of proceedings raising a point of constitutionality and legality before the Constitutional Court of Yugoslavia shall be determined by federal law.

Art. 250. If in proceedings on a point of constitutionality and legality the Constitutional Court of Yugoslavia finds that the law or other provision in question is not at variance with the Constitution of Yugoslavia or with federal law, it may for purposes of enforcement of the provision establish the interpretation which conforms to the Constitution or federal law.

Art. 251. The jurisdiction and procedure of the Constitutional Court of Yugoslavia, and the legal scope of its decisions shall be determined in detail by federal law.

The Constitutional Court of Yugoslavia shall autonomously determine its organization and work.

CHAPTER XIV. NATIONAL DEFENCE AND THE YUGOSLAV PEOPLE'S ARMY

Art. 252. It is the inalienable right and duty of the peoples of Yugoslavia to safeguard and defend the independence and territorial integrity of the Socialist Federal Republic of Yugoslavia.

Defence of the country shall be the right and duty of the citizens, of the working and other organizations, and of the Federation, republic, commune, and other social-political communities.

The Federation shall be responsible for the preparation and organization of the Yugoslav People's Army, and the Federation, republic, commune and other social-political communities shall be responsible for the organization of civil defence, preliminary military training and the general preparation and organization of the defence of the country.

In matters of national defence the rights, duties and responsibilities of the citizens and of the working and other organizations shall be determined by federal law.

Art. 253. Military service of the citizens shall be universal.

The beginning of service in the Yugoslav Pelope's Army and the cessation of service, as well as the special rights and duties of the members of the Yugoslav People's Army in regard to service in the Army shall be determined by federal law.

Art. 254. No one shall have the right to sign or to acknowledge capitulation or the occupation of the country on behalf of the Socialist Federal Republic of Yugoslavia. Such an action is unconstitutional and shall be punishable by law.

High treason is a crime against the people and shall be punished as a grave criminal offence.

Art. 255. The Yugoslav People's Army is the basic armed force of national defence of Yugoslavia.

The Yugoslav People's Army shall protect the independence, constitutional order, inviolability and integrity of the territory of the Socialist Federal Republic of Yugoslavia.

Art. 256. The Commander-in-Chief of the Armed Forces of Yugoslavia shall command and be in charge of the Yugoslav People's Army, and shall determine the bases of plans and preparatory measures for the defence of the country.

The Commander-in-Chief shall appoint, promote and relieve of duty generals and admirals and other military officers designated by Federal law.

The Commander-in-Chief shall appoint and remove the president, judges and lay judges of military courts, as well as the military prosecutors.

The Commander-in-Chief may have a deputy, who shall act in his stead in those affairs of command and jurisdiction over the Yugoslav People's Army designated by the Commander-in-Chief.

Art. 257. The Council of National Defence shall attend to the organization and mobilization of the resources and forces of the country for the requirements of national defence.

The members of the Council of National Defence shall be nominated and removed by the Federal Chamber upon the proposal of the President of the Republic.

The President of the Republic shall be chairman of the Council of National Defence.

PART THREE

TRANSITIONAL AND CONCLUDING PROVISIONS

Art. 258. A special constitutional law shall be enacted to implement the Constitution and to provide for transition to its application.

Art. 259. The Constitution shall be promulgated by the Federal People's Assembly.

APPENDIX

ANDORRA

Note

Andorra, rather than a state in the international sense of the term, is a "fief" under a special legal regime which is a survival from medieval times. Its status was established by the Act of *Paréage* of September 8, 1278, which placed the Valleys under the joint suzerainty of the Bishop of Urgel and the Count of Foix. The latter's rights passed to the French Crown at the accession of Henri IV through the fusion of the families of Foix and Béarn. Since that time the French Head of State has exercised the right of co-suzerainty. A Decree-Law of March 27, 1806, renewed the ties with the Valleys which had been abolished in 1793 when the Convention abolished feudal decrees and proclaimed Andorran independence. The Plan of Reform of 1866 fixed the general lines of local organization and administration; on July 17, 1933, the right to vote, previously held only by the heads of families, was extended to all male Andorrans over 25 years of age and this was reestablished, after suspension during the War, by Decree of the Viguiers of August 23, 1947.

The organization of Andorra is as follows:

1. The Permanent Delegates represent the two co-princes in the exercise of their rights of sovereignty *vis-à-vis* the Andorran authorities and each other. This office was established in 1882. The Permanent Delegate of France is the Prefect of the Eastern Pyrenees, of the Bishop of Urgel is traditionally his Vicar-General; their seats are at Perpignan and the Seu d'Urgel. Legislative power in most important matters is exercised through their decrees. The French Permanent Delegate exercises important functions in the sphere of technical assistance, education, posts and telecommunications.

2. The two Viguiers. This office has existed since the middle ages. They are the personal representatives of each co-prince and in them is vested the sovereign power, especially in matters of justice and the maintenance of order. They exercise criminal justice and their decisions are final. The Viguier of France is a member of the High Court of Andorra, the final court of appeal in civil cases.

3. The Bayles. This office has existed since the middle ages. One Bayle is nominated by each Viguier from Andorran nationals for three years from a list of six names proposed by the six parishes of Andorra. The Bayle is a judge of the first instance in civil matters and has certain police powers. He executes decisions of the administrative and judicial authorities.

4. The local assemblies consist of (a) 44 Councils of *Cuart* (the villages); (b) 6 Councils of the Parish who administer the parishes under the authority of the Viguiers; (c) the General Council of the Valleys composed of 24 members, four from each parish, elected for four years by universal male suffrage. It is presided over by a Syndic-General assisted by a Vice-Syndic, both appointed by the Council for a term of three years, renewable once only. It exercises administrative and budgetary functions by delegation of power of the co-princes.

The area of Andorra is 465 square kilometres, its population (1964) approximately 11,000. The official language is Catalan. The capital is Andorra-la-Vella.[1]

[1] Most information kindly supplied by the Viguier of France in September 1966. Ed.

SELECTIVE BIBLIOGRAPHY

ALBANIA

Hasluck, M. *The unwritten law in Albania.* Ed. J. H. Hutton. Cambridge 1954.

AUSTRIA

Adamovich, *Die Bundesverfassungsgesetze.* 8th ed. Österreichische Staatsdruckerei. Vienna 1953.
Adamovich-Spanner. *Handbuch des österreichischen Verfassungsrechts.* 5th Ed. Vienna 1957.
Clute, R. E. *The international legal status of Austria 1938–1955.* The Hague 1962.
Draxler-Weiler. *Freiheit und Recht – Eine Einführung in den Text und des Gedankengut der österreichischen Bundesverfassung.* Österreichischer Bundesverlag, Vienna 1964.
Ermacora. *Der Verfassungsgerichtshof.* Graz-Vienna-Cologne 1955.
Ermacora. *Handbuch der Grundfreiheiten und der Menschenrechte, Ein Kommentar zu den österreichischen Grundrechtsbestimmungen.* Vienna 1963.
Ringhofer. *Der Verwaltungsgerichtshof.* Graz-Vienna-Cologne 1955.
Werner. *Die österreichischen Bundesverfassungsgesetze.* 2nd Ed. Vienna 1963.
Werner-Klecatsky. *Das österreichische Bundesverfassungsrecht.* Vienna 1961 (supplement published 1962).

BELGIUM

Damoiseaux, M. *Les institutions nationales de la Belgique.* Louvain 1945.
Mast, A. *Overzicht van het Belgisch grondwettelijk recht.* Ghent 1963.
Senelle, R. *The political and economic structure of Belgium. Memo from Belgium,* No. 73, 74, 75, 1966.
Wigny, P. *Droit constitutionnel, principes et droit positif.* Brussels 1952.

DENMARK

Andersen, P. *Danish constitutional law.* Copenhagen 1964.
Harder, E. "La constitution danoise de 1953." *Revue internationale des sciences administratives,* 22:1956.
Heckscher, K. "La monarchie parlementaire danoise après la révision constitutionnelle de 1953." *Revue internationale d'histoire politique et constitutionnelle,* 4:1954.
Marcus, F. "Danemark. Die dänische Verfassung vom 5 Juni 1953 und das Thronfolgegesetz vom 27 Mars 1953." *Zeitschrift für ausländisches öffentliches Recht und Volkerrecht,* 15:1953/54.
Robert, J. "Danemark. La constitution du 5 juin 1953." *Revue du droit public et de la science politique,* 60:1954.
Ross, Alf. *Danish constitutional law* I–II. Copenhagen 1959–1960.

FINLAND

Merikoski, V. *Précis du droit publique de la Finlande.* Helsinki 1954.

FRANCE

Aron, R. *France, the new Republic.* New York 1960.
Burdeau, G. *Droit constitutionnel et institutions politiques conforme au programme des facultés de droit et écoles d'enseignement supérieur.* 9th ed. Paris 1962.

Chatelain, J. *La nouvelle constitution et le régime politique de la France*. Paris 1959.
Chevallier, J. J. *Histoire des institutions et des régimes politiques de la France moderne (1789–1958)*. Paris 1967.
Documentation Française. *Les Institutions politiques de la France*. 2 vols. Paris.
Duguit, L. *Les constitutions et les principales lois politiques de la France depuis 1789*. Paris 1952.
Duverger, M. *Constitutions et documents politiques*. Paris 1964.
Duverger, M. *La Cinquième République*. Paris 1959.
Duverger, M. *Les Constitutions de la France*. "Que Sais-je." Paris 1962.
Godfrey, E. D. *The government of France*. New York 1961.
Gonidec, P. F. *Constitutions des états de la Communauté*. Paris 1959.
Pickles, W. *The French Constitution of October 4, 1958*. London 1960.
Pickles, D. *The Fifth French Republic*. London 1960.

GERMANY

Bericht über den Verfassungskonvent auf Herrenchiemsee vom 10.–23. Aug. 1948. Hrsg. v. Verfassungsausschuß der Ministerpräsidenten-Konferenz der westlichen Besatzungszone. Munich 1948.
Brunn, W. *Die rechtliche, politische und wirtschaftliche Lage des Berliner Sowjetsektors*. Berlin 1954.
Bundesverfassungsgerichtsgesetz mit Nebengesetzen. Kommentar V.: Maunz, Sigloch, Schmidt-Bleibtreu, Klein. Munich 1965.
Das Bundesverfassungsgericht. Hrsg. vom Bundesverfassungsgericht. Karlsruhe 1963.
Dennewitz-Abraham. *Kommentar zum Bonner Grundgesetz* (Bonner Kommentar) Hamburg 1950.
Forsthoff, Ernst. *Einleitung zum Bonner Grundgesetz*. Printed together with Rothe, W. *Die Grundrechte der Deutschen*. Gerabronn 1953.
Giese-Schunck. *Grundgesetz für die Bundesrepublik Deutschland vom 23. Mai 1949*. 7th Ed. Frankfurt a/M. 1965.
Glum, F. *Die staatsrechtliche Struktur der Bundesrepublik Deutschland. – Bund und Länder – Parlament und Regierung*. Bonn 1965.
Golay, J. F. *The founding of the Federal Republic of Germany*. Chicago 1958.
Grosser, A. *La Démocratie de Bonn 1949–1957*. Paris 1958.
Hamann, A. *Das Grundgesetz für die Bundesrepublik Deutschland. Kommentar für Wissenschaft und Praxis*. 2nd Ed. Berlin 1961.
Ipsen, H. P. *Über das Grundgesetz*. Hamburg 1950.
Liebholz-Rinck. *Grundgesetz für die Bundesrepublik Deutschland. Kommentar an Hand der Rechtsprechung des Bundesverfassungsgerichts*. Cologne 1966.
Mampel, S. *Die Verfassung der Sowjetischen Besatzungszone Deutschland; Text und Kommentar*. Berlin 1962.
v. Mangoldt,-Klein. *Das Bonner Grundgesetz*. 2nd Ed. Vol. 1, 2. Berlin 1957/1964.
Merki, P. *The origin of the West German Republic*. London.
Nawiasky, Hans, *Die Grundgedanken des Grundgesetzes für die Bundesrepublik Deutschland*. Stuttgart 1950.
Nettl, J. P. *The Eastern Zone and Soviet Policy in Germany 1945–1950*. New York 1951.
Neumann-Nipperdey-Scheuner. *Grundrechte. Handbuch der Theorie und Praxis der Grundrechte*. Berlin 1954.
Plischke, E. *Contemporary government of Germany*. Boston 1960.
Schafer, H. *Der Bundesrat*. Cologne 1955.
Schulz, W. *Die Verfassung der Deutschen Demokratischen Republik*. Munich-Frankfurt/M. 1959.
Weber, W. *Die Verfassung der Bundesrepublik in der Bewahrung*. Göttingen 1957.
Weber, W. *Spannungen und Kräfte im westdeutschen Verfassungssystem*. 2nd Ed. Stuttgart 1958.

GREECE

Bacopoulos, G. T. *Outline of the Greek Constitution; political systems since the Greek Revolution of 1821*. Athens 1950.
Christides, Chr. Tó 'Ελληνικό Σύνταγμα Athens 1965.

Dagtoglou. "'Η συνταγματική ἐξέλιξις ἀπό τῆς εἰσαγωγῆς τοῦ ἰσχύοντος Συντάγματος μέχρι τοῦ θανάτου τοῦ Βασ. Παύλου" E.E.N. 1966. In German in *Jahrbuch des öffentlichen Rechts 1965. Bonn.*

Kyriakopoulos, "Die griechische Verfassung vom 1 Jan. 1952." *Jahrbuch des öffentlichen Rechts*. Bonn.

Manesis, A. "La nouvelle constitution hellénique." *Revue International de Droit Comparé*. (vol. 6) Paris 1954.

Svolos-Vlachos. Τό σύνταγμα τῆς Ελλάδος 2 vols. Athens 1954.

Sgouritsa, Chr. Συνταγματικόν Δίκαιον. 3 vols. Athens 1956, 1962, 1966.

Vlachos, G. "L'histoire constitutionnelle récente de la Grèce." *Revue Internationale d'Histoire Politique et Constitutionnelle*. 1952. Paris.

HUNGARY

Beér-Kovacsà. *A Magyar Népkoztarsasag Alkotmanya* [The Constitution of the Hungarian People's Republic]. Budapest 1959.

Eckhart, Ferenc. *Magyar Alkotmany-es jogtörténet* [A history of the Hungarian Constitution and law] Budapest 1946.

Kovacs, Istvan. *A szocialista alkotmanyfejlodés uj elemei* [New elements in the socialist constitutional development] Budapest 1962.

Sarlos, Marton (Ed.). *A Magyar Tanacskoztarsasag allama es joga* [The state and law of the Soviet Republic of Hungary] (Essays) Budapest 1959.

ICELAND

Thoroddsen, G. *The Constitution of Iceland*. London 1946 (15 pp.).

IRELAND

Batelli, M. *Le premier ministre au Canada et en Irlande*. Geneva 1943.

Chubb, B. *A source book of Irish government*. Dublin 1964.

Delaney. "The Constitution of Ireland, its origins and developments". *University of Toronto Law Journal* Vol. 12, 1957.

Grogan, V. "Irish constitutional development." Dublin: *Studies*, Vol. XL No. 160, 1951.

Kelly, J. M. *Fundamental rights in the Irish law and Constitution*. Dublin 1961.

Kohn, L. *The Constitution of the Irish Free State*. London 1932.

McCracken, J. L. *Representative Government in Ireland; a study of Dail Eireann, 1919–1948*. London 1958.

McDunphy. *The President of Ireland*. Dublin 1945.

ITALY

Amorth, A. *La Costituzione italiana*. Milan 1948.

Azzariti. *Problemi attuali di diritto costituzionale*. Milan 1951.

Balladore-Pallieri. *Diritto costituzionale*. Milan 1959.

Calamandrei and Levi. *Commentario sistematico alla Costituzione italiana*. Florence 1950.

Carullo, V. *La costituzione della Repubblica italiana*. Milan 1954.

Esposito. *La Costituzione italiana*. Saggi-Padova 1954.

Kogan, N. *The government of Italy*. New York 1962.

Mortati. *Istituzioni di Diritto pubblico*. Padua 1962.

Tesauro. *Corso di diritto costituzionale*. Naples 1948.

Virga. *Diritto costituzionale*. Palermo 1955.

LUXEMBOURG

Hammes, Ch.-Léon. "Le gouvernment du Grand-Duché. Essai sur son évolution." *Livre Jubilaire du Conseil d'Etat*. Luxembourg 1957.

Majerus, P. *L'Etat luxembourgeois, Manuel de droit constitutionnel et de droit administratif*. Luxembourg 1959.

Pescatore, P. *Conclusion et effet des traités internationaux selon le droit constitutionnel, les usages et la jurisprudence du Grand-Duché de Luxembourg*. Luxembourg 1964.

Weber, P. *Histoire du Grand-Duché de Luxembourg*. 3rd Ed. Luxembourg 1957.

NETHERLANDS

Belinfante, A. D. *Beginselen van Nederlands staatsrecht*, Amsterdam, 1964.

Colenbrander, H. T. *Ontstaan der Grondwet. Bronnenverzameling.* Eerste deel 1814. 's-Gravenhage, 1908.
Colenbrander, H. T. *Ontstaan der Grondwet. Bronnenverzameling.* Tweede deel 1815. 's-Gravenhage, 1909.
Fockema Andrea, S. J. *De Nederlandse staat onder de Republiek.* Amsterdam, 1961.
Fruin, R. *Geschiedenis der staatsinstellingen in Nederland tot den val der republiek.* Uitgegeven door H. T. Colenbrander. 's-Gravenhage: 1922.
Hasselt, W. J. C. van. *Verzameling van Nederlandsche staatsregelingen en grondwetten.* Herzien door P. R. Böhtling, aangevuld door J. C. Somer, Alphen aan de Rijn, 1964.
Pot, C. W. van der. *Handboek van het Nederlandse staatsrecht.* Zwolle, 1962.
Raalte, E. van *De ontwikkeling van het minister-presidentschap in Nederland, België, Frankrijk, Engeland en enige andere landen.* With an English summary. Avec un sommaire français. Leiden: 1954.
Raalte, E. van. *De Nederlandse Staat, wat hij is en hoe hij werkt.* The Hague 1966.
Raalte, E. van *Het Nederlands parlement.* 's-Gravenhage, 1960.
Rengers, W. J. van Welderen. Bijgewerkte uitgave door C. W. de Vries en W. H. Vermeulen. *Schets eener parlementaire geschiedenis van Nederland van 1849 tot 1918.* 4 vols. 's-Gravenhage: 1948–1955. 5e dl. 1940–1945, door L. S. J. Kortenhorst. 's-Gravenhage, 1956.
Thorbecke, J. R. *Bijdrage tot de herziening der grondwet.* (1848). Nieuwe uitgave met notitie en bijlagen van C. W. de Vries. 's-Gravenhage: 1948.
Verhagen, D. R. C. *L'influence de la révolution française sur la première constitution hollandaise du 23 avril 1798.* Utrecht: 1949.
Voorduin, J. C. *Geschiedenis en beginselen der grondwet voor het Koninkrijk der Nederlanden.* Utrecht: 1848.

NORWAY

Andenæs, J. *Statsforfatningen i Norge.* Oslo 1962.
Arven fra Eidsvoll. *Norges grunnlov.* Av Paal Berg, Frede Castberg (og) Sverre Steen. Oslo 1945.
Bergsgård, A. *Aret 1814.* V.1: Grunnlova. Oslo 1943.
Bjornberg, A. *Parlamentarismens utveckling i Norge efter 1905.* Uppsala 1939.
Castberg, F. *Juridiske stridsspørsmal i Norges politiske historie.* Oslo 1964.
Colban, E. *Stortinget og utenrikspolitikken.* Oslo 1961.
Grunnloven vår. Utg. for selvstudium ved Tonnes Andenæs. Oslo 1964.
Opsahl, T. *Delegasjon av Stortingets myndighet.* Oslo 1965.
Stavang, P. *Parlamentarisme og maktbalanse.* Oslo 1964.
Steen, S. *Det frie Norge.* V.1: 1814. Oslo 1951.
Storing, J. A. *Norwegian democracy.* Oslo 1963.

POLAND

Burda, A. *Polskie prawo panstwowe* (Le droit constitutionnel polonais). Warsaw 1962.
Constitution of the Polish People's Republic. Introduction by Prof. A. Burda. Warsaw 1964.
Izydorczyk, J. "The Parliament of the Polish People's Republic." *Inter-Parliamentary Bulletin* 1959.
"The Polish Diet". *Arkady,* Warsaw 1959.
"Le régime et les institutions de la République Populaire de Pologne." *Centre national pour l'étude des pays à régime communiste,* 8° p. XI, 139. Brussels 1959.
Rozmaryn, S. "La loi, le règlement et l'arrêté dans le droit constitutionnel polonais." *Revue international de droit comparé* 1961, No. 3.
Rozmaryn, S. *La Pologne.* Paris 1963.
Rozmaryn, S. *The Seym and People's Councils in Poland.* Warsaw 1958.
Wlodyka, S. *Organizacja wymiaru sprawiedliwosci w PRL* L'organisation de la justice en R.P.P. Warsaw 1963.

SPAIN

Candela Martinez, J. *El fuero de los Españoles.* Granada 1954.
Candela Martinez, "El orden de las leyes fundamentales de España, desde la perspectiva de la Ley de Sucesión." *Revista de Estudios Politicos,* no. 69, Madrid 1953.

Castan Tobenas, J. *Perspectivas filosóficos-jurídicas del pensamiento contemporaneo y de la Ley Fundamental española de 17 de mayo de 1958*. Madrid 1958.
Conde, F. J. *Representación política y régimen español*. Madrid 1945.
Fraga Iribarne, M. *Así se gobierna España*. Madrid 1949.
Fraga Iribarne, M. *El reglamento de las Cortes españolas*. Madrid 1959.
Fraga, Iribarne, M. *Horizonte Español*. Madrid 1965.
Lojendio, I. M. de, *Régimen político del Estado Español*. Barcelona, 1942.
Sanchez Agesta, L. *Derecho constitucional comparado*. Madrid 1965.
Sanchez Agesta, L. *Historia del constitucionalismo español*. Madrid 1955.
Serrano Serrano, I. *El fuero del Trabajo, doctrina y comentario*. Valladolid 1939.
Sevilla Andres, D. *Historia constitucional de España (1800–1966)*. Valencia 1966.

SWEDEN

Andren, Nils. *Modern Swedish Government*. Stockholm 1961.
Hastad, Elis. *The parliament of Sweden*. London 1957.
Heckscher, G. *The Swedish Constitution 1809–1959. Tradition and practise in constitutional development*. Stockholm 1959.
Malmgren, R. *Sveriges grundlagar och tillhorande forfattningar*. Stockholm 1961.

SWITZERLAND

Bridel, M. *Précis de droit constitutionnel et public suisse*. Lausanne, 1959, 1965.
Favre, A. *Droit constitutionnel suisse*. Fribourg, 1966.
Hughes, C. *The federal Constitution of Switzerland*. Oxford 1954.
Sauser-Hall, G. *Guide politique suisse*. 7th ed. Lausanne 1965.

UKRAINE

Allen, W. E. D. *The Ukraine, a history*. London 1940.
Chamberlin, W. H. *The Ukraine*. New York 1945.
Doroshenki, D. *History of the Ukraine*. 2nd Ed. Edmonton 1941.
Grushevski, M. S. *A History of the Ukraine*. New Haven 1941.
Manning, C. A. *Twentieth Century Ukraine*. New York 1951.

UNITED KINGDOM

Anson, W. *Law and custom of the Constitution*. Oxford.
Benemy, F. W. G. *The elected Monarch: the development of the power of the Prime Minister* London 1965.
Chalmers and Hood Phillips. *Constitutional laws of Great Britain*. 6th Ed. London 1946.
Dicey, A. V. *Introduction to the Study of the law of the constitution*. 10th Ed. London 1959.
Emden, C. S. *Principles of British constitutional law*. London.
Forrest, G. A. *Constitutional law*. 8th Ed. London 1950.
Harvey, J. and Bather, L. *The British Constitution*. London 1963.
Heuston, R. F. V. *Essays in Constitutional law*. London 1961.
Jennings, W. I. *Law and the Constitution*. London.
Joliffe, J. E. A. *Constitutional History of Medieval England*. 4th Ed. London 1962.
Keir, D. L. *Constitutional history of modern Britain 1485–1951*. 5th Ed. London 1953.
Keith, A. B. *Constitutional law*. 7th Ed. London 1939.
Mackenzie, K. *The English Parliament, a study of its nature and historic development*. Penguin 1950.
Mackintosh, J. P. *The British Cabinet*. The Hague 1962.
Maitland, F. W. *The constitutional history of England*. Cambridge 1961 (paperback of 1908 edition).
May, T. E. *Parliamentary practise*. London
Wade, E. C. S. and Phillips, G. G. *Constitutional law; an outline of the law and practises of the Constitution, including central and local government and the constitutional relations of the British Commonwealth;* London, 6th Ed. 1961.
Wheare, K. C. *The Statute of Westminster and dominion status*. London 1949.

VATICAN CITY STATE

D'Avack, P. A. *Chiesa, S. Sede e Città del Vaticano nel jus publicum ecclesiasticum*.
Cammeo, F. *Ordinamento giuridico dello Stato della Città del Vaticano*. Florence 1932.

Jemolo. "Carattere dello Stato della Città del Vaticano," *Rivista Di Diritto Internazionale,* 1929.

Miele. *Santa Sede e Città del Vaticano.* Rome 1933.

Pacelli, C. "Lo Stato della Città del Vaticano," *Il Vaticano.*

Pallieri, B. "Il rapporto fra Chiesa Cattolica e Stato Vaticano secondo il diritto ecclesiastico e il diritto internazionale," *Rivista Internazionale di Scienze Sociali,* 1930.

Rousseau. "Etat de la Cité du Vatican." *Revue Générale de droit international public,* vol. XXXVII, 1930.

Ruffini. "Lo stato della Città del Vaticano" *Atti della Accademia delle Scienze di Torino,* vol. LXVI, disp. 15.

GPSR Compliance

The European Union's (EU) General Product Safety Regulation (GPSR) is a set of rules that requires consumer products to be safe and our obligations to ensure this.

If you have any concerns about our products, you can contact us on ProductSafety@springernature.com

In case Publisher is established outside the EU, the EU authorized representative is:

Springer Nature Customer Service Center GmbH
Europaplatz 3
69115 Heidelberg, Germany

Batch number: 10830941

Printed by Printforce, the Netherlands